PRINCIPLES OF FEDERAL INCOME TAXATION OF INDIVIDUALS

Eighth Edition

Donald B. Tobin

Dean and Professor of Law
University of Maryland
Francis King Carey School of Law

Samuel A. Donaldson

Professor of Law
Georgia State University College of Law

CONCISE HORNBOOK SERIES™

WEST ACADEMIC PUBLISHING

COPYRIGHT © 1983, 1989, 1993, 1997 WEST PUBLISHING CO.
© West, a Thomson business, 1998, 2003
© 2005 Thomson/West
© 2017 LEG, Inc. d/b/a West Academic
     444 Cedar Street, Suite 700
     St. Paul, MN 55101
     1-877-888-1330

Printed in the United States of America

ISBN: 978-0-314-28786-1

For Dan Posin, the original author of this treatise.
His wit and love of tax lives on here.

DBT

To the students in my courses, especially those
that didn't drop the class.

SAD

"Where there is an income tax, the just man will pay more and the unjust less on the same amount of income."

—Plato, The Republic, bk K, 343-D

"Taxes are what we pay for civilized society."

—Oliver Wendell Holmes, Jr.
Compania de Tabacos v. Collector, 275 U.S. 87, 1000 (1904)

Special Note and Acknowledgments

Earlier editions of this book were written by the late Professor Daniel Q. Posin. Much of his wit and erudition remains in this Eighth Edition. For the best glimpse into Professor Posin's playful and insightful mind, we invite readers to read his classic discussion of the time value of money, presented intact as Appendix A in this Eighth Edition.

We would like to thank our families, colleagues and students who have been extremely helpful in completing this project. A special thanks to Leigh Tobin, who read several drafts of the book.

Highlights

The book includes analysis of cases and concepts in the leading casebooks, and provides easy to understand explanations of all the major topics in the field of Federal Income Tax. The Hornbook also includes graphs and drawings to help readers weave their way through the intricacies of the Internal Revenue Code and associated authorities.

Other highlights include:

- Tax ethics and the ethical responsibilities of tax lawyers
- Corporate tax shelters and the economic substance doctrine
- Capital gains
- Section 1031 exchanges
- Taxation of home-run baseballs
- Stock options
- Tax breaks for education—including law school
- Liberalizing the home office deduction
- Child care credit
- IRAs and other retirement options

Summary of Contents

Table of Contents

Table of Illustrations

PRINCIPLES OF FEDERAL INCOME TAXATION OF INDIVIDUALS

Eighth Edition

INTRODUCTION

Individuals are often intimidated by the thought of studying "tax law." It frequently makes judges, practitioners and students wish they had a clear resource to guide them through the complexities of the Internal Revenue Code. This book aims to be that guide.

The apprehension surrounding the study of tax is misplaced. The major theories and principles involved in the study of tax law are the same principles that are the foundation of the law in other subjects. In addition, unlike some other legal subjects, most people have a basic understanding of the tax system just by their familiarity with our society. We know many of the essential tax principles simply by our everyday experiences.

First, because of all the debate about tax policy in the headlines, we know that our federal income tax system is *progressive* and based on a principle of ability to pay. A progressive system is one in which the tax rates rise as income increases. A *regressive system* is one in which the tax burden on lower income individuals as a percentage of their income is higher than it is on higher income individuals. In order to achieve a progressive system of taxation, we utilize *marginal tax rates.* The marginal rate of tax refers to the tax on the last dollar of income that the taxpayer earns. That means that as income rises the percentage of income that must be paid in tax increases. For example, in 2015, if you are single and had taxable income of $50,000 a year, the first $9,225 of taxable income would be subject to tax at 10%, the next $28,225 would be taxed at 15%, and the remaining $12,550 would be taxed at 25%. Thus, a taxpayer's *effective tax rate*, the proportion of total income payable in tax, would not be the taxpayer's highest marginal tax rate, but would be based on the amount actually paid divided by total income.[1] In this example, the effective tax rate would be 16.5% (total tax due ($8,294) / taxable income ($50,000)).

Another intuitive principle in taxation is the *time value of money*. If your employer offered you a bonus of $1,000 on January 1, or the same bonus six months later, which would you choose? You would, we hope, take the money today. Why? Because a dollar today is worth more than a dollar in six months. At the very least you can put the $1,000 in savings and earn interest on the money. The fact that a dollar today is worth more than a dollar in six months is referred to as the *time value of money* (see discussion of time value of money in the appendix). Moreover, just as a dollar earned today is

---

[1]   See ¶ 1.02(1)(f).

worth more than a dollar earned in the future, so is a dollar saved. Thus the time value of money explains why a tax deduction today is beneficial even if you must pay tax on the amount deducted in the future. This is referred to as *tax deferral*. Deferring taxes is beneficial because not having to pay tax on income today is the equivalent of a dollar earned now that does not have to be paid back until the future.

Now let's take a look at how the tax system actually works. Assume you have a salary of $50,000 a year, earn interest on your deposits of $2,000 a year, and have two children. The total amount of income you have for that year is $52,000. The Code refers to this amount as *Gross Income*.[2] Section 61 of the Code defines gross income (somewhat unhelpfully) as "all income from whatever source derived." This includes, among other things, compensation for services, interest, rents, dividends, and gains from the sale of property. It also includes some items that people often do not think of as income. For example gambling winnings, prizes, and in-kind services all constitute income. However, some items that we might think would come under this definition of gross income are specifically excluded from gross income by other provisions of the Code. These items are referred to as *exclusions*. For example, profit on the sale of your personal residence may be excluded from income if you meet the requirements of § 121.[3]

But we do not pay tax on our gross incomes. The Code provides that certain amounts may be deducted from gross income prior to calculating the tax. Some of these items are deemed by Congress to be so important, either for policy reasons or to clearly reflect income, that they are taken before any other calculation is done. The income that is left after these items are subtracted is referred to as *Adjusted Gross Income*.[4] These deductions, those that take you from gross income to adjusted gross income, are also referred to as *above-the-line* deductions.[5]

Since one of the major goals of our tax system is to tax people on their ability to pay, the Code makes other adjustments to income that are designed to clearly reflect income. Thus, the Code provides for a *personal exemption* and an *exemption for dependents*. The personal exemption applies to the individuals filing the return (so a single

---

[2]   See ¶ 2.01.

[3]   See ¶ 4.05.

[4]   Section 62 defines Adjusted Gross income as gross income minus the deductions listed in § 62(a). These deductions include, among others, trade or business deductions, losses from the sale or exchange of property, retirement savings, alimony, moving expenses and interest on education loans.

[5]   These deductions are referred to as "above-the-line" deductions because they are taken before other credits and deductions, and they used to appear above a dark black line on the Form 1040.

taxpayer claims one exemption and a married couple filing a joint tax return claims two exemptions). The exemption for dependents applies to each person in taxpayer's family for whom the taxpayer provides at least half of the total support during the year.[6] These exemptions provide that an amount of your income is exempt from tax based on the number of people in your family.

At this point on your return, you have only received above-the-line deductions and personal and dependency exemptions, but you still have not had the benefit of other deductions. Here, you must make a choice. Section 63 provides for a *standard deduction*, a set amount that you are allowed to deduct from income regardless of your other expenditures, or for *itemized deductions*, the amounts spent on specific expenses authorized by the Code as deductions. Some familiar itemized deductions include home mortgage interest, property taxes, charitable contributions, casualty losses, and medical expenses.[7] In deciding whether to take the standard deduction or itemized deductions, you will generally want to choose the one that is bigger.

In addition, some itemized deductions are better than others. Section 67 limits the deductibility of aggregate *miscellaneous itemized deductions* to the amount that exceeds 2% of adjusted gross income. Miscellaneous itemized deductions include unreimbursed employee expenses (such as travel or professional journals), and expenses of investment advice for investing in stocks and bonds.[8] Itemized deductions that are not subject to the 2% "haircut" may be referred to as *regular itemized deductions*. There is one additional limitation on itemized deductions of which you should be aware: if a taxpayer's adjusted gross income exceeds a threshold dollar amount (adjusted annually for inflation), the amount of deductible itemized deductions is phased out; in the worst case scenario, this *phase out* can cause 80% of the otherwise deductible amount of itemized deductions to be disallowed.

Now, we are almost done. You started with gross income, and then took the above the line deductions to get to adjusted gross income. From there you took the applicable personal and dependency exemptions. You then took either the itemized deductions or the standard deduction, only to arrive, finally, at *taxable income*. Taxable

---

[6]   This is a simplistic overview of the dependency exemption. For further discussion of the requirements to be entitled to an exemption for dependents see ¶ 7.04.

[7]   Each of these deductions may be limited by the Code provisions that authorize them. In addition, as we will see in ¶ 7.01, a portion of the total of itemized deductions may be phased out for high income earners.

[8]   For a further discussion of miscellaneous itemized deductions see ¶ 7.02.

income is the amount of income upon which the amount of tax you owe is calculated. You are not done yet, however.

In addition to deductions and exemptions, you may also qualify for *tax credits*. Credits are different than deductions in that a credit usually reduces, dollar for dollar, the tax you owe. In the case of the child tax credit, for example, the amount of the credit is subtracted from the amount you owe in tax. Since the credit is subtracted from what was your final bill, you get a dollar for dollar reduction in your tax bill for every dollar your receive as a credit. A tax credit is therefore much more valuable than a deduction, because a deduction only reduces your income, and thus your tax bill, by the amount of your marginal tax rate. The marginal tax rate, recall, is the percentage of tax that you pay on the next dollar earned. For example, if you were a 25% bracket taxpayer, a $1,000 deduction would be worth $250. A $1,000 tax credit, however, would be worth $1,000.

Now you really are almost done. Just subtract the amount of any applicable credits from your initial tax liability and the final result is the amount you owe in tax.[9] The following chart gives you the basic framework for how this works.

---

[9]   For a detailed description of the structure of federal income taxation see ¶ 6.01.

INTRODUCTION TO TAX

Gross Income

minus

"Above the line" deductions

Adjusted Gross Income

minus

Personal and dependency exemptions

minus

Standard or itemized deductions —— Miscellaneous itemized deductions subject to the 2% limitation

Taxable income

Calculate the tax owed

minus

Credits

Amount of Tax

There is one last issue that we need to cover before we send you on your way. It is easy to determine income when it is earned as salary, but what if it is derived from the sale of property? Suppose in addition to receiving a salary, you also sell an asset you held for investment. If you sell the asset for $100,000 and paid $40,000 for the property, you intuitively know that you should have $60,000 of income and not $100,000. Why? Because you did not make $100,000 on the sale, you made $60,000. In tax terminology, your cost in the property is called *basis*. The amount you sell the property for is the *amount realized*. The difference between your basis and the amount realized is your *gain*. Furthermore, if the property is a *capital asset*, defined as all property held by the taxpayer *except* inventory, depreciable or real property used in his trade or business, certain copyrights and artistic compositions, accounts receivable and certain other types of property,[10] then the gain from the sale of the capital asset is referred to as *capital gain*. Capital gain, generally speaking, is taxed at a lower rate than other income.[11]

The basic concepts of federal income tax have been covered in the above brief description. Everything else is merely perfecting these basic concepts. If you hang on to your common sense, at least most of the time, the complexity of the Code will fall into place, and you too will enjoy the adventure of working with the Internal Revenue Code.

---

[10]   Section 1221(1)–(4). For the special treatment of depreciable or real property used in the trade or business, see ¶ 4.06(3)(a)(iv). The particular reach of the definition of "capital assets" is discussed in detail at ¶ 4.06(3).

[11]   See a discussion of capital gains see ¶ 4.06.

Chapter 1

HISTORY, POLICY AND STRUCTURE

Table of Sections

Para.

¶ 1.01 A BRIEF HISTORY OF INCOME TAXATION

(1) In General

Taxes are a building block of civilization. They pay for "public goods," such as the cost of government administration or military defense of the state. These "public goods" are of great benefit to society as a whole, and each person in society benefits from them. Since individuals in society benefit from these expenditures whether or not they pay for them, each individual has a great incentive to avoid paying taxes and let his neighbors carry the burden. In economic terms, this is referred to as the *free rider problem*. Each member of society has an incentive to be a free rider on the rest of society.

It is not surprising, then, that in the first organized society of record, ancient Sumer, the failure to pay taxes carried with it great religious sanction to overcome the human disinclination to pay. The Sumerians were organized in temple-communities in which the farmers produced a food surplus paid to the priests. In Sumerian theology the priests had the power to communicate with the Gods and were themselves supernatural beings. Moreover it was also part of Sumerian theology, conveniently for the priests, that man was a slave of the Gods destined to work indefatigably for them or face the threat of drought, flood, and starvation.[1]

---

[1]   Falkenstein, "La Cité-temple sumérienne," Cahiers d'histoire mondiale 791; (1954) 4 Schneider, "Die Anfänge der Kulturwirtschaft: Die sumerische Tempelstadt," Staatswissenschaftliche Beitrage (Essen, 1920). But see Oppenheim, "A Bird's-Eye View of Mesopotamian Economic History," in Polyanyi, Trade and Market in the Early Empires 27–37 (1957), indicating that there were some farming communities in Sumer that did not depend on a temple.

Even in the Golden Age of Greece, the heavy taxes imposed upon the Athenian upper classes by the democratic vote of its citizens precipitated coups d'état in 411 B.C. and 404 B.C.[2] The taxes imposed by the central administration in the Roman Empire were essential to financing further conquest, but ultimately their excessiveness was a significant factor in the Empire's disintegration.[3]

From the time of their earliest settlements, the American colonies of Britain evinced a healthy resistance to paying taxes to the mother country.[4] The first taxes levied by Great Britain on her colonies were the Acts of Trade and Navigation which provided for customs duties. These Acts raised little revenues for two reasons: first, they were only intended to direct the flow of commerce; second, they were widely ignored anyway. Indeed, through the mid-eighteenth century, the Americans were unique among the British colonies in being virtually exempt from taxation by the mother country. This was true notwithstanding that Great Britain incurred some significant expenses in maintaining the colonies, such as driving the French out of America during the Seven Years' War. (Most of the colonies refused to contribute troops to this war effort, flouted commercial regulations, and traded extensively with the enemy.)[5]

Thus at the conclusion of the Seven Years' War, in 1763, the British came to the reasonable decision not only to lay taxes upon the colonies but actually to collect them. The Revenue Act of 1764 (the "Sugar" Act) imposed a moderate system of customs duties on the Americans. In 1765 the British promulgated the Stamp Tax which required the payment of a fee, evidenced by the affixing of a stamp, on all commercial uses of paper, such as in legal and business documents and newspapers. Such a stamp tax for raising revenue was placidly assented to in Great Britain and employed by most of the countries of Europe. However, it aroused such violent opposition in the American colonies that it was repealed the following year. In 1767 Parliament, still endeavoring to come up with a tax tolerable to the Americans, promulgated the so-called "Townshend Duties," which imposed customs on American imports of paper, paint, lead, and tea. After another uproar this was repealed. The only element of

---

[2]   McNeil, The Rise of the West p. 289 (1963).

[3]   Id. at 344; Palmer and Colton, A History of the Modern World (1960). The religious aspect of taxation in Renaissance Italy is displayed in the Brancacci Chapel in Florence, Italy. The fresco "Rendering of the Tribute Money," shows the gods approving the Florentine income tax.

[4]   Except as otherwise indicated, the discussion of the taxation of the American Colonies is based on Palmer & Colton, note 3 supra, at 324–326.

[5]   1 Morrison and Commager, The Growth of the American Republic 9 (1937).

the "Townshend Duties" Parliament retained was the impost on tea, as a symbol of its power to tax the colonies.

The outcome to this point was something of a standoff. The colonies had in fact resisted taxation. Great Britain had, however, still maintained the principle that it could tax them. Great Britain had, moreover, the legitimate argument that it incurred substantial expenses in administering the colonies. To this the Americans answered with some force that since they were not represented in Parliament, it had no authority to tax them. The British response to this was that members of Parliament did not represent merely local constituencies but spoke for the entire empire. Thus the argument ran that the Americans enjoyed "virtual representation," as did the British City of Manchester, which was also not represented in Parliament. To this the Americans replied that if Manchester was not represented it ought to be, an argument which found a sympathetic ear in Manchester. (Indeed this controversy spawned a general drive to reform the means of selecting the members of the House of Commons.)

These relatively recondite arguments were rendered moot by the Boston Tea Party. One evening in 1773 in Boston harbor a party of men in disguise boarded several ships of the British East India Company and threw a number of chests of tea overboard. Although the motivations of this act are somewhat obscure, it was apparently a protest both against the tea tax and the granting by Parliament to the East India Company of the right to sell its tea directly in the colonies, by-passing American merchants. The British thereupon closed the port of Boston (threatening the city with economic strangulation), and forbade local elections and the holding of town meetings. Although the British response here seems excessive, it must be admitted they had been tolerating a good deal from the colonies for a long time.

After this point taxation receded as an issue and other more broadly-based justifications for the American Revolution came to the fore.[6]

(2) The American Income Tax

The dominant source of revenues of the new central government of the thirteen states, created by the adoption of the Constitution in 1789, was receipts from customs—which was of course the most

---

[6]   Cf. "It is repugnant to reason—to suppose that this continent can long remain subject to any external power . . . There is something absurd in supposing a continent be perpetually governed by an island. In no instance hath nature made the satellite larger than its primary planet; and as England and America, with respect to each other, reverse the common order of nature, it is evident that they belong to different systems, England to Europe, America to itself." T. Paine, Common Sense (1776).

inconspicuous method of taxing an undoubtedly recalcitrant populace.[7] Early in this period, excise taxes were also levied on carriages, whiskey and other distilled spirits, snuff, sugar, and other items.[8]

The American people, consistent with their attitude under the British, immediately resisted these taxes. One of the more engaging manifestations of this resistance was the so-called "Whiskey Rebellion" in Western Pennsylvania in 1794 when the home of General John Neville, the regional inspector of the excise, was burned to the ground. The resultant turmoil led ultimately to the occupation of several western counties of Pennsylvania by the army.[9] A somewhat more sober approach for resisting the excise taxes was the argument that they were direct taxes not apportioned among the States by population and thus violative of the new Constitution.[10] However, these taxes were held constitutional in the first of a number of Supreme Court cases on this subject.[11]

In 1797 a stamp tax was successfully promulgated that was similar to the one which had caused an outcry 30 years earlier when imposed by the British. In 1798 a property tax was levied on houses, land and slaves. When Thomas Jefferson became President, he abolished all these taxes. They reappeared to help finance the War of 1812 and were abolished again in 1817. During this period the British set an example by enacting an income tax to help pay for the Napoleonic wars. It was abolished in 1816 but came back permanently in 1842. Moreover, in 1815 the United States' Secretary of the Treasury suggested that an income tax might ultimately be necessary. The British experience and this suggestion were, however, the only small warning clouds on the horizon and indeed there were no taxes again in the United States other than customs until the Civil War.

In addition to the other tragedies wreaked upon this country by the Civil War, it also gave rise to the first federal income tax in 1862. This tax was graduated, providing for a levy of 3% on income up to $10,000 and 5% on income over $10,000. The first $600 of income was

---

[7]   Except as otherwise indicated this discussion of the history of the American income tax is based on the following materials: Myers, A Financial History of the United States (1970); Bureau of Internal Revenue, History of the Internal Revenue Service, 1791–1929 (1930); Ratner, American Taxation, Its History as a Social Force in Democracy (2d 1967); Blakely, The Federal Income Tax (1940); Paul, Taxation in the United States (1954); Annual Reports of the Commissioner of Internal Revenue.

[8]   The "Carriage Tax", March 3, 1791, as amended, 1 Stat. 373.

[9]   Brackenridge, History of the Western Insurrection (1859).

[10]   United States Constitution, Art. I, § 2, cl. 3. For a general discussion of this constitutional issue, see text accompanying notes 13–15 infra.

[11]   Hylton v. United States, 3 U.S. (3 Dall.) 171, 1 L.Ed. 556 (1796).

exempt from tax so (given the deflated dollar values of that time) only about 1% of the population was subject to the income tax. The rates were increased somewhat in 1864 and later years, and were reduced when the war ended. The income tax was then repealed in 1872.

Though the income tax was gone, it was not forgotten. It became a rallying cry of the agrarian, labor, and small business organizations of the South and West. In 1892 one of the proposals of the Populist Party was a graduated income tax. Since the tax was seen as a way of raising revenues by taxing the rich, the numbers inevitably favored the proponents of the tax. These pressures in Congress finally led to the passage of the Income Tax of 1894.

The 1894 tax was 2% on individual income over $4,000 (thus reaching only the highest individual incomes at that time) and 4% on corporate income. Significantly, included in income was personal property received by gift or inheritance.[12]

This income tax was, unsurprisingly, immediately challenged in the courts as being a "direct" tax and thus violating the Constitution's requirement that "direct" taxes must be apportioned among the states by population.[13] The issue was joined in the case of *Pollock v. Farmers' Loan and Trust Co.,*[14] involving a stockholders' suit to restrain payment of the corporate tax by the corporation's directors.

Past precedent was not on the opponents' side and their arguments appeared weak. They argued that it would be difficult to apportion an income tax among the states by population. Each state would have to ascertain its share of the total income tax due and reapportion it among its citizens by their incomes. Even if this could be done, it would lead to an oppressive result in a state with large population and low incomes. Opponents argued that it was unlikely the Constitution would require such an anomalous result.

But the fact that it would be difficult to apportion the tax was a major reason why the prior Supreme Court decisions addressing the question had unanimously found that a tax difficult to apportion was not a direct tax. There was dictum in the *Hylton* case that only poll taxes and taxes on land were direct taxes, and that a tax difficult to

---

[12]   Cf. ¶ 3.08.

[13]   Article 1, Section 2, Clause 3 of the Constitution provides:

"(D)irect Taxes shall be apportioned among the several States which may be included within this Union, according to their respective Numbers . . ."

Article 1, Section 9, Clause 4 of the Constitution provides:

"No Capitation, or other direct Tax shall be laid, unless in Proportion to the Census or Enumeration herein before directed to be taken."

[14]   157 U.S. 429, 15 S.Ct. 673, 39 L.Ed. 759 (1895), reh'g denied 158 U.S. 601, 15 S.Ct. 912, 39 L.Ed. 1108 (1895).

apportion would not be considered a direct tax by the Constitution.[15] The Court had early upheld the 1864 gross receipts tax on insurance companies on this ground.[16] The 1866 tax on the issuance of bank notes had been upheld as not a direct tax for historical reasons and because it would be difficult to apportion.[17] In addition, one ground for upholding the estate tax of 1864 was because, the Court said, it was indistinguishable from an income tax which was not a direct tax.[18]

The Court had found the income tax of 1864 valid on the grounds that it was an excise tax. Direct taxes, the Court said, could consist only of capitation taxes and taxes on real estate.[19]

Faced with this overwhelming array of argument and legal precedent, the counsel opposing the 1894 income tax salted their arguments with a little rhetoric:

> "I look upon this case with very different eyes from those of either the Attorney General or his associate who has just closed . . . The act of Congress which we are impugning is communistic in its purposes and tendencies, and is defended here upon principles as communistic, socialistic—what shall I call them—populistic as ever have been addressed to any political assembly in the world . . .
>
> I do not believe that any member of this court ever has sat or ever will sit to hear and decide a case the consequences of which will be so far-reaching as this—not even the venerable member who survives from the early days of the civil war, and has sat upon every question of reconstruction, of national destiny, of state destiny that has come up during the last thirty years [Field] . . .[20]

The Court struck down the tax. In one of its less distinguished moments in history, the Court reasoned that the tax on rental income from land was a tax on land and thus a direct tax which had to be apportioned, likewise as to a tax on income from personal property. Since so much of the income tax was invalid, the whole scheme was rejected.[21]

---

[15] Hylton, 3 U.S. (3 Dall.) at 174.

[16] Pacific Insurance Co. v. Soule, 74 U.S. (7 Wall.) 433, 19 L.Ed. 95 (1868).

[17] Veazie Bank v. Fenno, 75 U.S. (8 Wall.) 533, 544–545, 19 L.Ed. 482 (1869).

[18] Scholey v. Rew, 90 U.S. (23 Wall.) 331, 347–348, 23 L.Ed. 99 (1874).

[19] Springer v. United States, 102 U.S. (12 Otto) 586, 602, 26 L.Ed. 253 (1880).

[20] Pollock v. Farmers' Loan & Trust Co., 157 U.S. 429, 532, 553, 15 S.Ct. 673, 674–675, 679, 39 L.Ed. 759 (1895) (argument of Joseph H. Choate).

[21] Pollock v. Farmers' Loan & Trust Co., 158 U.S. 601, 637, 15 S.Ct. 912, 920–921, 39 L.Ed. 1108 (1895). Dissenting were Justices Harlan, White, Jackson and

Though a single breaker might recede, the tide was coming in. In the years following *Pollock*, pressures from the agrarian, populist and Progressive groups continued to build for Congress to pass another income tax and give the Supreme Court a chance to overrule *Pollock*. It seemed likely the Court would reverse itself as the *Pollock* rationale was being eroded by subsequent decisions. The inheritance tax of 1898 was upheld on the grounds *Pollock* had not overruled *Scholey v. Rew*,[22] which had found the 1864 inheritance tax valid.[23] The 1898 gross receipts tax on corporations engaged in sugar refining was sustained on the reasoning it was an excise tax and thus not within the purview of *Pollock*.[24]

In 1909 a coalition of western, progressive Republican and Democratic members of Congress appeared finally to have the votes to pass another income tax. The eastern Republicans and President Taft proposed as a compromise a corporate income tax and the Sixteenth Amendment to the Constitution sanctioning an income tax in general. The compromise was accepted. Though this appeared to be a victory for the supporters of the income tax, in fact it was a testament to the adroitness of its opponents, since the cumbersome process of the states ratifying an amendment to the Constitution would delay the imposition of an individual income tax by several years.

The Payne-Aldrich Tariff Act of 1909 resulted from this compromise, imposing a tax on corporate net income, with an exemption of $5,000. It was held constitutional in *Flint v. Stone Tracy Co.*[25] (a decision which further demonstrated the limited vitality of *Pollock*, although that question was by this time moot). In 1913 the Sixteenth Amendment, providing that Congress shall have the power to lay and collect taxes on income without apportionment among the states, was formally ratified. The 1913 Income Tax was then enacted posthaste. It imposed a 1% tax on net incomes of individuals above $3,000 ($4,000 for married persons) and an additional surtax of 1% on incomes above $20,000, graduated up to 6% on incomes of more than $500,000.

Brown. In the majority were Chief Justice Fuller, writing the opinion, and the venerable Justice Field, Justices Brewer, Shiras and Gray.

[22]   Scholey, 90 U.S. (23 Wall.) at 347–348.

[23]   Knowlton v. Moore, 178 U.S. 41, 20 S.Ct. 747, 44 L.Ed. 969 (1900).

[24]   Spreckels Sugar Refining Co. v. McClain, 192 U.S. 397, 24 S.Ct. 376, 48 L.Ed. 496 (1904).

[25]   220 U.S. 107, 31 S.Ct. 342, 55 L.Ed. 389 (1911).

Thus on account of the *Flint* case the constitutionality of the corporate income tax does not depend on the Sixteenth Amendment.

And still the struggle was not ended. Back into the courts went the opponents of the income tax.[26] This time they argued that the due process clause of the Fifth Amendment and the requirement that taxes must be uniform[27] were violated by the exemptions and graduated rates. However, it was the end of the line. In *Brushaber v. Union Pacific Railroad Co.*[28] Chief Justice White, a dissenter in *Pollock,* writing for the unanimous court (McReynolds not participating), held the income tax valid. The Court held that the Fifth Amendment was not violated because there was not an arbitrariness that amounted to confiscation;[29] as to uniformity, that requirement was only geographical.[30] Moreover, the Court recognized broadly that the purpose of the Sixteenth Amendment was to relieve income taxes of the *Pollock* requirement of apportionment.[31]

The income tax had arrived. In the years since *Brushaber* the story has not been of its constitutionality but of its ever-broadening reach and its constantly increasing complexity. In 1920 there were 5½ million individual income tax returns in a U.S. population of 106 million. In the late 1990's there were nearly 100 million income tax returns filed annually in a U.S. population of over 200 million.[32] The Income Tax of 1913 was 14 pages[33]—compare to the immoderately-sized tome that comprises the present Internal Revenue Code.

The present income tax is extraordinarily complex, and that is due to many forces. In the first instance there is the fact that the income tax is imposed on a very complex society. Thus a great deal of the complexity of the Internal Revenue Code will inevitably flow from that. Beyond that, there are the special interests who—having lost the constitutional battle—still engage in hand-to-hand fighting, with respect to various code sections, to escape the brunt of the graduated rates. There are the reformers, attempting to plug the "gaps" the special interests have opened. There are the planners, who attempt to use the Code to encourage "socially desirable" behavior. And finally, the income tax is used as an instrument of national economic

---

[26] Cf.: "In the fell clutch of circumstance, I have not winced nor cried aloud; Under the bludgeonings of chance My head is bloody, but unbowed."

—William Ernest Henley, Echoes (1888). IV, In Memoriam R.T. Hamilton Bruce ("Invictus"), st. 1, 2.

[27] Article 1, Section 8, Clause 4 of the Constitution requires that " . . . all Duties, Imposts and Excises shall be uniform throughout the United States."

[28] 240 U.S. 1, 36 S.Ct. 236, 60 L.Ed. 493 (1916).

[29] Id. at 24, 36 S.Ct. at 244.

[30] Id.

[31] Id. at 19, 36 S.Ct. at 242.

[32] See generally Annual Reports of the Commissioner of Internal Revenue.

[33] 38 Stat. 166–180 (1913).

policy, with rate changes, rebates, credits, deductions, and surtaxes all designed to affect the country's rates of growth, inflation and unemployment.

Thus since 1913 the income tax, serving many purposes and many masters, has evolved into a massive, grotesquely complex statute. And, since each new piece of tax legislation adds materially to the Code's complexity, the end of its wanton growth is not yet in sight.

¶ 1.02 THEORETICAL ASPECTS OF INCOME TAXATION

Oppressive and omnipresent as the income tax is, it naturally has provoked a good deal of discussion concerning how its operation might be improved. The themes around which this discussion has revolved relate to the capacity of the tax to raise revenues, its fairness, the effect the tax has on the use of resources in the economy, and its complexity. These themes arise in the context of particular issues discussed below.

(1) Progressivity, the Marginal Rate of Tax and the Effective Rates of Tax

We talk a lot in this book about the *tax base*. The tax base refers to what is taxed and what is not taxed. That is indeed the most complicated aspect of the field. But it is also necessary to understand the tax rate structure and how it works. The key concepts here are the *marginal rate of tax* and the *effective rate of tax*. The marginal rate of tax refers to the tax on the last dollar of income that the taxpayer earns. The effective rate of tax refers to the proportion of the taxpayer's total income that he has to pay in tax. These two rates are not the same in a system of progressive taxation.

Take a gander at § 1(a) of your favorite Code. This sets forth the tax on married couples filing joint returns. You see that as income goes up, the percentage applied to the higher amounts of income goes up. The lower amounts remain taxed at the same lower level. The percentages are the marginal rates of tax, that are applied to the top levels of a taxpayers income. The effective rate of tax is the average of the marginal rates as income moves up through the brackets. Thus, where the marginal rates are always rising, as in § 1(a), the effective rate of tax is always less than the marginal rate of tax, since it is the weighted average of the previous lower marginal rates.

Our system of "progressive taxation," as described above, can be usefully compared with "proportional taxation." Under "proportional taxation," everyone would pay the same proportion of his income, say 10%. In a 10% proportional system obviously an individual with $1 million of taxable income pays more ($100,000) than a person with $30,000 of taxable income ($3,000). But in this proportional system both of these taxpayers have a marginal and an effective rate of 10%.

However, a "progressive" system takes a bigger bite from higher incomes. In a "progressive" system, the higher-income individual not only pays more but pays a higher percentage of that income in tax. The effective rate is higher on the higher income individual. With a progressive system, the tax system is serving (to one degree or another) to redistribute the wealth.

We are presently in an era in which the rate structure is not very progressive. There have been times in the past when the marginal rate on very high amounts of income has been as high as 70% or 90%. Obviously, if marginal rates increase steeply, effective rates also go up but not as fast.

It should also be noted that the tax rates are "indexed" for inflation, see § 1(f). As a taxpayer's income goes up, the taxpayer would generally move up through the brackets, attracting a higher and higher marginal rate. But if the income increase is matched by an equal amount of inflation, then the taxpayer has not had a true increase in income and therefore it would seem to be unfair to hit that taxpayer with a higher marginal rate of tax. The inflation adjustment rules of § 1(f) take care of that problem.

These inflation adjustment rules, however, create problems of their own. If every financial transaction in the country were indexed for inflation, this would create an increased possibility of "hyper-inflation," as all transactions would "ratchet up" to keep up with inflation, thereby creating more inflation.

(2) Alternatives to the Income Tax

The boldest critique of the income tax is, of course, to suggest it be done away with altogether. Assuming, however, this society is not suddenly transformed into an island paradise in which the populace gathers coconuts for sustenance, the government will continue to need to raise substantial revenues. There are other possible sources of these revenues. Examining them provides insight into the strengths of the income tax.

(a) Value Added Tax

Several proponents of tax reform have advocated that the United States move from an income tax to a consumption tax. One form of consumption tax is a *value-added tax* (VAT), which imposes a tax on the increase in the value of a product at each step in the production-distribution chain. It is ultimately paid by the consumer.[34] VATs are effective. They are used all over the world and in every country in Western Europe. Since you pay VAT when you purchase a good, like you pay a sales tax, a VAT taxes consumption. By taxing consumption, the Government increases the cost of consumption. Many reform advocates support consumption-based taxes because they believe it will increase savings. Taxing income, by contrast, discourages saving (which produces income) and encourages consumption. It is highly questionable, however, whether the VAT can raise enough money by itself to substitute for the income tax.

(b) Net Worth or Wealth Taxes

In those few countries which have used it, a net worth tax imposes a levy, usually not more than 1%, on the value of property held by the taxpayer.[35] The net worth tax cannot raise a substantial amount of revenue, since the rate can never exceed the income from the property or the property will be abandoned.[36] Other problems with the net worth tax include difficulties in valuation, high cost of enforcement,[37] and lack of liquid assets on the part of the taxpayer to pay the tax.[38] In the United States the only forms of wealth tax in effect are real estate taxes and estate and gift taxes. Both of these taxes have evidenced the problems described above and neither appears capable of raising enough revenues to take the place of the income tax.[39]

(c) Head Tax

A head tax imposes a flat amount of tax on each person in the society, regardless of income, deductions or expenses. There can be

---

[34]   Thus it is a form of sales tax.

[35]   The net worth tax has been used in, among other countries, Germany, India, Sweden, Norway, Denmark, Finland, Columbia. See generally World Tax Series, Harvard Law School with respect to these countries.

[36]   Cf. generally Tait, The Taxation of Personal Wealth, 1967; C. T. Sandford, J. R. M. Willis, D. J. Ironside, An Annual Wealth Tax, 1975; Cooper, Taking Wealth Taxation Seriously, 34 Record of the Association of the Bar of the City of New York 24 (1979). Posin, "Toward a Theory of Federal Taxation: A Comment," 50 Journal of Air Law and Commerce (Southern Methodist University Law School) 907 (1985), excerpted in Oliver and Peel, Readings and Materials on Tax Policy, Foundation Press, 1996; excerpted in Caron, Burke, and McCouch, Federal Wealth Transfer Tax Anthology, Anderson Publishing (1997).

[37]   See Wheatcraft, "The Administrative Problems of a Wealth Tax", Brit. Tax Rev. 410–22 (1963).

[38]   Speaking more technically, it could be said that the net worth tax causes property to be converted to uses which return money income rather than imputed income, as only money income can be used to pay the tax. Thus, the old homestead, which gives a great deal of pleasure to its owners, might be sold out to be subdivided for a suburban development. Cf. A. Chekhov, The Cherry Orchard (1904).

[39]   See generally Annual Reports of Internal Revenue Service, and see Posin, Making Too Much of the Property Tax, Newsday, June 21, 1973, p. 62.

an exemption for the ill, elderly, and children. Though this tax sounds strange, there are some arguments in its favor. The law is simple. There would be almost no tax bar or tax accountants. No expensive treatises would be required to explain the law. (Wait, forget that. That's an argument against a head tax!) The bureaucracy needed for administering the law would be sharply reduced. The public would be spared the periodic Congressional agony over "tax reform." Reams of editorials on the subject would not be written.

Despite all these advantages, the head tax is ultimately unacceptable as an alternative to the income tax because of its extreme regressivity. The person with little (or no) income pays the same tax as the person making $1,000,000 a year. It might be suggested that a correction be made for levels of income. But that then converts the head tax into an income tax. Then arguments would be advanced to allow deductions for various expenses. The appeal of the head tax is its inflexibility. Once the door is opened to considering aspects of income, the whole structure of the income tax comes thundering in.

(d) Consumption or Cash Flow Tax

The concept of taxing consumption rather than income has a long and distinguished record of support from economists and lawyers concerned with taxation. This approach in essence involves taxing a base of income reduced by saving. At first blush it might appear that this approach is regressive, as in the case of a sales or value-added tax (see ¶ 1.02(2)(a)), since people in lower brackets allocate a greater percentage of their income to consumption than do people in higher brackets. However, a consumption type tax contemplates a steeply graduated rate structure, based on levels of annual consumption, so that the overall system can be quite progressive. Moreover, deductions and exemptions can be allowed for consumption of necessities. The consumption tax may appear unfair in that, for example, a person with an income of $100,000 who consumes $10,000 worth of goods and services and saves $90,000 will be taxed at the same level as a person with an income of $15,000 who consumes $10,000 and saves $5,000. However, a proponent of the consumption tax could answer that the two individuals are each enjoying the same standard of living and are thus fairly taxed at the same level. At such time as the high-income individual's savings are drawn down for consumption, that individual will be taxed upon it. Moreover, the proponents argue, the consumption tax encourages saving compared to the income tax, and increased saving has its own social benefits.[40]

(e) The "Flat Rate Tax"

Recently proposals have been made to have a "flat rate tax" system in place of the present system. The flat rate tax would involve having one flat rate tax, such as 20%, on all income rather than the present graduated bracket system. In addition, these proposals also contemplate doing away with many special deductions, exclusions, credits, and other special computations. (See ¶ 1.02(3)(b), relating to the Comprehensive Tax Base.)

It should be pointed out that the complexity of the Internal Revenue Code and the existence of a graduated bracket system are two independent issues. The complexity of the Internal Revenue Code does not arise from the existence of the graduated rate structure. The graduated rate structure takes only a few pages of the Internal Revenue Code to set forth. The other (1,000+) pages of the Internal Revenue Code are concerned with various special deductions, exclusions, credits, and other special computations that are designed in many cases to promote the fairness of the income tax. As just one example, the deduction for depreciation involves some complexity. Yet it would be manifestly unfair to tax the income from an asset without allowing some form of a deduction for the cost of that asset while it is being used. There are many examples of such necessary provisions, as illustrated throughout the pages of this book.

Nevertheless, it would be possible to simplify the Internal Revenue Code considerably. The favorable treatment of capital gains, as discussed in Chapter 4, by itself may account for one-third of the size of the Internal Revenue Code. There is, obviously, much room for improvement in reducing the complexity of the Internal Revenue Code. But the American economy is a sophisticated one, with a wide variety of complicated transactions to be taxed. It is unrealistic to expect that the income tax on such a sophisticated economy can be set forth in a one- or two-page statute, as some of the more

---

[40] The major modern economic work on this subject is N. Kaldor, An Expenditure Tax (1955). However, economists dating back to Alfred Marshall and John Stuart Mill (see J.S. Mill, Principles of Political Economy 545–46, Laughlin Ed.1884) have supported the idea. The application of this concept to the American tax system has been developed in Andrews, "A Consumption-Type or Cash Flow Personal Income Tax," 87 Harv.L.Rev. 1113 (1974). See also Graetz, "Implementing a Progressive Consumption Tax," 92 Harv.L.Rev. 1575 (1979); Warren, "Would a Consumption Tax Be Fairer Than An Income Tax?" 89 Yale L.J. 1081 (1980); Gunn, "The Case for an Income Tax," 46 Univ. of Chicago L.Rev. 370 (1979); McNulty, "Flat Tax, Consumption Tax, Consumption-Type Income Tax Proposals in the United States: A Tax Policy Discussion of Fundamental Tax Reform," 88 Cal. L. Rev. 2095 (2000).

enthusiastic proponents of flat rate tax proposals have suggested. Thus, wholesale simplification of the Internal Revenue Code is not possible if the variety of sophisticated transactions in the society are to be taxed in a rational fashion.

A second interesting aspect of flat rate tax proposals relates to the incidence of the income tax if such proposals were adopted. It is not at all clear who would pay more taxes and who would pay less if (1) the graduated rate structure were replaced by a single percentage flat rate of tax, and (2) a wide variety of special deductions, exclusions, credits and other special computations were eliminated. If the federal government is going to raise the same amount of revenue with a flat rate tax system as it raises under the present system, it is going to have to get the money from someplace. While a flat rate tax of, say, 20% may not sound very high, it will inevitably be imposed on a much broader base of income than is presently used. Thus, for example, if the deduction for interest on a home mortgage is eliminated; if Social Security payments are made fully taxable; if profits on the sale of a taxpayer's home are taxable no matter whether the taxpayer buys another home; and if medical expenses are not deductible, then that 20% rate on taxable income may produce a significantly higher tax burden for a large portion of the populace. The probable result of many flat tax proposals would be to lower the taxes paid by those in higher brackets and raise the taxes paid by those in middle and lower income brackets.[41] Whether that is a desirable result, and whether that is the result that is desired by the proponents of flat rate tax proposals are questions beyond the scope of this work.

(3) Problems with the Income Tax

Although the income tax is very likely here to stay, it could be improved. A number of criticisms have been advanced concerning the workings of the income tax. These criticisms raise a wide range of difficult problems. What the income tax does to the economy and how it might be improved are questions which have provoked a rich debate.

(a) Allocation of Resources: Imputed Income

At the loftiest level of discussion is the assertion that the income tax distorts the allocation of resources in the economy. The argument is that the income tax imposes a cost on income but not on leisure. So, people will tend to substitute leisure for work to an excessive degree. More generally, there is said to be a "deadweight loss" with

---

[41]   See Nordhaus, "A Proposed Flat Tax for Fat Cats," New York Times, Nov. 28, 1982, p. F3 (criticizing the flat tax proposal of Stanford University Economists Robert Hall and Alvin Rabushka).

regard to taxing money income and not imputed income. Here's an example of the argument:[42]

> *Example, deadweight loss caused by income tax:* Suppose that a paralegal can earn $50 per hour. That means that $50 per hour is the value that society places on the paralegal's services. If the paralegal's tax rate is, say, 40% (combined federal and state), the paralegal gets, after taxes, only $30 per hour. Suppose that a gardener charges $40 per hour. This is, again, the value that society places on those services. Assume that the paralegal can do gardening just as fast and efficiently as the gardener. The paralegal does not mind doing it—at least not any more than working overtime as a paralegal. Given the paralegal's after-tax income, the paralegal will be better off to do his or her own gardening. The paralegal only gets $30 per hour for working as a paralegal. So why should the paralegal work an extra hour at the office to earn $30 (after tax) in order to pay a gardener to work an hour at a cost of $40? The paralegal is better off not working overtime as a paralegal but rather gardening. Society is the loser, though. Society will pay the paralegal $50 an hour to work as a paralegal. But the paralegal does not choose to do it. Rather, the paralegal chooses to do work that society values at $40 per hour. This is the "deadweight loss" to society imposed by the income tax. So the argument goes. This is called the *substitution effect* brought on by the income tax. Activities generating nontaxable imputed income are substituted for activities generating taxable income. Thus the income tax discourages the paralegal from working as a paralegal.

> *Comment:* If the paralegal were also taxed on the imputed income of working in the garden (that's a good one—the IRS collects tax when you putter around in your begonias), then this distortion would not occur. The after-tax "income" from gardening would be 60% of $40 or $24. That $24 is less than what the paralegal gets after tax if the paralegal works in the office ($30). So the paralegal goes back to the office and hires the gardener.

> *Comment:* This analysis is all right as far as it goes. Unfortunately, it does not go far enough. In addition to the *substitution effect* described in the example, there is also something called an *income effect*. The income effect says the paralegal wants to maintain a certain level of income.

---

[42]   See, e.g., Posner, Economic Analysis of Law, 2d Ed. 373–374 (1977); cf. Aaron and Pechman Eds., How Taxes Affect Economic Behavior (Brookings, 1981).

So if the paralegal is taxed on the income from working at the office, the paralegal will work overtime to make up the difference. (Got to keep up those car payments.) Thus the income tax encourages working as a paralegal—the gardening doesn't make the car payments. The *income effect* might be as great or greater than the *substitution effect*. We don't know. As usual, in these theoretical discussions, there is no answer.

Also, if you really want to beat this discussion to death, there are many distortions in the economy in addition to the income tax: excise taxes, monopolies, license fees, collective bargaining agreements, tariffs, government price supports and subsidies. All of these (and there are many others) distort the true price of goods and services in the economy. They all therefore lead to a distortion in the allocation of resources of the economy. The important conclusion here is that it has been shown that elimination of one of these distortions, while the rest still remain, does not necessarily improve the allocation of resources in the economy and might well worsen it. *Thus if the distortions created by the income tax were eliminated but all of the other distortions remained, the allocation of resources in the economy would not necessarily be improved and might well be worsened.*[43]

Other similar criticisms of the income tax are fallacious for the same reason. For example, it is often asserted that the income tax distorts allocation of resources in the economy because it fails to tax the income from services of a spouse who stays at home and does not have formal employment. The argument is that the stay-at-home spouse is benefitting by doing her or her own housework and thus should be taxed on the fair value of that income. Such a tax would, it is argued, eliminate the distortion that is involved in taxing income

---

[43]   A full-fledged treatment of the subject of the allocation of resources in the economy is beyond the scope of this work, but putting the argument a little more technically: the economy is in an efficient condition when no resource can be reallocated and no product redistributed so as to make any one individual or business firm better off without making some other individual or business firm worse off. This is the condition of so-called Paretian Optimality, Pareto, Manuel d'Economie Politique (Paris: V. Giard and E. Briere, 1909). If there is one distortion, such as for example a tax on one commodity or an income tax, the Paretian conditions are not met, since relative prices of goods and services in the economy will not reflect their true economic price. Paretian optimality can only be reached by removal of the distortion. However, if there are *several* distortions in the economy and they cannot all be removed, removal of *one* of the conditions will not necessarily move the economy toward Paretian optimality, and may indeed worsen the situation. This result was demonstrated by Lipsey and Lancaster, "The General Theory of Second Best", 24 Rev.Econ. 11 (1956); and see also Stiglitz and Boskin, "Some Lessons from the New Public Finance", 67 Am.Econ.Rev. 295, 298 (1977); Baumol and Bradford, "Optimal Departures from Marginal Cost Pricing", 60 Am.Econ.Rev. 265–283 (1970). This conclusion illustrates the fallacy of "piecemeal welfare economics"—that is, suggesting that certain distortions in the economy should be removed because that will improve the allocation of resources in the economy, when in fact many distortions still remain in the economy.

received from an outside job and not taxing income arising from performing household services.[44] If the stay-at-home spouse were taxed on that income, though, then one would have to allow that spouse various deductions for expenses incurred in performing those services (cleaning supplies and such). A related problem is taxing the working spouse on earnings and not allowing deductions for paying for household help. The child care credit, discussed in Chapter 10, is an attempt to give some recognition to this problem, but it is inadequate. Again, since there are many distortions in the economy which interact with each other in complex ways, it cannot be said *a priori* that elimination of this particular distortion would improve the overall allocation of resources in the economy; indeed it might well worsen it.[45] Moreover, once one starts down the slippery slope of imputed income, it is difficult to know when to stop. Giving oneself a shave, painting one's porch, shining one's shoes, and doing one's own tax return all generate "income" in that sense. It is not to be expected that the Commissioner of Internal Revenue will be pushing the public to pay tax on these items any time soon.

This issue has policy implications. If the income tax is seen as truly a tax on all income, leading to distortions in the economy if all income is not reached, then great effort might be made to reach all income. Such efforts may raise severe administrative problems but it might be deemed worth undergoing these administrative problems to avoid any "distortion."[46]

---

[44]   See, e.g., Marsh, "The Taxation of Imputed Income", 58 Pol.Sci.Q. 514 (1943), Posner, note 16 supra at 374.

[45]   See Posner, supra note 9. In addition to the reasons advanced in the text for not taxing imputed income from household services, such a tax raises the practical problem of how it would be paid. Since the income the housewife generates from performing household services is not in monetary form, she could have difficulty coming up with the cash to pay the tax. One can easily imagine an outraged housewife faced with a $1,500 tax bill on the imputed income she received for doing her own housework—to satisfy some economist's idea about allocation of resources. She could well argue that if the Service is going to tax her on this kind of income, she can pay the same way, and she can offer to come down and sweep out the offices of the Internal Revenue Service once a month.

[46]   In this note we can say a little more about imputed income of owner-occupied housing. It is often urged that it should be taxed, because if the house were rented out, it would generate taxable rental income. By living in the house the owner receives tax-free rental income (i.e., his own rent that he pays to himself). Such imputed income, it is argued, should be taxed to eliminate the "distortion" in favor of owner-occupied housing over rental housing. See, e.g., Reforming the Federal Tax Structure, Commission to Revise the Tax Structure (Fund for Public Policy Research) 18 (1973). But taxing imputed rent raises the difficult problem of valuation and puts a burden on the taxpayer who does not have the cash to pay the tax. Moreover, if such a tax were imposed, one would also have to allow the homeowner to deduct his/her expenses of keeping the house up, such as maintenance and depreciation. The British imposed a tax on imputed income from owner-occupied housing until 1963, when the tax was abandoned due to difficulties presented in valuation. See Goode, The Individual Income Tax 121 (1964). Compare Helvering v. Independent Life Insurance Co., 292

However, once it is realized that the way the income tax is imposed cannot have great significance for the overall allocation of resources in the economy, the income tax can be seen for what it really is: a government device for raising revenues by taxing *some forms* of income. Those forms of income which are taxed are generally those which it is comparatively easy to reach, for example wages (which can be withheld against) and market transactions in property (which do not present problems of valuation or liquidity and which are reported). But any attempt to reach novel forms of income solely for the purpose of improving the overall allocation of resources in the economy seems futile and a waste of effort.[47]

(b) Comprehensive Tax Base

The preceding discussion has shown that allocation of resources in the economy is not helpful as a criterion for evaluating or improving the income tax. But can the criterion of fairness be usefully employed? It would seem reasonable to argue that people with about the same income should pay about the same tax, so-called *horizontal equity*.[48] But what is income? Unless it is possible to ascertain what constitutes income it is difficult to determine whether the income tax is fair.

Those who criticize the income tax as being unfair usually start with a list of items which seem clearly to constitute income but which are, for various reasons, exempted from tax. Examples of items exempted from tax include interest from municipal and state obligations, income earned from foreign sources by United States citizens living in foreign countries, much of social security and railroad retirement payments, and employee death benefits. All these

---

U.S. 371, 378–379, 54 S.Ct. 758, 759–760, 78 L.Ed. 1311 (1934) (*dicta* that taxing imputed income from owner-occupied housing is unconstitutional as being a direct tax requiring apportionment and not protected by the Sixteenth Amendment, Cf. ¶ 1.01).

[47] Attempts to improve the overall allocation of resources in the economy should be distinguished from attempts to use the tax system to encourage certain specific kinds of behavior. The former are futile for the reasons stated in the text. The latter, such as accelerated depreciation (see ¶ 6.02(120)), are effective in encouraging the desired activity for the very reason that they *do* distort the taxpayer's choice in favor of the desired activity. However, for the reasons stated above, such "distortions" do not necessarily worsen the overall allocation of resources in the economy; they may indeed improve it.

[48] It is also relatively reasonable to argue that the graduated rate structure is fair, that people with higher incomes should pay a greater percentage of that income to support the government. There are those, however, who would strongly disagree, see Friedman, Capitalism and Freedom 174 (1962). Cf. Blum and Kalven, The Uneasy Case for Progressive Taxation (1953); Steurle and Hartzmark, "Individual Income Taxation 1947–1979," 34 Nat'l Tax J. 145 (1981); Blum, "Revisiting the Uneasy Case for Progressive Taxation," 60 Taxes 16 (1982).

It would, however, be fallacious to argue that the progressive rate structure is undesirable because it distorts the allocation of resources in the economy. See the preceding discussion.

can be criticized as undermining the fairness of the tax system, since they all seem to constitute income.[49] Moreover, certain other items are treated favorably even though they do not escape taxation entirely, such as the variety of lower rates on long-term capital gains,[50] or delay in payment of tax on certain transactions in property.[51] Also some deductions—such as for rapid depreciation[52] or intangible drilling costs[53]—may be argued to be unjustifiably attractive. All of these are ways in which the income tax has been regarded by critics as unfair.[54]

However, the goal of creating a comprehensive tax base and imposing a tax on all income is virtually impossible to reach. There is, for example, a vast array of federal, state and local government programs which benefit many taxpayers and therefore constitute income to them in an economic sense. These are programs such as rent subsidies, road building and maintenance, Medicare and Medicaid protection, government guarantees of loans to businesses or individuals, government scholarships and fellowships, garbage collection and so on and on. Moreover, there are more public benefits, such as dams, providing cheap electric power, flood control, and recreation, as well as schools, public institutions of higher learning, libraries, and national defense. All of these confer benefits. All of these are income. But most of these are not likely subjects for imposition of tax, because to do so is either impossible or unpalatable.[55]

In addition, there are many other untaxed items of income, which do not emanate from the government: imputed income (the

---

[49]   The most widely accepted definition of income is the so-called Haig-Simons definition, which is: "Personal income may be defined as the algebraic sum of (1) the market value of rights exercised in consumption and (2) the change in the value of the store of property rights between the beginning and end of the period in question," H. Simons, Personal Income Taxation at 50, 61–62 (1938). Another way of stating it is to say that any item which increases the net worth of the taxpayer is income. If this approach were followed, a vast array of exclusions, exemptions and special deductions in the Code would be abolished.

[50]   See ¶ 4.06.

[51]   This would include unrealized appreciation in value of property held (see ¶ 4.02), stock received in corporate reorganizations (see §§ 368, 354, 355, 356, 351, D. Posin, Corporate Tax Planning: Takeovers, Leveraged Buyouts and Restructurings, Chapters 6–13, 1990, and certain other transactions in property see ¶ 4.05).

[52]   See ¶ 6.02(12).

[53]   See ¶ 6.02(13).

[54]   See Tax Revision Compendium of Papers on Broadening the Tax Base, House Committee on Ways & Means (1959); Blum, "Federal Income Tax Reform—Twenty Questions", 41 Taxes 672 (1963); Galvin, "Progress in Substantive Tax Reform", 1965 U.So.Cal.Tax Inst. 1; Blueprints for Basic Tax Reform (U.S. Treasury Dep't, 1977); Pechman, Federal Tax Policy (3rd Ed.1977).

[55]   See Bittker, "A 'Comprehensive Tax Base' As a Goal of Income Tax Reform", 80 Harv.L.Rev. 925 (1967).

rental value of consumer durables owned by the taxpayer, or services performed by the taxpayer for himself[56]), transfer payments from private charities or foundations, proceeds of life insurance,[57] gifts and bequests,[58] and appreciation in the value of assets that have not been sold.[59] Most of these too are unlikely candidates for imposition of tax because it would be unpalatable or impractical.[60]

Beyond even this there are non-pecuniary benefits in some jobs—e.g. the opportunity to be creative, or to exercise power—which are not taxed, although they may confer great psychic income. In contrast, the person who has a very unattractive or hazardous job and is paid a high wage to make up for it is fully taxed on that high wage.[61]

In view of all these considerations it seems impossible to create a truly fair income tax, which reaches *all* income, and which imposes the same tax on people with about the same income. Does this mean that any attempt to make the income tax more fair is futile? Is this situation like the question of allocation of resources in the economy? That is to say is there any guarantee that any single step taken to make the income tax more fair will not, through interactions too complex to trace, make it less fair? There seems to be no study that has answered this question.[62] It is possible that any one step taken to make the income tax more fair might make it less fair because of the sheer complexity of interactions in the system.[63]

Does this then mean that no attempt should be made to make the income tax more fair? Is fairness, like allocation of resources, not useful as a guide for acting on the income tax? There does seem to be a fundamental difference between allocation of resources and fairness. Allocation of resources in the economy is not of significance to the public. The public does not grasp that concept and is not interested in it. The public is, however, very interested and believes it understands fairness.[64] Since the success of the self-assessment

---

[56]   See R. Goode, The Individual Income Tax, 117–125 (revised edition 1976).

[57]   See ¶ 3.06 for proceeds of life insurance.

[58]   See ¶ 3.08.

[59]   See ¶ 4.02.

[60]   See Bittker, "A 'Comprehensive Tax Base' As a Goal of Income Tax Reform", 80 Harv.L.Rev. 925 (1967). Other problems, discussed by Bittker, with creating a comprehensive tax base include treatment of various deductions, the installment method of accounting, and the extent to which the tax system should take account of family relationships.

[61]   See Friedman, supra note 21, at 162.

[62]   Cf. Musgrave, "In Defense of an Income Concept," 81 Harv.L.Rev. 44 (1967).

[63]   See Bittker, "Comprehensive Income Taxation: A Response," 81 Harv.L.Rev. 1032, 1043 (1968), and see Bittker, "A 'Comprehensive Tax Base' As a Goal of Income Tax Reform", 80 Harv.L.Rev. 925, 985 (1967).

[64]   See e.g. P. Stern, The Rape of the Taxpayer (1972).

system ultimately depends on the confidence of the public that the income tax is roughly fair, that confidence must be maintained (or revived).

Therefore, steps to improve the apparent fairness (as opposed to improving the actual fairness which is perhaps impossible) of the income tax seem justified. The public is relatively easily satisfied in this matter. It does not demand that each person be taxed on his share of income from national defense. But the public may well demand that interest from state and municipal bonds be taxed or that tax shelters be limited.

As discussed in the preceding section, the income tax is a device for raising government revenues by taxing some forms of income: those that are relatively easily reached, visible, and relatively easily valued. Within that limited range of items of income there may be some items that seem unjustifiably exempt from taxation. They should be subject to tax to maintain the public's confidence in the system. That is why even though it is true that a comprehensive tax base cannot ultimately be achieved, those pressing for the changes in the income tax that concern the public are embarked on a worthwhile course.[65]

Public consensus as to what is fair is, therefore, the touchstone. Although there is a perfect system that imposes a tax on all income, that system is not reachable in this world. As to this world, Professor Boris Bittker seems right when he says, "(T)he income tax structure cannot be discovered, but must be constructed."[66] And it must be constructed by working through a number of controversial issues so that the appearance of fairness can be attained even though actual fairness probably cannot be reached.

(c) Tax Expenditures

An important aspect of the debate on the apparent fairness of the income tax is the concept of tax expenditures. The concept involves three components: (1) the regressive effect of deductions, exclusions and certain other provisions which benefit taxpayers; (2) compilation of a list of deductions, exclusions and other beneficial provisions which are not "necessary" to arriving at true taxable income; and (3) an estimate of revenue loss from these "unnecessary" provisions. Although proponents of the tax expenditure concept tend

---

[65]   Cf. Galvin, "More on Boris Bittker and the Comprehensive Tax Base: The Practicalities of the Tax Reform and the ABA's CSTR," 81 Harv.L.Rev. 1016 (1968).

[66]   Bittker, "A 'Comprehensive Tax Base' As a Goal of Income Tax Reform," 80 Harv.L.Rev. 925 (1967), at 985.

to advance these components together,[67] they can be regarded separately.

With respect to the first component, a clear contribution of the tax expenditure concept to the debate on the fairness of the income tax is highlighting the fact that deductions, exclusions and certain other favorable provisions are regressive in that they benefit those in higher brackets more than those in lower brackets. For example, suppose the maximum tax rate is 40%. If tax-exempt interest from a state or municipal bond (to take a favorite whipping-boy) in the amount of $100 is received by a taxpayer in the 40 percent bracket, that exemption has saved the taxpayer $40 in tax liability. If that same $100 of exempt interest is received by a taxpayer in the 15 percent bracket, the exemption has saved the taxpayer $15 in tax liability.

Moreover, the tax expenditure analysis would go further to make the point that this result is functionally equivalent to selling bonds with *taxable* interest but making available high yield bonds to taxpayers in high brackets and low yield bonds to taxpayers in low brackets. Thus if the interest on state and municipal bonds were taxable, the taxpayer in the 40 percent bracket would have to receive $167 of taxable interest to end up with $100 after taxes, whereas, the taxpayer in the 15 percent bracket would need to receive only $118 of taxable interest to wind up with $100 after taxes. If both taxpayers have bought a bond for $2,360, the taxpayer receiving $118 of interest has a 5 percent rate of return; the taxpayer receiving $167 of interest has a rate of return of 7 percent. This is, the proponents of the tax expenditure concept argue, a bizarre result and dramatizes the inequity of excluding state and municipal bond interest from taxation.

A similar analysis shows the regressive effect of deductions. Again, suppose a maximum tax rate of 40 percent. A deduction of $100 of home mortgage interest saves the taxpayer in the 40 percent bracket $40 in tax liability and saves the taxpayer in the 15 percent bracket $15 in tax liability. This is functionally equivalent to not allowing the deduction at all but paying a government subsidy to those with home mortgages. The terms of the hypothetical subsidy would be that those in high brackets get large subsidies and those in low brackets get low subsidies. Again, according to the proponents of the tax expenditures concept, this is a bizarre outcome.[68]

---

[67] See Surrey, "Tax Expenditures as a Device for Implementing Government Policy: A Comparison with Direct Government Expenditures," 83 Harv.L.Rev. 705 (1970); S. Surrey, Pathways to Tax Reform (1973).

[68] Id.

This analysis is correct and exceedingly interesting as far as it goes, but the question is what is to be done about it. This regressive effect arises inevitably from any exclusion or deduction because of the graduated rate structure. But as the discussion of the comprehensive tax base, supra, has demonstrated, it is impossible to include in taxable income all items of income in an economic sense. Imputed income from owner-occupied housing, income from unrealized appreciation in assets held, or income from national defense are, for various good reasons, not included as taxable income. Their exclusion also inevitably benefits those in high brackets more than those in low brackets. Thus, given a graduated rate structure, the only way to avoid completely the regressive effects described above is to impose a tax on a comprehensive base of all items of economic income (and to allow only the most narrowly defined business deductions). This is obviously an impossibility.

The proponents of the tax expenditure concept do not, however, advocate the elusive goal of a comprehensive tax base.[69] Rather, as the second component in the tax expenditure concept, they compile a list of *some* deductions, exclusions, and other provisions. Such a list is now published annually in The United States Government's Budget.[70] A sampling of just a few of the many items included on the list is exclusion of interest on state and municipal bonds, deductibility of interest on home mortgages, deductibility of charitable contributions, immediate deductions of research and development expenditures and so forth. The implication of such a compilation is to suggest that some of these provisions should be reconsidered and perhaps abolished in light of their regressivity.[71]

The problem with this list is that it is incomplete, as indeed it must be unless the proponents wish to support a comprehensive tax base. But the proponents of the tax expenditure concept explicitly do not wish to be viewed as advocating a comprehensive tax base. Since the list of tax expenditures is incomplete, it lacks the moral force that

---

[69]   For a very worthwhile exchange on this matter see Bittker, "Accounting for Federal 'Tax Subsidies' in the National Budget," 22 Nat'l Tax J. 244 (1969); Surrey and Hellmuth, "The Tax Expenditure Budget—Response to Professor Bittker," 22 Nat'l Tax J. 528 (1969); Bittker "The Tax Expenditure Budget—A Reply to Professors Surrey and Hellmuth," 22 Nat'l Tax J. 538 (1969).

[70]   As required by the Congressional Budget Act of 1974, Pub.L. 93–344, July 12, 1974; 88 Stat. 297. See also J. Pechman, Ed., Setting National Priorities: The 1979 Budget (Bookings 1978) 315–319; Congressional Budget Office Report, Tax Expenditures: Current Issues and Five Year Budget Projections.

[71]   In some cases, according to the proponents of the tax expenditure concept, the abolished exclusion or deduction could be replaced by a system of government subsidies which would accomplish the same goal as the exclusion or deduction without its regressive affect. See, e.g., McDaniel, "Federal Matching Grants for Charitable Contributions: A Substitute for the Income Tax Deduction," 27 Tax Law Rev. 377 (1972).

a list which purports to extirpate all regressive exclusions and deductions would have. Why then is the incomplete list compiled in the Budget or compiled by proponents of the tax expenditure concept better than any other list or, indeed, better than no list?[72]

The third component of the tax expenditure concept involves attaching dollar estimates of revenue loss to each of the tax expenditures listed. The items are broken down by the Budget into various categories, such as Commerce and Housing, Health, and National Defense. The theory of this tax expenditure budget is that it facilitates comparison of tax expenditure amounts with ordinary direct federal government expenditures for these same categories. The conclusion drawn is that the tax expenditure amounts are very large, sometimes equaling or even exceeding direct expenditures for these categories. Presumably the implication is that tax expenditures are a greater drain on the Treasury than is generally realized.

However, these dollar estimates of tax expenditures are arrived at under unrealistic assumptions: It is assumed that if income from an excluded activity were suddenly subject to tax, the activity would continue at the same level; it is also assumed that if deductible expenditures were suddenly not deductible they would continue unabated. These estimates also ignore the profound effect on the economy of removing all of these tax expenditures simultaneously. For all of these reasons the estimates of the revenue loss from the Budget's list of tax expenditures are probably greatly overstated.[73]

Although the Budget in a several-page discussion acknowledges these methodological shortcomings,[74] the dollar estimates continue to be published. One consequence of publishing such overstated estimates is that they tend to be picked up and used by popular writers who fail to understand the significance of the estimates.[75]

In summary, the tax expenditure concept is subject to some methodological complexity. Notwithstanding that, it is a tool that usefully highlights the effect of various tax provisions on the overall

---

[72]   See Andrews, "Personal Deductions in an Ideal Income Tax," 86 Harv.L.Rev. 309 (1972).

[73]   See e.g. Feldstein, "The Effects of the Charitable Deduction on Contributions: I and II", 28 Nat. Tax J. 81 and 209 (1975) for an analysis that suggests the Treasury's tax expenditure budget overestimates the revenue loss of the charitable contribution by more than 40 percent.

[74]   The Budget has in recent years attempted to correct for this problem.

[75]   See, e.g., Newfield and Greenfield, A Populist Manifesto 100 (1972); Cowan, "Washington and Business—Closer Look at Tax Loopholes," New York Times, January 26, 1978, p. D3. Cf. Bittker, "Tax 'Loopholes' and Political Rhetoric", 71 Mich.L.Rev. 1099 (1973) for a discussion of the effect on the public of the rhetoric of the tax expenditure debate.

budget process. The Budget's estimate of revenue loss attributable to tax expenditures is probably too large.[76]

(d) Complexity

One of the most outstanding features of the present income tax is its complexity. As indicated in ¶ 1.02(2),(3), this complexity arises from many forces: the fact that the income tax is imposed on a complex society, the impact of special interests, the impact of those who would "reform" the tax system, the impact of planners who would use the Code to foster "sociably desirable behavior," and the fact that the income tax is used as an instrument of national economic policy. Thus it is not surprising that the income tax is complex; it could not be otherwise.[77]

That is not to say that the Code need be this complex. Since the passage of the Tax Reform Act of 1986, where Congress simplified the tax code, Congress and the President have continued to add more and more provisions to the Code. Some of these are meritorious and others superfluous, but almost all of them have increased complexity. At the same time, those politicians often call for tax reform and tax simplification. Perhaps because of this duplicity, few think meaningful simplification is on the horizon.

(e) Recovery of Capital: A Major Theme in the Field

(i) Methods of Recovering Capital

One of the major problems running throughout the field of federal income taxation is the problem of allowing a taxpayer to recover his initial investment in an enterprise before taxing him on the profits from it. This sounds like a simple problem, but in fact it is of immense dimension. If you can see it whole and recognize the problem every time it crops up, that will help you a great deal.

Consider the problem with the following example: Taxpayer Matilda purchases a single premium life annuity. She pays $200,000

---

[76]   See in addition to the other materials cited, Woodworth, "General Policy Considerations Affecting the Choice of a Particular Tax Base," 30 National Tax Journal 225 (1977); Uilman, "Tax Policy" 29 Nat'l Tax J. 2 (1976); Thower "Preserving the Integrity of the Federal Tax System," 33 NYU Institute on Federal Taxation 707 (1975); Congressional Budget Office, Tax Expenditures: Five Year Budget Projections for Fiscal Years 1982–1986 (1981). For a very effective defense of the tax expenditure concept and description of its uses, see Surrey and McDaniel "The Tax Expenditure Concept: Current Developments and Emerging Issues," 20 Bost.Coll., Ind. & Comm'l Law Rev. 225 (1979); see also Kahn, "Accelerated Depreciation—Tax Expenditure or Proper Allowance for Measuring Net Income," 78 Mich.L.Rev. 1 (1979); Cohen, "Tax Expenditures in Troubled Times: The Failure of Tax Incentives for Low Income Housing," 30 Univ. of S.Cal.L.Instit. on Fed'l Taxation 971 (1978).

[77]   See Samuel A. Donaldson, "The Easy Case Against Tax Simplification," 22 Va. Tax Rev. 645 (2003).

for it when she is 65 years old. The terms of the annuity are that she immediately begins receiving annual payments from it for her lifetime. The payments will be based on the taxpayer's life expectancy at age 65. Let us say that is 20 years—so that the taxpayer is expected to live to 85.[78] The payments made for 20 years will be made out of this $200,000 fund. As the payments are made, the amounts remaining in the fund will grow at 9% per year compounded. This is an after-tax interest rate.[79] A computer (not you in the coffee room) can calculate the annual payment each year that will exhaust the fund after 20 years though the remaining amounts in the fund continue to grow as the payments are made. That annuity payment so calculated is $20,100 per year.

Let us say, to keep the facts simple, that Matilda dies right on her 85th birthday. Thus the payments go for exactly 20 years.[80] Here is an interesting point: What is the total amount Matilda receives under this arrangement? Obviously it is 20 times $20,100 or $402,000. She puts in $200,000. She starts getting payments immediately and ultimately she gets a total of $402,000. Where does the extra money come from? As pointed out above, while she is getting payments, the money remaining in the account is growing. Now we get a tax question (at last).

Here is our question: How do we deduct the $200,000 cost of this transaction against the $402,000 payoff? The taxpayer has made an investment here and it has turned a profit. She put in $200,000 and when she reaches age 85, the deal finally pays off a total of $402,000. Therefore it is a profit of $202,000. If we assume a tax rate of 40%, we have a tax due on this deal of 40% of $202,000 profit or $80,800 tax. *When* we deduct the cost will not affect the overall amount of tax. The profit is always going, ultimately, to be $202,000 taxed at a 40% rate. *When* we deduct the cost will, however, affect the timing of when we pay the $80,800 tax. As we know from the discussion of the time

---

[78]   It is true that the life expectancy of a female when she is born is about 77. However, once the female reaches 65, the life expectancy stretches out somewhat.

[79]   The after-tax rate is assumed here in order to keep the numbers straightforward for purposes of the discussion. It can sometimes be the case that amounts set aside in this fashion will compound at the pre-tax rate, if they are in a pension fund for example.

[80]   In a life annuity what the annuitant buys is a guarantee that the payments will go for his or her life, whatever that lifespan may prove to be. The insurance companies calculate the amount of the payment based on mortality tables. Thus if Matilda lived longer than 20 years she would continue to receive payments and get what is known in the business as a "mortality gain." If she died in less than 20 years she would undergo a "mortality loss." So that we do not fog up the discussion in the text with this, let us assume she lives her exact statistical life expectancy. For a complete discussion of annuities, see Chapter 3. See also the discussion of the *Drescher* case in Chapter 2.

value of money in the introduction, *when* that $80,800 is paid has major dollar implications for the taxpayer.

Let us consider the various possibilities for deducting the cost of this annuity. The payments are coming in every year for 20 years. They are therefore presumptively taxable in full unless the taxpayer is taking a deduction of the cost of the deal to offset some or all of the payment received. So how should we time the deductions of the cost of the annuity? The theoretical possibilities are:

1)   Allow the deduction of the entire cost immediately upon entering into the deal: *Immediate Deduction or "Expensing"*;[81]

2)   Allow the deductions up to the amount received on the deal each year (until the full cost of the deal has been deducted) then tax the remaining payments in full: *Open Treatment* (see also ¶ 8.03 discussing the *Logan* case);

3)   Prorate the deduction of the cost of the premium over the 20 years that the annuity pays out: *Installment Treatment*;

4)   Take the deduction at the end of the 20 years after the payout has stopped: *Stupid Treatment.*

Comment: The last approach is stupid because there is no really good reason to require the recovery of cost at the end of the 20 year period.[82] We mention it because it actually provides a basic insight into what is going on in the deal.

5)   Attribute most of the early payments to taxable interest and a small amount to non-taxable principal, with these amounts gradually altering in proportion over the term of the annuity: *Loan Amortization Treatment*. This is like a basic home mortgage. This treats the premium payment as though it were a loan from Matilda to the insurance company. It certainly looks like a loan, with the

---

[81]   We use the term "expensing" to indicate that the cost of the deal is treated as an "expense," which is to say it is immediately deductible. This is contrasted with a "capital expenditure" which is not immediately deductible (it is "capitalized"). The deduction of the capital expense may then be spread out over time (see Chapter 6).

[82]   The taxation of corporate dividends often follows the Stupid Treatment. When dividends are paid, they are often taxed in full, although for taxable years 2003–2008 at a preferential rate, with no offsetting deduction of basis. Only when the stock is sold is the cost or basis of the stock deducted from the amount realized on the sale: this constitutes Stupid Treatment. However, corporate distributions of cash to shareholders are not always taxed when paid. The distributions are only taxed if they are "out of" earnings and profits of the company. If the distribution occurs when the company has no earnings and profits, it is treated as a recovery of capital and not taxed. §§ 301(c), 312, 316.

insurance company undoubtedly paying Matilda back interest and principal.

6) Deem the present value of each payment at the beginning of the transaction to be its cost. Deduct that cost from the full amount of each payment as it comes in: *Economically Accurate Treatment*. This method is a sophisticated method carrying present value analysis to its extreme conclusion. It is by far the most economically accurate method. Naturally no one dreams of using it.

For pedagogical reasons we consider these methods in a particular order. Let us look first at alternative number 4), *Stupid Treatment*. The reason this treatment is stupid is that there is really no tax principle that justifies it. If the cost is paid at the beginning of the deal, and amounts are received over 20 years from the deal, then there is no reason to defer the deduction until the end of the deal. Nevertheless, *Stupid Treatment* helps us to understand the problem of recovery of capital. So let us see what happens under it.

There is, as we have calculated, a $202,000 gain at the end of the transaction. If we (stupidly) take the deduction for the cost of the transaction at the end of the deal, then Matilda will be taxable in full on each of the $20,100 payments as they come in each year. At a 40% rate, that produces a tax on each payment of $8,040. Thus the net cash flow is $20,100 − $8,040 = $12,060 each year. In the 20th year, Matilda also gets a $200,000 deduction, which saves her $80,000 in taxes.[83] Note that the total amount of taxes Matilda pays is still the same $80,800 that we calculated before. Matilda is paying tax of $8,040 for 20 years or $160,800. Matilda then saves $80,000 in taxes the last year so that her net tax is $160,800 − $80,000 = $80,800.

Let us now consider then what happens to Matilda on a *cash-flow basis* under *Stupid Treatment*. On a cash-flow basis, she gets $12,060 a year (after taxes) for 20 years. In the 20th year she gets $80,000 (from taxes saved). So what is the present value of this deal to Matilda? It is clearly the present value of $12,060 per year for 20 years plus the present value of $80,000 twenty years from now. All of this is calculated at our assumed interest rate of 9%. Firing up the computer, we find that the present value of $12,060 per year for 20 years is $120,000. The present value of $80,000 twenty years from now is $14,300. Thus, the total *present value* of *Stupid Treatment* is

---

[83] · This assumes that Matilda has enough other income that she remains in the 40% marginal bracket even after taking this large deduction. The astute reader may also point out that in the 20th year that deduction of $200,000 more than offsets the $20,100 of income in that year. That is true and for computational purposes we could treat the 20th year as a net deduction of $179,900. However it is mathematically the same to treat the two cash flows separately and it is clearer conceptually to do so.

$120,000 + $14,300 = $134,300. Let's see how that compares to some of our other possibilities.

Let us next take alternative number 3), prorating the deduction of the cost of the premium over the 20 years that the annuity pays out: *Installment Treatment*. Unlike *Stupid Treatment*, prorating has good logic behind it. It involves matching the deductions of the deal over time with the income of the deal over time.[84] To do that, we divide $200,000 by 20 years, which gives us $10,000 per year. We subtract that $10,000 from the $20,100 annual payment. This yields us a taxable gain of $10,100 per year.[85] And what is the tax Matilda pays? That is 40% of $10,100 or $4,040. Let's just keep checking ourselves. What is $4,040 times 20—i.e. the annual tax times the number of years it is paid? Turns out it is $80,800. So Matilda is still paying the same amount in tax as in *Stupid Treatment*.

Let's take a look at the *cash flow* results of the *Installment Treatment*. This one is easy to do; as a cash matter Matilda is receiving $20,100 per year less a tax of $4,040 per year. Thus the net cash flow per year is $20,100 − $4,040 = $16,060 per year. What is the present value of that? The *present value* of $16,060 per year for 20 years is $159,800. This is substantially more than the $134,300 of *Stupid Treatment*.

Let us now look at alternative 2), allow the deductions up to the amount received on the deal each year (until the full cost of the deal has been deducted): *Open Treatment*.[86] What this means is that as the $20,100 comes in each year, the $200,000 basis or cost of the annuity is taken against each $20,100 until the $200,000 is exhausted. After the $200,000 cost is exhausted, there is of course no more deduction. The effect is that there is no tax at all on the earlier payments until the $200,000 cost deduction is exhausted. The $200,000 taken against the $20,100 per year means that for the first 9 years there is no tax on the $20,100 per year. After 9 years $180,900 of the $200,000 is exhausted. Thus $19,100 is left to apply to the $20,100 in the tenth year. Applying that means that $1,000 in the tenth year is subject to tax. The tax is 40%. Thus after nine years of tax-free receipt of $20,100 payments there is a $400 tax in the tenth

---

[84]   In the major area of depreciation, we see the installment or proration method being used. It is called straight line depreciation. So-called accelerated depreciation is a variation of the proration method except that the deductions are "front-loaded" using various formulas (see Chapter 6). See also ¶ 8.03 on deferred payment sales, which is in effect what we are talking about here.

[85]   Just to check our work, we find that a profit of $10,100 per year for 20 years = 20 × $10,100 = $202,000. So we have got the right amount of profit.

[86]   "Open Treatment," especially for property sold for payments to be received in the future, has historically been a part of the tax law, although it is not widely used today. See Chapter 8, and the discussion there of Burnet v. Logan, 283 U.S. 404, 51 S.Ct. 550, 75 L.Ed. 1143 (1931).

year. In years 11 through 20 the payments are taxed in full. Thus in years 11 through 20, the tax is 40% of $20,100, or $8,040. Thus the after tax payments received in years 11 through 20 are $20,100 − $8,040 = $12,060. Let us check on the total amount of tax paid. It is $400 plus 10 × $8,040. That is $400 + $80,400 = $80,800. So once again we are on the money with the same amount of tax being paid as in the other above alternatives.

Let us look at the *cash flow* results of the *Open Treatment*. For the first 9 years, Matilda pays no tax on the $20,100 payments received, so there is $20,100 for years 1 through 9. In year 10 the net cash flow is the $20,100 less the $400 tax or $19,700. In years 11 through 20 the net after tax cash flow as computed in the preceding paragraph is $12,060. The *present value* of this stream of cash payments is $161,500. This is more interesting than you might think. Since the open treatment involves more up-front deductions than the prorated treatment it produces a more attractive result. But the difference is not great. It is only about $1,700 on our numbers. This is only 0.8% of the profit on the deal. The tax on that at the 40% rate is only 0.32% of the deal. This minor difference is not due to anything odd in our numbers. Rather, the reason that the difference is not that great is that the two methods are rather similar in pattern even though they are very different in concept. Both methods just spread out the cost deduction. They just do so in modestly different ways.

What makes this interesting is that the Service and the statute require the much more complex installment method to be used on transactions such as the sale of property for payments to be received over time (see Chapter 8). The conventional wisdom is that the open treatment is much more favorable to taxpayers than the installment method. In fact, our present value analysis demonstrates that the difference between the two methods is not very large. In that event, given the great complexity of the installment method of reporting gain on sales of property for future payments, it is questionable whether the increase in tax revenue to the fisc gained by using the installment method is worth the cost of increased complexity.[87]

Let us turn to alternative 1), allow the deduction of the cost immediately upon entering into the deal: *Immediate Deduction or "Expensing."* Under this method, Matilda deducts $200,000 the year she acquires the policy. This $200,000 deduction saves her 40% of that amount or $80,000 in taxes right away. Having then deducted her full cost, she pays tax in full on the 20 payments.[88]

---

[87]   For further discussion of the installment method, see ¶ 8.03(2).

[88]   As in the case of the last year of *Stupid Treatment* we treat the deduction and the payment as separate items to keep the discussion simpler. This approach does not affect the results. Matilda's ability to save $80,000 in taxes from a $200,000 deduction

From a *cash flow* standpoint, here is how *Immediate Deduction* shakes out. In the first year there is $80,000 from tax savings. Also in years 1 through 20 there is a payment of $20,100 which is subject to a 40% tax. As we have calculated, that tax is $8,040. Thus the after-tax cash flow with respect to the annual payments is $20,100 − $8,040 = $12,060, as we have calculated before. Thus the *present value* of this deal equals $80,000 plus the present value of $12,060 per year for 20 years, with a 9% interest rate. That turns out to be $80,000 + $120,000. The total is $200,000, substantially more than any of the other methods. This shows the attractiveness of an early deduction.

We now move to some more sophisticated approaches. Let us look at alternative 5), attribute most of the early payments to taxable interest and a small amount to non-taxable principal, with these amounts gradually altering in proportion over the term of the annuity: *Loan Amortization Treatment*. This is the familiar home mortgage or car mortgage schedule. Matilda is in effect the lender here. Most of what Matilda receives in the early years is taxable interest. The following table shows how this looks. Notice in particular the heavy amount of early income Matilda has. The repayment of principal by the insurance company to her is her basis or cost, which is not taxed. Notice that all the basic numbers are still the same: Cost, Profit, Tax Paid. The only thing different is present value because of the timing of the tax paid depending on the method of cost recovery.

---

depends, of course, on the fact that she has enough other income that she is still in the 40% bracket even after such a huge deduction.

LOAN AMORTIZATION METHOD OF RECOVERY OF COST OF SINGLE PREMIUM 20-YEAR ANNUITY @ 9% INTEREST RATE

Year of Payment	Years from Present	Payment	Interest Paid at 9% on Principal	Principal Paid (Payment − Interest)	Remaining Principal at End of Year	Tax @ 40% of Interest Income	Net Cash Flow Payment Tax	Present Value of Net Cash Flow
1	0	$20,100	$16,191	$3,909	$200,000	$6,476	$13,624	$13,624
2	1	$20,100	$15,839	$4,261	$196,091	$6,336	$13,765	$12,628
3	2	$20,100	$15,456	$4,644	$191,829	$6,182	$13,918	$11,714
4	3	$20,100	$15,037	$5,063	$187,185	$6,015	$14,085	$10,877
5	4	$20,100	$14,582	$5,518	$182,122	$5,833	$14,267	$10,107
6	5	$20,100	$14,085	$6,015	$176,604	$5,634	$14,466	$9,402
7	6	$20,100	$13,544	$6,556	$170,588	$5,418	$14,683	$8,755
8	7	$20,100	$12,954	$7,146	$164,032	$5,182	$14,919	$8,161
9	8	$20,100	$12,311	$7,789	$156,886	$4,924	$15,176	$7,616
10	9	$20,100	$11,610	$8,490	$149,097	$4,644	$15,456	$7,116
11	10	$20,100	$10,845	$9,255	$140,606	$4,338	$15,762	$6,658
12	11	$20,100	$10,013	$10,087	$131,351	$4,005	$16,095	$6,237
13	12	$20,100	$9,105	$10,995	$121,264	$3,642	$16,458	$5,851
14	13	$20,100	$8,115	$11,985	$110,268	$3,246	$16,854	$5,498
15	14	$20,100	$7,037	$13,063	$98,283	$2,815	$17,285	$5,173
16	15	$20,100	$5,861	$14,239	$85,220	$2,344	$17,756	$4,875
17	16	$20,100	$4,579	$15,521	$70,981	$1,832	$18,269	$4,601
18	17	$20,100	$3,182	$16,918	$55,459	$1,273	$18,827	$4,351
19	18	$20,100	$1,660	$18,440	$38,541	$664	$19,436	$4,120
20	19	$20,100	$0	$20,100	$20,101	$0	$20,100	$3,909
Totals			$202,006	$200,000				$151,274

Let us turn finally to alternative 6), deem the present value of each payment at the beginning of the arrangement to be its cost. Deduct that cost from each payment as it comes in: *Economically Accurate Treatment*. Here's the deal. Matilda paid $200,000 for the annuity. The annuity is worth $200,000 at the time it is purchased. Its value, like the value of any investment, grows over time. We therefore allocate the $200,000 over the 20 payments to be received in the future. That gives each payment to be received in the future. Then as we receive each payment we would deduct that cost or basis allocated to each payment to get the net profit on each payment. So far this sounds like the prorated or installment method above. But the cost is calculated differently. The payments to be received in years 1 through 20 each have a different present value. Therefore, we need to ascertain the present value of each payment of $20,100. (Their total present value will add up to $200,000—since that is what we paid for the policy and that is what the payments are presently worth in total). We then deduct that present value from each payment as it eventually comes in. That difference gives us the taxable income associated with each payment. We then apply the 40% tax rate to each amount of taxable income, giving us the tax associated with each payment. We subtract that tax from the face amount of each payment and that gives us the net after-tax amount of each payment. We then ascertain the present value of each after-tax amount and sum them. That sum gives us the present value of the deal. This is all done in the table below.

ECONOMICALLY ACCURATE RECOVERY OF COST OF SINGLE PREMIUM 20-YEAR ANNUITY @ 9% INTEREST RATE

Years Left	Payment	Present Value or Cost of Payment	Income: Payment— Cost	Tax @ 40% of Income	Net Cash Flow: Payment— Tax	Present Value of Net Cash Flow
19	$20,100	$3,909	$16,191	$6,476	$13,624	$2,650
18	$20,100	$4,261	$15,839	$6,336	$13,764	$2,918
17	$20,100	$4,644	$15,456	$6,182	$13,918	$3,216
16	$20,100	$5,063	$15,037	$6,015	$14,085	$3,548
15	$20,100	$5,518	$14,582	$5,833	$14,267	$3,917
14	$20,100	$6,015	$14,085	$5,634	$14,466	$4,329
13	$20,100	$6,556	$13,544	$5,418	$14,682	$4,789
12	$20,100	$7,146	$12,954	$5,182	$14,918	$5,304
11	$20,100	$7,789	$12,311	$4,924	$15,176	$5,881
10	$20,100	$8,490	$11,610	$4,644	$15,456	$6,529
9	$20,100	$9,255	$10,845	$4,338	$15,762	$7,257
8	$20,100	$10,087	$10,013	$4,005	$16,095	$8,077
7	$20,100	$10,995	$9,105	$3,642	$16,458	$9,003
6	$20,100	$11,985	$8,115	$3,246	$16,854	$10,049
5	$20,100	$13,063	$7,037	$2,815	$17,285	$11,234
4	$20,100	$14,239	$5,861	$2,344	$17,756	$12,579
3	$20,100	$15,521	$4,579	$1,832	$18,268	$14,107
2	$20,100	$16,918	$3,182	$1,273	$18,827	$15,846
1	$20,100	$18,440	$1,660	$664	$19,436	$17,831
0	$20,100	$20,100	$0	$0	$20,100	$20,100
Totals		$200,000	$202,000			**$169,164**

The payments that are furthest away in time (i.e. 19 years left) have the smallest present value ($3,909.) They therefore are allocated the lowest basis ($3,909). When time passes and they are finally paid, there will be the largest amount of income in the year of payment ($16,191).

Thus the economically accurate method involves only a small amount of taxable income in the early years, increasing as time goes on and later payments in the schedule are made.

This is the economically accurate way to recover the cost of this investment. It shows the present value of the investment to be different from any of the other methods used. It is unquestionably the economically accurate way to handle transactions with payments to be received in the future, whether annuities or any other kind of investment. Does anyone seriously suggest actually using this method? No, naturally. Why not? It might be because it's too complicated, but since when has that ever been a barrier to enacting provisions into the Internal Revenue Code? If you're going to have a complicated Code, you at least ought to get the answers right.

Note the symbiotic relationship between the economically accurate method and the loan amortization method. Observe that the column in the loan amortization method labeled "interest paid" has the same numbers in it as the column in the economically accurate method labeled "income = payment – cost." In both cases that is what is taxed to the annuitant. But there is one major difference. In the loan amortization method the big numbers start in the early years and go down to the small amounts in the later years. This hits the annuitant with taxes earlier than in the economically accurate method. In the economically accurate method, the amounts start with the small amounts in the early years and go up to the large amounts in the later years. They are the same numbers all the way; they just occur in the opposite order.[89] This can be seen by looking at the column on the left of each chart referencing "years left" in the economically accurate method and "years from present" in the loan amortization method. The numbers are in opposite order.

Thus a sideline result that cranks out of this analysis is that the usual method in the financial community for amortizing home mortgages and other loans (as exemplified by our loan amortization model) is not correct. The payor of a home mortgage (as represented by the insurance company in our example) or a homeowner in a home mortgage should be paying small amounts of deductible interest in the early years, with these deductible amounts gradually rising. This is clearly shown by the economically accurate method.

Another effect of this analysis is to put at least a second nail into the coffin of the installment method of reporting gain. The installment method is complicated. We have already shown that it

---

[89] A technical note: for the convenience of readers who may be using their own computers or amortization tables to check our numbers, we have assumed throughout this discussion of the recovery of capital methods that payments are made at the beginning of the period for which they are attributable rather than at the end of the period. The usual approach for loan amortization is to figure that payments are made at the end of the period. We wanted, however, to have the loan amortization approach to be consistent with the other methods of recovering capital, where we used the beginning of the period. Paying at the beginning rather than the end of the period changes the numbers somewhat but in no way affects the principle being discussed.

does not give a much different answer from the much simpler open treatment. Now we also see that the installment method (whose claim to fame at least was that it was accurate) does not give the right answer either. As a matter of fact, at least on these numbers, the Open Treatment comes closer to the Economically Accurate Treatment than does the Installment Treatment.

It is important to get the right answer for the present value of the arrangement. This is so taxpayers may correctly view their investment choices, without having their choices distorted by the tax rules.

The table below compares the method of recovering basis and the present value of the annuity.

Comparison of Basis Recovery Methods for $200,000 Premium 20-Year Life Annuity at 9% Annual Interest Compounded.

Total Amount Deducted in Each Case $200,000; Total Profit in Each Case $202,000; Total Tax Paid in Each Case $80,800

Method	Present Value
Immediate Deduction	$200,000
Open Treatment	161,500
Installment Treatment	159,800
Loan Amortization	151,274
Stupid Treatment	134,300
Economically Accurate	169,164

In tax, as in figure skating, timing is everything. Verify for yourself the fact that as the deduction of the cost of the premium is deferred more and more, the present value of the deal to the annuitant goes down.

You will see these methods used (except for the Economically Accurate Treatment) throughout the field of federal income taxation. Note that Stupid Treatment is notable for grossly discouraging investment in this transaction.

As pointed out in the footnote accompanying discussion of Stupid Treatment above, corporate dividends are often taxed according to

Stupid Treatment. This discourages investment in corporate stock. For example, suppose a taxpayer were faced with the choice of investing in either an annuity with the numbers above, or dividend-paying blue chip corporate stock with the same numbers (i.e. $20,100 dividends per year with little risk). The taxpayer would choose the annuity just because the basis recovery rule is unfavorable for corporate stock dividends. Is this the way to encourage investment in corporate America?[90]

When you see cost or basis being deducted in this field, be aware which of these methods is being used.[91]

(ii) Application to Easements: Inaja Land

Let us apply the principles we have supposedly learned in the preceding section to the issues presented by the case of *Inaja Land.*

INAJA LAND CO. V. COMMISSIONER[92]

Facts: In 1928, the taxpayer, a stock corporation, bought 1,236 acres of land together with water rights for $61,000. The land had a stream and was located on the banks of the Owens River in Mono County, California. The land was acquired by taxpayer to be used as a private fishing club. In 1940, as part of a water project, the City of

---

[90] It might be argued that corporate stock is not a "wasting asset," the way an annuity is. That is, corporate stock has a perpetual existence. So that after 20 years the annuity stops paying out whereas the corporate stock continues to pay dividends. Thus, it could be argued that Stupid Treatment is correct for corporate stock, since until the taxpayer sells the stock we do not know for how long it will produce dividends for him. That argument, while superficially appealing, does not really stand up. We do not know how long an annuitant with a life annuity will live, yet we have no trouble using mortality tables to ascertain how to apply the proration or installment method to annuities (see Chapter 3). By the same token we do not know how long a taxpayer will hold the corporate stock but it is safe to say he will not hold it after he dies. Thus we could use literally the same mortality tables for calculating cost recovery for corporate stock as we do for annuities. Or better yet we could use the Economically Accurate Treatment for both. It might be objected to these approaches that the corporate stock continues in existence after the stockholder dies, whereas the annuity expires with him. Thus the corporate stock's basis should continue in the hands of the heirs. However, the heirs of the holder of corporate stock take a new basis of the fair market value of the stock when the decedent dies (see Chapter 4). This new basis in the hands of the heirs has nothing to do with the basis of the stock in the decedent's hands; thus the basis rule we use for the decedent has no effect on the basis of the stock in the hands of the heir. This same analysis could be applied—if we wanted to make economic sense—to any other nonwasting assets, such as undeveloped land. Also, when you combine this treatment of dividends with the stringent rules against deducting net capital losses (see ¶ 4.06(1)), you have tax rules that severely discourage investment in the stock market.

A great deal of the disincentive to invest in corporate stock is taken away by the capital gains rules, which tax gains on the sale of corporate stock, among some other assets, at an attractively low rate, see ¶ 4.06.

[91] This analysis feeds directly into the discussion of depreciation, at ¶ 6.02(12).

[92] 9 T.C. 727 (1947), acq. 1948–1 C.B. 2. See also Rev.Rul. 70–510, 1970–2 C.B. 159.

Los Angeles built a tunnel that diverted contaminated water into the Owens River upstream of the taxpayer, rendering taxpayers's land unusable for fishing. Taxpayer threatened to sue, and the city paid $50,000 for a perpetual easement to divert waters into the Owens River. The taxpayer incurred $1,000 in legal fees.

Question: Is the net $49,000 settlement amount received taxable income in full or does taxpayer's basis offset or eliminate part of the gain?

Service's arguments: 1) The net $49,000 is compensation for lost present or future income and consideration for release of many meritorious actions against city. Hence the $49,000 is ordinary income. 2) Taxpayer did not allocate the proceeds between taxable and nontaxable income (it did not allocate any of its basis against the $49,000 of income), so it failed to meet its burden to show error.[93]

Taxpayer's arguments: 1) The language of the instrument and circumstances show that the consideration was for an easement. Loss of present or future income was not considered. 2) Character of easement renders it impractical to apportion basis to it. Since sum received is less than basis of property the entire amount should be excluded from tax.

Held: Judgement in favor of taxpayer. 1) The payment was for an easement. 2) Since on these facts apportionment of basis is not possible, the full amount of payment is excluded from income.

Comment: Under the court's holding, taxpayer's basis in his property would be reduced by $49,000, since that amount of basis would have been used to offset the payment.

Based on our extensive discussion above, which method of cost recovery is used here? Answer: Open Treatment. Take the basis against payments as they are received.[94] No income until (and unless) basis is recovered in full. *Inaja Land* comes in for a lot of criticism for a failure to apportion just part of the basis against the $49,000 and have some of the $49,000 be income. But, as our discussion above has shown, open treatment is not always unreasonable. In this instance, however, open treatment may provide for indefinite or at least long-term tax deferral. Why is that so here

---

[93]   Prior to the IRS Reform and Restructuring Act, P.L. 105–206, taxpayer had the burden of proving that the Commissioner's determination was false. As part of the RRA, the burden of proof in civil tax cases was shifted from the taxpayer to the IRS in certain circumstances. See § 7482. This provision makes no sense in that the taxpayer is the party with all the information. In at least slight recognition of this point, the provision, only applies if the taxpayer has "fully cooperated" with the IRS during audit and internal IRS appeals.

[94]   Indeed the court cited the leading open treatment case, Burnet v. Logan, 283 U.S. 404, 51 S.Ct. 550, 75 L.Ed. 1143 (1931), discussed and graphed at ¶ 8.03.

and not in the annuity example discussed above? The reason is that here, there is no continued income stream. Inaja Land will only receive additional proceeds if its sells the property. Thus, under *Inaja Land* the result is no tax until some indefinite time in the future. Since Inaja Land must reduce its basis by the $49,000 received, it will have to pay tax on its gain when it sells the property. But if Inaja Land holds on to the property, the gain will never be taxed.

What approach was the Commissioner arguing for? Stupid Treatment. Everything is income first. Take a deduction for full basis when (and if) the property is sold. Note that the numbers are all the same here. There's $49,000 of receipts and a basis of $61,000. This is a fight about timing.

(f) Inflation: Kerbaugh-Empire

A hallmark of modern industrial society is inflation, either low-grade or sometimes rampant. Without presenting you with a treatise on the subject it can be said that the causes of inflation appear to relate to the fact that wages and prices are "sticky downward." Workers do not like to take pay cuts. Monopolistic or oligopolistic businesses may be able to resist price cuts. Large government budget deficits pump too much money into the economy. Whatever the reasons, we've got inflation, in varying degrees at varying times. What impact, if any, does that have on the federal income tax system?

There was actually a case that explored that problem, albeit inadvertently. That case was *Kerbaugh-Empire Co.*

BOWERS V. KERBAUGH-EMPIRE CO.[95]

Facts: Kerbaugh-Empire borrows money in U.S. dollars from a German bank. Under the agreement, Kerbaugh-Empire must pay the loan back in German marks. Kerbaugh-Empire then invested the money in a losing venture. While Kerbaugh-Empire held the loan, the value of marks relative to the dollar dropped. Kerbaugh-Empire thus made money, in a sense, by playing the currency market. Although Kerbaugh-Empire made a profit on the loan repayment, it lost more money on the venture than it gained in the currency transaction.

Question: Did Kerbaugh-Empire have income on the loan repayment?

Service's argument: Repaying the debt in depreciated marks meant taxpayer had a profit on the loan transaction and thus it had income on the loan repayment.

---

[95]   271 U.S. 170, 46 S.Ct. 449, 70 L.Ed. 886 (1926).

Supreme Court held: No income because the loss on the losing venture was greater than the gain on the loan repayment.

Comment: With all due respect, the Court was dead wrong on this one. There were two transactions. They should not be combined. There was income on one and loss on the other. They occurred in different years. So it is completely wrong to say no income on loan repayment, see *Burnet v. Sanford & Brooks Co.*[96]

Comment: It was significant that the Court did concede that income could result from currency transactions.[97]

Kerbaugh-Empire opens a door into the murky problems of inflation and the income tax. What happened in this case was that there was high inflation in Germany during the period of this deal.[98] Inflation means that it takes more of the currency to buy the same product. Hence the currency is worth less. Thus marks could be bought with fewer dollars.

You do not need, however, international borrowing transactions to have inflation giving you problems with the income tax. Consider the following example:

> **Example:** There is a world of just two commodities, which uses dollars as its currency. The two commodities are undeveloped land and bacon. That's all anybody wants to use or cares about. Bette buys as an investment undeveloped land subdivided into 100 plots. She buys the land for $100,000, so each plot is worth $1,000. Kevin buys a 100 packages of bacon. He pays $100,000, so each package is worth $1,000 (some pigs!). Immediately after these transactions, Bette sells Kevin one of her plots for $1,000 cash. Very soon thereafter, Kevin sells Bette one of his bacon packages for $1,000 cash.
>
> Time passes. Over the course of the year, the land goes up in price by 30%. The bacon goes up in price by 10%. At the end of the year, Bette sells Kevin one of her plots for $1,300 cash. Kevin sells Bette one of his bacon packages for $1,100. Kevin says, "Hold the phone. Suddenly, I'm short $200." The IRS says it's worse than that, fella. You just sold

---

[96]   282 U.S. 359, 51 S.Ct. 150, 75 L.Ed. 383 (1931), discussed and diagramed at ¶ 9.02(1).

[97]   In modern international business transactions, companies usually protect themselves from currency value fluctuations by hedging in the currency markets.

[98]   This transaction took place in the early 1920's during the period of the Weimar Republic in Germany. The Weimar Republic experienced heavy inflation, which contributed to the social dislocation of the time, see e.g. B. Brecht, and K. Weill, *Die Dreigroschenoper* ("The Three Penny Opera") (1928).

that sandwich for a $100 gain. At our tax rate of 33% you owe us $33. Kevin blows up.

Kevin's problem is, of course, inflation. The consumer price index in this simple economy, assuming we weigh land and bacon equally, went up 20%. There is a 20% inflation rate. It costs (on average) 20% more dollars to buy products in this economy. Kevin suffered because he held property that rose in price by less than the inflation rate. Kevin suffered a loss in purchasing power. Bette's property, for whatever reasons, went up in price by more than the inflation rate. Bette enjoyed a gain in purchasing power. She no longer needs to sell a full plot of land to buy a package of bacon.

Since the tax law in our little world is blind to this problem, it gets it wrong as to Kevin, as we have seen. And it also gets it wrong as to Bette. The IRS would say that Bette had a gain of $300 in selling her plot at the end of the year. They are saying she can buy 1.30 packages of bacon when she sells a plot of land. But she cannot. She can buy only 1.27 packages of bacon when she sells a plot of land.[99] She has a gain, but not as much as the IRS thinks.

That is exactly the problem with inflation in our income tax. It is a massive, widespread, and distortive problem. What do we do about it?

Many people suggest that what is needed to deal with this problem is to give favorable treatment for capital gains (indeed we have several different low rates for capital gains in our present system, see Chapter 4). That is to impose a lower tax on gains from sales of property than we have on other forms of income such as salaries. Thus we would, say, cut the tax rate on sales of property in our little society from 33% to 15%. This idea is like taking a guy with a cold and giving him open-heart surgery. Not only is it the wrong thing, it's also too much of it.

Let us see how cutting the tax rate would play out on our example. Kevin would pay a tax of $15 instead of $33 on his "gain." Would he still blow up? Of course. Suppose we imposed no tax at all on Kevin. Would he still blow up? Yes. Kevin's problem is that he has actually suffered a loss in purchasing power. When he sells one package of bacon after a year, he has enough money to buy 85% of a plot of land.[100]

Suppose the price of land had remained constant. Suppose, then, the price of bacon had fallen to $85 per package. On selling a package of bacon, Kevin can now buy 85% of a plot of land. He would certainly

---

[99] $300 (Bette's money gain) is 27% of $1,100 (the new price of a package of bacon, the real gain corrected for inflation).

[100] $110/$130 = 85%.

be entitled to a $15 loss on the sale of his land, would he not? Why should this case be treated any differently from our original case?

So what do we do? Answer: we need to index the basis of assets held for the inflation rate. On our original example, the inflation rate was 20%. Thus the basis of plots of land and packages of bacon needs to rise by 20%. Kevin now has a basis of $120 in each package of bacon. He sells it for $110 and has a loss of $10, reflecting his true loss in purchasing power. Bette has a basis of $120 in her plots of land. She sells one for $130, she has a gain of $10, reflecting her true gain in purchasing power.

Will this be enacted? There's been talk about it over the years, but so far nothing has been done, although the problem is severe when one considers the effects of even modest inflation over long periods of time.

(g) Other Theoretical Problems

There are other theoretical problems in income taxation more conveniently dealt with elsewhere in this work. For the issues involved in the preferential treatment of capital gains, see ¶ 4.06. The debate on using various tax provisions as incentives to business is discussed at ¶ 6.02(12). The problem of treating activities which involve both business and personal aspects is considered at ¶ 6.02. The problem of the appropriate family unit on which to impose the tax is considered at chapter 15.

¶ 1.03 STRUCTURE OF THE INTERNAL REVENUE CODE

There is an underlying rational structure to the Internal Revenue Code. This structure may often not be honored, but nonetheless it still is useful to comprehend it. This structure is represented in the one-page diagram that appears at various places in this book. Set forth below is a simplified verbal statement of the structure:

The formula for computing federal income tax liability under the Internal Revenue Code is as follows:

Steps in Computing Tax Liability

1.   Gross Income (including compensation for services and other items of income).

2.   Less: most business deductions and some non-business deductions (as provided by § 62).

3.   Yields: adjusted gross income.

4.   Less: the greater of itemized deductions or the standard deduction (itemized deductions being most non-business deductions and business deductions not allowed in step 2 above).

5.   Less: deductions for personal and dependency exemptions.

6.   Yields: taxable income.

7.   Apply tax rate to taxable income.

8.   Yields: potential tax liability.

9.   Less: tax credits.

10.   Yields: tax liability.

Chapter 2

INCOME IN GENERAL; COMPENSATION FOR SERVICES

Table of Sections

¶ 2.01 WHAT CONSTITUTES INCOME IN GENERAL: *CESARINI, OLD COLONY TRUST, GLENSHAW GLASS* AND *DRESCHER*

Section 61 of the Internal Revenue Code defines gross income broadly and powerfully as "all income from whatever source derived," including, but not limited to, fifteen particular sources—ranging from obvious items like compensation for services, dividends, royalties, gross income derived from business,[1] and gains derived from dealings in property, to less likely candidates, such as alimony, pensions, and income from discharge of indebtedness. In advancing this sweeping definition of income, § 61 is the driving heart of the income tax. With § 61, Congress exerted the full measure of its taxing power, intending to tax all gains without regard to source except those specifically exempted.[2] It is with this heavy inclusive presumption that an item is income that all further analysis must contend.

A leading example of the breadth of the income concept is the case of *Cesarini v. United States*.[3] In that case taxpayers husband and wife in 1957 purchased a used piano at an auction sale for approximately $15. In 1964, while cleaning the piano, taxpayer

---

[1]   In a manufacturing, merchandising, or mining business, "gross income" means the total sales less the cost of goods sold, Reg. § 1.61–3(a).

[2]   Commissioner v. Glenshaw Glass, 348 U.S. 426, 429, 75 S.Ct. 473, 476, 99 L.Ed. 483 (1955); Commissioner v. Kowalski, 434 U.S. 77, 98 S.Ct. 315, 54 L.Ed.2d 252 (1977).

[3]   296 F.Supp. 3 (N.D.Ohio 1969) aff'd per curiam 428 F.2d 812 (6th Cir.1970).

discovered $4,467 in old currency. Taxpayers paid tax on the amount and then filed a claim for a refund of their $836.51 tax on the found money. Taxpayers argued in the alternative that the found money was 1) not income; 2) if it was income, it was income in 1957 and the statute of limitations has now run on that year and 3) if it was income, it should be taxed at the favorable capital gains rate. The court held that the found money was income in the year that it was found. The concept of income is broad enough to cover this, since Congress intended to exert the full measure of its taxing power under the Sixteenth Amendment. Regs. § 1.61–14 provides that treasure trove is income in the year when it is reduced to undisputed possession. Under Ohio state law, the money is reduced to possession when it is actually found. The court also rejected the capital gains argument.

Another major case in the income area *is Old Colony Trust Co. v. Commissioner.*

OLD COLONY TRUST V. COMMISSIONER[4]

Facts: Taxpayer, William Wood, was President of American Woolen Company. The Company pays Mr. Wood salary and commissions totaling $1 million in 1918, and $548,133 in 1919. The Company also agrees to pay Mr. Wood's 1918 and 1919 federal income taxes. These amounted to $681,169 in 1918, and $351,179 in 1919 due to the extremely high marginal rates at the time (due to World War I).

Question: Was the payment by American Woolen of Wood's federal income taxes income to Wood?

Taxpayer's argument: He never laid hands on the money; it was sent directly to the IRS.

Held: The over $1 million in tax paid by Wood's employer on Wood's behalf represents income to Wood. The Court held that "The discharge by a third person of an obligation to him is equivalent to receipt by the person taxed." Wood's wealth was increased by the payment, and the payment was compensation for his services to the company. The payments were not a gift.

Comment: This $680,000 of federal income taxes for 1918 would, of course, be paid in 1919, and the 1919 taxes would be paid in 1920. Under the Court's holding, this creates further taxable income to Wood of $680,000 in 1919 (in addition to his regular salary and commissions). This additional $680,000 of income in 1919 would generate further tax to Wood of $462,400 (assuming the same effective rate of 1918). The Company would then, under its

---

4   279 U.S. 716, 49 S.Ct. 499, 73 L.Ed. 918 (1929) 36 B.T.A. 838 (1929).

agreement with Wood, pay this additional $462,400 of income taxes for 1919 in 1920, generating additional income to Wood of $462,400 in 1920. This would generate additional tax liability for 1920 of $314,432, which would be payable in 1921 and so forth. Is this a problem? No. The Company could easily "gross up" the salary paid to Wood so that, after tax, Wood would end up with the desired amount of after-tax income. In fact, this is a common practice.

Comment: Why did Wood and American Woolen engage in this deal? Do you think they hoped to avoid taxes by arranging affairs this way? It was a less sophisticated time. Note the case went to the Supreme Court. Compare this case to Drescher and Benaglia, below, where once again we see a "beleaguered" upper-level employee "forced" to accept some major benefit which is thought not to be taxable.

The result in Old Colony is clearly correct. Obviously Wood's wealth was increased by this arrangement. Thus we learn that if one's debt is discharged, one is wealthier. The transaction was in the nature of compensation for services, which is explicitly taxable under § 61(a)(1).[5]

The breadth of the income concept is further illustrated in the leading case of *Glenshaw Glass*.

COMMISSIONER V. GLENSHAW GLASS[6]

Facts: Glenshaw Glass involved two consolidated cases. In both cases, the plaintiffs sued for fraud and treble damages under the federal antitrust laws. In the first, Glenshaw Glass Co. sued Hartford-Empire and settled the suit for $800,000. It was determined that $324,529 represented punitive damages for fraud and antitrust violations. In the second case, William Goldman Theatres, Inc., a corporation operating motion picture houses, sued Lowe's, Inc., and was awarded $500,000, $375,000 of which were for punitive damages. Glenshaw Glass and William Goldman Theatres did not pay tax on the proceeds that were considered punitive damages, claiming that they were not income.

---

[5]   As *Old Colony* shows, taxpayer cannot exclude from income his employer's payment of his taxes. It is also the case that the taxpayer cannot deduct payment of his own income taxes. § 275. He can deduct the payment of his state income taxes against his income as computed for federal purposes, § 164.

[6]   348 U.S. 426, 75 S.Ct. 473, 99 L.Ed. 483 (1955), reh'g denied 349 U.S. 925, 75 S.Ct. 657, 99 L.Ed. 1256 (1955). For an in-depth look at Glenshaw Glass, see Joseph M. Dodge, The Story of Glenshaw Glass: Towards a Modern Concept of Gross Income, in Tax Stories (Paul L. Caron ed. 2003). The book Tax Stories provides an in-depth look at 10 of the most important tax cases decided by the Supreme Court. The book looks at the briefs, the oral arguments, the historical settings for the cases, and the implications the cases have had for both tax law and legal thought more generally.

Question: Is the ⅔ of the award that is attributable to punitive damages includible in income?

Taxpayer's argument: The punitive damages are a windfall under the antitrust laws and thus not income under *Eisner v. Macomber. Macomber* held that "income is defined as gain derived from labor, from capital, or from both combined."[7]

Held: Not only are the compensatory damages taxable but so are punitive damages. The punitive damages are "accessions to wealth." "Congress applied no limitations as to the source of taxable receipts . . ."

Comment: The Court declared (much to everyone's surprise) its previous definition of income that set out in *Eisner v. Macomber* (that "income is defined as gain derived from labor, from capital, or from both combined") was not the exclusive test for income. The punitive damages here would not be income under the *Eisner v. Macomber* definition. Instead, the Court shifted to an "accession to wealth" test. The Court, in what is now often quoted language, indicated "Here we have instances of undeniable accessions to wealth, clearly realized, and over which the taxpayers have complete dominion. The mere fact that the payments were extracted from the wrongdoers as punishment for unlawful conduct cannot detract from their character as taxable income to the recipients." This definition is very broad and is a touchstone for analysis of what is income.

Comment: Does it really matter? Will not the parties in future negotiations on the settlement of antitrust claims take into account that the plaintiff's punitive damage award is taxable? Thus will not the plaintiff hold out for more to make up for it after this case? Thus will not the defendant pay all or some of the tax? This would seem to be the case.

This powerful presumption of income as exemplified by the *Glenshaw Glass* case is limited in two important respects, however. First, as the discussion in Chapter 1 has indicated, there are a number of items which are income in an economic sense that § 61 does not reach even under *Glenshaw Glass.* Second, even though an item is covered by § 61 it may be specifically excluded from income by some other provision of the Code. As will be seen, these two kinds of limitations restrict the broad sweep of § 61 with respect to the various items of gross income.

One of the most important items of gross income is, of course, compensation for the rendering of personal services. The rich variety

---

[7]   Eisner v. Macomber, 252 U.S. 189, 40 S.Ct. 189, 64 L.Ed. 521 (1920). See Chapter 4 for further discussion of this major case.

of ways in which people are compensated for rendering services has provoked an equally rich response from the Code, Regulations, rulings, and case law. The great bulk of compensation for services is paid in the form of money wages and salaries (including bonuses, fees and commissions). These payments are clearly income and usually present no problems.

Difficulties arise, however, where the compensation is not directly in the form of wages.

For example, take a look at the case of *Drescher:*

UNITED STATES V. DRESCHER[8]

Facts: Drescher was an officer and director of Bausch & Lomb Optical Company. The company purchased a single premium annuity contract for $5,000 that named Drescher as the annuitant. Drescher would receive benefits under the policy once he turned 65 years old. The annuity was non-forfeitable, but the company retained possession of it until Drescher retired. Drescher's salary was not reduced, and he was not given the option of taking cash instead of the annuity. However, Drescher could change the beneficiary, accelerate the payment date and if Drescher died, his beneficiary would receive the payments.

Question: When is the $5,000 premium includible in Drescher's income? If it was income, was Drescher required to include it at the time the annuity was purchased, or at the time when the annuity started paying out?

Taxpayer's argument: Not income at the time premium was paid because the taxpayer could not realize present cash benefits from the policy.

Service's argument: Drescher was better off for having received the policy. He had income at the time the annuity was purchased.

Held: Taxpayer had income when the annuity was purchased. The annuity had a present value. It was worth less than the $5,000 paid by the company (because it had restrictions), but more than zero. Reverse judgement in favor of taxpayer and remand.

Comment: In previous cases, taxpayers had lost on this issue primarily because the annuitant realized immediate cash from the deal. Drescher presumably did not control the annuity until he retired. Should this make a difference? The court rejected Drescher's assertion that control mattered. The annuity was non-forfeitable and it therefore had a value to Drescher at the time of grant. The court

---

   [8]   179 F.2d 863 (2d Cir.1950), cert. denied 340 U.S. 821, 71 S.Ct. 53, 95 L.Ed. 603 (1950).

recognized, however, that the fact that Drescher did not have full rights to the annuity made the annuity less valuable. This fact went to the value of the annuity, not whether Drescher received income when it was granted. We will see many of these same issues—control, valuation, forfeitability—return when we discuss the taxation of stock options in Chapter 2.[9]

Why did Bausch & Lomb and Drescher set up the transaction this way? Is it likely that Drescher was advised that previous cases of this kind were lost because of the annuitant's ability to realize immediate cash from the deal? Is it possible therefore Drescher consented to these fundamentally meaningless restrictions in order to attempt to avoid current taxation on the deal? Probably so.

Note this case is about timing of income. The amount of income is not seriously in dispute. Anyone who thinks timing does not matter, read the discussion of time value of money, *infra* Appendix A.

Further discussion: Note that the $5,000 would have grown in 20 years to be substantially more. Assuming a 7% growth or interest rate, the $5,000 would, after 20 years, have been worth $19,348. If he had lost and included the $5,000 now, then he would have paid tax on the $5,000 and acquired a basis of $5,000 in the policy. Then when he had to include the $19,348 into income, he would have the $5,000 basis to offset against it, for income when he includes it of $14,348. This shows how basis is used to keep track of past events so that we don't count income twice.

If Drescher had won hands down and included nothing, then he would have no basis in the policy. Thus, 20 years later when he would include the whole $19,348 into income, he would have no basis to offset. In both cases the total amount included is $19,348. The question in the case is just the timing of the $5,000.

As proof that timing is everything, let's run the numbers to see what is at stake for Drescher. Let us assume a 40% tax rate. If Drescher has to take the $5,000 into income immediately, his tax is $2,000. He has to pay the amount immediately. Suppose instead he does not have to take the $5,000 into income immediately but instead takes it into income 20 years hence. Assume the tax rate is still the same 40% rate. Thus $2,000 is his tax on the $5,000 20 years later. But what is the present value of a $2,000 tax payment 20 years from now. Assume, as we have above, that the after-tax rate of interest that Drescher can invest his money at is 7%. We now know enough to ask the computer to crank out the answer. The present value of $2,000 20 years from now with an interest rate of 7% is $517. Thus, nearly three-quarters of the tax payable is saved. Here is another

---

[9]   See ¶ 2.03.

way of saying it: If Drescher wins, he needs to set aside only $517 now. If he loses he needs to set aside (i.e. pay) $2,000.[10]

More on Finds

We saw in *Cesarini* the cash found in a piano is income. But what about when you find a less liquid asset like a rare coin, or when something of value drops into your lap?

How Much Is a Baseball Worth?

In 1998, Mark McGwire and Sammy Sosa were in a race to see if either of them could break Roger Maris's home run record of 61 home runs.[11] As McGwire got closer to breaking the record, a market emerged for the home run balls. The theory was that these balls would be very valuable sports memorabilia. In fact, it was estimated that the ball that broke the record would be worth over $1,000,000.[12] So what are the tax implications to a fan who catches a ball worth $1,000,000?

Well some poor fella at the IRS made the mistake of speaking to a newspaper reporter. The spokesman confirmed that the "giver of a gift is required to file the gift tax return." The implicit position was that the ball belonged to the recipient and that giving the ball to McGwire would subject the donor to gift tax. No, it can't be, you say. People went crazy. Members of Congress introduced legislation to exempt baseballs from the gift tax. They claimed that this was a perfect example of what is wrong with the IRS.[13] Well ... actually. ...

Let's look at this problem in two parts. First, the income side. The person who is sitting in the stands just got something of value— a baseball worth $1,000,000. Why is that not taxable as income? If he won the lottery it would be income. If he received an award it would

---

[10]   By the way, if you think they're fighting about small change—what's $1,500 after all—remember that *Drescher* came up in 1950. Inflation has worked its toll. As a matter of fact, if there is an inflation rate of 6%, then $1,500 in 1950 is worth $21,647 now.

[11]   For a nice summary of the events surrounding the home run chase see, Darren Heil, 52 Tax Law. 871 (1999).

[12]   Bill Dedman, Fan Snaring No. 62 Faces Big Tax Bite, N.Y. Times, September 7, 1998, at D1.

[13]   See Lawrence Zelenak and Martin McMahon, Jr., Taxing Baseballs and Other Found Property, 84 Tax Notes 1299 (Aug. 30, 1999), quoting Athelia Knight & Eric Pianin, IRS Chief Say No. 62 Has Free Return, The Washington Post, Sept. 9, 1998, at C5 ("the mere possibility that the baseball might be taxed was 'a prime example of what is wrong with our current tax code' "); see also H.R. 4522, 105th Cong., 2d Sess. (1998). The bill was limited and applied only to the 1998 baseball season and only if the batter had hit at least 61 home runs. Now that is a great argument for tax reform isn't it?

be income. Why is it not income just because it is a baseball? The answer is, it probably is income.[14]

Now what about the gift tax? If the fan catches a ball that is now his, and he decides to give it to someone else, why wouldn't that subject the fan to gift tax? It was his ball and he gave it to someone else. Seems like a taxable event, doesn't it?

Well the IRS is not as crazy as you might think. It quickly backpedaled and said that if a fan gave back the ball there would be no tax implications analogizing it to refusing a gift.[15] But, fans rarely just gave back the ball. When they do, they do not give it back to major league baseball; instead they give it back to the player. In other words, by choosing to give the ball to the player, they exercise dominion and control over the ball.

Now consider that some fans do not merely give back the baseball. Some get something in exchange, like free tickets to baseball games or baseball memorabilia. Those fans do not simply refuse a gift. They bartered the product away for some benefit.[16]

From a pure tax theory standpoint the question is not really that hard. If you catch the ball and throw it back on the field—no tax. If you keep it, and then give it to someone else, you likely have taxable income on receipt and owe gift tax on the transfer.

Some scholars have argued that the receipt of the ball should not be considered a recognizing event and that the recipient should not have to include the ball into income until he sells it.[17] The scholars compare the baseball to found treasure, and argue that we do not currently tax found treasure until it is sold. They concede that there are currently regulations that require that found treasure be included in income, but point out that these regulations are not enforced. They argue that the IRS is right not to enforce these regulations and argue that by analogy, the IRS should not enforce provisions allowing it to tax baseballs. Their main point is that the

---

[14]   In fact, the person who caught the home run baseball hit by Mark McGwire on September 8, 1998 (his 62nd home run of the season, then an all-time record), was Tim Forneris, a groundskeeper at Busch Stadium. Does any of this analysis change now that we know Forneris is an employee of the stadium (or perhaps, the St. Louis Cardinals, the team for whom McGwire played)?

[15]   I.R.S. News Release 98–56, 1998 WL 566879 (IRS); see Rev.Rul. 75–374 (an individual who refuses to accept a prize is not required to include the prize in income).

[16]   Heil, supra n. 78.

[17]   Lawrence Zelenak and Martin McMahon, Jr., Taxing Baseballs and Other Found Property, 84 Tax Notes 1299 (Aug. 30, 1999). Zelenak and McMahon also argue that there is a strong argument that the treasure trove regulations are invalid.

baseball is similar to self-created property, or imputed income, and that as such it should not be taxed until it is sold.[18]

Underlying this whole discussion appears to be a concern about equity, not taxes. Generally, it upsets us that someone who might want to keep the baseball, or do a good deed and return it, will have to pay tax even though he or she not received "cash" and has no money with which to pay the tax. We probably would not be thinking about this issue if Mark Zuckerberg had caught the ball. After all he can pay the tax if he wants to keep the ball.

Another lesson to take from this discussion is that the tax code is not consistent with how it treats non-liquid assets. Sometimes it requires payment immediately, sometimes it allows the tax to be pro rata as the income is produced, and sometimes it waits until the asset is liquid. Keep this timing issue in mind as we consider various provisions throughout this book.

One last question. What about McGwire? If the fan gives him a ball worth $1,000,000 why doesn't McGwire have to pay tax on it? Shhh. Don't tell anyone. He probably does!

From an ethical point of view, what would you advise McGwire if you were his attorney?

¶ 2.02 FRINGE BENEFITS

(1) Miscellaneous Benefits Under § 132

In addition to paying money wages or salaries, the employer may provide fringe benefits to the employee as compensation for services rendered. Under the general broad principles of § 61, the presumption is that such benefits are income. Thus, the employee has the burden of presenting some authority or other reason why any of these benefits should be excluded from income.

Section 132 provides for fairly comprehensive treatment of fringe benefits. Under § 132, gross income does not include any fringe benefit which qualifies as 1) no-additional-cost service, 2) qualified employee discount, 3) working condition fringe, 4) de minimis fringe, 5) transportation fringe, 6) qualified moving expense reimbursement, or 7) qualified retirement planning services. Any fringe benefit not excluded by these rules or other provisions of the Code is included in income. Extensive definition and detailed special rules are provided, allowing among other things non-taxability of on-premises athletic

---

[18]   Id.; For a thorough response to Zelenak and McMahon see, Joseph M. Dodge, "Accessions to Wealth, Realization of Gross income, and Dominion and Control: Applying the 'Claim of Right Doctrine' to Found Objects, including record-setting baseballs, 4 Fla. Tax. Rev. 685 (2000)."

facilities and employee parking. Detailed rules as to the taxability of personal use of the employer's copying machine are provided.

These types of excludible fringe benefits are described in more detail below:

The following fringe benefits are excludible:

(1) A no-additional-cost service—§ 132(b). This is any service provided by an employer to an employee for use by the employee, if two conditions are satisfied: 1) the service is offered for sale to customers in the ordinary course of the line of business of the employer in which the employee is performing services; and 2) the employer incurs no substantial cost (including foregone revenue) in providing the service to the employee (determined without regard to any amount paid by the employee for the service). The classic example of a no-additional cost service is an airline employee receiving free stand-by tickets on a flight.

(2) A qualified employee discount—§ 132(c). This is any employee discount with respect to qualified property or services to the extent the discount does not exceed certain limits. With respect to a discount on a product, the discount cannot exceed generally the difference between the sales price of the product and its cost to the employer. With respect to a discount on a service, the discount cannot exceed 20% of the price at which the services are offered by the employer to customers. In these cases, if the discount is greater than these limits only the amount of the discount which does not exceed these limits is excludible and the balance is includible in the income of the employee.

Moreover, only certain types of property or services may qualify for this limited exclusion. As to property, the property cannot be real property or personal property of a kind which is held for investment (i.e. stocks given to an employee of a brokerage firm would not qualify). Furthermore, the discount must be offered on property or services which are offered for sale to customers in the ordinary course of the line of business of the employer in which the employee is performing services.

Note on (1) and (2): The no-additional-cost service and the qualified employee discount will be excludible with respect to any officer, owner, or other highly compensated employee only if the fringe benefit is available to other employees on a substantially nondiscriminatory basis. If these two fringes are not provided on a nondiscriminatory basis, then the fringe will still be excludible to rank and file employees but will not be excludible to the officers, owners, or other highly compensated employees.[19]

Reciprocal agreements wherein employers provide services to each other's employees will qualify for exclusion, subject to the limits described above, provided that the reciprocal agreement is embodied in a written agreement between the employers and provided that neither employer incurs any substantial additional cost (including foregone revenue) in providing the service. Thus airlines may provide travel at a discount to each other's employees and still qualify for the exclusion.

(3) A working condition fringe—§ 132(d). This is any property or services provided to an employee of the employer to the extent that, if the employee paid for such property or services, such payment would be allowable as a deduction to the employee under § 162 (ordinary and necessary business expense, see ¶ 6.02(1)(a)) or § 167 (depreciation, see ¶ 6.02(12)).

(4) A de minimis fringe—§ 132(e). This is any property or service the value of which is (after taking into account the frequency with which similar fringes are provided by the employer to the employer's employees) so small as to make accounting for it unreasonable or administratively impracticable.

A special rule here provides that the operation by an employer of any eating facility for employees shall be treated as a de minimis fringe if (A) the facility is located on or near the business premises of the employer (compare the discussion of § 119, at ¶ 2.02(2) of the text); and (B) the revenue derived from the facility normally equals or exceeds the direct operating costs of the facility. This last provision regarding eating facilities only allows for exclusion if with respect to any officer, owner, or highly compensated employee access to the facility is available to other employees on a substantially nondiscriminatory basis.[20]

(5) A qualified transportation fringe—§ 132(f). This is qualified parking, transit passes, or transportation in a commuter highway vehicle (vehicle that seats at least 7 people) provided by the employer to the employee. A qualified transportation fringe may not exceed $105 per month for the aggregate of transportation passes and amounts spent on commuter highway vehicles, and $200 per month for qualified parking.[21]

---

[19]   See § 132(j)(1).

[20]   See American Airlines v. United States, 204 F.3d 1103 (Fed.Cir.2000) ($50 American Express credit given to employees by employer was not de minimis).

[21]   Section 132(f)(2)(B) provides for a $175 exclusion for qualified parking. Section 132(f)(6), however, requires that this amount be adjusted for inflation. In 2015, the

(6)   A qualified moving expense reimbursement—§ 132(g). This is any amount received from an employer in reimbursement for moving expenses that would have been deductible under § 217 if they had been paid by the employee.

(7)   A qualified retirement planning services—§ 132(m). This provision excludes retirement planning services provided by an employer to its employee regarding a qualified employer retirement plan. This provision applies to highly compensated employees only if such services are available on substantially the same terms to other employees who qualify for the retirement plan.

Other comments on § 132

But what happens if your spouse or children receive fringe benefits from your employer? Why should you have all the fun? If you are an airline pilot, can your children fly free? Section 132 provides that certain individuals are treated as employees for purposes of these provisions. For example, § 132(h)(1) provides that retired and disabled employees and surviving spouses are treated as employees for purposes of subsections (a)(1) and (2). In addition spouses and dependent children are treated as employees under § 132(h). Even parents of an airline employee can receive free stand-by tickets under § 132(h)(3).

Section 132 even provides a special rule for gyms in this health conscious era. A special rule provides that in any event gross income does not include the value of any on-premises athletic facility provided by an employer to his employees, their spouses and dependent children.[22]

BE CAREFUL, § 132 is not the only provision that deals with fringe benefits for employees. For example, there are also some special rules for tuition reduction plans for employees of educational institutions under § 117(d). The general rule here is that gross income does not include any "qualified tuition reduction." A "qualified tuition reduction" is the amount of any reduction in tuition provided to an employee of an educational institution for the education below the graduate level at the institution or at another educational institution. The tuition reduction may be provided to the employee or any retired or disabled former employees, the surviving spouse of the employee or the spouse and dependent children of the employee.

---

exclusion for qualified parking, as adjusted for inflation, is $250. See Rev. Proc. 2014–61.

[22]   See § 132(j)(4). The facilities must be located on the business premises, operated by the employer, and substantially all the use must be by employees, their spouses and their dependent children.

The exclusion of the reduction in tuition will only apply to any officer, owner, or highly compensated employee if the tuition reduction plan is available on substantially the same terms to other employees on a nondiscriminatory basis. § 117(d). See also ¶ 3.09(2).

The major other fringe benefit items are discussed below.

(2) Meals and Lodging

Under the general principles discussed in Chapter 1, meals and lodging provided by an employer to an employee would constitute income to the employee. After all, the employer is providing a significant compensatory benefit to the employee. But is the employee really receiving a benefit? If an employer required you to live above a funeral home to answer the phone at all hours of the evening, are you really receiving a benefit?[23] Or if you are given a free apartment in an apartment building so you can be on call to make repairs at any hour, is it really worth it? Sometimes it might have significant value and other times it might be a real pain. How should we treat these benefits? And if they are taxable, how do we value what is received?

As we will we see below, a common law doctrine determined that these benefits were not gross income to the recipient. There was some notion that these benefits did not have a real economic benefit to the employee because the "benefit" was paid at the convenience of the employer. In a sense, the courts determined that these benefits had no value to the employee because they were a direct part of the job. (We do not tax a lifeguard for getting to sit in the sun all day).

After a series of cases on this subject, Congress amended the Code and provided for the exclusion of meals and lodging provided for the convenience of the employer. Section 119 provides that meals and lodging furnished by the employer are excluded from the income of the employee if certain tests are met. As to meals the tests are: (1) the meals must be furnished for the convenience of the employer; and (2) the meals must be furnished on the business premises of the employer.[24] As to lodging, the tests are: (1) the lodging must be furnished for the convenience of the employer; (2) the lodging must be furnished on the business premises of the employer; and (3) the employee must be required to accept the lodging as a condition of his employment.[25]

---

[23] See *Herbert G. Hatt*, 28 T.C.M. (CCH) 1194 (1969), aff'd per curiam 457 F.2d 499 (7th Cir.1972). The Tax Court held that free lodging in a funeral home was not income. It was for the convenience of the employer and he was required to accept the lodging in order to be able to properly perform the duties of his employment.

[24] Section 119(a)(1); Reg. § 1.119–1(a).

[25] Section 119(a)(2).

The Supreme Court has stated that § 119 pre-empts the field and therefore the fair market value of meals and lodging which do not literally meet these tests are income.[26]

But does this doctrine really make sense? Does free room and board have some value that should be included income? We examine these questions by looking at the leading case in this area.

BENAGLIA V. COMMISSIONER[27]

Facts: Benaglia was the manager for the Royal Hawaiian Hotel and several other resort hotels in Hawaii (including the Moana and the bungalows and the Waialae Golf Club). His employer provided Benaglia and his wife with a suite at the Royal Hawaiian and free meals. Benaglia also received a salary fixed without reference to meals and lodging.

Taxpayer's argument: Living at the hotel was for the convenience of the employer. Taxpayer could not perform his duties as manager without living on premises.

Service's argument: These were significant items transferred by employer to taxpayer as employee. He did not have to pay for his own meals and lodging and was therefore wealthier because of the arrangement.

Held: Taxpayer could exclude these items, as they were provided for the convenience of the employer.

---

[26]   Commissioner v. Kowalski, 434 U.S. 77, 98 S.Ct. 315, 54 L.Ed.2d 252 (1977). "Meals" must be in kind, Reg. § 1.119–1(c)(2). If a cash allowance for meals is provided, it does not meet the literal terms of § 119 and will be included in income, *Kowalski, supra.* (Cash meal allowances to state troopers). The Supreme Court in *Kowalski* specifically declined to decide whether the long-standing exclusion for supper money to employees working overtime was still viable. Although, as the Court pointed out, this exclusion is not supported by the statute, the Court seemed to hold open the possibility that the exclusion might be justified on other grounds—*Kowalski*, 434 U.S. at 81, n. 28. One such ground could be as a courtesy of small value. The Court's statement could also be interpreted as simply an invitation to the Service not to press the issue. The Service early ruled that supper money to employees working overtime is not income, O.D. 514, C.B. 2, 90 (1920), but then did not follow its own ruling in successfully maintaining in Fogle, 18 T.C.M. 1032 (1959), that supper money was income. The Court in *Kowalski* also explicitly declined to decide whether sporadic meal reimbursements may be excluded from income (Cf. ¶ 2.02(1) supra).

Cf. Sibla v. Commissioner, 611 F.2d 1260 (9th Cir.1980), holding that where firemen were assessed a flat amount to finance organized firehouse lunch mess whether or not they actually participated in the mess, firemen could either exclude or deduct the amount of the assessment. If the employee brings home the bacon in the form of free groceries furnished by the employer, the rule seems to be that constitutes meals for purposes of the statute. Compare Jacob v. United States, 493 F.2d 1294 (3d Cir.1974) (groceries are meals, thus qualifying for the exclusion) with Tougher v. Commissioner, 51 T.C. 737 (1969), affirmed 441 F.2d 1148 (9th Cir.1971), cert. denied 404 U.S. 856, 92 S.Ct. 103, 30 L.Ed.2d 97 (1971) (groceries are not meals).

[27]   36 B.T.A. 838 (1937).

Comment: If taxpayer's presence was so necessary in the Royal Hawaiian, why was he able to manage the Moana and bungalows, and the Waialae Golf Club without living at them? Also the facts indicate that Benaglia was absent from the hotel for about 5 months in 1933 and over three months in 1934.

Note that, unlike the *Drescher* case but like *Glenshaw Glass*, this case involves a now-or-never proposition. Either the items are taxable or they are not.

It might be asked why "convenience of the employer" should be the test here at all. Presumably, it is "convenient" for the employer to hire the employee or the employer would not do so. It might be answered that in-kind items which the employee must accept to help perform the job deprive the employee of choice. After all, no matter how swanky the accommodations at the Royal Hawaiian are for Benaglia, the retail cash value of those accommodations would have been better. Why? Then he could have chosen the Royal Hawaiian or something more modest and saved the difference. So no taxation. Poor Benaglia and Drescher, "compelled" by their employers to accept luscious perks. Is this real? Perhaps a more realistic approach in this area would be to require inclusion but at less than fair market value (such as 60%), to reflect the possible lack of choice.

(3) Group Term Life Insurance

Under general principles the employer's payment of premiums on a life insurance policy of the employee will generally constitute income to the employee.[28] However, to encourage the provision of life insurance, the Code provides that payment by the employer of premiums on an employee life insurance policy for up to $50,000 of life insurance will not constitute income to the employee.[29] Unlike the case of meals and lodging, supra, where the exclusion seemed grounded to a large extent on fairness, this exclusion is a clear example of using the Internal Revenue Code to encourage socially desirable behavior.[30] (Treatment of the receipt of proceeds of life insurance—as opposed to the payment of the premium—is discussed at ¶ 3.06 infra.)

The basic rule is that employer payment of the premium on a standard group term life insurance policy for its employees does not constitute income to an employee unless his coverage exceeds $50,000.[31] This exclusion has come to be of great significance in the field of labor law where the amount of group life coverage for

---

[28]   Reg. § 1.61–2(d)(2)(ii)(a).

[29]   Section 79. Such payments will, of course, still be deductible by the employer.

[30]   See the discussion of "tax expenditures," ¶ 1.02(3)(c) supra.

[31]   Section 79(a).

employees is the subject of collective bargaining. The Regulations are drafted to facilitate collective bargaining.

(4) Employee Death Benefits

Employee death benefits paid to the beneficiary or the estate of the deceased employee are included in gross income.

(5) Accident and Health Benefits

The employer may receive a deduction for funding a health plan for employees. Provided certain requirements are met, employer contributions to such plans will not be included in the employees' incomes. The payments made under such plans to employees for personal injuries or sickness may also, under certain conditions, be excluded from the employees' income. As an alternative, the employer may make direct payments to employees in the event of personal injuries or sickness. Under some conditions these direct payments too may be excluded from the employees' income.[32]

¶ 2.03 BARGAIN PURCHASES OF STOCK OR OTHER PROPERTY AND STOCK OPTIONS

The employer may confer compensation on the employee (or independent contractor) by allowing him to buy property or stock at less than its market price (a "bargain" price) or by providing the employee with stock options.[33] The employer may confer this benefit through either unrestricted or restricted property.

(1) Unrestricted Property

Dealing with unrestricted property (excluding stock options) is usually very easy. The taxpayer has received a clear benefit—the purchase of property for less than fair market value—and the amount of the benefit should be subject to tax.[34] Where the property that is purchased at the bargain price is not subject to any restrictions (such as, for example, that the employee must render substantial future services or return the property—see (2) infra), the

---

[32] Sections 104(a)(3), 105, 106.

[33] Independent contractors may also receive stock or other property at a bargain price. The entire analysis in the text applies to independent contractors as well as employees. Note that bargain purchases of stock are provided to independent contractors in a wide variety of situations: underwriters in a "firm commitment" distribution of a new issue of securities; organizers of a corporation who take stock at less than the price sold to outside investors; lawyers and other corporate consultants may also be able to buy stock at less than its market value.

[34] Bargain purchases usually involve the purchase of stock in the employee's company at a bargain price. If, however, the employee is entitled to purchase at a discount products that are sold by his employer, the purchases may qualify as a nontaxable fringe benefit under § 132(a)(2). See ¶ 2.02(1) infra.

employee has taxable ordinary income at the time of purchase.[35] The amount of the taxable compensation income is the value of the property less the price the employee paid for it.[36] Thus, where an employer gave an employee two new cars in exchange for two used cars, the employee had compensation income.[37]

Usually, however, the bargain purchase is of stock of the corporate employer.[38] A major issue in this area of bargain purchases of unrestricted stock or other property is whether the "bargain" is really due to services rendered or to be rendered, or whether the bargain is due to other factors, thus rendering the transaction not taxable—or indeed whether there was any bargain at all.[39]

The basis (or cost) of the property received in a bargain purchase giving rise to compensation income is the amount paid for the property increased by the amount included in income.[40]

(2) Restricted Property

(a) General Rule

Employers generally use two types of property when trying to confer a restricted benefit on an employee. First, employers may provide an employee with an opportunity to purchase property at a bargain price, but that property carries with it conditions that might require that the property be forfeited back to the employer. These transfers usually involve stock of the employer and are generally engaged in to give the employee an interest in the future growth of the company. The transfers will generally provide that the employee may buy stock at a bargain price but must forfeit or sell back the stock to his employer if the employee leaves the company within a certain number of years. These transactions are controlled by § 83,

---

[35] See § 83(a), Reg. § 1.61–2(d)(2)(i).

[36] Section 83(a), Reg. § 1.61–2(d)(2)(i).

[37] Strandquist v. Commissioner, 29 T.C.M. 387 (1970).

[38] Mason v. Commissioner, 125 F.2d 540 (6th Cir.1942), cert. denied 317 U.S. 657, 63 S.Ct. 56, 87 L.Ed. 529 (1942) (cash bonus to employee required to be immediately used to purchase stock of the corporate employer at less than market value. This is a technique that can be used to circumvent state law disallowing a direct issuance of stock for future services).

[39] Aspegren, Jr., 51 T.C. 945 (1969) (nonacq.) (taxpayer not aware he was getting stock at a bargain not taxable); Smith, 24 T.C.M. 899 (1965) (bargain purchase of second mortgage attributable to seller's distress hence not taxable); Berckmans, 20 T.C.M. 458 (1961) (contingencies depressed the value of the stock of a company bought by its organizers; hence they did not have a bargain purchase). The SEC turns over all registration statements and offering circulars to the Internal Revenue Service so that they may be analyzed to see if compensation of underwriters and promoters has been properly reported, I.R.–454, February 16, 1962.

[40] Reg. § 1.61–2(d)(2)(ii). See ¶ 4.03(2), for discussion of "basis."

which deals with property transferred in connection with the performance of services.

The second major way that employers use their stock to compensate their employees is through the issuance of stock options. Stock options are a major way for corporations to provide their employees with the potential to have significant gains from the growth of the company's stock. By providing employees with stock options, employers are able to make their employee's compensation packages look smaller, and still provide employees with significant benefits. Stock options also provide employees with an incentive to increase the value of their company. The theory is that if employees share in the gain of the corporation, they will work harder for the corporation.

The first question to consider is whether a transaction involves the grant of property (either for free or at a discount) or stock options. If the transaction involves the transfer of property, § 83 controls. If the transaction involves stock options, then you need to determine whether the options are incentive stock options under § 422 or non-qualified arrangements pursuant to § 83. These provisions help us understand how to tax the transfer of stock or stock options to an employee.

(i)   Incentive Stock Options

Section 422 covers incentive stock options. Incentive stock options are easy to identify because they must comply with a very strict statutory scheme. The reward to the employee if the options comply is that the incentive stock options receive favorable tax treatment.

Section 422 sets out four major requirements for incentive stock options:

1.   The recipient must not dispose of the stock within two years of the grant of the option, and must retain the stock for at least one year after the option is exercised.[41]

2.   The option price must not be less than the fair market value of the stock at the time the option is granted.[42]

3.   The option must be granted pursuant to a plan approved by the stockholders.[43]

4.   To the extent that the aggregate fair market value of stock with respect to which incentive stock options are

---

[41]   Section 422(a)(1).

[42]   Section 422(b)(4).

[43]   Section 422(b)(1).

exercisable for the first time by any individual during the calendar year exceeds $100,000, the amount over $100,000 is not treated as incentive stock options.[44]

If a stock option qualifies as an incentive stock option, the recipient pays no tax upon receipt and the corporation receives no deduction.[45] The employee then pays capital gains tax on the amount of gain when the stock is sold.

(ii) Section 83

Section 83 applies to both stock and stock options. The initial discussion applies equally to stock and stock options. The treatment of stock options, however, may be a little trickier. As we will consider in subsection (iii) below, § 83 does not apply to stock options without a readily ascertainable fair market value. The following are general rules applicable to both stock and stock options.

Section 83 deals with the taxation of stock transferred to an employee for a bargain price and subject to restrictions. (As indicated above, if the stock were transferred for a bargain price and not subject to restrictions, the result would be immediate compensation income of the bargain element.) Typical of the restrictions on such stock transfers would be a provision that the bargain purchase must be rescinded if the employee does not perform substantial future services for the employer within a specified time.[46] Other examples of risks of forfeiture include: a provision that the stock purchased at a bargain price by an underwriter participating in a public offering must be returned to the issuing company for the original purchase price if the underwriting is not successful;[47] and a provision that the stock purchased at a bargain price must be returned if the total earnings of the employer do not increase.[48]

---

[44]   Section 422(d)(1).

[45]   Section 421.

[46]   Reg. § 1.83–3(c)(1) and (2).

[47]   Id.

[48]   Id. This list is not exclusive. A substantial risk of forfeiture also exists generally when the bargain transfer is conditioned on "the occurrence of a condition related to a purpose of the transfer, and the possibility of forfeiture is substantial if such condition is not satisfied," Reg. § 1.83–3(c)(1). Reg. § 1.83–3(c)(2) gives as an example of a condition which does not constitute a substantial risk of forfeiture a requirement that the property be returned to the employer if the employee is discharged for cause or for committing a crime.

A risk that the property will decline in value is not a substantial risk of forfeiture nor is an arrangement whereby a retiring employee is transferred stock at a bargain price on the condition he render consulting advice when asked if the likelihood that he will be asked is low. A covenant not to compete might constitute a substantial risk of forfeiture. This regulation provides some further discussion of the factors that will be used in ascertaining whether a condition constitutes a substantial risk of forfeiture.

If the risk of forfeiture is *substantial* (and the Regulations agree that the preceding examples do generally constitute substantial risks of forfeiture),[49] then the employee does not have to include the bargain element of the transaction in income at the time of the transaction but can postpone inclusion in income until the substantial risk of forfeiture is lifted. This makes sense from a policy standpoint. If the employee had to include the income at the time the property is received, the employee might have difficulty coming up with the money to pay the tax, since property subject to a substantial risk of forfeiture is not very marketable. At the time the forfeiture is lifted, the employee includes as ordinary income the value of the stock at the time the forfeiture is lifted—not the value at the time of the transfer. This income amount is reduced by the employee's purchase price.[50] See discussion infra for additional rules on valuing the stock or other property transferred. If the pattern of stock ownership of the corporation is such that it is unlikely that the forfeiture will be enforced against the employee (e.g. because the employee owns a controlling amount of stock in the corporation), then in no event will the condition be regarded as a substantial risk of forfeiture, and the employee will have to include the bargain element of the transaction in income at the time of the transaction.[51]

As a further important qualification on this treatment, if the property is received by the employee subject to a substantial risk of forfeiture, under the criteria discussed above, but can nonetheless be transferred to a third party who will hold the property free of the risk of forfeitability, then the bargain element in the transaction must be included in the employee's income at the time of the transfer.[52] This is because, under the statute, the property in these circumstances is "transferable," and hence immediate inclusion of the bargain element in income is required notwithstanding that the property is subject to a substantial risk of forfeiture.[53]

---

[49]   Id.

[50]   Section 83(a). This is for transfers of restricted property occurring after June 30, 1969, § 83(i). The rules for transfers of restricted property prior to that time were considerably more lenient, providing generally that no tax was imposed until the restriction was lifted, at which time only the value of the stock at the time it was transferred was ordinary income; subsequent appreciation was capital gain. Congress felt this liberal treatment provided an end-run around the rules for qualified stock options at that time, Senate Report 91–552 accompanying the Tax Reform Act of 1969, 1969–3 C.B. 423, at 500.

The rules described in this section do not apply to qualified stock options and stock purchase plans, qualified pension and profit sharing plans, qualified annuity plans, or the transfer of an option without a readily ascertainable fair market value, § 83(e).

[51]   Reg. § 1.83–3(c)(3), containing extensive discussion and examples on this enforceability question.

[52]   Section 83(a), 83(c)(2), Reg. § 1.83–3(d).

[53]   Id.

As an example of this transferability issue, suppose an employer transfers stock to an employee at a bargain price but for a two-year period the stock can be forfeited to the employer if the employee does not perform substantial services. The arrangement further provides, however, that if the employee transfers the stock to a third party within the two-year period, the third party will not forfeit the stock even though the employee does not perform substantial services. Under such conditions, the bargain element of the transaction would be included in the employee's income at the time of the transaction, notwithstanding that it is subject to a substantial risk of forfeiture, because it is "transferable."[54]

As indicated above, the amount that is included in income when the substantial risk of forfeiture is lifted is the value of the stock at the time the substantial risk of forfeiture is lifted less the price the employee paid for the stock, and this amount is ordinary income.[55] Particularly if the stock is of a closely-held corporation, the question of the value of the stock at the time the risk of forfeiture is lifted will present the usual controversy between the Service and the taxpayer concerning valuation. In this area, however, the statute provides a rule which may bear heavily on the question of valuation: if at the time the substantial risk of forfeiture is lifted, the stock is still subject to some other restriction which by its terms will never lapse (a "non-lapse restriction"), the restriction will be a major factor on the question of valuation.[56]

A "non-lapse restriction" is generally a condition subjecting the stock to a permanent right of first refusal, usually in favor of the employer or the other stockholders, in the event the employee would like to sell the stock.[57] The price at which the right of first refusal may be exercised, fixed by a formula or a flat price, will be considered the value of the stock unless the Service can carry the burden of establishing a higher value.[58]

If the non-lapse restriction is canceled by the employer, the employee has compensation income in the amount of the increase in the value of the property unless the employee can carry the burden

---

[54] According to the legislative history, if the risk of forfeiture is not legended on the stock, so that the transferee would have no notice of it, the stock is considered transferable, regardless of the intent of employer and employee, Senate Report 91–552 note 12 supra at 502.

[55] As opposed to being a capital gain, see ¶ 4.06.

[56] Section 83(a)(1), Reg. §§ 1.83–3(h), 1.83–5(a) and (c).

[57] Reg. § 1.83–3(h).

[58] Reg. § 1.83–5(a).

of showing (1) that the cancellation was not compensatory and (2) that the employer will not take a deduction for the cancellation.[59]

If, instead of being sold, the substantially non-vested property is forfeited by the employee because of the occurrence of the forfeiting event (such as the failure to render substantial services), the tax consequence is that the difference between the amount paid (if any) for the property and the amount received (if any) upon the forfeiture will be treated as ordinary gain or loss.[60] The Regulations describe in relatively lucid fashion the tax consequences of a number of other possible transactions with substantially non-vested and substantially vested property (such as gifts, transfers at death, forfeiture even after substantial vesting, etc.).[61]

The employer in the bargain purchase setting is allowed to deduct the amount includible in the employee's income.[62] As discussed, the employee will have income on the occasion that the substantially non-vested property has become substantially vested or because a non-lapse restriction has been canceled. The employer's deduction is allowed under §§ 162 or 212, and hence must meet their requirements as to reasonableness, etc.

If property is transferred either free or at a discount, § 83 provides that the fair market value of the property (determined without regard to restrictions that will lapse) minus the amount paid for the property is included in income when the rights to the property are transferable *or* are not subject to a substantial risk of forfeiture. For example, assume you purchase stock from employer for $10 when the stock is worth $40. You have clearly received a $30 benefit. But assume instead that when you purchase the stock, you agree not to transfer the stock for two years and agree to forfeit the stock if you do not work for the company for two years. Assume further that two years later you are still working for the company and the stock has increased in value to $100. You have $90 of ordinary income in year

---

[59]   Section 83(d)(2), Reg. § 1.83–5(b)(1)(i)–(iii). Whether the cancellation was compensatory depends on the facts and circumstances, as discussed at Reg. § 1.83–5(b)(1)(iv).

The regulations set forth further discussion and examples of non-lapse restrictions. Notable in this discussion is the fact that stock sold under an exemption to the registration requirements of the federal securities laws, such as the private placement exemption, and thus restricted as to resale, is not considered to be stock subject to a non-lapse restriction. Of course once various information, volume and holding period requirements are met, stock sold under exemptions to the federal securities laws can be freely re-sold by subsequent transferees.

[60]   Reg. § 1.83–1(b)(2). This treatment does not apply where the election, discussed infra, has been made to include the substantially non-vested property in income immediately upon its receipt.

[61]   See generally Regs. §§ 1.83–1, 1.83–4.

[62]   Section 83(h), Reg. § 1.83–6(a)(1).

two. It is the first year in which the stock is not subject to a substantial risk of forfeiture.

(b) Election

Where, in connection with the rendering of services, the employee or independent contractor has made a bargain purchase of substantially non-vested property (as defined above), he or she may elect to include the bargain element of the transaction as compensation income immediately, rather than following the general rule of deferring inclusion in income until the property has become substantially vested.[63] Under the election, the amount includible in income would be the fair market value of the property received, determined without regard to restrictions except restrictions which by their terms will never lapse,[64] less the price paid for the property.[65] If this election is made, the substantial vesting rules described above will not apply to this property—no further amount will be included in income when the property becomes substantially vested.[66] The basis of the property subject to this election will be the amount (if any) paid for it increased by the amount included in income on its receipt.[67] The holding period of property subject to the election commences just after its receipt.[68] A gain on subsequent sale of the property will not be treated as compensatory but will be capital gain (assuming, as would usually be the case, the property is a capital asset in the hands of the employee).[69]

If, instead of being sold, the property subject to the election is subsequently forfeited back to the employer, because of the occurrence of the forfeiting event, no deduction of the amount previously included in income is allowed.[70] However, a deduction would be allowed equal to the excess of the amount paid (if any) on

---

[63]   Section 83(b), Reg. § 1.83–2(a). The election must be made not later than 30 days after the transfer. Reg. § 1.83–2(b)–(f) provide rules concerning the manner of making the election and revocation.

[64]   See discussion in text above.

[65]   Section 83(b)(1), Reg. § 1.83–2(a).

[66]   Id.

[67]   Reg. § 1.83–2(a).

[68]   Reg. § 1.83–4(a).

[69]   Reg. § 1.83–2(a). A loss would also be capital. Trap for the unwary: suppose the employee receives substantially non-vested stock but pays the fair market value for it, without regard to the restrictions. Making the election would then appear to be an idle gesture and therefore it might not be made, since there would be no amount to include in income at the time of the transfer. However, if the stock appreciates and is later sold for a profit, that profit will be compensatory, since the election was not made. Letter Ruling 7829007. Presumably also under these facts the appreciation would be taken in as compensatory income if, instead of being sold, the stock was held until it became substantially vested.

[70]   Section 83(b)(1).

the original bargain purchase less the amount received (if any) on the forfeiture.[71] Under the example above, $30 would be income in year one taxable as ordinary income, and $60 would be income in year two (if you sold the stock), taxable at the lower capital gains rate.

Thus the calculus for ascertaining whether to make the election runs as follows: If it is expected that the stock will appreciate, it is probably most attractive to make the election so that the subsequent gain will be capital gain. However, even though the stock is expected to appreciate, several considerations could still cut in favor of not making the election. First, the employee may not have the wherewithal to pay any tax immediately—and it is probably difficult to sell the substantially non-vested stock to raise the money to pay the tax. Secondly, even though the employee has the cash to pay the tax, the employee may still prefer to defer payment of any tax (so as to have use of the money or because the employee will later be in a lower bracket) though the gain will ultimately all be ordinary income. Third, if there is a significant possibility that the stock or other property will be forfeited on account of the occurrence of the forfeiting event, making the election is disadvantageous because no deduction is allowed for the previous inclusion in income.

REMEMBER: The provisions in § 83 excluding stock options without a readily ascertainable fair market value does not apply when dealing with property. You cannot avoid § 83 by claiming that the transfer of property does not have a readily ascertainable fair market value.

(i)   Stock Options Under § 83

Section 83(e)(3) provides that § 83 does not apply to the transfer of an option without a readily ascertainable fair market value. Regulation 1.83–7 provides that a stock option has a readily ascertainable fair market value if it is actively traded on an established market.[72] If the option is not traded on an established market, the option will be considered to have an ascertainable fair market value if: 1) the option is transferable by the optionee, 2) the option is exercisable immediately, 3) the option is not subject to a restriction that has a significant effect upon its value, and 4) the fair market value of the "option privilege" is readily ascertainable.[73]

---

[71]   Reg. § 1.83–2(a). See generally, Rosenberg, "The Tax Impact of Section 83 on Planning for Executive Compensation," 32 NYU Instit. Fed'l Taxation 1031 (1974); Johnson, "Tax Models for Nonrecourse Employee Liability," 32 Tax L.Rev. 359 (1977); Nasuti "New Twists for Nonstatutory Stock Options: How They Work; How They're Viewed by IRS," 53 J. of Tax. 142 (1980).

[72]   Reg. § 1.83–7(b).

[73]   Reg. § 1.83–7(b)(3) defines the option privilege and considers whether the value of the property subject to option can be ascertained, the probability that the value of

What happens if the option lacks a readily ascertainable fair market value? Since § 83(e)(3) provides that § 83 does not apply, the grant of the option is not taxed. However, once the option is exercised, § 83(e)(3) will no longer apply (because it will be stock not a stock option), and the stock is then subject to § 83. Thus, the optionee pays tax on the stock option once it is exercised.

This graphic summarizes the rules for bargain purchases of property:

---

the option will increase or decrease, and the length of the period during which the option can be exercised.

BARGAIN PURCHASES OF PROPERTY

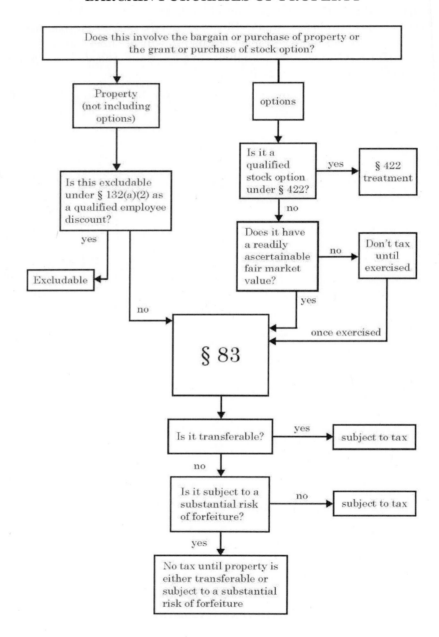

(3) How Not to Pay Tax on a Billion Dollars: Deferred Compensation Goes Better with Coke

For a dazzling example of how the late Mr. Robert Goizueta, former chief executive of the Coca Cola company, employed § 83 to defer taxes on almost $1 billion of restricted stock, see ¶ 8.04(2)(a).

¶ 2.04 OTHER ITEMS OF COMPENSATION INCOME

Taxable compensation may be received other than in the form of wages in the course of a regular job. Thus the Code and Regulations cast a broad net, specifying a number of items in the nature of compensation as income: fees, commissions, tips, bonuses, severance pay, rewards, jury fees, marriage fees, pay of persons in the armed forces, and pensions.[74] As discussed below, some of these items and other items in the nature of compensation present further problems.

(1) Tips

Although the regulations specify tips as a form of compensation, an initial question might be raised concerning this treatment since the person paying the tip is usually not legally bound to pay it. Hence it might be questioned whether the tip is a gift and hence not taxable.[75] However as the discussion of the *Duberstein*[76] case (¶ 3.08) indicates, a payment arising in a business setting can constitute income notwithstanding that there was no legal obligation to make the payment.[77] The authorities are clear that all tips are income.[78]

Taxpayers receiving tips must report them monthly to the employer, and the tips are then treated as wages subject to withholding and social security taxes. Indeed, "large food and beverage establishments" must meet extensive reporting requirements with respect to their gross receipts and reported tip income of their employees. If the tip income reported by the employees is less than 8% of the gross receipts, then the employer must under most circumstances allocate additional tip income to the employees for purposes of reporting to the IRS. These reporting requirements in no way preclude the IRS from proving that the

---

[74]   Section 61(a), Reg. § 1.61–2(a)(1).

[75]   Section 102(a) and see ¶ 3.08 infra.

[76]   363 U.S. 278, 80 S.Ct. 1190, 4 L.Ed.2d 1218 (1960), conformed to 283 F.2d 949 (6th Cir.1960).

[77]   See ¶ 3.08 infra. See also IR–284, April 4, 1959.

[78]   Reg. § 1.61–2(a)(1). Cf. Olk v. United States, 536 F.2d 876 (9th Cir.1976), rev'g 388 F.Supp. 1108 (D.Nev.1975) (tips to casino croupiers are income notwithstanding that croupiers are usually prohibited from rendering extra services to the tipper and only 5 to 10 percent of casino customers tip).

employee received a higher amount of tip income than that reported.[79]

Congress's concern with the apparently low level of taxpayer compliance in reporting tip income led to these rather stringent reporting requirements.[80] Thus does Congress attempt to penetrate the so-called "underground economy" and recover some of its lost tax revenues. There will still no doubt continue to be a rather significant number of cases in which the IRS attempts to ascertain the amount of tip income that has been received by a taxpayer. A variety of formulas, based on the percentage of sales made by the tippee and other factors have been used by the Service to estimate tip income and have been upheld in the courts.[81]

(2) Strike Payments

Payments by a union to striking or locked out employees are, under the general weight of authority, income. This is because usually these payments are made to the striking employees without regard to their relative need, and often picketing duties are required of the recipients.[82] However, in United States v. Kaiser[83] the Supreme Court upheld a determination by a jury that under the facts of a particular case, strike benefits were a non-taxable gift. Deferring to the lower court's fact-finding, under the principles espoused in *Duberstein,*[84] decided the same year, the Court found that the jury's determination that the payments were a gift was supported by the evidence, including the facts that the taxpayer was not a member of the union when he started to receive the payments, assistance was granted on a need basis, and picketing was expected but not required.

The Service, in an apparent attempt to limit the reach of Kaiser, has stated that in facts "substantially like those in the *Kaiser* case" it will regard the payment as non-taxable gifts, but that "other cases

---

[79]   Sections 6053(a) and 6053(c), General Explanation of the Revenue Provisions of the Tax Equity and Fiscal Responsibility Act of 1982, pp. 199–202. Form 1070 may be used for reporting tips. The taxpayer may also use a pamphlet, Treasury Document 5635, for keeping a record of tips.

[80]   Id.

[81]   See e.g. Cesanelli, 8 T.C. 776 (1947) (percentage of sales of waiter or waitress), Meneguzzo, 43 T.C. 824 (1965) (ratio of total tips to total wages in the business). See also United States v. Fior D'Italia, 536 U.S. 238, 122 S.Ct. 2117, 153 L.Ed.2d 280 (2002) (IRS may use the aggregate method to determine, assess, and collect the employer's share of Federal Insurance Contribution Act (FICA) taxes on tips received by its employees).

[82]   A leading case is Woody v. United States, 368 F.2d 668 (9th Cir.1966) (Strike benefits income to member of newspaper workers union where union made no inquiry into financial need).

[83]   363 U.S. 299, 80 S.Ct. 1204, 4 L.Ed.2d 1233 (1960), arising out of the bitter strike against the Kohler Company in Wisconsin in the mid-1950's.

[84]   See ¶ 3.08(2).

will be scrutinized to determine whether the payments constitute gross income . . ." However, according to the Service, that benefits are paid only to union members will not in itself render the payments income.[85]

(3) Other Miscellaneous Items of Compensation Income

Unemployment compensation payments paid by state or federal governments are taxable if they exceed certain levels.

Payments by employers to employees for violation of Title VII of the Civil Rights Act of 1964 outlawing discrimination in employment based on race, religion, sex, or national origin are generally taxable.[86] See also discussion of damages at ¶ 3.11.

"Cafeteria plan" benefits are not taxed under § 125. This does not refer to an employee lunchroom but rather to a fringe benefit compensation scheme in which an employee has the right to choose between a particular benefit and the equivalent amount of cash. Under the law prior to the enactment of § 125, such an arrangement would give rise to a tax to the employee even if he chose under the plan a fringe benefit that would otherwise have been non-taxable (such as accident and health insurance). The principle was that where cash (which is always taxable if chosen) is an alternative the employee is viewed as having taken the cash and used it to purchase the alternative benefit. Section 125 insures that employees who select the otherwise non-taxable fringe benefit under a cafeteria plan will not be taxed on it. To qualify for this treatment the cafeteria plan must be written and cannot discriminate in favor of highly compensated individuals.

---

[85]   Rev.Rul. 61–136, 1961–2 C.B. 20, at 21.
[86]   Rev.Rul. 72–341, 1972–2 C.B. 32.

Chapter 3

OTHER ITEMS OF INCOME AND EXCLUSIONS FROM INCOME

Table of Sections

The concept of income, of course, stretches well beyond the receipt of compensation for the rendering of personal services. It reaches a great many items which, though not in the nature of compensation, increase the wealth of the taxpayer.[1] As the discussion in Chapter One indicated, the outer limits of the concept of income are far from clear. Nonetheless, items not in the nature of compensation have been established to be income by statute or case law. Moreover because of the broad reach of the income concept, the Code, for various reasons, specifically excludes some items from income under some circumstances. These problems are the topic of this chapter.

---

[1]   Section 61, and see ¶ 1.02(2)(b) relating to the comprehensive tax base.

¶ 3.01 INTEREST

(1) In General

The general rule is that interest is taxable income.[2] Interest can only arise out of a bona fide indebtedness.[3] However courts will use a "substance over form" analysis to find a loan and hence interest income despite a taxpayer's assertion that the transaction is a sale and repurchase, hence giving rise to capital gain.[4]

Where the agreement is bona fide and negotiated at arm's length the Service and the courts will generally defer to the intent of the parties as to how much of a particular repayment of an indebtedness is interest and how much is principal.[5] This is clearly because the lender and the borrower have adverse interests on the question of how much of a particular loan payment is denominated "interest." To the extent the lender delays the receipt of interest income and all of the first payments are ascribed to principal, the borrower is deprived of an interest deduction. Hence in one ruling the Service even respected a loan arrangement in which, by agreement of the parties, all repayments to the cash method taxpayer were first to be credited to the principal.[6]

While this "hands-off" approach appears logical, it is not fully persuasive. Though the lender and the borrower may be at arm's length, one party or the other may have no particular motivation to negotiate on the question of the timing of the interest payment. The borrower, for example, may already be running losses, and therefore have no great use for the interest deduction, and hence be willing to let the lender have its way on the matter. Or, though the parties are

---

[2]   Section 61(a)(4).

[3]   Taylor, 27 T.C. 361 (1956), aff'd 258 F.2d 89 (2d Cir.1958). But see United States v. Williams, 395 F.2d 508 (5th Cir.1968) (dicta that "interest" as a "compensation for advance payment" could exist notwithstanding that the underlying transaction was not a loan but a prepayment of rent). Cf. Franklins' Estate v. Commissioner, 544 F.2d 1045 (9th Cir.1976), & 8.02(4), denying an interest *deduction* in the tax shelter setting in the absence of a bona fide debt.

In the category of "last laugh" is the long-standing rule that where the taxpayer gets a refund of tax from the Treasury, the interest on that refund is taxable, I.T. 2210, C.B. IV–2, 43 (1925), Rev.Rul. 62–160, 1962–2 C.B. 139.

[4]   Comtel Corp. v. Commissioner, 376 F.2d 791 (2d Cir.1967), cert. denied 389 U.S. 929, 88 S.Ct. 290, 19 L.Ed.2d 280 (1967), recounting the complex tale of the Zeckendorf Hotels Corporation's attempt to purchase the Commodore Hotel financed through what the court found in substance to be a loan from Comtel Corp., giving rise to interest income to Comtel instead of the capital gain the taxpayer sought. The maneuver of attempting to create capital gain instead of interest income is of great significance under current law, where capital gains are very favorably treated, with several very low rates. See ¶ 4.06.

[5]   Rev.Rul. 63–57, 1963–1 C.B. 103; Huntington-Redondo Co. v. Commissioner, 36 B.T.A. 116 (1937) (acq.).

[6]   Rev.Rul. 63–57, supra note 5, at 105.

at arm's length, they may not have equal bargaining power, and
hence one side may be able to have its way on the question of how the
loan repayments are denominated.[7] However, the Service's "hands-
off" approach as to the reporting of interest, with the exceptions noted
below, is very well established.

(2) Tax Exempt Interest

As a major refuge from the progressive rate structure for the
high income taxpayer, interest on most obligations of any state,
territory or possession of the United States, or any political
subdivision thereof, or of the District of Columbia is excluded from
gross income.[8] This exclusion for interest on government obligations
has been in the tax law since the first income tax statute in 1913[9]
and may rest on constitutional grounds.[10] The exclusion, of course,
increases the after-tax yield on state and municipal bonds. The
higher the taxpayer's bracket the more attractive the tax-exempt
bond becomes because the tax savings increases. Thus for a taxpayer
in a 15% bracket, the yield on a tax-exempt bond paying 7% is equal
to the yield on a taxable bond paying 8.24%. For a taxpayer in a 40%
bracket, however, the yield on a tax exempt bond paying 7% is equal
to the yield on a taxable bond paying 11.67%.

Tax-exempt state and municipal bonds have therefore come to
be a major target of those who would "reform" the Internal Revenue
Code, as discussed in ¶ 1.02(3)(c), relating to the comprehensive tax
base and tax expenditures. Whatever the merits of the argument to
tax the interest on state and municipal bonds (and there is something
to be said on both sides), there are many political interests who favor
the exemption—not only high income taxpayers and their advisors,
but also states and municipalities themselves who can therefore
issue bonds at lower interest rates, bond counsel, investment banking

---

[7] The widespread custom in the home mortgage and other consumer finance
areas is, of course, to have most of the early repayments denominated interest. For an
analysis suggesting this treatment is in error, see ¶ 1.02(3)(e).

[8] Section 103(a). If the "interest" is not really interest, the exemption will not
apply, however.See Rev.Rul. 58–536, 1958–2 C.B. 21 (citing a number of other
authorities for the proposition that where an underwriter detaches an interest coupon
from a tax exempt bond as compensation for marketing the issue, collection on the
coupon constitutes taxable compensation, not tax free interest; moreover, and most
curiously, the "taint" remains, and any subsequent purchaser of the interest coupon
also has taxable ordinary income on collection).

The Tax Equity and Fiscal Responsibility Act of 1982 imposed a 10% withholding
requirement on the payers of interest and dividends subject to certain exemptions and
limitations, effective for payments paid or credited after June 30, 1983.

Original issue discount on tax-exempt government securities is treated as tax-
exempt interest, Rev.Rul. 73–112, 1973–1 C.B. 47.

[9] 63 Stat. 168 (1913).

[10] There is a debate as to whether this exemption is commanded by the
Constitution. See e.g. H.R.Rept. 413, 91st Cong., 1st Sess. pt. 1 at 172–174, 1969.

firms, public works contractors, etc. Hence it seems clear the exemption will remain in the tax law for the foreseeable future, as a form of revenue sharing between the federal government and the states.

Since this is a type of revenue sharing, interest on federal government obligations does not enjoy the exclusion.[11] Nor does the interest on "arbitrage bonds"—in general bonds sold by states or municipalities whose proceeds are reinvested in securities which pay a materially higher yield than the bonds sold.[12]

(3) Private Activity Bonds; Qualified Bonds

In the late 1940's and early 1950's, private businesses started taking advantage of the exclusion for interest on state and local bonds. Under the typical arrangement, a state or municipality would issue a so-called "industrial development bond" and the proceeds would be used to purchase or construct a facility to be leased to a private corporation. The bonds would be secured by the facility and amortized out of the rents paid by the corporation.[13] The state or municipality's tax-exempt bonds were in effect used to finance private businesses, at a lower interest rate than if the businesses had to finance themselves with taxable bonds.

In the 1950's the Service began to grapple with this problem, issuing a series of rulings designed to limit the tax exemption to those industrial development bonds which were financing projects of a public nature.[14] Eventually the Service announced that it was going to issue proposed regulations that would deny the interest exemption to all industrial development bonds.[15]

At this juncture Congress stepped in for the express purpose of barring the Service's aspirations in this area.[16] Congress enacted legislation that more or less codified the Service's earlier rulings, which allowed the interest exemption for bonds financing projects of an essentially public nature.

---

[11]   Reg. § 1.103–4(b).

[12]   Section 103(c).

[13]   Senate Report No. 1014 on Tax Adjustment Act of 1968, March 15, 1968, 1968–2 C.B. 790, at 794.

[14]   Rev.Ruls. 54–106, 1954–1 C.B. 28; 57–187, 1957–1 C.B. 65; 63–20, 1963–1 C.B. 24.

[15]   Tech. Information Rel. 972, March 6, 1968.

[16]   ". . . The Committee on Finance is concerned that the Treasury Department in taking this action (denying the interest exemption) is, in effect, legislating on this subject. It does not believe that change should be made in the status of the interest on these bonds without specific legislative action on the part of the Congress." Senate Report, supra note 19, at 794.

The field is now covered heavily by § 141. One can make a career as a bond counsel shepherding bond issues through to qualify for the tax exempt interest. It's a comfy living, and it could happen to you.

¶ 3.02 ORIGINAL ISSUE DISCOUNT

(1) Background

The present value analysis of this area is set forth extensively in Appendix A. As pointed out there, understanding original issue discount is a key to understanding the field of time value of money in taxation. This discussion complements the analysis in the appendix by giving a background on the development of the legal rules in this area. It is interesting to see how far we have come from the primitive attempts to understand and tax original issue discount decades ago.

Recapitulating the meaning of original issue discount: Where a corporation or other entity issues bonds or notes, the interest stated on the obligations may be insufficient, given prevailing market conditions. Hence the only way to sell the obligations may be to offer them at less than their face value. Thus a note which will be paid $100 at maturity, plus 6% interest annually may have to be sold at $97 because the 6% interest is inadequate. The extra $3, called original issue discount, is economically the same as interest: for the use of the $97 the issuer of the obligation has to pay the 6% interest annually plus the extra $3 at maturity.

Many obligations are sold with original issue discount. This is because there is inevitably a time lag between the time the debt arrangements (face amount and interest rate) are finalized and the time the debt issue is finally marketed. In that intervening time interest rates may have increased somewhat, necessitating that the debt issue be sold at a discount from face value in order to remain competitive. (Should interest rates drop during the period between printing and sale, the issue would be marketed at a premium price in excess of the face amount. This then raises the question of how the issuer should amortize this premium as a cost of capital—see § 171 and see discussion infra). In addition to these factors, much short-term commercial paper is offered without any stated interest at all but is as a matter of course marketed at a discount from its face price. As discussed in the appendix, in the past long-term debt not carrying interest has been issued to finance corporate takeovers. Thus for all these reasons a great many long-term and short-term debt obligations are marketed with original issue discount.

Although it has long been undisputed that original issue discount was functionally the same as interest, treatment of it has given the courts, the Service and Congress a good deal of trouble over the years. As an initial matter the problem grew up under the 1939 Code, which provided that favorable capital gains treatment would arise on the sale or exchange of a capital asset.[17] This led to a great deal of wrangling over whether original issue discount was a capital asset for purposes of the statute, notwithstanding its economic equivalence to interest.[18]

Matters took a bleak turn for the Service in the case of *Caulkins v. Commissioner*[19] in 1943 in which the Tax Court, later affirmed by the Sixth Circuit, held that the gain on retirement of ten-year non-interest bearing certificates marketed at a discount was capital under the statute. The Service reacted to this setback by first nonacquiescing to *Caulkins* in 1943, then acquiescing in 1944, then reinstating its original nonacquiescence retroactively 11 years later in 1955.[20]

The Supreme Court in 1965 spoke definitively on the matter in United States v. Midland-Ross,[21] dealing with pre-1954 code tax years, holding that original issue discount as the functional equivalent of interest was not a capital asset; hence gain attributable to it was ordinary income on sale of the bond. In the 1954 Code, Congress had provided the same result. Although at first blush this appeared to lay the problem to rest, there still remained a debate over *when* would the discount properly be income: spread out ratably over the life of the notes (i.e., as "earned" in some sense) or only when the notes were sold or retired? The court in *Midland-Ross* assumed without discussing it that the discount was income only when the notes were sold—and this was the legislative treatment in 1954. Yet, if original issue discount were to be truly treated as interest, it should be taken into income over the life of the bond.

Congress enacted some apparently reasonable rules in this area in 1969, providing for the accrual of original discount ratably over time. Thus, for example, a ten-year bond with a face amount of $100 issued at $90 would accrue $1 of taxable original issue discount per year; the basis of the bond would also go up by $1 per year to reflect this inclusion in income.

After these rules had been in effect for some years, it became apparent that they did not accurately reflect the economics of original issue discount. In particular, the 1969 rules did not reflect the fact that the holder of an original issue discount bond does not in fact

---

[17]   1939 Code § 117(a), the predecessor to § 1221 of the 1954 Code.
[18]   See S.Rep. No. 1622, 83rd Cong., 2d Sess. p. 112 (1954).
[19]   1 T.C. 656 (1943), aff'd 144 F.2d 482 (6th Cir.1944).
[20]   Rev.Rul. 55–136, 1955–1 C.B. 213, at 214.
[21]   381 U.S. 54, 85 S.Ct. 1308, 14 L.Ed.2d 214 (1965).

receive the cash represented by the original issue discount until the bond matures. In effect the holder of the bond is re-lending the interest to the issuer, indeed at further interest. In short, the 1969 ratable accrual rules ignored the effects of compounding.

It can be shown mathematically (see Appendix A ¶ 1.4.5) that when account is taken of the effect of compounding, the holder of the bond has relatively small income in the early years and relatively large income in the later years of the life of the bond. Similarly, the issuer of the original issue discount bond should not deduct the OID ratably over the life of the bond, as the 1969 rules had provided. Rather, the issuer should take a relatively small deduction in the early years of the life of the bond and a relatively large deduction in the later years.

During the period after the issuance of the 1969 rules, particularly in the late 1970's (during a time of high interest rates), corporations began to take full advantage of this weakness in the 1969 rules by issuing deeply discounted bonds. They were then taking very large deductions attributable to this discount.

Congress responded in the Tax Equity and Fiscal Responsibility Act of 1982 by providing rules for the taxation of original issue discount to reflect the effect of compounding. These rules dramatically reduce the deduction available in the early years to the issuer of an original issue discount bond. And the new rules dramatically reduce the taxable income to the holder of the OID bond in its early years. Both income and deductions are "back-loaded" by the new rules to take account of the effect of compounding. See the charts at Appendix A ¶ 1.4.5.

(2) The 1982 Rules

As the discussion above has indicated, the fundamental change in the original issue discount rules effected by the Tax Equity and Fiscal Responsibility Act of 1982 was to take account of the compounding that occurs when the holder of an original issue discount bond in effect re-lends the interest to the issuer. The holder of an original issue discount bond, issued after July 1, 1982, includes in his income the ratable portion of original issue discount computed with reference to the yield to maturity determined on the basis of compounding.[22] The basis of the bond is increased to reflect this inclusion in income. This inclusion in income and upward basis adjustment is deemed to be done daily. See the mathematical and graphical analysis at Appendix A ¶ 1.4.5.

---

[22]   Sections 1271–1275.

The issuer of the discount bond similarly computes its deduction by reference to compounding—thus the amortization of the discount bond will give rise to a relatively small deduction in the early years of the bond and a relatively large deduction in the later years.

Where the bond is sold and the subsequent holder pays more for the bond than the basis of the original holder (as adjusted upward to reflect the daily inclusion in income), the subsequent holder will reduce the daily ratable inclusion into income of original issue discount by the ratable portion of the excess of what the subsequent holder paid over the basis of the seller at the time of the sale. This approach insures that the subsequent holder will have a basis equal to the face amount of the bond at maturity.

A buyer who pays less than the seller's basis for the bond will make no such correction. The buyer will simply include the usual daily ratable amount into income and increase the buyer's basis by that same amount. At maturity, the buyer will have a further gain.[23]

¶ 3.03 DIVIDENDS AND OTHER DISTRIBUTIONS TO STOCKHOLDERS

Section 61(a)(7) provides that gross income includes income from dividends. Prior to 2003, dividends from stocks were taxed as ordinary income. Opponents of the taxation of dividends argued that these dividends should not be taxed at all since they are the proceeds of corporate profits that had already been taxed. This is referred to as the "double taxation" of corporate profits. Although thorough discussion of this topic is saved for a course in corporate tax, the basic complaint was that a corporation was required to pay tax on its profits (the first incidence of tax), and the shareholders who received those profits as dividends were also required to pay tax on those profits (the second incidence of tax). Some commentators argued that this "double tax" was unfair and that dividends should not be taxed.

---

[23] These new rules do not apply to obligations issued by individuals, state and local tax-exempt obligations, U.S. Treasury Bills, U.S. Savings Bonds, and (of course) bonds purchased at a premium rather than a discount.

As a historical curiosity, while passing these original issue discount rules under the Tax Equity and Fiscal Responsibility Act of 1982, Congress also took the occasion to close up a tax avoidance maneuver known in the trade as "coupon stripping." This was actually a maneuver developed by Michael Milken, among his many other exploits. This involved the holder of a bearer bond separating the unmatured interest coupon from the bond and selling either the coupon, the bond, or both. Taxpayers engaging in this maneuver argued that they should receive certain attractive treatment with respect to the computation of the basis of the bond and the coupon. They also argued that the original issue discount rules did not apply to the coupon and the stripped bond, which allowed them to defer gain on these instruments until maturity. The Tax Equity and Fiscal Responsibility Act closed the door on this maneuver.

Commentary abounds on this issue,[24] but one concern about eliminating the tax on dividends was that some corporations had no taxable income. Due to either proper deductions or tax shelters, corporations often have positive cash balances despite tax losses. If the reason for not taxing dividends was the double taxation issue, the issue only exists when corporations had paid tax on the amount distributed. Although some proposals have advocated tracking whether in fact the corporation has paid tax on the amount distributed, doing so is very difficult. The ultimate compromise was to lower the tax rate on dividends to the same tax rates applicable to adjusted net capital gain (currently 0% for low-income taxpayers, 15% for middle-income taxpayers, and 20% for high-income taxpayers).

How does this actually work? Section 1(h)(11) of the Code redefines the term "net capital gain" as net capital gain plus qualified dividend income.[25] Basically, you calculate "net capital gain" without regard to dividends and then add dividend income to that amount. The capital gains rates then apply to net capital gain.

Now that we know how dividends are taxed, you need to know what a dividend is. The characterization whether a distribution to shareholders is a dividend is a central topic when studying corporate tax. We will provide only a brief discussion of the issue here.

The stockholder of a corporation may receive payments from the corporation with respect to the stock. These payments may be in the form of cash, property, or additional stock of the corporation. The stockholder may also have some or all of the stock redeemed by the corporation, or the corporation may be liquidated. In all of these transactions, the questions are whether the stockholder has received any amount that is taxable; and, if so, whether the amount received is taxable as dividend income or as capital gain.[26]

---

[24]   Reuven S. Avi-Yonah, Corporations, Society, and the State: A Defense of the Corporate Tax, 90 Va. L. Rev. 1194, 1254 (2004); Michael J. Graetz and Alvin C. Warren Jr., Introduction to Integrating Corporate and Individual Taxes, Tax Notes Today (Sept. 27, 1999); Jeffrey L. Kwall, "The Uncertain Case Against the Double Taxation of Corporate Income," 68 N.C. L. Rev. 613 (1990); Halperin, Daniel I., "Will Integration Increase Efficiency?—The Old and New View of Dividend Policy," 47 Tax Law Review 645–651 (1992); Hubbard, R. Glenn, "Corporate Tax Integration: A View From the Treasury Department," 7 Journal of Economic Perspectives, 115–132 (1993); U.S. Department of the Treasury, Integration of the Individual and Corporate Income Tax Systems, Taxing Business Income Once, Jan. 1992.

[25]   See § 1(h)(11). Technically, the definition provides that " 'net capital gain' means net capital gain (determined without regard to this paragraph) increased by qualified dividend income." This prevents a circular definition.

[26]   Other major transactions which corporations may engage in which have ramifications for the stockholders are the formation of the corporation, various corporate combinations (mergers, acquisitions of assets, acquisitions of stock), corporate divisions (spin-offs, split-offs, and split-ups), and recapitalizations

An individual who is a stockholder of a corporation may receive a payment from the corporation in the form of cash (or other property) or in the form of the corporation's stock. Where the payment is in the form of cash or property, it is taxable and added to "net capital gain" to the extent of the earnings and profits of the corporation. If the amount of the distribution exceeds the earnings and profits, the excess will reduce the taxpayer's basis in the stock. This basis treatment is known (in this book) by the sobriquet "Stupid Treatment," see ¶ 1.02(2)(e)(i). If the distribution exceeds both earnings and profits and the stock's basis, that excess will be treated as a capital gain, taxed at the preferential capital gain rate as long as it was held longer than 12 months, see ¶ 4.06.

If the distribution to the stockholder is of the corporation's own stock, a different set of rules are triggered. From early in the history of the tax law, stock dividends created problems for the Service and the courts. In the seminal case of Eisner v. Macomber[27] the Supreme Court held that a stockholder in receipt of a 50% stock dividend declared by Standard Oil to all shareholders had no taxable income, because no gain had been realized: ". . . The essential and controlling fact is that the stockholder has received nothing out of the company's assets for his separate use and benefit; on the contrary, every dollar of his original investment, together with whatever accretions and accumulations have resulted from employment of his money and that of the other stockholders in the business of the company, still remains the property of the company, and subject to business risks . . . (the taxpayer) has received nothing that answers the definition of income . . ."[28]

This theme that a pro rata stock dividend does not give rise to income was eventually picked up by the Code.[29] However, there are now variations on that theme. Where the stock distribution is not pro rata—where, for example, some stockholders get a distribution of stock and the others get a distribution of cash—the stock received is taxable as a cash payment under the principles discussed above, to the extent of its fair market value.[30] This is because, unlike in *Macomber,* the stockholder in receipt of a stock dividend which other stockholders have not received has enjoyed an increase in the

---

(reshuffling of the corporation's capital structure). These transactions also present the questions for the stockholders of whether anything taxable was received, and if so whether it is taxable as ordinary income or capital gain.

[27]   252 U.S. 189, 40 S.Ct. 189, 64 L.Ed. 521 (1920). See ¶ 4.02(1).

[28]   Id. at 195, 40 S.Ct. at 211.

[29]   Section 305(a).

[30]   Section 305(b). The cash dividend is also, of course, taxable on the principles discussed above.

percentage ownership of the corporation's assets. This is an event of economic significance and is thus an occasion to impose tax.

Where the stockholder has some or all of the stock redeemed (i.e., bought back) by the corporation for an amount greater than the stockholder's basis in the stock, there is no doubt that the stockholder has taxable gain. This transaction is simply a sale or exchange of the stock, which is an occasion to impose tax.

A liquidation is a complete termination of all stockholders' interests in the corporation and generally gives rise to gain (or loss) from, in effect, a sale of the stock.

¶ 3.04 RENTS

Rent is income,[31] whether received in the form of cash or property.[32] Payments may be held to be rent, though not so denominated.[33]

For discussion of the case where a lessee makes improvements to leased property which are then received by the lessor on the termination of the lease, see ¶ 4.02(1).

¶ 3.05 ROYALTIES

(1) In General

Royalties are income.[34] Royalties can arise from books, stories, plays, copyrights, trademarks, formulas, patents, and from the exploitation of natural resources, such as coal, gas, oil, copper, or timber.[35] Royalty and other income from the discovery and exploitation of natural resources enjoy a number of favorable tax rules, on the theory that such favorable treatment will stimulate new production.[36] Payments received on the transfer of patent rights may

---

[31]   Section 61(a)(5).

[32]   C.G. Meaker Co., Inc., 16 T.C. 1348 (1951) (landlord corporation's receipt of its own stock back for renewal of a lease constituted rental income in the amount of the value of the stock.).

Payments which are not even directly received at all may constitute rent to the landlord. Thus to the extent the lessee pays the property tax and insurance etc. on the leased property, the lessor will have rental income, Reg. § 1.61–8(c).

[33]   Commissioner v. Riss, 374 F.2d 161 (8th Cir.1967) (amounts in addition to rent for airplane paid as a deposit against contingency that plane would have to be overhauled were rent in year it was established plane would not have to be overhauled); Kennedy, 33 T.C.M. 655 (1974) (receipts from sharecropping rent); cf. Washington Fireproof Building Co., 31 B.T.A. 824 (1934); Waggoner v. Commissioner, 15 T.C. 496 (1950) (payments for damages above ordinary wear and tear were return of capital, not rent).

[34]   Section 61(a)(6).

[35]   Reg. § 1.61–8(a).

[36]   These favorable rules for natural resources include: percentage depletion (allowing the taxpayer to deduct more than his original cost of the property—not

under some circumstances constitute capital gain instead of ordinary royalty income.[37]

(2) Advance Royalties: It's Only a Paper Moon

Analogous to the rent area, advance royalties are taxable as ordinary income on receipt.[38]

Notwithstanding this general rule it appears possible under some circumstances to structure the advance royalty transaction as a loan and thereby avoid taxation on the advance payment. In the interesting case of *Arlen v. Commissioner*[39] the taxpayer, a songwriter, was given a $50,000 interest-free loan[40] by his publisher, repayable at $5,000 a year, in exchange for the taxpayer assigning the publisher renewal rights to copyrights on his songs. The publisher could, but did not have to, apply royalties due to the taxpayer against the $5,000 annual repayments. To the extent the publisher did not choose to credit the royalties against the $5,000 annual payments or to the extent the royalties were insufficient to cover the annual payments, the taxpayer was personally liable for the $5,000 annual payments. The loan was evidenced by negotiable promissory notes, and treated as such on the publisher's books. The taxpayer's royalty history indicated his royalties would be more than $5,000 a year. The publisher did indeed amortize the loan by applying $5,000 of royalties against the annual repayments.

Against the Service's challenge that the arrangement was in substance a $50,000 advance against future royalties taxable in full on receipt, the Tax Court held that the arrangement was really a loan. There was, the Tax Court found, a valid business purpose for structuring the transaction as a loan, because under the copyright law, in the event of the death of Arlen and his wife more than a year earlier than the renewal date of the copyright of any of the songs, an assignment of the copyright of such song to the publisher *might* be

---

available for large oil and gas operators); election to deduct intangible drilling and development costs, and election to deduct exploration and development costs (costs which under ordinary rules would be capitalized, see ¶ 6.03(4) and then depreciated). See generally, Subchapter I of Subtitle A of the Internal Revenue Code. See also Miller, "Percentage Depletion and the Level of Domestic Mineral Production," 15 Natural Resources Journal 241 (1975), suggesting that percentage depletion may discourage rather than encourage natural resource production.

[37]   Section 1235 and see ¶ 4.06(3)(a)(vi).

[38]   See ¶ 3.04 supra. Holbrook v. United States, 194 F.Supp. 252 (D.Or.1961) (advances against author's royalties income on receipt, based on analysis of intention of the parties).

[39]   48 T.C. 640 (1967) (acq.).

[40]   For current treatment of interest-free or below-market interest loans, see ¶ 5.04(3)(b).

void. With the transaction in the form of a loan, the publisher would then be able to recoup his payment.

However, the transaction was taking place within a year of the renewal date of half the songs. Hence the assignment could not be void as to them. If Arlen *or* his wife survived only a few more years, the assignment of at least another quarter of the songs could not become void. Therefore, despite the Tax Court's finding that the entire $50,000 was a loan, the business reason for structuring the entire transaction as a loan was not overpowering.[41]

Nonetheless, the Service acquiesced in this decision.[42] This decision meant that rather than being taxed on the entire $50,000 when received, the taxpayer was taxed on the $5,000 or so royalties earned each year and paid to him and/or applied against the loan. The advantage here was in the deferral of tax liability (see the Appendix) and the spreading of the tax liability out over a number of years, possibly resulting in application of lower rates, since the taxable income would not be bunched in one year.

Several factors were crucial to the Tax Court's finding of a loan in *Arlen:* (1) the possibility of the copyright assignments becoming void, as found by the Tax Court; (2) the taxpayer's personal liability to repay the loan in the event the royalties proved to be insufficient; and (3) the holding by the lender of negotiable notes of the taxpayer. These notes could, of course, have been sold to a third party for collection against the taxpayer without regard to whether the royalties were earned.

An author, composer, or artist wishing to receive a substantial payment in the nature of advance royalties tax-free would apparently have to plan the transaction to meet these conditions. Meeting these conditions, however, would be relatively difficult. It would be hard to build into the typical royalty situation the potential failure of consideration that existed in *Arlen* with respect to the possible voiding of the copyright assignments. Probably few authors, composers, or artists would be willing to bind themselves to repay the advance payment in the event the project did not earn sufficient

---

[41] Therefore, notwithstanding that Harold Arlen wrote "I've Got a Right to Sing the Blues," (1932), he most certainly did not in this instance. On the contrary, he proved that though "It's Only a Paper Moon" (1933), it isn't make believe if the Tax Court believes in you. The Internal Revenue Service was, on the other hand, constrained to hum "It's Fun to be Fooled" (1934). See 48 T.C. at 642.

[42] 1968–2 C.B. 1. Cf. Estate of Stranahan v. C.I.R., 472 F.2d 867 (6th Cir.1973) (allowing taxpayer to accelerate future dividend income by selling stock to his son, to take advantage of a large interest deduction in the year of sale, rejecting the Service's argument that the transaction was in substance a loan); Martin, 56 T.C. 1255 (1971), aff'd 469 F.2d 1406 (5th Cir.1972) (finding a loan and disallowing the acceleration of income on similar facts). See generally Chapter 5. Cf. also § 636, regarding this issue in the oil and gas area.

royalties. Most formidable of all perhaps would be the necessity of executing negotiable notes to repay.

Notwithstanding these difficulties, the author, composer or artist who is about to receive a substantial advance payment and who is confident his royalties will earn out may be willing to meet these conditions in order to receive the advance payment as a tax-free loan. For those taxpayers with the temerity to follow him, songwriter Harold Arlen's Tax Court case may prove to be his finest melody.

¶ 3.06 PROCEEDS FROM LIFE INSURANCE

Although as a broad general rule proceeds from life insurance contracts are taxable,[43] a very important exclusion from income is carved out for proceeds of life insurance payable by reason of death of the insured.[44] Although this exclusion almost swallows the general rule, it should be noted that the general rule of inclusion will still bite in several circumstances. If, as discussed below, the proceeds of the life insurance are not paid by reason of death of the insured but prior to that time, they may be included in income.

The exclusion from income of the proceeds of life insurance paid by reason of death of the insured is of major importance to many taxpayers and to the insurance industry. The extent to which this exclusion is justified can be explored by considering an example: Suppose the insured takes out a $100,000 ordinary life policy at age 45. The insured then dies twenty years later at age 65. Using typical figures,[45] the net premiums paid after 20 years will amount to $60,000. When the beneficiary receives the $100,000 face amount of the policy, it will all be excluded from gross income.

If one wished to take a hard-line "tax reform" position, how much of these proceeds might be argued to be includible in the beneficiary's income? It is clear that, as in calculating the gain on any asset, the beneficiary-taxpayer is entitled to offset the cost of the asset against the proceeds received.[46] Hence, even under the most hard-nosed "tax reform" view of the matter, the most that could possibly be included in the beneficiary's income would be $40,000 ($100,000 amount received less the $60,000 cost of the policy). However, the matter is not quite so simple.

This $40,000 "profit" is made up of two elements: the pure insurance element (also called "mortality gain") and the accumulated

---

[43]   Section 61(a)(10).

[44]   Section 101(a)(1).

[45]   These numbers are adapted from Goode, The Individual Income Tax (1964).

[46]   See ¶ 4.03, for a discussion of computing gains and losses on sales or exchanges of property.

interest earned on the portion of the premiums paid in as a savings element on the ordinary life policy (the so-called "inside buildup"). Looking first at the mortality gain, the insured died early in an actuarial sense. Although the insured's life expectancy may have been age 65 at birth, when the insured was 45 the life expectancy was by then to live to a considerably older age. Thus, by dying early the insured was a "winner" in the pure insurance lottery and the beneficiary "wins" a substantial amount of mortality gain. This amount was taken from the premiums of those mortality "losers" in the pure insurance lottery who lived to ripe old ages beyond their life expectancies. Again, using typical figures, of the $40,000 profit on the life insurance policy, about $27,700 would be mortality gain paid to the beneficiary because the insured was a "winner." The balance of the $40,000 profit, $12,300, would be interest earned on that portion of the overall premium paid in as a savings element, inside buildup.

Under general income tax principles,[47] both these elements of the $40,000 profit, the mortality gain and the interest, would be income, as constituting net increases to wealth. However, it might be argued as a matter of tax policy that these two elements should be treated differently. It could be asserted, for example, that the death of the insured is a time of economic and emotional hardship for the family, and is therefore not an appropriate time to levy a tax. However, a number of other taxes, including federal estate taxes, can be levied at the time of the death of the family breadwinner.

Even if this hardship argument is accepted as to the mortality gain, perhaps the interest element inside buildup should still be taxed. However, it is not. Not only is the interest received free of tax, it also compounds in the policy tax free.[48]

Cutting the other way is the argument that the mortality gain proceeds are usually to replace the lost earnings of the insured, and as such they should be subject to tax as would the earnings have been. An answer to that is that since the lump-sum insurance payment is received all in one year, it will be taxed at a very high marginal rate. There are, however, attractive options, discussed below, for spreading out the payment of the insurance proceeds.

The law disfavors a mortality "loser," i.e., one who lives beyond one's life expectancy. The "disfavor" comes from the fact that the long-lived insured will have paid more in premiums for pure insurance protection (taking account of foregone interest) than the beneficiary finally gets in insurance proceeds when the insured

---

[47]   See ¶ 1.02(2)(b).

[48]   However, to the extent money has been borrowed to fund the payment of the premium, no deduction is allowed for the portion of the interest attributable to the inside buildup, § 264(f).

finally does kick the bucket. But this loss is not deductible. And the insurance premium is not deductible.

The IRS comes out about even on this: undertaxing people who die early and overtaxing people who live long. So there is no net loss in tax revenues. But individual taxpayers are playing a lottery with the Service in addition to the lottery they are playing with the insurance company.

Consider also the case of the interest element paid to the policyholder who lives longer than expected. At this point the policyholder can receive the face amount of a matured policy. This constitutes simply a refund of the policyholder's savings element in the policy plus accumulated interest. The rule is that the amounts received are income to the extent they exceed the total premiums paid for the policy.[49] This treats the long-lived less generously than the short-lived in that some of the interest is taxed when received by the long-lived.[50]

Finally, perhaps the most telling argument is that society wishes to encourage the purchase of insurance, to promote financial security. The favorable treatment of employee group term life insurance[51] suggests that policy. Hence, the argument goes, the mortality gain proceeds should be tax-free. Nonetheless, this might still suggest the interest element should be taxed.

However these arguments balance out, it seems fair to say that the argument for excluding the interest element is not as strong as the argument for excluding the mortality gain. Note that even if the interest element were taxed, it would be taxed presumably only on the payment of the proceeds, not as earned and compounded over the life of the insured (i.e. no current tax on the inside buildup)—still an attractive deferral treatment.

One policy argument in favor of the exclusion of life insurance proceeds is that it serves as a substitute for allowing depreciation of human capital. The idea is that an individual with a career is gradually wearing out (we can vouch for this). This career or life that is going downhill should be allowed a deduction, since it does produce income along the way. But no such deduction is allowed directly. However, excluding the proceeds life insurance paid by reason of death of the insured, as well as the favorable treatment of pension

---

[49] Section 72(e)(2).

[50] However, cutting the other way, some of the interest earned, under the terms of the policy, might have been used to pay the premium for the insurance element of the policy. In that way the policy allows in effect the deduction of premiums for term insurance. Another insured who is simply buying term life insurance may not deduct the premium as that is a non-deductible personal expense.

[51] See ¶ 2.02(3).

plans may provide something like a deduction for the taxpayer's declining human capital.[52]

This exclusion of the interest element suggests some tax avoidance maneuvers for the very wealthy. The very wealthy often do not need the mortality gain protection of life insurance. Nonetheless they may find it attractive to purchase life insurance which provides a very small amount of mortality gain protection and a very large amount of savings and interest income. Since the interest is part of an insurance policy, it will be tax-free when paid on the death of the insured. The logic of this investment thus becomes similar to the logic of investing in tax-free municipal bonds—the higher the bracket, the more attractive the arrangement.[53]

Taxpayers' exploitation of this possibility through the use of so-called "Universal Life Insurance" policies, offered by many insurance companies, led Congress to enact guidelines in this area as part of the Tax Equity and Fiscal Responsibility Act of 1982. These guidelines specify the relative size of the premiums, cash surrender value and death benefits allowable for policies to qualify for the exclusion. These guidelines prevent policies that have loaded up on savings features and that offer minimal pure life insurance protection from qualifying for the exclusion.[54]

The very rich have found other ways to use life insurance as a mechanism of avoiding taxes. Split dollar life insurance is an accepted form of life insurance that allows the premiums and/or benefits to be split between different parties. Such arrangements are often used by corporations as part of the compensation package for highly paid employees. In a standard arrangement, the employer and employee jointly purchase a life insurance policy on the life of the employee. The employer and employee then allocate by agreement the policy benefits. As we discuss supra ¶ 2.02, the life insurance benefits to the employee are included in income. Therefore, in a split dollar situation the employee must be able to determine the benefit received. This is where it gets tricky. In Revenue Ruling 64–328, the IRS ruled that in split-dollar life insurance arrangements, the employee must include in income the value of the insurance protection in excess of the premiums paid. In determining the value of the insurance protection, the IRS allowed employees to use premium rates established by the IRS (Table 2001) or the insurer's lower published premium rates that are generally available.[55]

---

[52]   See also the discussion of treatment of personal damages, below at ¶ 3.11(2).
[53]   See ¶ 3.01(2).
[54]   Section 101(f).
[55]   See IRS Notice 2002–59.

Wealthy taxpayers have used the theory described above to create what is called a "reverse split-dollar" life insurance policy (who said tax lawyers aren't creative).[56] Reverse split-dollar policies allow taxpayers to split life insurance policies into two parts. The owner keeps part of the policy (usually the term-insurance value) and then transfers the remaining value of the life insurance policy to a trust. The owner pays very high premiums for the policy, thus building up tremendous equity in the policy. The owner then places a high value on the part of the life insurance retained and a low value on the part of the policy transferred to the trust. The beneficiaries of the trust receive the insurance proceeds tax free upon the death of the insured (and remember, the insurance has a large payout based on the huge premiums payed), but the taxpayer does not have to pay gift tax because of the low value assigned to the part of the policy that was transferred.

The result was that taxpayers were able to transfer large amounts of their estates to a trust for the benefit of their children without having to pay estate or gift tax. This was obviously not the intent of the statute, so the Treasury eventually issued guidance that such transactions would not be respected for tax purposes.[57]

¶ 3.07 ANNUITIES

An annuity is an arrangement whereby a taxpayer makes a premium payment, often one lump amount, to an insurance company (or other party) in exchange for which the insurance company agrees to make periodic payments to the taxpayer commencing on a particular date for the rest of the taxpayer's life.[58] This, of course, is a method for the taxpayer to guarantee an income for life. The amount of the annuity payments is calculated with reference to the taxpayer's premium and life expectancy. Thus annuities for life are the inverse of life insurance: where the taxpayer dies earlier than expected, there is a mortality loss on the annuity; the beneficiaries receive, however, a mortality gain on the life insurance.[59] Where the taxpayer dies at an age beyond life expectancy, the taxpayer reaps a mortality gain on the annuity, but the payments to the life insurance beneficiaries are less than the premium payments plus interest—a mortality loss.

---

[56]   David Cay Johnston, Death Still Certain, but Taxes May Be Subject to a Loophole, N.Y. Times, July 28, 2002, at A1.

[57]   Notice 2002–59, 2002–2 C.B. 98.

[58]   The annuity may also be for a fixed period, rather than life. The analysis of such limited period annuities is similar to that given in the text of life annuities.

[59]   See ¶ 3.06.

Income from annuities is unquestionably taxable;[60] the problem in the field is accounting for the fact that a substantial portion of amounts paid as an annuity represent a return of the taxpayer's premium which should not be taxed. (The taxable balance, of course, is interest earned on the premium.)

The problems in the field of annuities can be illustrated by the leading case of *Egtvedt*. (No, that's not a typo.)

EGTVEDT V. UNITED STATES[61]

Facts: Taxpayer purchased four annuity policies for $100,000. In return, taxpayer received the right to receive approximately $5,000 a year for life. Taxpayer was 45 years old when he purchased the annuity, and he had a life expectancy of 27 years.

Question: How should payments under the annuity be taxed? In particular is the statutory rule that 3% of the cost of the annuity be included in income constitutional?

Taxpayer's argument: The 3% rule is unconstitutional. Under the rule, 3% of $100,000 is $3,000. Thus $3,000 of the $5,000 annual payment must be included in income. Therefore only $2,000 of the annual $5,000 payment is return of capital. Hence taxpayer must live 50 years (i.e., to age 95) to recover capital.

Service's argument: The statute is constitutional.

Held: The statute is constitutional. The court reasoned that Congress set the 3% figure after full investigation and that it was not so arbitrary as to violate the Sixteenth Amendment.

At ¶ 1.02(3)(e) in Chapter One we have an extensive discussion of the various ways one could recover basis in the case of an annuity. It will be recalled that those various ways were:

1) Immediate deduction or expensing

2) Open treatment

3) Installment treatment

4) Stupid treatment

5) Loan amortization treatment

6) Economically accurate treatment

These are all the possible ways to recover basis in a deal that extends over time. The economically accurate method uses present value analysis (see ¶ 1.02(3)(e) and Appendix A). Under the economically accurate method, the results are that only relatively

---

[60]　Sections 61(a)(9), 72(a).

[61]　112 Ct.Cl. 80 (1948).

small amounts of income are reported in the earlier years of the transaction. In the later years of the transaction, large amounts of income are reported.

You should review this discussion at ¶ 1.02(3)(e) at this time. Making reference to that discussion, what type of method is the 3% rule? It is a dumb form of the proration or installment rule (No. 3). Dumb in that its assumptions about life expectancy for Egtvedt were wildly off the mark.

The current rule is a more intelligent form of the proration method, with realistic assumptions about the life expectancy for the annuitant.

Historically, the first way annuities were handled was to provide that the first annuity payments represent entirely a non-taxable return of the premiums, until the full amount of the premium has been recovered. Subsequent payments from the annuity were then taxable in full ("open treatment" as at ¶ 1.02(3)(e)).[62] This method, while clear and giving a precise result, has the disadvantage (from the point of view of the government) of postponing the time at which the taxpayer begins to pay a tax on his annuity until he has recovered his cost.

Hence, the current rule is to apply a more sophisticated version of the installment method, using realistic assumptions about taxpayers' life expectancies. This of course results in some of every annuity payment being taxed.

Where, as is often the case, the annuity payments are to be made for the life of the annuitant, the procedure is to exclude a certain proportion of each annuity payment ("exclusion ratio") from the annuitant's income and impose a tax on the rest. The proportion of each payment that is excluded is the same proportion that the total premium of the annuity bears to the total amount that will be paid under it.[63] With respect to an annuity for life the total amount that will be paid under it (the "expected return") is ascertained by multiplying the amount that will be received by the annuitant each

[62]   See House Report No. 704, 73rd Cong., 2d Sess., p. 21 (1939–1 C.B., Part 2, pp. 554, 569–570). This method was changed in 1934 to require an annuitant to include in his annual annuity income an amount equal to 3% of the cost of the annuity, as a rough method of accounting for income and basis simultaneously, Revenue Act of 1934 (48 Stat. 680).

[63]   Section 72(b) and (c) Reg. § 1.72–1(a). The total amount that will be paid under the annuity is of course greater than the premium because of the interest earned on the premium. Cf. the installment method of reporting gain on the sale of property, ¶ 8.03(2).

year by the annuitant's life expectancy as of the date the annuity starts.[64]

To take a numerical example:

The annuitant, a male age 50, purchases a single premium annuity for $10,000, which will pay him $1,000 a year for life, payments to start immediately. Making reference to the tables at Reg. § 1.72–9, this annuitant, as an actuarial matter, may expect to live about another 25 years.[65] Hence, the expected return of the annuity is $1,000 times 25 or $25,000. The total premium was $10,000; hence the proportion of each annual payment that is excluded (the exclusion ratio) is $10,000/$25,000, or 40%. Thus, of each $1,000 payment received annually, $400 will be excluded as a return of capital and tax will be imposed on the other $600. If the annuitant lives precisely the expected 25 years, he will have excluded precisely his cost of $10,000, and have been taxed on his income of $15,000.

If our annuitant in the above example lives beyond his life expectancy, he is thereafter taxed in full on his annuity payments, since he has recovered the cost of his annuity. If the life annuitant lives less than his life expectancy, and hence does not recover his cost, he may deduct his unrecovered cost of the annuity on his final tax return.[66]

If the annuity is not for life but for a limited term, an analogous calculation is made, substituting the term of the annuity for the annuitant's life expectancy.[67]

Modifications of the basic principle for taxing annuity income are used to calculate taxable income on specialized types of annuities, such as annuities with a refund feature, temporary life annuities, increasing and decreasing life annuities, joint and survivor annuities, variable annuities and permutations and combinations of these.[68]

Integrated Summary of Annuity and Life Insurance Rules

Where proceeds of an insurance policy are just simply paid to a beneficiary by reason of death of the insured, the proceeds are excluded from the beneficiary's income, § 101(a)(1). If the beneficiary leaves the proceeds with the insurance company and the company

---

[64]   Section 72(c)(3)(A), Regs. §§ 1.72–4, 1.72–9.

[65]   The actual life expectancy is 25.5 years, but 25 years has been used to simplify the computations.

[66]   Section 72(b).

[67]   Section 72(c)(3)(B).

[68]   See generally the regulations under § 72. Where an insurance company is involved, it will generally make these calculations.

pays the beneficiary interest on the proceeds, the interest is fully taxable to the beneficiary, § 101(c). We can illustrate the interaction of these rules with those related to annuities in the following four examples.

(1)   Suppose Marvin leaves $150,000 of insurance proceeds paid to him by reason of death of his uncle with Rock Solid Insurance Company. The agreement is that Rock Solid will pay Marvin $15,000 per year for Marvin's life. At the time the contract is entered into, Marvin's life expectancy was 30 years. In that event, the original amount of proceeds is spread out over Marvin's life and is excluded. Thus, $5,000 per year is excluded ($150,000/30). The balance of the annual payment, $10,000, is included in Marvin's income each year. It is interest on the $150,000 and is therefore taxable.

If Marvin lives beyond his 30 year life expectancy, he can continue to exclude $5,000 of the $15,000 payment, Regs. § 1.101–4(c). This is an odd result, since it allows Marvin to exclude more than the original $150,000 of insurance proceeds. If this were a straight annuity instead of being constructed out of life insurance proceeds, Marvin would not be able to continue the exclusion, see discussion below.

(2)   Zastro Corporation purchases $5 million of "key-man" life insurance on its chief executive officer, Irving Finster, because Finster is absolutely essential to the corporation's success. Under these facts Zastro Corporation would have an "insurable interest" in Irving Finster's life. If Finster dies, Zastro Corporation would be able to exclude the insurance proceeds paid to it by the insurance company, § 101(a)(1). If Zastro bought a fully paid up policy (perhaps from Finster) on Finster's life, then it would be able to exclude only the amount it paid for the policy (its basis). Amounts in excess of the cost of the policy would be included in Zastro's income, § 101(a)(2). Thus it is much more advisable to purchase a new rather than an existing policy. If Finster is a shareholder in Zastro Corporation, then the entire proceeds of the policy are excluded from Zastro's income even if Zastro bought the policy from Finster, § 101(a)(2)(B).

(3)   George purchases an insurance policy on his life for $25,000. Seven years later he sells it to his wife Martha for $50,000. George has $25,000 income realized but no income recognized on the transaction, § 1041(a), and Martha takes George's basis in the policy § 1041(b)(2). See ¶ 4.02(2). When George dies and Martha receives the insurance proceeds of $250,000, she will be able to exclude the entire amount of the proceeds, § 101(a)(2)(A).

(4)   Friebisch purchases an annuity on his life for $200,000. His life expectancy is 40 years. The contract provides he will receive

$16,000 a year for life. In effect § 72(b) spreads the $200,000 basis out over the 40 years and allows that amount to be excluded each year. The balance of the payment is included in income. Thus $5,000 a year is excluded and $11,000 per year is taxed, § 72(b)(2).

If Friebisch lives past his life expectancy he will be taxed in full on the annuity payments, thus income of $16,000 per year starting in the 41st year of the annuity. If Friebisch dies after 20 years of annuity payments, he will receive a deduction for his last taxable year of the investment in the annuity which he had not yet excluded, in this case $100,000, § 72(b)(3), Regs. § 1.72–4(a)(2) Example. This deduction will also be treated as though it arose in Friebisch's trade or business for purposes of generating a net operating loss deduction which could be carried to other years, § 72(b)(3)(C).

Suppose Friebisch and his wife had purchased the annuity described above, as a joint and survivorship annuity, with their joint life expectancy being 40 years. The same numbers would apply: exclusion of $5,000 and income of $11,000.

¶ 3.08 GIFTS AND INHERITANCES

(1) Rationale for Excluding

Ever since the Income Tax of 1913, gifts and inheritances have been excluded from income.[69] Without this specific exclusion, gifts and inheritances would probably be included in income, given the general broad sweep of the concept of income. This seemingly simple exclusion raises some puzzling theoretical questions. One who receives a gift or inheritance has certainly enjoyed an increase in wealth. Why should the fact that the recipient has not worked for the gift or inheritance be a reason to exempt the bounty from tax?[70]

Cutting the other way is the donor's circumstance. A donor with dominion over wealth may spend it on a vacation, buy a car, confer a gift or leave it to heirs. Why should the latter transactions give rise to an income tax? Perhaps the matter is best viewed as a question of the appropriate taxable unit. Gifts and inheritances generally occur among family members. Perhaps the taxable unit is the family[71] and gratuitous transfers among its members should not give rise to income, even as imputed income from services rendered by members of the family to each other is not taxed. That analysis is, perhaps,

---

[69]   Section 102(a) is the present exclusion. The exclusion in the 1913 Income Tax was embodied in § IIB., c. 16, 38 Stat. 167.

The basis of property received by gift or inheritance is treated at ¶ 4.03(2).

[70]   A federal estate and gift tax may be imposed on gifts and inheritances.

[71]   See ¶ 5.02.

persuasive; except perhaps what if the gift is of $250,000 of marketable securities?

See also Chapter 4, ¶ 4.03(2)(c)(i) regarding treatment of gifts of appreciated or depreciated property.

(2) Definition of "Gift": Duberstein

In any event, these theoretical questions have not given taxpayers or their advisors much pause. Rather, the question in the field has been, ever since 1913, what kinds of transfers qualify as a "gift" for purposes of the exclusion? (Indeed the first case ever reported by the Board of Tax Appeals dealt with this question.[72])

The leading case on this subject, and one of the best-known cases in the field, is *Duberstein*.

---

[72]   Appeal of Parrott, 1 B.T.A. 1 (1924).

COMMISSIONER V. DUBERSTEIN[73]

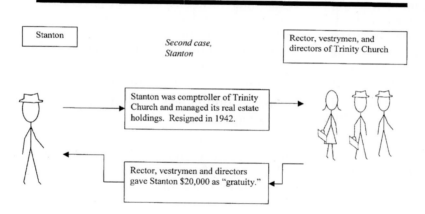

Facts: This case involves two consolidated cases involving Duberstein and Stanton. Duberstein was the president of an iron and metal company. He referred customers to Berman who was president of Mohawk Metal Company. In 1951 Berman gave Duberstein a Cadillac because information Duberstein gave Berman was very helpful. Duberstein claimed the Cadillac was a gift and not taxable.

In the second case, Stanton was the comptroller of Trinity Church in Manhattan and managed the church's real estate holdings. He resigned in 1942, but the facts indicate that the resignation may have not been completely voluntary. The Rector, vestrymen and

---

[73]   363 U.S. 278, 80 S.Ct. 1190, 4 L.Ed.2d 1218 (1960), opinion conformed 283 F.2d 949 (6th Cir.1960).

directors gave Stanton $20,000 as a "gratuity" in appreciation of his
past services rendered. They also indicated that they "gave" him the
money because he was well liked. Stanton claimed that the payment
was a gift and not subject to tax.

It should come as no surprise, that in both cases, the IRS argued
that the amount transferred was taxable.

Question: Are the transfers in these cases gifts, thus excludible
from income?

Held: Appellate court must defer to trier of fact. As to
Duberstein, the Tax Court was not clearly erroneous in its findings
that the Cadillac was at bottom a recompense for services and an
inducement for more services. As to *Stanton,* the district court's
finding of a gift was not explained sufficiently. Hence, the appellate
court vacated the judgment and remanded case to the district court
for further proceedings.

Reasoning: The "mere absence of a legal or moral obligation" to
make a transfer does not make it a gift. The transfer is income if it
proceeds from "the incentive of anticipated benefit." And the most
famous phrase: "A gift in the statutory sense . . . proceeds from a
'detached and disinterested generosity,'" made out of "affection,
respect, admiration, charity, or like impulses," citing Commissioner
v. LoBue. Thus the issue turns on the state of mind of the donor.

Comment: On remand, Stanton was found to have received a
gift.[74] But Duberstein had income.

Comment: The famous phrase "detached and disinterested
generosity" means that a gift does not stem from any *financial*
interest. A transfer that comes from affection, indicating a high
degree of *personal* interest, would be a gift.

Comment: Having the question of taxability to the donee turn on
the state of mind of the donor seems like a bad idea from the point of
view of administration of the tax laws. Note that taxability turns not
on what the donee thinks the donor thinks. It turns on what the donor
actually thinks. This may be something the donee cannot find out.
Indeed it may be something no one can find out. Is this any way to
run a tax system?

The weakness of the *Duberstein* approach was demonstrated in
the almost unbelievable case of *Harris.*

---

[74] Stanton v. United States, 186 F.Supp. 393 (E.D.N.Y.1960), aff'd 287 F.2d 876
(2d Cir.1961), Lumbard, C.J. concurring because of the nature of appellate review but
stating that he thought a contrary inference should have been drawn from the
undisputed facts, id. at 877.

UNITED STATES V. HARRIS[75]

Facts: Taxpayers, Leigh Ann Conley and Lynnette Harris, were twin sisters who resided with David Kritzik, a wealthy individual who was "partial to the company of young women." Before his death, Kritzik gave both Conley and Harris, either directly or indirectly, more than half a million dollars each. Letters given to each of the sisters indicated that Kritzik gave the money to them because he loved them. Kritzik, however, only claimed a small amount of the money on his gift tax returns. In separate criminal trials, Harris and Conley were convicted of "willfully evading" their income tax obligations. Harris was sentenced to ten months in prison, followed by two months in a halfway house and two years of supervised release. She was also fined $12,500. Conley was sentenced to five months in prison, followed by five months in a halfway house and one year supervised release. She was also fined $10,000 and ordered to pay a $4,100 assessment.

Questions: Were the amounts given by Kritzik to Harris and Conley income to them? What was Kritzik's intent when he gave the money? What did Harris and Conley think Kritzik's intent was when he gave them the money? Harris's and Conley's intent is important since this was a criminal prosecution for "willful evasion" of their income tax obligations, which requires Harris and Conley to believe the items are income.

Held:

Case as to Conley and Harris: This case is a criminal case and therefore different than most of the other cases discussed in this book. The Government not only has the burden of proof, but it must show that the defendants "willfully" violated the statute. The court found that the Government's evidence failed to prove either that the money Conley and Harris received was income or that they acted in knowing disregard of their obligations (as required for a criminal prosecution for willfully failing to file a return).

Comment as to Conley: The court recognized that Kritzik's intent that some of payments not be considered gifts is evidenced by his gift tax returns in which he identified as gifts to Conley substantially less than the amounts he transferred to her, suggesting the balance was income. Kritzik was now dead, however, and the court noted that he could have just underreported his gifts. The court also acknowledged that Kritzik told an IRS agent in an affidavit before his death that he regarded Harris and Conley as prostitutes, but concluded that he could have been lying to avoid paying civil and criminal penalties for

---

[75]   942 F.2d 1125 (7th Cir.1991).

failure to pay gift taxes. In any event, the district court excluded this affidavit under the hearsay rule and the Confrontation Clause. The court found, however, that this evidence was insufficient to prove that Conley knew that the money she received was income.

Comment as to Harris: At trial, Harris tried to introduce as evidence three letters that Kritzik wrote. In the letters to Harris, Kritzik indicated the he loved Harris and that he got great pleasure in giving her things. In a second letter to an insurance company, Kritzik indicated that he gave jewelry to Harris as a gift. The district court excluded the letters as hearsay and under Fed. R. Evid. 403 because the possible prejudice exceeded their probative value. The court of appeals concluded that these letters were not hearsay because they were offered to prove Harris' lack of willfulness, not for the truth of the matter asserted. Even if Kritzik was lying, the letters could have caused Harris to believe in good faith that the things he gave her were intended as gifts.

The conclusion that Harris should have been allowed to present letters as evidence would ordinarily lead the court to remand the case for retrial. The court found this unnecessary, however, because it concluded that the current law on the treatment of mistresses provided Harris with no fair warning that her conduct was criminal. Indeed the authorities favor Harris' position that the money was a gift. With the authorities in that posture, Harris cannot possibly willfully evade tax. See Green v. Commissioner, 54 T.C.M. 764 (1987), order aff'd 846 F.2d 870 (2d Cir.1988), cert. denied 488 U.S. 850, 109 S.Ct. 131, 102 L.Ed.2d 104 (1988) (Marvin v. Marvin palimony not income); Reis v. Commissioner, 33 T.C.M. 1333 (1974) (long-term payments as a mistress to nightclub dancer Lillian Reis held a gift, despite Reis' statement that she "earned every penny" of the money).

Conclusion: Remand with instructions that the indictments against Harris and Conley should be dismissed.

Comment: Pending the appeal, Harris and Conley served most of the sentences under the convictions that were now reversed. This was because their counsel apparently failed to show "by clear and convincing evidence that the person is not likely to flee or pose a danger to the safety of any other person" and "that the appeal is not for the purpose of delay and raises a substantial question of law or fact likely to result in reversal or an order for a new trial," 18 U.S.C.A. § 3143(b).

Comment, "willfulness" in criminal tax cases: "Willfulness" may work as a concept in situations of murder or arson. But in criminal prosecutions under the tax laws, the concept of willfulness can at times be troublesome. As discussed in connection with the *James* case at ¶ 3.13(2), are we to believe that potential tax evaders read the advance sheets in order to ascertain their legal position? It was very important to the court that the precedents in the field favored Harris and Conley. But suppose the precedents had not been favorable. Are Harris and Conley really reading Tax Court Memo cases before they decide not to file tax returns or not to report income? And if Harris and Conley are not to be supposed to be reading these cases, then what is the meaning of the concept of willfulness in the prosecution of criminal tax fraud cases?

Comment: How did this mess happen anyway?

Why this ghastly muddle of a case, leading to two women serving time for convictions that were reversed? Why did the IRS bring this case in the first place? Why didn't it just bring a civil case against Conley and Harris? If the case was really as bad as it appears, how did the Government convince a jury to convict both Conley and Harris?

Comment on the implications of Harris:

Although Harris and Conley were able to obtain a reversal of their convictions, the case presents a real problem for nontraditional couples. In the marriage context, we routinely treat payments by one spouse to the other as support. We would never think of taxing a stay-at-home dad on the money he received from his working spouse. But at least technically, the Government's position in *Harris* implies that such transfers between non-married couples might be taxable. Thus, a person who works and economically supports a non-married partner would theoretically be providing the supported partner with income. While it appears the IRS has not attempted to enforce the statute in such a manner, the *Harris* case is strong evidence that it could attempt to do so. Does that mean that non-married couples where one member provides support to the other should file returns claiming transfers between them as income? Does it mean that such couples constantly run the risk, even if small, of criminal prosecution? One could argue that the problem could easily be taken care of by simply marrying the partner. Is there or should there be some doctrine of "support" that treats these payments neither as a gift nor as income?

This concern is not far fetched. In a nationally syndicated advice column, the columnists, at least one of whom is a lawyer, advised a woman who was thinking of moving in with a man that there would be tax ramifications from such a move.[76] The columnists claimed that

---

[76]   See, e.g., Jan Collins and Jan Warner, *Living Together requires plan to account for taxes, gifts*, Columbus Dispatch, October 17, 2002, at F2.

any amounts he paid to support her (she did not plan on working) would either be considered income or gifts. If the money was considered a gift, there might be gift tax implications to the donor. If the money was not a gift, the columnists concluded that it would be considered income to her. Does this really make sense?

Comments on Duberstein in the Employer-Employee context:

Section 102(c) of the Code now provides in the employer-employee context that there shall not be excluded from income any amount transferred by an employer to an employee, except for *de minimis* gifts under the § 132 fringe benefit rules. In short, in the employer-employee setting § 102(c) provides a conclusive presumption of income. This would clearly change the result in *Stanton* (although not in *Duberstein*) no matter how affectionately the vestrymen regarded Stanton (and there was indeed some question about that as his departure was in fact occasioned by a bit of a tiff over the status of another employee). Section 102(c) would not have been of help in *Harris.*

Section 102(c) therefore clarifies matters in the employer-employee setting, but outside that setting there is still a confusing welter of facts that must be used to decide, under *Duberstein's* fact-based approach, whether a particular transfer is a gift.

Section 274(b) clarifies the situation as far as deductibility to the transferor is concerned. It provides that no deduction is allowed for gifts to recipients in amounts of more than $25. Prior to this section, transferors were often deducting the transfer as a business expense while the transferee was calling the transaction a gift (otherwise known as having it both ways). Indeed this was attempted in *Duberstein*, with Berman deducting the Cadillac, while Duberstein attempted (ultimately unsuccessfully) to exclude it. Thus under § 274, once over the $25 threshold, taxpayers have to make up their minds. Either the transferor can take a business deduction for the transfer, in which case the transferee must take the item into income, or the transferor must forego the deduction, in which case the transferee can assert it is a gift.

After *Duberstein,* gratuitous transfers in a business setting have almost always been found to be income,[77] notwithstanding that the

---

[77]   Rhodes v. Commissioner, 36 T.C.M. 149 (1977) (gratuitous transfer of real estate to taxpayer for his role in bringing together buyer and seller of tract of land held not a gift but income notwithstanding an agreement that taxpayer would receive no commission); Thrower v. Commissioner, 21 T.C.M. 1540 (1962), aff'd 330 F.2d 614 (5th Cir.1964) (liquor given to members of state liquor board by distilleries did not arise from "detached and disinterested generosity,"). Cf. Mesinger v. Commissioner, 31 T.C.M. 1127 (1972) (rent-free use of an apartment held gift where no special business favors done).

Duberstein Court later in its opinion purported not to be laying down any presumptions in the matter. The implications of *Duberstein* have radiated out into many areas, including employee death benefits,[78] tips,[79] and strike payments.[80]

Many gift cases post *Duberstein* have concerned family members doing business together, where gratuitous transfers between them can carry both heavy business and personal connotations. Thus in a family quarrel, a mother transferred cash and securities to her son after he had threatened both to put the family business into bankruptcy and to report her to the IRS on account of alleged violations. Subsequently, the mother successfully sued the son for conversion of the cash and securities and for punitive damages. On these facts the Second Circuit found the mother's transfer of cash and securities to the son to have been "prompted by something less than maternal affection . . . " and found the transfer to be income to the son.[81] Other transfers in the family business setting have not been quite so easy to decide and the cases have gone off on their particular facts.[82]

(3) Gifts of Income from Property

Instead of making an outright gift of property, the donor may confer the income from property as a gift. In such an event, the income from the property is taxable to the donee, notwithstanding that the transaction is indisputably a gift by the standards discussed above.[83] While this may seem inconsistent with the exclusion from income of the outright gift of property, discussed above, this statutory scheme makes sense. In the case of the excludible outright gift of property, there is no doubt that income subsequently derived from the property given (i.e. rent from given real estate or interest from given money) is income to the donee.[84] That being the case, it would be consistent to say that where only the income is given, it will be taxed to the recipient. Without such a rule, of course, great amounts

---

[78]   See ¶ 2.02(4).

[79]   See ¶ 2.04(1).

[80]   See ¶ 2.04(2).

[81]   Altman v. Commissioner, 475 F.2d 876, 878 (2d Cir.1973).

[82]   E.g. Dexter v. United States, 306 F.Supp. 415 (N.D.Miss.1969) (transfer of real estate to daughter by father in exchange for daughter's past performance of services held income, not a gift); Kass, 33 T.C.M. 239 (1974) (father's transfer of stock in family corporation to son held a gift to son, who was on salary, although as a result of the transfer, son declined an offer to work for his wife's business).

[83]   Section 102(b)(2).

[84]   Section 102(b)(1) Reg. § 1.102–1(b). This rule of inclusion in income would also cover appreciation in the value of the given property in the hands of the donee, when realized on subsequent sale. Indeed, the donee is even liable for the tax on the appreciation in the hands of the donor! See ¶ 4.03(2)(c)(i).

of income would be lost from taxation because they had once been the subject of a gift.

If the gift takes the form of periodic payments from specified property, it is taxable to the recipient to the extent the payments are out of income from the property and excludible to the extent the payments must be made from principal,[85] a rule consistent with the above analysis. However, according to an old Tax Court case, a gift payable "in a single lump sum in any event" out of either income or principal is not taxed to the beneficiary, though ultimately paid out of income.[86] Though the Service has acquiesced in this holding, it seems possible, given the paucity of recent authority, that the Service might choose to reconsider this question. In the meantime the lesson is clear: where a gift of income from property is contemplated, the most attractive technique is to couch the gift in terms of a lump sum payable, in any event, out of income or principal.

Where gifts of income from property or gifts of the underlying property itself are made, a more profound question can be raised: whether any gift was made at all. When, for example, a high-bracket taxpayer purports to make a gift of income or property and income to a low bracket taxpayer, the Service may attack the transaction on "assignment of income" principles and attempt to tax the income to the donor. This topic is discussed in Chapter 5.

(4) Inheritances

(a) In General

Property acquired by bequest, devise or inheritance is excluded from income. In the Supreme Court case of *Lyeth v. Hoey*,[87] the question presented was whether property received by the taxpayer from the estate of a decedent in compromise of his claim as an heir is taxable income. Taxpayer died in 1931 leaving as her heirs four surviving children and the taxpayer and his brother who were sons of a deceased daughter of the decedent. The decedent in her will gave the heirs small legacies. The residuary estate she gave to a complex trust the purpose of which was to preserve "the records of the earthly life of Mary Baker Eddy," the founder of the Christian Science religion. The heirs challenged the will on the grounds of lack of testamentary capacity and undue influence. The controversy was subsequently settled for $141,484 payable to the taxpayer. The Commissioner treated this as taxable income and assessed a tax of $56,389.

---

[85]   Section 102(b) flush language; Reg. § 1.102–1(c).

[86]   Lindau v. Commissioner, 21 T.C. 911 (1954) (acq.).

[87]   305 U.S. 188, 59 S.Ct. 155, 83 L.Ed. 119 (1938).

The Court disregarded state law decisions in the area holding that amounts received in settlement of a will contest are income. The Court said the matter was a federal question and held that the amounts received in compromise were excluded from income.[88] The same policy considerations that underlie the exclusion of gifts (however they might be resolved (see ¶ 3.08(1)) underlie this exclusion).

There have, of course, been a healthy number of disputes concerning what qualifies for this exclusion. As in the gift area, though a transfer may in form qualify for the exclusion, it will be included in income if it is in substance compensation. In the leading case of *Wolder*,[89] taxpayer, an attorney, entered into a written agreement with his client to forego billing for past and future legal services in exchange for the client's bequest to him of a substantial amount of stock. Though the transfer was a bequest under New York law (and was treated as such in ancillary state court litigation) the Second Circuit, taking a leaf from the book of *Duberstein,* found the arrangement to be in substance compensation.[90]

While this principle seems plain enough, a line of bequest-to-executor cases has raised some problems. An executor of course may receive a bequest tax-free. However, where the bequest is contingent upon the performance of services as an executor, it seems clear that the bequest is taxable compensation, and the courts have so held.[91] Where, however, the bequest is contingent only on the taxpayer's acceptance of the role of executor but is not contingent on the taxpayer's performance of the duties of executor, the Supreme Court held in the old case of *Merriam*[92] that the bequest will be excluded.

This analysis in *Merriam* was severely criticized by the Second Circuit in *Wolder* as not withstanding economic analysis, but until

---

[88] Section 102(a). It is clear that by these terms Congress meant to exclude from income all property, real and personal, which passes by reason of death of the decedent, Lyeth v. Hoey, 305 U.S. 188, 59 S.Ct. 155, 83 L.Ed. 119 (1938).

The sales proceeds of an expected inheritance from a living parent are income, Rev.Rul. 70–60, 1970–1 C.B. 11.

[89] Wolder v. Commissioner, 493 F.2d 608 (2d Cir.1974), cert. denied 419 U.S. 828, 95 S.Ct. 49, 42 L.Ed.2d 53 (1974).

[90] See also Rev.Rul. 67–375, 1967–2 C.B. 60. To hold otherwise would, of course, invite widespread tax avoidance by tax advisors and their elderly clients.

Where taxpayer receives an amount in settlement of a claim for compensation for services rendered the decedent, the payment is income, where the taxpayer is not an heir or legatee, Braddock v. United States, 434 F.2d 631 (9th Cir.1970).

[91] Ream v. Bowers, 22 F.2d 465 (2d Cir.1927).

[92] United States v. Merriam, 263 U.S. 179, 44 S.Ct. 69, 68 L.Ed. 240 (1923) (interpreting the will of Alfred C. Vanderbilt), followed by Rev.Rul. 57–398, 1957–2 C.B. 93; cf. Bank of New York v. Helvering, 132 F.2d 773 (2d Cir.1943) (although bequest formally contingent on services, underlying facts suggested none was contemplated).

such time as the Supreme Court reverses itself, an attractive method to pay executors is to make cash bequests to them "in lieu of all compensation or commission to which they would otherwise be entitled as executors or trustees" (the *Merriam* Court language), being careful not to state further that *services* as an executor or trustee are required.[93]

Where there is a will contest, payments in settlement are treated as though they were acquired under the will and, hence, are excludible.[94]

(b) Transfers in Trust: Irwin v. Gavit

Some fascinating problems are presented if, say, $300,000 of securities is transferred under a decedent's will so that the decedent's spouse gets the income for life and then the remainder goes to the decedent's child. How does the exclusion of bequests of § 102 apply in that circumstance? These problems are illustrated by the case of *Irwin v. Gavit:*

IRWIN V. GAVIT[95]

Facts: Taxpayer, E. Palmer Gavit, was the son-in-law of the deceased, Anthony N. Brady. Brady's will provided that a portion of the property in his estate should be placed in trust. A portion of the income from the trust would go to Gavit's daughter, and a portion was to be distributed to Gavit. The payments to Gavit, however, terminated once his daughter died or turned twenty-one. Since his daughter was six at the time, the longest Gavit's interest could last was 15 years.

Question: Are the payments to Gavit excluded as a bequest under § 102 or are they not excluded since they are income from property which was the subject of the bequest?

Taxpayer's argument: The amounts left to Gavit are installment payments of a bequest of property measured by income from the property. As a bequest, the payments are therefore excluded.

Held: (Holmes, C. J.) Reversing lower courts, the payments to Gavit are taxable as income from the bequest. The property which was the subject of the bequest produces the income from it. "Day and night, youth and age are only types . . . the distinction is not hard to draw . . . this is a gift of income from a very large fund of income."

---

[93]   This arrangement would seemingly mean the estate will not get an income tax or estate tax deduction for the payments, generally § 2053.

[94]   Lyeth v. Hoey, supra. If the payment comes out of estate income it may be taxable, see Delmar, 25 T.C. 1015 (1956).

[95]   268 U.S. 161, 45 S.Ct. 475, 69 L.Ed. 897 (1925).

Comment: The Court here was interpreting the predecessor of § 102(a) which excludes bequests from income and the predecessor of § 102(b)(1) which taxes income from property which has been excluded as a bequest. Section 102(b)(2) was subsequently enacted to explicitly tax income from property which is the subject of a bequest. Thus § 102(b)(2) confirms the holding in *Gavit.*

This holding was undoubtedly correct. If Gavit had won, then not only would bequeathed property not be taxed but so would the income from it if the income were bequeathed to a different party. By contrast, there was no doubt that if property and income from it were bequeathed to the same person that only the property and not the income from it would be excluded. Thus a huge tax shelter would be created where everyone would be encouraged to leave divided interests in property to their heirs.

There is another fascinating time value of money issue in this case. After all, this whole deal does play out over a number of years. To get a handle on this problem, let us simplify the facts a little by saying that Gavit got all the income from the property and there was none paid for Marcia's support. Let us say that Gavit gets the income for life and that his life expectancy is 15 years. There are no other contingencies that cause Gavit to stop getting the income other than his own death. On Gavit's death, his daughter Marcia gets the trust corpus.

This alteration of facts clearly draws the problem as the classic one of an income beneficiary for life and a remainderman (or in this case remainderwoman).

Let us also specify that the trust corpus is $500,000 of investment-grade corporate bonds, paying an interest rate of 10%, or $50,000 per year.

Now what is the problem? We have two people each with an interest in the trust property. We have Gavit with his income interest and Marcia with her remainder interest. Gavit is taxed in full on his interest and Marcia is not taxed at all on her interest either at the date of death or later when she gets her interest. Thus Marcia gets the full amount of the exclusion and Gavit gets none of it. That is the current law. That is fine, but there is another way to look at it: Gavit had a point in the case. He did have an inheritance. The inheritance was of $50,000 per year for 15 years.[96] As we know, due to the time value of money, the deal has a value. That value is the present value of a stream of earnings of $50,000 per year for 15 years, assuming a 10% interest rate. The present value of that is $380,300.

---

[96]   He might live longer or shorter than 15 years but we use his life expectancy for these discussion purposes.

What about Marcia? What did Marcia really inherit? Well she inherited the right to get $500,000 in 15 years. What is that worth now? Turns out the value of what Marcia got is $119,700. Adds up with Gavit's interest to $500,000, of course. The income plus the remainder equals the total bequest and the total bequest was $500,000.

Thus why not have a rule that actually reflects reality? Why don't we say that Gavit inherited something with a fair market value at the date of death of $380,300 and Marcia inherited something with a fair market value at the date of death of $119,700? Since that's what really happened, it might be nice to treat it that way.[97]

Thus what we would do is say that that is what they each inherited and that neither is taxed on the value of his or her inheritance, under § 102. Their two exclusions taken together then exhaust the total $500,000 exclusion (fair market value of the corpus) to which the heirs are entitled. In short, the heirs have each inherited a slice of that $500,000 corpus.

If we push this analysis further, what do we do? Take Gavit. He's got a basis of $380,300. Here is a critical point. That $380,300 basis that Gavit has is like his capital now. He's entitled not to be taxed on it in the future just as surely as if he had purchased this right to receive $50,000 payments per year for 15 years as an annuity. So the discussion is now in terms of recovery of capital, and how you are entitled not to be taxed on your capital, see Chapter One, ¶ 1.02(3)(e).

Therefore, let's look at Gavit. He's receiving payments of $50,000 per year for 15 years. This looks, walks, and quacks like an annuity. Recall the treatment of annuities in Chapter One at ¶ 1.02(3)(e) and in this chapter at ¶ 3.07.

What we do is somehow offset Gavit's basis against the annual $50,000 payments. Then we tax the net amount as income. In that way, Gavit is allowed to exclude his basis in his inheritance and be taxed on income from his inheritance over time.

For example, if we took the usual annuity rules, we would spread his basis of $380,300 over 15 years. That would mean he could deduct $25,333 per year against $50,000 per year. Thus he would have taxable income of $24,667 per year. If we took the economically accurate approach of recovering capital that we discussed in

---

[97] One side-line effect of this present value analysis is to throw a light on what the parties really got. One might have thought off the top that it would have been better to be Marcia than to be Gavit. After all $500,000 sounds like a lot more than $50,000 a year. But it turns out that what Gavit got was much more valuable. Remember, Gavit can reinvest his income stream every year for 15 years compounded. Marcia's bequest was deferred. If you are advising clients on estate planning, you might like to bear such things in mind.

¶ 1.02(3)(e), then the result would be that we would be giving Gavit larger deductions of his basis in the early years and smaller deductions in the later years, as the calculations in ¶ 1.02(3)(e) demonstrate.

What about Marcia? Her basis in her remainder interest is, as we have calculated, $119,700. As in the case of Gavit, Marcia has income over time from her interest. How do we see that? Marcia's future interest of $119,700 is becoming larger as time passes. This is because as time passes, her future payment is getting closer and closer to the present. When we finally hit 15 years out and Marcia takes her remainder interest,[98] what is it worth at that time? Well of course it is worth $500,000. So Marcia, over the course of 15 years, has had her interest grow to the point where she has total income over the period of $500,000 − $119,700 or $380,300 (no surprise there).

So how do we tax Marcia on this income? We could do it pro rata—namely, $380,300/15 = $25,353 per year. Or we could do it more economically accurately by understanding that her economic interest of $119,700 is growing by the prevailing interest rate of 10% compounded. It turns out that $119,700 growing at 10% compounded annually grows to $500,000 in 15 years. This economically accurate approach would be like the treatment of original issue discount. For example Marcia's interest would grow in the first year by 10% of $119,700 or $11,970.

Is Marcia taxed on this? She is not getting her hands on any money at this point. This is very much like holding appreciated property. We could therefore easily choose not to tax her on the grounds that she has not had a "realization," see ¶ 4.02. However, just to be nasty about it, let's say she is taxed on it. If she is taxed on this 10% compounded increase per year, then she is entitled to raise her basis in her remainder interest by that amount. This is to insure that she will not be taxed on it again. She has in effect "earned" the right to that increase in basis by paying tax. Let's see how things work out.

Now we're ready for some complications. Suppose Gavit kicks the bucket after five years. This looks like it messes up our calculations, but in fact we can handle it. If Gavit is using the annuity system for recovering his basis, then after five years he would have deducted 5 × $25,333 = $126,665. Thus he would have $380,300 − $126,665 or $253,635 of unrecovered basis. In his final tax return

---

[98] Assuming Gavit dies exactly on his birthday 15 years from now so as not to complicate our example. We'll give him a little drink of something.

that is taken as a deduction, as in the annuity rules generally. So that works out.

Then, as a result of Gavit's untimely demise, Marcia gets her remainder interest early. She gets $500,000 of securities. If she is using the economically accurate or original issue discount approach for paying tax and increasing basis, she then has a basis in her remainder interest of $119,700 increased by 10% compounded annually for 5 years. That comes out to be a total of $192,778. So, Marcia gets $500,000 less her basis of $192,778, or $307,222 of income on the early receipt of her remainder interest.[99]

That is a way to do it instead of the approach of the current law, as exemplified by *Gavit*. One argument in favor of the *Gavit* approach is that it is less complicated. A strong argument in favor of the present value analysis approach is that it is economically accurate.

One objection that might be raised to the present-value approach is that we do not know what interest rate to apply to value the life interest and remainder. Would it depend on the type of property held by the trust? This is not a big problem. We can pick some interest rate amount that is somewhat above the prevailing risk-free rate, as the Internal Revenue Code does now for many time value of money questions. Doing that certainly gets you closer to an economically accurate answer than does the completely inaccurate *Gavit* approach.

Integrated Summary of Inheritance Rules

Money or property received from a decedent by will or by intestate succession is excluded from income, § 102(a).

Amounts received in settlement of a will contest are also excluded from income under § 102(a), Lyeth v. Hoey, 305 U.S. 188, 59 S.Ct. 155, 83 L.Ed. 119 (1938).

The rules can be illustrated with an example. Nicole leaves $100,000 to her close friend Faye in thanks for Faye's companionship and support through turbulent years. This would still be excluded from Faye's income and would not trigger a *Wolder* analysis to find income.

But if Nicole had left $100,000 to Faye under a written agreement in which Faye promised to care for Nicole and provide her with therapeutic services and medicine, the $100,000 would be income to Faye, under *Wolder*. Note that § 102(c) would not apply

---

[99]   If we had not taxed Marcia on her 10% a year compounded return, then she would have her original basis of $119,700. Then her gain on the early receipt of her remainder interest would be $500,000 − $119,700 = $380,300.

here since Faye would not be an employee of Nicole but more in the nature of an independent contractor.

Suppose there was this same written agreement, but Nicole died suddenly without a will. If Faye then successfully sued Nicole's estate on the claim, the amounts Faye received would be income.

If Faye settled her claim with the estate for $75,000, the $75,000 would be income.

Suppose Nicole appointed Faye as executrix of her estate and Nicole's will stated that Faye would receive $60,000 for these services. Again under *Wolder*, the $60,000 would be income.

Alternatively, Nicole's will provides that Faye will be the executrix of her estate and will receive a bequest of $60,000 "in lieu of compensation or commissions to which she would otherwise be entitled as executrix." In that case, *Wolder* suggests that the $60,000 would be income, but the older case of *Merriam* holds that where the bequest is contingent only on the taxpayer's acceptance of the role of executrix but is not contingent on the performance of the duties of executor, the bequest is excluded. As discussed in the text above, the Supreme Court's holding in *Merriam* was criticized in *Wolder*, but until the Supreme Court reverses itself, using the *Merriam* language quoted above is an attractive way to compensate executors.

In general suits against an estate for services rendered in which there is payment or a settlement based on any contractual theory would give rise to income to the recipient.

Section 102(c) is not necessarily applicable in *Wolder* situations because *Wolder* situations involve not only employer-employee relationships but also independent contractor relationships, to which § 102(c) has no application.

Suppose Nicole leaves $2 million in trust with income to Ronald and following Ronald's death the remainder to Denise. Assuming Ronald survives Nicole, the income paid to Ronald under the trust instrument would not be excluded. This is because where a bequest is of income from property, it is not excluded, Irwin v. Gavit, discussed above, § 102(b)(2).

¶ 3.09 PRIZES, SCHOLARSHIPS AND FELLOWSHIP GRANTS

(1) Prizes: McDonell

Prizes and awards are included in income under § 74(a). This includes everything from the Nobel and Pulitzer Prizes to a door prize at a keno parlor. There are limited exceptions to the inclusion of prizes in income for prizes transferred to charities, § 74(b), and certain employee achievement awards, § 74(c). The leading prize case of *Allen J. McDonell v. Commissioner*,[100] which involved the question whether the expenses of a trip to Hawaii taken by the taxpayer and his wife and paid for by his employer were income to the taxpayer and, if so, whether the amounts were deductible by him. Taxpayer was sent as something of a chaperone for salesmen who were sent to Hawaii as an award for meeting certain sales quotas. He was selected out of eligible supervisors by drawing names out of a hat. At the time he was selected, he was told that he and his wife were expected to go. Those selected to go received no cut in pay and did not lose vacation time. Those not chosen received no substitute benefit. Taxpayer was told he was to consider this trip an assignment and not a vacation. Taxpayer and his wife did not have spare time for swimming or shopping. The court held that taxpayer had no income on this trip, that it was taken to carry out duties assigned to the taxpayer by his employer.

Much ado was made in 2004 when Oprah Winfrey started giving away property to people in her studio audience. First, Oprah (really Pontiac) gave away a free car to guests in her studio audience. The interesting tax issue was whether the car was taxable to the audience member. The clear answer is yes. The car is not a gift. It has not been given out of detached and disinterested generosity, and it does not fit within any exclusion provision. It is simply income under § 61.

The problem for contestants was that they may not have the cash to pay the tax on the prize. If we assume the car was worth $30,000 and the taxpayer was in the 25% bracket, the taxpayer would have a tax bill of $7,500. A middle income taxpayer might not have $7,500 of cash sitting around to pay the bill.

Should we feel sorry for the taxpayer? Not in our book. The audience member now has an asset worth $30,000. If the recipient doesn't have the money to pay the tax then the recipient can sell the car, or take out a $7,500 loan secured by the car. The taxpayer is still better off.

Oprah caused a stir again several months later when she gave property valued at approximately $13,000 to teachers in her audience. This time Oprah also provided an additional $2,500 cash to the recipients to cover the federal tax bill. Tax commentators were once again abuzz about how Oprah saddled her guests with a big tax bill. But in this case, the controversy may have been much ado about nothing.

---

[100]   26 T.C.M. 115 (1967).

Assuming the property and cash were worth $15,500, a 15% taxpayer would have incurred $2,325 in federal income tax. That number might be slightly higher depending on the state tax rate (but remember state income taxes would be deductible and would reduce the federal income tax liability), but it was very close to the $2,500 that Oprah provided. It was only married taxpayers with taxable incomes over $58,100 (that likely means incomes of at least $80,000) that would pay more tax since they would be in a higher tax bracket. Oprah probably assumed that most of the teachers were in the 15% tax bracket, and if they were not, they could afford to pay the added tax.

In any event, the prize winner is in control. If the teacher wanted the payment to cover the total tax bill, the teacher could always refuse a portion of the prize.

The important fact to realize is that this type of prize should be taxed. The taxpayers are receiving a windfall, and there is no reason to exempt that windfall from tax. If anything, a windfall is one of the most appropriate items to tax. The tax provides almost no economic detriment because it has no impact on behavior. Who would you rather see pay extra tax, the teacher who makes $25,000 a year, or the teacher who makes $25,000 a year and receives a $15,000 prize from Oprah?

(2) Scholarships and Fellowship Grants

There is an exclusion for degree candidates[101] for scholarships which the recipient establishes are for tuition and related expenses (such as fees, books, supplies, and equipment required for courses of instruction).[102] There is no exclusion for amounts received for teaching, research, or other services required of the student as a condition for receiving the scholarship.[103]

An exclusion is also allowed for a qualified tuition reduction, which is defined as a reduction in tuition provided to an employee of an educational institution for the education of the individual or his spouse or dependents. The exclusion is available also for tuition reduction plans at other educational institutions (these are often

---

[101] A "degree candidate" is a graduate or undergraduate pursuing studies or conducting research to meet the requirements for an academic or professional degree. The definition also includes a student who receives a scholarship for study at a secondary institution. Reg. § 1.117–3(e). This regulation does not mention students at elementary schools, although indeed often private elementary schools do grant substantial scholarships to students.

At the other end of the educational spectrum, a doctor in a psychiatric residency program is not a degree candidate, Bergeron, 31 T.C.M. 1226 (1972).

[102] Section 117(a) and (b).

[103] Section 117(c).

exchange programs). The exclusion is available to highly compensated employees only if the reduction program does not discriminate in favor of highly compensated employees.[104] See also ¶ 2.02(1).

The exclusion for scholarships raises some interesting questions. Why should tuition scholarships be excluded from income? Presumably, it is to go easy on the recipients who are struggling students. But if that is the case, note also that students who go to state universities and pay very low tuition are getting a subsidy. Not taxing them on that subsidy is, perhaps, consistent with not taxing the recipient of a scholarship. That still leaves the working student out in the cold.

The exclusion of scholarships and fellowship grants is best viewed in the context of a wide range of other assistance to education such as free schooling, low tuition at state universities and federally subsidized low-interest student loans. See ¶ 10.07 for a full recap of assistance to education. Since these other very real benefits are not considered income (see generally ¶ 1.02(2)(b) relating to the comprehensive tax base) perhaps the exclusion of scholarships and fellowship grants simply equalizes the situation for students receiving this particular form of educational assistance. The only problem with that analysis is that it omits the student who gets no scholarship but is working to pay for school. Should that student get to deduct tuition payments (which is functionally equivalent to an exclusion)?[105] Or do we mean to go harder on the student who works to pay for school than the student who gets a scholarship?[106]

If a grant is in the form of a scholarship or fellowship but is in reality compensation for services, it will be treated as such and included in income. This is consistent with the treatment of other areas such as gifts and prizes and awards, supra, where the exclusion will be denied if the transaction is at bottom compensatory.[107]

To those who would be rude enough to suggest that the scholarships that college athletes receive are income, because of the expectation they will participate in intercollegiate sports, the Service has ruled to the contrary. Under NCAA rules, once an athletic scholarship is granted for a particular year it cannot be revoked even

---

[104]   Section 117(d)(3).

[105]   Several tax provisions now help the working student as well. Section 25A provides tax credits for certain higher education expenses. Moreover, § 222 provides a limited deduction for education expenses. See ¶ 10.07 for further details.

[106]   See, e.g. Commission to Revise the Tax Structure, Reforming the Federal Tax Structure (Fund for Public Policy Research, 1973). Cf. ¶ 6.03(3)(b) relating to the deductibility of education expenses.

[107]   Bingler v. Johnson, 394 U.S. 741, 89 S.Ct. 1439, 22 L.Ed.2d 695 (1969).

though the recipient chooses not to play sports. Hence the theory of the ruling is that the scholarship is not awarded in exchange for playing sports. The apparent flaw in this reasoning is that if the recipient does not choose to play sports, the scholarship need not (and probably will not) be renewed for the following year. Thus, in reality, in order to keep the scholarship going from year to year, the recipient must play sports. That certainly seems to make the scholarship income under general principles.[108]

Integrated Summary of Scholarship and Fellowship Grant Rules

Scholarships for tuition and books for a student who is a degree candidate at an educational institution are excluded from the student's gross income, § 117(b)(2)(A). Scholarships covering room and board are not excluded from income. Payments to the student for doing research are included in the student's income.

If the student receives a scholarship for room and board for, say, $5,000 but is required to do 500 hours of research to receive it (where the going rate for compensated research is $10 per hour), then the scholarship is included in income for two independent reasons: 1) room-board scholarships are always included in income and 2) the room-board scholarship was in effect payment for the research services.

Suppose a student receives a $10,000 scholarship which covers $5,000 tuition and books and $5,000 room and board. Suppose further the student is required to render 500 hours of research services (value $10/hour) to get this $10,000 scholarship. If the research is deemed to be for receiving the tuition-books scholarship, then that $5,000 tuition-books scholarship is included in income. In addition the $5,000 room-board scholarship is included in income because room-board scholarships are always included in income. If the $5,000 of research services is deemed to be for receiving the room-board scholarship, then the $5,000 tuition-books scholarship is not included in income and the $5,000 room-board scholarship is still of course included in income.

The moral of the story is that the educational institution should specify that the research services are required for receiving the room and board scholarship and not the tuition-books scholarship. The results above are not changed even if all students are required to render 500 hours of research in order to get their degree. As discussed above in the text, the traditional athletic scholarship does not

---

[108] Rev.Rul. 77–263, 1977–2 C.B. 47. Ruling that athletic scholarships are income would tend to suggest that big time college athletes are basically underpaid professionals. Perish the thought.

constitute income to the recipient because failure to participate in sports does not cause the scholarship to be withdrawn for the current year.

It is fairly common that several educational institutions in an area agree to give tuition scholarships to spouses of their employees attending one of the other institutions. As long as the plan is not discriminatory, the tuition scholarships are not includible in the recipient's gross income, § 117(d)(3).

Suppose Phil, an engineer for Westinghouse, goes back to Carnegie Mellon University for a Ph.D. in mechanical engineering. Westinghouse pays $15,000 toward tuition and books for the course of study on the condition that Phil return and work for Westinghouse. As discussed above, tuition payments here would be income, because what Westinghouse is doing is paying compensation for future services, which is taxable, see Regs. § 1.117–4(c), Prop. Reg. § 1.117–6(d)(2) and (5). Even if Phil was not required to come back to Westinghouse, the tuition payments could be income as payment for past services.[109]

¶ 3.10 DISCHARGE OF INDEBTEDNESS

(1) General Rule and Background: Old Colony Trust; Clark; Kirby Lumber; Zarin

Before you get out of debt, of course, you have to get in debt. The way you do that is by borrowing. What are the tax consequences of borrowing? Money is, after all, flowing from one party to another. Taking an annual accounting or cash flow view of the matter, the borrower could be regarded as being in receipt of income when he borrows and entitled to a deduction when he pays back the principal. The rule in fact, however, is that borrowing does not give rise to income to the borrower and repaying the debt does not give rise to a deduction.[110]

The usual reason given for this treatment is that borrowing creates an immediate offsetting deduction to repay and therefore the borrower is not wealthier than he was before the borrowing. That answer is surprisingly inadequate, however. The tax law is rife with circumstances where taxpayers are taxed in transactions where they have not enjoyed an increase in wealth. For example, the simple act of selling appreciated stock is such a case. The taxpayer is not wealthier the day after selling stock than the day before. The

---

[109] But see I.R.C. § 127 (providing that employer provided educational assistance may be tax exempt.)

[110] The interest paid on the debt is deductible, subject to various exceptions and limitations. See ¶ 7.01(3).

taxpayer has merely changed the form of the investment to cash.[111] The wealth came from the previous rise in the value of the stock. That previous rise in the value of the stock, which did make the stockholder richer, was not taxed. And it would never be taxed if the taxpayer never sold the stock, even though the taxpayer was much wealthier because of it.

As another example, a stockholder in a corporation who receives a distribution of cash is taxed on that distribution, even if the stock has not appreciated in the stockholder's hands. In fact the stockholder has income on the cash distribution even if the stock has gone down in price.[112]

What this discussion seems to show, if it shows nothing else, is that an increase in wealth is not necessarily the touchstone of taxation.[113]

Thus we are still left trying to explain why the borrower does not have income at the time of borrowing. The borrower certainly has the funds to pay the tax. We might say that the borrower has an amount realized of the amount of the loan. But then we could also say that the borrower has a basis equal to the amount of the loan, since the borrower is now obligated to repay the loan. Thus the reason there is no income from borrowing is that there is no gain realized, since amount realized equals basis, see ¶ 4.03.

Whatever the confusion on the rationale, the cold rule of law on the subject is clear: The borrower does not have income on borrowing and does not have a deduction on repayment. Similarly, the lender does not have a deduction on making the loan[114] and does not have income on repayment.

Let us turn now to the question of what happens when the taxpayer is discharged from a debt. One of the early cases, *Old Colony Trust* presented an interesting set of facts, as discussed in ¶ 2.01.

Old Colony spawned an interesting case about 10 years later in the Board of Tax Appeals (the predecessor of the Tax Court), holding that the payment by an employer of an employee's taxes was income to the employee.

---

[111]   In the jargon he has undergone a "realization," see ¶ 4.02.

[112]   The cash distribution is taxable as a dividend as long as the corporation has something, as an accounting matter, called "earnings and profits." These "earnings and profits" could have been earned long before the stockholder owned stock in the company. §§ 301(c), 312, 316. See ¶ 3.03.

[113]   For a discussion of just what *is* the touchstone, see ¶ 4.02.

[114]   We could explain that by saying that the lender in making the loan has undertaken a capital expense in the amount of the loan. The loan is a capital asset that will create income (i.e. interest). The basis of the capital asset will be amortized against repayment of the loan principal leading to no net gain there.

This was *Clark:*

CLARK V. COMMISSIONER[115]

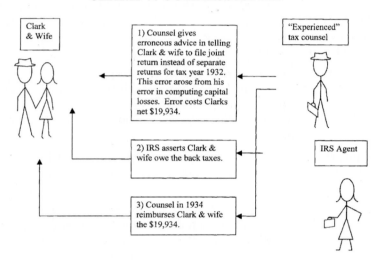

Facts: Taxpayer, Edward H. Clark and his wife, upon the advice of experienced tax counsel, filed a joint tax return. The taxpayers were subsequently audited, and the IRS claimed taxpayers owed additional amounts of money. This additional sum was imposed because the taxpayers' counsel erred in computed the amount of capital losses that could be deducted from income. The taxpayers' counsel admitted that if he had advised them to file separate returns instead of joint returns, they would have had to pay $19,941.10 less in tax. Counsel then paid the taxpayer the $19,941.10.

Question: Was the reimbursement of the taxes by the Clark's counsel income to the Clarks?

Service's theory: Counsel paid Clark's taxes and thus it is income, citing *Old Colony.*

Taxpayer's theory: The reimbursement was compensation for damages and thus constituted a return of capital and not income (see ¶ 1.02(3)(e) on return of capital). He took no deduction for the earlier payment.

Held: The reimbursement was not "derived from capital, from labor or from both combined." The reimbursement was a return of capital and was not income.

Comment: The holding in *Clark* that the payment was not income because it was not derived from capital, labor or both

---

[115]   40 B.T.A. 333 (1939), acq. 1957–1 C.B. 4.

combined no longer applies. See the discussion of *Glenshaw Glass* ¶ 2.01. The result in *Clark*, however—that this is a return of capital—still applies. The IRS has taken the position that *Clark* applies when taxpayers pay "more than their minimum proper federal income tax liabilities based on the underlying transactions" and are reimbursed by a third party for those amounts. The IRS has distinguished *Clark* from other cases where the payment "of additional federal income tax was not due to an error made by the attorneys on the return itself but on an omission to provide advice that would have reduced your federal income tax liability."[116] It appears that the Service's logic is that repayments for mistakes on a return are a repayment of capital, but mistakes in tax planning are not. Is this distinction really satisfying?

Consider *Old Colony,* discussed at ¶ 2.01, and this case. We see that the fact that a third party discharges debt of the taxpayer does not decide the question of taxability. We must know the reason for the discharge. Was it compensatory in nature, as in *Old Colony* or was it a return of capital as in *Clark*?

No doubt *Clark* is correctly decided. It can be viewed as a damage case. As we learn in ¶ 3.11(2), damages are taxed by what they substitute for. Here the damage payment by counsel to the Clarks was for loss of capital that he caused to the Clarks. The particular loss of capital involved (the necessity to pay federal income taxes) was not deductible. Since the obligation to pay the taxes was not deductible, the Clarks had a basis in the payment. Hence when they received the reimbursement, it was not taxable up to the amount of their basis. Had Counsel also paid them interest on the $19,934 (which would have been appropriate to do) the Clark's would have had income to the extent the payment exceeded their basis of $19,934. This logic would equally apply, however, when an accountant makes an error in setting up a transaction, and it appears that at least the Service would not allow a deduction in such a case.

The classic case in the field of cancellation of indebtedness is *Kirby Lumber*.[117]

---

[116] See Priv. Ltr. Rul. 9833007 (distinguishing the facts in Clark and Rev.Rul. 57–47 from the facts in the revenue ruling on the grounds that taxpayer did not misstate a deduction on the return).

[117] For an in-depth look at Kirby Lumber see Deborah H. Schenk, The Story of Kirby Lumber: The many Faces of Discharge of Indebtedness Income, 97–129 (Paul L. Caron ed. 2003).

UNITED STATES V. KIRBY LUMBER CO.[118]

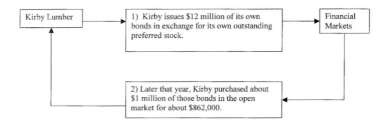

Facts: Taxpayer, Kirby Lumber Co., was a company that, in July of 1923, issued approximately $12 million of bonds in exchange for its own outstanding preferred stock on which there were dividend arrearages. Later in 1923, the taxpayer purchased back approximately $1,000,000 of these bonds for approximately $862,000. Thus, taxpayer bought the bonds back for $138,000 less than the price at which they were issued.

Question: Is the $138,000 difference in price that Kirby repurchased its own bonds for includible in Kirby's income?

Taxpayer's argument: In *Bowers v. Kerbaugh-Empire* (see ¶ 1.02(3)(f)) repayment of a debt in German marks which had fallen in value did not give rise to income.

Held: In *Kerbaugh-Empire*, unlike here, the overall transaction produced a loss. Here there was no diminution of assets. There was an accession to income and the difference is taxable.

Comment: Apparently Kirby was able to repurchase these bonds for less than the original issue price because interest rates had risen in the economy. Rising interest rates drive bond prices down because richer yields are available throughout the financial markets.

The Court made reference to *Kerbaugh-Empire*.[119] In that case, the proceeds of a loan denominated in dollars were repaid in depreciated German marks. Thus there was a profit on the repayment. The taxpayer in *Kerbaugh-Empire*, however, invested the proceeds of the loan in a losing venture and therefore the overall transaction netted to a loss. Suppose Kirby Lumber had invested the proceeds of the bonds it later repurchased in a venture that lost $200,000. Would the Court have followed *Kerbaugh-Empire* and have netted the $138,000 gains on the bond repurchase against the (say) $200,000 loss on the venture to find a net loss of $62,000?

---

[118]   284 U.S. 1, 52 S.Ct. 4, 76 L.Ed. 131 (1931).
[119]   Bowers v. Kerbaugh-Empire, 271 U.S. 170, 46 S.Ct. 449, 70 L.Ed. 886 (1926), discussed at ¶ 1.02(2)(f).

We received some insight into those questions in the case of *Commissioner v. Jacobson*.[120] This case presented similar facts to *Kirby* in that the taxpayer repurchased its debt at a discount. The reason it was able to do so, however, was not because there was a general rise in interest rates. Rather, the taxpayer had come upon straitened financial circumstances. Since it was less creditworthy, its bonds were regarded as riskier by the financial markets and fell in price. *Jacobson* thus presented the *Kerbaugh-Empire* issue: the taxpayer was a loser overall but was making money on the particular repayment transaction. The Court held that there was income on the repurchase.

This is certainly the right answer. If the taxpayer is suffering other losses it may take them as appropriate. Let us ascertain tax liability one transaction at a time.

Now that we have staggered through to the truth, we find that Congress changed the rules on us anyway. Congress apparently found cases like *Jacobson* deserving of relief. Here, after all, is a taxpayer struggling along on the verge of collapse. It manages to pull a deal to help itself a little (repurchase its own obligations at less than face value) and then the big bad IRS comes along and knocks the taxpayer back down again.

This led to the passage of § 108, which provides that cancellation of debt income ("COD income" in the argot) is excluded if the discharge occurs in a bankruptcy case or when the taxpayer is insolvent. The exclusion is temporary in that the taxpayer benefitting from it has to suffer in other ways. In particular it has to reduce other favorable "tax attributes," such as net operating loss carryovers, by the amount of COD income excluded.[121] Eventually, then, the taxpayer will pay more in tax because of the loss of these favorable attributes. Section 108, therefore, is best viewed as *deferring* (not *forgiving*) the inclusion of income.

COD income and § 108 have assumed major importance with respect to some large companies. Some companies are staggering under a heavy debt load. Their very shakiness causes their debt to collapse in price. They then often repurchase their depreciated outstanding debt and still try to keep their net operating losses alive. This is a good place to remind ourselves that the provisions we study are not just for individuals. Most of the provisions we study are used as well by, for example, large publicly-held corporations.[122]

---

[120]   336 U.S. 28, 69 S.Ct. 358, 93 L.Ed. 477 (1949).

[121]   108(b). See discussion below at ¶ 3.10(2).

[122]   In addition, there are specialized corporate tax provisions. See Internal Revenue Code, Subchapters C and S.

The problems in the discharge of indebtedness field were highlighted by the fascinating case of *Zarin*.

ZARIN V. COMMISSIONER[123]

Facts: Taxpayer, David Zarin, was an engineer who often gambled in Atlantic City. The taxpayer initially asked for and was granted a gambling credit line of $10,000 with Resorts Hotel. The taxpayer quickly developed a reputation as a high roller, was provided with many privileges and complimentary services, and had his credit line increased to $200,000. The taxpayer lost and paid in full $2,500,000 during this time period. The New Jersey Division of Gaming Enforcement then told Resorts Hotel that they could not extend the taxpayer any more credit. Resorts evaded the order through the use of alternative credit devices such as "considered cleared" credit and "this trip only" credit. Both devices were later found to be illegal by the Commission and Resorts was fined. The taxpayer racked up $3,435,000 in gambling debts. The personal checks he wrote to pay off the debt were dishonored. Resorts then filed suit against the taxpayer and eventually settled with him for $500,000.

Question: Does Zarin have $2,935,000 of cancellation of indebtedness income?

Service's argument: Resorts' advance to Zarin of $3,435,000 in chips was a loan. The settlement for $500,000 constituted a cancellation of the remaining indebtedness.

Held: The debt Zarin owed to Resorts was unenforceable as a matter of New Jersey law, because of Resort's violation of the Casino Commission rules regarding extending Zarin credit. Thus the debt was not one for which the taxpayer is liable as required by § 108(d)(1)(A). Thus cancellation of the debt did not give rise to income.

Comment: Zarin had the defense that he was insolvent (liabilities exceed assets) at the time of the purported cancellation of debt income; thus he would not be taxable, § 108(a)(1)(B). However, Zarin's first attorneys failed to raise this issue. After losing his case and hiring a new attorney, Zarin made a motion to reconsider his case and raised the § 108(a)(1)(B) issue. The Tax Court denied his motion to reconsider the case. Zarin later sued his first attorneys for malpractice but lost.[124]

---

[123] 916 F.2d 110 (3d Cir.1990).
[124] Zarin v. Reid & Priest, 184 A.D.2d 385, 585 N.Y.S.2d 379, 382 (N.Y. App. Div. 1992).

Comment: If Zarin subsequently failed to pay the $500,000 settlement amount, he then probably would have cancellation of debt income of $500,000.

The court also held that the unenforceability of the debt meant there was a legitimate dispute as to the amount of the debt and thus that cancellation of it could not give rise to income.

The question that might be asked here is what would have happened if the facts were the same as in Zarin, except that Resorts did not violate any of New Jersey's gaming rules? The debt then would be enforceable under New Jersey law. Zarin was a resident of New Jersey. Cancellation of the debt would then appear to be income. Resorts' egregious conduct was clearly a factor in this case, so *Zarin* can certainly not be read as standing for the proposition that cancellation of gambling debts never gives rise to income.

A number of commentators have advanced some imaginative arguments that even though the gambling debt was unenforceable, Zarin still could have had income on other grounds. This would be that Zarin had a benefit of entertainment from Resorts equal to his $2.9 million cancelled debt. Since he did not pay for it, he had income of that amount. This line of reasoning finds support in the *Tufts* case (see Chapter 4). *Tufts* held that when a taxpayer benefits (in that case taking depreciation) from borrowed funds and then does not pay the debt back in full, there is still income in the amount not paid back. Another possible approach is that cancellation of the debt was in effect a punishment to Resorts for its violations of gambling regulations. As such the cancellation of the debt was tantamount to the receipt of punitive damages by Zarin, which is taxable under the leading case of *Glenshaw Glass*, see Chapter 2.

Another possibility is that the cancellation of the debt was in the nature of compensatory damages to Zarin for the casino's injuries to him in preying on and aggravating his compulsion to gamble. Compensatory damages are not taxable, see ¶ 3.11. It could also be argued that there was no cancellation of debt because the settlement payment equaled the actual size of the debt. This argument is that the $3.5 million in chips advanced by Resorts were not really worth their face amount. The chips were not negotiable and could not be used outside the casino. Moreover, it is unlikely that Zarin could have turned the chips in for cash given the size of his debt to the casino. Another way of saying it was that there was no serious expectation that the full amount of the debt would be paid. One problem with this analysis is that if Zarin had experienced a winning streak and won the $3.5 million back, the casino would have been obligated to pay him in cash the full face value of the chips. Cutting the other way is that over an extended period of play, a winning streak of that magnitude against the house percentage was virtually impossible. There is also the intriguing argument that because Zarin was a compulsive gambler, the cancellation of $2.9 million of debt did not have that value to Zarin.

One possible problem with these imaginative approaches is that they are leaving the facts of the case and the statute behind. In point of fact the debt was unenforceable under New Jersey law. Thus it was not a true debt. Therefore there was nothing to cancel and there could not be cancellation of debt income. That's all she wrote.

It would seem a stretch to say that Zarin had $2.9 million of psychic income from gambling in the casino for which he should be taxed. No doubt everyone in a casino is having more fun than what they are losing or they would not be there. Shall we tax everyone who enters a casino's portals for their net psychic pleasure? And why limit it to casinos? In any event, Zarin, a compulsive gambler, would seem to be the last person to whom this argument could apply. It also seems a stretch to bring *Tufts* into this case. There was no depreciation founded on nonrecourse debt in this case. Unless one wants to read *Tufts* as saying that anyone who benefits in some way is taxed (certainly not our system), *Tufts* would seem to be inapposite. The same problem exists for the argument that the cancellation of the debt was in effect punitive damages exacted from Resorts and thus income to Zarin under *Glenshaw Glass*. This was not a punitive damages case; this was a cancellation of debt case. It is true that everything can be analogized to everything else at some level of abstraction. But our system does not go off on simply whether we can find a benefit somewhere and then tax it because in some other completely unrelated set of circumstances someone else who benefitted was taxed.

The imaginative arguments as to why Zarin did not have income also suffer from this infirmity of leaving the facts and the statute behind. To say, for example, that the cancellation of debt was compensatory damages to Zarin and thus not taxable is to ignore the facts of the case. The debt was not enforceable because of Resort's violations of regulations. The failure to enforce the debt was not intended by anyone involved to compensate Zarin for the psychological damages he suffered. It is supposition that he suffered any such damages at all. This compensatory damages argument also flatly contradicts the psychic income argument, showing the weakness of both approaches. The argument that the chips were not worth their face amount is similarly shaky. Just because the chips were not negotiable outside the casino does not mean they were not worth their face amount. In the course of play Zarin's chips were being turned over with the chips of other gamblers who were cashing chips in for their face amount at will. Did these fungible chips suddenly depreciate in value the minute they touched Zarin's fingers? Zarin was playing the same game the others played with the same chips.

Curiously, the one thing the commentators seem not to want to do is to take the case at face value: To have cancellation of debt income, there needs first to be a valid debt.[125] Because of Resorts' violations, the debt was not valid. Since it was not a valid debt it could not be cancelled by Resorts and there was no cancellation of debt on the settlement payment.

On a theoretical level, however, this does not seem to be the right result. Even if the debt was not enforceable, Zarin actually received $3.5 million. He neither had to pay it back, nor include it in income. If Resorts had no claim against Zarin because the debt was not enforceable, then Zarin had income when he received the chips. He received something worth $3.5 million with no concurrent obligation to pay it back. The payment by Resorts to Zarin was clearly not a gift. It might simply be a windfall, but windfalls are taxed. Thus, if Zarin did not have discharge of indebtedness income, he likely had income when he received the chips. The court finds the fact that Zarin did not really own the chips because he would have to pay any winnings back to the casino as relevant. But Zarin, at least while he was in the Casino, could do what he wanted with the chips. He could make large bets, give huge tips to dealers and the wait staff, or even give the chips to other gamblers.

Consider the same facts except assume that Zarin is worth $200 million. He still refuses to pay because he says the debt is unenforceable. Does it still make sense not to tax him on either that amount he received in income when he obtained the chips or on the debt forgiven?

Another way of fleshing out these arguments is to take another case like *Zarin* except that the New Jersey casino does not violate any regulations. The gambler is a New Jersey resident. The debt is enforceable. Because the gambler is hysterical and because of the fear of bad publicity the casino settles a $3.5 million debt for $0.5 million. What happens to the fancy arguments now? Under the statute it's income. That is not even a particularly heartless decision unless the gambler is insolvent or bankrupt, in which case the insolvency or bankruptcy exceptions to the statute would spare him from being taxed.[126] If the gambler is worth $2 billion, who's to worry that we're taxing him on $3 million of cancellation of debt income?

---

[125] Section 108(d)(1)(A).

[126] Section 108(a)(1)(A), (B).

That being the analysis, you don't need the fancy psychic income arguments to give Zarin income. As to the arguments that this is not income, they would fall by the wayside too on this new set of facts. Consider the arguments that settlement of the debt constitutes non-taxable compensatory damages, or that the chips aren't worth their face amount. Are those arguments going to be taken seriously in the face of having income cold under the statute?

Postscript: In an interview, Zarin's attorney indicated that his client had given up gambling and spoke regularly at Gamblers Anonymous gatherings.[127] Mr. Zarin died in 2005. If you are fascinated by the Zarin case and want more information, one of his former lawyers published an article, with Zarin's permission, detailing the situation behind the case.[128]

(2) Insolvent or Bankrupt Debtor

If a debtor's liabilities exceed the debtor's assets, the debtor is insolvent. The insolvent debtor may or may not choose to file a petition under the Bankruptcy Code.[129] As mentioned above, if an insolvent debtor receives a discharge from indebtedness by virtue of a Bankruptcy Code case, the amount of income from discharge of indebtedness is excluded from the debtor's income.[130] That amount of income so excluded is applied to reduce the "tax attributes" of the debtor ("tax attributes" for this purpose being net operating losses and loss carryovers, and certain other credit carryovers, capital losses and capital loss carryovers, the basis of the debtor's assets, and the foreign tax credit carryover).[131] In the alternative the debtor may elect to apply the amount of income excluded to reduce the basis in depreciable property or real property held as inventory, rather than have the excluded amount reduce his "tax attributes."[132] Accordingly, the subsequent disposition of property with a reduced basis under these provisions will give rise to income to the extent of the basis reduction, under the rules of §§ 1245 and 1250.[133]

---

[127] Wayne E. Green and Ann Hagedorn, The Wall Street Journal, Oct. 12, 1990, at B6.

[128] See Theodore Seto, Inside Zarin, 59 SMU Law. Rev. 1762 (2006), which is written, with permission, by one of Zarin's former lawyers.

[129] 11 U.S.C.A. § 301. A solvent debtor may file a petition in bankruptcy, but it would make little sense for him to do so inasmuch as he would in any event have to surrender his assets to the extent required to pay his creditors; but see the petition in bankruptcy of the solvent Manville Corporation, filed out of concern for asbestos litigation claims.

[130] Sections 108(a)(1)(A), 108(d)(2).

[131] Sections 108(b)(1), 108(b)(2), 1017(a)(2).

[132] Sections 108(b)(5)(A), 1017(b)(3)(A) and (E).

[133] Section 1017(d)(1).

If the debtor is insolvent but not, as in the discussion above, in a bankruptcy proceeding, then discharge of indebtedness income will be excluded from the debtor's income to the extent the debtor is insolvent.[134] The amount of excluded income is applied to reduce the debtor's "tax attributes" in the same way as in the case of a debtor in a bankruptcy case, described above, including the option to reduce basis of property instead of reducing "tax attributes."[135]

Integrated Summary of Discharge of Indebtedness Rules

Let's illustrate the applicable rules through several examples.

(1) Borrower borrows $100,000 from Lender and then pays the debt off for $85,000. (Lender accepts the payoff because Borrower is somewhat shaky financially and Lender figures that this is the best deal under the circumstances). Borrower has $15,000 of cancellation of debt income ("COD income" in the argot). See *Kirby Lumber, Zarin*, supra.

(2) Same as (1), but Borrower pays off the debt in full just with land that cost $60,000 and worth that same amount, Borrower would have COD income of $40,000. If the land had a value of $60,000 but a "basis" (or cost see ¶ 4.03(2)) in Borrower's hands of $40,000, Borrower would have both $40,000 of COD income and $20,000 of income due to satisfying a legal obligation with appreciated property, see ¶ 4.02 and the discussion of the *Davis* case.

(3) Same as (1), but Borrower does $100,000 worth of legal work for Lender who then cancels the debt. Borrower then has $100,000 of income, since Borrower is effectively receiving compensation for services in the form of COD income. If Borrower's legal work is worth only $50,000 and Lender still cancels the $100,000 debt for it, then Borrower still has $100,000 of income. It is made up of $50,000 of compensation income and $50,000 of COD income.

(4) Same as (1), but Borrower's Aunt Moneybags pays off the $100,000 loan. The nature of Aunt Moneybags's payment must be examined. If the payment is a gift, then the repayment is excluded, § 102. If the payment is compensatory (i.e. if Aunt Moneybags stated that the loan repayment was in exchange for $100,000 of work from Borrower), then Aunt Moneybags's repayment would be income to Borrower.

(5) Felix purchases undeveloped land for investment for $50,000. It rises in value to $100,000. Felix then borrows $75,000 from Windsor Bank, secured by the property, but Felix also remains

---

[134] Section 108(a)(1)–(3).

[135] Section 108(b).

personally liable on the loan (in the argot, that's a "recourse liability"). Subsequently the property drops in value to $60,000. The liability is still $75,000. Felix transfers the property to Windsor and Windsor cancels the full debt of $75,000. The results to Felix are analyzed in two steps:

First, he has gain of $10,000 with respect to the transfer of the property. That is, the transfer of the property to the Windsor Bank has cancelled the debt to the extent of $60,000. Thus Felix has $10,000 of gain with respect to the transfer of the land ($60,000 amount realized less $50,000 basis.)

Second, he has $15,000 of discharge of debt income, since the bank discharged the remaining $15,000 of this recourse debt. Since this is recourse liability, the other $15,000 of debt was not necessarily cancelled by the transfer of the land. But when in fact Windsor chose to cancel it, Felix has $15,000 of discharge of debt income.[136]

The significance of splitting this transaction into two steps is that only the gain in the first step could qualify for capital gains treatment, since only that gain occurred with reference to the sale or exchange of property, see ¶ 4.06.

The qualified real property business debt exception of § 108(a)(1)(D), providing that discharge of debt is not included in income, does not apply to exclude any of this discharge of debt from income because that exception only applies to debt incurred with respect to real property used in a trade or business, and this property is held for investment, § 108(c)(3). To qualify for the real property business debt exception, the debt must be qualified acquisition indebtedness—debt incurred to acquire, construct, or improve the property, § 108(c)(4).

(6)   Same as (5), but Felix borrowed on a nonrecourse basis. Here the full amount of the liability would be discharged by the transfer of the property to Windsor Bank. Thus Felix would have an amount realized of $75,000, taken against his basis of $50,000 for a gain realized of $25,000. See discussion of the *Tufts* case at ¶ 4.03(2)(b)(iv). Note the nonrecourse liability situation produces the same amount of gain as the recourse liability situation—$25,000. But in the nonrecourse liability situation, the gain is computed in one step, not two steps as in the recourse liability situation.[137]

(7)   Felix borrows $2 million from Venture Capital to help finance the purchase of a casino to operate in Mississippi. The riverboat is his only asset. At a time when the riverboat casino has a

---

[136]   Regs. §§ 1.1001–2(a)(1), 1.1001–2(a)(2), 1.1001–2(c) Example 8.
[137]   See Regs. §§ 1.1001–2(a)(4)(i), 2(b).

basis in Felix's hands after depreciation of $500,000, it runs into financial problems. Venture Capital agrees to have the $2 million debt paid off for $1 million. Assuming that Felix is solvent, the result would be that Felix has discharge of indebtedness income of $1 million, under *Kirby Lumber*. *Kirby Lumber* is the general rule and there is no applicable exception in § 108(a)(1).

(8) Same as (7), but Felix borrowed his $2 million from the Lucky 7 Riverboat Casino Manufacturing Company, from whom he bought the boat. Now a settlement by Felix of the $2 million debt for $1 million is treated as a reduction in the purchase price of the boat he bought from Lucky 7 and is not income to him.[138] The basis of the riverboat in the hands of Felix would then be lowered from $500,000 (after depreciation) to $0. That lowering of the basis to $0 accounts for $500,000 of the $1 million debt discharge. And Felix would have $500,000 in income under *Kirby*. That accounts for the remainder of the $1 million debt discharge.

(9) Same as (7), but Felix has another $1,700,000 in debt in addition to the $2 million he borrowed. Thus he is insolvent in that his liabilities ($3.7 million) exceed his assets ($2 million—the riverboat). Then a discharge of the $2 million loan for $1 million triggers § 108(a)(1)(B) exception to the *Kirby Lumber* rule. Thus $1 million is excluded. With this exclusion, § 108(b) provides for a concomitant reduction in tax attributes. If Felix has none of the tax attributes described in § 108(b)(2)(A) through (D), then a reduction of his basis of $500,000 is required under § 108(b)(2)(E). However, as an exception to this rule, note that Felix has other liabilities (in addition to the $2 million of debt that was settled) remaining of $1,700,000. This would mean that the amount of those remaining liabilities is greater than his basis in the riverboat casino ($500,000 after depreciation). Section 1017(b)(2) provides that in an insolvency (or Title 11 case), the aggregate basis of the taxpayer's property shall not be reduced below the aggregate amount of the liabilities. Since in this case the amount of aggregate basis is already below the amount of the aggregate liabilities, there is no further basis reduction. There are no further tax consequences. On these facts, Felix got an exclusion from income without a concomitant reduction in tax attributes (of which he had none) or reduction in basis (which was already less than the liabilities). It might be noted that there is no strong logical relationship between the amount of liabilities and the basis of assets in the taxpayer's hands. Nonetheless, the statute uses a comparison between the two as a test for whether basis will be lowered after an exclusion of discharge of debt income.

---

[138] Section 108(e)(5).

(10) Same as (9), but Felix also had a net operating loss of $100,000. In that event, the $1 million of debt discharge would be excluded from income (because Felix is insolvent) and the $100,000 net operating loss would be eliminated. There would be no reduction of basis because of § 1017(b)(2), as discussed in the preceding paragraph. In this situation, Felix could elect, under § 108(b)(5), to reduce the basis in his depreciable property (the riverboat) instead of reducing the net operating loss carryover. If the § 108(b)(5) election is made, then the § 1017(b)(2) limitation, discussed in the preceding paragraph, does not apply, see § 1017(b)(2) last sentence. Thus making this election means that $500,000 of basis is wiped out and $100,000 of net operating loss is preserved. Not making the election means that $100,000 of net operating loss is wiped out and $500,000 of basis is preserved. Clearly on these numbers not making the election is preferable.

(11) Felix has liabilities of $775,000 and assets of $700,000. If a creditor discharges $200,000 of Felix's debt for $100,000, there is potential *Kirby* discharge of debt income of $100,000. However, Felix is insolvent by $75,000. Thus, under § 108(a)(1)(B) it appears that he can exclude the entire $100,000. However, § 108(a)(3) provides that the insolvency exclusion is limited to the amount of the insolvency. Hence on these numbers Felix excludes $75,000 and includes $25,000.

A discharge of debt can constitute a gift or income, depending on the surrounding circumstances. Where A fails to file a claim on a debt against B and the statute of limitations runs on the claim, the result is probably income. If A affirmatively renounces the debt in a setting of friendship, then the discharge would probably be a gift. Similarly a decedent in a will frequently discharges debts of relatives. These bequests, absent *Wolder* issues (discussed above) constitute non-taxable gifts and are thus exceptions to the *Kirby Lumber* doctrine.

The cancellation of indebtedness issue has also arisen with regard to child support payments. Should a parent who fails to pay child support payments have discharge of indebtedness income? If the parent has a legally binding obligation to make the payments, and refuses to do so, why shouldn't the deadbeat parent have to claim the discharge as income? Under current law, the failure to pay child support does not create COD income. See ¶ 7.02(6)(a) for a discussion of this issue as it relates to the custodial parent who must pay the child's expenses without receiving the support payments.

¶ 3.11 RECOVERY OF DAMAGES TO THE PERSON OR BUSINESS

(1) In General

A taxpayer may suffer damages arising out of a personal or business tort, breach of contract, breach of fiduciary duty, violation of the antitrust laws, violation of the securities laws, violation of the civil rights laws, patent, copyright or trademark infringement, etc. Recovery of these damages must be analyzed under various special rules to determine their ultimate includability in income.[139] In order to answer this question, the character and classification of the award is important. It could be, among other things, a return of capital, compensation for lost profits, or compensation for personal injury. Each of these characterizations may have different tax consequences. In determining the character or classification of an award, it is traditional to examine in lieu of what were damages paid.[140]

(2) Damages from Personal Injuries

The rules here have become extremely difficult. The way the field now lays out there are two fundamental kinds of damages—damage to the person and damage to the business.

Section 104(a)(2) provides that damages (other than punitive damages) that are received on account of personal physical injuries or physical sickness are excluded from income. The regulations further provide that the term "damages received" means an amount received through prosecution of a legal suit based upon a tort or tort-type right, or a settlement entered into in lieu of such prosecution.[141] In *Commissioner v. Schleier*,[142] the Supreme Court clarified that the statute and regulations create a two-part test. First, the damages

---

[139] The relationship between these special rules and the tax benefit rule (¶ 9.02(3)) is that if the analysis under these special rules indicates the recovery should be excluded from income, nonetheless the recovery will be included in income if it is attributable to a deduction taken in an earlier year which gave rise to a tax benefit. As an example of this set of facts, a taxpayer may suffer a business casualty loss, for which he properly takes a deduction in a particular year, § 165(c). The deduction benefits him. Reimbursement by insurance proceeds in a later year would then be includible in income under the tax benefit rule, notwithstanding that under the special rules for the recovery of damages the reimbursement is a non-taxable return of capital.

[140] See United States v. Gilmore, 372 U.S. 39, 83 S.Ct. 623, 9 L.Ed.2d 570 (1963) (origin of the claim test); Woodward v. C.I.R., 397 U.S. 572, 577, 90 S.Ct. 1302, 25 L.Ed.2d 577 (1970) (same); Anchor Coupling v. United States, 427 F.2d 429, 433–434 (7th Cir.1970) (classification of proceeds determined by nature of the action settled); Canal-Randolph v. United States, 568 F.2d 28, 33 (7th Cir.1977) (same); Gail v. United States, 58 F.3d 580, 582 (10th Cir.1995) ("Our general rule for characterizing the proceeds of a judgment for tax purposes focuses upon what the judgment replaces").

[141] Reg. 1.104–1(c).

[142] 515 U.S. 323, 115 S.Ct. 2159, 132 L.Ed.2d 294 (1995).

must be received on account of personal injuries or sickness, and second, the underlying cause of action giving rise to the recovery must be based on a tort or tort-type right.

Prior to 1996, there was a tremendous amount of litigation under § 104(a)(2) regarding whether a particular cause of action was on account of personal injuries or sickness. Taxpayers sought to exclude damage payments received for various causes of action such as libel,[143] discrimination,[144] and breach of duty of fair representation.[145] In 1996, Congress amended the statute and added the term "physical," not once but twice. This clarified (perhaps redundantly) that only those damages that were received on account of *physical* injury or sickness were excluded from income.

Thus, compensatory damages received on account of physical injuries or physical sickness are generally excluded from income.[146] This includes both direct damages, such as a broken arm in a car crash, and indirect damages, such as lost wages. Everything is excluded as long as the damages are on account of the physical injury. In addition, although damages from emotional distress are generally not excluded from income, they are excluded if they are on account of the physical injury.[147] Punitive damages, on the other hand, are always included.[148] The key here is that the damages must be *on account of* or *because of* the physical injury.

It was clearly Congress's hope that the insertion of the word "physical" would reduce the litigation in this area. But it hasn't answered all questions. For example, are damages for sexual harassment excludible from income? Does this question turn on the amount of actual contact between the parties? Is this conflict an imaginary one conjured up in the minds of crazy law professors? No. In a Private Letter Ruling,[149] the Service addressed this specific issue. The taxpayer was a victim of sexual harassment on several occasions. During the first period of her work, her employer made

---

[143] See e.g., Bagley v. C.I.R., 121 F.3d 393 (8th Cir.1997).

[144] Schleier, 515 U.S. 323, 115 S.Ct. 2159, 132 L.Ed.2d 294 (1995) (ADEA suit not on account of personal injury or sickness); United States v. Burke, 504 U.S. 229, 112 S.Ct. 1867, 119 L.Ed.2d 34 (Title VII action is not a tort or tort-type right).

[145] Banks v. United States, 81 F.3d 874 (9th Cir.1996) (Union's breach of duty of fair representation was on tort-like and excludible under 104(a)(2)).

[146] Section 104(a)(2).

[147] Section 104(a)(2), flush language, last 2 sentences.

[148] Section 104(a)(2).

[149] Priv. Ltr. Rul. 200041022. Remember private letter rulings (PLRs) are rulings the IRS provides to taxpayers regarding the Service's view of a particular tax problem. If a taxpayer requests a PLR and then follows it, the PLR is binding on the IRS, absent a change in the law or a misstatement by the taxpayer. It is not, however, precedent and other taxpayers may not rely on the ruling. But, PLRs still provide tremendous insight into the Service's position on many issues.

lewd remarks and touched her. The touching, however, did not result in observable bodily harm or cause extreme pain. During the second period of her work, the harassment intensified and her employer physically assaulted her causing extreme pain (termed "the first pain incident" by the Service). During the third period of her work, the harassment became constant and extremely abusive. He physically and sexually assaulted her and on at least one occasion cut her. The taxpayer filed suit alleging sex discrimination, battery, and intentional infliction of emotional distress.

The Service concluded that damages received prior to the "first pain incident" were not excludible from income since the employer's actions did not result in any observable harms or cause the taxpayer pain. The Service concluded, however, that the damages attributable to the second and third period of employment (after the first pain incident) were excludible because they were linked to physical injuries suffered by the taxpayer.

Another example of a case involving a mix between physical injury and non-physical injury involved a suit against Dennis Rodman, a professional basketball player.[150] During the course of a basketball game, Rodman landed on Mr. Amos, a photographer sitting courtside, and twisted his ankle. Rodman then kicked Amos in the groin area. Amos was treated at a hospital for his injuries, but they were not serious.

Amos sued Rodman for personal injuries and received a settlement for $200,000. The IRS asserted that the $200,000 was not excludable under section 104(a)(2) because it was not on account of personal injuries. The IRS argued that Amos's injuries were minimal and that the payment of $200,000 was not made because of the injury. (Presumably it was made to protect Rodman's reputation or to avoid having Amos cooperate with authorities in a criminal prosecution). Amos of course argued that the entire amount was paid on account of personal physical injury under section 104(a)(2).

The Tax Court applied the two-part test in *Commissioner v. Schleier*. The Tax Court determined that it "is the nature and character of the claim settled, and not its validity, that determines whether the settlement payment is excludable from gross income." The court concluded that there was a dual purpose for the payment. The dominant purpose was to compensate Amos for his personal injury, but the court recognized that there was also a secondary purpose. The settlement agreement required Amos not to "1) defame Mr. Rodman" (It seems odd to compensate Amos for agreeing not to do something the law doesn't allow him to do anyway), "2) disclose

---

[150]   Amos v. Commissioner, T.C. Memo 2003–329 (2003 WL 22839795).

the existence or terms of the settlement, 3) publicize facts relating to the incident, or (4) assist in any criminal prosecution against Mr. Rodman with respect to the incident." The Tax Court thus allocated the money between the injury claim ($120,000) and the remainder of the settlement agreement ($80,000).

This is another bizarre case. Most settlement agreements contain language similar to this one. Are taxpayers now going to have to dissect and allocate proceeds to every provision in a settlement agreement? Obviously, Amos would not have received the settlement but for the personal injury. Should that be enough for exclusion? It generally had been prior to this case. In other words, though the IRS lost, it may have won. Maybe the court just couldn't believe Amos received $200,000 for being kicked in the groin?

This raises another issue under § 104(a)(2). How do you allocate damages among claims? If there is an actual jury award allocation is easy. The allocation is based on the award. If there is a settlement, the courts will generally accept an allocation contained in the settlement agreement,[151] but the Service contends that when a settlement agreement is not arrived at in a bona fide, arm's length transaction, or when the settlement is inconsistent with the true substance of the claim, it not bound to respect the allocation of the payments in a settlement.[152] The Service argues that in allocating the payments, one should look at the best evidence under the circumstances.[153] But the Service often concludes that the best evidence is the relative percentages alleged in the complaint.[154]

In the "be careful what you wish for department," lawyers often forget § 104(a)(2) when they originally file a complaint. In a complaint, a lawyer may ask for compensatory as well as punitive damages, even though the likelihood of receiving punitive damages is very low. Often the punitive damages figure is very high in order to scare the defendant or to encourage the defendant to settle. Since punitive damages are not excludible under § 104(a)(2), any amount of a future settlement allocated to punitive damages would be taxable. Since the Service often views the best evidence for the allocation of a settlement as the percentages set out in a complaint,

---

[151] See Bagley v. Commissioner, 105 T.C. 396, 406 (1995), aff'd 121 F.3d 393, 395 (8th Cir.1997) ("When assessing the tax implications of a settlement agreement, courts should neither engage in speculation nor blind themselves to a settlement's realities"); McKay v. Commissioner, 102 T.C. 465 (1994).

[152] Field Service Advisory (FSA) 200146008, 2001 WL 1451882 (IRS FSA).

[153] Rev.Rul. 85–98, 1985–2 C.B. 51.

[154] Rev.Ruls. 85–98 (finding complaint best evidence to determine allocation between punitive and compensatory damages was the complaint), 58–418 (best evidence relative percentages in the complaint).

a taxpayer may find himself unable to exclude a large portion of the damages he receives.

For example, assume you are in car accident. You sue for $50,000 in compensatory damages and $1,000,000 in punitive damages. You settle the case for $45,000. You obviously would argue that the entire $45,000 is compensatory and thus excludible under 104(a)(2). But why should that be so? Your complaint indicates that 5% of the damages you seek are for personal injury. The remaining 95% is for punitive damages. Why should that allocation not apply to the settlement?

Does this seem fair? The Service's argument that the complaint is the best measure of how to allocate the proceeds is preposterous. In any suit, the chance of receiving punitive damages is much less than the chance of receiving compensatory damages. An attorney just needs a reasonable basis to ask for punitive damages, but that does not mean the likelihood of succeeding on the punitive claim is very high. At the very least the Service should discount the punitive damages percentage by some factor involving the likelihood of success on the claim.

That brings us to three suggestions for future plaintiffs' attorneys. First, don't ask for punitive damages unless your client deserves them. Second, if your client does deserve them, make sure you document the likelihood of success on the claim for punitive damages. And lastly, always allocate any settlement proceeds in the settlement agreement.

(3) Damages from Injuries to Business; Raytheon

Injuries to taxpayers in their business do not qualify for the broad-scale exclusions of § 104(a)(2). The major principles in the field of damages from injuries to business are illustrated by the leading case of *Raytheon*:

RAYTHEON PRODUCTION CORP.
V. COMMISSIONER[155]

Facts: Taxpayer, Raytheon Production Corp., was involved in the production of tubes for radios. The taxpayer brought suit against Radio Corporation of America (RCA) for antitrust violations and eventually settled the suit for $410,000. As part of the settlement, Raytheon agreed to give RCA patent license rights and sublicensing rights to some thirty patents. The parties, however did not allocate

---

[155]   144 F.2d 110 (1st Cir.1944), cert. denied 323 U.S. 779, 65 S.Ct. 192, 89 L.Ed. 622 (1944).

the settlement proceeds between the patent license rights and the amount attributable to damages due to anti-trust violations.

Questions: 1) Are the damages for a) recovery of capital for damage to good will or b) for lost profits? 2) If for recovery of capital, what is the treatment if Raytheon can't prove basis?

Held: Damages are for recovery of capital; hence, not taxable to extent of basis. Unfortunately Raytheon cannot prove its basis in goodwill. The burden is on the taxpayer to prove basis. In absence of proof, basis taken to be zero and amounts are taxable in full. If the current provisions to shift the burden of proof to the IRS in litigation (see discussion at ¶ 1.03(2)) had applied to Raytheon, does that mean taxpayer would have won?

Comment: Raytheon's goodwill probably arose from its own business rather than having been purchased.[156] Since it arose from its own business, Raytheon had no basis, since most of the costs of generating the goodwill would have been deducted. Allowing an exclusion from income after expenses of producing the goodwill had been deducted would have been an unjustified double benefit. Any capital expenditures (see ¶ 6.03(4)) involved in generating goodwill would, however, have gone to produce basis in the goodwill.

Comment: The transaction would be treated as a sale or exchange. Since good will is a capital asset, Raytheon would qualify for capital gain treatment. Had the damages been for lost profits, favorable capital gain treatment would not have been available. (See Chapter 4 for discussion of capital gains).

As background, the general rule is that where a taxpayer is injured in his business, the gross income inclusion of damages received depends on what gave rise to the damages.[157] The damages may be attributable to a recovery of capital, lost profits (past, present, or future), or they may be punitive damages. If the damages are attributable to a recovery of capital, they will not be income unless the amount received exceeds the basis of the capital.[158]

---

[156]   See ¶ 4.06(3)(b) for examples of how a basis in good will may be established.

[157]   This is often referred to as the origin of the claim doctrine. See United States v. Gilmore, 372 U.S. 39, 83 S.Ct. 623, 9 L.Ed.2d 570 (1963), supra ¶ 6.02; Woodward v. Commissioner, 397 U.S. 572, 577, 90 S.Ct. 1302, 25 L.Ed.2d 577 (1970).

[158]   In that event they will be § 1231 gain, discussed at ¶ 4.06(3)(iv). See also Boehm v. Commissioner, 146 F.2d 553 (2d Cir.1945), cert. granted 325 U.S. 847, 65 S.Ct. 1556, 89 L.Ed. 1969 (1945) (payments for loss in value of stock a return of capital where taxpayer had taken no prior deduction); IR 401, Sept. 29, 1961 (compensation to persons of Japanese ancestry, paid under the American-Japanese Evacuation Claims Act, 62 Stat. 1231 (1948) for loss of property arising from the evacuation of such persons from various western states during World War II a return of capital).

On a superficial level this seems like a reasonable approach. One might be concerned, though, that the damages arise from an involuntary transaction, thus forcing the taxpayer to pay tax on gains at a time not of his choosing. The possible harshness of this is mitigated by § 1033, which allows the taxpayer to postpone the taxation of any gain if he reinvests the proceeds of his damage award in property "similar or related in service or use."[159]

The difference between recovery of capital (tax-free to the extent of basis) and recovery of lost profits (fully taxable) approaches the metaphysical, inasmuch as capital is only significant because it produces profits. Hence any recovery of capital is in some sense a recovery of lost profits and any recovery of lost profits is in some sense a recovery of capital. Taxpayers, of course, want to argue that the damages received are a tax-free recovery of capital; the Service, of course, asserts the damages are a taxable recompense for lost profits. Lacking a meaningful economic standard for allocating between the two, the courts have rendered decisions in this area that have been somewhat erratic in rationale and result; often the approach of the underlying transaction is important.[160]

Similar agonizing problems are presented where the allocation of a damage award is between recovery of capital and punitive damages. This issue arises most frequently in the antitrust field, where statutory provision is made for punitive treble damages in civil suits.

The principle that the includability in income of business damages received depends on to what the damages are attributable has been used to ascertain the treatment of damages for a number of other types of claims, including patent infringement (ordinary income or return of capital),[161] breach of employment contract

---

[159] Section 1033(a)(1). See ¶ 4.05(3).

[160] See, e.g., *Raytheon,* supra (lost profits used to measure the damage to the good will); Specialty Engineering Co., 12 T.C. 1173 (1949) (acq.) (adopting allocation of underlying judgment); Basle v. Commissioner, 16 T.C.M. 745 (1957), aff'd per curiam 256 F.2d 581 (3d Cir.1958) (ignoring allocation of settlement agreement where taxpayer otherwise failed to prove loss of good will); Kendall, 31 T.C. 549 (1958) (acq.) (adopting allocation of condemnation award that the entire proceeds were for capital).

[161] W.W. Sly Manufacturing Co., 24 B.T.A. 65 (1931) (payment of patent infringer's profits to taxpayer is ordinary income to taxpayer); Big Four Industries, 40 T.C. 1055 (1963) (acq.) (damages were ordinary income, return of capital and capital gain); Mathey v. Commissioner, 177 F.2d 259 (1st Cir.1949), cert. denied 339 U.S. 943, 70 S.Ct. 797, 94 L.Ed. 1359 (1950) (damages for lost profits ordinary income).

(ordinary income),[162] and breach of contract to purchase property (ordinary income).[163]

(4) Damages to Capital

When damages are received on account to damage to capital, the damages may be considered either gain (subject to tax) or a return of capital (not be subject to tax).

In *Dye v. United States*,[164] the taxpayer sued her stockbroker alleging improprieties regarding her brokerage account. Her allegations involved claims that would produce both ordinary and capital income. For example, she alleged that she lost interest on bonds and dividends, which would have produced ordinary income, and she alleged diminution in the value of her investments, and excessive commissions and fees, which would have been capital in nature.

The taxpayer claimed that all of her income was capital in nature and the government claimed it was all ordinary, contending that Dye had not allocated her proceeds between capital and ordinary. For our purposes, however, what is important is that the court concluded that if the origin of the claim was capital, the proceeds would be treated as "capital in nature." Presumably, this means that the proceeds should be treated as a return of capital, and not taxed, for amounts needed to restore the basis of the asset, and capital gain for the remainder.

An easy example will illustrate the point. Suppose Taxpayer owns a shipping company and has one ship with a basis of $100,000 and a fair market value of $500,000 (assume for simplicity the ship has not been depreciated). Due to negligence of a third party the ship is ruined. Taxpayer sues and settle the claim for $500,000. The $500,000 only represents compensation for damage to the vessel. The

---

[162] Knuckles v. Commissioner, 349 F.2d 610 (10th Cir.1965) (taxpayer executive found incompetent by board of directors was fired but refused to knuckle under and sued for breach of employment contract. Held: amounts received were ordinary income for breach of employment contract over taxpayer's claim that some of the award was non-taxable recompense for personal injury.). See also, Coats, 36 T.C.M. 1650 (1977), and Priv. Ltr. Rul. 7737061 (payment in settlement of suit under Title VII of the Civil Rights Act, 1964, barring discrimination in employment on the basis of race, sex, religion or national origin, 42 U.S.C.A. 2000(e–2) *et seq.* held ordinary income as a recovery of back pay).

[163] Smith v. Commissioner, 50 T.C. 273 (1968), aff'd 418 F.2d 573 (9th Cir.1969) (damages for breach of contract to purchase stock and real estate were ordinary income, since the sale was not completed). Republic Automotive Parts, Inc. v. Commissioner, 68 T.C. 822 (1977) (ordinary income for damages paid for suit for inducing breach of contract to distribute auto parts for a royalty).

[164] 121 F.3d 1399 (10th Cir.1997).

first $100,000 of damages would not be taxed, and the remaining $400,000 would be gain.

¶ 3.12 ALIMONY AND SIMILAR PAYMENTS

To the extent payments made incident to a divorce are income to the spouse receiving them, they are deductible to the spouse making them. This subject of alimony and similar payments made incident to a divorce is discussed in detail at ¶ 6.02(14).

¶ 3.13 MISCELLANEOUS ITEMS OF INCOME AND EXCLUSIONS FROM INCOME

(1) In General

As the discussion in Chapters 1 and 2 has indicated, gross income is a far-reaching and open-ended concept. In general, the presumption is that a net accretion to wealth will be included in income, whether it is from an orthodox or an unorthodox source. The statute is broad enough to cover income from sources unimagined at the time the statute was drafted. As § 61 states: ". . . gross income means all income from whatever source derived . . ." There are many exceptions, limitations and special treatments, as Chapter 2 and the other sections of Chapter 3 have shown. Beyond these topics is a range of miscellaneous transactions and events reaching across the fullness of the society which, because they apparently involve a net accretion to wealth, could be regarded as giving rise to gross income. A representative listing of these variegated items and the authority for their inclusion or exclusion from income is set forth below.

One puzzling example is illegal income.

(2) Illegal Income: The Fantastic Saga of Wilcox, Rutkin and James

The Supreme Court's opening shot in the murky area of illegal income was *Commissioner v. Wilcox.*[165] The Court held that embezzled funds were not income to the perpetrator because he had an obligation to restore the funds to the victim. In that sense the transaction was analyzed as being roughly like a loan (see the discussion of treatment of loans at ¶ 3.10).

This presented some policy difficulties. Why should hard-working folks pay tax on their incomes if thugs and embezzlers do not have to pay tax on their stolen loot? This very idea may have led the Court to take a different approach in *Rutkin v. United States.*[166]

---

[165]   327 U.S. 404, 66 S.Ct. 546, 90 L.Ed. 752 (1946).

[166]   343 U.S. 130, 72 S.Ct. 571, 96 L.Ed. 833 (1952), reh'g denied 343 U.S. 952, 72 S.Ct. 1039, 96 L.Ed. 1353 (1952).

The Court there held that an extortionist's ill-gotten gains were income. This was fine except that the *Rutkin* Court explicitly refused to overrule *Wilcox*. Thus as matters stood after *Rutkin*, income from embezzlement was not taxable but income from extortion was.

This was not a state of affairs that could continue. The *Wilcox* case was decided in 1946. The *Rutkin* decision was in 1952. It was clear after *Rutkin* to any observer of the Court that the next embezzler decision that came down the road would see *Wilcox* overruled. This proved to be the case in the celebrated case of *James v. United States*.[167] The Court in that case overruled *Wilcox* and settled the matter that illegal income was income.

There was just a teeny little loose end. The *James* case involved not only the question whether embezzled funds were income but also the prosecution of the taxpayer in that case for tax fraud. "Fraud" under the statute required willfulness. As to that issue, the Court held that the Government could not prove willfulness since the interpretation of the statute at the time the incident occurred did not require embezzled funds to be included in income.[168]

This raised some really interesting questions. Are potential embezzlers reading Supreme Court cases? And if they are, how good a job are they doing of it?[169]

---

[167] 366 U.S. 213, 81 S.Ct. 1052, 6 L.Ed.2d 246 (1961).

[168] Id. at 222–223, 81 S.Ct. at 1057.

[169] See also the case of *Harris*, discussed at ¶ 3.08, also raising the question of willfulness in criminal tax fraud cases.

¶ 3.14 OVERVIEW

STRUCTURE OF FEDERAL INCOME TAXATION

Gross Income (GI)

"All income from whatever source derived" (§61), including salaries, tips, gains from dealings in property, gains from business, interest, rents, royalties, dividends, alimony, annuities & pensions (prorated amounts), income from discharge of debt, cancellation of debt (unless bankrupt or insolvent), winnings, treasure trove. Excludes life insurance proceeds, gifts, bequests, imputed income, interest on state and local bonds.

less   Adjustments to Income

Trade or business deductions by others than employees; major limit is capital expenses not deductible; major deductions include depreciation, and ordinary and necessary business expenses including wages. §162 (subject to limits on entertainment etc. deductions (§274) depreciation; losses from sales of property; deductions attributable to investments producing rents or royalties; alimony. §62 places these deductions as coming from GI but does not create original authority for them, which must be sought in other provisions.

yields   Adjusted Gross Income (AGI)

AGI is an intermediate step in computing taxable income. AGI is used to compute the limits on certain deductions such as charitable contributions. Deductions allowed in arriving at AGI are always allowed in addition to the standard deduction. §62 does not create authority but just places deduction. Ex.-- the original authority for the deduction for interest is §163. One must first meet §163's requirements. Once having met §163's requirements, the deduction for interest is taken in arriving at AGI if it is attributable to borrowing for a trade or business. But it is deductible in arriving at TI below if it is home mortgage interest.

less
Itemized Deduction or
Standard Deduction

Take the larger of the Standard Deduction or itemized deductions.

Major itemized deductions include home mortgage interest (§163) subject to a limit of interest on debt of lesser of original basis or $1 million, plus $100,000 home equity; property taxes on taxpayer's home (§164); state income or sales taxes; §164; charitable contributions; §170; unreimbursed employee expenses; deductions attributable to investment income such as interest and dividends (§212). Unreimbursed casualty losses (§165) and medical expenses (§213) are subject to such severe limits keyed to AGI that they are rarely available.

less   Deductions for Personal
      Exemption and exemption
      for dependents

The personal exemption applies to the individuals filing the return. The exemption for dependents applies to each person in your family for whom you provide at least half of the person's total support during the year.

yields   Taxable Income (TI)

yields Tax

less   Credits & Withholding

yields   Tax Owed or Refund

Cutting through all this is the major issue of Time Value of Money. This affects amounts and timing of items.

Gains and losses from dealings in property involve major subroutine: calculate by "amount realized" or received less "adjusted basis", §1001. Basis is cost for purchased property, §1012; donor's basic for gift property, §1015; fair market value for property received from decedent, §1014. Basis is adjusted down for depreciation and up for capital expenditures, §1016. Gain so calculated may not be recognized (i.e., taxed) if it falls within limited group of "nonrecognition" provisions – such as §1031 like kind exchange, Gain recognized may qualify for special capital gain treatment. Gains and losses from depreciable and real property used in trade or business get special "double boiler" treatment of §1231 to ascertain if capital gain or not. Under §1231: if gains exceed losses, transactions capital; if losses exceed gains, transactions ordinary.

Unreimbursed employee expenses (such as union dues, professional journals) and investment expenses are so-called "miscellaneous itemized deductions" and are only allowed to the extent they exceed 2% of AGI, §67.

Ascertain tax by applying tax rates of §1 to taxable income. From that tax subtract amounts already withheld and credits such as child care, §21.

Chapter 4

INCOME FROM DISPOSITIONS OF PROPERTY

Table of Sections

¶ 4.01 OVERVIEW

Gains derived from dealings in property are includible in gross income. § 61(a)(3). It should be noted that it is not the gross receipts received on dealings in property that are included in gross income but the "gains" derived from dealings in property—a net concept. As discussed at ¶ 2.01, normally gross income as defined by § 61 encompasses only the gross amount of wages, dividends, interest, rent, etc. received by the taxpayer undiminished by any deductions attributable to such income. Those deductions that are allowed would then be subtracted from gross income to arrive at adjusted gross income, § 62 (see ¶ 6.01). However, when it comes to "dealings in property" (i.e., sales, exchanges or other dispositions, including sales of inventory), gross receipts are offset by the basis of the property to arrive at the gain; it is that gain that is included in *gross* income.[1]

When property is sold or otherwise disposed of, a complex statutory scheme involving several steps is triggered for arriving at the amount of taxable gain (or deductible loss). The several steps of the statutory scheme will first be set forth here in outline. This will be followed by a detailed discussion of each of these steps.

The first step in analyzing whether there has been a taxable gain or deductible loss is determining whether there has been a *realization event,* generally a sale or other disposition of the property

---

[1]   Section 61(a)(3), Reg. § 1.61–6(a).

for consideration.[2] If there has been a realization event, the next step is to compute the *gain* or *loss realized*.[3] This is done by ascertaining the *amount realized*[4] on the sale or other disposition of the property and subtracting from it the *adjusted basis* of the property.[5] The gain realized may (in relatively rare circumstances) be *excluded* from income. And any loss might well be *disallowed*. In the case of such exclusion or disallowance, that is the end of the process.[6] Otherwise, having computed the gain realized and not excluded or the loss realized and allowed, the next step is to ascertain whether the gain or loss will be *recognized*. If a gain or loss is recognized, it will be given immediate significance on the taxpayer's tax return. If, in the alternative, the gain or loss is not recognized, it will in general be deferred until some later year.[7] Once it is ascertained that the gain or loss will be recognized, the next step is to determine the *character* of the gain or loss—whether capital or ordinary.[8] Historically capital gains are taxed under favorable rules and capital losses are taxed under unfavorable rules. So-called "net capital gains" are taxed at rates lower than those that apply to ordinary income, and "net capital losses" are subject to unfavorable rules not applicable to ordinary losses. Finally, there can on occasion be a further *timing* question of the taxable year in which the gain or loss will be reported.[9]

This analysis may be boiled down to a series of questions that should be answered, in order, when analyzing the taxation of any disposition of property. These questions, and the related issues they spawn, are represented in the accompanying graphic. The issues mentioned in this graphic are the subject of the ensuing discussion.

---

[2]   Section 1001(a) and (b).

[3]   Section 1001(a).

[4]   Section 1001(b).

[5]   Sections 1001(a), 1011.

[6]   Sections 165(c), 183, 121. As discussed at ¶ 4.04 the disallowance of a broad range of losses is of major structural significance in the Code. The exclusion of gain is much rarer and not of great structural significance. See § 121, relating to the exclusion of gain on the sale of a taxpayer's personal residence, discussed at ¶ 4.04(5).

[7]   Section 1001(c) and see ¶ 4.05. As discussed in ¶ 4.05, nonrecognition sometimes means permanent exemption.

[8]   Sections 1221, 1222, 1231, are the main authorities.

[9]   See ¶ 8.03 and Chapter 9.

GAINS AND LOSSES FROM DEALINGS
IN PROPERTY

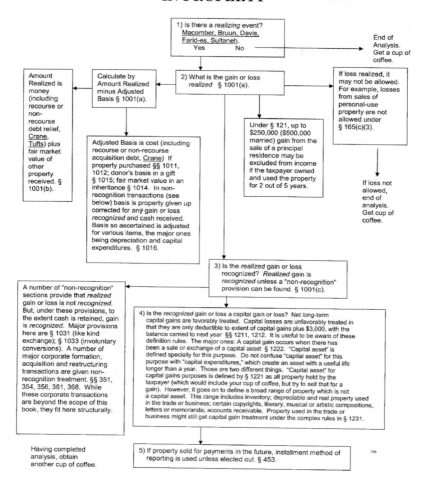

(1)   Has there been a realization event? If the answer is no, that is the end of the process.

(2)   What is the realized gain or realized loss? This is computed by the formula: amount realized minus adjusted basis.

(3)   If there is a realized loss, is the loss allowed? If the loss is not allowed, this is the end of the process. (On rare occasions a gain will be excluded from income, which would also be the end of the process.)

(4)   Is the realized gain or loss recognized? Generally, realized gain will be recognized unless a so-called "non-recognition" or

deferral provision applies. On the other hand, only three types of realized losses are deductible.

(5) What is the character of the recognized gain or loss? Some gains and losses are capital gains and losses to which special rules apply, generally treating capital gains favorably and capital losses unfavorably.

(6) In what taxable year is the gain or loss to be reported? This is less frequently a problem than the other steps but can be a significant issue.

The workings of this structure can be illuminated by an example of a purchase and sale of marketable securities. Suppose securities are purchased as an investment on January 21, Year One for $1,000 and sold January 22, Year Two for $5,000. The following is the treatment of this transaction: The sale is clearly a realization event. The amount realized is the $5,000 received; the adjusted basis is the cost, or $1,000. Hence the realized gain is $4,000. The gain will be recognized, since no non-recognition provision applies to this transaction. The character of the gain on these facts will be a long-term capital gain, thus qualifying for the favorable tax treatment of capital gains. In particular, on these facts the gain would be taxable at a maximum 20 percent rate and possibly as low as zero percent.[10] The proper time to report this gain would be the year of sale.

This structure works comparatively simply in the case of a sale of marketable securities. If, however, the transaction had involved the sale of a mortgaged building subject to depreciation used in the taxpayer's trade or business in consideration for which was received another mortgaged building and cash (not an uncommon transaction), many of the steps above would have been much more complex, although the underlying structure would have been the same.[11]

Each of the steps in the structure can often be resolved simply. However, each step can on occasion raise exceedingly complex problems. It is to these steps that the discussion now turns.

---

[10] Prior to the American Taxpayer Relief Act of 2012, the maximum rate of tax was 15 percent. You may from time to time see references to this 15-percent rate in materials written between 2003 and 2013. Let that be a helpful lesson: always check the date on which material was written, for it may refer to laws that are no longer current. How often does this happen in tax research? All. The. Time.

[11] For treatment of this complicated transaction, see ¶ 4.05(2)(b).

¶ 4.02 THE REQUIREMENT OF A REALIZATION

(1) In General: Macomber, Bruun, Cottage Savings

The first step in ascertaining the taxability of dealings in property is determining whether a gain or loss has been realized. The concept that income from property must be "realized" before it can be taxed is one of the most venerable in the tax law. It is clear that when property appreciates in value, the owner of that property has in some sense enjoyed income: the owner's net wealth has increased. The owner could borrow against this appreciation, or simply not save other funds because the owner knows there is the nest egg of appreciation already stashed away. Thus the owner can use the funds that would have been saved for a vacation or to party it up. In that way appreciation gives rise to an immediate tangible benefit just as surely as if the taxpayer had received an increase in salary.

According to the classic definition of income advanced by the economist Henry Simons, the taxpayer holding appreciated property certainly has income. According to Simons, "Personal income may be defined as the algebraic sum of (1) the market value of rights exercised in consumption and (2) the change in the value of the store or property rights between the beginning and end of the period in question."[12] Yet the tax law has been loath to tax appreciation on property which continues to be held by the owner.

What is the reason for this? Some say mere appreciation is untaxed because it is difficult to make annual appraisals to ascertain how much appreciation has occurred. This should not itself be a problem, however. The price of marketable securities can be easily ascertained. Real estate (the other major asset people hold for investment) can also be appraised annually; heck, it already is for state property tax purposes.

Others say unrealized appreciation is not taxed because the taxpayer lacks the money to pay the tax. If the appreciation is in marketable securities, however, it would be easy enough to sell some of the securities to pay the tax. Moreover, the statute certainly taxes substantial amounts of compensation income in kind, as discussed in Chapter 2. Thus the fact that unrealized appreciation is not reduced to cash does not seem to be a defense to taxing it. Furthermore, if the appreciation is in an illiquid asset such as real estate, the taxpayer could apparently borrow against the property to pay the tax. People might, however, take offense at a tax system that compels them to go

---

[12]   H. Simons, Personal Income Taxation 50 (1938).

into debt (particularly since most people are already in substantial debt).

However, even in the case of real estate, the rules could be tighter than they now are. Where a taxpayer holding appreciated real estate mortgages the property without personal liability to the lender (nonrecourse borrowing), that could be an occasion for imposing a tax on the mortgage proceeds. There are several arguments to support this. First, the nonrecourse mortgage bears some of the earmarks of the sale, since the taxpayer can choose to forfeit the property to the lender without any more money changing hands between them. Also, there is no valuation problem, since the tax can be imposed on the mortgage proceeds to the extent they exceed the taxpayer's basis in the property. Nor is there a liquidity problem since the taxpayer clearly has the funds. Were such a tax to be imposed the basis of the property would be increased *pro tanto*. This issue was addressed in *Woodsam Associates, Inc. v. Commissioner*, 198 F.2d 357 (2d Cir.1952), where the court rejected the argument that nonrecourse financing of property held by the taxpayer was a realizing event. The *Woodsam* case and the issue it raises are discussed extensively at ¶ 4.03(2)(b)(iii) below.

It should be noted that the failure to tax unrealized appreciation in assets held constitutes a huge tax break to those lucky enough to hold highly appreciated assets. It should be recognized that failure to tax unrealized appreciation is a time value of money issue. Let us take a quick example:

Lucy purchases undeveloped land for $100,000 when she is 20 years old. (Don't waste time imagining how a 20 year-old has $100,000 lying around.) One year after she buys it oil is struck on a neighboring parcel. Her land shoots up in value to $500,000. Oil is never found on Lucy's land, but there is that potential. The land remains at the value of $500,000 for the next 40 years. Lucy sells the land when she is 61 years old. Assume a tax rate of 40%.

Now if Lucy had to pay tax right away on that $400,000 gain, she would pay a tax of 40% of $400,000 or $160,000.

But Lucy, under our system of not taxing unrealized appreciation, doesn't have to pay a tax on that gain right away. On our facts, Lucy holds the property for another 40 years and then pays her $160,000 tax.

Let us say that Lucy, being a planner, knows she is going to hold the property until she is 61. So she sets aside money when she was 21 that will grow to be enough to pay the $160,000 tax 40 years later. If the money grows at an after-tax rate of 8%, what amount of money does Lucy have to set aside when she is 21 to have $160,000 when she is 61? Answer is $7,365. Once again we see the staggering power of time value of money.

So "mere" deferral saved Lucy $152,635. She saved 95% of her tax through "mere" deferral. That $152,635 that Lucy does not pay is $152,635 that the rest of us, who don't own appreciated assets, do have to pay.

Anybody like to reconsider the unrealized appreciation issue?

Notwithstanding this lucid analysis, the courts, the Congress, and the Service have in their combined wisdom through the ages imposed the requirement that before the appreciation in value of property can be taxed, there must be a "realization event." The property must be disposed of, usually sold or exchanged for money or other property, before the appreciation in its value can be taxed. (Similarly a decline in the value of property may only be deducted upon the "realizing event" of sale or other disposition.)

The seminal case in this area is Eisner v. Macomber.[13]

EISNER V. MACOMBER[14]

Facts: Taxpayer, Myrtle Macomber, was the owner of 2,200 shares of Standard Oil Company stock. Standard Oil then ordered a fifty percent stock dividend, meaning that the taxpayer was issued an additional 1,100 shares of stock.

Question: Was the stock dividend taxable to Macomber where the statute specifically taxed stock dividends?

Held: No. The stock dividend did not constitute a realization event, as required by the Constitution. Hence the statute is unconstitutional here. To have income the gain must not accrue to capital, but it must be severed from the capital, or derived from the capital, for the taxpayer's separate use, benefit and disposal (Holmes, Brandeis, Day and Clarke dissenting).

Brandeis dissent: The present transaction has the same effect as if Standard Oil had offered stock to its shareholders to be purchased pro rata and had at the same time declared a cash dividend of the

---

[13]   For an in-depth look at Macomber see Marjorie E. Kornhauser, The Story of Macomber: The Continuing Legacy of Realization, in Tax Stories 53–96 (Paul L. Caron ed. 2003).

[14]   252 U.S. 189, 40 S.Ct. 189, 64 L.Ed. 521 (1920). See also Gray v. Darlington, 82 U.S. (15 Wall.) 63, 21 L.Ed. 45 (1872) (appreciation in value of property not taxable under Income Tax of 1867); Lynch v. Turrish, 247 U.S. 221, 38 S.Ct. 537, 62 L.Ed. 1087 (1918).

price of the stock. There is no doubt that this latter transaction would have been taxable.

Comment: As pointed out, the Supreme Court's theory in this case was that the stock dividend was not a gain severed from the capital of the corporation but simply represented the shareholder's continued investment in the corporation. Standard Oil had in fact been profitable and the stock dividend was backed by an appropriate accounting transfer from earned surplus to capital account. Nonetheless, the Court found that to tax the pro rata stock dividend would be to in effect tax the appreciation in value of the shareholder's investment, rather than to tax the income from the investment. Taxing the appreciation in the value of the capital, rather than income derived from the capital was, in the Court's view, unconstitutional; whereas there was no question that a cash dividend would have been taxable.[15]

Taxability of stock dividends is now handled by § 305, which in important respects follows the basic *Macomber* rule. The basis of stock received as a dividend is ascertained under § 307, which provides that a proportionate amount of the basis of the old stock is transferred to the new stock. In the *Macomber* case one-third of the basis of the old stock would have been allocated to be the basis of the new stock. Pro rata stock dividends, not taxable under current law, are widely used by corporations to lower the value of their stock to a more convenient trading range. The only effect of a stock dividend is to lower the price of the corporation's outstanding stock. This is for the same reason that when you cut a piece of pie into more pieces, the pieces are inevitably smaller and you don't have any more pie.

It is useful to focus in detail on the meaning of *Macomber*. It is clear that the day after the pro rata stock dividend, the shareholder was no wealthier than the day before, because of the "pieces of pie" effect. The existence of the new shares in the hands of the shareholders of the corporation inevitably reduced the value of the original shares. Thus the value of the new shares plus the original shares in the hands of the shareholder was equal to the value of his original shares the day before the stock dividend—the taxpayer still had the same percentage interest in the same corporation.[16]

This, however, was *not* the basis of the Court's decision. Nor could it have been. For it is also evident that if the corporation had paid a pro rata *cash* dividend, the stockholders would have been no

---

[15]   252 U.S. at 211, 40 S.Ct. at 194.

[16]   It is well established in stock market trading that when a stock dividend is paid (or a stock splits), the stock price immediately drops to the appropriate new price; and the overall market value of the shareholders' holdings does not change as a result of the stock split or stock dividend. This indeed happened in the *Macomber* case.

wealthier the day after than the day before such a cash dividend was paid. The value of the stockholder's shares just after he received the cash dividend would be reduced *pro tanto* on account of the distribution of cash from the corporation. Thus in both cases—the stock dividend and the cash dividend—the shareholder's wealth does not increase on account of the transaction. But in the *Macomber* view of the world the shareholder in receipt of a cash dividend has experienced a taxable event, because there has been a severance of the income from the capital of the corporation—there has been a realization event. And in the *Macomber* view such a realizing event is constitutionally required, for the Sixteenth Amendment only speaks to a tax levied on income, and, in the *Macomber* view, income only arises when there has been a severance from capital.[17]

Is it still the case that Congress is constitutionally barred from imposing an income tax on appreciation in value of assets? We get some insight into this question with the well-known case of *Helvering v. Bruun*:

HELVERING V. BRUUN[18]

1) July 1, 1915, leased land and building for 99 years to Tenant.

2) In 1929 tenant demolishes existing building and constructs new building.

3) July 1, 1933, tenant defaults. Lease is cancelled. Bruun gets possession of land and building. Fair market value of new building at this time $64,245. Bruun's basis in demolished building was $12,811.

Facts: The taxpayer, Bruun, was the owner of certain real property that he leased to another individual for ninety-nine years

---

[17] 252 U.S. at 211, 40 S.Ct. at 194. Indeed, in distinguishing income from capital, the Macomber Court employed the "fruit and tree" metaphor (*id.* at 206), which was traded upon heavily later in the assignment of income area for somewhat analogous purposes. See ¶ 5.02.

[18] 309 U.S. 461, 60 S.Ct. 631, 84 L.Ed. 864 (1940), mandate conformed 112 F.2d 573 (C.C.A.8 1940).

starting in 1915. The lease provided that the lessee might, at any time subject to certain restrictions, remove and replace the building that was on the land. In 1929, the lessee demolished the old building and built a new one. In 1933, the lessee defaulted on the lease and the taxpayer regained possession of the property. (Remember the Great Depression?) At that time, the new building had a fair market value of $64,245.68. Bruun's basis in the demolished building was $12,811. The net gain to Bruun was about $51,434.

Question: Is the net gain on reacquisition of the building income to Bruun?

Service's position: Bruun has gain of $51,434 in 1933 on reacquisition of the building.

Taxpayer's position: The improvements became part of the realty. The gain is not derived from capital nor severed from capital. There has, in short, not been a realization event, citing *Macomber.*

Held: For IRS. Gain was realized in 1933. "The fact that the gain is a portion of the value of property received by the taxpayer in the transaction does not negative its realization." The forfeiture was a realization event.

Comment: Even though the new building was worth more than Bruun's basis in his old building, probably the land in 1933 (the depths of the Great Depression) was worth less than it was in 1929. Thus did Bruun really have an economic gain of $51,434 in 1933? It was likely much less than $51,434, if any at all. Does that mean the Court's holding is wrong? No. If there was a realization event, then this is like the case where a corporation pays a cash dividend and concomitantly its stock drops severely in value due to other market forces. The cash dividend is still taxable as a realizing event. To realize the loss in the underlying capital it would be necessary, for example, to sell it.

There are enough ways to analyze this fact pattern to choke a horse. Think of all the ways and times we could tax a *Bruun*-type transaction with respect to the building constructed by the lessee.[19]

---

[19]   This footnote is a side trip for those who want to O.D. on this present value stuff. Those who are just trying to get through can pass this one up.

Consider a fancy way of treating the rental payments. On signing this 99-year lease in 1915, Bruun could be taxed on the present value of his rental payments over the lease term. Say the lease payments were $3,000 per year for 99 years. The present value of $3,000 per year for 99 years, assuming a 10% interest rate, is $29,998. We could tax him on that. Eventually, as the lease payments came in, he would get more than that, of course. He gets in total $99 \times \$3,000$ or $297,000. Once we tax him on the $29,998, we then spread that new basis out against the lease payments in some way (see Chapter One ¶ 1.02(3)(e) on recovery of capital). For example, if we spread it out in a straight line fashion, we would deduct $29,998/99 = \$303$ per year. This would result in his finally being taxed on the full amount of his $297,000. Thus as the lease

1) *Tax the new building at the front end and the back end.* Tax the value of the new building on signing of the lease and on termination of the lease. Take this hypo: landlord and tenant sign a 15-year lease on undeveloped land. They agree the tenant will pay rather low rent but the tenant will also construct an office building at a cost of $20 million. The building will have a useful life of 30 years. If constructing the new building is part of the lease deal, then the construction of the new building looks like rent. What is the amount of the rent? This would be the value of the building at the end of the lease term. If it's worth $20 million when constructed, then let us say it is worth $10 million at the end of the 15–-year lease term (which is half the building's useful life). What is the present value of $10 million 15 years from now, with an interest rate of 10%? That present value cranks out to be $2,393,920. We then tax lessor on that amount at lease signing, treating the building as pre-paid rent. When the lease expires, the landlord gets a building worth $10 million. We subtract the landlord's basis (i.e., the amount of gain on which tax has already been paid) of $2,393,920, giving us further income at lease termination of $10,000,000 − $2,393,920 = $7,606,080. Then (we're not through yet) we have to let the landlord depreciate the building with a basis of $10 million over the building's remaining useful life.

2) *Tax new building at the front end and during lease term.* Another way to go on this would be to once again sock the landlord with the $2,393,920 on signing the lease. Then, say, the landlord has income every year as the time for getting the new building approaches. What we'd be saying is that the landlord's $2,393,920 is increasing in value at 10% compounded annually. That will take us to $10 million after 15 years (trust us, actually it's just the reverse of the calculation above). See the discussion of *Irwin v. Gavit* in Chapter 3. Once again there would be a $10 million basis for depreciation for the landlord at the end of the lease.

3) *Tax the building at the back end only.* Just sit around and tax the landlord on nothing with respect to the building until the lease terminates. Then tax the landlord on $10 million. Thereafter the landlord has a basis for depreciation of $10 million.

4) *Don't tax the building at all.* Keep believing *Macomber*. There is no realization at any time during the signing or termination

_____

payments came in, Bruun would be taxed on $3,000 − $303 or $2,697 per year. He would also, as the owner of the property, be able to take other deductions with respect to the property as well, such as depreciation and maintenance. This is economically what is happening. But this is crazy, right? Nobody does this. Our tax system is not going to operate at this level of sophistication. We tax people on rents as they are paid as a cash method. We are not going to do this present value stuff. It is interesting to see how inadequately our tax system reflects true economic income.

of the lease. The landlord has no income, but the landlord has no basis in the building and therefore gets no depreciation deduction thereafter.

Notice, very importantly, that all four of these methods involve a net of zero when we're all through. The first three methods involve $10 million taxed and $10 million deducted for a net of zero. Method 4 is a net of zero by having nothing taxed and nothing deducted. The only difference among them all is timing.

Which method should we use? Much of the discussion in this area and the history of the treatment of this problem has focused on administrative convenience. It is said to be difficult to value the building many years from now. Thus methods 1 and 2 are discredited. In fact, however, if the estimate of the value of the building proves to be off, it could be corrected with a further offsetting deduction or inclusion in income. In any event, historically methods 3 and 4, which do not require any advance estimates of the building value, were favored.

It looks otherwise like these methods are all pretty much the same. But what this administrative convenience approach fails to appreciate is the immense time value of money implications of the method chosen.

Let's explore that a little. Which method would the landlord prefer? You should be able to answer this one. The method that gives the most deferral! That's 4. You have no income on signing the lease or during the lease term or at the end of the lease. What is the price paid? It is no depreciation over the last 15 years of the building's useful life. So with Method 4 you have the good news (no income) early and the bad news (no depreciation) later.

Which method would the IRS prefer from a revenue standpoint? The method which taxes the most up front! That's Method 2, tax up front and during the lease term. Method 2 is also the most economically accurate method.

How much difference does it make which method we use, applying our present value analysis?

The table below shows the present value of the unfavorable (to the landlord) Method 2. It will not surprise us to learn that if the landlord pays $4 million in tax over the course of the first 15 years of the lease and then gets $4 million in tax savings over the last 15 years of the lease, the landlord is under water as far as tax consequences go over the term of the lease. Indeed, this method of reporting income costs the taxpayer almost a million dollars in present value terms, or nearly 5% of the value of the entire project.

ECONOMICALLY ACCURATE METHOD
OF TAXING *BRUUN*

Present Value of Method 2): determine present (negative) value of paying tax on growth in first 15 years and present (positive) value of taking depreciation deductions in last 15 years. Net the two numbers together for net present value (using 10% growth rate).

Annual Present Value of Building	Annual Before-Tax Growth	Tax on Annual Growth @ 40%	Present Value of Tax on Annual Growth	Year No.
$2,393,920	$2,393,920	$957,568	($957,568)	0
$2,633,312	$239,392	$95,757	($87,052)	1
$2,896,643	$263,331	$105,332	($87,052)	2
$3,186,308	$289,664	$115,866	($87,052)	3
$3,504,938	$318,631	$127,452	($87,052)	4
$3,855,432	$350,494	$140,198	($87,052)	5
$4,240,975	$385,543	$154,217	($87,052)	6
$4,665,073	$424,098	$169,639	($87,052)	7
$5,131,580	$466,507	$186,603	($87,052)	8
$5,644,738	$513,158	$205,263	($87,052)	9
$6,209,212	$564,474	$225,790	($87,052)	10
$6,830,133	$620,921	$248,368	($87,052)	11
$7,513,146	$683,013	$273,205	($87,052)	12
$8,264,461	$751,315	$300,526	($87,052)	13
$9,090,907	$826,446	$330,578	($87,052)	14
$9,999,998	$909,091	$363,636	($87,052)	15
Totals	$10,000,000	$4,000,000	**($2,263,343)**	

Basis of Building After Depreciation	Annual Depreciation	Tax Savings from Depreciation 40% Rate	Present Value at Beginning of Lease of Tax Savings Due to Depreciation	Years Out
$10,000,006	$666,667	$266,667	$122,163	16
$9,333,339	$666,667	$266,667	$116,346	17
$8,666,672	$666,667	$266,667	$110,806	18
$8,000,005	$666,667	$266,667	$105,529	19
$7,333,338	$666,667	$266,667	$100,504	20
$6,666,671	$666,667	$266,667	$95,718	21
$6,000,004	$666,667	$266,667	$91,160	22
$5,333,337	$666,667	$266,667	$86,819	23
$4,666,669	$666,667	$266,667	$82,685	24
$4,000,002	$666,667	$266,667	$78,747	25
$3,333,335	$666,667	$266,667	$74,998	26
$2,666,668	$666,667	$266,667	$71,426	27
$2,000,001	$666,667	$266,667	$68,025	28
$1,333,334	$666,667	$266,667	$64,786	29
$666,667	$666,667	$266,667	$61,701	30
$0				
Totals	$10,000,000	$4,000,000	**$1,331,412**	

Net Present Value of Method 2   **($931,930)**

The net present value of negative $931,930 is equal to the negative $2,263,343 present value of taxing the appreciation in value of the building plus the $1,331,412 present value of taking depreciation later on the building.

By contrast Method 4 has a net present value of zero, as far as the method of tax reporting is concerned. There is no $4 million in taxes in the early years and there is no $4 million in deductions in the later years. There is just nothing at all. Thus you don't need to be a rocket scientist to see that the net present value of reporting on this method is zero. That is $931,930 better than Method 2. When the Service allows Method 4 to be used, it is giving away nearly $1 million in taxes. Maybe the administrative convenience argument should be reconsidered.

Method 3, tax the building at the lease termination and then allow depreciation thereafter, was the one taken by *Bruun*. It is not quite as favorable to the taxpayer as 4, but still a lot more favorable to the taxpayer than the economically accurate Method 2. In cases prior to *Bruun*, Method 4 was often used on the grounds that there was no realization under *Macomber*.

After all this, Congress modified the result in *Bruun* by statute. Guess which method they took? Number 4. That is money in the landlord's pockets (and money out of the pockets of the rest of us). Section 109 provides that there is no tax at all on the termination of a lease with respect to the value of property erected or other improvements made by the lessee. Under § 1019, the basis of such property so received back and not taxed under § 109 will be zero. There's number 4, do not tax or depreciate. We know that is the most favorable method for taxpayers.

The only relatively minor exception to this rule is the parenthetical language in § 109 which provides that the exclusion does not apply if the improvements by the tenant were intended as rent. If that is true (and the lease agreement would have to reflect that), then the improvements are included in income at the time of the lease termination. The amount of income would be the fair market value of the improvements. In that event the lease improvements would also be accorded a basis of their fair market value under § 1019. This is Method 3.

So, under the statute, you usually get Method 4, unless the improvements are intended as rent, in which case you get 3. Methods 1 and 2 are never heard from.

As far as the constitutional issues raised in *Bruun* are concerned, it is doubtful today that Congress would be regarded as constitutionally barred from imposing an income tax on appreciation in the value of assets. However, the issue does not usually arise because Congress has for the most part required there to be a realization event before tax can be imposed on appreciation in the value of assets, or before a deduction will be allowed on the decline in the value of assets.[20]

Some fascinating further questions in this area were presented by the Supreme Court case of *Cottage Savings*.

---

[20] See Surrey, "The Supreme Court and the Federal Income Tax: Some Implications of the Recent Decisions" 35 Ill.L.Rev. 779 (1941); Fellows, A Comprehensive Attack on Tax Deferral, 88 Mich. L. Rev. 722 (1990); Jeff Strnad, Periodicity and Accretion Taxation: Norms and Implementation, 99 Yale L. J. 1817 (1990); Shakow, Taxation Without Realization: A Proposal for Accrual Taxation, 134 U. Pa. L. Rev. 1111 (1986). See also IRC § 951, which provides for the taxation of undistributed income of controlled foreign corporations. Compare the "mark-to-market" rule for certain tax straddles as a result of the Economic Recovery Tax Act of 1981. See ¶ 4.06(2)(c)(vi).

COTTAGE SAVINGS ASSOC. V. COMMISSIONER[21]

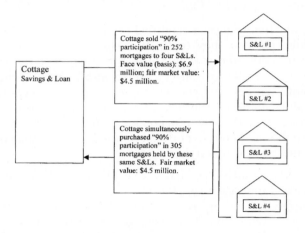

Facts: The taxpayer, Cottage Savings Association, was a savings and loan association that loaned out large sums of money for many long-term mortgages. Due to a rise in interest rates, these mortgages declined in value. Had the taxpayer sold the mortgages it would have been able to take a tax-deductible loss. However, under accounting regulations, they would have also had to record the losses on the books. Since the savings and loan industry was in serious trouble at the time, actually taking the losses at issue might have caused serious problems for the stability of Cottage Savings. The Federal Home Loan Bank Board (FHLBB) then issued Memorandum R–49 that stated that savings and loan associations did not have to report losses associated with mortgages if they were exchanged for substantially identical mortgages held by other lenders. The FHLBB was attempting to allow savings and loans to take tax losses while not having to account for those losses on their books. (That fish you smell isn't tuna—there was some funny bookkeeping here.)

The taxpayer then sold 90% participation in 252 mortgages to four savings and loan associations and purchased 305 mortgages from those associations.[22] All the loans involved in the transaction were secured by single-family homes, most of which were in the Cincinnati area. The fair market value of the interests exchanged by each side was $4,500,000. The face value of the interests that the taxpayer relinquished was $6,900,000.

---

[21]   499 U.S. 554, 111 S.Ct. 1503, 113 L.Ed.2d 589 (1991).

[22]   A loan participation is a transaction whereby a bank makes a loan to a borrower and then sells or transfers some portion of that loan to another bank. Banks usually do this in large transactions to reduce the risk that any one particular loan will go into default.

Question: Did Cottage Savings realize its losses through the transaction? For there to be realization under § 1001(a), there must be "a sale or other disposition." The parties concede that the transactions engaged in did not constitute a "sale," because ownership was not surrendered. So did the transaction constitute a "disposition of property"?

Service's argument: An exchange of property can only be a disposition if the properties exchanged are "materially different." Since the underlying mortgages were essentially economic substitutes, the participation interests exchanged by Cottage Savings were not materially different from those received by Cottage Savings from the other S & L's. In addition, property is "materially different" only if so regarded by the parties, the evaluation of the interests by the secondary mortgage market, and the views of the FHLBB.

Cottage Savings' argument: The participation interests exchanged were materially different because the underlying loans were secured by different properties.

Held: The participation interests exchanged by Cottage Savings and the other S & L's derived from loans that were made to different obligors and secured by different homes. Thus the interests did embody legally distinct entitlements. Cottage Savings thus realized its losses. There is no reason not to treat the exchange of these interests as a realization event, even though the FHLBB treats them as "substantially identical" for its purposes.

Reasoning: The Service has by regulations construed § 1001(a) to require that gain or loss is realized on an exchange only if the property received differs materially either in kind or in extent from the property exchanged.[23] This is a reasonable interpretation of § 1001 and we therefore defer to it. The question is what really constitutes a "material difference" for these purposes. Look, therefore, to the established case law in this area: *Macomber* (see above) and other older Supreme Court cases involving corporate reorganizations. These cases stand for the proposition that properties are "different," in the sense that is "material" for purposes of the Internal Revenue Code, so long as their respective possessors enjoy legal entitlements that are different in kind or extent. Thus if a corporate reorganization results in the shareholders surrendering stock in exchange for stock giving them "the same proportional interest of the same character in the same corporation," then the new stock received is not materially different from the stock surrendered. However, if the stock received is issued by a different corporation, or

---

[23]   Reg. § 1.1001–1.

if it confers different rights and powers in the same corporation, then it is materially different. Case law does not support the Service's more elaborate approach and that approach is also administratively unworkable. Also the existence of the nonrecognition of gain or loss for like-kind exchanges for property held for productive use in trade or business or investment suggests that Congress contemplated that the exchange of similar properties would be a realization event.

Comment, is that then and this now? Do corporate reorganization cases decided six decades ago under law long since changed really throw light on the sophisticated transactions involved in this case? Consider, as the dissent pointed out, what was not "materially different" with regard to the properties exchanged: the retention of the 10% interests, so that the transferors could keep servicing their loans; the borrowers' lack of knowledge of the transaction; the lack of attention paid by the transferors to the factors cited by the majority as "differences," including no credit checks or appraisals; the selection of the loans to be exchanged by computer; the absence of names of the borrowers on the closing agreements. Could it not be said that if the term "material" means anything in the test of "material difference" that these differences were not "material." Thus does the dissent argue for "realities."

Comment, but what is reality? Isn't the *real* reality that these Savings & Loans had undergone substantial losses as a result of the drop in value of their mortgages due to the increase in interest rates? Maybe what's unrealistic in the tax field is the realization requirement itself, for it prevents appreciation or depreciation in the value of assets held from being given tax effect. If that's true, then perhaps the realization requirement should be penetrated whenever possible so that tax results more clearly mirror true economic results. That can certainly be an interpretation of the early reorganization cases: that the Supreme Court, having enunciated the requirement of a realization in *Macomber*, then proceeded to cut back on it and find realization of gain in most of the subsequent cases.[24]

Comment, we're talking big time: We're not just debating doctrine here, we're talking about major transactions. The promulgation of the rules by the FHLBB in the early 1980's allowing swaps of mortgage interests without requiring the recognition of accounting losses triggered the exchange of billions of dollars of depreciated mortgage interests among S & L's.

Comment, the S & L catastrophe: Far from allowing the nation's beleaguered S & L's to exchange mortgages without recognizing

---

[24]   See Daniel Posin, Taxing Corporate Reorganizations: Purging Penelope's Web, 133 U. Pa. L. Rev. 1335 (1985).

accounting losses, the FHLBB should have required them to recognize unrealized depreciation in the mortgages they held. This would have put everyone on notice that the S & L industry was in deep trouble much earlier and have averted a major catastrophe. Ignoring reality in financial transactions is always hazardous.

(2) Gifts, Charitable Contributions, and Straddles

As to other transactions, it is well established that gifts and bequests are not realizing events and therefore do not give rise to income to the transferor. The treatment of abandonment of property and the surrender of mortgaged property has, however, presented problems in this area and is discussed in the margin.[25]

The Supreme Court has held that where a donor gives a gift on the condition that the donee pay the gift tax, a realizing event— namely a sale—has occurred. The donor has income to the extent the gift tax paid by the donee exceeds the donor's basis, *Diedrich v. Commissioner*, 457 U.S. 191, 102 S.Ct. 2414, 72 L.Ed.2d 777 (1982), discussed at ¶ 4.03(2)(b)(iv).

The Tax Court has ruled that a charitable contribution of property encumbered by nonrecourse indebtedness is a sale that can give rise to a taxable gain, *Guest v. Commissioner*, 77 T.C. 9 (1981).

The realization requirement was suspended in the case of certain "tax straddles" under the Economic Recovery Tax Act of 1981. In this case, a "mark-to-market" rule was enacted, requiring taxpayers to treat regulated futures contracts that they hold as sold for their fair market value on the last business day of the taxable year, causing unrealized gain or loss to be taken into account. The purpose here was to foreclose tax avoidance "spread" transactions.

---

[25] Abandonment of property, although not a sale or exchange, is a realizing event, Reg. § 1.165–2(b). This is usually attractive to the taxpayer, since the loss on abandonment will therefore not be subject to the limitations on capital losses, Reg. § 1.165–2(b), and see ¶ 4.06(2)(b)(ii). Special rules apply for the retirement or abandonment of depreciable property, see ¶ 6.02(12). See also CRST, Inc. v. Commissioner, 909 F.2d 1146 (8th Cir.1990) (motor carrier's operating authorities held not abandoned as a loss under § 165).

The surrender of property subject to a mortgage indebtedness in exchange for extinguishment of the indebtedness is a realizing event, with the mortgage indebtedness constituting the amount realized, whether or not the indebtedness was with personal liability (Parker v. Delaney, 186 F.2d 455 (1st Cir.1950), cert. denied 341 U.S. 926, 71 S.Ct. 797, 95 L.Ed. 1357 (1951)), see ¶¶ 4.03(2)(b)(iv), 8.02(3). Surrender of property in extinguishment of a nonrecourse mortgage greater in amount than the value of the property is discussed below at ¶ 4.03(2)(b)(iv).

(3) Marital Property Settlements and Other Satisfactions of Obligations: Davis; Farid-Es-Sultaneh

In most areas it is usually clear whether there has been a realizing event and the issue does not give rise to a dispute. It is also well established that the transfer of appreciated property to satisfy a pre-existing obligation is a realizing event. However, where property is transferred incident to a divorce or separation, some tricky questions are raised. The leading case in this area is *Davis:*[26]

UNITED STATES V. DAVIS[27]

Facts: As part of a separation agreement prior to divorce, Thomas Davis transferred to his estranged wife, among other things, 1,000 shares of DuPont stock.[28] "The then Mrs. Davis" accepted the stock and other items transferred "in full settlement and satisfaction of any and all claims and rights against the husband whatsoever (including . . . dower and all rights under the laws of testacy and intestacy)."

Questions: 1) Was the transfer of DuPont stock a taxable event? 2) If so, how much taxable gain resulted?

Taxpayer's argument: The transaction is like a nontaxable division of property between two co-owners.

Service's argument: The transaction is a taxable transfer of property in exchange for the release of an independent legal obligation.

Held: 1) Under controlling local law of Delaware, a wife's inchoate rights in her husband's property "do not even remotely reach the dignity of co-ownership." The wife's rights are merely a personal liability against the husband rather than a property interest. Thus this was a realization event, not a nontaxable division of property between two co-owners. 2) The gain to the husband is measured by the fair market value of what he received (satisfaction of rights) less the basis in the stock transferred. Though it is difficult to value the satisfaction of marital rights, the Court assumed the parties bargained at arm's length, so it then assumed the value of the marital rights equaled the fair market value of the transferred stock.

---

[26]   For an in-depth look at Davis, see Karen B. Brown, The Story of Davis: Transfers of Property Pursuant to Divorce, in Tax Stories 13–154 (Paul L. Caron ed. 2003).

[27]   370 U.S. 65, 82 S.Ct. 1190, 8 L.Ed.2d 335 (1962), reh'g denied 371 U.S. 854, 83 S.Ct. 14, 9 L.Ed.2d 92 (1962).

[28]   Davis actually transferred 500 shares in 1955 and the remainder in 1955. Only the 1955 tax year was before the court.

Comment: Under the Court's rationale, a division of property in a community property state would lead to a different result: no tax to the husband. This would be the case because the transaction would then constitute a division of property among two co-owners. The Court conceded that under its reasoning results would vary depending on the state.[29]

Davis thus applied in a mechanical way the well-established proposition that transferring appreciated property to satisfy a debt is a taxable event.[30] Suppose Davis had owed a debt to his lawyer (which he undoubtedly did; indeed, there was a subsidiary issue about legal fees in the *Davis* case). Suppose also the debt was $100,000. Transferring $100,000 worth of stock that happened to have appreciated from when Davis bought it at $70,000 would undoubtedly mean there was a realization event. His gain would be $30,000. The question was whether it was appropriate to apply that paradigm to transfers of property incident to a divorce.

The *Davis* case leaves some other fascinating questions hanging. What about the treatment of the wife on these facts? Although it was not before the Court, the question remains how the wife handles this transaction. The *Davis* Court did tell us that the wife would take a basis of the fair market value of the stock transferred to her. This makes some sense. Her "cost" for these purposes is the value of the property she gave up, the value of her marital rights. Those rights, the Court has found, are equal to the fair market value of the stock she received. So we seem to know everything we need to know about the wife. But we're missing one item of information. What is the wife's basis in her marital rights? Is it zero, in which case she has a gain equal to the fair market value of the stock she receives?

---

[29]   Thus, *Davis* spawned two lines of cases: cases holding that in a common law state the marital property settlement is a realizing event and cases holding that in a community property-type state the marital property settlement is not a realizing event.

For common law states, see for example, Wiles v. Commissioner, 499 F.2d 255 (10th Cir.1974), cert. denied 419 U.S. 996, 95 S.Ct. 310, 42 L.Ed.2d 270 (1974); Wallace v. United States, 439 F.2d 757 (8th Cir.1971), cert. denied 404 U.S. 831, 92 S.Ct. 71, 30 L.Ed.2d 60 (1971).

For community property states, see Imel v. United States, 523 F.2d 853 (10th Cir.1975) (property settlement non-taxable where case law had established that under Colorado law the rights of the wife in the marital property had vested at the time of the filing of the divorce suit and before the transfer); see Rev.Rul. 81–292, 1981–2 C.B. 158 (No gain or loss realized on division of jointly owned property in common law state, despite fact that each spouse took some parcels outright.).

This somewhat anomalous situation is reminiscent of the old case of Poe v. Seaborn, 282 U.S. 101, 51 S.Ct. 58, 75 L.Ed. 239 (1930) which held that the effectiveness of assignment of income (see Chapter 5) between husband and wife turned on state law. To cure this disparity Congress enacted the federal joint return.

[30]   See Kenan v. Commissioner, 114 F.2d 217 (2d Cir.1940).

Another major case in this area is *Farid-Es-Sultaneh.*

FARID-ES-SULTANEH V. COMMISSIONER[31]

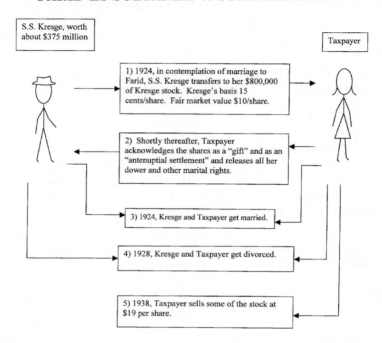

S.S. Kresge, worth about $375 million

Taxpayer

1) 1924, in contemplation of marriage to Farid, S.S. Kresge transfers to her $800,000 of Kresge stock. Kresge's basis 15 cents/share. Fair market value $10/share.

2) Shortly thereafter, Taxpayer acknowledges the shares as a "gift" and as an "antenuptial settlement" and releases all her dower and other marital rights.

3) 1924, Kresge and Taxpayer get married.

4) 1928, Kresge and Taxpayer get divorced.

5) 1938, Taxpayer sells some of the stock at $19 per share.

Facts: In 1923, the taxpayer, then unmarried, and S. S. Kresge, then married, were contemplating their future together. Kresge transferred to her 700 shares of stock in the S. S. Kresge Company.[32] The stock was valued at $290 per share at the time of the transfer. Due to stock splits, the value of the stock and each party's basis in the stock was reduced. Kresge's basis in the stock was 15 cents a share. The transfer was for her benefit and protection in case Kresge died prior to their marriage. Kresge was later divorced from his first wife and in 1924 delivered an additional 1,800 shares of stock to the taxpayer for her benefit.[33] The taxpayer then executed an antenuptial settlement wherein she accepted the shares and his promise to marry in exchange for her release of all dower and other

---

[31]   160 F.2d 812 (2d Cir.1947).

[32]   Sebastian Kresge founded the S.S. Kresge Co. in 1899. The company became a retail giant and owned Kmart and other retail stores. In 1977 it officially changed its name to Kmart Corporation. In 2001, Kmart filed bankruptcy. See e.g. "Kmart Through the Years," Chicago Sun-Times, January 23, 2002, at 57.

[33]   The total value of the stock received was approximately $800,000. That would be the equivalent of 8,467,840 in 2002. Not a bad deal. At the time, however, Kresge was worth $375,000,000. Her dower and intestacy rights, had he still agreed to marry her without the pre-nuptial, would have been worth far more than $800,000.

marital rights. They were married in 1924 and were divorced in 1928.[34] In 1938, the taxpayer sells some of the stock.

Question: How should the taxpayer's gain on the sale of the stock in 1938 be calculated?

Service's argument: The taxpayer's stock was acquired by gift and hence she took Kresge's basis of 15 cents per share, § 1015(a).

Held: The stock was transferred in consideration of the taxpayer's promise to relinquish her rights in Kresge's property she would acquire by the marriage. The transaction was therefore a sale. The taxpayer's basis in the stock was her cost of acquiring it, and that was equal to the fair market value of her marital rights. And the value of her rights was equal to the fair market value of the stock at the time of the transfer. Hence her basis was $10 per share, not 15 cents per share.

Comment: Kresge undoubtedly treated the transfer of the stock as a gift. But under the rationale of *Davis*, he should treat it as a sale. Note that *Davis* was decided 15 years after *Farid-Es-Sultaneh.*

Comment: How does Farid treat the transfer of her marital rights for the stock? Is it a taxable gain to her? What is her basis in her marital rights? Zero? The fair market value of the stock (so there is no gain)? Drop us a line if you get the answer.

These two marital property settlement cases are important for probing the outer contours of the realization requirement. They are correctly decided. A benefit of real legal significance was acquired by the transferor of the stock in both cases. Indeed, in *Farid-Es-Sultaneh*, the taxpayer's inchoate interests in the property of her husband greatly exceeded the value of the stock transferred to her.

These transactions are different from transfers of property between married or unmarried individuals that are truly gifts, for which no consideration is received. *Davis* and *Farid-Es-Sultaneh* are also different from bequests. The only possible problem with these cases was that, under *Davis,* the tax treatment of transfers in exchange for marital rights varied depending on state law. But of course that just reflected that state law really was different, and the

---

[34]   In a somewhat hostile obituary, the New York Times provided us with a small look into Princess Farid-Es-Sultaneh's life. Interestingly, the obituary does not mention her tax dispute, which has made her famous to generations of budding tax lawyers. The obituary does note, however, that she received $3,000,000 from Kresge in settlement of all claims against him. She later met and married Prince Farid of Sadri-Azam, a nephew of the former Shah of Iran. In 1936 the marriage ended. She continued to use the name Farid-Es-Sultaneh and the title "princess." This has nothing to do with the case but is interesting. Who says tax law lacks intrigue? Princess Farid-Es-Sultaneh, 74, Ex-Wife of S.S. Kresge, Dead, N.Y. Times, August 13, 1963, at 31.

rights of the parties to a marriage really are different in different states.

Notwithstanding that these cases are sound, Congress changed the law in this area in 1984. It provided in § 1041(a) that no gain or loss is recognized on a transfer of property to a spouse (or to a former spouse if the transfer is incident to the divorce). This overrules *Davis*. Congress provided in § 1041(b) that the basis of the property so transferred is the transferor's basis.[35] This does not reach *Farid-Es-Sultaneh* which was a pre-nuptial case. So in the pre-nuptial setting we still have the *Farid* problem.

Section 1041 gives a truly inaccurate answer in this area. Modify the *Farid* facts as an example. Say Kresge transferred the stock to Farid on the occasion of their divorce. This brings the transaction within the ambit of § 1041, which applies to spouses and former spouses but not to intended spouses. On these modified facts, then, Kresge transfers $800,000 of stock with a basis of 15 cents and a fair market value of $10. This means he transferred 80,000 shares of stock with an aggregate basis of $12,000. For that he satisfied a legal obligation of at least $800,000. Why should he not be taxed on this tremendous gain of $788,000?

Put it this way: If Kresge wanted to make a lump sum payment to satisfy his marital obligations and you were his advisor, what would you tell him? Should he pay $800,000 cash or pay with $800,000 of very appreciated stock? If he pays with cash, he is still stuck with the appreciated stock that has a locked in gain of $778,000. At a 40% tax rate, that is a pending tax liability of $315,200. If, however, he pays with the appreciated securities, then there is no tax paid. He still has the $800,000 cash and he's got no pending tax liability.

It is true that under the basis rule of § 1041(b), the obligation for paying the $778,000 of appreciation is taken over by the wife here. So the appreciation is still subject to tax. But why allow a transferor who has under general tax principles undergone a realization to escape taxation?

For other federal income tax aspects of separation and divorce, see ¶ 6.02(14).

---

[35] Even if the fair market value of the property is less than the basis at the time of the transfer, the basis is still the transferor's basis. Thus the rule here is different than in the straight gift area. No "notch" transaction and all that, see this Chapter ¶ 4.03(2)(c).

¶ 4.03 COMPUTATION OF GAIN OR LOSS REALIZED

Once it is ascertained that a realization event has occurred,[36] the second step in taxing dispositions of property is to compute the amount of realized gain or loss. The Code explicitly sets forth the formula for making this computation.[37] In substance the formula is first to ascertain the "amount realized" on the transaction and subtract from it the "adjusted basis" of the property. If the result is positive, there is a realized gain; if the result is negative, there is a realized loss.[38] The critical terms in the formula are, of course, "amount realized" and "adjusted basis."

The Code provides further definitions of these terms. The "amount realized" from the sale or other disposition of property is the sum of money received plus the fair market value of the property received.[39] The "adjusted basis" of the property is generally the cost of the property, adjusted further for such things as depreciation or capital expenditures.[40] Actually the ascertainment of the "amount realized" and the "adjusted basis" can be a good deal more complex than these definitions suggest; hence it is useful to discuss each of these terms in turn.

(1) Amount Realized

Amount realized is an essential component in computing realized gain or loss. As a matter of clarity, the "amount realized" should be distinguished from the "realized gain." (Don't worry—this vocabulary is confusing for everyone at first. But it's crucial to read and use these terms carefully.) As the discussion above has indicated, "realized gain" is a net term; the difference between the amount realized and the adjusted basis. "Amount realized" is the gross amount of the money plus the fair market value of the property received on the transaction.

Usually the amount realized will be clear. Sometimes there can be a problem in ascertaining the fair market value of property received, where the property is not traded frequently and no market values exist. Valuation under these circumstances requires some degree of estimation. There is a rich debate among the cases, the commentators and the Service concerning the best techniques to

---

[36]   As discussed in ¶ 4.02, a realizing event, although required by the statute in most cases, is not of constitutional dimension.

[37]   Section 1001.

[38]   Section 1001(a).

[39]   Section 1001(b).

[40]   Sections 1011, 1012, 1016.

employ for this purpose—such as capitalization of future earnings, replacement value, book value, liquidation value and cash flow. Notwithstanding the existence of these various techniques, it is sometimes conceded—even by the Service—that some types of property, often involving payments contingent on future events, cannot be valued at the time of the transaction.[41] In such rare cases reporting of gain realized may be deferred to future years, as discussed at ¶ 8.03.

Also questions can arise concerning what is the amount realized in tax shelter type situations, where, for example, recourse or nonrecourse debt is involved. The tax shelter field is discussed at ¶ 8.02.

A leading case in the area of amount realized is *International Freighting Corporation, Inc. v. Commissioner.*[42] The Second Circuit, speaking through Judge Frank, held that when an employer gave stock with a fair market value greater than its basis to its employees as compensation, the employer had a realized gain in the amount of the difference between the basis of the property and its fair market value. What was received that was taxed was the fair market value of the services of the employees, even though the statute (§ 1001(b)) says that the amount realized is the fair market value of the money or property received. The value of the stock furnished to the employees was a good indicator of the value of the services received. In effect, the transaction was the same as if the employer had sold the stock and transferred the cash proceeds to the employees.

(2) Adjusted Basis

(a) Background

Adjusted basis is the other essential component in computing realized gain or loss. Without a concept like adjusted basis, the taxpayer would be taxed on the gross amount received on sale or other disposition of the property, without being able to subtract the previous cost of acquiring the property or some other substantial expenditures made with respect to the property—a manifestly unjust result.

Hence it is intuitively apparent that a major factor in determining basis is the cost of the property to the taxpayer. However, cost is far from being the whole story. Where the property

---

[41]   See e.g. Dewing, Financial Policy of Corporations (1953), Vol. I, pp. 281–282, 287–292, 390–391; Perlman v. Feldmann, 154 F.Supp. 436 (D.Conn.1957).

For "open" treatment, see Rev.Rul. 68–194, 1968–1 C.B. 87. See also the classic case in this area, Burnet v. Logan, 283 U.S. 404, 51 S.Ct. 550, 75 L.Ed. 1143 (1931), discussed at ¶ 8.03.

[42]   135 F.2d 310 (2d Cir.1943).

is not acquired by purchase, but in a tax-free exchange or by gift, inheritance, or other non-market transactions, techniques other than cost will have to be used to establish basis in order to compute gain or loss properly on a subsequent disposition. Moreover, once basis is established, it will often be subject to further adjustments upward or downward to account for such things as capital expenditures, depreciation, casualty losses and so forth.[43]

Pay close attention here, for basis is one of the most important concepts in the tax law. The taxpayer should always know or be able to ascertain easily the basis of property, not only for the purpose of computing gain or loss on disposition but also as a point of departure in making other adjustments to the basis. Ascertaining the basis of property is important in a number of types of transactions, besides sales or exchanges, discussed at various points herein.[44] Indeed ascertaining the basis is important in almost every transaction involving property. The various methods for establishing basis are discussed below.

(b) Cost Basis

(i)   In General

The dominant rule for establishing the taxpayer's basis of property is the cost of acquiring the property. More precisely, the basis of property is its cost, unless another rule specifically provides otherwise.[45] The cost of acquiring the property is generally the amount paid for the property in cash and/or property, plus acquisition costs.[46]

For example in *Philadelphia Park Amusement Co. v. United States*,[47] Philadelphia Park Amusement Co (PP), in 1889, had a 50-year franchise to operate a passenger railway in Fairmount Park, Philadelphia. PP constructed the Strawberry Bridge over the Schuylkill River for use by its streetcars. In 1934 PP sold the bridge to the city in exchange for a 10-year extension of its franchise. Then

---

[43]   The precise statutory formulation is: Section 1011 provides that the adjusted basis shall be the basis, determined generally under § 1012. Section 1012 provides that the basis shall be the cost of the property—except as otherwise provided in certain cases discussed below. Section 1016 provides that once basis is established by cost or other rules, it shall be adjusted for a number of items, such as capital expenditures and depreciation, see ¶ 4.03(2)(g).

[44]   This is by no means an exhaustive list: see ¶ 6.02(12) relating to depreciation; ¶ 4.05(6), relating to wash sales of stock or securities; ¶ 4.06(2)(c), relating to holding periods for capital gains and losses; ¶ 3.02, relating to original issue discount; ¶ 2.03, relating to employee bargain purchases of property.

[45]   Section 1012.

[46]   Reg. § 1.1012–1(a), see ¶ 6.03(4) for discussion of acquisition costs, such as brokerage fees and commissions.

[47]   126 F.Supp. 184 (Ct.Cl.1954).

in 1946, PP abandoned the 10-year extension of the railway franchise and instead employed bus transportation for its passengers. PP attempted to take depreciation deductions with respect to the 10-year extension of the franchise as well as a loss deduction on its abandonment. This raised the question of PP's basis in the franchise, since (as we will learn) deductions for depreciation and loss with respect to property cannot exceed the taxpayer's basis in the property.

The essential problem in the case was that it appeared that the fair market value of the bridge was much less than the fair market value of the 10 year extension at the time the taxpayer exchanged the bridge for the extension. This created a problem in figuring out what the taxpayer's basis in the extension was.

The court pointed out that there are two theories as to what is "cost" in cases where the property was acquired by exchange for other property. One theory of cost is that the basis of property acquired in an exchange is the fair market value of the property *given* in the exchange. The other theory is that the basis of property acquired in an exchange is the fair market value of the property *received* in the exchange. (Of course one would usually expect the two to be the same, but as pointed out that was not the situation in this case).

The court held that the proper approach is that the cost is the fair market value of the property received in the exchange.

As the court pointed out, this is a problem that rarely arises, since ordinarily the values of two properties exchanged in an arm's-length transaction are equal or presumed to be equal. Thus, the court said that the fair market value of the 10-year extension should be ascertained and that will be its basis in PP's hands for further transactions. If, the court said, the value of the 10-year extension cannot be ascertained, one would then look to the value of the bridge. Once the value of the bridge is established it can be assumed that it was the same as that of the extension. Since the case was not prosecuted on this theory, the court remanded the case.

(ii) Mortgages and Other Debts of the Purchaser or Seller: Crane

Where the property is purchased for a down payment plus debt obligations of the purchaser, the usual rule is that the basis is the full amount of the purchase price even though some of it is not yet paid.[48] However, where the purchaser is not personally liable on the debt obligations because they are only secured by the property purchased, problems can arise in ascertaining basis. On a theoretical level, obligations of the purchaser without personal liability should

---

[48]	Edwards, 19 T.C. 275 (1952) (acq.); Martin, Jr., 23 T.C.M. 1217 (1964).

probably be included in basis, since they do represent in some sense the "cost" of the property.

But the problem here is that the purchaser may very well succumb to the temptation to pay a very high price for the property, financed by nonrecourse obligations, in order to create a high basis from which to compute depreciation.[49] This is, of course, a classic tax shelter—a field which is now covered like a blanket by the Code.[50]

However, even prior to the onslaught of tax shelter legislation, there was an occasional judicial foray against tax shelter-type arrangements, disallowing the creation of artificially high basis with nonrecourse debt.[51] And such judicial attacks on artificially high basis have continued contemporaneously with the enactment and implementation of the tax shelter legislation[52]—which, as noted, approaches the matter from the point of view of disallowing losses rather than not respecting the debt. Thus a tax shelter may founder on either the legislative or judicial shoal. See ¶ 8.02 for a detailed treatment of tax shelters.

Closely related to the question of the treatment of mortgage obligations of the buyer of property is the question of the treatment of mortgage obligations of the seller for which the buyer takes some responsibility. For example the seller may not have as yet paid off the original purchase money or other mortgage on the property before conveying the property to the buyer. If the buyer, in addition to whatever other consideration paid for the property, assumes personal liability on the seller's mortgage, that mortgage will properly be

---

[49]   See ¶ 6.02(12) for depreciation.

[50]   See §§ 465, 469 and see ¶ 8.02.

[51]   Marcus, 30 T.C.M. 1263 (1971) (contingent obligations disregarded for basis purposes.) But see Mayerson, 47 T.C. 340 (1966) (acq.) allowing nonrecourse mortgage debt to be used in computing taxpayer's basis for purposes of depreciation, notwithstanding that the mortgage was for 99 years and most of the amount was due in a balloon payment at the end of the term, thus allowing the taxpayer (or his heirs) to walk away from the property after having enjoyed the depreciation deductions. Although the Service acquiesced in this case (1969–1 C.B. 21), it emphasized that its acquiescence was based on the particular facts in *Mayerson* and could "not be relied upon in the disposition of other cases except where it is clear that the property has been acquired at its fair market value in an arm's length transaction creating a bona fide purchase and a bona fide debt obligation," Rev.Rul. 69–77, 1969–1 C.B. 59.

[52]   Estate of Franklin v. Commissioner, 544 F.2d 1045 (9th Cir.1976), a lineal descendant of *Mayerson,* above, in which the court disallowed deductions of depreciation and interest arising from a purported sale and leaseback of a motel financed by a nonrecourse mortgage with a balloon payment at the end of 10 years because the selling price was for more than the fair market value of the property. See also Rev.Rul. 78–29, 1978–1 C.B. 62 (excluding from cost basis a very large nonrecourse note where taxpayer failed to prove that the fair market value of the property being purchased at least approximately equaled the note).

considered to be part of the buyer's cost basis of the property.[53] Similarly the buyer's assumption of personal liability for any other non-mortgage liabilities of the seller as consideration for the property would be part of the buyer's cost basis of the property.[54]

The harder question is when the buyer takes the property from the seller subject to a mortgage on the property but does not assume personal liability on the mortgage. The considerations here are, of course, essentially the same as in the case where the buyer issues his or her own nonrecourse obligation in consideration for the property. In one sense nonrecourse mortgage is still a "cost" of the property, since the buyer is motivated to pay off the debt or lose the property. However where the taxpayer has issued a nonrecourse mortgage, the taxpayer has the option to walk away from the property if it declines in value below the amount of the mortgage. This makes the nonrecourse mortgage different from the recourse mortgage. Whether this difference should matter to the tax law is another question.

A large proportion of commercial mortgages (those financing shopping centers, apartment buildings and office buildings) are nonrecourse.[55] Thus for all these reasons it becomes important to understand the treatment of nonrecourse debt for tax purposes.

The seminal case in this area is *Crane v. Commissioner*.[56] Given the immense importance of *Crane* in the field, it requires careful attention:

---

[53]   United States v. Hendler, 303 U.S. 564, 58 S.Ct. 655, 82 L.Ed. 1018 (1938), reh'g denied 304 U.S. 588, 58 S.Ct. 940, 82 L.Ed. 1548 (1938). See also Old Colony Trust v. Commissioner, 279 U.S. 716, 49 S.Ct. 499, 73 L.Ed. 918 (1929) (the classic case holding that an employer's payment of an employee's taxes is income to the employee, cf. ¶ 2.01). If, however, the liabilities assumed are quite contingent and indefinite, they will not be included in basis, Rev.Rul. 55–675, 1955–2 C.B. 567.

[54]   United States v. Hendler, 303 U.S. 564, 58 S.Ct. 655, 82 L.Ed. 1018 (1938), reh'g denied 304 U.S. 588, 58 S.Ct. 940, 82 L.Ed. 1548 (1938).

[55]   Indeed, part of the problem in the savings and loan catastrophe was that many of the loans made by the failed savings institutions were on a nonrecourse basis. When real estate values collapsed, the savings institutions could not proceed personally against the borrowers to recoup their losses.

[56]   For an in-depth look at Crane see George K. Yin, The Story of Crane: How a Widow's Misfortune Led to Tax Shelters, in Tax Stories 207–257 (Paul L. Caron ed. 2003).

CRANE V. COMMISSIONER[57]

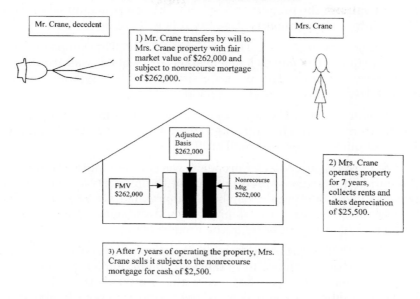

Facts: Taxpayer, Mrs. Crane was the sole beneficiary of her late husband's will. As such, Mrs. Crane received property from her husband's estate that was subject to a nonrecourse mortgage whose principal and interest outstanding totaled $262,000. The property's fair market value at the time was also $262,000. Mrs. Crane continued to operate the property for the next seven years, which included collecting rents and taking deductions, including $25,500 in depreciation. When the mortgagee threatened to foreclose, Mrs. Crane sold the property to a third party for $2,500 cash and assumption of the mortgage.

Question: How is Mrs. Crane's gain or loss computed on the sale of the property?[58]

Comment: This seems like a straightforward question but in fact it carries a great deal of baggage. To compute the gain we need to know the amount realized and the basis. Those numbers are not given in the facts and it is not immediately clear what they are.

---

[57]   331 U.S. 1, 67 S.Ct. 1047, 91 L.Ed. 1301 (1947).
[58]   The numbers in this case have been simplified a little to clarify the issues.

Comment: It is but a coincidence that the mortgage and the fair market value of the property are exactly the same amount when Mrs. Crane inherits the property. Usually this will not be the case.[59]

Taxpayer's argument: The gain was $2,500. The "property" sold was her equity. Her equity had a basis of zero when it was acquired—i.e., there was no equity on acquisition. The equity was sold for $2,500. Her gain was therefore $2,500.[60]

Comment: Mrs. Crane's having a zero basis in her property is inconsistent with her having taken $25,500 in depreciation—but hey! Let's not quibble over the small stuff.

Service's argument: Her property was not her equity, but instead the building. Her gain was the value of the property at the time of transfer ($264,500) minus her basis (approximately $236,500). The Service believed that the depreciation deductions were properly taken and reduced her basis in the property.[61]

Held: I) The property here is the physical property, not the equity. The basis is the value of the land and buildings undiminished by the mortgage. II) Since the basis in the property is the value of the land and buildings it was proper for the taxpayer to take depreciation deductions. III) The amount realized is the sum of any money received plus the fair market value of the property transferred. The term "property," in this context, means the same as it does when talking about acquisition and depreciation of property—namely the physical property undiminished by mortgages.

Reasoning: I) The first question is to determine the basis of the property. As the Court held the basis of the property is the physical property or the owner's rights undiminished by the mortgage. This result is clear for several reasons: 1) This is the ordinary, everyday usage of the term "property." Equity is something else, the value of the property above the total liens. 2) This interpretation of the word "property" is also consistent with administrative practice for estate tax purposes. In estate cases the appraised value of the property should be reported and the mortgages deducted separately. 3) In many other parts of the Code, the language has been clear in distinguishing "property" from "equity." 4) If we took equity as the property, the computation of depreciation would be a mess. It would

---

[59] Apparently what really happened is that the appraiser put the value of the building at the amount of the debt. Appraisers of real estate are well known to fudge their numbers somewhat for the convenience of their clients.

[60] Taxpayer also claimed her gain was a capital gain which, under the law at that time, allowed her to exclude one-half the gain, giving her a taxable amount of $1,250. The capital gain aspect of the case is not significant and will be ignored.

[61] Note: These numbers do not work out exactly because of rounding and because other factors also impacted taxpayer's basis.

be an unrealistically low number. It would also be complex, since the equity changes every year as the mortgage is paid off. Also the taxpayer would gain control over the timing of the deductions. If the taxpayer paid off more of the mortgage, the equity would increase, causing the depreciation base to increase. Depreciation from equity has never been contemplated in the tax laws. Thus the proper basis is the value of the property undiminished by the mortgage or $262,000.

II) Since the property is the building and the land, it was appropriate for the taxpayer to take depreciation on the building. Taxpayer's basis therefore must be reduced by the amount of depreciation taken under the usual rules.

III) The amount realized, under the statute, is the sum of any money received plus the fair market value of the property received. Since Mrs. Crane received only $2,500 cash, she must have received something else in addition for this property, and that was relief from the mortgage. Relief from a nonrecourse debt is thus part of the amount realized.

If the mortgage had been recourse (where taxpayer was personally liable for the loan) the result was well settled prior to this case. In that event, if the buyer assumed personal liability on the mortgage, getting relief from the mortgage would constitute an amount realized in the amount of the mortgage.[62] If a mortgagor has property mortgaged on a nonrecourse basis in an amount less than the fair market value of the property, the mortgagor will treat the mortgage the same way as if it was a mortgage with personal liability, for if the mortgagor does not make timely payments on the mortgage, the property (worth more than the amount of the debt) will be lost.

The Court states as follows in famous footnote 37: "Obviously, if the value of the property is less than the amount of the mortgage, a mortgagor who is not personally liable cannot realize a benefit equal to the mortgage. Consequently, a different problem might be encountered where a mortgagor abandoned the property or transferred it subject to the mortgage without receiving boot. That is not this case."

The Court's analysis continues here to say that what taxpayer seeks here is a double gain. She took depreciation but seeks to have the computation of gain on the sale of the property made without reduction of basis.

---

[62]   United States v. Hendler, 303 U.S. 564, 58 S.Ct. 655, 82 L.Ed. 1018 (1938), reh'g denied 304 U.S. 588, 58 S.Ct. 940, 82 L.Ed. 1548 (1938). Ed. note: This is in the nature of cancellation of debt income (see ¶ 3.10).

Comment: Putting it a little more succinctly, *Crane* held, in effect, that the amount of a nonrecourse liability incurred on acquisition of property is included in the basis. (Thus the basis was $262,000). And the amount of a nonrecourse liability is included in the amount realized on sale of the property. Thus if the mortgage was still $262,000 at the time of sale, then Mrs. Crane's realized amount was $262,000 + $2,500. Her adjusted basis would be $262,000 less the $25,500 depreciation she took, or a gain of $28,000.

This is depicted in the accompanying graphic:

THE COURT'S DECISION IN *CRANE*

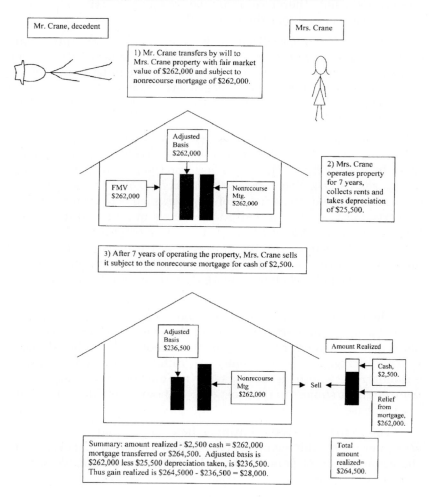

Comment: It is easy to see from this graphic that the crucial lesson from *Crane* is that the mortgage must be included in both sides of the transaction; that is, debt must be included both in the amount realized and in the adjusted basis. If the mortgage is not included in the basis but is included in the amount realized, then we get a taxable gain on the sale of $264,500, which has no relation to economic reality. If the mortgage is included in the basis but not in the amount realized, then we have a deductible loss on the sale of the property of $234,000 ($236,500 basis against $2,500 amount realized). This also does not make economic sense. The only other logical possibility is to exclude the mortgage both from basis and amount realized. That would mean the basis is zero and thus no depreciation would be allowed until some of the mortgage is paid off. As the *Crane* Court pointed out, this is administratively unattractive. We don't want the depreciability of property to depend on the property's financing.

Comment: This all seems complicated superficially, but the underlying theory is simple. We are calculating gain on sale of property by reference to the formula: amount realized minus adjusted basis. The hassle with *Crane* is figuring out how to compute amount realized and adjusted basis when property is subject to nonrecourse debt.

Comment: Another short-hand way of describing *Crane* is to say that you treat nonrecourse debt the same way that you treat recourse debt: include the debt incurred in acquisition of the property in basis and include being relieved of the debt in amount realized.

Comment: Yet another way to look at it is to say that mortgages are just money going the other way. If you incur a mortgage on acquisition of property, it's like you paid money of that amount, pumping up your basis. If you get relieved of a mortgage on selling property, it's like you received money, pumping up your amount realized.

Comment: The footnote 37 issue: Crane may well be the most famous tax case ever decided, but footnote 37 of the *Crane* decision is easily the most famous footnote in the tax field. You can go up to a tax lawyer at a cocktail party and out of the blue say "I've been thinking about the footnote 37 problem," and the tax lawyer will know what you mean. The tax lawyer will still judge you for your inability to set aside work issues at a social occasion, but at least he or she will understand you.

In footnote 37 the *Crane* Court declined to consider the case of what would happen if, at the time of the property's sale, the property had a fair market value less than the amount of the mortgage. Obviously this can only happen if the property has declined in value after a mortgage has been put on it.

This situation undermines a major ground of the Court's decision. Key to the *Crane* rationale is that a taxpayer with a nonrecourse mortgage in an amount less than the value of the property has more or less the same motivation to pay off the mortgage as a taxpayer who has a mortgage with personal liability. What would happen in the case where the mortgage exceeds the fair market value of the property at the time of sale? This is a question that plagued the tax profession for decades. Since we had to wait over four decades to get the answer, you can wait a few pages to get the answer too (we always like a cliffhanger).

Comment: Observe that a major preoccupation of the court was that depreciation should be correctly calculated. The court felt that it would not be correctly calculated unless the mortgage were included in the basis. But as we show in ¶ 6.02(12), the usual methods of calculating depreciation—straight line or declining balance techniques—do not give the economically correct results in any event. The economically correct method of depreciation is sinking fund depreciation. It is a little ironic that after all this struggle in the *Crane* case to get depreciation right, in fact it is still calculated wrong.

The holding in the *Crane* case was amplified in the First Circuit case of *Parker v. Delaney.*[63] The facts were similar to *Crane,* except that the property was acquired by purchase rather than by inheritance. The court had no trouble applying the principles of *Crane* and finding that when a mortgage is used to finance the purchase of property, that mortgage goes into the basis of the property. Then on subsequent foreclosure on the property by the lender, which is treated as a sale, the mortgage goes into the amount realized. Thus the gain is calculated by the amount realized minus the basis (which will be reduced by any depreciation taken).

Okay, you may say, the *Crane* case was interesting, although a little turgid. But what makes it such an important case? It would indeed be hard to overstate the importance of the *Crane* case to the field of federal income taxation. As Professor Daniel Posin observed, "If Helen of Troy had the face that launched a thousand ships, Beulah Crane had the case that launched a thousand tax shelters." By winning the case and causing Mrs. Crane's nonrecourse debt to be included in her basis, the government gave birth to the tax shelter industry. This is an example of tunnel vision litigation strategy, for the government has obviously lost far more money in tax shelters over the decades than they ever won in the *Crane* case. See Chapter 8 for discussion of tax shelters. *Crane's* principles are still widely

---

[63]   186 F.2d 455 (1st Cir.1950), cert. denied 341 U.S. 926, 71 S.Ct. 797, 95 L.Ed. 1357. See also Blackstone Theatre Co., 12 T.C. 801 (1949).

used not only in taxation of individuals but also in the fields of corporate and partnership taxation, where mortgages are involved. If you wish to pursue those fields, you can do no better than to start by mastering *Crane*.

(iii) Mortgaging Property Held: Woodsam

(A) Basic Rules. Suppose Janice purchases Blackacre, a parcel of undeveloped land, for $500,000 cash. Three years later, when the property is worth $1,000,000, she takes out a nonrecourse mortgage on the property for $750,000. To keep it simple let us say it is a standing mortgage, meaning the principal remains the same and the only payments are for interest. So she puts $750,000 in her pocket, secured by the property but without personal liability. What are the tax consequences?

First, is the $750,000 taxable to Janice?

"No!" you say, laughing. "The transaction is obviously a loan." But is that so obvious? Suppose, six years later when the mortgage is still in an amount of $750,000, real estate values start to sink. The value of the property is now $600,000. Now does the deal look like income? No?

Well, suppose Janice stops paying interest on the mortgage. She says to the bank: "The property is yours. I have nothing to lose by you taking it. I'll keep the $750,000." The bank takes the property. Janice takes a world cruise. Does it look like income now? (It better!)

These issues were presented in the leading case of *Woodsam Associates.* To clarify the issues involved, the facts and numbers in *Woodsam Associates* have been changed and simplified to pick up the numbers we have just been discussing.

WOODSAM ASSOCIATES, INC. V. COMMISSIONER[64]

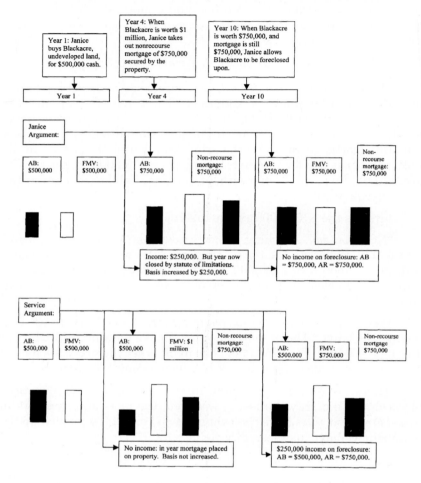

Facts: Woodsam Associates was a corporation owning property transferred to it by Mr. and Mrs. Wood. One piece of property so transferred was a piece of land with a brick building on it. This property had initially been purchased by Mrs. Wood for $101,400 in cash and a pair of mortgages worth $195,000 ($296,400 total). Mrs. Wood subsequently refinanced the property and took it subject to a $325,000 mortgage (she was personally liable on the mortgage). Then, Mrs. Wood obtained an additional mortgage on the property, bringing the total mortgage to $400,000. However, under the new structure, Mrs. Wood was not personally liable on the mortgage. Finally, Mrs. Wood transferred the property to the taxpayer in a tax-

---

64   198 F.2d 357 (2d Cir.1952).

free exchange. The mortgage still had a remaining balance of $381,000 when it was foreclosed upon.

Question: What is Mrs. Wood's gain in the year of transfer to the taxpayer?

Mrs. Wood's argument: The mortgaging of the property was a realization event, giving rise to an amount realized of $750,000. Taking that against the adjusted basis yields gain of $250,000. Thus her basis increased from $500,000 to $750,000 to reflect the $250,000 gain. Mrs. Wood concedes that she did not pay tax on that $250,000 at the time of the financing, but that year is now barred by statute of limitations, so Mrs. Wood doesn't want to get into that.[65] The point is that at the time of the transfer to the taxpayer Mrs. Wood's basis is $750,000. Thus her gain from the transfer is as follows: Amount realized: $750,000 debt relief. Subtract an adjusted basis of $750,000 (for reasons argued above). Thus gain realized is $0.

Comment: Obviously Mrs. Wood is trying to pull a fast one here. When you cut through all the funny paper flying around, what happened was that Mrs. Wood bought the property for $500,000 and later sold it for $750,000. She should therefore be taxed on $250,000, but is not taxed at all on her argument. Note too how Mrs. Wood extracted her gain out of the property. First she mortgaged the property on a nonrecourse basis for $750,000. The first $500,000 of that amount could be viewed as a recovery of her basis or capital. The next $250,000 represents a gain. But she denies having to pay tax on the mortgaging in the prior year because the statute of limitations has closed.

Held: The nonrecourse mortgaging of already-held property is not a realization event. Hence Janice does not have income from the receipt of the mortgage proceeds in excess of basis. And her basis does not increase. At the time of the transfer, then, her basis is $500,000. Her amount realized is $750,000, comprised of the $750,000 debt relief. Her taxable gain is $250,000.[66]

---

[65]   Under current law, the statute of limitations is not so easily avoided. Under current law where the taxpayer takes a position in the current year that is inconsistent with a position that he took in a year closed by the statute of limitations, the closed year may be opened, see §§ 1311–1314.

[66]   To take a variation, if the property had been worth $1 million in the year of transfer, then Janice could have sold it for $250,000 cash plus $750,000 debt relief. Her amount realized would then be $750,000 (debt relief) plus $250,000 (cash) = $1 million. Adjusted basis equals $500,000. Thus gain is $500,000.

Incidentally, we don't recommend reading the *Woodsam Associates* case straight up. The court succinctly summarized its holding: " . . . the lien of a mortgage does not make the mortgagee a cotenant; the mortgagor is the owner for all purposes; indeed that is why the 'gage' is 'mort', as distinguished from a 'vivum vadium,'" Woodsam Associates, Inc. v. Commissioner, 198 F.2d 357, 359 (2d Cir.1952).

Comment, relationship to Crane: Note we're learning a little more than you might think. In *Crane* we learned that acquisition debt *does* increase basis. Now we learn that mortgaging property subsequent to its acquisition *does not* increase basis. With both acquisition mortgages and after-acquired mortgages, getting relieved of them *does constitute* an amount realized.

Comment, foreclosure: As indicated from the discussion above, a foreclosure is treated as a sale.[67] What is the amount realized on the "sale?" It is the amount of the mortgage.

Okay, we learned the basic teaching of the *Woodsam* case, but there's more. You're still sneering at us for thinking that the first step in the process, the placing of the mortgage on the property, might have been income right there.

If the mortgage had been with recourse, of course the receipt of the mortgage proceeds would not be income. But nonrecourse financing is a little bit different. Admittedly *Crane* treated it like recourse financing for the particular purposes of its facts. But the nonrecourse mortgagor has got something going that the recourse mortgagor does not. The nonrecourse mortgagor can take a hike on the deal any time he or she wants. When Mrs. Wood borrowed the $750,000 on a nonrecourse basis, she not only got the loan proceeds, she also in effect got an option to sell the property to the bank for the $750,000. If real estate values shift downward, Mrs. Wood has the option to call up her banker and say "Hey, Bank, you just bought some property at $750,000 and I'm out of here." This right to sell at a particular price is called, in financial lingo, a "put."[68] This is not something a borrower with recourse can do.

A put can be economically attractive. For example, if real estate values continue to fall so that the property is worth $600,000, it is very economically attractive for Mrs. Wood to be able to force the Bank to buy the property at $750,000. Whereas, if the property goes up in value to, say, $1,200,000, Mrs. Wood does not exercise the put, but keeps the more valuable property by continuing to make her mortgage payments.[69]

That all being the case, it might be said that placing a nonrecourse mortgage on property the taxpayer holds is moving closer to a sale than placing recourse liability on the property. Why shouldn't we tax Mrs. Wood at this point? She is richer. By hypothesis

---

[67]   Helvering v. Hammel, 311 U.S. 504, 61 S.Ct. 368, 85 L.Ed. 303 (1941).

[68]   As in "puts and calls" that are traded in the financial markets. In those cases the puts and calls are on stock or other financial instruments rather than real estate, but the principle is the same.

[69]   What the bank gives Mrs. Wood in return for this put is a higher interest rate on the mortgage than it would charge if the loan were with recourse.

the property has appreciated from $500,000 to $1,000,000—or at least to $750,000. Moreover Mrs. Wood obviously has got the cash to pay the tax. There's real income here.

What is stopping us from taxing Mrs. Wood? It is not enough that taxpayer is richer; we need a realization event. And what is that? See our discussion at ¶ 4.02. A "realization event" is not just a sale. It could be other things as well, such as trading property, abandoning property or a foreclosure. A "realization event" is what the courts say it is. It is not a concept that has economic content. So what about mortgaging nonrecourse?

As stated before, we can view Mrs. Wood's nonrecourse mortgaging of her property as a loan plus an option to sell (or a put). There's another way to look at it, though. We could look at it as a sale plus an option to buy it back. That is, when Mrs. Wood mortgages her property on a nonrecourse basis, we could say that she has sold the property for $750,000. But she has the right to pay back the $750,000 and get the property back. This option to buy is called, in financial terminology, a "call." So now the transaction really starts to look like a taxable event.

Suppose we did tax it. What would we do then? Well, the "sale-plus-a-call" model tells us. For the sale part, we have amount realized of $750,000 and adjusted basis of $500,000. So we have a gain of $250,000, on which tax is paid. That part of the transaction is done. Then let's say that Mrs. Wood exercises her option to call the property back. That is, she repays the $750,000 to the bank. Now she owns the property all over again. What is her basis? It has to be $750,000, since that is what she paid for it when she exercised the call. That is, as you see, just another statement of taxpayer's argument in *Woodsam Associates*.

Now we can put it all together. We now know what to do if we want to treat Mrs. Wood's placing a nonrecourse mortgage on property as a taxable event. We would tax Mrs. Wood on the loan proceeds less her basis in the property. We would then also raise her basis in the property by the amount of that gain. That is the same thing as treating the transaction as a sale with a call which is exercised.

Which approach would the Service favor? Well, you would think the Service would favor treating the nonrecourse mortgage as a realization event, so that it collects the tax up front. If, alternatively, the transaction is treated as a loan, then the Service gets no tax at the time of the transaction and perhaps never, if the loan is paid back. The basis in the property would remain low, so the Service would get its tax at a later time when the property sold. Also depreciation is less. Moreover, the property might be held by the taxpayer until death, with consequent tax-free step up in basis.[70] Thus the Service might never collect a tax.

But, in the *Woodsam Associates* case the Service took the opposite approach. It favored not treating the nonrecourse financing as a taxable event. That was because the year in which the nonrecourse financing occurred was barred by the statute of limitations.

This may be another example of "tunnel vision" litigation policy on the part of the Service. Instead of realizing that on a time value of money basis it was better for the fisc to have nonrecourse financing be taxed, the particular litigators for the government probably sought to win their particular case on its unusual facts.

So how do *Crane* and *Woodsam Associates* work together? The following example will illustrate.

> Michelle buys Whiteacre, a tract of undeveloped land, from Herbert for $50,000. Michelle gets the $50,000 to pay Herbert by putting down $10,000 of her own money and borrowing the other $40,000 on a nonrecourse basis from Belly-Up Savings and Loan, which issues a check to be used for payment at the closing. The transaction goes smoothly.
>
> • Michelle's basis in Whiteacre: $50,000.
>
> Time passes. Since Whiteacre is undeveloped real estate it is not depreciated so we don't have to worry about the basis changing on account of that.[71] After five years, Whiteacre has appreciated to a value of $100,000. At this time Michelle has paid off $10,000 of the mortgage, so the remaining mortgage is now $30,000.
>
> • The partial pay off of the mortgage has no impact on her basis in Whiteacre: it's still $50,000.
>
> At this time, Michelle borrows another $35,000 on Whiteacre on a nonrecourse basis and uses the loan proceeds to finance various personal expenses unrelated to Whiteacre.
>
> • Impact of the after-acquired mortgage on Michelle's basis: nothing. Her basis is still $50,000.

---

[70] Section 1014, and see ¶ 4.03(2)(e).

[71] See ¶ 6.02(12).

- Over the next two years, the property drops in value from $100,000 to $85,000.

- Impact on Michelle's basis of the drop in value of the property: nothing. Her basis is still $50,000.

Two years later Michelle sells the property. She has paid off no further principal on the mortgages. She gets $10,000 at the closing and the buyer takes the property subject to the mortgages. What is her gain or loss?

Her amount realized is total debt relief of $65,000 plus $10,000 cash, for a total of $75,000. Her basis is still $50,000. Her gain is $25,000.

Comment: Does this make sense? Take a strict cash flow analysis: Michelle put in originally cash of $10,000. She then paid off $10,000 on the mortgage. So she put in a total of $20,000. How much cash is jingling around in her pockets now that the deal is over? She borrowed $35,000 after she had held the property. She also received $10,000 on the sale. That amount went into her pocket. Thus she got a total of $45,000. Balance that against the $20,000 she put in. So she's ahead $25,000. That is the amount on which she is taxed. Good news: the system works!

(B) Nice Work if You Can Get It. Crane and *Woodsam Associates* also work together in another way that leads to some very attractive results. Unlike most of the tax advice given in this book (which is either too theoretical, obvious, or out of date), this piece of advice actually works. As we have seen, what *Crane* and *Woodsam Associates* teach us is that debt incurred to acquire property is included in basis and debt incurred later on property is not. Both kinds of debt are included in amount realized when the property is sold or otherwise disposed of.

Here's the gimmick, illustrated by an example:

Murgatroyd acquires a small apartment building for $200,000. He puts $20,000 down and borrows the other $180,000 nonrecourse. As we know, his basis is $200,000. Three years later, the apartment building has appreciated to a value of $400,000. Murgatroyd borrows another $150,000 nonrecourse against the $200,000 of appreciation. Under *Woodsam Associates* he is not taxed the receipt of the $150,000, and it does not go into his basis. He then uses the $150,000 to make some major capital improvements to the apartment building. As a result the $150,000 as a capital expense does go into his basis. It can therefore be used to increase his depreciation deduction.[72] So he gets the best of both worlds: the $150,000 is not taxed but increases his basis for depreciation purposes. This is a nice little move.

Comment: What you need for this maneuver to work, of course, is to buy real estate which will go up sharply in value. That should be no problem (!!). See how useful this book is?

(iv) The "Footnote 37" Problem: Tufts; Diedrich

(A) "Phantom Gain". Crane, as discussed above, held that acquisition nonrecourse indebtedness is included in basis and in the amount realized from a sale or other disposition of the property. In footnote 37 of that opinion, recall, the *Crane* Court declined to consider what would happen if at the time of the sale of the property, the property had a fair market value of less than the amount of the mortgage. Obviously this can only happen if the property has declined in value after the mortgage has been put on it, since no lender would lend more than the fair market value on property.

This is a highly significant issue. Since the *Crane* Court left the issue open, lawyers for taxpayers who sold property subject to nonrecourse debt of more than the value of the property argued that the amount realized could not exceed the value of the property. This thus lowered their clients' tax bill. This issue was addressed by the leading case of *Tufts*. The facts have been simplified a little to get to the point.

---

[72] See ¶¶ 6.03(4) and 6.02(12) for discussion of depreciation and capital expenditures.

COMMISSIONER V. TUFTS[73]

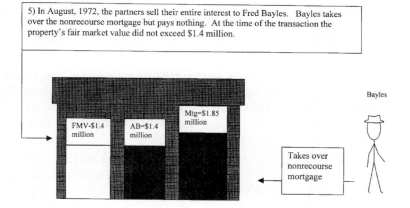

Facts: Mr. Tufts and others represent individuals and a corporation that formed a general partnership in order to obtain financing for the building of an apartment complex. None of the partners initially contributed money into the partnership. The taxpayers obtained a nonrecourse loan in the amount of $1,851,500 to build the complex. After completion of the project, the taxpayers contributed some capital and took their allocable shares of ordinary losses and depreciation. This combined activity left the partnership with an adjusted basis in the property of $1,455,740. After an

---

[73]   461 U.S. 300, 103 S.Ct. 1826, 75 L.Ed.2d 863 (1983), reh'g denied 463 U.S. 1215, 103 S.Ct. 3555, 77 L.Ed.2d 1401.

economic downturn in the area, the partnership was unable to pay its mortgage payments, so all the taxpayers sold their interest to a third party who agreed to assume the mortgage as full payment. At the time of sale, the fair market value of the complex was not more than $1,400,000.

Question: What was the gain realized by Tufts and the other partners on the sale of the property to Bayles?

Service's argument: They realized a gain because the $1.85 million nonrecourse mortgage (included in the amount realized, remember) exceeds the $1.4 million adjusted basis by $450,000.

Taxpayer's argument: The transaction is calculated by using an amount realized of $1.4 million, the fair market value of the property, less the $1.4 million adjusted basis. Hence there is no gain or loss.[74]

Comment: Observe the injustice if taxpayers prevail. They use the nonrecourse debt to pump up their basis for purposes of taking $450,000 of depreciation. Then when they sell, they don't want to hear about the nonrecourse debt to the extent it exceeds the fair market value of the property.

Held: The full amount of the nonrecourse mortgage is an amount realized to the taxpayers on sale of the property even though it is greater than the fair market value of the property. Thus the partners had a realized gain of $450,000.

Thus borrowing with and without recourse are treated the same way for basis and amount realized purposes. Once you take the position that recourse and nonrecourse debt are to be treated the same, then cancellation of debt principles[75] enter to put the full amount of the mortgage into income.

Comment, cash flow: Note the numbers crank out correctly on a cash flow basis also. The amount of gain is equal to the depreciation deduction taken ($450,000) less the amount of cash invested ($0). Since, on a cash flow basis, the depreciation deduction was unjustified, it has to be taken back into income on disposition of the property.

Comment, time value of money: The taxpayers in *Tufts* still got the benefit of the time value of money—although in this case it was only over two years. Thus even after *Tufts*, tax shelters are alive and well. Deferral, which is money in the bank, is still available. Tax shelters are more difficult due to the anti-tax shelter legislation, but as we will see in Chapter 8 they are still with us.

---

[74]   We have rounded the numbers for convenience.

[75]   See ¶ 3.10.

Comment, an alternative view: Justice O'Connor's concurring opinion argued that the transaction could instead be analyzed in two steps. 1) There was a sale of the apartment building for $1.4 million and 2) There was cancellation of debt income of $450,000 (see ¶ 3.10). The difference in Justice O'Connor's approach is that there is no attractively taxed capital gain on the transaction if the $450,000 is viewed as cancellation of debt income since there is no sale or exchange of a capital asset associated with that step. This view ultimately did not prevail, but it has substantial merit. And the Service later decided to use the same approach when it comes to the discharge of recourse debt in excess of the collateral's fair market value.

Comment, what about Bayles? Why did Bayles want to take the property over when it was subject to a nonrecourse mortgage of $1.85 million and had a fair market value of $1.4 million? There are a couple of possibilities. First note that Bayles has nothing to lose. The mortgage is, of course, nonrecourse. Bayles does have to make mortgage payments or face foreclosure. But he may have been able to say something to the lender Farm & Home Savings along the lines of "Don't push me. You want this property now you can have it." Having thus fended off Farm & Home, he might then hope to be a sharp enough operator to do some cosmetic fix ups and hope that the Dallas economy turns around. Then he might be lucky enough to sell the property for more than the $1.85 million mortgage and walk away a clear winner.

Alternatively Bayles might have been intending to assert under *Crane* that his basis in the property included the full amount of the nonrecourse mortgage or $1.85 million. Thus Bayles would hope to take depreciation deductions from that inflated amount.

This would appear not to work, however. There is case law holding that where the amount of a nonrecourse indebtedness exceeds the fair market value of the property, the debt will not be respected for tax purposes.[76] Both depreciation and interest deductions founded on the debt will be lost.

Comment, the role of the value of the property: A major lesson to be drawn from all this concerns the role of the value of the property subject to a nonrecourse debt. On acquisition of the property, the value seems to matter a great deal. If the nonrecourse debt is greater than the value of the property, it will not be respected. Once valid nonrecourse financing is in place, however, we cease to care about the value of the property. On disposition of the property, the entire amount of nonrecourse debt is included in amount realized,

---

[76]   See ¶ 8.02(4) and the discussion of the *Franklin* case.

regardless of the value of the property. The treatment of nonrecourse debt must be symmetrical.

Comment, tax jargon: Tufts provides some major additions to tax jargon. The gain from circumstances on the pattern of *Tufts* is called "phantom gain" or "Tufts gain." That is to say, the effect on the taxpayer of a *Tufts* type pattern is, in a narrow sense, shocking. The taxpayer has a failed investment. The taxpayer gets rid of the property and gets nothing for it. Still, the taxpayer gets hit with a big tax. You can only explain it to your client using words like "phantom gain," or "*Tufts* gain." Even if you pour on this gibberish, your client will not be a happy camper. You might also try to explain to your client that he got "phantom deductions" in the form of depreciation founded on the nonrecourse debt. But they usually don't want to hear about that.

Comment, relevance for partnership taxation: If you are considering going on in federal income taxation, a course in partnership taxation would be a likely candidate. *Tufts* gain is a major concept at some of the most critical points in that field. Have *Tufts* well in mind going in and it will help.[77]

(B) Can You Give It Away? How can you dodge the "phantom gain" in the *Tufts* type situation? That is a question that many taxpayers and their advisors started asking before the ink on the *Tufts* decision was dry. Instead of selling the property to an erstwhile investor such as Bayles, what about giving it away? Since we're not getting anything for the property on a sale in the *Tufts* setting, let us give it away and perhaps avoid the "phantom gain." This issue was presented in the leading case of *Diedrich*.

DIEDRICH V. COMMISSIONER[78]

Facts: Taxpayers, Victor and Frances Diedrich, transferred 85,000 shares of stock to their three children on the condition that their children pay the resulting gift taxes. The taxpayers' basis in the stock at the time of transfer was $51,073; the gift tax paid by the children was $62,992.

Question: Do Victor and Frances have income to the extent that the gift tax paid by the children exceeds their basis in the stock?

Service's argument: Victor and Frances have income of $10,000, computed by an amount realized of $60,000 gift tax paid less their basis of $50,000.[79]

---

[77]   It will indeed be noted that taxpayers in *Tufts* did business as a partnership.

[78]   457 U.S. 191, 102 S.Ct. 2414, 72 L.Ed.2d 777 (1982).

[79]   We have rounded the numbers for computational convenience: the actual basis was $51,073 and the actual gift tax was $62,992.

Taxpayer's argument: They have made a "net gift" of the amount by which the fair market value of the stock exceeds the gift tax paid. Thus they have no income; the amount of the gift is simply reduced by the gift tax paid by the children.

Held: The transaction is a part sale, part gift. The sale price is the amount of the gift tax. The donors' gain is the amount of the gift tax paid less their basis in the property. Thus the Service's treatment prevails, as it better relies on *Crane, Bruun, and Old Colony.*

Comment, relationship to Tufts: The gift tax is imposed on the donor.[80] Thus this is not a nonrecourse debt situation. But the gift tax is a debt. The way that *Diedrich* informs the *Tufts* decision is to tell us that a gift of property subject to a liability is a realizing event. You will recall that the general rule for gifts is that they are not realizing events.[81] Thus it might be hoped by people in the *Tufts* fix that they could give the property away subject to the large nonrecourse liability and not have to take the liability back into income. After *Diedrich* it is clear that the gift of property subject to a liability is a realizing event to the donor to the extent of the liability. The balance of the value of the property above the liability (if any) is still treated as a gift. Thus the transaction is a part sale, part gift.

The significance of this case is very great and bears repeating: *Tufts* gain cannot be escaped by giving the property away, whether to a family member or a charitable organization or whomever.

We dwell on this because there is a second issue in the *Diedrich* case which gets a great deal of attention from the commentators, but that issue is not nearly as important as the *Tufts* gain issue.

Comment, second issue, how to compute the gain: The Service and the Court concluded that Victor and Frances had a gain of $10,000 computed by subtracting the basis in the stock of $50,000 from the gift tax liability which is the amount realized of $60,000. But is there something strange about this computation?

Take an alternate approach: Suppose that Victor and Frances had sold $60,000 of stock in order to pay the gift tax themselves and then had given the balance of the stock to their children. What would have happened then? They would have had to compute gain on the sale of that stock in the usual fashion. Since they would be selling 1/5 of their stock ($60,000 of $300,000) their basis would be 1/5 of their total basis in their stock. That would be $10,000 (1/5 of $50,000). Thus their gain would be $50,000 ($60,000 − $10,000).

---

[80]   Section 2502(d), the theory being apparently that if the donor has got such big bucks that he can make the gift, he can share a little of it with the Government.

[81]   See ¶ 4.02.

Instead, according to the method employed by the Service and the Supreme Court, the gain was only $10,000. Curious, no? This approach opens the door to some tax planning. Making a conditional "net" gift is better than selling the stock and paying the tax. Not surprisingly, then, there has been a great increase in conditional gifts since *Diedrich*.

(v) Adjustment of the Purchase Price

Negotiations between the buyer and seller of property may lead to an agreement on a certain price. If subsequent negotiations may cause the price to be reduced, then obviously the cost basis will be the new lower price. Close questions can arise as to whether the whole transaction should be regarded as a reduction in purchase price or rather a discharge of indebtedness of the buyer, resulting in immediate income. See ¶ 3.10.

(vi) Bargain Purchases of Property by Shareholders or Employees

If a corporation allows its shareholders to buy corporate property for less than the fair market value of the property, then the excess of the fair market value of the property over its adjusted basis in the hands of the corporation will be considered to be a dividend to the shareholder.[82] The basis of the property in the hands of the shareholder will be its fair market value.[83] Thus the basis in this situation is the cost of the property plus a step up to its fair market value. This is the appropriate basis, because the shareholder, having "paid the price" of a dividend treatment on the transfer, is now entitled to a fair market value basis on the property for future transactions. If the basis were not "stepped up" to account for the inclusion in income, the taxpayer would be taxed again on the income when the taxpayer later sells the property.

This same general "cost plus a step-up to fair market value" approach is applied to the case of employees getting a bargain purchase of property from an employer. The bargain element of the purchase in this case is considered compensation and is so taxed at the time of the transfer.[84] Often the property purchased for a bargain price by the employee is subject to a condition that it might have to be forfeited back to the employer on the happening of some future contingency—such as the employee's failure to render future services to the employer. There is an elaborate statutory treatment of employee purchases of such restricted property, including specialized

---

[82]   Reg. § 1.301–1(j).

[83]   Reg. § 1.301–1(h).

[84]   See ¶ 2.03.

rules for ascertaining the amount included in income and the basis of the property. See ¶ 2.03(2) for a discussion of this area.

(vii) Miscellaneous Problems

The basis of goodwill is established either by showing that the goodwill was purchased as part of an ongoing business,[85] or by establishing that certain non-deductible expenditures were made to attempt to improve the prospects of the business.[86]

If a sale of property involves installment payments over time bearing little or no interest, the Service may impute an amount as interest.[87] To the extent a purchaser's payments are imputed to be interest, his basis in the property purchased will be reduced.

If a purchaser obtains a number of different properties for one lump sum, the price paid must be allocated among the properties to establish the basis of each property.[88] The allocation of purchase price set forth in the sales contract is not necessarily dispositive; it may be self-serving in that, for example, too much is allocated to depreciable assets. In such a circumstance the Service may reallocate the purchase price to prevent substantial tax avoidance.[89] These problems arise frequently on the sale of a sole proprietorship going business, where it becomes necessary for the purchaser and seller to allocate the sales price among many types of assets. This particular problem is discussed more fully at ¶ 4.06(3)(b).

---

[85]   Grace Brothers, Inc. v. Commissioner, 173 F.2d 170 (9th Cir.1949). See also ¶ 4.06(3)(b) on the process of allocating purchase price to goodwill. See also ¶ 6.02(13)(d) regarding the amortization of goodwill.

[86]   Cf. Cooperative Publishing Co. v. Commissioner, 115 F.2d 1017 (9th Cir.1940) (dicta); cf. also Welch v. Helvering, 290 U.S. 111, 54 S.Ct. 8, 78 L.Ed. 212 (1933) (payments by taxpayer to creditors of a bankrupt corporation with which he was formerly associated to improve his business standing held nondeductible capital expenditures. Hence should this taxpayer subsequently sell his business, these payments would go into his basis for his goodwill). Section 197 provides that goodwill acquired through the purchase of a company may be amortized over a 15-year period.

[87]   Section 483.

[88]   Reg. § 1.61–6(a).

[89]   Rev.Rul. 77–168, 1977–1 C.B. 248 (first in, first out technique required for ascertaining basis of fungible property acquired on different dates at different prices; see ¶ 4.03(2)(f) regarding special basis rules for securities); Rev.Rul. 77–413, 1977–2 C.B. 298 (basis of real property sold allocated between the 20-year possessory interest retained and the interest sold).

(c) Carryover Basis

(i) Gifts; Taft

The problems here are illustrated in the case of *Taft v. Bowers*. This leading Supreme Court case presented the problem as a hypothetical:[90]

TAFT V. BOWERS[91]

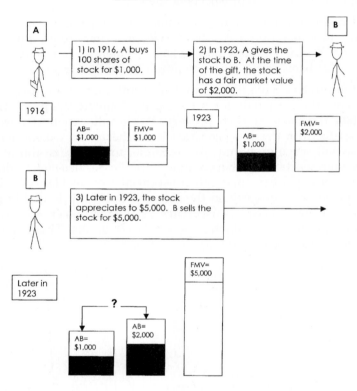

[90]   It is interesting that the Supreme Court used hypothetical numbers in this case. The court of appeals decision indicated that the stock given to Mrs. Taft was worth $42,350 at the time of the gift. She sold approximately 1/4 of the stock about 1 year later for $11,708 more than it was worth the year before. In today's dollars, the original gift would be almost $450,000 today. Mrs. Elizabeth Taft, the plaintiff in the case, was the daughter-in-law of Henry W. Taft, who was the brother of then Chief Justice William Howard Taft. See AMERICAN PRESIDENTIAL FAMILIES 584 (MacMillan Publishing Co. 1993). Henry Taft represented Elizabeth Taft. The Chief Justice of course did not take part in the case. Professional courtesy may, however, have influenced the Justices to use hypothetical numbers thereby not publicizing the amount of the gift, or they may have just wanted to use clearer facts. In any event, we are all the beneficiaries of this gesture since the hypothetical facts set out by the Court are far easier to understand. For a better factual discussion of the case see *Bowers v. Taft*, 20 F.2d 561 (2d Cir.1927).

[91]   278 U.S. 470, 49 S.Ct. 199, 73 L.Ed. 460 (1929).

Facts: Taxpayer, Elizabeth Taft, received a gift of 100 shares of stock from her father. Her father had purchased the stock in 1916 for $1,000 and held it until 1923, when its fair market value was $2,000. He then gave the property to the taxpayer who sold it in 1923 for $5,000.

Question: How much gain is B to be taxed on, $4,000 or $3,000?

Service's argument: The statute [the predecessor to § 1015] says that B must take A's basis and thus pay tax on $4,000—the entire amount of the appreciation of the property.

Taxpayer's argument: It is unconstitutional to tax me on gain that did not occur in my hands. I should not be taxed on the $1,000 the property appreciated in A's hands. Thus I should be taxed on $3,000.

Held: B takes A's basis and is taxed on $4,000, as the statute provides. The statute is constitutional.

Comment: See also ¶ 3.08 for discussion of what constitutes a "gift."

As this case illustrates, where property is transferred as a gift, the cost-of-acquisition approach discussed in the previous section cannot appropriately be used for establishing the basis of the property in the hands of the donee. Since the donee's cost is zero, this approach would result in a zero basis in the gifted property. But a zero basis would mean that the donee would be taxed in full on the entire value of the property upon a later sale. This result is manifestly inconsistent with the exclusion of gifts from the donee's income of § 102 (see ¶ 3.08). That exclusion is more than just a mere deferral provision.

The upshot of *Taft* is that what is excluded on a gift is the donor's basis. Appreciation above that amount, whether in the hands of the donor or the donee, will be taxed eventually to the donee when he sells the property.

Another possibility for handling gifts would be to say that a gift is a realizing event (see ¶ 4.02). In that event, on the *Taft* facts, A would be taxed on $1,000 at the time of the gift. B would take a basis of $2,000. On sale of the property for $5,000, B would have a $3,000 gain.

The present rule is more favorable to taxpayers in general in that the tax on $1,000 of appreciation in A's hands is deferred until B sells the property. The present rule, however, invites taxpayers to game the system. That is, if A has appreciated property, A may give it to family-member B who is in a lower tax bracket. B could then sell soon thereafter (as indeed happened in the *Taft* hypothetical). As a result, the tax on the family unit is less than if A had sold the property and given B the proceeds. Conversely, if the property has declined in value since the donor bought it, A would sell the property, and take a deduction for the loss. This deduction is more valuable to A because A is in a higher bracket than B. A could then give the cash proceeds to B.

No particular larger social purpose is served by allowing taxpayers to play games of this kind. Thus it would appear that the better rule would be to make gifts a realizing event. In addition, this proposed rule would reduce the donee's administrative problems. Under the present rule, the donee has to ascertain the donor's basis, which may be difficult to do if the donor has held the property for decades. The donor's cooperation is required to ascertain the donor's basis. With the proposed rule, the donee takes the fair market value at the time of the gift. This is something the donee can establish without the cooperation of the donor, at the time of the gift or later.

The fair market value approach received a bad name as a historical matter. This is because the original rule in this area was that the donee takes a basis of the fair market value of the property given.[92] However—and this was a fatal omission—the donor did not pay tax on the appreciation in his hands at the time of the gift. As a result, this approach erred too much in the other direction. Under this flawed fair market value approach, if the donor gave the donee highly appreciated property, that appreciation would not be taxed to the donor, since the gift was not considered a realizing event. But if the donee took a basis of the fair market value at the time of the gift, then the donor also would never pay tax on the appreciation in the hands of the donor. The appreciation in the hands of the donor would, therefore, forever escape taxation in anyone's hands. Taxpayers thus abused the rule by giving appreciated property back and forth among family members.

This carryover basis of the property in the hands of the donee is, of course, subject to further adjustments, such as depreciation or capital expenditures that may occur during the period the donee holds the property.[93]

---

[92] Wilson Brothers & Co. v. Commissioner, 124 F.2d 606 (9th Cir.1941).

[93] The donee's holding period of the property received by gift includes the holding period of the donor, IRC § 1223(2). The holding period of property is important for the capital gains rules.

A similar carryover basis rule is used for transfers of property in corporate organizations and reorganizations. See IRC §§ 362(a) and (b) and see, Bittker and Eustice, FEDERAL INCOME TAXATION OF CORPORATIONS AND SHAREHOLDERS (1987) § 14.33. The same rule is also used in the formation of partnerships, ¶ 723.

See ¶ 4.03(2)(g) regarding adjustments to basis. The basis of the gift in the hands of the donee may also be increased by some of the gift tax paid, IRC § 1015(d)(6).

Change the facts of *Taft* somewhat and we get ourselves into a surprising muddle. Suppose that A bought the stock for $2,000 and then made the gift at a time when the fair market value was $1,000. B then sells the stock for $300. Being rational (which is your first mistake), you would think that B would take A's basis of $2,000 and thus have a loss of $1,700 ($2,000 basis; $300 amount realized).

Not so. The statute reacts here much like an elephant might when a mouse crawls up its leg: screaming and jumping up at this savage attack. This is because on these facts A is seen as "giving away a loss." This smacks of "tax avoidance" and "trading in losses."

So the statute takes away that built-in loss. It does so by providing that, on our facts, B would take a basis of the fair market value at the time of the gift, or $1,000. Thus B's loss would be $700 ($1,000 basis; $300 amount realized) instead of $1,700. B can only deduct the loss that occurs while the stock is in B's hands. On these facts, the loss that A suffered is never deducted. Which is to say that giving away depreciated property is not a very good idea.

Stating the rule more generally, then: If the donee receives property with a fair market value less than the basis at the time of the gift, then for purposes of calculating further loss in the donee's hands, the donee shall use that fair market value as his basis.[94]

The astute reader might then ask, suppose the facts are these: A buys the stock for $2,000, gives the stock to B at a time when the stock has a fair market value of $1,000. B then sells the stock for $1,500. What result to B? Now we're really in a pickle. If we take the fair market value at the time of the gift as a basis for B, that would be $1,000. But using $1,000 as a basis generates a gain when B sells the property for $1,500. But this basis of fair market value at the time of the gift rule is only supposed to be used to compute a loss for B. On our numbers there is a gain.

So we go back to the usual rule: B takes A's basis. That is $2,000. When B goes to sell the stock now for $1,500, there is a loss. But when B has a loss and the property had a fair market value at the time of the gift of less than the basis, we are supposed to use that fair market value as B's basis.

So, wait a second. This is where we came in. The answer is that, on our numbers, any sale by B of the stock between the price of $1,000 and $2,000 yields no gain or loss. This is weird. This is the so-called "notch" transaction.[95]

---

[94]   Section 1015(a).
[95]   Reg. § 1.1015–1(a)(2) Example.

There are a couple things to be said about this "notch" transaction. 1) If you don't like this at all—if you are getting nauseous—then tax may not be the field for you, because there's a lot of rules like this in the field. Then again, any field of law with complex statutes may not be for you. 2) Conversely, if you like the fantasy aspect of this, then tax may be a good field for you. 3) We see here the roots of complexity. By promulgating an artificial rule divorced from economic reality—that the basis on a gift of depreciated property is the fair market value at the time of the gift— we get ourselves into further difficulty. This requires promulgation of further rules that get even more divorced from reality and more complex.

The accompanying graphic attempts to summarize the gift rules we have been discussing:

GIFT RULES: ONCE MORE WITH FEELING

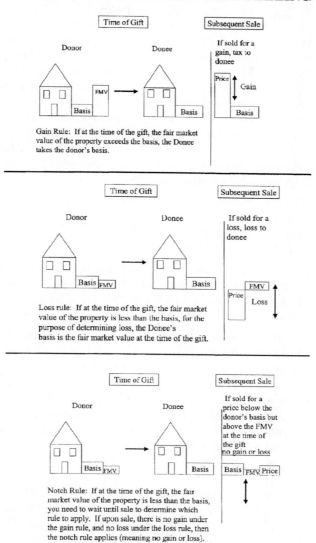

Gain Rule: If at the time of the gift, the fair market value of the property exceeds the basis, the Donee takes the donor's basis.

Loss rule: If at the time of the gift, the fair market value of the property is less than the basis, for the purpose of determining loss, the Donee's basis is the fair market value at the time of the gift.

Notch Rule: If at the time of the gift, the fair market value of the property is less than the basis, you need to wait until sale to determine which rule to apply. If upon sale, there is no gain under the gain rule, and no loss under the loss rule, then the notch rule applies (meaning no gain or loss).

One final point: Where the donee is or was the donor's spouse, the donee always takes the donor's basis in a gift, if the transfer is incident to divorce.[96]

Instead of making an outright gift, a transferor may confer a benefit by selling property to a transferee at a price substantially below the property's fair market value. In such a case the transferor

---

[96]   Section 1041(a)–(c).

has effected a transaction "in part a gift and in part a sale."[97] The transferee's basis in a "part gift, part sale" is the greater of the amount paid by the transferee or the transferor's basis for the property at the time of the transfer.[98] Where the property involved in a part gift, part sale is depreciated (fair market value less than transferor's basis at the time of the transfer) then as a further limitation on the part gift, part sale basis rule, the transferee's basis for determining *loss* on a subsequent sale cannot be greater than the property's fair market value at the time of the transfer.[99] Thus do the exigencies of developing a reasonable rule for a part gift, part sale combine with the prohibition against giving away losses to create a somewhat complex overall rule in this area. Some examples, adapted from the Regulations, will illustrate:[100]

> (1) A transfers property to his son for $60,000. At the time of the transfer the property has a basis in A's hands of $30,000 and a fair market value of $90,000. The basis in the hands of the son will be $60,000.

> (2) A transfers property to his son for $30,000. At the time of the transfer the property has a basis in A's hands of $60,000 and a fair market value of $90,000. The basis in the hands of the son will be $60,000.

> (3) A transfers property to his son for $30,000. At the time of the transfer the property has a basis in A's hands of $60,000 and a fair market value of $45,000. The basis of the property in the hands of the son will be $60,000 for the purpose of determining gain on a subsequent sale by the son and $45,000 for the purpose of determining loss on a subsequent sale by the son. Sales for a price between $45,000 and $60,000 will yield no gain or loss.

(ii) Transfers in Trust

If a transfer of property to a trust is a gift, the gift rules discussed above apply for ascertaining the basis of the property in the hands of the trust.[101] If the transfer in trust is for consideration, the basis of the property in the hands of the trust is the same as the basis in the hands of the transferor, increased by the amount of gain

---

[97] Reg. § 1.1015–4.

[98] This basis might be increased by a portion of the gift tax paid, (if any). § 1015(d)(6).

[99] Reg. § 1.1015–4(a). As with the other bases derived above, this basis will be increased by any gift tax paid, Reg. § 1.1015–4(a)(2) and will be subject to further adjustment in the hands of the transferee.

[100] Reg. § 1.1015–4(b) Examples 1–4.

[101] Reg. § 1.1015–1(a)(1).

or decreased by the amount of loss recognized to the transferor on the transfer.[102]

(d) Substituted Basis

There is a class of transactions in which basis in property acquired in a transaction is determined with reference to the basis in property given up in the deal. The major examples of this class of "substituted basis" transactions are tax-free exchanges of property[103] and involuntary conversions of property into other property.[104] The theory of these transactions is that the taxpayer remains invested in generally the same type of property after the transaction as before the transaction; hence the transaction should not be an occasion to recognize gain (or loss).[105] The substituted basis technique is then used to ensure that the gain which has escaped tax at the time of the transaction will be taxed at some later time. For example, if a taxpayer has a building with a basis of $20,000 and a FMV of $100,000 and exchanges it for a building with a basis of $70,000 and a FMV of $100,000, taxpayer will have a basis of $20,000 in the new building. The old basis becomes the new basis in the new building. Nonrecognition transactions like this one and their concomitant substituted basis rules are discussed more fully at ¶ 4.05.[106] To the extent the taxpayer *does* cash out of the investment and thus recognizes some gain, however, appropriate basis correction will be made.

(e) Fair Market Value Basis: Property Acquired from a Decedent

(i) Present Rule

The basis of property acquired from a decedent is its fair market value at the date of the decedent's death.[107] This rule allows

---

[102]   Section 1015(b).

[103]   Section 1031, see ¶ 4.05(2).

[104]   Section 1033, see ¶ 4.05(3).

[105]   See ¶ 4.05.

[106]   As with the carryover basis, the substituted basis technique has very important use in the corporate organization and reorganization area. See Subchapter C, Parts III and IV.

[107]   Section 1014. Where the executor of the decedent's estate elects the alternate valuation date (six months after death or the date of disposition of the property if disposed of within six months after death) for estate tax purposes, the value of the property on the alternate valuation date will be the basis of the property in the hands of the heir, §§ 1014(a), 2032(a).

The holding period of property acquired from a decedent will be considered to be more than 12 months even if it is disposed of within that time, in order for the sale to qualify for the attractive 15 percent capital gains rate. See ¶ 4.06(2)(b)(i).

Other exceptions to the fair market value at date of death rule for property acquired from a decedent include: (1) a gift in contemplation of death of the decedent, which is appreciation in the hands of the decedent to escape taxation forever. Contrast this with the gift rule, ¶ 4.03(2)(c)(i) above, where tax on the appreciation in the hands of the donor is only deferred but not permanently exempted. Thus, a major estate planning technique is for the taxpayer to sell loss property and hold gain property until death.

One owning appreciated property might be tempted to give that property to a relative who is obviously in ill health. The plan would be that upon the relative's death, the relative's will would transfer the property back to the donor. The donor's theory would be that the property was acquired from a decedent, thus allowing for a freshly "stepped-up" basis. This macabre bit of tax planning is foreclosed by § 1014(e), which provides that in such circumstances the property will retain its original basis in the hands of the donor if the property is received back by either the donor or the donor's spouse.

(ii) Property Acquired from a Decedent: The Saga of Carryover Basis

As discussed just above, the basis of property acquired from a decedent by will or by the laws of intestate succession is the fair market value of the property at the date of death.[108] This rule allows unrealized appreciation in the hands of the decedent to forever escape income taxation.[109] The appreciation is not taxed to the decedent or the decedent's estate at death because a bequest or inheritance is not a taxable event to the decedent, see ¶ 4.02. It is often the case that on inheritance some unrealized appreciation forever escapes income taxation.[110] This rule is, not surprisingly, of major importance in the income tax and estate tax planning of taxpayers who hold great amounts of appreciated property. In

---

included in the estate of the decedent for estate tax purposes, where such property is sold or exchanged before the decedent's death. In such a case the donee uses a carryover basis under §§ 1015, 1014(a); (2) items which are income in respect of a decedent pursuant to § 691.

[108] An alternate valuation date, at the election of the executor, is available if also used for estate tax purposes §§ 1014(a), 2032.

[109] The property may, of course, be subject to estate tax, but that is not relevant to the question of what is the proper treatment for purposes of income taxation. Many taxes—sales taxes, property taxes,—are imposed in the society, but their imposition does not properly excuse not imposing an income tax on the same property or transaction.

[110] Moreover, even if the property has not in fact risen in value, it may have been subject to the allowance for depreciation deductions, which would have lowered the basis (¶ 6.02(12)) and hence it would still be property with potential, unrealized gain.

Of course, it is possible that the property has declined in value in the decedent's hands to the extent that the fair market value is less than the decedent's basis at the date of death. In that event the fair market value basis rule for inheritances is disadvantageous to taxpayers, since there will then never be an opportunity to deduct the loss.

general the approach is to sell loss property before death so as to realize the loss and to hold gain property so that the heirs would benefit from the basis step-up.

A major theme during President George W. Bush's 2000 presidential campaign was the elimination of the estate tax. President Bush claimed the estate tax should be repealed because it hurt small businesses and family farms.[111] It was recognized, however, that if the estate tax was repealed *and* property from a decedent received a stepped-up basis large amounts of revenue would be lost and wealthy taxpayers would receive an extremely lucrative tax benefit. Under the current rules, at least, the benefit of receiving a stepped-up basis is at least somewhat countered by having to pay estate tax (if your gross estate exceeds a statutory threshold).[112] But if the estate tax was repealed there would be no reason for providing a stepped-up basis at death.

Congress at least partially agreed with this logic. In 2010, the year the federal estate tax was eliminated, each taxpayer receives only a limited step-up in basis (if you can call an aggregate step-up of over $5 million a limited one). Here is how it works. Section 1022 provides that property acquired from a decedent dying in 2010 shall be treated as if transferred by gift. Therefore, the basis in the property is the lesser of the adjusted basis of the decedent or the fair market value of the property at the date of death. The provision provides for a "basis increase," however, for certain property. In other words, a certain amount of the decedent's property will receive an adjusted basis. The statute provides that the decedent's basis in property may be increased up to $1.3 million. In addition, the basis in property transferred to one's spouse may be increased by $3 million. And since the surviving spouse still has his or her own $1.3 million adjustment, the basis in the property can be increased once again.

Therefore, a decedent with assets worth $5 million and a basis of $700,000 can plan to ensure that all property will receive a step up in basis. If the decedent gives $1.3 million to children and $3 million to a spouse, and the property has a basis of $700,000, the amount of basis adjustment allowed is $4.3 million. Thus, the beneficiaries

---

[111] See 38 Weekly Comp. Pres. Doc. 14 (April 4, 2002), available at 2001 WL 14297386 (President Bush applauding the House of Representatives action in repealing the estate tax claiming that it is unfair to family farms and small businesses.) It is unclear why a complete elimination is necessary to protect family farms and small businesses. A proposals to keep the estate tax but to raise the estate tax exemption to $4 million to protect small businesses and family farms was rejected by the Senate by a vote of 43 to 56. 147 Cong. Rec. S5255 (daily ed. May 21, 2001).

[112] Section 2010 generally provides for an exclusion of $5,000,000 per person, but this number is adjusted annually for inflation. In 2016, for example, the exclusion was $5,450,000 per person.

effectively receive the property with a stepped-up basis. So, while Congress claims the rule is that you get the decedent's basis, the rule only applies in a limited number of situations when there are extremely large estates.

While this provision allows a tremendous amount of wealth to be transferred without tax, some type of basis adjustment was probably necessary. If one did not exist, the wealthiest among us would get a very large benefit from the estate tax repeal while middle income taxpayers would actual pay more. Why? Because people with estates under $5,000,000 do not pay tax, and they get the benefit of the stepped-up basis. If one eliminated the estate tax and eliminated the step-up in basis, middle income taxpayers would find that their tax bill increased. They would not receive the benefit of the estate tax repeal, but they would suffer the consequences in the form of having to pay tax on inherited property.

(f) Special Rules for Stock, Securities and Mutual Fund Shares

Stock and securities are acquired or transferred in a variety of unique transactions that occasion the use of special rules for ascertaining basis. Substituted and carryover basis techniques are used in the corporate organization, reorganization and division areas.[113] A substituted basis is used in wash sale transactions.[114] A "cost plus taxable income" approach is used for stock transferred as compensation for services.[115]

Where a taxpayer has bought identical shares of stock at different times for different prices, there is a problem when the taxpayer sells some but not all of the taxpayer's holdings. The size of the realized gain or loss and its character (long term or short term) may well depend on which of block of shares is deemed to have been sold. The Regulations provide that unless the taxpayer can in fact identify the particular shares sold, the taxpayer is deemed to have sold the shares purchased earliest in time.[116] The Regulations set forth steps the taxpayer can take to identify the particular shares being sold, whether the taxpayer holds the certificates outright or through a broker.[117] Unless such steps are taken to identify the shares sold, the Service's "first-in first-out" rule will apply.

---

[113]   Sections 358, 361.

[114]   Section 1091 and see ¶ 4.05(6).

[115]   Section 83 and see ¶ 2.03. As these authorities indicate, the cost plus taxable income approach is used to ascertain the basis of any property received as compensation for services.

[116]   Reg. § 1.1012–1(c)(1).

[117]   Reg. § 1.1012–1(c)(2) and (3).

Similar problems are presented where the taxpayer has purchased shares of an open end mutual fund at different times for different prices. A redemption or sale of some but not all of the holdings leads to questions of which shares were redeemed or sold. Here again there are two basic possibilities. If the taxpayer can in fact identify the actual mutual fund shares disposed of, then actual cost will be used as basis. If the shares, as will often be the case, have been left by the taxpayer in the custody of a transfer agent, then the taxpayer may elect to use an average cost approach to ascertain basis.[118]

(g) Adjustments to Basis: The Basis as History

Once basis is ascertained by any of the methods discussed above, it does not necessarily remain unchanged while the property is held by the taxpayer. On the contrary, it may well be adjusted on account of a wide variety of items while the property is held by the taxpayer, such as capital expenditures, casualty losses, and depreciation.[119]

As indicated, the basis of property may be treated specially (carried over to another taxpayer, or substituted on to another piece of property) if the property is disposed of in a nonrecognition transaction. Thus in some sense the basis traces the history of a piece of property, always recording what has happened to it and informing what the results will be on future transactions. Applying with equal significance to all types of property from vacant land to variable annuities, and serving as a point of departure not only for calculating gain or loss on disposition but also for computing further adjustments to basis, the basis is a central concept in the tax law.

¶ 4.04 DISALLOWANCE OF SOME LOSSES AND EXCLUSION OF SOME GAINS

(1) In General

As indicated in the above discussion, the first step in approaching sales and other dispositions of property is to determine whether there has been a realization event. If there has been a realization event, the second step is to compute the amount of the realized gain or loss, as discussed in the preceding section.

---

[118] Reg. § 1.1012–1(e), also providing for the option to treat all shares together or to maintain separate accounts for shares held for various long-term periods and shares held for a short term.

This average cost method would, as discussed in the text, apply only to open-end mutual fund shares, Regs. § 1.1012–1(e)(1)(ii)(a). Shares of a closed-end fund, traded as they are over a securities exchange or over the counter, would be treated under the rules for stock, above.

[119] Section 1016, also listing a number of other adjustments to basis; see 6.03(4).

Realized gains and losses might still not be reflected on the taxpayer's tax return. A realized gain, for example, might still be excluded from the taxpayer's income by some other provision of the Code. Similarly a realized loss might not be allowed as a deduction by some other provision of the Code. If a realized gain is so excluded or a realized loss is so disallowed, then that is the end of the process for the transaction. No further issue is or need be raised with respect to recognition or characterization (as discussed below).

There is at present only one Code provision (discussed below) permanently excluding from income a realized gain from the sale or exchange of property; it applies to a relatively narrow range of transactions and is not of great significance in terms of the structure of the Code. It is of great significance, however, for anyone thinking about selling a home.[120]

The more problematic situation involves losses. A broad range of realized losses from the sale or other disposition of property are permanently disallowed by the Code and this disallowance is of great significance in the structure of the Code.[121] Thus the discussion will deal first with the disallowance of realized losses and then with the exclusion of realized gain.

With respect to losses incurred on sales or other dispositions of property, the Code takes a two-level approach. The general rule is that such losses are allowed.[122] However, there are provisions specifically disallowing losses incurred on certain types of transactions. These provisions are treated below. (Note that the topic of allowance of losses on sales or other dispositions of property is only a part of the larger topic of allowance of losses of all kinds—such as casualty losses or losses from bad debts, etc.).

(2) Losses from Sales of Residence or Other Personal-Use Property

As indicated, the general rule with respect to the allowance of losses from sales or other dispositions of property is that the loss is allowed. However, an important exception to this rule is where the loss arises from the sale or other disposition of property held solely by the taxpayer for his personal use. The loss realized from sale or other disposition of the taxpayer's personal-use property is not

---

[120] See ¶ 4.04(5).

[121] See ¶ 4.04(2).

[122] Section 165(a). The amount of the loss allowed is limited to the basis of the property, § 165(b); this limitation is also inherent in the process of computing gain or loss realized, see ¶ 4.03.

allowed.[123] Thus the loss on sale of taxpayer's personal-use property—such as a personal residence,[124] jewelry,[125] or a horse[126]— is not allowed. The situation is not symmetrical, however, as realized gains on the sale of personal-use property are usually taxed.[127]

Since losses on the sale of personal-use property are not allowed, but losses on the sale of investment or business property are allowed,[128] there can naturally arise a healthy dispute over whether particular property that was sold at a loss was personal-use or investment property. This issue arises most frequently on the sale of a taxpayer's personal residence which may have been converted at some point to rental or other income-producing use. Fairly specific principles have been evolved by the courts and the Service for dealing with this problem.[129]

---

[123] Section 165(c)(3). A loss would be allowed with respect to personal use property if it arose from a casualty above certain floor amounts. See ¶ 7.01(5)(a).

[124] Reg. § 1.165–9, Newton, 57 T.C. 245 (1971) (loss on mortgage foreclosure of personal residence disallowed).

[125] Winkler v. Nunan, 143 F.2d 483 (2d Cir.1944) (jewelry not bought for investment).

[126] Clarence W. Daugette, Jr., 36 T.C.M. 252 (1977) (distinguishing between horses held for business and a personal-use horse that was not depreciated).

[127] Section 61(a)(3); ¶¶ 4.01–4.03. See ¶ 4.04(5) for discussion of exemption of gain on sales of personal residences. See ¶ 4.06 for discussion of capital gains.

[128] See ¶ 7.01(5).

[129] The received wisdom in this field was handed down in Heiner v. Tindle, 276 U.S. 582, 48 S.Ct. 326, 72 L.Ed. 714 (1928) which involved a property that had been used as the taxpayer's personal residence for 9 years and then rented for 19 years and then sold at a loss. The Court held that the loss would be allowed since at the time of the renting the property ceased to be held for personal use and was devoted exclusively to the production of income.

This rule has now been adopted by the Regulations, Reg. § 1.165–9(b)(1). To benefit from this *Tindle* rule, the property must in fact be converted from personal to business or investment use. Renting the property out, as held in *Tindle* and Reg. § 1.165–9(b)(1), constitutes such a conversion. Putting the property up for sale does not constitute such a conversion. Unsuccessfully attempting to rent the property out does not constitute such a conversion, and a loss on property sold after an unsuccessful attempt to rent will not be allowed, Phipps v. Helvering, 124 F.2d 292 (D.C.Cir.1941) (Senator Lawrence Phipps of Colorado denied a deduction for loss on his sale of the Colorado home he vacated after his election to the United States Senate).

Once the property has been rented, the fact that it later becomes vacant apparently will not destroy the loss deduction, as long as personal use is not made again of the property, see McBride, 50 T.C. 1 (1968) (acq.) (loss on demolition of previously rented property allowed).

The amount of the loss allowed is the lesser of the cost of the property or the fair market value of the property at the time of conversion (reduced by depreciation taken), less the amount realized on sale of the property, Reg. §§ 1.165–9(b)(2) and 1.165–9(c), providing examples and see *Tindle* above. Of course if such property is sold at a gain, the usual basis rules apply. Presumably if property is sold at a price that would yield gain if the loss rules were applied and a loss if the gain rules were applied, then no gain or loss is realized. Cf. the "notch" transaction in the gift area, ¶ 4.03(2)(c)(i).

Even if the property is clearly held for investment-type purposes, the taxpayer must believe that there is at least some remote chance of making a profit for a loss on sale

(3) Losses from Sales of Property in Activities Not Engaged in for Profit

Some taxpayers engage in activities—most typically "gentleman farming" or the breeding and racing of horses—which are a hobby rather than a serious business or investment. When such activities generate losses, the difficult problem is to sort out the true farm or racehorse business which can legitimately take loss deductions from the recreational farmer or racehorse breeder who may seek to take loss deductions arising from what is essentially a hobby or pastime. This problem has long-plagued the tax law.[130]

The present treatment of deductions from hobby-type activities not entered into for profit is discussed fully at ¶ 6.02(9). A part of that treatment is the disallowance of losses from sales of property arising from activities not entered into for profit.[131]

(4) Disallowance of Losses Versus Nonrecognition of Losses

In addition to the two provisions discussed above disallowing losses on sales or other dispositions of personal-use property or property used in activities not entered into for profit, there are two other provisions of the Code which purport to "disallow" losses on sales or other dispositions of property. These are § 267, disallowing losses on transactions between related taxpayers, and § 1091, disallowing losses from "wash" sales of stock or securities. However, §§ 267 and 1091 do not permanently disallow the loss involved but rather, through basis adjustment, preserve the loss so that it may be claimed at some later time. Thus, though couched in terms of "disallowance of loss," §§ 267 and 1091 really smell more like nonrecognition transactions. They are therefore discussed at ¶ 4.05.[132]

---

or abandonment of the property to be allowed. King v. United States, 545 F.2d 700 (10th Cir.1976) (worthless oil leases abandoned in the aftermath of the collapse of the King Resources Company and the IOS mutual fund complex of Bernard Cornfeld held deductible, as taxpayer's intent was to make a profit). Cf. Knetsch v. United States, 364 U.S. 361, 81 S.Ct. 132, 5 L.Ed.2d 128 (1960) and Goldstein v. Commissioner, 364 F.2d 734 (2d Cir.1966), cert. denied 385 U.S. 1005, 87 S.Ct. 708, 17 L.Ed.2d 543 (1967) discussed at ¶ 6.03(6)(b).

[130] Senate Report 91–552, 1969–3 C.B. 423, 489–491.

[131] Sections 183(a)–(c); Reg. § 1.183–1(b). See Bessenyey v. Commissioner, 379 F.2d 252 (2d Cir.1967), cert. denied 389 U.S. 931, 88 S.Ct. 293, 19 L.Ed.2d 283 (1967).

[132] See also discussion at ¶ 4.05(1), note 3.

(5) Exclusion of Gain from Sale of Residence

At present the only permanent exclusion of realized gain is in § 121, relating to a taxpayer who sells a principal residence.[133] If this gain is excluded, no further steps in the process (relating to recognition or characterization, etc.) are taken.

Section 121(a) provides that gross income does not include up to $250,000 of gain from the sale or exchange of property if, during the five-year period ending on the date of the sale or exchange, the property has been owned and used by the taxpayer as the taxpayer's principal residence for periods aggregating two years or more. The exclusion is not available if the individual engaged in another sale of a principal residence resulting in exclusion of gain within the preceding two years.[134]

The $250,000 exclusion escalates to $500,000 for married individuals filing joint returns, if the couple meets the following conditions:

a)   *Either spouse* meets the requirement of owning the property for two years out of the five years prior to the sale.

b)   *Both spouses* meet the requirement of using the property as their principal residence for two years out of the five years prior to the sale.

c)   *Neither spouse* is ineligible for the exclusion due to engaging in another sale of a principal residence resulting in exclusion of gain within the last two years.

If a taxpayer does not meet the ownership or residence requirements a pro rata amount of the $250,000 or $500,000 exclusion may be allowed if the sale or exchange is due to a change in place of employment, health, or unforeseen circumstances.

Regulations elaborate on the above exclusions. First, in order to qualify for an exclusion based on a change in place of employment, health problems, or unforeseen circumstances, the qualifying reason must be the primary reason for the sale or exchange.[135] Whether one

---

[133]   The Taxpayer Relief Act of 1997, which introduced this rule, also repealed the provisions that allowed non-recognition of gain on sale of a residence if the proceeds were rolled over into another residence, and repealed the provision allowing an exclusion of some gain on sale of a residence to taxpayers who had attained the age of 55. Still, a generation after its enactment, you'll occasionally see references in the popular media to the need to "roll over" the gain from the sale of a home or that an exclusion is limited to individuals aged 55 or older. Sometimes journalists aren't good at keeping up to date on the law.

[134]   Sales prior to May 7, 1997 do not count in this. So everyone gets a fresh start on the two-year period commencing May 7, 1997, § 121(b)(3)(B).

[135]   Temp. Reg. § 1.121–3T.

qualifies is once again determined based on the facts and circumstances of the situation. Factors that are relevant for determining taxpayer's primary reason include: (1) whether the sale and the reasons for the change are proximate in time, (2) whether the suitability of the property as a principal residence materially changes, (3) whether the taxpayer's financial ability to afford the residence materially changes, (4) whether the taxpayer used the property as a residence during the period of ownership, (5) whether the circumstances giving rise to the sale or exchange were foreseeable, and (6) whether the circumstances giving rise to the sale or exchange occurred while taxpayer used the property as a principal residence.[136]

The regulations also create certain safe harbors. First, the sale or exchange will be considered primarily due to a change in employment if the change in employment occurs while taxpayer is living in the property as his or her principal residence, and the new place of employment is at least 50 miles farther from the residence sold than was the former place of employment.[137] Second, the sale or exchange will be considered by reason of health if the primary reason for the sale is to "obtain, provide, or facilitate the diagnosis, cure, mitigation, or treatment of disease, illness, or injury [for you or a family member]" or "to obtain or provide medical or personal care for a [family member] suffering from a disease, illness, or injury." There is a further safe harbor in this provision that provides the health exception is satisfied if a physician recommends a change of residence for health reasons.[138]

The last, and probably most interesting exception, is the "unforseen circumstances" exception.[139] A sale or exchange is because of "unforeseen circumstances" if the primary reason is due to "the occurrence of an event that the taxpayer does not anticipate before purchasing and occupying the residence."[140] There are wonderful safe harbors here including: (i) the involuntary conversion of a residence, (ii) natural or man-made disasters, including acts of war, (iii) death of the taxpayer or a family member, (iv) cessation of employment for which the individual qualifies for unemployment compensation, (v) change in employment that causes taxpayer to no longer be able to afford housing expenses, (vi) divorce or legal separation, (vii)

---

[136]　Temp. Reg. § 1.121–3T(b)(1–6).

[137]　Temp. Reg. § 1.121–3T(c).

[138]　Temp. Reg. § 1.121–3T(d)(2).

[139]　Until the release of the temporary regulations, the IRS had indicated that because it has not yet issued regulations regarding what constitutes "unforeseen circumstances" a taxpayer could not rely on that exception. See IRS Publication 523 at 12.

[140]　Temp. Reg. § 1.121–3T(e).

multiple births from the same pregnancy, and (viii) other great things the Commissioner thinks up.[141] Interestingly, neither marriage nor adoption is listed as an unforeseen circumstance. While those events are certainly within the control of most taxpayers, it's not like the events treated as unforeseen circumstances are truly unforeseen. After all, neither death nor multiple births from the same pregnancy is exactly "unforeseen."

Example 1:

Alex bought a house in Florida for $250,000 and took a job as a scuba instructor. Six months after his arrival he decides that Florida is too hot and that scuba diving is not for him. Alex then receives an offer to work as a ski instructor in Utah. He jumps at the chance and sells his home for $350,000. He owned and used the home for six months. Alex is single. What are the tax consequences of this transaction?

Since Alex did not own and use the property for two of the last five years, he is not eligible for the $250,000 exclusion. But, since the reason for the sale of his home was because of a change in his employment, Alex is entitled to a pro-rata exclusion. See § 121(c)(2)(B). The ratio is calculated based on the number of months Alex lived in the property divided by the 2 year requirement (for math ease use 24 months). Thus here Alex is entitled to 6 (months he owned and used the property)/24 (total months) multiplied by the exclusion amount ($250,000) or .25 × $250,000. Alex's exclusion amount is therefore $62,500. Since he had $100,000 gain, Alex must pay tax on $37,500. (More importantly, how did Alex realize a 40% gain on his property in just six months?

Example 2:

Assume the same basic facts except that while in Utah, Alex meets a wonderful woman, Jennifer, and gets married. He had previously bought a house in Utah on February 27, 2000. On February 28, 2001, they get married and Jennifer moves in with Alex. On January 28, 2002, they decide they need a bigger house. They sell the house on February 28, 2002 and have a $300,000 profit. What are the tax consequences?

1.   Alex and Jennifer meet the ownership test under § 121(b)(2)(A)(i) (providing that only one spouse must meet the ownership requirement).

2.   Alex, but not Jennifer, meets the use requirement of § 121(a). See 121(b)(2)(A)(ii).

---

[141] Id.

3.   Under § 121(b)(2)(B), they are entitled to exempt the aggregate of Alex's and Jennifer's individual benefits. Alex is entitled to $250,000 (he owned and used the house for 2 years.) Since Jennifer did not use the property for 2 years and did not move for business or health reasons, so her exclusion amount is zero. Thus as a couple, they can exclude $250,000 of the gain.

Notice also that the statute refers to gain from the sale of a "principal residence," not just a "residence." A determination regarding whether a property is a principal residence is based on a facts and circumstances approach. The factors include (i) the taxpayer's place of employment, (ii) the principal place of abode of the taxpayer's family, (iii) the address listed on taxpayer's tax returns, (iv) the mailing address for bills and correspondence, (v) the location of taxpayer's banks, and (vi) the location of religious organizations and other clubs with which taxpayer is associated.[142] Moreover, if a taxpayer has two residences, the principal residence will generally be the one at which the taxpayer spends the most time. Thus, if a taxpayer owns a vacation home in Florida and lives in it five months out of the year, the taxpayer could easily meet the ownership and use tests (since the taxpayer would have owned and used the property for two out of the last five years), but the gain from the sale of the second home would not be excludible from income.

Vacant land will be considered part of the principal residence if it is adjacent to the dwelling, and the land was owned and used as part of the taxpayer's principal residence. Thus, if your house sits on 100 acres, you may be able to exclude both the sale of the house and the sale of the land from income.[143]

See how a seemingly easy rule can become very difficult with a little bit of work? The main result of this rule, however, is that most people will not have a taxable gain when they sell their home. It relieves many taxpayers of the burden of keeping track of the cost of capital improvements to their homes which would increase basis and affect gain that might otherwise be taxable. Nevertheless, there are a number of taxpayers that are not protected by this provision and would therefore have to maintain records. Examples would of course be taxpayers who fail to meet the requirements concerning ownership, use, or prior sales. In addition, it is possible that the gain on a home could be larger than the excluded amount, in which event one would have to know what the gain actually is, in order to

---

[142]   See Reg. 1.121–1.
[143]   Reg. 1.121–1(b)(3).

ascertain the amount that is taxed above the $250,000 (or $500,000) exclusion.

¶ 4.05 RECOGNITION OF GAIN OR LOSS

(1) In General

Having determined the amount of realized gain or realized loss, the issue then becomes whether the realized gain or loss will be recognized. "Recognition" of a gain or a loss means that the gain or loss will in fact be taken into account in computing the taxpayer's taxable income. The powerful presumption of the Code is that all gains or losses realized are recognized.[144] Indeed, most gains and losses on dealings in property are recognized without further problems. However, in an important category of transactions, Congress has provided that the gains (and sometimes losses) realized will not be recognized at the time of the transaction but will be deferred until some later time. Insuring that the deferred gain or loss will be accounted for later is accomplished by appropriate adjustment of the basis of the property involved in the transaction. Bear in mind that the gains or losses not recognized by these provisions are only deferred. The idea is that they will be recognized at a later time.

The rationale behind these nonrecognition provisions of the Code varies somewhat from provision to provision. Roughly, however, it can be said as to many of them that Congress has determined that a taxpayer who has engaged in this class of transactions has not changed the nature of his investment sufficiently to warrant a tax being imposed on his realized gain. Tax-free exchanges of like-kind property can be explained on this basis, as can the tax-free treatment of certain corporate mergers and acquisitions.[145]

Some other nonrecognition provisions can be explained on the basis that the taxpayer is in a difficult spot and we should not impose a tax at that exact time. Involuntary conversions and transfers of property between spouses incident to a divorce[146] are examples of this type.

---

[144] Section 1001(c). See also Reg. § 1.1031(a)–1(a). Of course the loss might be disallowed or the gain might be excluded as discussed in ¶ 4.04. In such an event the question of recognition of the gain or loss, of course, is never reached. For convenience in this section, when realized gains and losses are discussed, it will be assumed that the gains are not excluded from income and that the losses are allowed. (As discussed in ¶ 4.04 it is usually the case that a realized gain will not be excluded. However, a number of realized losses may in fact be disallowed).

[145] See D. Posin CORPORATE TAX PLANNING: TAKEOVERS, LEVERAGED BUYOUTS AND RESTRUCTURINGS, Chapters 7–9 (1990).

[146] See ¶ 4.02.

It should also be noted that these nonrecognition provisions are not always "taxpayer-friendly." For example, suppose a taxpayer owns some stock on which there is an unrealized loss. The taxpayer may wish to continue holding the stock because the taxpayer believes in the company. But the taxpayer may still wish to get a deduction for the loss. The taxpayer might think of selling the property (thereby creating a realization event) and then buying it back ten minutes later. The Code does not like tricks like this. The loss on this maneuver, known as a "wash sale," will not be recognized.[147]

Even supposedly "taxpayer-friendly" provisions can be seized by the Service and used to beat the taxpayer over the head. Thus the nonrecognition rule for like-kind exchanges carries a bite because it also applies to disallow the recognition of losses. As such, like-kind treatment has been imposed on taxpayers—to their surprise—in some transactions to bar a loss.[148]

The nonrecognition of gain accords the taxpayer, of course, the great advantage of deferral of tax on a realized gain. As previously discussed, deferral of gain is money in the bank to the taxpayer. Time value of money issues are at the core of nonrecognition transactions.[149]

As indicated above, nonrecognition can be a double-edged sword. The taxpayer may prefer recognition of gain where the taxpayer is in a relatively low marginal tax bracket at the time of the transaction or where the taxpayer has another recognized loss to offset against the gain. Depending upon the particular nonrecognition provision involved, the taxpayer may not be able to escape nonrecognition treatment when so desired. Indeed, taxpayers scrambling to get into or out of these nonrecognition provisions have given rise to a good deal of litigation and complexity in this area.[150]

---

[147] See ¶ 4.05(6) below. If, instead, the taxpayer tries to sell the loss stock to a family member, another nonrecognition provision will bite, see ¶ 4.05(7) below.

[148] See ¶ 4.05(2)(c).

[149] It is indeed possible that the deferral of gain will ripen into a permanent exemption if the taxpayer dies and his heir takes a fair market value basis in the property. See ¶ 4.03(2)(e). For more on the rationale of nonrecognition transactions, see Commissioner v. Wheeler, 324 U.S. 542, 65 S.Ct. 799, 89 L.Ed. 1166 (1945), reh'g denied 325 U.S. 892, 65 S.Ct. 1182, 89 L.Ed. 2004.

[150] It might be noted that the same results of postponing gain or loss on the various types of nonrecognition transactions could have been accomplished by providing in the Code that no gain is *realized* on them. Accounting for the deferral could still be accomplished by appropriate basis correction. This would have had the advantage of keeping the overall structure simpler.

It should also be noted that the Code is not consistent in its use of the term "recognition". Although the provisions discussed in this section involve postponing gain or loss, some corporate tax provisions which are phrased in terms of "non-recognition" in fact allow permanent exemption from taxation. See e.g. § 1032.

Finally, for those of you planning to take other courses in the field, it should be noted that much of corporate taxation is concerned with nonrecognition transactions. The formation of a corporation is often accomplished on a tax-free basis.[151] Likewise, many corporate mergers and acquisitions are structured on a tax-free basis.[152]

Corporate taxation builds on the structure of individual income taxation that we have been discussing here. When there is a corporate transaction, it runs the gauntlet of the steps in this Chapter regarding whether there is a realization event and calculating the realized gain or loss. When we get to the question of recognition, we consider various corporate nonrecognition provisions at this nonrecognition step. So keep that relationship in mind and it should help in the advanced classes.

(2) Tax-Free Exchanges of Business or Investment Property of "Like Kind"

(a) Overview

The granddad of all tax-free exchanges is exchanges of business or investment property of like kind, as provided in § 1031. The basic operation of § 1031 is fairly straightforward. If a taxpayer who holds property used in business[153] or for investment[154] exchanges that property for property of like kind, no gain or loss will be recognized to the taxpayer on the transaction. This will be so, notwithstanding that the taxpayer may have a substantial realized gain (or loss) on the transaction (as measured of course by the difference between the fair market value of the property received and the adjusted basis of the property surrendered).[155]

There are definitional problems up front. One question is whether a transaction is an "exchange" at all, as exemplified by the case of *Bloomington Coca-Cola Bottling Co. v. Commissioner*.[156] Section 1031 requires an "exchange" of property; a "sale" will not

---

[151]   Take a look at § 351.

[152]   If you have some interest in this, you might take a gander at §§ 368, 354, 356, 362, 358.

[153]   For example, in a business for which expenses are deductible under § 162, see ¶ 6.02(1).

[154]   For example, in an activity for which expenses are deductible under § 212, see ¶ 6.02(3).

[155]   Excluded from this non-recognition treatment are inventory; stocks, bonds or notes; other securities or evidences of indebtedness or interest; interests in a partnership; and certain other intangible property, § 1031(a)(2). The exclusion of stocks and securities from non-recognition treatment under § 1031 can be regarded as the basis for the entire field of corporate reorganizations, which, as mentioned above, provides its own complex nonrecognition rules in this area. This non-recognition is mandatory if the requirements are met.

[156]   189 F.2d 14 (7th Cir.1951).

qualify. *Bloomington* held that if the taxpayer receives both like-kind property and a small amount of money for his property, the taxpayer will still be regarded as having engaged in an "exchange" of the property and thus qualify for treatment under § 1031. *Bloomington* recognized that "Border-line cases arise where money forms a substantial part" of the consideration, the implication being that if money is a substantial part, then perhaps an "exchange" has not occurred and that the transaction is instead a sale. In the event the transaction is a "sale," § 1031 would not apply.

Another question can be whether property involved in an exchange is of "like kind." This question is discussed in detail at ¶ 4.05(2)(c). The case of *Commissioner v. Crichton*[157] provides an example of the kind of problems that can be encountered. In *Crichton*, the taxpayer and her children owned, in undivided interests, a tract of unimproved country land and an improved city lot. Taxpayer effected an exchange of interests with her children. The children transferred to taxpayer their undivided interest in the city lot, worth $15,357.77. Taxpayer transferred in exchange an undivided 3/12 interest in the oil, gas and other minerals in the country land. Taxpayer's basis in the mineral interest was zero, so she was looking at $15,357.77 of taxable gain. Thus she argued that the transaction fit within § 1031. Under local Louisiana law, mineral rights are interests in real and not personal property. As discussed at ¶ 4.05(2)(c), the regulations broadly hold that all real estate is "like kind." As a result, the Fifth Circuit affirmed the lower court and found that the transaction qualified as an exchange of like-kind property and therefore the gain was not taxed.

Another danger spot is whether the property is held "primarily for sale," even if it is not held for sale "in the ordinary course of business." In *Neal T. Baker Enterprises, Inc. v. Commissioner*, 76 T.C.M. 301 (1998), taxpayer put up a sign offering the property for sale before engaging in the § 1031 transaction. The posting of the sign was held to be enough to disqualify the transaction for § 1031.

Once the transaction qualifies for § 1031, the realized gain on the transaction is not recognized. Although this realized gain is not recognized at the time of the transaction, the gain is not permanently exempted from tax. Rather, the basis rules insure that the gain (or loss) will be accounted for on subsequent disposition of the new property. This is done by substituting the basis of the old property onto the new property.[158]

---

[157]   122 F.2d 181 (5th Cir.1941).

[158]   Another thing that happens is that the holding period of the property exchanged is added on to the holding period of the property received, § 1223(1). This is of great importance given that extremely attractive low rates are available on a

For example, suppose Ferdinand exchanges an office building with a fair market value of $200,000 and an adjusted basis of $120,000 for an apartment building, also with a fair market value of $200,000.[159] An apartment building is considered "like kind" to an office building for purposes of the statute, see discussion below. On the transaction Ferdinand realizes $80,000 of gain. Note that the gain is realized in that this exchange is a realizing event, as discussed at ¶ 4.02. However, because we come within the nonrecognition rule of § 1031, no gain is recognized.[160] The basis of the apartment building received is the same as that of the office building exchanged, or $120,000. Thus the unrecognized gain on the office building is preserved on the apartment building. When the apartment building is subsequently sold, the $80,000 gain will be recognized at that time. The graphic "§ 1031: A Simple Exchange" illustrates this transaction.

---

subsequent sale of the property. The most attractive rate is 15% on property held longer than 12 months. See ¶ 4.06(2)(b)(i).

[159]   The property received would of course have to have the same fair market value as the property exchanged or the parties would not do the deal. Where the properties involved in the transaction do not have the same fair market value, money can be used to even up the deal. The treatment of that is discussed below.

[160]   Section 1031(a).

§ 1031: A SIMPLE EXCHANGE

When two parties wish to exchange property, it is in fact unlikely that their two properties will have exactly the same value. Hence it is common that some cash is used to even up the transaction. The cash is often termed "boot" in the lexicon of tax professionals (as in "I'll give you my property plus cash 'to boot.'").

Recall that the theory of § 1031 exchanges is that the taxpayer receiving like-kind property has not changed the form of the investment sufficiently to warrant paying a tax. However, where some cash is received, that theory does not hold up. The taxpayer has "cashed out" in part. Hence when some cash is received, that will trigger recognition of realized gain to the extent of the cash.[161]

Thus in our example, suppose Ferdinand exchanges his office building with a fair market value of $200,000 for an apartment building worth $180,000, and $20,000 of cash. Ferdinand will still have a realized gain of $80,000. He will recognize that realized gain to the extent of the cash, or $20,000. This will leave him with $60,000 of unrecognized gain. The basis in the apartment building received

---

[161]   Section 1031(b).

will preserve that unrecognized gain. To do that, the basis will be $120,000. The graphic "§ 1031: An Exchange With Cash" illustrates this transaction.

§ 1031: AN EXCHANGE WITH CASH

Note that even if the subsequent sale of the office building is not for $180,000 but for some other number, the gain preservation rules still work. That is, Ferdinand is always $60,000 under water. His gain will always be $60,000 more than it would be if his basis were $180,000. Or any subsequent loss will always be $60,000 less than it would be if his basis were $180,000. Thus for example if Ferdinand sells the office building three years later for $340,000, his gain will be $340,000 − $120,000 or $220,000. If his basis had been the fair market value of the apartment building at the time it was acquired of $180,000, then his gain on sale at $340,000 would be $160,000. Thus he is still hit with the extra $60,000 gain that he did not recognize on the earlier transaction.

The preceding example required a relatively small amount of cash to even up the transaction. But the relative values of the buildings being exchanged might require a large amount of cash to even up the transaction. In particular the cash might be for more than the realized gain. How does that play out?

To vary our example once again, suppose that Ferdinand exchanges his apartment building with a basis of $120,000 and a fair market value of $200,000 for an office building worth $110,000, and $90,000 of cash. Ferdinand still has a realized gain of $80,000. He recognizes that realized gain to the extent of the cash, or $80,000. Note: don't fall into the trap of thinking that he recognizes $90,000 of gain—i.e., the amount of the cash.

It's fundamental that you cannot recognize more gain than you realize. The realized gain is Ferdinand's true economic gain on the disposition of his apartment building. His entire realized gain is $80,000. That is all he will recognize.

What will be his basis then in the office building he receives? Observe that since Ferdinand has recognized all of his realized gain, the basis rule should not lock in any gain. The basis of the office building received should therefore be its fair market value of $110,000. This is the result the statute gives. In effect, what the statute does is give the office building the basis of the apartment building, reduced by the $10,000 that the cash received exceeds realized gain.[162] However, you can just view the matter as saying that since all the realized gain was recognized, the basis of the property received should be its fair market value. The graphic "§ 1031: An Exchange With Lots of Cash" illustrates this transaction.

---

[162] Section 1031(d). For more discussion of the mechanics of the basis rule, see below.

§ 1031: AN EXCHANGE WITH LOTS OF CASH

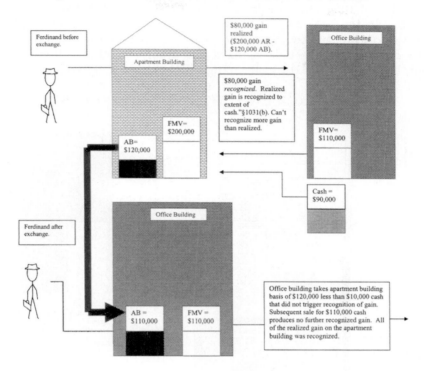

Be clear with regard to these transactions involving cash: *receiving boot* triggers recognition of gain. *Giving boot* does not. The taxpayer giving boot simply adds the fair market value of the boot to the basis of the property he is receiving.[163]

It can also happen that Ferdinand would receive not only like kind property but also other property, which is not like kind. Thus in the exchange of the apartment building for the office building, Ferdinand could receive not only the office building but also a pickup truck. In that event, the pickup truck, not being like kind to the office building exchanged, is considered to be boot (or "other property" in the lexicon of the statute). As far as recognition of gain is concerned then, the pickup truck triggers recognition of realized gain to the

---

[163] Sections 1031(a) and (b), W.H. Hartman Co., 20 B.T.A. 302, 1930 WL 266 (1930) (acq.) (no gain recognized on exchanging old printing press plus money for a new printing press). This result, of course, makes sense inasmuch as the taxpayer, far from cashing out, has increased the amount of his investment in the like-kind property. This would also have the effect of increasing his basis in the property received. In this circumstance, of course, gain may be recognized to the other party in the transaction, as the recipient of "boot", see Allegheny County Auto Mart, Inc., 12 T.C.M. 427 (1953), aff'd 208 F.2d 693 (3d Cir.1953) *dicta* that a taxpayer who gives boot might be able to recognize a loss on a § 1031 exchange.

extent of the fair market value of the pickup truck. As far as basis is concerned, the pickup truck gets a basis of its fair market value. That is to say the basis of "other property" or "recognition property" is always its fair market value. The basis of the nonrecognition property received locks in the unrecognized gain (if any). All this is illustrated in the graphic: § 1031: An Exchange With "Other Property."

§ 1031: AN EXCHANGE WITH "OTHER PROPERTY"

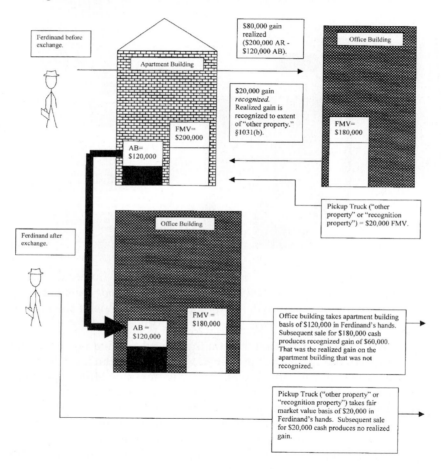

Another possibility is that Ferdinand enters the transaction with a loss on his apartment building. Say, for example, that Ferdinand's basis in his apartment building is $200,000 and the fair market value of the apartment building is $150,000. Ferdinand exchanges the apartment building for an office building with a fair market value of $120,000 plus $30,000 cash. Ferdinand's realized loss is $50,000. But under § 1031, Ferdinand's loss is not recognized.[164] The basis rule preserves the realized loss on the apartment building; thus the basis of the office building is $170,000.[165]

Mechanics of the Basis Rule: The preceding analysis has shown how the basis rule in a § 1031 transaction works to lock in any realized gain that was not recognized. A further word needs to be said about how the basis rule accomplishes this task. There were two ways the statute could have been drafted to preserve the right amount of gain on the property received in a § 1031 transaction: 1) The easy way to understand; and 2) the virtually impossible way to understand. Naturally, the statute chose the second way.

The easy way to understand would have been for the statute to say, simply, that the basis of the nonrecognition property received will be equal to the fair market value of the nonrecognition property received less any unrecognized gain on the property exchanged.[166] As is apparent from the above analysis, this is what we are doing. And, as a matter of fact, we would even suggest that you could just do that and you would always get the right answer.

However, you should be aware that the statute does not actually do it that way, although it gets to the same result. Instead, the basis rule, as provided in § 1031(d), provides that as to the property received, "the basis shall be the same as that of the property exchanged, decreased in the amount of any money received by the taxpayer and increased in the amount of gain . . . that was recognized on the exchange."[167]

Now you may ask, "What on earth is all this down and up stuff!" Well, as the saying goes, it's just so crazy it works. We will now explain why this rule is the way it is and why it works. You actually need not read this explanation. We would suggest that those interested in going on in the field of taxation should read it, however. A number of corporate and partnership tax basis rules work on this approach of going down and up. It is therefore useful for you to be familiar with it.

---

[164]   Section 1031(c).

[165]   Section 1031(d).

[166]   If the property exchanged is loss property, then the rule would be that the basis of the property received is the fair market value of the property received increased by the amount of any unrecognized loss.

[167]   The portion of the statute omitted in this quote states that the basis shall go down by the amount of any loss to the taxpayer that was recognized. As we have discussed above, taxpayers do not recognize any loss on § 1031 transactions. However, § 1031(d) is also serving as the basis rule for several other nonrecognition provisions (§§ 1035, 1036, and 1037) which do recognize losses.

Those of you bailing out of this field after this course could easily skip the ensuing discussion, although you might find it interesting. You know how to get the right basis on a tax free-exchange. You don't need to know the complicated way the statute gets the same answer you can get (and it is always the same answer).

Advanced Explanation of Mechanics of Basis Rule: May Be Omitted by Students Not Going On in the Field

Okay, to explain the down and up rule for those few of us still reading here: First we will explain how it works and then we will explain why it works. Finally, we explain the mechanics when "other property," i.e., recognition property such as the truck, is received.

How it works

Take our first example of a simple exchange (refer to the first § 1031 graphic). According to the literal terms of § 1031(d) the basis in the office building received is the basis of the apartment building exchanged ($120,000), down by money received ($0), so we're still at $120,000, and up by gain recognized ($0), so we're still at $120,000. Thus the basis in the office building received is $120,000, which is the correct answer. The $120,000 basis preserves the $80,000 unrecognized gain on the $200,000 apartment building. It was a strange way to get the right answer but it did work.

Take our second example of an exchange with cash (the second § 1031 graphic). According to the literal terms of § 1031(d) the basis of the office building received is the basis of the apartment building exchanged ($120,000), down by money received ($20,000), taking us down to $100,000, and up by gain recognized ($20,000), taking us back up to $120,000. Thus the basis in the apartment building received is $120,000, which is the correct answer. The $120,000 basis preserves the $60,000 unrecognized gain on the $180,000 office building. It's weird, but it's working.

Take our third example of an exchange with lots of cash. Once again according to the literal terms of the statute, the basis of the office building received is the basis of the apartment building exchanged ($120,000), down by money received ($90,000), taking us to $30,000, and up by gain recognized ($80,000), taking us back up to $110,000. This turns out to be the right answer again. The $110,000 basis is the same as the fair market value of the office building received. No gain or loss is preserved on the office building, nor should there be. All the $80,000 realized gain was recognized on the exchange. Once again, the strange basis rule worked.

Why it works

Here is why the rule works: We start with the basis in the property exchanged. We go down by money received. What we are really doing is moving some of our basis onto the money. This is the case because money must always take a basis of its face value. (You can't have a basis of 90 cents in a dollar and then have a gain of 10 cents when you spend it). That explains why we go down by money received. We go up by gain recognized, because we always increase basis of property when we recognize gain with respect to it, so that we won't recognize the same gain again. If we pay a tax with respect to property, we're entitled to raise our basis on it.[168]

Treatment of "other property"

Where "other" (i.e., recognition) property is in the deal, we in effect treat it like money, explained above. We take enough basis from the property exchanged and apply it to equal the fair market value of the recognition property. That then becomes the basis of the recognition property. In other words, the basis of recognition property (such as the truck in our example above) is always its fair market value. The remaining basis of the property exchanged is then applied to be the basis of the property received, subject to the down and up rules described above.[169]

(b) Mortgages

Another possible form of a § 1031 exchange is the case where one or both properties is subject to a liability. Where real estate is concerned that is a likely possibility. Where property is transferred subject to a liability in a § 1031 exchange, being relieved of the liability is treated as receiving money. This is the *Crane* rule (we told you to study it, remember). Treating the debt relief as money, you crank out your results from there, using the money rules discussed above. The following example illustrates:

Example: A holds for investment Whiteacre, undeveloped land with an adjusted basis of $750 in his

---

[168]   Recall for example the discussion of the *Woodsam* case, ¶ 4.03(2)(b)(iii) above, where the taxpayer argued that nonrecourse financing should be a taxable event with a concomitant increase in basis.

[169]   Section 1031(d).

hands and a fair market value of $1,500. Whiteacre is subject to a nonrecourse liability of $500. A, in a § 1031 transaction, exchanges Whiteacre for Blackacre, owned by B, B taking Whiteacre subject to the mortgage. Blackacre has a fair market value of $1,000 and is unencumbered by any liabilities.[170]

A has a gain realized on the transaction of $750. This is arrived at as follows: A's amount realized was $1,000 (the fair market value of Blackacre) plus $500 (the debt relief) or $1,500. A's adjusted basis was $750. Hence, the gain realized is $750. Since A received boot of $500 (the debt relief), $500 of the $750 realized gain is recognized. A's basis in Blackacre is $750 (the original basis of $750 reduced by the $500 boot and increased by the $500 gain recognized). This basis of $750 makes sense. A entered this transaction with a potential gain of $750, of which $500 was recognized. A now has a basis of $750 in Blackacre which has a fair market value of $1,000; the $250 unrecognized gain has been preserved.

In the circumstance that both properties in the § 1031 exchange are encumbered with liabilities and cash is also present in the transaction, matters become interesting indeed. Although such a transaction may sound esoteric at first blush, it is not such an unlikely event, particularly in the real estate area where property is often mortgaged. The treatment of such a transaction involves netting the liabilities against each other. The party being relieved of the larger liability will have boot to the extent the larger liability exceeds the smaller.

As a policy matter it seems reasonable to treat mortgages in this way. As we have discussed above in connection with the *Woodsam* case, an argument exists that mortgaging property nonrecourse in excess of basis constitutes a realizing event. The argument is even stronger in the § 1031 setting. In the § 1031 setting, being relieved of a mortgage means that the taxpayer has withdrawn funds from the investment, at some earlier date, and now does not have to pay them back. Recognition appears to be appropriate. This analysis would hold even if the debt on the property exchanged were acquisition debt. On the acquisition debt, the taxpayer has had the advantage of borrowing money and now does not have to pay it back. Recognition seems appropriate.

---

[170] This deal makes economic sense for the parties. The economic value of Blackacre is clearly $1,000 and the economic value of Whiteacre, net of liabilities, is $1,000.

Such is the basic framework of § 1031. A number of difficult definitional problems arise in the practical working out of transactions under § 1031. These problems are discussed in turn.

(c) The Requirement That the Property Be of "Like Kind"

(i) Real Property; Jordan Marsh

The Regulations state "the words like-kind have reference to the nature or character of the property and not to its grade or quality. One kind or class of property may not . . . be exchanged for property of a different kind or class. The fact that any real estate involved is improved or unimproved is not material, for that fact relates only to the grade or quality of the property and not to its kind or class."[171] Examples of real estate exchanges in which the property was "like kind" include: city real estate for a ranch or farm;[172] exhausted timberland for virgin timberland;[173] a tenant in common interest in three parcels of property for a 100% ownership interest in one of the parcels;[174] a remainder interest in one tract of farm land for a remainder interest in another tract of farm land.[175] Note that real property in the United States and real property located outside the United States are not like kind properties.[176]

In most of these examples the real estate received was put to generally the same use as the real estate exchanged. Moreover, the Regulations provide the property must be put to the same use.[177] However the Regulations' example above of an exchange of city real estate for a ranch or farm suggests possibly a broader principle. The matter therefore is somewhat unclear.[178]

An important unresolved area with respect to exchanges of real estate relates to exchanges of real property owned in fee for long-term leases of real property. The Regulations provide that an exchange of real estate for a lease of real property with 30 years or more to run is an exchange of like kind.[179] However where the transaction is a sale

---

[171] Reg. § 1.1031(a)–1(b).

[172] Reg. § 1.1031(a)–1(c).

[173] Rev.Rul. 72–515, 1972–2 C.B. 466; see also Rev.Rul. 76–253, 1976–2 C.B. 51.

[174] Rev.Rul. 73–476, 1973–2 C.B. 300. Cf. note 13 below.

[175] Rev.Rul. 78–4, 1978–1 C.B. 256, compare Rev.Rul. 72–601, 1972–2 C.B. 467, holding a transfer of a life estate in one parcel of real estate in return for a remainder interest in another does not qualify as a like-kind exchange. See also Letter Ruling 7943136.

[176] Section 1031(h).

[177] Reg. § 1.1031(a)–1(c).

[178] Cf. ¶ 4.05(3) relating to the test of "property similarly or related in service or use" for purposes of nonrecognition of gain on reinvestment of proceeds of involuntary conversions.

[179] Reg. § 1.1031(a)–1(c).

and leaseback for more than 30 years of the same real property, case law is in conflict as to whether the transaction will be accorded nonrecognition.

This problem has arisen in particular where the taxpayer has a substantial unrealized loss on business property and engages in a sale and leaseback for a long term of the property in order to gain a tax advantage by realizing the loss on the sale while in fact retaining possession of the property for use in business. Where the leaseback has been for longer than 30 years, the Service has sought to impose § 1031 treatment on the transaction, thereby disallowing any loss.[180] The courts have split on whether the loss will be allowed.[181] The well-advised taxpayer seeking to realize a loss on his business property will, of course, effect the transaction with a leaseback for less than 30 years.[182] The fact that the leaseback for less than 30 years is with a related party (who might be expected to renew the lease) will not necessarily bar the loss.[183]

A leading case in this area is *Jordan Marsh.*

---

[180]   Section 1031(c).

[181]   Century Electric Co. v. Commissioner, 192 F.2d 155 (8th Cir.1951), cert. denied 342 U.S. 954, 72 S.Ct. 625, 96 L.Ed. 708 (1952) (applying § 1031 and disallowing the loss on a sale and 95 year leaseback); allowing the loss are Leslie Co., 64 T.C. 247 (1975) (nonacq.), aff'd 539 F.2d 943 (3d Cir.1976) (leasehold had no capital or premium value; hence the transaction was a sale and not a § 1031 exchange, discussed in the text below). City Investing Co. & Subsidiaries, 38 T.C. 1 (1962) (nonacq.) (sale and leaseback a bona fide sale; hence § 1031 not applicable). The Service announced in 1960 it would not follow *Jordan Marsh,* Rev.Rul. 60–43, 1960–1 C.B. 687 and its nonacquiescences in the more recent *Leslie* and *City Investing* indicate its opposition to these loss cases remains undiminished. See also Crowley, Milner & Co., 76 T.C. 1030 (1981), aff'd 689 F.2d 635 (6th Cir.1982) (loss allowed on sale leaseback).

[182]   Reg. § 1.1031(a)–1(c). See also Standard Envelope Manufacturing Co., 15 T.C. 41 (1950) (loss on sale and leaseback for 24 years allowed as a bona fide sale. Transaction not attacked as being an § 1031 exchange).

[183]   This pattern was allowed in Capri, Inc., 65 T.C. 162 (1975) (10-year leaseback to related party not considered automatically renewable and hence not equivalent to 30 year leaseback).

There are a number of types of exchange transactions in the oil, gas and other mineral rights area, see e.g., Commissioner v. P.G. Lake, 356 U.S. 260, 78 S.Ct. 691, 2 L.Ed.2d 743 (1958), reh'g denied 356 U.S. 964, 78 S.Ct. 991, 2 L.Ed.2d 1071 (1958), holding that an exchange of an oil payment for an interest in realty does not involve like-kind property. For the assignment of income aspects of *P.G. Lake,* see ¶ 5.04(1).

JORDAN MARSH CO. V. COMMISSIONER[184]

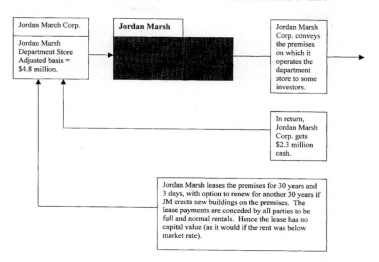

Facts: Taxpayer, Jordan Marsh Co., sold two properties with an adjusted basis of $4,800,000 to an unrelated party for $2,300,000 (generating a $2.5 million loss). Taxpayer then leased back the properties for a term of thirty years and three days with the option to renew the lease for an additional thirty years if it erected new buildings on the properties. The rent paid under the leases were fair and normal rentals.

Question: Could Jordan Marsh deduct its $2.5 million loss on the department store?

Taxpayer's argument: The transaction was a sale followed by a lease back. Hence the sale generated a deductible $2.5 million loss.

Service's argument: The transaction was in substance a like-kind exchange. Under regulations, a fee ownership is like-kind to a lease for more than 30 years.[185] Thus under the rules of § 1031(a), no loss is recognized.

Comment: This is the kind of case you come upon in practice. Complicated as the mechanics of calculating gain and basis seem at first blush in § 1031, they are not a problem in practice. The problem is figuring out whether your deal fits into the statute at all.

Held: This was a sale and not a like-kind § 1031 exchange. Taxpayer cashed out in full and received full value. Also an "exchange" means a swapping of one piece of property for another,

---

[184]   269 F.2d 453 (2d Cir.1959).
[185]   Regs. § 1.1031(a)–1(c).

not a swap of a greater interest in a piece of property for a lesser interest. The rentals were full and normal; thus taxpayer received no capital value back in the leasehold. Thus taxpayer received nothing to which § 1031 could apply.

Comment: Why the taxpayer got such exquisitely poor advice as to make the leaseback for just over 30 years rather than just under 30 years (in which event it could have indisputably taken its loss without having to litigate to the Second Circuit) is a tantalizing question.[186]

Another leading case presenting a sale and leaseback was *Leslie Co. v. Commissioner.*[187] On facts similar to *Jordan Marsh,* the Third Circuit held that the leasehold had no capital or premium value. Hence there was no exchange of property on the sale of the property and the leaseback for 30 years. Thus the transaction was a sale and not a § 1031 exchange and taxpayer was able to deduct a loss on the transaction. See *Bloomington Coca-Cola Bottling Co.* above.

(ii) Personal Property

The same principles of the Regulations that govern real property like-kind exchanges govern personal property like-kind exchanges, namely, that the words "like kind" have reference to the nature or character of the property and not to its grade or quality, and moreover that one kind or class of property may not be exchanged tax free for property of a different kind or class.

Thus a used car or truck exchanged for a new car or truck which will be put to the same use involves like-kind property.[188] "Like-kind" property also includes all the business assets of one telephone company exchanged for all the business assets of another telephone company;[189] exchanges of contracts of professional football (and presumably other sports) players;[190] and, it is interesting to note, an exchange of bullion-type, non-circulating gold coins of one country for

---

[186] Especially in light of the earlier holding in Century Electric v. Commissioner, 192 F.2d 155 (8th Cir.1951), cert. denied 342 U.S. 954, 72 S.Ct. 625, 96 L.Ed. 708 (1952) (exchange of fee for 95-year lease with cash was § 1031 exchange).

[187] 64 T.C. 247 (1975) (nonacq.), aff'd 539 F.2d 943 (3d Cir.1976).

[188] National Outdoor Advertising Bureau v. Helvering, 89 F.2d 878 (C.C.A.2, 1937) (disallowing a loss on the exchange).

[189] Rev.Rul. 57–365, 1957–2 C.B. 521, citing Williams v. McGowan, 152 F.2d 570 (2d Cir.1945) ¶ 4.06(3)(b), which suggests that the mass exchange of the assets of any company for the assets of another company in the same line of business would qualify. This transaction was in effect a form of corporate reorganization—an "assets for assets" reorganization; cf. § 368(a)(1)(C), regarding the stock for assets form of reorganization.

[190] Rev.Rul. 71–137, 1971–1 C.B. 104.

an exchange of bullion-type, non-circulating gold coins of another country.[191]

Congress has decreed that livestock of different sexes is not property of like kind, for purposes of § 1031.[192]

(d) The Requirement That the Property Be Held for Productive Use in Trade or Business or for Investment

In addition to being like-kind, property involved in an § 1031 nonrecognition exchange must be held by the taxpayer for productive use in a trade or business or for investment.[193] This test is applied with reference to each party to the transaction. Thus, for example, if property given up and received is held for productive use by one party, § 1031 will apply even though the property is dealer or inventory property to the other party to the transaction.[194] Also, property held for productive use in the trade or business may be exchanged for property held for investment and vice versa.[195] Thus, apparently, land held by the taxpayer for productive use in a trade or business may be exchanged tax free under § 1031 for land held by

---

[191]   Rev.Rul. 76–214, 1976–1 C.B. 218 (Mexican 50-peso coins can be exchanged tax free for Austrian 100-corona gold coins, since both are bullion-type rather than numismatic-type coins held for investment); compare Rev.Rul. 79–143, 1979–19 I.R.B. 19 (exchange of collector-type United States gold coins for South African Krugerrands did not involve like-kind property, because value of the U.S. coins was determined by aesthetic considerations, whereas value of the Krugerrands is determined by metal content). Rev.Rul. 82–166, 1982–40 I.R.B. 9 (exchange of gold bullion for silver bullion is not like-kind, reversing earlier private letter ruling 8128102); Rev.Rul. 82–96, 1982–1 C.B. 113 (individual taxpayer who is not a dealer exchanged gold bullion held as an investment for Canadian Maple Leaf gold coins. Held: transaction qualified as tax-free exchange since Canadian Maple Leaf gold coins, though legal tender, were more valuable for their gold content than face amount, hence were bullion type coins.)

See also Rev.Rul. 74–7, 1974–1 C.B. 198 (taxpayer who was not a currency dealer exchanged U.S. currency for foreign currency while on a trip and then at the conclusion of his trip reconverted his foreign currency back to U.S. currency. Held: a gain on the reconversion would not qualify as a tax-free exchange because the currency is not property held for productive use in a trade or business or for investment, see ¶ 4.05(2)(d)).

[192]   Section 1031(e). The legislative history of this provision is as follows: " . . . There appear to have been representations that male calves can be traded for female calves tax free as a like-kind exchange. The importance of this arises from the fact that ordinarily the ratio of males to females in a calf crop is approximately 50-50. Since few males are normally retained in a typical cattle operation, the remaining male calves are castrated and sold as steers at ordinary income rates. If a tax-free trade of male calves for female calves were allowed, a breeding herd of females could be built up more quickly without tax consequences . . ." Senate Report 91–552, Pub.L. 91–172, 1969–3 C.B. 489. See also Martin McMahon,Taxation of Equine Sales and Exchanges, 75 Ky.L.J. 205 (1986).

[193]   Section 1031(a).

[194]   Section 1031(a), Reg. § 1.1031(a)–1(a). The other party in this case would, of course, not qualify for § 1031 treatment.

[195]   Reg. § 1.1031(a)–1(a).

the taxpayer for investment.[196] Where the taxpayer has a plan to sell or is attempting immediately to sell property given up or received in an exchange, the property is then not held for productive use in a trade or business or for investment and § 1031 will not apply. This will be so even though the taxpayer is not a dealer with respect to the property.[197]

(e)   Three-Cornered Exchanges

At first blush, § 1031 looks like it is of limited significance. This is because it seems to require that two people get together, each of whom has property that the other wants, and that the two pieces of property are roughly of the same fair market value (although disparities in fair market values can be evened up through the use of "boot," as we have seen above). However, the Service allows for a so-called "three-cornered deal," which has opened up the possibilities for using § 1031 to a far greater scale than had hitherto been permitted. In *Revenue Ruling 77–297*[198] the Service approved the following pattern, under § 1031: A enters into a written agreement with B to sell to B a ranch (the first ranch) for $100,000. Pursuant to the agreement, B places $10,000 into escrow and agrees to pay at closing an additional $80,000. In addition the agreement provides that B would cooperate with A to effect the exchange should A locate suitable property. A locates another ranch (the second ranch), owned by C. B enters into an agreement with C to purchase the second ranch for $100,000. Pursuant to the agreement B placed $4,000 into escrow, agreed to pay at closing $96,000. C could not look to A for specific performance on the contract, so B was not acting as A's agent in the purchase of the second parcel of property.

At closing B purchased the second ranch as agreed. After that purchase B exchanged the second ranch with A for the first ranch.

The Service ruled that as to A the exchange of ranches qualifies for nonrecognition of gain under § 1031. As to B the transaction does not qualify for nonrecognition, since B did not hold the second ranch for productive use in a trade or business or for investment. But B did not realize gain or loss on the transaction since the amount realized

---

[196]   The land involved would still, of course, have to be of "like kind," which seems to mean the property must be put to the same "use." Query whether the "like kind" test, which seems to require that the property involved be put to the same use, is inconsistent with the "productive use or investment test," which seems to suggest the property exchanged can be put to a different use than the property received.

[197]   Regals Realty Co. v. Commissioner, 127 F.2d 931 (2d Cir.1942). However, unproductive real estate held by one other than a dealer for future use or future realization of the appreciation in value is held for investment and not primarily for sale, Reg. § 1.1031(a)–1(b).

[198]   1977–2 Cum.Bull. 304.

equalled the basis, inasmuch as B only held the property for a short time.

The upshot is that A was able to sell his property to B under a § 1031 transaction when B did not initially own like kind property, but A was able to find and designate like kind property for B to acquire and exchange.

Starker v. United States[199] approved a similar pattern. A transferred appreciated real estate to B. B promised in return to locate and purchase parcels of real estate for A within five years and to pay any remaining balance in cash. As to the property that A received within the five year period, the court held § 1031 applied. In short, simultaneous transactions were not required in a § 1031 exchange.

Section 1031(a)(3), enacted after the *Starker* case, substantially cut back on non-simultaneous exchanges. This section still allows three-cornered transactions, but requires that the property received in the exchange must be identified within 45 days after the date the taxpayer seeking § 1031 treatment transfers his property. Moreover the taxpayer must also receive the new property either within 180 days after the date he transfers his old property or by the due date of his tax return for the year of the transfer, whichever is earlier. Further rules are provided concerning the manner of identifying the property to be received.

(3) Tax-Free Involuntary Conversions Where Proceeds Reinvested (Condemnations, Casualties)

(a) General Rules

Occasionally it may come to pass that a taxpayer's property may be condemned or otherwise taken against the taxpayer's will, or it may be subject to fire, flood, theft, or other casualty.[200] These involuntary conversions are taxable events.[201] Gain or loss on involuntary conversions is computed under the usual rules, namely that the basis of the property involuntarily converted is offset against any insurance proceeds or other compensation received.[202] Therefore, if the insurance proceeds or other compensation exceeds the taxpayer's basis in the property, the taxpayer will have a gain on the

---

[199]   602 F.2d 1341 (9th Cir.1979).

[200]   Cf. " . . . time and chance happeneth to them all." Ecclesiastes 9:11.

[201]   See generally ¶¶ 4.02, and 7.01(5), regarding taxable events and casualties respectively.

[202]   See ¶¶ 4.02 and 4.03, and see Rev.Rul. 73–408, 1973–2 C.B. 15.

involuntary conversion. This gain, unless some nonrecognition provision applies, will of course be taxable.[203]

Taxing an involuntary conversion could be regarded as a hardship on the taxpayer inasmuch as the taxpayer, by the very nature of involuntary conversions, did not mean to cash in the investment at that particular time and sustain a tax. To alleviate this problem, § 1033 provides generally that if the taxpayer reinvests the proceeds of the "involuntary conversion" (essentially condemnations, threats of condemnations, casualties and thefts), within two years in other property "similar or related in service or use" then, at the election of the taxpayer, no gain will be recognized.[204]

---

[203]   Section 1001(c).

[204]   Section 1033(a)(2)(A). Section 1033 does not apply to losses, and losses sustained on an involuntary conversion will be recognized. If the property is converted directly into other property similar or related in service or use (not a likely event), the nonrecognition of gain is mandatory, § 1033(a)(1). If instead of purchasing the replacement property outright the taxpayer purchases at least an 80% interest in a corporation owning such similar property, then the election to enjoy nonrecognition may still be made, § 1033(a)(2)(A) and (D).

Examples of property held to be "similar or related in service or use": Rev.Rul. 59–8, 1959–1 C.B. 202 (standing crop of grain replaced another standing or harvested crop of grain); Compare Maloof, 65 T.C. 263 (1975) (inventory replaced by depreciable property not qualify); Rev.Rul. 76–319, 1976–2 C.B. 242 (bowling alley burned down and replaced by billiard center not qualify). For more detailed treatment of involuntary conversions in the real estate area, see ¶ 4.05(3)(b).

If the taxpayer does not evince an "intent" to come within the rule, he will not enjoy nonrecognition, even though the replacement property is purchased within the requisite time, Feinberg v. Commissioner, 377 F.2d 21 (8th Cir.1967) (unimproved property for unimproved property not qualify for lack of intent).

Just in case you thought § 1033 was some kind of a backwater provision, it was once employed to attempt to avoid $1 billion in taxes. This arose from the celebrated contract case between Texaco and Pennzoil. In late March, 1988, Pennzoil collected a staggering $3 billion from Texaco in settling its case for Texaco's interfering with Pennzoil's contract to purchase Getty Oil. The amount would be reduced by legal fees of about $400 million. Taxes on the award, regarded as lost profits, were expected to be in the $1 billion area.

Pennzoil attempted to use § 1033 as follows: It would first argue that Texaco's action in contract interference was a "theft." A theft qualifies as an "involuntary conversion," which is what is required under § 1033. Pennzoil would then purchase assets similar to those of Getty Oil. If all this held together, Pennzoil would be within the protection of § 1033 and thus be able to defer the $1 billion in taxes indefinitely (without paying any interest).

An advance ruling by the Service that this works would be required. Subsequently Pennzoil acquired 8.8% of Chevron Corporation's outstanding stock for $2.2 billion, pursuant to this plan. Chevron was not happy at this major purchase and decided to try to break Pennzoil's chops on the § 1033 issue. Chevron argued that the passive nature of the investment meant that the transaction could not qualify for § 1033. This was because Pennzoil's 49% interest in Getty Oil, which it lost to Texaco, was obviously actively managed. Thus Chevron's stock would not be similar to Getty's stock for § 1033 purposes. Pennzoil responded by raising its stake in Chevron to 9.4% and obtaining an extension of time from the Service to try to establish that the Chevron stock was similar to the Getty stock for § 1033 purposes. See D. Posin, CORPORATE TAX

This is, of course, analogous to § 1031 exchanges; in both instances the idea is that to the extent a taxpayer winds up invested in roughly the same kind of property as before the transaction, the taxpayer will not be taxed. If the taxpayer reinvests some but not all of the proceeds from the involuntary conversion, the realized gain will be recognized to the extent that the amount realized on the conversion exceeds the cost of the new property.[205] (This too is closely analogous to the approach under § 1031). To the extent that the taxpayer does not reinvest the proceeds of the involuntary conversion, the taxpayer has cashed out the investment and is therefore properly taxed *pro tanto* on the realized gain.[206] Appropriate basis rules are provided to insure that the deferred gain will ultimately be recognized on the disposition of the new property.[207]

Section 1033 only applies to defer recognition of gain on an involuntary conversion and reinvestment.[208] Losses are always recognized even though the proceeds received may be fully invested in new property. It might be supposed that this is an attractive result to the taxpayer, namely that losses are always recognized immediately, whereas gains may be deferred. However, this is a mixed blessing. If a loss were not recognized on a § 1033 transaction, then the basis of the new property would inevitably be higher. This would, in the case of depreciable property, lead to higher depreciation

---

PLANNING: TAKEOVERS, LEVERAGED BUYOUTS, AND RESTRUCTURINGS 1084–1086 (1990).

[205] Section 1033(a)(2)(A). Thus for example suppose T has a building with an adjusted basis of $50,000 and a fair market value of $100,000 which is completely destroyed by fire. T receives $80,000 of insurance proceeds, $60,000 of which T uses to purchase a building similar or related in service or use to the destroyed building. T has a *realized* gain of $30,000 ($80,000 insurance proceeds amount realized minus $50,000 adjusted basis). Since T's amount realized exceeds the purchase price of the new building by $20,000, $20,000 is the amount of gain recognized. If the facts had been the same as above except that T's basis in the building was $70,000 rather than $50,000, then T would have a gain realized of $10,000. T's recognized gain would then be $10,000, since recognized gain cannot exceed realized gain.

[206] The unreinvested proceeds here play the role of "boot." See discussion at ¶ 4.05(2)(a).

[207] In the usual case where the taxpayer receives money on the involuntary conversion and uses it to purchase replacement property, the basis of the replacement property is the cost of the replacement property decreased in the amount (if any) of the realized gain not recognized, § 1033(b). This is a "backward" version of the § 1031(d) rule. Indeed all substituted basis rules could be drafted in this way, which would have the advantage of making it more clear that the purpose of the substituted basis rules is to preserve unrecognized gain. Cf. §§ 358, 722. If more than one piece of property is purchased as replacement, the overall basis is allocated among them in proportion to their costs, § 1033(b).

The holding period of the replacement property includes the holding period of the converted property, § 1223(1)(A). This is for purposes of ascertaining long-term capital gains.

[208] Section 1033(a), Reg. § 1.1033(a)–1(a).

deductions against ordinary income.[209] Immediate recognition of the loss on a § 1033 pattern can, however, lead to the loss being treated as an unfavorable long-term capital loss, under § 1231.[210]

The foregoing has set forth the general rules of § 1033. Particular problems have arisen in connection with involuntary conversions, especially condemnations, of real property. That topic is taken up next.

(b) Involuntary Conversions of Real Estate

The bulk of the problems and litigation in the § 1033 field have come in the area of involuntary conversions of real property. Where real property was involuntarily converted—condemned by the state or destroyed by a casualty—and the taxpayer reinvested the condemnation or insurance proceeds in other real property, the question would arise whether the replacement property was "similar or related in service or use" to the property converted in order for the transaction to qualify for nonrecognition under § 1033. The Service early on took a very strict view of what constituted property "similar or related in service or use" for these purposes. In essence, the Service took a "functional" approach, that the physical characteristics and the end use of the converted and replacement property by the taxpayer had to be similar, and some early court decisions supported that view. Thus it was held that the test is not met if unimproved real estate is converted into improved real estate, a barge is substituted for a tug, property used in a trade or business is substituted for rental property, or city real estate is replaced by a farm or ranch.[211]

Dissatisfied with this restrictive view, Congress in 1958 prospectively made the "like-kind" standard of § 1031[212] applicable to § 1033 condemnations of real estate held for productive use in a trade or business or for investment.[213] This was regarded as a

---

[209] See ¶ 4.06(3)(a)(vii).

[210] See ¶ 4.06(3)(a)(iv) for discussion of § 1231.

[211] Reg. § 1.1033(a)–2(c)(9); S.Rept. No. 1983, 85th Cong., 2d Sess. 1958–3 C.B. 993. See also McCaffrey, 31 T.C. 505 (1958), aff'd 275 F.2d 27 (3d Cir.1960), cert. denied 363 U.S. 828, 80 S.Ct. 1598, 4 L.Ed.2d 1523 (1960) (rental parking lot replaced by rental warehouse space did not meet the test).

[212] See ¶ 4.05(2)(c).

[213] Section 1033(g) S.Rept. No. 1983, supra note 398, at 993. The "similar or related in service or use" test remains applicable to involuntary conversions of real estate not involving condemnations or the threat or imminence thereof, such as casualties and thefts. Reg. § 1.1033(f)–1(a) cross references to § 1031 for principles in determining what is like-kind property. To the same effect is Rev.Rul. 67–255, 1967–2 C.B. 270. The like-kind standard only applies to realty which is held for productive use in a trade or business or for investment—not to realty which is inventory or for personal use, § 1033(g)(1). The reinvestment period under this rule is 3 years, § 1033(g)(4).

liberalization, since the "like-kind" standard of § 1031 had clearly allowed a wider range of transactions (including some of those enumerated above) to pass muster tax free.[214]

In the meantime, a number of cases concerning condemnations of real estate began to find their way into the circuit courts. Since these cases involved taxable years prior to 1958, the applicable standard for nonrecognition was still that the replacement property be "similar or related in service or use" to the property condemned. The Service's restrictive "functional" interpretation of this standard, discussed above, uniformly took a beating in the circuit courts in these cases. Rather, with some variations, the circuit courts held that the standard "similar or related in service or use" related to the similarity in the services or uses which the original and replacement properties bore to the taxpayer-owner. This was particularly relevant to the case where the taxpayer was a lessor and his rental property was condemned. Reinvestment of the condemnation proceeds in a different kind of rental property (such as a rental office building to replace a rental apartment building) was held by the circuit courts to meet the "similar or related in service or use" standard since the new piece of property bore the same general relationship to the taxpayer as did the original property, in terms of demands made on the taxpayer by the property and the use he made of the property.[215]

Therefore the Service, always able to perceive when it is licked, threw in the towel in a revenue ruling and conceded that insofar as rental property was concerned the "similar or related in service or use" test related to the relationship the old and new property bear to the taxpayer-owner, rather than to the tenant-user.[216] Thus, to take an example from the ruling, where the taxpayer is a lessor of property used for a light manufacturing plant and the property is involuntarily converted, the reinvestment by the taxpayer of the proceeds of the conversion in a wholesale grocery warehouse which he rents out could meet the test, if the taxpayer maintained the same general lessor relationship with the property. However, where the taxpayer is a lessor as to the converted property but an owner-

---

In a bow to the recent concern for environmental quality, Congress has decreed that condemnation of billboards and their replacement with real property may come within this like-kind rule, § 1033(g)(3).

[214]   See ¶ 4.05(2)(c).

[215]   Liant Record, Inc. v. Commissioner, 303 F.2d 326 (2d Cir.1962), on remand 22 T.C.M. 203 (1963) (replacement of office building with three apartment buildings met test); Loco Realty Co. v. Commissioner, 306 F.2d 207 (8th Cir.1962) (replacement of light manufacturing building by warehouse and office space met the test); Pohn v. Commissioner, 309 F.2d 427 (7th Cir.1962). See also Davis v. United States, 589 F.2d 446 (9th Cir.1979).

[216]   Rev.Rul. 64–237, 1964–2 C.B. 319.

operator as to the replacement property, the test is not met even though the two properties are otherwise of the same kind or class.[217]

Thus in sum, the Service's restrictive view of what constituted "similar or related in service or use" for § 1033 purposes provoked both a legislative and judicial response. The legislative response was the more liberal "like kind" standard for condemnations of real estate; the judicial response was the more liberal interpretation of "similar or related in service or use" for rental property.

These two possibilities remain at the present time. The "similar or related in service or use test" applies to all involuntary conversions; the "like kind" test applies to condemnations of real property. Therefore, where real property is condemned and the taxpayer reinvests the proceeds, the transaction can be tested under either standard. Moreover where the converted and replacement property are rental real estate, the "similar or related in service or use" test is particularly liberal.

As an example of these possibilities consider a taxpayer whose 5,000 acres of unimproved rental farmland were condemned. Taxpayer invested the proceeds of the condemnation in constructing a commercial rental building on other land the taxpayer owned. The taxpayer was not responsible for maintenance of the rental farmland but was responsible for maintenance of the commercial building. Hence the transaction does not qualify under the "similar or related in service or use" test for rental property, since the services the taxpayer rendered on the two pieces of property were different.[218] Moreover, the transaction does not qualify under the "like kind" test, because the leased commercial building is not "like kind" to the leased unimproved farmland.[219]

---

[217] Rev.Rul. 70–399, 1970–2 C.B. 164 (rental resort hotel destroyed by fire and replaced by resort hotel which taxpayer operated himself did not meet the test. As the text discussion indicates, had this property been condemned rather than destroyed by fire, the "like-kind" test would have applied and probably have been met).

See also Rev.Rul. 70–466, 1970–2 C.B. 165 (investment of proceeds of condemned residential housing in personal-use housing did not meet the "similar or related in service or use" test); Rev.Rul. 79–261, 1979–35 I.R.B. 13 (reinvestment of insurance proceeds from destruction of a rental office building in a new office building partly rented to tenants and partly owner-occupied met the test to the extent of the portion of the building rented to tenants); Rev.Rul. 70–144, 1970–1 C.B. 170 (lessee of a condemned building who uses his share of the proceeds to purchase property similar or related in service or use to the leased premises can qualify for non-recognition of gain).

[218] Rev.Rul. 76–391, 1976–2 C.B. 243.

[219] Id. See also Rev.Rul. 76–84, 1976–1 C.B. 219 (transaction flunked both tests because replacement property was used for personal use).

(4) Other Tax-Free Transactions

Nonrecognition-employing principles similar to those discussed above are also accorded to the exchange of insurance policies,[220] and reacquisition of mortgaged real property.[221] Exchanges of common stock for common stock in the same corporation, or preferred stock for preferred stock in the same corporation are also tax free.[222] In all of these cases the deferred gain is preserved by an appropriate basis correction.

(5) Wash Sales of Stock or Securities

Consider a taxpayer owning 100 shares of stock in X Corporation. Taxpayer has a cost basis in the stock of $50 per share; the stock in the few months since the purchase has dropped in price to $30 per share. Notwithstanding this drop the taxpayer may still think highly of X Corporation and intend to hold the stock for a number of years. However, it would appear that the taxpayer can wrest a tax advantage from this immediate drop in the price of the stock. Suppose the taxpayer engages in a "wash sale"—the taxpayer sells the 100 shares of X stock and then a few days later repurchases 100 shares of X stock, thereby realizing the loss without actually giving up ownership of the X stock for any significant period. Of course had the stock risen in price after his original purchase the taxpayer would never engage in a wash sale to realize his gain! Thus it would appear generally that with marketable securities the taxpayer can realize losses but not gains—and all the while effectively maintain ownership of the stock or securities involved.

Naturally this power of the taxpayer to load the tax dice in the taxpayer's favor in the holding of marketable securities has not gone unnoticed by the Congress. The supposed neutralizer for this maneuver is the wash sale provision, § 1091, which disallows the loss deduction on the sale of old stock or securities where the taxpayer has purchased substantially identical new stock or securities within the period beginning 30 days before and ending 30 days after the sale for loss of the old stock or securities.[223]

---

[220] Section 1035.

[221] Section 1038.

[222] Section 1036. The whole field of corporate reorganizations involves many kinds of exchanges of stock for stock and stock for assets tax free, with appropriate basis correction. See §§ 368, 354, 356, 361, 355.

[223] Section 1091(a), also providing a "purchase" of substantially identical stock or securities would encompass any exchange in which all gain is recognized, and would cover any option or contract to acquire substantially identical stock or securities. The loss will be allowed to one who is in the trade or business of buying and selling stock or securities or to a corporation which is a dealer in stocks or securities and the transaction is made in the ordinary course of business, §§ 1091(a) and 165(c).

As a theoretical matter, therefore, where the taxpayer sells stock or securities for a loss in a § 1091 situation, the taxpayer clearly has a taxable event,[224] and the taxpayer can calculate the realized loss under the usual rules.[225] Section 1091, however, overrides these normal rules and disallows the loss so calculated on a wash sale transaction. The loss is not permanently disallowed, only deferred. Appropriate correction is made to the basis of the new stock or securities to insure that the loss will ultimately be taken advantage of on a subsequent sale.[226]

The strictures of § 1091 are triggered if the taxpayer purchases securities "substantially identical" to the securities sold for a loss within the prescribed 30-day forward and back period. Stock or securities are not "substantially identical" if they are from two different issuers, even though in all other ways they may be very similar.[227] Stock or securities from the same issuer which are dissimilar in fundamental terms are not "substantially identical."[228] A well-known and effective maneuver in this area is to sell and buy stock of companies in the same industry. Thus where a taxpayer has a loss on his X Company Oil stock, the taxpayer could sell it and immediately buy Y Company Oil stock, rather than wait 30 days and risk that the oil group might move upward during that period. Similarly with respect to the holding of long-term bonds, when interest rates move higher the bondholder will have significant unrealized losses. Selling such bonds and reinvesting the proceeds in bonds of another issuer of the same quality will be effective to create a deductible capital loss. At the same time the interest income will

---

[224] See ¶ 4.02.

[225] See ¶ 4.03.

[226] Section 1091(d), which provides the unadjusted basis of the new stock or securities is the basis of the old stock or securities increased or decreased, as the case may be, by the difference between the price at which the new stock or security was acquired and the price at which the old stock or security was sold. For example:

> A buys 100 shares of stock of X Corporation, traded on the New York Stock Exchange, at $50 per share. The price soon drops to $30. A sells his 100 shares at $30. Within 30 days of the sale, A buys 100 shares of stock of X Corporation at $35. The loss on the sale of X Corporation is disallowed. However, A's basis in the new X Corporation stock is $50 plus $5 or $55. Thus should A later sell his stock for $35 A will get his loss of $20.

Had A repurchased the new X Corporation stock at $25, A's basis in it would have been $45.

The basis of the new stock will also include acquisition costs such as brokerage fees, see ¶ 4.03(2)(b). The holding period of the new stock will include the holding period of the old stock, § 1223(4). Though a loss in sale of stock or securities may escape the limitation of § 1091, it may still be subject to the limitations of §§ 267 and 1211. See ¶¶ 4.05(7) and 4.06(2)(b)(ii) respectively.

[227] Rev.Rul. 59–44, 1959–1 C.B. 205 (bonds with virtually the same maturity dates and interest rates issued by different local housing authorities are not "substantially identical.").

[228] Rev.Rul. 58–210, 1958–1 C.B. 523.

continue uninterrupted. It is true that the bondholder will have a lower basis in the new bonds and might have a gain when the bonds are ultimately retired at face. (See ¶ 4.06(3)(a)(xii) for treatment of retirement of bonds). However the bondholder on this maneuver has enjoyed the benefit of deferral—a capital loss now at the price of a capital gain many years hence.

Another effective technique for avoiding the wash-sale rules is "doubling up." A taxpayer who has a loss on some stock and would like to realize it but not actually cash out of the stock can simply buy a second lot of the stock to double the taxpayer's holdings. Then the taxpayer would wait more than 30 days and then sell the original loss shares. That capital loss is deductible; the provisions of § 1091 have not been triggered. Taxpayer got a deductible loss while maintaining a position in the stock at all times.

Where the taxpayer has engaged in a number of purchases and sales of the same stock or securities, special rules are provided. In general the approach is to match the stock or securities sold first in time with the stock or securities bought first in time. All of this occurs under a moving 30-day forward and back period in which sales or purchases occurring within that period are matched against each other. However, an acquired share of stock or security can only be matched against a loss once. Appropriate basis rules account for these transactions.[229] All of this taken together can provide a rather interesting tableau, as the following example illustrates:

> T, who did not previously own any shares of Y Corporation stock, engages in the following transactions in Y Corporation common stock during the taxable year:
>
> May 16   buys 1000 shares at $50 per share
> June 1   sells 300 shares at $40 per share
> June 20   buys 500 shares at $37 per share
> June 25   sells 300 shares of those acquired on May 16 at $32 per share

> Had there been only the May 16 and June 1 transactions, T would have been allowed his loss. Although the May 16 purchase comes within 30 days of the June 1 sale at a loss, the June 1 sale was of some of the original stock purchased on May 16. Nothing, of course, in § 1091 prohibits selling the original stock or securities at a loss within 30 days of their purchase. It is only when substantially identical stock or securities are purchased

---

[229]   Reg. § 1.1091–1(b), (c) and (d); Reg. § 1.1091–1(h).

within the 61-day period to "wash out" the effect of the loss sale that § 1091 comes into play.

The June 20 purchase causes the June 1 loss sale to be disallowed. With respect to the June 25 sale, T has a realized loss of $18 per share on the 300 shares. Within 30 days of that June 25 sale, namely on June 20, T had bought "substantially identical" stock. Hence it might appear that the loss will be disallowed in its entirety. However 300 of the 500 shares purchased on June 20 have already been matched against the June 1 loss sale. Thus the loss on only 200 of the 300 shares sold on June 25 will be disallowed.[230]

Query what would happen if T asserted and could show by identifying the share certificates that the June 25 sale was of shares bought on June 20? Then could T assert that the wash sale rule did not apply, since T bought and sold the same shares, not engaging in a wash transaction using "substantially identical" shares? Nevertheless, where the shares are fungible and T owns a block of shares from an earlier purchase, perhaps any buying and selling transactions within 30 days of one another will be deemed to be within the wash-sale rule. There is no direct authority on this matter.[231]

(6) Losses on Sales and Exchanges Between Related Taxpayers

(a) In General

The taxpayer who holds property which has declined in value is often sorely tempted to realize that loss by selling the property. However for business or other reasons the taxpayer may also wish to keep control of the property. This dilemma has often propelled taxpayers into tricky maneuvers such as selling the property and buying back substantially identical property or selling the property to a related individual or an entity controlled by the taxpayer.

The maneuver of selling property and immediately buying back substantially identical property is most easily available for stock or securities, where vast accessible markets for such property exist. The disallowance of losses on such wash sales is discussed at ¶ 4.05(5).

---

[230] The basis for the various lots of stock would be as follows: The lot purchased on May 16 would of course take a cost basis of $50 per share (plus acquisition costs). Three hundred shares of the lot purchased on June 20 would take a basis of $47 per share. The other 200 shares would take a cost basis of $37 until June 25 (Reg. § 1.1091–1(c), (d)). On June 25 these 200 shares would take a basis of $55.

[231] See Krane, "Losses From Wash Sales of Stock or Securities", 4 J. CORP. TAX. 226 (1977).

With respect to other kinds of property, such as real estate or tangible personal property, the more likely maneuver would be to sell the property to a buyer whom the taxpayer controls. Disallowance of loss on this latter maneuver is generally the object of § 267; § 267 will allow an appropriate basis correction to the buyer to preserve the loss as discussed below.

Section 267 covers all property,[232] unlike the "wash sale" provision § 1091, which covers only stock or securities. Thus should a taxpayer sell depreciated stock or securities to a related buyer, the loss would be barred by § 267. However a taxpayer could engage in a "wash sale" of property that was not stock or securities, such as selling depreciated rental real estate and buying similar rental real estate.[233] Such a maneuver would be effective to create a deductible loss for the taxpayer (assuming the effort of locating the new property, the closing costs, and other headaches were worth it).[234]

(b) "Related Taxpayers" and Constructive Ownership Rules

The related or controlled persons between whom losses on sales or exchanges are not allowed are: the taxpayer and the taxpayer's siblings, spouse, ancestors, and lineal descendants;[235] losses are also disallowed on sales or exchanges between an individual and a corporation of which the taxpayer owns more than 50 percent of the

---

[232] Section 267(a)(1).

[233] Indeed the taxpayer could up the ante and sell depreciated real estate to a buyer who would soon sell it back to the taxpayer. That bald an attempt to realize a loss is, of course, likely to be disregarded as a sham.

[234] The Service might attempt to interpret this transaction as a multi-party § 1031 transaction and bar the loss. See ¶ 4.05(2).

Another ploy with respect to marketable securities could be for the taxpayer to sell securities at a loss on an exchange and have a family member buy the same kind of securities also in an open market transaction. While this might be effective to skirt the wash-sale rule, the Supreme Court has held that this transaction constitutes a sale at a loss to a related party, coming within the strictures of § 267, McWilliams v. Commissioner, 331 U.S. 694, 67 S.Ct. 1477, 91 L.Ed. 1750 (1947). But see United States v. Norton, Jr., 250 F.2d 902 (5th Cir.1958) (sale of Magma Copper stock by taxpayer on New York Stock Exchange and purchase of Magma Copper stock by taxpayer's mother 28 days later did not result in disallowance of taxpayer's loss on the sale where there was no contemplation of the purchase at the time of the sale.). Cf. Merritt, Sr. v. Commissioner, 400 F.2d 417 (5th Cir.1968) (disallowing loss on taxpayer's stock which was seized by the Internal Revenue Service and then bought several months later by taxpayer's wife at a public auction, and discussing contrary authorities on this pattern), and see Hassen v. Commissioner, 599 F.2d 305 (9th Cir.1979).

[235] Section 267(b)(1) and (c)(4). Brothers and sisters may be of the half or whole blood. Marital property settlements can also raise the threshold question of whether there has been a realizing event at all. See ¶ 4.02(2).

stock,[236] two corporations where the same individual owns more than 50 percent of the stock of each and one or both of the corporations has been a personal holding company or a foreign personal holding company during the preceding year,[237] a grantor and a fiduciary of any trust,[238] as well as certain other related persons.[239]

In determining whether an individual owns more than 50 percent of the stock of a corporation for these purposes, constructive ownership rules apply. Stock owned, directly or indirectly, by a corporation, partnership, estate or trust is deemed owned proportionately by its shareholders, partners or beneficiaries.[240] *This is attribution from entities.* Thus for example:

> A sells property at a loss to X Corporation. A actually owns 30% of the stock of X Corporation. A owns 30% of the stock of Y Corporation. Y Corporation owns 80% of the stock of X Corporation. Therefore A is deemed to own constructively 24% (his proportionate share) of the stock of X Corporation on account of his ownership of Y Corporation stock. Therefore, taking A's actual ownership of X Corporation plus the constructive ownership of X Corporation together, A is deemed to own 54% of X Corporation. Hence A's loss on sale of property to X Corporation would be disallowed. The same sort of analysis would apply if Y had been a partnership, estate, or trust.

---

[236]   Section 267(b)(2). The stock ownership is measured by value. Constructive ownership rules are applied, see below. A loss on a distribution in liquidation of a corporation is allowed, however, § 267(a) parenthetical language.

[237]   Section 267(b)(3), also providing that the stock ownership is measured by value.

[238]   Section 267(b)(4).

[239]   The other related persons between whom sales or exchanges for a loss will be disallowed are a fiduciary of a trust and a fiduciary of another trust, if the same person is a grantor of both trusts, § 267(b)(5); a fiduciary of a trust and a beneficiary of such trust, § 267(b)(6); a fiduciary of a trust and a beneficiary of another trust if the same person is a grantor of both trusts, § 267(b)(7); a fiduciary of a trust and a corporation more than 50 percent in value of the outstanding stock of which is owned, directly or indirectly, by or for the trust or by or for a person who is a grantor of the trust, § 267(b)(8); a person and a tax-exempt organization which is controlled directly or indirectly by such person or by members of such person's family, § 267(b)(9).

Regarding partnerships, § 267 does not cover transactions between a partner and his partnership. Such transactions are governed by § 707, for which purposes the partnership is considered to be an entity separate from the partners, Regs. §§ 1.267(b)–1(b)(1)(i); 1.707–1. Any loss sale between a partnership and a person not a partner is considered as occurring between the person not a partner and the members of the partnership separately. Therefore if the non-partner and a partner are within any of the relationships described herein, no loss deduction will be allowed to the extent of the partner's interest in the transaction, Reg. § 1.267(b)–1(b)(1) and (2).

[240]   Section 267(c)(1).

Also, an individual is deemed to own stock owned, directly or indirectly, by his family.[241] *This is attribution from family members.* Thus for example:

> A sells property at a loss to X Corporation. A actually owns 25% of the stock of X Corporation. A's father owns 30% of the stock of X Corporation. Thus A is deemed to own constructively 30% of the stock of X Corporation on account of the father's ownership. Therefore, taking A's actual ownership of X Corporation plus the constructive ownership of X Corporation together, A is deemed to own 55% of X Corporation. Hence A's loss on sale of property to X Corporation would be disallowed.

Also if an individual actually owns stock in a corporation, or is deemed to own stock in a corporation on account of *attribution from an entity,* that individual will be deemed to own such additional stock in the corporation as is owned by the individual's partner.[242] *This is attribution from partners.*

Note that attribution from partners will only occur if the individual owns some stock actually in the corporation or is deemed to own some stock by attribution *from an entity.* If the individual only owns stock in a corporation by reason of attribution from a family member, then attribution from partners will not occur. For example:

> A sells property at a loss to X Corporation. A owns no stock in X Corporation. A's mother owns 10% of the stock in X Corporation. A's partner owns 48% of the stock in X Corporation. A is deemed to own only 10% of the stock in X Corporation on account of the mother's stock ownership and the loss on the sale of the property will be allowed. There is no attribution from the partner on these facts.

---

[241] Section 267(c)(2). An individual's "family" is defined to be his brothers and sisters (whether by the whole or half blood), spouse, ancestors, and lineal descendants, § 267(c)(4). See Arizona Publishing Co., 9 T.C. 85 (1947) for treatment involving community property. It is mildly interesting to note that the constructive ownership rules of § 318, used to ascertain whether a stock redemption will be treated as a sale or exchange, do not allow for attribution between siblings; they are also more restrictive in other ways.

Cf. also § 544(a)(2) which takes the more expansive approach of § 267 in ascertaining constructive stock ownership for purposes of determining whether a corporation is a personal holding company, and cf. the very limited attribution rules of § 1239, which change the character of gain from capital to ordinary on sales of depreciable property among related persons. The subtle differences among these sets of attribution rules for these various purposes can perhaps best be explained by a tax lawyer who also has an advanced degree in anthropology. For a valiant attempt in this area see Goldstein, "Attribution Rules: Undue Multiplicity, Complexity Can Create Liabilities", 15 Tul.Tax Inst. 384 (1965).

[242] Section 267(c).

Alternative: A sells property at a loss to X Corporation. A owns no stock in X Corporation. A trust of which A is 50% beneficiary owns 10% of the stock in X Corporation. A's partner owns 48% of the stock of X Corporation. A is deemed to own 5% of the stock in X Corporation on account of his 50% interest in the trust. In addition, A is deemed to own 48% of the stock in X Corporation on account of attribution from the partner. Hence A is deemed to own altogether 53% of the stock in X Corporation and the loss on the sale of property will not be allowed. There is attribution from the partner on these facts.

It is possible to have two-step or "foxtrot" attribution in some circumstances. Where the ownership of a block of stock has been attributed to an individual from an entity, ownership of that same block can then be reattributed to another individual under the rules of attribution from family members or attribution from partners.[243] For example:

A sells property at a loss to X Corporation. A owns no stock in X Corporation. A trust of which A's mother is sole beneficiary owns 60% of the stock of X Corporation. A's mother is therefore deemed to own 60% of the stock of X Corporation by the rules of attribution from entities. A is then deemed to own 60% of the stock of X Corporation by the rules of attribution from family members. Hence A's loss on the sale of property to X Corporation would be disallowed.

However, "foxtrot" attribution cannot occur where the first step is taken under the rules for attribution from family members or attribution from partners. For example:

A sells property at a loss to X Corporation. A owns no stock in X Corporation. A's brother-in-law owns 60% of the stock of X Corporation. By the rules of attribution from family members, A's sister is deemed to own 60% of the stock in X Corporation. Since two successive applications of the rules for attribution from family members is not allowed, A is not deemed to own any of the stock owned by the sister. Hence A is not deemed to own any of the stock of

---

[243] Section 267(c)(5). It is also possible that the same block of stock can be attributed to two or more individuals simultaneously. A's wife and son might make sales of property at losses simultaneously to a corporation all of whose stock A owns. The losses on both transactions would be disallowed.

X Corporation, and A's loss on the sale of property to X Corporation is allowed.[244]

(c)　Use of Disallowed Loss by Buyer

Section 267 is ultimately a "hybrid" provision—a cross between a pure deferral provision and a pure disallowance provision. If a loss on a sale to a related party is disallowed to the seller on account of § 267(a), the buyer will under some circumstances be able to take advantage of the disallowed loss on a subsequent transaction. Under other circumstances the disallowed loss will never be usable by the buyer, or anyone else.

If the recipient of property on which the loss has been previously disallowed subsequently sells the property at a gain, he or she will only be taxable to the extent (if any) gain exceeds the loss disallowed.[245] For example:

> A sells property with a basis in his hands of $100 to B, A's child, for $50. The loss is disallowed to A. B subsequently sells the property to C for $125. B has a taxable gain of $25.[246] B's holding period starts upon purchase of the property; B does not include A's holding period.[247]

If the buyer of property where the loss has been previously disallowed subsequently sells the property at a loss, only the loss accruing during actual ownership will be allowed. The previously disallowed loss, in other words, will have no effect. This is because § 267(d) acts only to exempt gain to the buyer on a subsequent transaction; it does not affect the buyer's basis.[248] For example:

> A sells property with a basis in his hands of $100 to B, A's child, for $50. The loss is disallowed to A. B subsequently sells the property to C, an unrelated party, for $30. B has a deductible loss of $20. The loss disallowed to A will never be used. Any subsequent disposition by C will be

---

[244]　Another arcane variation: A sells property at a loss to W Corporation. A owns no stock of W Corporation. X Corporation owns 60% of the stock of W Corporation. Y Corporation owns 100% of the stock of X Corporation. Z Corporation owns 100% of the stock of Y Corporation. A owns 100% of the stock of Z Corporation. By the rules of attribution from entities, Y Corporation is deemed to own 60% of the stock of W Corporation. Again by the rules of attribution from entities Z Corporation is deemed to own 60% of the stock of W Corporation. By the rules of attribution from entities A is deemed to then own 60% of the stock of W Corporation, and the loss on the sale of property is not allowed. This chain of attributions is alright, since successive application of the rules for attribution from entities is not barred, § 267(c)(5).

[245]　Section 267(d).

[246]　Reg. § 1.267(d)–1(a)(4) Example 1.

[247]　Reg. § 1.267(d)–1(a)(4) Example 1.

[248]　Reg. § 1.267(d)–1(a)(4) Example 2.

treated under usual rules, without reference to the fact that the property was once sold in a § 267 transaction.

If the buyer of the property in the § 267 transaction transfers the property to a third party by gift, the donee will be taxable in full upon a subsequent sale of the property at a gain (a sale at a loss will of course also be deductible in full).[249] For example:

> A sells property with a basis in his hands of $100 to B, A's child, for $50. The loss is disallowed to A. B subsequently gives the property to C. C later sells the property for $125. C has a taxable gain of $75. C's basis for determining gain was $50 on the gifted property. C's holding period of the property includes B's holding period.[250]

Suppose the buyer of the property in the § 267 transaction subsequently engages in a tax-free exchange[251] of the property. If the buyer later sells the property received in the exchange for a gain, he will only be taxable to the extent (if any) his gain exceeds the original loss disallowed the seller.[252] For example:

> A sells Blackacre with a basis in his hands of $100 to B, A's child, for $50. The loss is disallowed to A. B subsequently engages in a tax-free exchange with D, receiving Greenacre in exchange for Blackacre. B therefore takes a basis of $50 in Greenacre.[253] B later sells Greenacre for $75. B has no gain on the sale. If B had sold Greenacre for $125, B would have had a taxable gain of $25.

Finally, it should be noted that even sales to related parties at a gain will be penalized under certain circumstances, in that such gains may be deemed ordinary rather than capital.[254] This matter is discussed at ¶ 4.06(3)(a)(viii).

¶ 4.06 CHARACTER OF GAIN OR LOSS: CAPITAL GAINS

(1) The Preferential Treatment of Capital Gains

The last major step in the treatment of sales or other dispositions of property is characterizing the gain or loss as capital

---

[249] Reg. § 1.267(d)–1(a)(4) Example 3. See ¶ 4.03(2)(c)(i) for basis rules on gifts.

[250] Id.

[251] See ¶ 4.05(2).

[252] Reg. § 1.267(d)–1(a)(4) Example 4.

[253] Section 1031(d).

[254] Section 1239. For further background on § 267, see Cavagna, "Related-party Rule of § 267 Can, But Need Not, Upset a Client's Tax Planning," 15 Taxation for Accountants 368 (1975). See also generally Bittker, "Federal Income Taxation and the Family," 27 Stan.L.Rev. 1389 (1975).

or ordinary. (There can occasionally be the further question of the year in which the transaction is reportable, see ¶ 8.03). This step is important because long-term capital gains are generally taxed at a lower rate than ordinary gains.[255] Concomitantly, capital losses are generally less attractive from a tax point of view than ordinary losses.[256] Thus whether a taxpayer is glad any particular transaction is capital in nature will generally depend on whether there is a gain or a loss.

The advantage of capital gains under § 1(h) is that the tax rates on net capital gains (the excess of long-term capital gains over short-term capital losses as defined below) is capped at rates lower than the top rate on ordinary income. Net capital gains are currently taxed at 20% for taxpayers in the highest bracket, at 0% for taxpayers in the bottom two brackets, and at 15% for taxpayers in the middle brackets.[257]

Just to be clear, the issue of characterizing a gain or loss as capital or ordinary only arises as to recognized gains or losses. Obviously if a gain or loss is not recognized, there is no need to flavor it. Moreover, the process of ascertaining the flavor of a gain or loss has no impact on the *amount* of the gain or loss, which is computed independently, as discussed above.

The relatively complex mechanical details of the capital gain and loss rules and the planning implications thereof will be taken up in the next section. This will be followed by a discussion of the problems in defining what particular transactions are to be subject to the capital gain and loss rules. Finally there will be a discussion of the history and policy of capital gains.

---

[255] For a few years in the 1980's the favorable treatment of long-term capital gains was repealed.

It should also be noted that "capital gains and losses" do not have to do with "capital expenditures." Although the terminology is similar, the two concepts do not have a great deal to do with each other. For a discussion of "capital expenditures", see ¶ 6.03(4).

[256] This is a generalization. There are certainly times when a capital loss can be as attractive as an ordinary loss. See detailed discussion below.

[257] The preferential rate generates a great deal of litigation on the question whether various particular transactions can be treated as capital gains. It also fosters substantial innovative tax planning to try to achieve for the taxpayer capital gains rather than ordinary income treatment. These matters are discussed further at ¶ 4.06(3).

Corporations do not receive favorable treatment on capital gains. Estates and trusts are taxed under the same rules as individual for capital gains. Limited liability companies, partnerships, and S Corporations are not themselves taxable entities and so their capital gains flow through to be taxed to their investors.

(2) The Rules for Taxing Capital Gains and Losses

(a) Background

A capital gain or loss occurs if there has been a sale or exchange of a capital asset.[258] The two critical factors in this definition are "sale or exchange" and "capital asset." Both must be present for there to be a capital gain or loss. In analyzing a transaction, it is usually clear whether a sale or exchange has occurred (although problems on this score are discussed at ¶ 4.06(3)). Whether the asset sold or exchanged was a "capital asset," however, is a trickier problem. "Capital assets" are defined as all property held by the taxpayer *except* inventory, depreciable or real property used in his trade or business, certain copyrights and artistic compositions, accounts receivable, supplies used or consumed in the ordinary course of business, and certain other types of property.[259] A classic example of a capital asset under this definition is stock or securities held by a taxpayer who is not a professional dealer in stocks or securities. Another classic example of a capital asset is undeveloped land held as an investment by the taxpayer. Other examples of capital assets include a taxpayer's

---

[258] Section 1222.

[259] Section 1221(a). For the special treatment of depreciable or real property used in the trade or business, see ¶ 4.06(3)(a)(iv). More specifically with respect to some other kinds of property: a copyright, a literary, musical, or artistic composition, a letter or memorandum or similar property, held by a taxpayer whose personal efforts created such property are not capital assets. Moreover, in the case of a letter, memorandum, or similar property, even if the taxpayer's personal efforts did not create the property, if it is held by a taxpayer for whom it was prepared, it is not a capital asset. With respect to a copyright, a literary, musical, or artistic composition, a letter or memorandum or similar property, if the basis of such property (for purposes of determining gain) is ascertained by reference to the basis of such property in the hands of another taxpayer for whom the property was not a capital asset (for the reasons described above), then the property will not be a capital asset.

For example, a composer gives a copyright of his composition to his son. The son, as a donee, would ascertain his basis for determining gain on future transactions of the property by reference to his father's basis in the property (¶ 4.03(2)(c)(i)). Since the father's personal efforts created the copyright, the copyright is not a capital asset in the hands of the father. Therefore the copyright is not a capital asset in the hands of the son, § 1221(a)(3). Similar results would obtain for such property for transfers to partnerships, transfers in trusts, and transfers to controlled corporations, §§ 723, 1015(b), and 351.

Also not considered a capital asset are U.S. Government publications, including the Congressional Record, received from the U.S. Government other than by purchase, § 1221(a)(5).

home[260] and paintings or other artifacts.[261] The particular reach of the definition of "capital assets" is discussed in detail at ¶ 4.06(3).

(b) The Mechanics

The mechanics of capital gains and losses taxation are best approached as a series of steps which, if followed carefully, will lead to the correct results.[262] There are two branches in the approach. One branch of steps is followed when the taxpayer's capital gain and loss transactions add up to a net gain for the year—so called "capital gain net income." The other branch is followed when the taxpayer's capital gains and losses transactions add up to a net loss for the year. The series of steps involved when there is capital gain net income will be discussed first.

(i) Capital Gain Rules

The complex rules for taxing capital gains are presented in two ways: an Easy Overview and the Professional Level. Easy Overview should be sufficient for most basic tax courses, depending on the instructor. Professional Level is appropriate if you are particularly interested and want to see some examples of how the new rules work, want to go further in the field, are taking an advanced course, or are a practicing tax professional. In addition, after the Professional Level, we give a special explanation on the treatment of real estate that most people probably should read.

Easy Overview

Here is an easy explanation of the mechanics of capital gains and losses (well, relatively easy).

Step 1)   Decide which transactions give rise to capital gains and losses, under definitional rules discussed below. (A typical example of a capital gain is the gain from the sale of stock held for investment.)

---

[260] Note that if the home were sold at a loss, a deduction for the loss would not be allowed, ¶ 4.04(2). Thus the question of capital loss treatment would not arise. The first $250,000 of gain ($500,000 for married couples) on the sale of taxpayer's home is exempted entirely from tax, see ¶ 4.04(5). Any gain beyond that threshold would be a capital gain.

[261] A loss on the sale of such assets would not be allowed at all, unless the property were not held for personal use. Gain on these items as collectibles would fall into the 28% group, as discussed below. The taxpayer's personal-use car is also a capital asset; rare, however, is the taxpayer who sells his personal-use car for a gain.

[262] Another source for rules, to be followed blindly in this area, is Form 1040, Schedule D. While the Schedule D certainly yields the correct results, it is less clear what is really going on under the Schedule D approach than the approach taken in the text. Indeed the Service has announced that the form can be correctly filled out without the taxpayer understanding what is happening.

Step 2)   Net all of the capital gains and losses without regard to holding period (i.e., whether the gains and losses are "long-term" or "short-term"). If the net result is a gain, then you apply the gain rules. If the net result is a loss, then you apply the loss rules (discussed below at ¶ 4.06(2)(b)(ii).)

So let's say we net them together and get a gain. Then we will apply the gain rules.

Step 3)   The gain rules: Separate the transactions by holding period. Assets held longer than a year before sale or exchange are long-term gains or losses; assets held one year or less before sale or exchange are short-term capital gains and losses.

Step 4)   Look to see if you have something called "net capital gain." If you have this "net capital gain," then you qualify for special lower rates of tax. There is a pattern of capital gains that yields the "net capital gain." The pattern is given by the formula:

Net capital gain equals

Net Long-term Capital Gains minus Net Short-term Capital Losses (NLTCG – NSTCL = NCG) (see § 1222(11))

Note that the term "net capital gain" is a very specialized term. Importantly, it does not include (or event refer to) net short-term capital gains. If, for example, you have a pattern of transactions of $10,000 STCG and a $5,000 STCL, do you have a "net capital gain," under the statute?

No. Putting these numbers in the formula doesn't give you anything.

See:

Net Capital Gain = ($0) – ($0)

Net Capital Gain = $0.

Net Capital Gain is zero on these numbers, even though your capital gain transactions are positive. Net capital gain is very interested in net long-term capital gains and not at all interested in net short-term capital gains. Consequently, net short-term capital gains are taxed as ordinary income, like wages, with no special rates at all.

Step 5)   If you have a "net capital gain," as thus defined, it is at this point that the preferential rates kick in.

It will help you greatly in getting a grip on this material if you remember that there are only two kinds of income for these purposes: ordinary income and capital gains. Ordinary income is taxable under the usual progressive rate structure of brackets. Take a look at § 1(a). Capital gains are taxed at various lower rates, pursuant to § 1(h).

Now we take "net capital gain" calculated in Step 4 and break it into various subgroups. If the taxpayer has something called "adjusted net capital gain," then the maximum rate applied is 20 percent.[263] Typical examples adjusted net capital gain include stock or investment real estate (but not including the gain on previously deducted depreciation). Importantly the items in this group have to be held for more than 12 months to qualify for this attractive, low maximum rate.

If the taxpayer has something called "unrecaptured section 1250 gain," also called "25 percent group gain," the maximum gain applied to that group is 25 percent. The only item in this group is gain arising from previously deducted depreciation on real estate. For example, suppose a taxpayer buys an office building for $1 million and depreciates it under the straight-line method (the only method available for real estate) for 10 years, driving the basis down to $700,000 (see ¶ 6.02(12)). Then the taxpayer sells the property for $900,000. There is thus $200,000 gain, all of it due to the fact that the property spun off depreciation deductions. This gain goes into the netting process of § 1231 (see ¶ 4.06(3)(iv)). If this is the only transaction in § 1231 (or if the transactions in § 1231 net to a gain), then this $200,000 will be treated a long-term capital gain. But this $200,000 also meets the definition of "unrecaptured section 1250 gain." Indeed, this is the only way that "unrecaptured section 1250 gain" is created. The $200,000 gain will be taxed at 25%, assuming that is a preferential tax rate. If the taxpayer is in the 10- or 15-percent brackets, the unrecaptured section 1250 gain will be taxed like ordinary income (and thus at a rate lower than 25 percent). Note also that because of the way this group is defined, there are no losses in the "25 percent group."

If the taxpayer has something called "28 percent rate gain," the maximum tax applied to this group is 28 percent.

---

[263] Remember that if the taxpayer has "adjusted net capital gain," defined as gain that is not from collectibles, small business stock or unrecaptured § 1250 gain, and the taxpayer's marginal rate is 10% or 15%, the taxpayer's adjusted net capital gain is taxed at 0%.

This group includes gains and losses from collectibles (think stamps, artwork, coins, and antiques), the taxable portion of § 1202 stock gain (if any), net short-term capital losses, and long and short-term capital loss carryovers.[264]

Step 6) Add the amount of tax generated in Step 5 above from the various rate groups to the normal tax on the taxpayer's ordinary income. That total is the taxpayer's total tax.

We can put the preceding discussion together in the following chart, which pretty well covers everything:[265]

CAPITAL GAINS: EASY OVERVIEW

If your capital gain is from	Then the maximum rate of tax is
Collectibles or § 1202 stock	28%
Unrecaptured § 1250 gain	25%
Other sources, and your marginal rate is 39.6%	20%
Other sources, and your marginal rate is at least 25% but less than 39.6%	15%
Other sources, and your marginal tax rate is 10% or 15%	0%

Professional Level

In the *Professional Level*, the first four steps from the *Easy Overview* are the same. The only difference is that in Step 5 we provide a much more detailed discussion of how the whole process works, and what the technical problems are.

Here is the *Professional Level* explanation, a more elaborate explanation of Step 5:

---

[264] As under the previous law, if the amount of ordinary income does not fill up the first bracket amount of 15 percent, then the capital gain items get to slide in and take advantage of the low 15 percent rate. They do this in the following order: first unrecaptured section 1250 gain, then 28 percent group gain, then adjusted net capital gain. Moreover if adjusted net capital gain fits into the first bracket, it is taxed at only 5 percent rather than 15 percent. If you want to see how all this works, read the Professional Level treatment following this discussion.

[265] A chart similar to this one appears in IRS Publication 17 (2004) at p. 117. For a more detailed chart listing the various capital gains rates based on the type of asset, the holding period, and the taxpayer's marginal rate see Appendix II.C, infra.

Much of the complexity here comes from the concept of "adjusted net capital gain." Recall that it is defined as the taxpayer's net capital gain[266] reduced, by the other groups, described in more detail below. This definition means that gain included in adjusted net capital gain is net capital gain from capital assets held for more than one year. Since the wealthy in the society often own more of the capital, a reduction in capital gains rates is usually seen as benefitting top wealth holders in society at the expense of lower wealth holders. If the 20 percent rate applied to all taxpayers, taxpayers at the bottom, those in the 10% bracket, would actually have a higher rate for capital gain than for ordinary income. That simply does not seem right. Moreover, the reduction from the top marginal rate of 39.6% to 20% is very significant. A similar reduction from say, 25% to 15% doesn't seem so significant.[267] Congress was very attuned to the argument that capital gains rates favor the rich, and therefore provided a further reduction in those rates for taxpayers with marginal rates of 10% and 15%.

So, if the taxpayer has a marginal rate of 10% or 15% the adjusted net capital gain rate is 0%.[268]

The following items are not included in "adjusted net capital gain" group:

* *Unrecaptured Section 1250 Gain.* Unrecaptured section 1250 gain is long-term capital gain attributable to prior depreciation of real property and which is from property held for more than one year. The calculation whether the gain on the property is capital gain is made after consideration of § 1231, including the § 1231(c) "look-back rule."[269] Note that all the gain due to depreciation is recaptured at ordinary income rates on nonresidential real estate placed in service after 1980 and before 1987.[270] Thus this gain is not unrecaptured

---

[266] "Net capital gain," remember, is net long-term capital gain less net short-term capital loss, § 1222(11). For the purpose of defining net capital gain, "long-term" means a holding period of more than 1 year, and "short-term" means a holding period of not more than 1 year, §§ 1222(2) and (3).

[267] See Appendix for the current marginal rates for each year.

[268] Prior to 2008, the lowest preferential rate was 5%.

[269] For discussion of § 1231, see ¶ 4.06(3)(a)(iv).

[270] See James Edward Maule, Re-Use Gain Taxation Relief Keys: Unlock Section 1245(a)(5) Ordinary Income, 77 Tax Notes 733 (November 10, 1997), observing that the failure to provide relief on the taxation of this gain is probably a drafting error. However, it may not be a drafting error in that the 25 percent rate on unrecaptured depreciation with respect to real estate represents a rate increase compared to the 20 percent rate that was otherwise available for gain on assets held longer than 12 months. To provide a 25 percent rate to depreciable real estate placed in service after 1980 and before 1987 would constitute generally a rate cut to this property, which might be inconsistent with the approach of the statute of raising, if ever so slightly, the rate on depreciation recapture.

§ 1250 gain. Rather this gain retains its character as ordinary income on sale of the property.

Note that there are no losses included in the computation of unrecaptured § 1250 gain. While that may be true literally, one should not conclude that losses will not have an effect on the amount of unrecaptured § 1250 gain. Under some circumstances, they will reduce the amount of the gain. This comes about because, under the statute, the unrecaptured § 1250 gain cannot exceed the amount of the § 1231 gains.[271] For example, suppose a gain on real estate of $100,000 all of which is unrecaptured depreciation. If there were a loss of $40,000 on the sale of an artwork decorating a business office, the unrecaptured § 1250 gain would be $60,000, the amount of the net § 1231 gain.

Then consider the case where, in the previous example, the $40,000 loss occurs with property held more than 12 months, say, a parking lot used for a parking business. On the above figures, the unrecaptured § 1250 gain would still be $60,000. If we add to this example an $80,000 gain on artwork used in the office, that would be 28 percent rate gain (as discussed below), it seems that the better analysis is that the $40,000 parking lot loss does not go to offset the 28 percent artwork gain. Rather, the $40,000 parking lot loss is still taken against the $100,000 unrecaptured § 1250 gain. If this were not so, we would need a rule, within § 1231, to allocate the parking lot loss against the unrecaptured § 1250 gain and the artwork gain, raising the level of complexity to hitherto undreamed of heights. Thus the best analysis seems to be that losses with respect to real estate used in the trade or business do come into the unrecaptured § 1250 gain calculation to reduce the amount of that gain.

Another interesting case arises if the numbers from the above example are that the unrecaptured § 1250 gain is $40,000, the parking lot loss is $100,000 and the artwork gain is $80,000. According to the above analysis, what happens now is that the parking lot loss completely wipes out the unrecaptured § 1250 gain and the remainder of the parking lot loss reduces the artwork gain to $20,000. Thus on these numbers, all that would come out of § 1231 would be the $20,000 28 percent rate gain.[272]

---

[271]   Section 1(h)(7)(B).

[272]   1t should be noted that by providing that the amount of unrecaptured § 1250 gain that can come out of § 1231 is limited to the net § 1231 gain (as defined in § 1231(c)), § 1231 does more than simply characterize individual gains as capital or ordinary.

* *The 28-Percent Group*, which consists of the following items:

(1)   capital gains and losses from collectibles (works of art, rugs, antiques, precious and non-precious metals, stamps, coins, alcoholic beverages) held for more than one year;

(2)   long-term capital loss carryovers;[273]

(3)   net short-term capital losses including consideration of short-term capital loss carryovers;[274]

(4)   section 1202 gain.

Gains and losses are netted within each group (the 28-percent group, unrecaptured § 1250 gain, and adjusted net capital gain) to arrive at a net gain or loss for the group. If any group produces a net loss, that loss is taken first against the highest rate group that still has a gain, bringing that amount to zero and then netted against the next highest rate group and so forth. Thus, if there is a net loss in the 28 percent group, that loss is used first against the gain from unrecaptured § 1250 gain group, then against the adjusted net capital gain group. Similarly a loss from the adjusted net capital gain group is taken first against the gain in the 28-percent group and then against unrecaptured § 1250 gain. (As discussed above, the 25-percent group cannot generate a loss).

In discussing these rules, it is also convenient to make reference to "ordinary income," namely taxable income less net capital gain.

Having said that we can see that the Code then stacks ordinary income and the three types of capital gain—the adjusted net capital gain group, the unrecaptured § 1250 gain group and the 28-percent group—in four steps. A tax liability is calculated on each layer of the stacks, and the total is the total tax liability. The four steps are:[275]

1)   The "grab bag."[276] This step, alas, is the most complicated. This step taxes a "grab bag" of potentially all the types of income in the following order.

First, it taxes ordinary income at a progressive rate structure set out in § 1.

---

[273]   Notice 97–59, 1997–45 IRB.

[274]   Notice 97–59, 1997–45 IRB, states that a net short-term capital loss (including consideration of short-term capital loss carryovers) is first applied to reduce any net long-term gain from the 28-percent group, then to reduce gain from unrecaptured § 1250 gain and finally to reduce net gain from adjusted net capital gain. Since, as discussed below, a loss in the 28 percent group is applied first against the 25 percent group and then against adjusted net capital gain, the rule for short-term capital losses means in effect that they are in the 28 percent group.

[275]   See § 1(h)(1)(A)–(E).

[276]   The term "grab bag" has been introduced by the authors to clarify the explanation. It does not appear in the statute or the legislative history.

Second, it taxes unrecaptured § 1250 gain (the 25-percent group) at the 10 and 15 percent rates to the extent ordinary income has not filled up these brackets.

Third, it taxes collectibles and other property in the 28-percent group at the 28% rate (or at the 10, 15, and 25 percent rates to the extent there is room in those brackets after ordinary income and unrecaptured § 1250 gain have been taken into account).

Fourth, it taxes adjusted net capital gain at 0% if there is still room in the 10% and 15% brackets after ordinary income, unrecaptured § 1250 gain and 28-percent group gain is taken into account.

2) "Adjusted Net Capital Gain Beyond The First Bracket." This step taxes at a 15 percent rate the balance of adjusted net capital gain to the extent there is still room below the 39.6% bracket after application of step 1.

3) "Adjusted Net Capital Gain in the Highest Bracket." To the extent the sum of the taxpayer's ordinary income, unrecaptured § 1250 gain, and 28-percent rate gain pushes the taxpayer into the highest bracket (39.6%), that portion of the adjusted net capital gain will be taxed at 20%.

4) "Unrecaptured Section 1250 gain." This step taxes unrecaptured § 1250 gain at a maximum 25% rate to the extent that there was not room in the first two brackets to tax it in step 1 at a rate below 25%.[277]

5) "28-Percent Rate Gain" This final step taxes collectibles/etc. gain at a 28% rate to the extent there was not room after step 1 to tax it at the 10%, 15% or 25% rates.[278]

We now explore the operation of these rules through a series of examples. The following conditions hold for the examples discussed below:

* Taxpayer is a married individual filing a joint return, with tax liability calculated under section 1(a) and (h) with indexing to 2016.

* The standard deduction/itemized deductions and deductions for personal exemptions have been accounted for with offsetting other income.

* All transactions involve assets used in a trade or business or held for investment.

---

[277] Section 1(h)(1)(E).
[278] Section 1(h)(1)(F).

Example 1:

* $250,000 salary income;

* $100,000 gain from sale of stock held for 15 months;

* $15,000 gain from sale of stock held for 6 months.

Analysis: The long-term capital gain transaction yields a net capital gain of $100,000 (net long-term capital gain of $100,000 minus net short-term capital loss of $0). The $15,000 short-term capital gain is taxed as ordinary income. The $100,000 net capital gain is part of adjusted net capital gain.[279]

Thus for the year the taxpayer has $365,000 of taxable income; ordinary income of $265,000; adjusted net capital gain of $100,000.

Under the four steps, the tax is computed as follows:

Under the grab bag first step, the $265,000 of ordinary income yields tax of $62,863.

There is no further tax generated in the grab bag step since the 10- and 15-percent brackets are filled.

Under the adjusted net capital gain above the 10 and 15 percent bracket step, the $100,000 adjusted net capital gain is taxed at 15 percent yielding a tax of $15,000.

Under the unrecaptured section 1250 gain step, no tax is imposed, since there is no unrecaptured section 1250 gain on these facts.

There is no 28 percent rate gain.

Total tax liability is $62,863 (grabbag first step) + $15,000 (adjusted net capital gain above the 15% bracket step) = $77,863.

Alternative: No income from salary: If taxpayer has no income from salary, then the only ordinary income is the $15,000 short-term capital gain. There is $115,000 of taxable income. There is still $100,000 of net capital gain and $100,000 of adjusted net capital gain.

Under the four steps, the tax is computed as follows: under the grab bag step, the $15,000 of ordinary income yields tax of $1,500 (all at 10%).

Notice there is still $60,300 left in the 10- and 15-percent brackets ($75,300 cap to the 15% bracket less the $15,000 of ordinary income we just taxed). That gap is filled first with that amount of

---

[279]   See § 1(h)(3) and 1(h)(7) which in effect define adjusted net capital gain as net capital gain except collectibles gain, unrecaptured section 1250 gain, and section 1202 gain.

unrecaptured section 1250 gain, if any. Since there is no unrecaptured section 1250 gain, the gap is filled with the amount of 28-percent rate gain, if any. Since there is no 28 percent rate gain, that amount of adjusted net capital gain will fill the gap. In other words, we can tax $60,300 of the $100,000 adjusted net capital gain at 0%.

The 15% bracket is now filled, so no more gain is generated by the grab bag step. In the next step, there remains $39,700 as yet untaxed. It is taxed at the 15 percent rate, yielding a tax of $5,995.

Under the unrecaptured section 1250 gain step, no tax is imposed, since there is no such gain here.

There is no 28 percent rate gain.

The total tax liability, therefore, is $1,500 (ordinary income from the grab bag step) + $0 (adjusted net capital gain at the grab bag step) + $5,995 (adjusted net capital gain above the 15% bracket step) = $7,455.

Example 2:

   * $250,000 salary income;

   * $200,000 of gain from sale of vacant land held for investment for three years;

   * $90,000 of gain from sale of a painting held for three years;

   * $150,000 of loss from sale of a rare stamp held for 25 months;

   * $120,000 of gain from the sale of an option held for 20 months. The option was to buy property that would have been capital gain property in the taxpayer's hands.

Analysis: Taxable income is $510,000. The four capital gain and loss transactions produce a net capital gain of $260,000. Ordinary income is $250,000. Adjusted net capital gain is $320,000. This is arrived at by taking the net capital gain of $260,000 and removing the 28-percent rate gain items (the collectibles), which net to a $60,000 loss.[280] Removing a negative $60,000 from net capital gain is the same as adding $60,000 to it. There is no unrecaptured section 1250 gain. The 28-percent rate gain group is, as pointed out above, a $60,000 loss.

Since there is a loss in the 28-percent rate group, that $60,000 loss is netted first against gain, if any, in the unrecaptured section 1250 gain group. There is no gain in that group, so the $60,000 loss

---

[280]   See Notice 97–59, 1997–45 IRB 1.

is netted against the $320,000 adjusted net capital gain, bringing gain in that group to $260,000.

Computing tax, first under the grab bag step, the $250,000 ordinary income yields a tax of $57,913. The 15% bracket is filled so no further tax is generated by the grab bag step.

There is no unrecaptured section 1250 gain, so no tax is generated by that step.

There was a negative balance in the 28 percent rate gain group (which reduced the adjusted net capital gain), so no tax is generated by that step.

At this point, there is $260,000 of adjusted net capital gain but there is only $216,950 remaining in the brackets below 39.6% (the top bracket begins at $466,950). We thus tax $216,950 of the adjusted net capital gain at 15%, which yields tax of $32,543 (rounding up to the nearest dollar), The remaining $43,050 of adjusted net capital gain is taxed at 20%, resulting in tax of $8,610.

The total tax liability, therefore, is $57,913 from the grab bag step, plus $32,543 of adjusted net capital gain taxed at 15 percent, plus $8,610 of adjusted net capital gain taxed at 20 percent, or $99,066.

Alternative: If the taxpayer had no income from salary, then the four transactions produce $260,000 of taxable income; $0 ordinary income; $260,000 of net capital gain; and $320,000 of adjusted net capital gain, for the reasons discussed above. There is no unrecaptured section 1250 gain and $60,000 of loss in the 28-percent rate group.

Once again the netting of the groups produces adjusted net capital gain of $260,000 and $0 in the 28-percent rate group. The tax is computed as follows:

Under the grab bag step, the $0 of ordinary income yields tax of $0. There is no unrecaptured section 1250 gain. There is no 28-percent rate gain, so no tax is imposed on either of these in the grab bag step. There is room for $75,300 of adjusted net capital gain in the 10- and 15-percent brackets, and it is taxed at the very favorable rate of 0%.

Under the step of adjusted net capital gain beyond the 15% bracket, the remaining $184,700 of the $260,000 total adjusted net capital gain is taxed at the 15 percent rate, yielding a tax of $27,705.

Total tax liability is therefore $0 (grab bag) + $27,705 (adjusted net capital gain taxed at 15%) = $27,705.

Example 3:

Now for a grand finale let's consider the following:

* 1) $10,000 salary (ordinary income);

* 2) $10,000 gain from sale of stock held for 8 months (short-term capital gain);

* 3) $10,000 gain from sale of stock held for 19 months (adjusted net capital gain);

* 4) $20,000 gain from sale of antique furniture held for 25 years;

* 5) $10,000 gain from sale of building attributable to previously taken unrecaptured depreciation, held for 8 years, with taxpayer having no non-recaptured section 1231(c) losses (unrecaptured section 1250 gain).

Analysis: Taxable income is $60,000. Of this total, $20,000 will be taxed as ordinary income, the salary of $10,000 and the short-term capital gain of $10,000. This leaves net capital gain of $40,000. The adjusted net capital gain is the net capital gain reduced by the total of the 28-percent rate gain (the collectible), and the unrecaptured section 1250 gain. The adjusted net capital gain is $10,000. The unrecaptured section 1250 gain is $10,000. The 28-percent rate group gain is $20,000.

The tax computation consists of taxing the first $18,550 of ordinary income and the short-term capital gain in the 10% bracket to produce a tax of $1,855. The remaining $1,450 of short-term capital gain fall into the 15% bracket and yields a tax of $218 (rounding up). The unrecaptured section 1250 gain of 10,000 falls into the 15% bracket, and it results in a tax of $1,500. This leaves $45,300 of room in the 15% bracket (the cap on the 15% bracket is $75,300). The $20,000 of 28-percent rate gain is included in this bracket and taxed at 15 percent yielding a tax of $3,000. This leaves $25,300 left in the 15% bracket. Since the adjusted net capital gain does not exceed this amount, it is taxed at the preferential rate of 0%.

There is no remaining unrecaptured section 1250 gain.

Total tax is therefore $1,855 + $450 + $1,500 + $3,000 + $0 = $6,805.

(ii) Capital Loss Rules

The very attractive benefit of capital gains—particularly long-term capital gains—is counterbalanced by restrictive rules when the taxpayer has capital losses. The loss rules are of some complexity, although compared to the gain rules they're a walk in the park.

As a general overview, all capital losses occurring during the taxable year may be deducted by the taxpayer to the extent of all capital gains occurring during the year.[281] Thus if a taxpayer has $1 million in capital losses in a taxable year, the taxpayer may deduct that $1 million capital loss against $1 million of capital gains that also occurred during the year.

However, suppose the taxpayer has $1 million in capital losses but only $500,000 in capital gains. It is here that the restrictive rules bite heavily. Congress has decreed that a taxpayer may in general deduct capital losses in excess of capital gains only to the extent of $3,000.[282] Thus in the example above the taxpayer may in general take a deduction for only $503,000 of the $1 million in capital losses. Unused capital losses may be carried over and deducted the following taxable year, assuming the taxpayer has sufficient capital gains to absorb the carryover loss. If not, the carryover continues to the next year.

The particular technical steps that must be followed to ascertain the proper deduction for capital losses are set forth below.

The procedure is to net all capital gains and losses, without regard to how long the property was held before it was sold or exchanged. (This is the same first step as in the gains branch. It is in this step that the taxpayer ascertains whether to follow the gain rules or the loss rules.) If all the capital gain and loss transactions taken together without regard to holding periods give rise to a net loss, then it is appropriate to employ the capital loss rules. (If all the transactions taken together give rise to a gain, then the capital gain net income rules discussed above should be used).

If indeed all the transactions taken together yield a net loss, then nothing should be entered in gross income. This has the effect of allowing losses to be deducted to the extent of gains—the losses have washed out the gains.

Then the net capital loss can be deducted up to a limit of $3,000. This is not much given that the taxpayer might have a net capital loss of several million dollars. Remaining losses beyond the $3,000 limit are carried forward to the following year, retaining their character as long term or short term.

Thus suppose Myrtle, with $100,000 of salary income, realized a $300,000 short-term capital loss in year 1 and had no other capital

---

[281]   Section 1211(b)(1), Reg. § 1.1211–1(b)(1). See ¶¶ 4.04 and 4.05 for discussion of whether a loss is deductible at all.

[282]   Section 1211(b)(1) and (b)(2)(B). This discussion applies only to non-corporate taxpayers. Corporate taxpayers may deduct capital losses only to the extent of capital gains, § 1211(a), with excess capital losses carried over to other years, § 1212(a).

transactions. She could deduct $3,000 of that loss in year 1 and would carry over $297,000 of short-term capital loss to year 2. If in the years thereafter she never had another capital gain or loss transaction, she would continue to carry forward this short-term capital loss, deducting $3,000 per year. It would take 100 years to deduct the short-term capital loss in full. Since capital loss carryovers die with the taxpayer, the only way Myrtle would be able to deduct this loss in full is if she incurred it when she was very young and she exercised a lot.

Note that when the loss rules are in effect, we do not worry about the various special types of capital gains (i.e. adjusted net capital gain, unrecaptured section 1250 gain, and the 28-percent group), which are only relevant when employing the gains rules.

(c) Planning Implications

A study of the capital gain and loss rules suggests a number of planning techniques for the taxpayer who holds capital assets. Many of these techniques are most likely to be used at the end of the taxable year, when the taxpayer is most conscious of improving the taxpayer's tax position. However, many of these techniques are appropriate at any time in the year and indeed some of them, to be effective, have to be undertaken at a time other than at the end of the taxable year.

(i)   Holding Appreciated Property Indefinitely

Looking at the capital gains rules first, the most obvious technique is to be sure to hold an appreciated capital asset for longer than 12 months before selling it, in order that the gain be taxed at a preferential rate.[283] While there is certainly merit to this idea, an even better idea is not to sell the appreciated asset at all and incur no tax on it whatsoever. The extreme version of this approach involves the taxpayer never selling the asset and dying in possession of it, at which point the basis of the asset is adjusted to its fair market value in the hands of the taxpayer's heirs.[284] Thus the appreciation in the asset would never be taxed.[285] Even if this extreme approach is not taken, a taxpayer may be very well advised to hold an appreciated asset well beyond 12 months or one year in order to defer payment of tax as long as possible.[286] These techniques, of course,

---

[283] Similarly, one should also be conscious of the one-year holding period with regard to the 28-percent group and unrecaptured § 1250 gain.

[284] Section 1014. See ¶ 4.03(2)(e).

[285] There are, of course, various rollover and nonrecognition techniques available for a taxpayer to change the property he holds without paying a tax. See ¶ 4.05.

[286] See the appendix and ¶ 8.02(1) for a discussion of the very great advantage of deferral of tax, particularly for the high income taxpayer.

derive not from the capital gains taxation rules but from the more fundamental principle that unrealized appreciation in the value of assets held is not taxed.[287]

(ii) Holding an Appreciated Capital Asset Longer than Its Required Holding Period

Tax considerations, however, do not always rule the world. Notwithstanding that, the best tax advice, all other things equal, is to hold an appreciated asset indefinitely. The taxpayer, however, may well at some point desire to sell appreciated property, either because the taxpayer needs the cash for business or personal use or because the taxpayer wants to invest in a different asset. In the latter instance, the new investment should be significantly superior to the old investment in order to compensate for the fact the net proceeds available for the new investment will be diminished by the tax paid on the gain from the old investment.

If the appreciated property the taxpayer wishes to sell is not a capital asset, then it does not matter how long it is held; the gain will be taxed at ordinary income rates, since the transaction does not involve the sale or exchange of a capital asset.

(iii) Selling Property That Has Declined in Value

Considerations are just the reverse, of course, when the property held by the taxpayer has declined in value so that there is an unrealized loss. Just as unrealized appreciation in value of assets held is not taxed, so too is it the case that unrealized losses are not deductible.[288] Therefore the well-advised taxpayer wants to realize losses as soon as possible so as to receive the tax benefit early. This ability of the investment-oriented taxpayer to realize losses early and postpone realization of gains is a powerful, and perfectly legitimate, tax avoidance tool.

Where the loss property held is a capital asset, the loss picture is not as attractive as with an ordinary asset, because of the limit on amount of deduction of net loss from capital transactions. Although the unused balance of capital losses can be carried over to subsequent years, it may take many years for the full tax benefit of a large capital loss to be received. This suggests that the taxpayer with a large unrealized loss on a capital asset may want to continue to hold the asset in the hope that it will ultimately go up in value, since the tax benefit from selling the property will not be substantial.

---

[287] This is the case even though unrealized appreciation is indisputably income, in an economic sense. For further discussion of this issue as it relates to the comprehensive tax base, see ¶ 1.02(3)(b).

[288] Cf. ¶ 4.02.

(iv) Combined Gains and Losses

The considerations discussed above may well be different where the taxpayer has had (or anticipates having) several capital gain and loss transactions during his taxable year.

Importantly, note that the following discussion holds with respect to the first three steps in the capital gain process which are used to arrive at the amount of net capital gain.

Moreover, for purposes of the following discussion the phrase "short term" means one year or less and the phrase "long term" means longer than a year. As discussed above, in the first three steps of the analysis of capital gains, the only relevant holding period is whether an asset has been held longer than a year.

Thus in the first three steps, where the taxpayer has already realized, say, a $50,000 capital gain, the taxpayer need not hesitate in realizing, say, a $35,000 capital loss, insofar as the $3,000 limit is concerned. The taxpayer will get the full benefit of the $35,000 loss (whether it is short-term or long-term) since the excess capital loss rules only bite to the extent capital losses exceed capital gains. Capital losses are always deductible in full to the extent of capital gains. Similarly where the taxpayer has already realized, say, a $40,000 capital loss, the taxpayer may be less hesitant to realize a capital gain, of, say, $60,000, since a large part of the gain, $40,000, will be washed out by the loss, leaving only the balance to be taxable.

The formula for ascertaining what gets the favorable capital gains rate will yield surprising results under some circumstances. Consider a taxpayer with a long-term capital gain of $4,000, short-term capital gain of $1,000, and one other capital loss of $500. The $500 capital loss could be either short-term or long-term, depending on when during the taxable year the taxpayer decides to sell the property. The question is whether it matters if the taxpayer sells the property early in the tax year as a $500 short-term capital loss, or whether the taxpayer sells the property late enough in the tax year so that it becomes a $500 long-term capital loss. At first blush one might expect that it would not matter whether the $500 loss is short-term or long-term, since overall the gains exceed the losses, so the losses are fully deductible, whether short-term or long-term. However, the capital gain formula has the effect that it is more attractive if the loss is taken as a short-term loss, under these conditions.

This is the case because if the $500 loss is taken as a long-term loss, the amount available for the favorable capital gains rate is $3,500 − $0. (Net long-term capital gain of $3,500 minus net short-term capital loss of $0). If the $500 loss is taken as a short-term loss, the amount available for the favorable rate will be $4,000 (net long-term capital gain of $4,000 minus net short-term capital loss of $0).

Thus, the lesson that can be drawn from this is that: *It is preferable that a loss be taken as a short-term loss for any loss up to the amount of the short-term gain, where the taxpayer also has a net long-term gain.* This is because where the loss is short-term it will be consumed by the short-term gain and therefore not enter into the formula to diminish the amount eligible for the favorable capital gains rate.

The formula for computing the amount eligible for the favorable capital gains rate yields another surprising result. Consider a taxpayer with a long-term capital gain of $4,000, a short-term capital loss of $2,000, and one other capital gain of $1,000. The $1,000 capital gain could be either short-term or long-term, depending on when during the taxable year the taxpayer decides to sell the property. In the first instance one might expect that it would be preferable to hold the property later into the year in order to take the $1,000 gain as a long-term capital gain. After all, long-term capital gains are eligible for the favorable rate. However, under these particular conditions, it does not matter whether the $1,000 capital gain is taken as a long-term or a short-term gain.

This is the case because if the $1,000 gain is taken as a long-term capital gain, the amount available for the favorable rate will be $3,000 ($5,000 net long-term capital gain minus $2,000 net short-term capital loss). If the $1,000 gain is taken as a short-term capital gain, the amount available for the favorable rate will also be $3,000 ($4,000 net long-term capital gains minus $1,000 net short-term capital loss). Thus under these particular conditions, it does not matter whether the $1,000 capital gain is taken as a short-term or a long-term gain.

The lesson that can be drawn from this is that: *Where the taxpayer has a short-term loss and a net long-term gain larger than the short-term loss, it does not matter whether any gain up to the amount of the short-term loss is short-term or long-term.* This is because under these conditions the gain increases the amount of the amount available for the favorable capital gains rate by the same amount whether it is short-term or long-term. It does so by either decreasing the amount of the net short-term capital loss or increasing the amount of the net long-term capital gain.

A variation of the rule above is also true: *Where the taxpayer has a short-term loss and no long-term transactions at all, it does not matter whether a gain up to the amount of the short-term loss is short-*

term or long-term. This is because in either case the gain will not qualify for the favorable rate for capital gains.

The above discussion has indicated that the conventional wisdom of how capital transactions should be handled does not always hold up when capital transactions occur in particular combinations. Thus a taxpayer with several capital transactions in one year should study the options carefully before deciding on the holding period of any particular gain or loss.

(v)   Holding Period Problems; Short Sales

As the preceding discussion has indicated, the holding period is a key factor in determining how a taxpayer will be taxed on capital gains and losses. A taxpayer may generally control the length of time property is held. The statutory scheme in this area clearly invites the taxpayer to decide, purely on tax considerations, how long to hold his property. That a taxpayer has held onto property for longer than a year solely for the purpose of enjoying the various favorable rates on long-term capital gains will not be a ground for the Service or the Courts to disallow the favorable treatment on the basis that the transaction was "tax-motivated" or had no "business purpose." This is in sharp contrast to some other areas of the tax law, where the taxpayer's failure to show non-tax motivations or failure to show a "business purpose" will be a reason to deny favorable treatment.[289]

Usually there is no doubt as to whether a taxpayer has held property longer than one year to qualify for favorable treatment. However, occasionally a taxpayer will sell property held for right around the required holding period and it becomes necessary to count carefully months or days (if not minutes) to ascertain the proper treatment.[290]

In general, the holding period is the period the taxpayer has owned the property usually with reference to state law.[291] In determining this, consideration must be given not only to the dates on which the bare legal title passes but also to the dates on which the

---

[289]   Cf. Knetsch v. United States, 364 U.S. 361, 81 S.Ct. 132, 5 L.Ed.2d 128 (1960) (purchase of annuities yielding interest of 2.5% financed by nonrecourse indebtedness bearing interest of 3.5%, resulted in denial of deduction for the interest because nothing of "substance" was realized by the taxpayer beyond a tax advantage.) See ¶ 6.03(6)(b). Evolving a theory of when it is necessary to show more than just a tax motivation for a transaction to be respected is beyond the scope of this work. See Blum, The Importance of Form in the Taxation of Corporate Transactions, 54 Taxes 613 (1976).

[290]   The holding period also determines whether property will qualify as § 1231 property, see ¶ 4.06(3)(a)(iv).

[291]   McFeely v. Commissioner, 296 U.S. 102, 56 S.Ct. 54, 80 L.Ed. 83 (1935), reh'g denied 296 U.S. 664, 56 S.Ct. 304, 80 L.Ed. 473 (1935); R. O'Brien and Co., Inc. v. United States, 56–1 U.S.T.C. ¶ 9261, 1956 WL 10399 (D.Mass.1956).

benefits and burdens of ownership are transferred in closed transactions.[292] This somewhat imprecise rule, grounded as it is in the vagaries of state law, can lead to some uncertainty.[293] In nonrecognition transactions, gifts, and certain other transactions, other rules will apply, usually involving lengthening the holding period to include the holding period of some other property or some other taxpayer.[294]

It is well established that in computing a period of time "from" or "after" a particular day, the day thus designated is excluded and the last day of the period involved is included.[295] Consistent with that practice, the Service has ruled that in measuring the period property has been held for capital gains and losses purposes, the day the property was acquired is excluded and the day the property is sold is included.[296] Moreover, the holding period is measured in terms of months, not total days.[297] Thus, if A buys property on November 7, Year 1, the first day of his holding period is November 8, Year 1. On December 8, Year 1, A has held the property for more than one month. If A sells the property on November 7, Year 2, A has not held the property for more than one year. If A sells the property on November 8, Year 2, A has held the property for more than one year. If B buys property on February 28 in a year which is not a leap year and sells it in the following year which is a leap year on February 29, B has not held the property for more than a year. B must sell the property on March 1st of the following year to have held the property for more than a year.[298]

Where the transaction involved is a short sale, the rules are a little more harsh. It is in fact very difficult for a taxpayer to enjoy a long-term capital gain on a short sale. Short sales usually involve securities or commodities futures traded on national or regional

---

[292]   Merrill v. Commissioner, 336 F.2d 771 (9th Cir.1964). Thus in the typical real estate transaction, the holding period would not begin at the time the parties go to contract, but could begin at the closing date, if title passes then under state law, and would certainly begin when the seller takes possession. See Rev.Rul. 54–607, 1954–2 C.B. 177.

[293]   See Morrison v. United States, 449 F.Supp. 654 (N.D.Ohio 1977).

[294]   For nonrecognition transactions, see ¶ 4.05. For gifts, see ¶ 4.03 (2)(c)(i). For property acquired from a decedent, see ¶ 4.03(2)(e). For holding period rules for bargain purchases of property by employees, see § 83(f) and ¶ 2.03. For the rule on worthless securities, see ¶ 7.01(6)(b).

[295]   See Sheets v. Selden's Lessee, 69 U.S. (2 Wall.) 177, 17 L.Ed. 822 (1864).

[296]   Rev.Rul. 70–598, 1970–2 C.B. 168, also providing that with respect to securities the dates of purchase and sale are the trade dates, not the dates payment and delivery are made. Where stock or a security is acquired from a corporation by the exercise of rights to acquire such stock or security, the date on which the right to acquire is exercised is included in the holding period, § 1223(6), Reg. § 1.1223–1(f).

[297]   Rev.Rul. 66–7, 1966–1 C.B. 188.

[298]   That is the clear implication of Rev.Rul. 66–7.

exchanges, although in principle they could involve any sort of property. As an example of a short sale, a seller will sell stock the seller does not own to a buyer, in a usual brokerage transaction. The seller will in effect borrow the stock from a broker (from its own inventory of the stock or from another customer or another brokerage house) for delivery to the buyer. At the time of the short sale the seller receives the proceeds of the sale, although they must be held in the brokerage account against the time when the transaction is closed. At some later date the seller closes or covers the short position by buying the stock to replace the borrowed stock. It is the seller's hope that when the seller covers the short position the seller will be buying the stock at a price which is lower than the price at which the seller sold short, thereby enjoying a profit. If the seller covers the position at a price higher than the price at which the seller sold short there is a loss.

Selling short raises a number of tax questions. The first question is when is the transaction taxable? The possibilities are that the transaction could be taxed at the time of the short sale itself, when the amount realized is received; or at the date the seller orders the broker to cover the transaction (trade date) or at the day the stock is delivered back to the lender to close the transaction. The well-established rule is that the date the stock is delivered back to the lender, or the closing date, is the date the transaction is deemed to have occurred.[299] Thus if a calendar year taxpayer is short some stock and orders a broker to cover the transaction on December 31, and the cost of the stock is fixed as of that date, but the purchased shares are not delivered to the lender until January 3 of the following year, a loss realized on that transaction would only be reportable in that following year.[300] While this rule is disadvantageous when the short seller realizes a loss, it is advantageous when there is a gain.

Regarding the character of gains or losses from short sales, the rule is that capital gain or loss results to the extent that the property used to cover the short sale is a capital asset in the hands of the

---

[299]   Hendricks v. Commissioner, 423 F.2d 485 (4th Cir.1970), Reg. § 1.1233–1(a)(1).

It is interesting from a theoretical point of view to consider taxing the transaction as of the time of the short sale. This presents a sort of reverse *Logan* situation (see ¶ 8.03) wherein the amount realized is known but the adjusted basis—the cost of the stock to cover the transaction—is not known. Roughly analogizing to *Logan,* the procedure could be to tax the amount realized at the time of the short sale and allow a deduction when the transaction is closed. This issue would only be significant, of course, if the short sale and the closing occurred in different taxable years. Cf. discussion in the text.

[300]   Essentially the facts *of Hendricks,* supra note 493. Note that this treatment is inconsistent with the treatment of long transactions, where the trade dates of both buying and selling securities are determinative of the timing of the transaction. See discussion above. The stated reason for this discrepancy is the supposed flexibility in delivery time of securities to cover a short position, *Hendricks,* above.

taxpayer.[301] Thus the typical investor engaging in short sales will have capital treatment.[302]

The stickiest problem in the area of short sales is the holding period. The holding period is not, as one might expect, the length of time between the short sale and the closing of the transaction. Rather, under the Regulations, the holding period is the length of time the taxpayer holds the property delivered to close the transaction.[303] Thus if a taxpayer sells X Corporation stock short on May 2, Year 1, and closes the position out on May 10, Year 2, with X Corporation stock bought for the purpose on May 5, Year 2 (a typical pattern), the transaction will give rise to a short-term capital gain or loss.

This rule seems unjust in that the taxpayer has undergone the risks of the short position, and has had to put up margin of at least 50% of the short-sale proceeds, for more than a year and yet is denied long-term capital gain treatment should the transaction turn a profit. The only explanation of this rule appears to be that the Service, along with the other financial powers that be, does not want to encourage short selling in the securities markets.[304]

The taxpayer's only escape is to close the transaction not by purchasing stock to cover the short position but by selling the short contract to someone else. The Tax Court in *dicta* has indicated that if the contract is a capital asset in the taxpayer's hands, as it likely would be, the holding period will be measured by the time elapsed between the date of the short sale and the date the contract was sold.[305] While selling the short position itself is a maneuver that may be available in the foreign exchange market and other specialized markets, it is not generally available in the securities markets and hence the typical taxpayer-investor will not easily be able to escape short-term treatment on closing short sales.

---

[301] Section 1233(a). Where a taxpayer has sold short, it may happen that a dividend is declared on the stock sold short. In that case, the taxpayer would have to make a payment equal to the dividend to the lender of the securities. That payment is deductible as an investment or business expense by the taxpayer, Rev.Rul. 72–521, 1972–2 C.B. 178.

[302] See ¶ 4.06(3) for discussion of capital assets.

[303] Reg. § 1.1233–1(a)(3).

[304] This rule is comparable to the rule on the major securities exchanges that short sales can only occur on an "uptick," or after an increase in the price of the stock. Thus do the securities laws and the tax laws discourage "bear raids."

[305] LaGrange v. Commissioner, 26 T.C. 191 (1956) (*dicta* discussing currency transactions).

This rule does not apply to "hedging transactions." There are special rules for commodity transactions. These matters are discussed below.

The plot thickens in the short sale area where the taxpayer engages in a short sale "against the box." This tax planning maneuver is foreclosed by § 1259. In understanding § 1259 it helps to examine the underlying transaction it was designed to prevent. This maneuver involves selling stock short where the taxpayer already owns the same stock—thus the taxpayer is "long" and "short" at the same time. In such a situation the taxpayer clearly is not at risk, since whichever way the stock price moves, the taxpayer will have a gain on one branch of his investment and a loss on the other. A reason a taxpayer might engage in such an apparently pointless investment is to extend the holding period on a gain without risk and thus obtain a long-term capital gain.

For example, suppose a taxpayer buys 100 shares of Y Corporation stock on January 5, Year 1, at $50. By July 10, Year 1, the stock has appreciated to $80. The taxpayer would like to sell the stock on July 10, but doing so would result in a less favorable short-term capital gain. The taxpayer, however, fears that if the taxpayer continues to hold the stock for longer than 12 months to qualify for preferential tax rates, the gain will evaporate. So on July 10, Year 1, the taxpayer sells short 100 shares of Y Corporation stock. Now the taxpayer is immune from further risk on the movement of Y Corporation stock. The taxpayer cannot make further gain from the movement of the stock, but also cannot lose the existing gain.[306]

On January 6, Year 2, the taxpayer closes out the short position by delivering the stock held long. The taxpayer's theory here is that there is a long-term capital gain of $30 no matter what the price of the stock. As discussed above the two positions always net out to a $30 gain, no matter what the price of the stock. Both positions are held more than 12 months, under the taxpayer's theory. The long position is more than 12 months because the taxpayer has in fact held the stock for more than 12 months. The short position is more than 12 months because it has been covered by stock held for more than 12 months. Thus the taxpayer secures a long-term capital gain without having borne the economic risk of the investment for the full 12-month holding period.[307]

Some time ago, Congress threw cold water on this short sale "against the box" insofar as holding periods are concerned. It provided that as to the short-sale branch of the transaction, any gain on the closing of a short sale will be short-term if, at the time of the

---

[306] There will be additional transaction costs, but they will be minimal compared to the tax advantages. Moreover, the brokerage commissions themselves can be offset against the gain. See ¶¶ 4.03(1), 6.03(4).

[307] Moreover, the taxpayer has also deferred realization of the gain until the following year.

short sale, "substantially identical" property has been held by the taxpayer for less than a year[308] (as in the example above). Any loss on the short sale branch will be capital (unattractive) under the general short sale rules discussed above. As to the long side of the short sale "against the box" transaction, Congress provided that the holding period of the stock held long at the time of the short sale commences on the date of the closing of the short sale, or on the date of any other sale or other disposition of the property, whichever occurs first.[309] This of course inevitably gives rise to a short-term gain

---

[308] Section 1233(b)(1). "Property" for the purpose of these rules includes only stocks and securities (including stocks and securities dealt with on a "when issued" basis) and commodity futures which are capital assets in the taxpayer's hands, Reg. § 1.1233–1(c)(1), cf. Corn Products Refining Co. v. Commissioner discussed at ¶ 4.06(3)(a)(ii). There are certain restrictions on the application of these rules to commodity futures, see text below. Options to sell property or "puts" are treated as short sales and the exercise or expiration is treated as the closing of the short sale for these purposes. This rule does not apply to an option to sell which is acquired on the same day as property identified as intended for use in exercising the option, as long as the option, if exercised, is exercised through the sale of such property, § 1233(c). Thus conventional "spreading" transactions are not subject to these special short sales rules. For more on arbitrage and spreading transactions, see the discussion below.

If the option to sell is not exercised, its cost is added to the basis of the property, id. Stock index options do not toll individual stock holding periods.

A variation on the short sale "against the box" is also precluded by § 1233. In the variation pattern, the taxpayer sells short first. The stock then declines in value giving the taxpayer an unrealized gain. To lock up the gain, the taxpayer buys the underlying stock. At such time as the taxpayer has held the long stock for more than a year closes the short position with the long stock. Again the taxpayer's theory might be that both positions are long-term, but the statute provides that both positions are short-term. Indeed, in a particularly harsh result the statute provides that both positions will be short-term, even if the taxpayer was short for longer than a year before purchasing the underlying stock.

[309] Section 1233(b)(2). Note that these specialized rules discussed in the text hold only for the particular conditions of the short sale "against the box," namely that the short sale has been engaged in at a time when substantially identical stock has been held for less than the long-term holding period.

Where a taxpayer engages in an "arbitrage transaction,"—for example buys warrants to purchase stock of X Company and sells the stock of X Company short, to profit from a premium in the price of the warrant—this arbitrage transaction, if clearly identified, will not affect the holding period of other X stock of X Company held by the taxpayer, § 1233(f), Regs. § 1.1233–1(f).

In ascertaining whether this rule shortening the holding period will apply, property held or sold short by the taxpayer and his spouse (unless they are legally separated) will be considered together, § 1233(e)(2)(C), Reg. § 1.1233–1(d)(3). This is a surprisingly limited ownership attribution rule, considering the large amount of taxpayer planning and maneuvering in this area. Thus where stock is held by a taxpayer and sold short by his son, the statutory rule will not apply. Similarly there is no attribution for transactions by siblings, or transactions by a taxpayer and his controlled corporation. Why a much narrower ownership attribution rule is used in this area than in other areas—such as disallowance of losses, disallowance of capital gains, treatment of stock redemptions—remains one of those mysteries that afflict the ownership attribution rules. See ¶ 4.05(7)(b).

or loss on the stock when it is used to close the short position.[310] Thus these short-sale rules have rendered the short-sale "against the box" technique ineffective as a method of extending the holding period of assets without any economic risk. The Regulations provide further examples.[311]

However, as described in more detail at ¶ 4.06(5), below, selling short against the box has still been used by well-heeled investors to in effect cash in their gains and terminate their risk without paying a tax. Section 1259 treats selling short against the box and similar transactions as a "constructive sale," resulting in recognition of gain.

The Service, in Revenue Ruling 78–182, 1978–1 C.B. 265–270, provides an extensive analysis of the tax consequence to the holders and writers of "puts," "calls," and related transactions and combinations of transactions entered into on national options exchanges. Where such options are exercised, the price of the option is added on to the price of the underlying stock.

The holding period for a commodity futures contract to qualify for a long-term capital gain (or loss) is six months.[312] This special treatment can be explained in part by the fact that the bulk of trading in commodity futures involves holding periods of less than a year.[313]

(3) Definition of Capital Gains and Losses

As discussed earlier, the fundamental transaction that gives rise to the operation of the capital gains and losses rules is the "sale or exchange of a capital asset."[314] The key definitional terms here of course are "sale or exchange," and "capital asset." The taxpayer with a transaction that yields a gain wishes to argue that there was a "sale or exchange," and that the property so sold or exchanged was a "capital asset." By the same token the taxpayer with a transaction

---

[310] To the extent that the taxpayer holds more stock long than he holds short, the normal holding period rules will apply to the excess. These specialized rules apply first to the stock bought earliest in time, § 1233(b)(2).

[311] Reg. § 1.1233–1(c)(6).

If a taxpayer engages in a short sale and then closes it during a time in which he has been long the same stock, any loss on the short sale will be long term, § 1233(d) and see Reg. § 1.1233–1(c)(4) and examples under § 1.1233–1(c)(6).

[312] Section 1222 flush language. The long-term holding period of any commodity itself is one year. It is only contracts to deliver the commodity in the future, where the commodity is subject to the rules of a board of trade or commodity exchange, that are subject to the shorter holding period. For the rules determining whether or not a commodity future is a capital asset, see ¶ 4.06(3).

[313] The legislative history also suggests that it is only agricultural commodity futures that are to be subject to the six-month holding period, but the statute applied it to all commodity futures. SeeGeneral Explanation of the Tax Reform Act of 1976, 1976–3 C.B. 1 at 439.

[314] Section 1222.

that yields a loss in general wishes to argue either that there was no "sale or exchange" or that the property involved was not a "capital asset" (or both). Note that the taxpayer seeking capital gains treatment must meet both tests to receive the favorable treatment accorded capital gains. The taxpayer seeking to avoid the restrictive capital loss rules need only fail one of the tests.

Capital gains are entirely a creation of the tax law. As discussed in more detail below, there is no underlying economic definition of capital gains. There is rather an ungainly and shifting collection of statutory and judicial rules which endow a certain group of transactions with the characteristic of being a "sale or exchange of a capital asset."

(a) Statutory and Judicial Rules

Section 1221(a) defines capital asset as any property held by the taxpayer, excepting from that definition a number of broad classes of property.[315] Therefore, any property held by the taxpayer which does not come within the enumerated exceptions is a capital asset. This somewhat strange definitional approach can favor the taxpayer seeking capital gains, in a close case, since any property not specifically excepted from being a capital asset is a capital asset.[316]

The exceptions to the § 1221(a) general rule are:

(1) Property in the nature of inventory, or property held by the taxpayer primarily for sale to customers in the ordinary course of his trade or business.[317]

(2) Depreciable personal or real property used in the trade or business and non-depreciable real property used in the trade or business.[318]

(3) A copyright, a literary, musical or artistic composition, a letter or memorandum, or similar property held by a taxpayer whose personal efforts created such property.[319] In the case of a letter, memorandum, or similar

---

[315] See also Reg. § 1.1221–1(a).

[316] This statutory tilt in favor of the taxpayer is counterbalanced somewhat by the courts' tendency to interpret the statute against the taxpayer, not finding a capital asset in a border line case when the transaction involves a gain and finding a capital asset when the transaction involves a loss. See Corn Products Refining Co. v. Commissioner, 350 U.S. 46, 76 S.Ct. 20, 100 L.Ed. 29 (1955), reh'g denied 350 U.S. 943, 76 S.Ct. 297, 100 L.Ed. 823 (1956) (discussed below); Surrey, "Definitional Problems in Capital Gains Taxation," 69 Har.L.Rev. 985 (1956). Chirelstein, "Capital Gain and the Sale of a Business Opportunity: The Income Tax Treatment of Contract Termination Payments," 49 Minn.L.Rev. 1 (1964).

[317] Section 1221(a)(1).

[318] Section 1221(a)(2). Reg. § 1.1221–1(b). See ¶ 6.02(12) regarding depreciation.

[319] Section 1221(a)(3)(A). Reg. § 1.1221–1(c).

property, if someone else prepared the material for the taxpayer who now holds it, the material is also not a capital asset.[320]

(4) Accounts or notes receivable acquired in the ordinary course of trade or business for services rendered or from the sale of property in the nature of inventory described above.[321]

(5) Certain U.S. Governmental Publications.[322]

(6) Certain "commodities derivative financial instruments"[323] held by a commodities derivative dealer.[324]

(7) Most "hedging transactions."[325]

(8) Supplies regularly used or consumed in the ordinary course of the taxpayer's trade or business.[326]

Beyond these exceptions are a number of other statutory and judicial exceptions. Therefore it would be fair to say that a capital asset is property held by the taxpayer, except for the property specified in § 1221(a)(1)–(8) and certain other property statutorily and judicially excepted. Beyond that it is also true that certain property which does not have capital asset status under these terms may still be endowed by the Code with capital asset status. These matters are all discussed below. The area is obviously far from simple. Indeed one would hardly expect it to be simple given the great stakes and pressures involved.

Before proceeding to these various definitions and exceptions, it is useful to bear in mind that all personal-use property held by the taxpayer—a residence, a painting on a wall at the residence, a car used for personal purposes, the lawnmower used for the home—are capital assets and the sale or exchange of them at a gain would in general trigger the favorable capital gain rules. Such property is "held" by the taxpayer and is not subject to being further excluded from the status of a capital asset. Note that if such personal-use property were sold or exchanged at a loss, the loss would be

---

[320] Section 1221(a)(3)(B). Reg. § 1.1221–1(c)(2). Where a taxpayer holds such property as a result of a gift or other nonrecognition transaction, the property will not be a capital asset as to the taxpayer, § 1221(a)(3)(C).

[321] Section 1221(a)(4). Reg. § 1.1221–1(d).

[322] Section 1221(a)(5), more specifically, U.S. Government publications held by a taxpayer who did not purchase them at retail.

[323] See § 1221(b)(1) for the definition of this term. An extensive discussion is outside the scope of this work, even in a footnote.

[324] Section 1221(a)(6).

[325] Section 1221(a)(7). Hedging transactions are defined in § 1221(b)(2).

[326] Section 1221(a)(8).

disallowed,[327] and hence the capital loss rules would not come into play.[328]

It is generally only when property is sold or exchanged that the definition of a capital asset becomes an issue. The various categories of property and transactions that are given special treatment with respect to the question of capital gain or loss status are discussed below, in turn. The large number of definitional rules in this area indicates the great taxpayer pressure (and countervailing governmental pressure) with respect to the favorable tax treatment of capital gains.

(i)   Inventory, Property Held Primarily for Sale to Customers

"Stock in trade ... inventory ... or property held by the taxpayer primarily for sale to customers in the ordinary course of his trade or business," is not a capital asset and its sale or exchange therefore yields ordinary gain or loss.[329] Thus the normal profits and losses of an ongoing business are accorded ordinary gain and loss treatment.[330]

There is a certain redundancy in the statute, inasmuch as "stock in trade," "inventory" and "property held by the taxpayer primarily for sale to customers in the ordinary course of his trade or business," all more or less amount to the same thing. Although the issue is usually clear there has been, over the years, a substantial amount of litigation over whether what the taxpayer has sold falls within this

---

[327]   See ¶ 4.04(2).

[328]   Thus the taxpayer is in a somewhat disadvantageous position with respect to his personal-use property. If sold at a gain, the taxpayer is generally taxed on that gain (albeit at capital gain rates); if personal-use property is sold at a loss, there is no deduction whatsoever.

[329]   Section 1221(a)(1). "Ordinary" gain or loss in this context means "non-capital" gain or loss; the taxpayer does not receive the favorable capital gains treatment on an ordinary gain and is not subject to the restrictive capital loss rules on an ordinary loss.

A taxpayer would like to characterize a gain transaction as capital and a loss transaction as ordinary. The Service, of course, takes just the opposite approach. Thus taxpayers and the Service will flip-flop their positions on a given type of transaction, depending on whether the particular case has yielded a gain or loss. This process tends to put a strain on the courts in their attempt to articulate consistent standards.

[330]   One reason for this (although it can be perilous to search for reasons for according or withholding capital gains treatment) may be the lack of a "bunching" effect of gain in an ongoing business. Cf. ¶ 4.06(4), discussing the history and policy of capital gains taxation. See also Malat v. Riddell, 383 U.S. 569, 86 S.Ct. 1030, 16 L.Ed.2d 102 (1966), vac'g and remanding 347 F.2d 23 (9th Cir.1965). Corn Products Refining Co. v. Commissioner, 350 U.S. 46, 76 S.Ct. 20, 100 L.Ed. 29 (1955), reh'g denied 350 U.S. 943, 76 S.Ct. 297, 100 L.Ed. 823 (1956); Burnet v. Harmel, 287 U.S. 103, 106, 53 S.Ct. 74, 75, 77 L.Ed. 199 (1932).

inventory-type class of property so as to give rise to ordinary gain or loss.[331]

This matter has been particularly vexing in the field of real estate. While it is hazardous to offer generalizations in this area, it could at least be said that the tendency of courts to find ordinary income on the sale of real estate will depend on the following factors: to the extent the taxpayer sells relatively many parcels in a given period of time, that will tend to suggest ordinary income treatment; to the extent the taxpayer engages in subdividing and otherwise improving the property, that will tend to suggest the taxpayer is in the real estate business and thus sales of the property will give rise to ordinary gain or loss; to the extent the taxpayer hires brokers, advertises, and engages in other promotional activity, that will tend to suggest ordinary gain or loss; and to the extent the taxpayer uses the sales proceeds to buy other similar realty, that will suggest a real estate business that yields ordinary gain or loss. Beyond that, other facts and circumstances may bear on the question.[332]

For example in *Mauldin v. Commissioner*[333] the taxpayer in 1924 bought a large tract of land originally for cattle ranching. Due to a poor cattle market, he subdivided the property for residential purposes, and prior to 1940 he sold some of the lots. At that time he was undoubtedly in the business of selling real estate lots. After 1940 he made no effort to promote sales but nonetheless sold many lots due to expansion of a nearby city. The court, pointing out that indeed he sold more lots in 1945 than he did in 1940, held that at all times he had lots for sale and that the volume depended on prevailing economic conditions. Notwithstanding that he was also in the lumber business after 1940, the court sustained the Tax Court's finding that taxpayer had ordinary income on the sale of his lots.

---

[331] See Malat v. Riddell, discussed in the text *infra*. See also Drybrough, 45 T.C. 424 (1966), aff'd per curiam 384 F.2d 715 (6th Cir. 1967) (inventory sold in bulk still accorded ordinary asset treatment); Continental Can Co. v. United States, 190 Ct.Cl. 811, 422 F.2d 405 (1970), cert. denied 400 U.S. 819, 91 S.Ct. 35, 27 L.Ed.2d 46 (1970) (property treated as inventory though at one time it had been held for rent); United States v. Winthrop, 417 F.2d 905 (5th Cir. 1969) (the court, confronted with the question whether inherited property that had been subdivided and sold gave rise to capital gain, observed: "Finding ourselves engulfed in a fog of decisions with gossamer-like distinctions, and a quagmire of unworkable, unreliable and often irrelevant tests, we take the route of ad hoc exploration to find ordinary income.")

[332] Id. Cf. Curtis Co. v. Commissioner, 232 F.2d 167 (3d Cir.1956) (improved property yielded capital gain; some unimproved property yielded capital gain and other unimproved property yielded ordinary income based on these various factors); Biedenharn Realty Co. Inc. v. United States, 526 F.2d 409 (5th Cir.1976), cert. denied 429 U.S. 819, 97 S.Ct. 64, 50 L.Ed.2d 79 (1976) (ordinary income found on sale of large number of lots notwithstanding lack of overt promotional activity).

[333] 195 F.2d 714 (10th Cir.1952).

In the leading Supreme Court case of *Malat v. Riddell*[334] the Supreme Court held that the word "primarily" in the definitional phrase ". . . property held primarily for sale to customers in the ordinary course of (taxpayer's) trade or business . . . ,"[335] means "of first importance." The implication of the Court's holding here is that if a taxpayer purchased and subdivided lots for the purpose of developing them and then, encountering financial difficulty, sold the lots off to various customers (approximately the facts of Malat), he would not hold the lots "primarily for sale to customers. . . ." Thus such a taxpayer would have capital gain or loss on the sale of the lots. The Court in fact vacated and remanded *Malat* for new findings of fact based on this standard. The taxpayer in *Malat* ultimately received capital gain on account of this standard.[336]

In the Supreme Court case of *Hort v. Commissioner*,[337] discussed also at ¶ 5.03, a lessor received a lump-sum payment from the lessee in cancellation of the lease. The taxpayer claimed a capital gain transaction, but the Court held that the amount received was ordinary income as a substitute for rent. As a corollary of the holding of ordinary income, the taxpayer could not offset basis of property against the amount received.

Metropolitan Building Co. v. Commissioner,[338] discussed also at ¶ 5.04(2)(b), involved a case where, under a rather unusual set of facts, the sublessor released the sublease to the landlord in exchange for a payment from the sublessee. The sublessee then entered into a new lease on the same property with the landlord. Since the sublessor was paid for the release by the sublessee, the facts conjured up *Hort* and ordinary income. But since the release of the sublease was to the landlord, the facts also suggested § 1231—capital gain treatment. The Ninth Circuit struggled with this problem and heroically came up with the solution that the sublessor enjoyed § 1231-type capital gain treatment, since the release of the sublease was to the landlord. The source of the payment was held to be irrelevant.[339]

Congress in 1954 attempted to bring a modicum of rationality to the real estate area by providing, in § 1237, some objective tests to be met in order for sales of real estate to be given capital gain treatment.[340] Section 1237, alas, is not the most useful provision ever

---

[334]   383 U.S. 569, 86 S.Ct. 1030, 16 L.Ed.2d 102 (1966).

[335]   See § 1221(a)(1).

[336]   275 F.Supp. 358 (S.D.Cal.1966).

[337]   313 U.S. 28, 61 S.Ct. 757, 85 L.Ed. 1168 (1941).

[338]   282 F.2d 592 (9th Cir.1960).

[339]   Id. at 597.

[340]   Section 1237 does not apply to corporations, § 1237(a). Section 1237 does not apply to losses. It cannot make what otherwise would be an ordinary loss a capital loss, Reg. § 1.1237–1(a)(4). Cf Buono, 74 T.C. 187 (1980) (acq.) 1981–5 I.R.B. 6

enacted into the Code. In general it provides that capital gain will be accorded sales of real property notwithstanding the sales are from a tract the taxpayer has subdivided if: (1) No part of the tract being sold in the year in question was ever held by the taxpayer for sale in the ordinary course of a trade or business;[341] (2) In the year the property is sold from the tract the taxpayer holds no other real property for sale to customers in the ordinary course of the taxpayer's trade or business; (3) No substantial improvement that substantially enhances the value of the parcel sold is made by the taxpayer on such tract, or is made by a contract of sale between the seller and the buyer;[342] (4) The lot or parcel sold has been held by the taxpayer for at least 5 years (unless the taxpayer inherited it);[343] and (5) In the year of the sale of the sixth lot, 5% of the selling price of all lots sold in that year and thereafter shall be treated as ordinary income.[344]

Section 1237 is not of great help. First of all it is not applicable if the tract involved was ever held by the taxpayer for sale in the ordinary course of a trade or business. That of course begs the very question that § 1237 is designed to answer. Second, it is not exclusive. The Regulations state that the tests of § 1237 do not automatically disqualify the taxpayer from enjoying capital gain treatment on sales of real property, if the taxpayer can otherwise make an argument based on the case law in the field.[345] Thus § 1237 does not particularly further the cause of certainty in this area. Finally, most anyone who could pass the relatively stringent tests of § 1237 probably would not need it. Such a person could rely on case law to secure capital gains treatment. Anyone who really needs § 1237 to get capital gains cannot meet its tests.

Thus § 1237 is just another factor in the mush of factors in this field. The cases keep coming but clarity on the question of discriminating between sales of investment real property and sales of inventory real property must, apparently, wait another time.

(Subchapter S corporation which subdivided property but ultimately sold 90% of it in one block had capital gain).

[341] Section 1237(a)(1), Reg. § 1.1237–1(a)(5).

[342] Section 1237(a)(2), Reg. § 1.1237–1(a)(5). Thus the buyer as well as the seller can make improvements on the property which would prevent the application of § 1237, Reg. § 1.1237–1(c)(2)(iii). Special rules are provided to help ascertain what is a "substantial improvement," § 1237(b)(3). Reg. § 1.1237–1(c)(3)(ii). See Rev.Rul. 80–216, 1980–2 C.B. 239, regarding the applicability of § 1237 to condominium conversions.

[343] Section 1237(a)(3); Reg. § 1.1237–1(a)(5).

[344] Section 1237(b)(1), Reg. § 1.1237–1(a)(5). Mitigating this already *de minimis* provision, the taxpayer may offset his selling expenses first against the ordinary income portion of the selling price, § 1237(b)(2), Reg. § 1.1237–1(e)(2)(ii) providing an example.

[345] Reg. § 1.1237–1(a)(4).

The difficulties in the real estate area are in contrast to the sale and purchase of securities. The ordinary taxpayer buying and selling securities (stocks, bonds, convertibles, warrants, etc.) holds these instruments as capital assets and has capital gain or loss on their sale.[346] This is the case regardless of how many transactions the taxpayer-investor engages in; the securities will still not fall into the inventory category.[347] Securities bought and sold by registered brokers or dealers are not capital assets.[348] However, a registered broker or dealer may enjoy capital treatment on securities by complying with certain identification rules and by not in fact holding the securities primarily for sale to customers in the ordinary course of a trade or business.[349]

It is curious that a taxpayer can engage in a virtually unlimited number of trades with securities and still not lose capital gain and loss treatment; whereas a taxpayer who engages in a relatively few sales of real estate will probably lose capital gain and loss treatment.[350]

---

[346] Section 1221; Wood, 16 T.C. 213, 220 (1951); Kemon, 16 T.C. 1026, 1032 (1951) (despite numerous transactions, taxpayer held not to be a dealer in securities). Rev.Rul. 74–293, 1974–1 C.B. 54; Rev.Rul. 71–253, 1971–1 C.B. 228.

[347] Mirro-Dynamics Corp. v. United States, 374 F.2d 14 (9th Cir.1967), cert. denied 389 U.S. 896, 88 S.Ct. 215, 19 L.Ed.2d 214 (1967) (though taxpayer, not a registered broker or dealer, engaged in thousands of securities transactions over a several-year period, it had capital losses on its losses).

The legislative history of § 1221(a)(1) also shows that the phrase "to customers" was added to the predecessor of § 1221(a)(1) to exclude from the definition of capital assets only those securities bought and sold by registered brokers or dealers. Securities traded by investors for their own account were not intended to be excluded from the definition of capital assets, H.Conf. Rep. No. 1385, 73rd Cong., 2d Sess., p. 22 (1939–1 C.B. (Part 2) 627, 632; Cf. S.Rep. No. 558, 73rd Cong., 2d Sess., p. 12 (1939–1 C.B. (Part 2) 586, 595.

Though a taxpayer is not a registered broker or dealer, the taxpayer may in fact be found to be a dealer for tax purposes, depending on the surrounding facts and circumstances, and thereby be denied capital gains treatment on the sale of securities, Frank v. Commissioner, 321 F.2d 143 (8th Cir.1963) (taxpayers previously had been registered brokers or dealers; their role in the transaction was to assist in raising capital; they owned a corporation which was a dealer in securities; they sold stock acquired in the transaction through this corporation to the public.) It is interesting to compare this result with the results in the securities law field, where an individual who is not a registered broker or dealer may still be regarded as a "statutory underwriter" by participating in the offering of securities to the public, and thereby meeting the disclosure requirements of the Securities Act of 1933. See Securities and Exchange Commission v. Chinese Consolidated Benevolent Association, Inc., 120 F.2d 738 (2d Cir.1941), cert. denied 314 U.S. 618, 62 S.Ct. 106, 86 L.Ed. 497 (1941).

[348] Section 1236 and see legislative history to § 1221, supra note 550.

[349] Section 1236, Reg. § 1.1236–1.

[350] In addition to the authorities discussed in this section, there has been a great deal of litigation over the capital asset status of many other kinds of property. The general principles discussed in this section would apply; but matters are often disposed of on a case-by-case basis.

(ii) "Corn Products" Assets

After the Supreme Court decided *Corn Products Refining Co. v. Commissioner*,[351] there was a question whether the Court had created an additional exception to capital asset treatment. *Corn Products* implied that there was an exception to capital asset treatment when the asset was used as an integral part of the taxpayer's business.

In *Corn Products*[352] the taxpayer was a manufacturer of starch, sugar and their by-products, as well as feeds and oil. The taxpayer made all these products from grain corn. Droughts in 1934 and 1936 caused a sharp increase in the price of spot corn. With only a three-week storage supply capacity, the taxpayer could not buy corn at a price that would enable it to compete successfully with sugar made from cane and beets. To avoid a recurrence of this problem, the taxpayer in 1937 instituted a program of establishing a long position in corn futures.[353] Then as shortages occurred and the price of corn rose, the taxpayer's profits on its corn futures contracts balanced the squeeze on its profits from sugar refining. If the price of corn would drop, presumably the taxpayer's losses on its corn futures would be made up by its increased profits from sugar refining. Thus, the taxpayer's futures transactions were in the nature of hedging: it did not seek to make a killing in the commodities markets but rather sought to protect its business operations. Taxpayer netted a profit of about $681,000 from its corn futures in 1940 and a loss from its corn futures of about $110,000 in 1942.

The problem in the case was that under the predecessor of § 1221[354] corn futures contracts were capital assets, at least on a literal reading of the statute. Corn futures were "property held by the taxpayer" but were not, strictly speaking, inventory or stock in trade held by the taxpayer primarily for sale to customers in the ordinary course of its trade or business.[355] The taxpayer was not in the business of selling corn futures. The corn futures were certainly also not depreciable property used in the trade or business or real

---

[351]   350 U.S. 46, 76 S.Ct. 20, 100 L.Ed. 29 (1955).

[352]   350 U.S. 46, 76 S.Ct. 20, 100 L.Ed. 29 (1955), reh'g denied 350 U.S. 943, 76 S.Ct. 297, 100 L.Ed. 823 (1956).

[353]   A corn or other commodity future is a contract to buy a fixed amount of the commodity at a fixed price at a future date. The purchaser of such a contract is said to be "long" and benefits from a rise in the price of the commodity. The seller of such a contract—who has thus agreed to sell the commodity at a fixed price on a future date— is said to be "short" and benefits from a drop in the price of the commodity. See ¶ 4.06(2)(c)(vi) for discussion of the treatment of taxpayers who engage in "spreads" and "straddles", i.e., go long and short at the same time.

[354]   Section 117(a) of the Internal Revenue Code of 1939, which for these purposes read approximately the same as the present § 1221.

[355]   See § 1221(a)(1).

property used in the trade or business.[356] Nor were corn futures contracts even close to fitting into any of the other exceptions to the capital asset definition under the predecessor to § 1221. Thus there was an argument at that time that the corn futures were a capital asset, whose sale gave rise to capital gain or loss.[357]

The Supreme Court, however, asserted that the definition of a capital asset must not be so broad as to defeat the purpose of Congress. The purpose of Congress, the Court felt, was clearly to deny capital gain or loss treatment to the profits and losses arising from the everyday operation of a business.[358] Thus it held that taxpayer had ordinary gain and loss on its corn futures transactions.

At the time of the decision in *Corn Products*, commentators generally believed that the Court had created a common law exception to capital asset treatment. There was an alternative reading of *Corn Products*, however, that saw the decision as merely expanding the definition of inventory in § 1221. In other words, *Corn Products* was not a common law exception to the definition of capital asset, but merely, a broad interpretation of the meaning of inventory.

When one reads the case, however, it appears that the Court was creating another exception from capital asset treatment. This interpretation of *Corn Products* created further problems. For example, where taxpayer has purchased stock in a company that supplies it with material for its manufacturing business, the subsequent sale of the stock has been held to yield ordinary loss, on the basis of *Corn Products*.[359] Similarly other investments to secure business prospects have yielded ordinary treatment, even though the asset bought was *prima facie* a capital asset.[360] Notably, the *Corn*

---

[356] See § 1221(a)(2).

[357] If the case arose today, of course, the future contracts would very likely be a "hedging transaction" and capital asset treatment would be foreclosed by § 1221(a)(7).

[358] 350 U.S. at 52, 76 S.Ct. at 24.

[359] Waterman, Largen & Co. v. United States, 419 F.2d 845 (Ct.Cl.1969), cert. denied 400 U.S. 869, 91 S.Ct. 103, 27 L.Ed.2d 109 (1970) (assuring a supply of yarn to yarn seller); Booth Newspapers, Inc. v. United States, 157 Ct.Cl. 886, 303 F.2d 916 (1962) (newspaper bought stock in newsprint supplier to assure source of supply during post World War II newsprint shortage); Windle Co., 65 T.C. 694 (1976), appeal dism'd for lack of jurisdiction 550 F.2d 43 (1st Cir.1977), cert. denied 431 U.S. 966, 97 S.Ct. 2923, 53 L.Ed.2d 1062 (1977) (stock purchased with a substantial investment purpose is a capital asset even if there is a more substantial business motive for the purchase and even if the investment purpose later disappears). Union Pacific Railroad Co., Inc. v. United States, 524 F.2d 1343 (Ct.Cl.1975), cert. denied 429 U.S. 827, 97 S.Ct. 83, 50 L.Ed.2d 89 (1976) (stock of subsidiary corporations treated as noncapital assets for purposes of computing taxpayer's excess profits credit, citing *Corn Products, Booth Newspapers,* and *Waterman, Largen & Co.;*) cf. Gulftex Drug Co., Inc., 29 T.C. 118 (1957), aff'd per curiam 261 F.2d 238 (5th Cir.1958) (stock bought originally to assure source of supply but subsequently held as an investment gave rise to long-term capital loss when sold).

[360] Steadman v. Commissioner, 424 F.2d 1 (6th Cir.1970), cert. denied 400 U.S. 869, 91 S.Ct. 103, 27 L.Ed.2d 109 (1970) (attorney who purchased stock in music

Products rule has been held not to apply to the purchase and sale of a partnership interest.[361]

Most of the cases decided in this area involve taxpayers with losses. It seems fair to surmise that taxpayers with *Corn Products* type investments who have gains on them are just reporting them as capital gains. Since the assets involved are *prima facie* capital assets—i.e., shares of stock or commodity futures, etc.—the reporting of their sale as a capital gain on the taxpayer's return would not in general give rise to inquiry by the Service. It is probable that it is only when the *Corn Products*-type investment gives rise to a loss that taxpayers point out the shares of stock or commodity futures, etc. were integrally related to its business, that the motive for the purchase was predominantly business and that, therefore, the transaction should give rise to ordinary loss treatment.[362]

The Supreme Court recognized these problems and clarified the scope of *Corn Products* in *Arkansas Best v. Commissioner,*[363] where the Court dealt with a case in which stock was received by the taxpayer from a troubled bank in exchange for the taxpayer making investments in the bank. The investments were designed to preserve the taxpayer's reputation by keeping the bank from failing. The Court held the loss on the sale of the stock was capital, explicitly rejecting the broad reading *Corn Products* had received in *Booth Newspapers,* and other circuit court cases. The Court's rationale was that in *Corn Products,* the corn futures were really a substitute for inventory, whereas the stock held by the taxpayer in *Arkansas Best* was not in any way inventory, since the taxpayer was not in the securities business. Thus, in *Arkansas Best,* the Court interpreted *Corn Products* not as creating a common law exception to capital loss

---

company to assure his position as general counsel had ordinary loss on his worthless stock when company went bankrupt); Rev.Rul. 58–40, 1958–1 C.B. 275 (describing three business situations in which the purchase and sale of stock, bonds, and debentures yields ordinary income treatment). Rev.Rul. 75–13, 1975–1 C.B. 67 (loss suffered by employee on employer's stock held capital notwithstanding that purchases of employer's stock were considered helpful to employee's career). Private Letter Ruling 7847004 *(Corn Products* will apply in currency transactions to give ordinary loss only when there is a direct relationship between the foreign currency transaction and a risk of exposure arising from the taxpayer's everyday business; moreover ordinary loss on short sales of foreign currency is allowed only where the corporation conducts its business in that country through a branch or division—not where the corporation conducts its business in the country through a subsidiary).

[361] Pollack, Jr., 69 T.C. 142 (1977). See Davis, "The Corn Products Doctrine and its Application to Partnership Interests," 79 Colum.L.Rev. 341 (1979).

[362] It is interesting to note in this connection that the *Corn Products* case itself involved a taxpayer with a net gain. Possibly the reason the transactions caught the eye of the Service was that the taxpayer in *Corn Products* first reported the transactions as ordinary income and then later changed its mind and reported them as capital gain, 350 U.S. at 49, 76 S.Ct. at 22.

[363] 485 U.S. 212, 108 S.Ct. 971, 99 L.Ed.2d 183 (1988).

treatment, but instead as taking a very broad definition of the term inventory.

See also Cenex, Inc. v. United States, 38 Fed.Cl. 331 (1997) in which taxpayer purchased stock in an oil refining company for the purpose of securing a source of supply for petroleum products for its customers. The taxpayer sold the stock for a loss and claimed an ordinary loss under *Corn Products*. The court rejected the argument under the *Arkansas Best* line of reasoning.

(iii) Depreciable and Real Property Used in a Trade or Business

Another major category of property excluded from the status of "capital asset" is depreciable property used in a trade or business and real property used in a trade or business[364] Sales or exchanges of such business property are, however, picked up along with some other transactions and put through a special capital gain-ordinary loss treatment under § 1231. Section 1231 is discussed below at ¶ 4.06(3)(a)(iv).

Prior to 1942, only depreciable property used in a trade or business was excluded from the definition of capital assets; real property used in a trade or business was considered a capital asset. This led to some difficult allocation problems where, for example, a manufacturing plant was sold. The building was not a capital asset but the land on which it stood was. This caused problems in allocating the purchase price. If the overall transaction was for a gain, the seller would want to allocate the bulk of the purchase price to the land (so as to enjoy a capital gain) and a relatively small amount of the purchase price to the building (which would give rise to ordinary gain). The buyer could very well take a contrary view, since the buyer would want a low basis in the nondepreciable capital asset (the land) and a high basis in the depreciable asset (the building).[365]

To eliminate this allocation problem, Congress in 1942 provided that all real property—whether or not depreciable—used in a trade or business would be excluded from capital asset status.[366] This maneuver is surprisingly unsuccessful in disposing of this allocation problem under the present statutory structure. To the extent there may be recapture of depreciation on the building,[367] the seller will still be interested in allocating the purchase price to the land. The

---

[364] Section 1221(a)(2).

[365] Cf. ¶ 4.06(3)(b) relating to current planning problems in the sale of a business. See ¶ 6.02(12) regarding depreciation generally.

[366] Section 1221(a)(2); H.R.Rep. No. 2333, 77th Cong., 2d Sess., 1942–2 C.B. 372, 414.

[367] See ¶ 4.06(3)(a)(vii).

buyer is still interested in allocating the bulk of the purchase price to the building for purposes of subsequent depreciation.

Depreciable personal property, as well as real property used in a trade or business, also comes within the purview of § 1221(a)(2) and is excluded from capital asset status. (Such property will be picked up by § 1231 as discussed below.) See ¶ 6.02(13)(d) for discussion of the wide variety of intangible personal property that is now subject to depreciation or amortization.

There are two critical definitional terms relating to this category of § 1221(a)(2) property. First, the property must be "used"—as opposed to lying idle. Second, the use must be in a "trade or business"—as opposed to an investment activity or a personal activity. Not surprisingly, close questions have spawned a significant amount of litigation with respect to these two definitional terms.[368]

(iv) Section 1231 Treatment

Although the class of "depreciable and real property used in the trade or business" is not regarded as a capital asset as discussed

---

[368] See Carter-Colton Cigar Co., 9 T.C. 219 (1947) (Taxpayer purchased unimproved lot for purpose of constructing on it a store, warehouse, and principal place of business. Construction plans were abandoned on account of the depression and due to the death of one of two major stockholders. On the ultimate sale of the property for a loss, taxpayer allowed to take an ordinary loss over the Service's argument that there should only be a capital loss, since the property was never "used" in the taxpayer's trade or business.); Davis, 11 T.C. 538 (1948) (Unimproved lot purchased for purpose of constructing on it a paint store ultimately sold at a loss upon discovery that the property was zoned exclusively for residential use. Held: the loss was capital, because the property could never have been used in the taxpayer's trade or business); Fackler v. Commissioner, 133 F.2d 509 (6th Cir.1943) (Renting of a multi-tenant building was a trade or business although landlord services provided through agents); Bauer v. United States, 144 Ct.Cl. 308, 168 F.Supp. 539 (1958) (*Dicta* that whether rental activity rises to the level of a trade or business so that a loss on sale of the property can be ordinary is a question of fact, citing other leading cases); Alvary v. United States, 302 F.2d 790 (2d Cir.1962) (Two rental apartment houses managed by an agent constituted a trade or business, thus taxpayer accorded ordinary loss); see Comment, "The Single Rental as a 'Trade or Business' Under the Internal Revenue Code," 23 U.Chi.L.Rev. 111 (1955).

The question whether property is used in the trade or business generally only arises in the case of individuals. By and large corporations are assumed to use their property in their trade or business, since presumably that is the only thing a corporation can do with its property, but see International Trading Co. v. Commissioner, 57 T.C. 455 (1971), rev'd and remanded 484 F.2d 707 (7th Cir.1973) (Corporation not allowed a loss on sale of property it held for personal use of its shareholders.)

Note therefore, that where an individual sells property at a loss, the stakes can be great indeed if a question is raised as to the use to which the individual put the property. If the property is regarded as "used in a trade or business," the taxpayer will generally get an ordinary loss (see discussion in the text below relating to § 1231); if the property is regarded as held for investment rather than used in a trade or business, the loss will be regarded as capital and subject to the capital loss limitations; if the property is regarded as used for personal use, the loss deduction will be completely barred, see ¶ 4.04(2).

above, the sale or exchange of this property may give rise to capital gain or loss treatment under certain circumstances. This is due to the rather unusual workings of § 1231, an extremely important as it deals with the taxation of depreciable plant and equipment.

In order to understand the workings of § 1231, it is useful to look briefly at the historical conflicts that led to its enactment.[369]

The saga begins with the Revenue Act of 1938, which excluded depreciable personal property from capital asset status. This provision, enacted in the later years of the depression, offered relief to those who sold their business assets at a loss—which was usually the case at that time—by providing ordinary loss treatment on such transactions. The purpose, among others, was to encourage replacement of obsolete equipment.

By 1942 economic conditions had, of course, changed dramatically. The demands of World War II caused business assets to have a significantly increased value. Congress wished to encourage businesses to dispose of business assets, particularly ships and boats, for use in the war effort. Because such assets were now deemed ordinary, sale or exchange of them gave rise to ordinary gain. Thus Congress became concerned with altering the treatment of business assets to encourage the disposal of these assets to benefit the war effort. Moreover, Congress wanted to provide an attractive tax treatment for the proceeds of condemnations of property to be used in the war effort. And Congress also wanted to give attractive tax treatment to insurance proceeds where private property was destroyed on account of the war.

Most of these transactions gave rise to gains. That is to say, the amount received on sale, condemnation, or casualty of property related to the war effort was usually greater than the basis of such assets. This led to great political pressure for legislation that these business assets be put back into the status of capital assets. However, there were a number of types of industries—notably the railroads— who continued to dispose of their business property at a loss. They of course would have been extremely unhappy with a return to capital status of business assets. Into this steaming caldron of the congressional consideration of this matter also came farmers, who regularly sold their business assets—breeding and dairy livestock— at a gain. They of course favored restoring business assets to capital status.

Putting all this together, Congress came up with a solution which demonstrated that the genius of the American political system

---

[369] See generally, Birkeland, "Section 1231: A Fading Star for the Business Taxpayer," 60 A.B.A.J. 845 (1974).

was still intact[370] even if the integrity of the income tax was, in the process, somewhat undermined. Congress's solution, roughly speaking, was to regard all these transactions that a taxpayer may have together. If all these transactions, taken together, give rise to a net gain, then each transaction considered separately will be considered capital in character. If all these transactions taken together break even or give rise to a loss, then each transaction considered separately will be considered ordinary in character. In addition there is a preliminary treatment of casualties before all the transactions are taken together.

In particular, § 1231 works like this:

> *Step 1, The Firepot:* Attention is first given to all casualties the taxpayer has sustained during the taxable year with respect to three classes of property—(1) depreciable property used in the taxpayer's trade or business and held more than one year, (2) real property used in the taxpayer's trade or business and held more than one year, and (3) capital assets held for more than one year in connection with a trade or business or a transaction entered into for profit. The gains and losses on all of these casualty transactions[371] are netted together. If that net result is a loss, then none of these individual casualty transactions enters further into the workings of § 1231.[372] Rather, they will be treated as casualties are normally treated. That is, they will be given ordinary gain and loss treatment.[373]

---

[370] See V.O. Key, Politics, Parties, and Pressure Groups (1967).

[371] A gain on a casualty would arise if, for example, the amount of the insurance proceeds received were greater than the adjusted basis of the property destroyed, see ¶ 4.03. In particular, casualties to personal-use property are only allowed as a deduction if as an aggregate they exceed 10% of the taxpayer's adjusted gross income. They must also exceed a $100 floor applied on a per casualty basis. With respect to personal-use property, only the few casualties that exceed these limits are eligible for § 1231 treatment. Casualties to business or investment property are deductible and go into § 1231 without having to meet these limits. See ¶ 7.01(5).

[372] Section 1231(a) flush language.

[373] Casualties normally give rise to ordinary gains and losses rather than capital gains and losses, because casualties do not involve a sale or exchange, Helvering v. William Flaccus Oak Leather Co., 313 U.S. 247, 61 S.Ct. 878, 85 L.Ed. 1310 (1941). In Rev.Rul. 82–74, 1982–1 C.B. 110, taxpayer, the lessor of an office building, paid a third party to burn it down so he could receive the insurance proceeds. The Service determined that the taxpayer's gain—measured by the insurance proceeds less his basis in the building—did not qualify for capital gain under § 1231, since the arson was not an involuntary conversion. Outside the workings of § 1231 the receipt of the insurance proceeds did not qualify for capital gains treatment since it did not arise from a sale or exchange; and see ¶ 7.01(5).

Therefore for example, even if there is a casualty gain with respect to a capital asset, the gain will be ordinary because although the asset involved was a capital

If the net result on all the casualties is to break even or is a gain, then all of the casualties—gains and losses—involved in this netting process pass into the "hotchpot."[374] This preliminary process of netting the casualties for these purposes can be conveniently termed the "firepot," as a fire is a type of casualty.

Step 2, The Hotchpot: The "hotchpot" also involves a process of netting transactions. The transactions that are netted in the hotchpot are the following: (1) All casualties, if they have netted to break even or a gain in the "firepot;" (2) Sales or exchanges of capital assets or depreciable property and real property used in the trade or business, held for more than one year;[375] (3) Condemnation of depreciable property and real property used in the trade or business, held for more than one year; (4) Condemnations of capital assets held more than one year which are held in connection with a trade or business or transaction entered into for profit.[376]

If all the transactions in the hotchpot net out to a gain, then each transaction in the hotchpot is considered to be a long-term capital gain or loss. These capital gains and losses arising from § 1231 are then combined with the taxpayer's other capital gains and losses arising from a sale or exchange of capital assets. All of these capital gains and losses are then treated under the normal rules for capital gains and losses, as described at ¶ 4.06(2)(b)(i). Note that

---

asset, there was no sale or exchange, see ¶ 4.06(2)(a) relating to the definition of a capital gain or loss. (If the casualty gain on the capital asset comes to pass into the "Main Pot" of § 1231, it could then be treated as a capital gain, as discussed in the text.)

[374]   Section 1231(a) flush language.

[375]   In the case of gains from depreciable property, only the gain not subject to recapture of depreciation goes into this netting process. Regs. §§ 1.1245–6(a); 1.1250–1(c). See ¶ 4.06(3)(a)(vii) for recapture of depreciation.

[376]   Section 1231(a), 1231(b). The gains and losses subject to § 1231 must, of course, all be recognized, § 1231(a), Reg. § 1.1231–1(d)(4), see also ¶ 4.01. Further, the losses must otherwise be allowed. Thus not included in § 1231 are losses which are not deductible under § 267 (relating to losses on transactions between related taxpayers) or § 1091 (relating to wash sales), Regs. § 1.1231–1(d)(1), see also ¶ 4.04. If gain on the sale of § 1231(b) property is reported on the installment method of § 453 (see ¶ 8.03(2)), only the gain reportable in any particular tax year is included in § 1231 for that year, Regs. § 1.1231–1(d)(3). Of course the limitation on capital losses of § 1211 does not apply in ascertaining the amount of loss includible in § 1231, Reg. § 1.1231–1(d).

Where the taxpayer engages in a relatively small amount of rental activity, the courts have had great difficulty in resolving whether the rental property involved is § 1231 property—giving rise to the capital gain-ordinary loss results discussed in the text—or whether the rental property involved is a pure capital asset. This matter is discussed and authorities are set forth in the discussion above.

an important effect here is that real estate sold for a gain attributable to previously taken depreciation that comes out of § 1231 gets special attention as constituting "unrecaptured § 1250 gain." Thus can § 1231 transform ordinary transactions into long-term capital gains and losses.

If all the transactions in the hotchpot net out to break even or to a loss, then each transaction in the hotchpot is considered an ordinary gain or loss.[377]

It used to be the case that the netting process here is only for the purpose of *characterization* of the gains or losses. The gains and losses otherwise remain as separate and distinct transactions. But after the complex changes to the capital gain rules, see ¶ 4.06(2)(b)(i), it may be that the gains in the various types of capital gain rate groups within § 1231 are netted against each other.

That is the end of the workings of § 1231. It should be noted that depreciable and real property used in the trade or business and held for more than one year is often denominated "§ 1231 property" or "§ 1231 assets," because it is the main class of property that is subject to § 1231 treatment.

In the belief that "A picture shows at a glance what it takes dozens of pages of a book to expound,"[378] the workings of § 1231 are presented on the following page. It is believed that this diagram presents the most helpful approach to § 1231.

---

[377] Section 1231(a).
[378] I.S. Turgenev, *Fathers and Sons* (1862), Ch. 15.

§ 1231: BUSINESS PROPERTY SALES, CASUALTIES AND CONDEMNATIONS

SUBHOTCHPOT ("FIREPOT")
§1231 gains from (a)(4)(C) involuntary conversions
and
§1231 losses from (a)(4)(C) involuntary conversions

if losses
exceed gains

if gains equal
or exceed losses

§1231 does not apply to
these gains and losses

MAIN HOTCHPOT
Other §1231 gains & losses
Condemnation gains & losses
(a)(4)(C) §1231 gains & losses

if gains equal
or exceed losses

if losses
exceed gains

long-term capital
gains & losses

ord. income &
ord. loss

Some problems of § 1231 are illustrated by the case of *Stephen P. Wasnok v. Commissioner*,[379] in which the question presented was whether the property the taxpayer disposed of constituted § 1231 property and thus produced. The property at issue was the taxpayer's residence that he had trouble selling when he moved from Ohio to California. The court held that taxpayer's activity with respect to the property namely, that he rented the property for four years, claimed depreciation and ultimately sold the property for a loss, established that the property was used in a trade or business. Thus the property was not a capital asset but an asset described in § 1231. Thus the loss was put into the netting process of § 1231 and produced an ordinary loss. The loss was sustained in the year of sale of the property of 1965, when, as it happened, the taxpayer had no other income that could absorb it. The loss was not capital, which could have been carried over to other years when the taxpayer did have income that could have been canceled out by this loss. This case is therefore unusual in that the taxpayer was arguing for what is usually unattractive for taxpayers (capital loss treatment) and the Commissioner was arguing for what is usually a favorable treatment for taxpayers (ordinary loss). The reason the parties switched positions is that the taxpayer had no taxable income to absorb the loss in the year of sale so the taxpayer sought capital loss treatment to get the carryover. The Commissioner naturally opposed.

The case of *Williams v. McGowan*,[380] discussed in more detail at ¶ 4.06(3)(b), held that the sale of a going business in a sole proprietorship form is treated as the sale of the collection of the individual assets of the business by the individual owner. As a result, § 1231 and other characterization sections come into play to characterize the gain or loss on the sale of the individual assets. The planning implications of this are discussed at ¶ 4.06(b).

Looking at the mechanics of § 1231, some examples are useful to illustrate its workings. It is assumed that all the property in the examples below has been held by the taxpayer for more than one year.

Example: One Casualty Loss—T owns gold bars held for more than one year for investment with a basis of $100,000 and a fair market value of $150,000. The bars are

---

[379]   30 T.C.M. 39 (1971).
[380]   152 F.2d 570 (2d Cir.1945).

stolen and he receives insurance proceeds of $80,000. Therefore T has a deductible loss in the amount of $20,000.[381] T has no other transactions subject to § 1231. This $20,000 goes into the firepot. Since it is the only transaction in the firepot, the losses exceed the gains in the firepot. Therefore the $20,000 loss does not drop into the hotchpot. Rather, the $20,000 is given ordinary treatment and is entered on the taxpayer's tax return as an ordinary loss deduction from adjusted gross income.[382]

Example: One Casualty Gain—The facts are the same as in the previous Example except the amount of the insurance proceeds received is $135,000. Therefore, the transaction is now a casualty gain of $35,000.[383] This $35,000 goes into the firepot. Since it is the only transaction in the firepot, the gains exceed the losses in the firepot. Therefore, this $35,000 gain drops down into the hotchpot. Since it is the only transaction in the hotchpot, the gains exceed the losses in the hotchpot. Hence the $35,000 gain is treated as a long-term capital gain. It is combined with T's other capital gains and losses transactions under the usual capital gains and losses rules.

Example: One Casualty Gain, One Loss on Sale of § 1231 Property—T has a casualty gain on the gold bars of $35,000, as in the previous Example. T has loss on sale of machinery used in T's small manufacturing business of $50,000. T has no other transactions subject to § 1231. The $35,000 casualty gain first goes into the firepot. Since it is a gain, it drops down into the hotchpot. In the hotchpot it is netted against the $50,000 loss on sale of § 1231 property. Since the two transactions net to a loss, the two transactions are each treated as ordinary. Thus the casualty gain goes into gross income as $35,000 of ordinary income. The loss on the § 1231 property is taken as a $50,000 ordinary loss deduction from gross income.

Example: One Sale of § 1231 Property for a Gain, One Sale of § 1231 Property for a Loss, One Condemnation of a Capital Asset for a Loss—X sells a building used in X;s trade or business for a $300,000 gain. X also sells some machinery used in X's trade or business for a $160,000 loss. A plot of vacant land held by X as an

---

[381]   Section 165(c)(2). See ¶ 7.01(5) regarding computation of casualty losses.

[382]   See ¶ 6.01 regarding whether deductions are from gross income or adjusted gross income.

[383]   See ¶ 7.01(5).

investment and not used in X's trade or business is condemned for a $100,000 loss.[384]

There are no casualties, so the only netting process goes on in the hotchpot. The three transactions in the hotchpot net out to a gain. Therefore each transaction is considered to be long-term capital. Thus there is a long-term capital gain of $300,000, a long-term capital loss of $160,000 and a long-term capital loss of $100,000. These are combined with X's other capital gains and losses (if any) from sales or exchanges of capital assets under the usual capital gain and loss rules. Note in particular that the gain on the building may be unrecaptured § 1250 gain.

There are certain implications that can be drawn from this cocktail-shaker approach to § 1231 transactions. First, it is clear that § 1231 always favors the taxpayer. The taxpayer who has a preponderance of gains in § 1231 transactions will prefer to have all those gains and losses treated as capital rather than all as ordinary—and they will all be capital. The taxpayer who has a preponderance of losses in § 1231 transactions will prefer to have all those gains and losses treated as ordinary rather than all as capital—and they will all be ordinary.[385]

Moreover, the workings of § 1231 suggest some active planning possibilities for the taxpayer who regularly has a number of § 1231 transactions during the year. The best way to handle § 1231 transactions is to group the losses and gains in separate years. If all the § 1231 losses are taken in one year and all the § 1231 gains are taken in another year, then all the losses will be ordinary (most attractive) and all the gains will be long-term capital (most attractive). This maneuver is, however, foreclosed by § 1231(c), which provides that capital gain coming out of § 1231 will be treated as ordinary to the extent that there have been ordinary losses coming out of § 1231 in the preceding five years (that have not already been applied to recapture capital gain as ordinary).

---

[384] A condemnation loss would result, of course, if the proceeds of the condemnation were less than the basis of the property condemned.

[385] Section 1231 treatment is sufficiently attractive that there has been interest in including certain transactions within its unique netting processes, even though those transactions would not otherwise have fit in on account of the property involved being in the nature of inventory. Thus Congress has specifically provided that property subject to § 1231 includes cut timber, and timber, coal, and iron ore royalties as well as unharvested crops § 1231(b)(2) and (4). § 1231 property also includes cattle and horses held by the taxpayer for draft, breeding, dairy, or sporting purposes, and held for more than 24 months, § 1231(b)(3)(A), as well as other livestock held by the taxpayer for these same purposes for at least 12 months, § 1231(b)(3)(B). § 1231 property does not include poultry, § 1231(b) flush language, so chicken farmers are out in the cold when it comes to enjoying the benefits of § 1231.

(v) *Copyrights, Literary or Other Artistic Compositions Created by the Taxpayer, Memoranda Held by the Taxpayer and Similar Property*

The categories of property excluded from capital asset status that have been discussed so far are inventory-type property, and depreciable and real property used in the trade or business. In addition, the special treatment accorded by § 1231 to depreciable and real property used in the trade or business has been discussed.

Another major category of property that is excluded from capital asset status involves copyrights, literary personal efforts created it;[386] (4) property described in (1)–(3) above if held by a taxpayer who received the property by gift or non-recognition transaction from a taxpayer described in (1)–(3) above.[387]

This class of property cannot be subject to § 1231. This would be true even though this type of property may in fact be depreciable and may in fact be used in the taxpayer-creator's trade or business.[388] Thus sale by the taxpayer-creator would always yield ordinary income or loss. If property of this type is used in the trade or business of one who acquired it by purchase (or inheritance where the step-up of basis applies), then sale of it will be eligible for § 1231 or capital asset treatment as the case may be.

Prior to the enactment of the predecessor of § 1221(a)(3), the treatment of the sale of a copyright or artistic composition by a taxpayer who created the property depended on the taxpayer's professional status. If the taxpayer were a professional, then the sale produced ordinary income; if the taxpayer were an amateur then the sale produced capital gain.[389] Drawing the line between professionals and amateurs produced problems; Congress therefore resolved to provide uniform ordinary income treatment for the sale of a product created by personal effort.[390]

A major definitional problem with the present statute relates to what is "similar property." The Regulations provide that "similar

---

[386] Section 1221(a)(3).

[387] Section 1221(a)(3)(C). Conversely, a taxpayer who acquired such property by purchase could hold the property as a capital asset, or as property used in the trade or business.

[388] Reg. § 1.1231–1(c)(1)(ii). Cf. Rev.Rul. 55–706, 1955–2 C.B. 300 (films created by a publicly-held corporation which paid fair market value for the multiplicity of skills of the many people involved in making the film were not held by the corporation as § 1221(a)(3) property, because the corporation had not "created" the films. Thus the films were properly subject to § 1231 on their sale.)

[389] See Senate Finance Committee Report, S.Rep. No. 2375, 81st Cong., 2d Sess. 43, 83–84 (1950); House Committee on Ways and Means Report, H.Rep. No. 2319, 81st Cong., 2d Sess. 54, 91–92 (1950).

[390] See § 210 of the Revenue Act of 1950, 64 Stat. 906, 933.

property" does include a theatrical production, a radio program, a newspaper cartoon strip, or any other property eligible for copyright protection (whether under statute or common law).[391] However, "similar" property does not include a patent, or an invention or design which may be protected only under the patent law and not under the copyright law.[392] Beyond that, the question of what is included in this category of non-capital assets has given rise to significant litigation.[393]

(vi) Patents

The life of the inventor is happier than the life of the artist, writer or musician in that the inventor has an excellent chance of enjoying long-term capital gains on the creations of the inventor's muse. If an inventor transfers for consideration "all substantial rights" or certain other interests to a patent, then under § 1235 the inventor will enjoy long-term capital gains on the transaction (regardless of how long the patent has been held), notwithstanding that the payments for the patent are (1) contingent on the

---

[391]   Reg. § 1.1221–1(c)(1). "Similar property" also includes a draft of a speech, a manuscript, a research paper, an oral recording of any type, a transcript of an oral recording, a transcript of an oral interview or of dictation, a personal or business diary, a log or journal, a corporate archive, including a corporate charter, office correspondence, a financial record, a drawing, a photograph or a dispatch, Reg. § 1.1221–1(c)(2). Many of these items listed above are of significance to former holders of high public office who may wish to sell or make a charitable contribution of their personal papers. See ¶ 7.01(8) regarding the charitable contribution of such material.

[392]   Reg. § 1.1221–1(c)(1).

[393]   See Cranford v. United States, 338 F.2d 379 (Ct.Cl.1964). In this case, taxpayer developed a format for a quiz program. He applied for copyright protection but was informed that a format for a quiz program could not be copyrighted. Taxpayer was nonetheless able to sell this format, and it ultimately became the radio program "Take It or Leave It" and the television program "The $64,000 Question." In seeking capital gain on the proceeds of the sale, taxpayer argued that since the format could not be copyrighted, it was not "similar property," under § 1221(a)(3), and hence it was not excluded from the definition of capital asset. The court held the format was "similar property" although it was not subject to copyright, and hence the taxpayer received ordinary gain.

See also Stern v. United States, 164 F.Supp. 847 (E.D.La.1958), aff'd per curiam 262 F.2d 957 (5th Cir.1959), cert. denied 359 U.S. 969, 79 S.Ct. 880, 3 L.Ed.2d 836 (1959) (sale of movie rights to the character "Francis the Talking Mule" gave rise to ordinary income because it was "similar property" regardless of its susceptibility to copyright); Commissioner v. Ferrer, 304 F.2d 125 (2d Cir.1962) (rights of actor-turned producer Jose Ferrer in the play production of the novel "Moulin Rouge" based on the life of Toulouse-Lautrec were not covered by § 1221(a)(3). As Judge Friendly noted, "The difficulties Mr. Ferrer must have had in fitting himself into the shape of the artist can hardly have been greater than ours in determining whether the transaction here at issue fits the rubric 'gain from the sale or exchange of a capital asset . . .' "); see Eustice, "Contract Rights, Capital Gain and Assignment of Income—The Ferrer Case," 20 Tax L.Rev. 1 (1964).

productivity of the patent or (2) coterminous with the transferee's use of the patent.[394]

Payments which are contingent on use and/or coterminous with use of the transferee look at first blush like royalties, giving rise to ordinary income treatment.[395] However, even outside of § 1235, where patents, copyrights, literary or artistic and similar property are transferred for contingent payments, or payments coterminous with use, the transaction will often be regarded as a sale.[396]

Just a sale or exchange is not enough to give rise to capital gain treatment to a transaction; there must be a sale or exchange of a capital asset.[397] It is in providing both capital asset status as well as the requisite sale or exchange that § 1235 insures long-term capital gains (or long-term capital loss), treatment for the transfers of patents within its ambit.

The purpose of this provision is to "provide an incentive to inventors to contribute to the welfare of the Nation."[398] Without this provision professional inventors, and possibly amateur inventors as well, would have the sale of their patents treated as ordinary gain.[399] Section 1235 makes it clear that professional as well as amateur inventors are entitled to capital gain treatment on the sale of all substantial rights in their patents.[400] In addition to the inventor, one who purchases the inventor's interest in the patent prior to the actual reduction of the invention to practice also will have long-term capital gain on the subsequent sale of the interest in the patent. This will be true regardless of how long the interest has been held and notwithstanding that on such subsequent sale the consideration is in the nature of royalties, payable over a period coterminous with the transferee's use or contingent on the productivity of the patent.[401] The inventor and the person who purchases his interest in the patent

---

[394]   Section 1235(a)(1) and (2); Reg. § 1.1235–1(a). "Patent" means a patent granted under the provisions of Title 35 of the United States Code, or any foreign patent granting rights generally similar to those under a United States patent. It is not necessary that the patent or patent application for the invention be in existence if the requirements of § 1235 are otherwise met, Reg. § 1.1235–2(a).

[395]   See ¶ 3.05.

[396]   See ¶ 3.05.

[397]   See ¶ 4.06.

[398]   S.Rep. No. 1622 83rd Cong., 2d Sess. 439 (1954). It might be argued that inventors already receive sufficient incentive by virtue of receiving the patent itself.

[399]   Cf. Edward C. Myers, 6 T.C. 258 (1946) (amateur inventor had capital gain on the transfer of all substantial rights in a patent notwithstanding consideration was contingent on quantity of articles sold under the patent). The acquiescence in this case was withdrawn, Mim. 6490, 1950–1 C.B. 9; Rev.Rul. 55–58, 1955–1 C.B. 97 (patents sold for royalty arrangements gave rise to ordinary income for years not covered by § 1235); United States v. Zacks, 375 U.S. 59, 84 S.Ct. 178, 11 L.Ed.2d 128 (1963).

[400]   Reg. § 1.1235–1(d)(3).

[401]   Section 1235(a) and (b)(2).

from the inventor are considered a "holder" of the patent for these purposes.[402]

Not just any transfer of patent rights by a "holder" will qualify for the long-term capital gain (or loss) treatment of § 1235. The transfer by the "holder" of the patent must be of either (1) "all substantial rights to the patent" or (2) an "undivided interest therein which includes a part of all such rights."[403]

"All substantial rights" to a patent means all rights (whether or not then held by the holder) which are of value at the time the rights to the patent are transferred. Thus "all substantial rights to a patent" would not be transferred if the grant of rights was limited geographically within the country of issuance, was limited in time to a period less than the remaining life of the patent, was limited to certain fields of use, or was limited to less than all claims or inventions covered by the patent which have value at the time of the transfer.[404]

An "undivided interest" in all substantial rights to a patent means the same fractional share of each and every substantial right to the patent. An "undivided interest" therefore would not include the right to income from a patent limited geographically or limited in time to less than the remaining life of the patent.[405]

---

[402] Section 1235(b). An "inventor" for the purposes of qualifying as a "holder" is one whose efforts created the patent property and who would qualify as the "original and first" inventor, or joint inventor, within the meaning of Title 35 of the United States Code, Reg. § 1.1235–2(d)(1)(i).

In order to qualify as a "holder" the purchaser of the patent must meet a number of tests. The purchaser cannot be the employer of the inventor at the time of the transaction, nor can the purchaser be related to the inventor, as defined, § 1235(b)(1) and (2), § 1235(d) (Regs. §§ 1.1235–2(d)(1)(ii), 1.1235–2). In addition the purchaser must have purchased the interest prior to its actual reduction to practice, Reg. § 1.1235–1(d)(1)(ii). "Actual reduction to practice" for these purposes has the same meaning as it does under § 102(g) of Title 35 of the United States Code. Generally, an invention is reduced to actual practice when it has been tested and operated successfully under operating conditions. This may occur either before or after application for a patent but cannot occur later than the earliest time that commercial exploitation of the invention occurs, Regs. § 1.1235–2(e).

Thus does the statute attempt to provide incentive to inventors and to those who would invest in the promotion of the patent before its commercial use becomes established. It is only they who qualify as holders and who can therefore enjoy capital gains under § 1235.

[403] Section 1235(a). Cf. Hooker Chemicals and Plastics Corp. v. United States, 219 Ct.Cl. 161, 591 F.2d 652 (1979) (reservation of right to sell in transferee's territory did not destroy "sale").

[404] Reg. § 1.1235–2(b), also providing that the circumstances of the whole transaction rather than the particular terminology used in the instrument of transfer shall be considered in determining whether or not all substantial rights to the patent have been transferred in a transaction. See Estate of Klein v. Commissioner, 507 F.2d 617 (7th Cir.1974), cert. denied 421 U.S. 991, 95 S.Ct. 1998, 44 L.Ed.2d 482 (1975).

[405] Reg. § 1.1235–2(c). See also S.Rep. No. 1622, 83rd Cong. 2d Sess. 439 (1954).

A "holder" of a patent for the capital gain purposes of § 1235 may only be an individual.[406] However, where a partnership owns the patent, each individual member of the partnership may be a holder as to his share of the patent owned by the partnership.[407]

This attractive treatment of the "holders" of patents under § 1235 is in contrast to the relatively unattractive treatment of their transferees. According to the Regulations, payments made by the transferee of patent rights in a transaction qualifying under § 1235 must be capitalized (and recovered through amortization) rather than immediately deducted.[408] Some case law has suggested techniques around this problem.[409]

(vii) Recapture of Depreciation

Yet another way in which the tax law provides special rules for characterizing transactions is in the area of so-called "recapture" of depreciation. The necessity for the specialized recapture rules arises from the fact that property subject to the depreciation deduction[410] is often sold for gain. This is the case because the taking of depreciation has caused the basis of the property to decline[411] while the fair market value of the property may not have declined as fast, or the fair market value may indeed have risen. The gain on the sale or exchange of such depreciable property will go into § 1231, where it could very well come out treated as a capital gain.[412] Thus has the taxpayer been able to take depreciation deductions, which reduce ordinary income, but pay a compensating tax at only capital gains rates. The advantage of this can be quite striking for the high bracket taxpayer.

As a numerical example: T, at all times in the tax 35% bracket due to high ordinary income, buys a machine for use in T's trade or business for $100,000. It has a useful life under the depreciation rules

---

Note that this "undivided interest" approach to ascertaining capital gains treatment is fundamentally inconsistent with the approach for ascertaining capital gains treatment in the assignment of income area. In the assignment of income area "vertical cuts" are what give rise to capital gains, whereas the "undivided interest" approach of § 1235 involves a "horizontal cut." See ¶ 5.03.

[406]   Section 1235(b).

[407]   Reg. § 1.1235–2(d)(2).

[408]   Reg. § 1.1235–1(d).

[409]   Associated Patentees, Inc., 4 T.C. 979 (1945) (acq.); Allied Tube & Conduit Corp., 34 T.C.M. 1218 (1975).

See generally, Morreale, "Patents, Know-How and Trade-Marks: A Tax Overview," 29 Tax Lawyer 533 (1976); Pansius, "Fruit and Roots: Transfers of Patents and the Shared Rights Test of Capital Gain," 54 Notre Dame Lawyer 846 (1979).

[410]   See ¶ 6.02(12).

[411]   Section 1016 and see ¶ 4.03(g).

[412]   See ¶ 4.06(3)(a)(iv).

of 10 years and may be depreciated under the straight-line method (see ¶ 6.02(12)).

At the end of the 10 years, when the machine has a basis of 0, T sells the machine for $100,000. As a matter of economic reality nothing happened to T on this transaction in terms of value. T bought a machine for $100,000 and sold it 10 years later for $100,000 because the market for this type of machine remained strong. But while nothing happened as a matter of economic reality, the tax consequences to T of this transaction were far-reaching indeed.

Over the course of the 10 years T took $100,000 of depreciation deductions. If T was in the 35% combined bracket over this period, these depreciation deductions saved $35,000 in taxes. The sale by T of the machine yields $100,000 of gain, since T's basis after the depreciation is now 0. The gain goes into § 1231 and could very well be long-term capital gain under that provision's netting processes (see ¶ 4.06(3)(a)(iv)). If there were no "recapture of depreciation," the $100,000 long-term capital gain is taxed at 15%, and the tax on the transaction is $15,000 (see ¶ 4.06(2)(b)(i)). Thus T has a net tax savings of $20,000 ($35,000 taxes saved by the depreciation deduction less $15,000 15 percent capital gains tax paid). Thus even if the machine produces no net income, the investment has been profitable simply on account of the ability to take depreciation deductions and pay only a compensating capital gains tax.[413] T in this sense is said to have "converted ordinary income into capital gains."

This attractive pattern has long been (and still is in some cases) a basic building block of tax shelters.[414] In order to try to close up this particular advantage Congress in 1962 enacted "recapture" provisions.

Various recapture provisions apply to various types of transactions, recapturing varying amounts of the gain attributable to depreciation. The major recapture provisions are § 1245, applying generally to depreciable personal property;[415] and § 1250, applying generally to depreciable real property.

The basic theory of recapture is that the gain on the sale of depreciable property which is attributable to previously taken depreciation is deemed to be ordinary gain.

Section 1245, added to the Code in 1962, applies to personal property (i.e. not real estate) such as machinery, equipment, and vehicles. Section 1245 provides that a taxpayer's gain from the sale

---

[413]   Beyond the advantages discussed in the text it should be noted that T has been able to defer payment of his taxes.

[414]   For more on tax shelters see chapter 8.

[415]   Section 1245(a)(3) and (4).

of property attributable to previously taken depreciation will taxed as ordinary income. Thus in our example above the entire amount of the $100,000 gain would be ordinary and taxed at the 35% rate, yielding a tax of $35,000. This makes sense inasmuch as the taxpayer took depreciation, with its tax advantages, and yet the machine did not actually decline in value economically. It is therefore only fair that the taxpayer pay tax in full on the gain on sale to make up for the previous economically inaccurate depreciation deduction.

As a further example consider the same facts as above except that T only depreciates the machine for 6 years (thus $60,000 of depreciation against ordinary income and a basis in the machine of $40,000) and then sells the machine for $130,000. Then T would have realized and recognized gain of $90,000 (amount realized of $130,000 less adjusted basis of $40,000). Under the recapture rule of § 1245, the character of the gain would be as follows. $60,000 is ordinary income, not involved in the netting process of § 1231. This is because of the $90,000 gain, $60,000 was due to previously taken depreciation. This is the automatic result, without reference to § 1231. The $60,000 of gain due to previously taken depreciation does not go into § 1231 or have anything to do with the netting procedures of that section. The remaining $30,000 of gain goes into the § 1231 hotchpot where it may turn out to be ordinary income or capital gain, depending on the other transactions in the pot. If there are no other transactions in the pot, then the $30,000 would be a capital gain under the usual § 1231 rules, qualifying for the 15 percent rate group in this case.

Section 1250, added to the Code in 1964, applies to real estate. It provides, in general, that the only gain recaptured on the sale of real estate is the excess of accelerated depreciation over straight line. Moreover, it is only meaningful prior to 1986. Since 1986, only straight line depreciation is allowed on real estate. However, there is still some real estate out there that has been held prior to 1986 on which some accelerated depreciation was taken. It is that pre-1986 excess of accelerated over straight line depreciation that § 1250 recaptures at ordinary income rates.

To illustrate what this means, consider this example. Assume T purchases an office building for $100,000 in 1975 and it has a useful life under the statute of 30 years. Suppose T can properly under the statute depreciate the building on the double declining-balance method. Straight line depreciation in the first year would be $3,333. Thus double declining balance would be $6,666. T then sells the building for $100,000 after one year. The gain is computed as the excess of the $100,000 amount realized over the $93,334 adjusted basis, or $6,666. Under the statute, the excess of accelerated depreciation over straight line for the first year is $3,333. This is the $6,666 of depreciation allowed on the accelerated method, less the $3,333 allowed on the straight-line method.

Thus on the sale of this building for $100,000, $3,333 of the gain would be ordinary and $3,333 would go into the § 1231 hotchpot. Note that if the building were instead a machine, then § 1245 would apply to this transaction and the entire gain of $6,666 would be ordinary. That is the difference between the "strong" recapture rule of § 1245, which applies generally to personal property, and the "weak" recapture rule of § 1250, which applies generally to real estate.

As pointed out above, in fact the present depreciation rule, since 1986, with respect to real estate is that it can only be depreciated under the straight-line method. Therefore, while § 1250 is on the books, it does not currently apply. However, it does apply to the gain attributable to the excess of accelerated depreciation over straight line on the sale of real estate which was put in service before 1986 and subjected to accelerated depreciation. Thus there could be some recapture of depreciation on real estate sold this year, if it had been subjected to accelerated depreciation prior to 1986. For an example of the complexities of taxing gains on real estate see ¶ 4.06(2)(b)(i)— Special Case of Real Estate.

Sections 1245 and 1250 generally do not affect the amount of gain or loss realized on a transaction. With respect to recognition, §§ 1245 and 1250 override some non-recognition provisions but not others.

With respect to like-kind exchanges under § 1031 and involuntary conversion rollovers under § 1033,[416] §§ 1245 and 1250 do not cause any additional gain to be recognized beyond that which would be recognized under § 1031 or 1033.[417] However, to the extent that realized gain is not recognized by virtue of § 1031 or 1033, §§ 1245 and 1250 provide that the remaining unrecognized gain subject to recapture will be preserved on the basis of the new property in the taxpayer's hands.[418]

As the previous discussion has indicated, with respect to the relationship to § 1231, the recognized gain subject to recapture comes out before consideration of § 1231. Only the recognized gain beyond that which is subject to recapture goes into § 1231.[419]

---

[416] See ¶¶ 4.05(2) and (3).

[417] Sections 1245(b)(3), 1250(d)(3).

[418] Regs. §§ 1.1245–2(c)(4); 1.1250–3(d)(5).

[419] Regs. §§ 1.1245–6(a); 1.1250–1(c)(1).

The workings of § 1245 are illustrated by the following further examples:

Example: Jones sells machine A that he has used in his trade or business for $20,000. Machine A had a basis in Jones' hands before the sale of $10,000. Jones' original cost basis for machine A was $16,000, the basis having been reduced to $10,000 by the taking of depreciation computed on the straight-line method.[420] Jones' gain realized on the transaction is $10,000. Since no non-recognition provision applies, all the gain is recognized. Since $6,000 of the gain is attributable to previously taken depreciation, $6,000 of the gain is characterized as ordinary by § 1245. The other $4,000 of gain goes into § 1231, where it may very well come out as capital, depending on the other transactions in § 1231. Had machine A been sold for $12,000, all the $2,000 gain would have been ordinary and nothing would have passed into § 1231.

Example: Smith exchanges machine B that she has used in her trade or business with a fair market value of $17,000 for machine C with a fair market value of $16,000 and $1,000 cash, in a transaction subject to § 1031. Before the transaction machine B had a basis in Smith's hands of $10,000. Smith's original cost basis in machine B was $15,000, the basis having been reduced to $10,000 by the taking of depreciation computed on the straight-line method. Smith's gain realized on the transaction is $7,000 (amount realized of $17,000 minus adjusted basis of $10,000). Smith's gain recognized on the transaction is $1,000 (the amount of the "boot" received in the § 1031 exchange). This $1,000 is ordinary gain, under § 1245. Nothing passes into § 1231. Smith's basis on machine C is $10,000.[421] The $4,000 unrecognized recapture is preserved on machine C. Smith holds machine C for one year, properly taking $1,000 depreciation on it, reducing her basis to $9,000. She then sells it for $16,500. Her gain realized on that transaction is $7,500 ($16,500 amount realized less $9,000 adjusted basis). All that gain is recognized, since no nonrecognition transaction applies to the sale. With respect to the character of the gain, $5,000 of the $7,500 gain will be ordinary. This is made up of the $4,000 preserved recapture from the § 1031 transaction and $1,000 recapture

---

[420] See ¶ 6.02(12).
[421] See ¶ 4.05(2).

from the one year's depreciation taken by Smith on machine C.[422] The rest of the gain goes into § 1231.

If the gain on the sale of property subject to recapture is reported on the installment method, recapture applies first, deeming all the gain first reported as ordinary.[423]

(viii) Sale of Depreciable Property to a Related Party

In general, if depreciable property is sold at a gain, that gain in excess of what is recaptured at ordinary rates will likely be capital.[424] The sale will of course result in a new basis to the buyer, who can use that basis for purposes of computing depreciation. This fortuitous circumstance could naturally lead the astute tax planner to engineer the following transaction: Taxpayer sells real estate for a substantial capital gain to Taxpayer's controlled corporation, which then rents the property out, having the advantage of a high basis for purposes of depreciation. Thus does the taxpayer reap the golden harvest of capital gain and deductions against ordinary income (while, it might be noted, still retaining control of the property). Such stratagems were available until 1958 when § 1239 came upon the scene to provide ordinary income treatment on the sale or exchange between related parties of property subject to the allowance for depreciation in the hands of the transferee.

Prior to the Tax Reform Act of 1976, the "related parties" for purposes of § 1239 were husband and wife, or individual and corporation where more than 80 percent of the value of the stock of the corporation was owned by the individual, his spouse, and his minor children and minor grandchildren. The Service and taxpayers were in dispute over sales between brother-sister corporations that were more than 80 percent owned by the taxpayer. The Service maintained that such transactions were "indirectly" sales between an individual and his controlled corporation and hence within the ambit of § 1239, but the case law went the other way.[425]

The Tax Reform Act of 1976 resolved this matter decisively in the Service's favor, providing that "related persons" includes two or more corporations where 80 percent or more in value of their stock is owned by or for the same individual.[426] Moreover, the Service's

---

[422]   See Reg. § 1.1245–2(c)(4)(iii) Example (1). The treatment under § 1033 is analogous.

[423]   Reg. § 1.1245–6(d).

[424]   Section 1231 will, of course, control the transaction, and if its "netting" process is positive, the gain in excess of recapture will be capital.

[425]   Miller v. Commissioner, 510 F.2d 230 (9th Cir.1975); 10-42 Corp., 55 T.C. 593 (1971), nonacq. 1972–2 C.B. 4; Rev.Rul. 69–109, 1969–1 C.B. 202.

[426]   Section 1239(b)(3).

legislative victory in this arena also included incorporation of the attribution rules of § 318 of the Code to ascertain whether or not 80 percent or more of a corporation's stock is owned by an individual.[427]

However, an individual's family for purposes of the attribution rules includes only the relevant party and spouse and the entity ownership attribution rules are applied without regard to the percentage limitations of § 318(a)(2)(C) (by virtue of § 1239(c)(2)).

The Committee Reports[428] provide an example of a way in which the constructive ownership rules could apply in the Section 1239 setting:[429]

> An individual who owns 80 percent of the stock of a parent company will also constructively own 80 percent of the wholly-owned subsidiary;[430] hence, the two corporations will be related parties, and transactions in depreciable property between the parent and the subsidiary will be governed by § 1239 rules.[431]

(ix) Accounts Receivable

In addition to the variegated transactions described above, there are a number of other transactions and types of property that are specially endowed by the Code with capital or ordinary character. Accounts receivable are, not surprisingly, regarded as ordinary assets and hence their sale will give rise to ordinary gain or loss.[432] This would be expected inasmuch as the sale of inventory yields ordinary income, as discussed above.

(x)   Transfers of Franchises, Trademarks and Trade Names

A transfer of a franchise, trademark, or trade name is not regarded as a sale or exchange of a capital asset if the transferor retains any significant power, right, or continuing interest with respect to it.[433] A significant power, right, or continuing interest includes various managerial powers,[434] as well as a significant right

---

[427]   Section 1239(c).

[428]   Staff of the Joint Comm. on Taxation, General Explanation of the Tax Reform Act of 1976 653 (1976).

[429]   Section 1239(c).

[430]   Section 318(a)(2)(C).

[431]   Sections 318(a)(2)(C), 1239(c).

[432]   Section 1221(a)(4).

[433]   Section 1253.

[434]   Section 1253(b)(2)(A)–(E).

to receive payments contingent on the productivity or use of the interest transferred.[435]

(xi) Cancellation of Lease or Distributor's Agreement

Amounts received by a lessee for the cancellation of a lease, or by a distributor of goods for the cancellation of a distributor's agreement (if the distributor has a substantial capital investment in the distributorship), are considered by the Code as amounts received in a sale or exchange for such lease or agreement.[436] This statutory sale or exchange does not, of course, guarantee capital gain or loss treatment. For such treatment the lease or distributorship must also be a capital asset in the hands of the lessee or distributor. This will depend on the individual facts of the case. The probability is that the lease or distributorship is not a capital asset but is depreciable property in the hands of the lessee or distributor used in a trade or business. In that event the statutory sale or exchange treatment of the cancellation will usually cause the transaction to be treated under § 1231, which applies to the sale or exchange of depreciable property used in the trade or business.[437]

(xii) Retirement of Bonds

The general rule is that the collection of a claim is not a sale or exchange and therefore cannot give rise to capital gain or loss treatment.[438] However the retirement of a corporate or government bond which is a capital asset in the hands of a taxpayer is accorded sale or exchange treatment.[439] Therefore capital gain or loss will result on such transactions measured as usual by the amount received on retirement (usually the face amount), less the taxpayer's basis. Compare in this connection the discussion of original issue discount at ¶ 3.02.

(xiii) Worthless Securities

When securities which are capital assets in the hands of the taxpayer become worthless, the loss is treated as a loss from the sale or exchange of a capital asset on the last day of the taxable year.[440]

---

[435] Section 1253(b)(2)(F). Such contingent payments would be deductible by the transferee, § 1253(d)(1). Any noncontingent payments in the transaction must be deducted according to particular rules, § 1253(d)(2).

[436] Section 1241.

[437] See ¶ 4.06(3)(a)(iv). Cf. Gray v. Commissioner, 642 F.2d 320 (9th Cir.1981) (payments in form for cancellation of lease of almond grove not governed by § 1241 but rather were a return of previously deducted advance rent and hence ordinary income, not capital gain.).

[438] See Fairbanks v. United States, 306 U.S. 436, 59 S.Ct. 607, 83 L.Ed. 855 (1939).

[439] Section 1271(a)(1).

[440] Section 165(g)(1).

"Securities" for this purpose are defined as a share of stock in a corporation, a right to subscribe to a share of stock in a corporation, or a bond, note, or other evidence of indebtedness issued by a corporation with interest coupons or in registered form.[441] This statutory sale or exchange, of course, leads to an unattractive result. The loss, instead of being ordinary, will be capital. Whether the capital loss is short-term or long-term will depend on whether the statutory "end of the year" holding period,[442] coupled with the period the taxpayer has actually held the security, will give rise to a short-term or a long-term holding period. In either event, of course, the result is less attractive than an ordinary loss.

(xiv) Bad Debts

A "business bad debt" is regarded as an ordinary loss,[443] whereas a "non-business bad debt" is treated as a less attractive short-term capital loss (regardless of the period of time of the debt's existence).[444] Where a taxpayer undergoes a bad-debt loss as an investor, the loss will be treated as a non-business bad debt. For the taxpayer to enjoy a business bad-debt deduction, the debt must arise out of a business in which the taxpayer is actively engaged.[445]

(xv) General Comments on the Sale or Exchange Requirement

As we have previously indicated, in order to receive capital treatment there must be a sale or exchange of a capital asset. The "sale or exchange" prong is often examined to determine whether there is an event that causes the need to recognize gain. However, in some very interesting instances, the sale or exchange requirement has also been used to argue for ordinary, instead of capital, treatment. For example, in *Nahey v. Commissioner*,[446] a business with a pending suit against Xerox for breach of contract was

---

[441] Section 165(g)(2).

[442] The purpose of this "end of the year" holding period is to obviate the necessity of determining on which particular day of the taxable year the security became worthless.

[443] Section 166(a).

[444] Section 166(d).

[445] Whipple v. Commissioner, 373 U.S. 193, 83 S.Ct. 1168, 10 L.Ed.2d 288 (1963), reh'g denied 374 U.S. 858, 83 S.Ct. 1863, 10 L.Ed.2d 1082 (1963) (losses on loans made by taxpayer to his closely-held corporation were nonbusiness bad debts, notwithstanding that he devoted time and energy to the corporation, the Court implying that the taxpayer would have had to be in the business of promoting and financing corporations to enjoy a business bad debt deduction); United States v. Generes, 405 U.S. 93, 92 S.Ct. 827, 31 L.Ed.2d 62 (1972), reh'g denied 405 U.S. 1033, 92 S.Ct. 1274, 31 L.Ed.2d 491 (1972) (test for a business debt is that the business motivation be dominant rather than just significant; on the facts, taxpayer's loan to his business found to be a nonbusiness bad debt).

[446] 196 F.3d 866 (7th Cir.1999), cert. denied 531 U.S. 812, 121 S.Ct. 45, 148 L.Ed.2d 15 (2000).

purchased by another company. The new company settled the suit and received approximately $6 million. The new company argued that it was entitled to capital treatment because the settlement proceeds were in fact part of the purchase price. (This assumes the new company knew it was going to receive the settlement and adjusted the price it was willing to pay accordingly). The Tax Court rejected capital gains treatment, not only because the character of the gain was ordinary, but also because there was no sale or exchange. The Tax Court held that the settlement was not a sale or exchange.[447]

The court of appeals upheld the Tax Court's decision but on other grounds. The Seventh Circuit concluded that the proceeds would have been ordinary income if received by the original owner, and that the sale of the company should not change the character of the gain. Thus, it is still open whether the settlement of a claim can lead to capital treatment. It seems, however, fairly clear that a settlement of a claim involving a capital asset should get capital treatment and the settlement of a claim involving ordinary income should be treated as ordinary income. This logically follows from the origin of the claim doctrine discussed, supra ¶ 6.02(3).

(b) Planning Implications: Sale of a Going Business

As the preceding discussion has indicated, the capital gains rules are far-reaching indeed. Capital gains taxation can have significant planning impact on major transactions, such as sale of a going business, choice of the form of doing business, and on a number of corporate transactions. Problems are particularly acute where a going business is sold.

There are four major forms of doing business—the corporation, the partnership, the limited liability company, and the sole proprietorship. When an ongoing business in corporate form is sold, it may be sold in one of two basic ways: either the stock of the corporation may be sold or the assets of the corporation may be sold. Where the stock is sold, the transaction in general gives rise to

---

[447] Some courts have taken a very strict view regarding the sale or exchange requirement. See Lee v. Commissioner, 119 F.2d 946 (7th Cir.1941) (settlement of obligation not a sale or exchange); Hale v. Helvering, 85 F.2d 819 (D.C.Cir.1936) (compromise of a promissory notes did not constitute sale or exchange); Towers v. Commissioner, 24 T.C. 199, 231 (1955) (amount received in satisfaction of a claim was not a sale or exchange); Ogilvie v. Commissioner, 216 F.2d 748 (6th Cir. 1954) (amount paid to third-party purchaser of a judgment in settlement of a judgment not a sale or exchange); Fahey v. Commissioner, 16 T.C. 105 (1951) (compromise of a note not a sale); Rosenzweig v. Commissioner, 1 T.C. 24 (1942) (amount received in settlement of copyright infringement suit is not capital gain because settlement is not sale or exchange of a capital asset).

capital gain (or loss) treatment to the shareholders.[448] Where the assets of the corporation are sold, the character of the gain or loss to the corporation will depend on the character of the various assets in the hands of the corporation. However, on subsequent liquidation of the corporation and distribution of the proceeds of the sale, the stockholders will in general enjoy capital gain (or loss) treatment. Thus as a general matter, when the business that is sold is in corporate form, the sale will ultimately give rise to capital gain (or loss) to the shareholders.

With respect to a business in a partnership form or limited liability form, it is also generally true that the sale of a partnership interest gives rise to capital gain (or loss) treatment to the selling partner, although this may be overridden in some circumstances.[449] The character of the gain on the sale of the partnership assets by the partnership is passed through to the partners, with much the result as described below for the sale of a sole proprietorship. Limited liability companies are treated the same as partnerships for tax purposes.

The sale of a going business in a sole proprietorship form is treated as the sale of the collection of the individual assets of the business by the individual owner, under the case of *Williams v. McGowan*.[450] Therefore the sale necessitates an allocation of the purchase price among the various assets of the business. As to important aspects of this allocation, the buyer and seller have adverse interests.

Often the sale of a going business sole proprietorship is negotiated for at an overall fixed price. Take the usual case where the business is operated for some years and is sold for a fixed price which is an overall gain to the seller. The task then becomes one of allocating that fixed price among the various assets of the business. These assets will involve some or all of the following: inventory, accounts receivable, cash, § 1231 assets, perhaps some undeveloped land held as an investment, covenant not to compete, and goodwill. Obviously, the sales price must be allocated to these types of property within some bounds of reality. However, within the bounds of reality, there may well be scope for negotiation between the parties as to how the sales proceeds should be allocated among their various types of property to gain tax advantage.

---

[448]   This would generally be the case, unless the corporation were found to be a collapsible corporation, see § 341.

[449]   Sections 741, 751.

[450]   152 F.2d 570 (2d Cir.1945).

The seller will want to allocate the bulk of the sales price to assets which yield a capital gain to take advantage of one of the several attractive capital gain rates, as opposed to an ordinary gain. This will conflict at least in some cases with the buyer's desire to allocate the bulk of the sales price to assets which yield ordinary gain—so as to minimize ordinary gain or give rise to an ordinary loss on subsequent sale. The buyer will also be interested in allocating a substantial amount of the sales price to depreciable or amortizable property, so as to maximize the basis for deducting depreciation.

What this means in terms of the particular assets involved would be the following: As to inventory, an ordinary asset,[451] the seller would wish to allocate relatively less to it and the buyer would wish to allocate relatively more to it. The same could be said for accounts receivable,[452] although the value of the accounts receivable will of course be heavily controlled by their face amount.

The parties would change points of view as to, say, undeveloped land held as an investment, or any other "pure" capital asset sold as part of the business. With respect to such "pure" capital assets, the seller would wish to allocate relatively more to them, so as to maximize the amount of the gain on the sale that is characterized as capital.[453] The buyer would wish to allocate relatively less to them. This would be the buyer's approach so that the buyer could have a low basis on his capital assets (rather than on the ordinary assets) in the event of subsequent sale. Even if the buyer does not anticipate a subsequent sale in the near future, the buyer prefers to have a low basis on pure capital assets—such as undeveloped land—which are not depreciable.

Regarding § 1231 property, it rolls out like this. If the seller expects a gain to result from § 1231 transactions[454] (as may well be the case), the seller may be happy to allocate a substantial amount of the sales price to the § 1231 assets. This would be because the seller would want to "tip" the workings of § 1231 to crank out to a gain, yielding capital gains. Furthermore, the seller would want to have more of the overall gain attributable to assets giving rise to capital

[451]   Section 1221(a)(1), ¶ 4.06(3)(a)(i).

[452]   Section 1221(a)(4), ¶ 4.06(3)(a)(ix).

[453]   Assuming the asset has been held for longer than one year so as to qualify for favorable treatment. Another example of "pure" capital assets that might be sold as part of the business in addition to undeveloped land held as an investment would be stock of a closely-held corporation. This would usually be a capital asset (see § 1221) and, since it is not traded on a securities market, its value would be open to negotiation between the parties.

If the stock were a "Corn Products asset", see ¶ 4.06(3)(a)(ii), it would then not be a capital asset, and the parties' points of view would be reversed.

[454]   See ¶ 4.06(3)(a)(iv).

gains. Since the buyer will often be depreciating the § 1231 property, the buyer too may be happy to allocate a substantial portion of the purchase price to § 1231 property. Thus it would not be surprising to find in many cases a relatively great portion of the sales proceeds allocated to § 1231 property. Where, however, the seller will undergo a substantial amount of depreciation recapture on the sale of § 1231 property, the seller will wish to allocate a relatively small amount of the sales price to the § 1231 property.[455]

Matters become exquisitely difficult when it comes to the covenant not to compete and goodwill. The giving of a covenant not to compete by the seller of a business gives rise to ordinary income to the seller.[456] This is generally on the theory that compensation not to work is very similar to compensation to work, and should similarly give rise to ordinary income. As to the buyer, a covenant not to compete for a period of years is amortizable over 15 years under § 197.[457]

Goodwill, by contrast, is a capital asset.[458] Therefore, the sale of goodwill for gain yields attractive capital gains to the seller. But under § 197 goodwill that is acquired (not goodwill you create) can also be written off over 15 years.

Thus the seller and buyer are not adverse in their view of how much of the sales price should be allocated to these two closely-related intangible assets, goodwill and covenant not to compete. The seller wants more allocated to goodwill (to get capital gain) and the buyer does not care (since the buyer deducts either goodwill or a covenant not to compete over 15 years). The result is that in these transactions we see large amounts allocated to goodwill and small amounts allocated to covenants not to compete.

Therefore, with regard to some of the property that is transferred in the sale of a going business, the buyer and seller are adverse in their view of how much of the overall fixed sales price should be allocated to each of the types of property. The places in

---

[455] See ¶ 4.06(3)(a)(vii) regarding depreciation recapture.

[456] Rev.Rul. 69–643, 1969–2 C.B. 10; Ullman v. Commissioner, 264 F.2d 305 (2d Cir.1959) (covenants not to compete executed in conjunction with the sale of stock of linen supply corporations gave rise to ordinary income).

[457] See ¶ 6.02(13)(d).

[458] Prior to the enactment of § 197 the traditional view of goodwill was that it is a capital asset because it does not come within any of the exceptions of IRC § 1221. See ¶ 4.06(3)(a). See generally Beghe, "Income Tax Treatment of Covenants Not to Compete, Consulting Agreements and Transfers of Good Will," 30 Tax Lawyer 587 (1977). After the enactment of § 197, providing for the amortization of goodwill, it is possible that goodwill has become a § 1221(a)(2)–§ 1231 asset. The discussion in the text will assume that goodwill continues as a capital asset.

which the buyer and seller may not have adverse views is the § 1231 property, and the covenant not to compete-goodwill dichotomy.

There is, therefore, a "three-cornered" game involved in the sale of a going business involving the buyer, the seller, and the Service. Varying approaches have been tried by the parties involved. For example, the buyer and the seller could report the allocation of the sales price inconsistently, each allocating it the way it chooses to attain maximum tax advantage. Where that occurs the Service can be expected to contest the allocation of either or both parties. The outcome of any such litigation could be similarly inconsistent— particularly if the cases arise in different courts, as they well might.[459] If the Service challenges both parties and wins in one case, it will generally concede in the other case so as to avoid collecting two deficiencies in inconsistent cases.[460] The Service may be expected to press for a victory in the case which has the most attractive precedential value.

The parties may well attempt to control their tax destinies in these cases by agreeing on an allocation of the purchase price of the business as part of the sales contract. The Service might respect this allocation since, as discussed above, the parties are adverse in some of their interests as to how the sales price will be allocated. However, if one party is in a substantially higher marginal bracket than the other, the parties may plan to give the tax benefits to the higher-bracket party in exchange for concessions by that higher-tax-bracket party on the sales price. In such an event, the Service can challenge the contractual sales price allocation.[461]

If, for various reasons, the allocation of the sales proceeds must be judicially determined, the greatest problem is presented in the allocation between the covenant not to compete and goodwill. Obviously, these two intangible assets are closely related: the goodwill of a purchased business may mean little if the seller opens a shop across the street. Moreover, the value of such intangible assets is obviously quite speculative compared to the value of the physical assets of the business. Therefore, it is not surprising that the problem of allocating a portion of the purchase price between a covenant not

---

[459]   Generally taxpayers may litigate in the Tax Court by filing a timely petition. Taxpayers may litigate in federal district courts or the Claims Court by paying their tax and suing for a refund.

[460]   Dixie Finance Co. v. United States, 474 F.2d 501 (5th Cir.1973). See ABA Tax Section, Final Report of Special Committee on Whipsaw, 30 Tax Lawyer 127 (1976).

[461]   A related problem arises if one of the parties is not represented by tax counsel during the sales negotiations and therefore unwittingly agrees to an unfavorable allocation of the sales proceeds. In that event it is possible for such a party to escape from being held to that allocation. The party in such a case, however, must carry an unusually heavy burden of proof, Ullman v. Commissioner, 264 F.2d 305 (2d Cir.1959); Commissioner v. Danielson, 378 F.2d 771 (3d Cir. 1967).

to compete and goodwill has spawned a good deal of litigation.[462] This litigation may be expected to continue since, as discussed above, after § 197 the parties will tend to conspire together to pick the Service's pocket.

(4) Policy Aspects of Capital Gains Taxation

Capital gains have, for most of the time since 1921, been taxed more favorably than ordinary gains. Concomitant with this favorable treatment of capital gains has gone a restrictive treatment of capital losses.[463] The type of favorable treatment for capital gains and restrictive treatment for capital losses has varied widely over the years. As the preceding discussion of the mechanics of capital gains and losses taxation has indicated, the treatment is now exceedingly complex. This complexity no doubt results from the fact that capital gains apparently do not exist as a concept separate from the Internal Revenue Code. In short, capital gains (and capital losses) are whatever the Internal Revenue Code says they are. Lacking any economic or other touchstone for defining capital gains, it is perhaps not surprising that Congress has floundered into a sea of complexity in defining them in the Code. Moreover, this lack of any definition of "real" capital gains makes discussion of the policy reasons for taxing capital gains favorably relatively difficult.

Nevertheless, there are a number of standard arguments that are advanced for according capital gains favorable tax treatment. Interestingly, there is no similar set of reasons for applying restrictive rules to capital losses. The literature appears to be devoid of any discussion of reasons why capital losses should be disfavored under the tax system. Apparently, all hands are content to accept the proposition that if capital gains are to be treated favorably, somehow capital losses should be treated restrictively to make up for it.[464] The lack of any serious independent reasons for restricting deductibility of capital losses may tend to undercut the reasons for favorably

---

[462] E.g. Proulx v. United States, 594 F.2d 832 (Ct.Cl.1979) (discussing various theories for making this allocation); Throndson v. Commissioner, 457 F.2d 1022 (9th Cir. 1972) (dental practice); Better Beverages, Inc. v. United States, 619 F.2d 424 (5th Cir.1980), rehearing denied 625 F.2d 1160 (buyer carries heavy burden of establishing a significant value in covenant not to compete where sales agreement makes no allocation).

[463] Revenue Act of 1921, P.L. No. 98, § 206(b), 42 Stat. 233; see also Revenue Act of 1924, § 206(a)(2).

[464] It might be argued that a reason for applying restrictive rules to capital losses is that capital losses are within the control of the taxpayer and therefore it is desirable to restrict the taxpayer's ability to "take advantage" of those losses. The problem with that argument is that capital losses can arise from involuntary conversions and indeed even casualty losses (see the discussion of IRC § 1231 at ¶ 4.06(3)(a)(iv)). Moreover, losses can also arise from the sale of property which is not a capital asset, in which case the loss is deductible in full, and the timing of which would be within the control of the taxpayer.

treating capital gains. The situation begins to partake of a game with certain benefits and costs—which taxpayers are invited to play if they so choose.

In any event, there are a number of traditional reasons advanced for the favorable treatment of capital gains. They are:

1. *The bunching of income.* This argument holds that gains from the sale of capital assets accrue over time but are only taxed at the point of sale. This, therefore, means that the gains will be bunched up in one taxable year and subjected to a higher rate of taxation, given the graduated rate structure. There are several possible answers to this argument. First of all, the sympathy for the taxpayer selling a capital asset which may have been held for many years and undergoing this bunching effect may be mitigated when it is noted that throughout the period that the taxpayer was enjoying this appreciation in the value of the capital asset, the taxpayer paid no tax at all. In short, the taxpayer holding an asset which has appreciated over many years has enjoyed the great advantage of deferral of what is, from an economic point of view, income. The taxpayer has, throughout this period, enjoyed the benefit of holding the appreciated asset. The taxpayer could have borrowed against its value or otherwise included it in financial planning.

A second reason for questioning the "bunching" argument is that many taxpayers enjoy capital gains every year and therefore their income is not "bunched up" in any one particular year on account of capital gains. A third reason for questioning the "bunching" argument is that many taxpayers who enjoy capital gains are already at the highest possible marginal tax bracket—without consideration of their capital gains and, therefore, the capital gains transaction does not in fact push them into any higher bracket. Finally, it may be said as to the "bunching" argument that many other taxpayers who have non-capital gains type income may also undergo wide fluctuations in their income.[465]

2. *The lock-in effect.* The lock-in argument is that since gains on the holding of capital assets are only taxed on their sale or other disposition, taxpayers holding highly appreciated assets may hesitate to sell them for fear of incurring a substantial tax. The lock-in argument is always advanced somewhat gingerly, however, since it may provide a rationale for taxing accrued gains on capital assets annually rather than waiting for them to be sold at all. Moreover, the lock-in argument would appear to hold at whatever rate taxable gains are taxed. There are no studies indicating what minimal rate

---

[465] Bunching can result from bonuses, lottery or gambling winnings, and sales of real estate that do not qualify for capital gains.

of tax would have to be applied so as not to discourage taxpayers from selling appreciated assets and reinvesting them in more productive property. One possible approach, if the lock-in effect is a serious problem, is to allow taxpayers to roll over gains on the sale of investment assets tax-free into other investment assets. Basis rules could be provided to insure the gain is ultimately taxed at full rates when the taxpayer cashes out.

3.   *Encouraging investment.* Treating capital gains favorably is often justified as an incentive to encourage investment in productive assets in the economy. The problem with this argument is that the incentive fostered by the capital gains rules is too broad. Is it part of national economic policy to encourage investment in paintings, antique furniture, stamps, and the like, which explicitly get from the statute the relatively favorable 28 percent rate? Enjoying gain due to previously taken depreciation is hardly part of national economic policy; yet it specifically gets the 25 percent rate. If the tax system is to be used to foster productive investment, apparently more refined techniques would be appropriate.

4.   *The inflation effect.* It is often argued that capital gains should be taxed more favorably since a significant portion of capital gains are illusory, in that they simply reflect the overall inflation rate in the economy. Since the gain due to the inflation is not "real," it should not be taxed so heavily. It might be answered as to this argument that many taxpayers suffer from this inflation effect. The taxpayer who has only compensation income may receive wage increases every year which do not actually increase the taxpayer's standard of living but simply keep the taxpayer in step with inflation. Such a taxpayer would be moved into higher tax brackets and pay higher taxes although the wage increase was not "real." Therefore, if the problem is that inflation is pushing taxpayers into higher brackets, a general solution to that problem should be found, instead of simply solving the problem for those who enjoy capital gains.

However these arguments finally come out, one thing is clear as to capital gains: The introduction of special treatment for capital gains into the Code creates a great deal of complexity. The rules for taxing capital gains are extremely complex (see ¶ 4.06(2)(b)(i)) and the existence of such favorable treatment puts heavy pressure on the extensive definitions of what is a capital gain (see ¶ 4.06(3)). Since there is no true economic definition of capital gains, anyone who regularly engages in a particular type of transaction may hope to have that transaction deemed a capital gain. This creates a great deal of pressure to broaden the definition of capital gains.[466]

---

[466] It is probably fair to say that the existence of capital gains is responsible for at least one-third of the size of the Internal Revenue Code.

Chapter 5

ASSIGNMENT OF INCOME: WHO IS TAXED AND THE NATURE OF THE TAX

Table of Sections

¶ 5.01 BACKGROUND

The previous chapters have considered what is included in gross income. Beyond what was said in those chapters is an additional set of problems found in that rather loosely connected body of cases and statutes that fall under the heading "assignment of income." There are two basic issues in the assignment of income field. One is who is the proper person on whom to impose a tax and the second is the character—whether capital or ordinary—of a particular item of income. While these two issues do not appear at first blush to be closely related to one another, when these two issues arise in the context of an assignment of income, the underlying concepts and problems are very similar.

Assignment of income—as the name itself implies—involves the transfer of income from one taxpayer to another before that income is received. There are two fundamental types of such assignments: gratuitous assignments and assignments for consideration.

Generally speaking the purpose of a gratuitous assignment of income is to shift income from a higher-bracket taxpayer to a lower-bracket taxpayer in the same family. The idea is to lower the tax on the income, while still keeping the income in the family. The purpose of an assignment of income for consideration is to attempt to get favorable capital gains treatment on the transaction.

Speaking a little more specifically, *gratuitous* assignments involve, for example, a cash-basis taxpayer who is owed compensation for personal services rendered attempting to assign the payment of that compensation to a member of the family, the fact pattern of the seminal case of *Lucas v. Earl*.[1]

The purpose of such a gratuitous assignment of income is to attempt to defeat the progressive tax system. This is done by shifting income from, say, the high-bracket parent to the lower-bracket child. Not surprisingly, the Service and Congress generally successfully oppose these maneuvers. In such a case the income is reattributed back to the person whose personal services earned the income.

In contrast to the personal service area, there is no problem whatsoever in gratuitous assignments of income from property. Thus Mildred can give dividend-producing stock to her son Freemantle. Freemantle, in a lower bracket, will be taxed at a lower rate on the dividends. The Service does not object to an outright gift of that kind. Moreover, as we discussed at ¶ 4.03(2)(c)(i), if the property transferred has appreciated in value, Freemantle rather than Mildred will also be taxed on that appreciation. Mildred's transfers were effective not only in shifting the future dividends to Freemantle but in also shifting past appreciation to Freemantle. Again, the Service takes no issue with this.

It really comes down to this, then, as classist as it might sound: those who own property can easily shift income to lower-bracket family members, but those earn their money by the sweat of their own efforts cannot.

In this context it should be noted that allowing all gratuitous assignments of income to be effective in shifting the tax burden would not, as is commonly thought, undermine the progressive tax system. Rather, it would simply lead to another progressive system, in which the taxable unit is the family, instead of individuals. Indeed, that is precisely what happened with the advent of the joint return, which imposes a tax on the married couple. This in effect allows all gratuitous assignments of income between married partners.

Assignments of income for *consideration* spring not from a desire to split income but from an urge to enjoy capital gains treatment on what would otherwise be ordinary income.[2]

Consider, for example, a taxpayer who owns property on which there is a lease, producing periodic rental payments to the taxpayer. For various business reasons the lessee wishes to be discharged from the lease. After negotiations the lessee pays the taxpayer a lump sum in exchange for cancellation of the lease. The taxpayer may be

---

[1]   281 U.S. 111, 50 S.Ct. 241, 74 L.Ed. 731 (1930).

[2]   Capital gains generates several very attractive low rates of tax. For a general discussion of capital gains see ¶ 4.06.

regarded as having effected an assignment of his rights on the lease for consideration. The question in cases of this nature is whether the transaction can give rise to capital gain rather than ordinary income.[3]

Similarly, the taxpayer could sell the right to receive future dividends, interest, royalties, or trust income—all with the hope of receiving capital gain in lieu of what would otherwise have been ordinary income, very attractive given the various low rates on capital gains. The Service would be expected to oppose such maneuvers, as discussed below.

Both of these types of assignments—the gratuitous assignment and the assignment for consideration—raise far-reaching questions in the tax law. Almost all types of income can be subject to them. Many of the areas are now covered by statute. There are, however, hoary cases, whose principles still bite. The doctrine of assignment of income spills out into many fields, including the taxation of trusts, family partnerships, and collapsible corporations. A classic case like *Old Colony Trust Co. v. Commissioner*[4] is fundamental to the field; ultimately the assignment of income area is a child of the great case of *Gregory v. Helvering*[5] and the doctrine of substance-over-form.

¶ 5.02 GRATUITOUS ASSIGNMENTS OF INCOME: BIRTH OF A METAPHOR

The early cases in the assignment of income field almost uniformly related to gratuitous assignments of income. The case which contributed the most in particular to the assignment of income field is, without doubt, *Lucas v. Earl,*[6] decided by the Supreme Court

---

[3]   These are essentially the facts in Hort v. Commissioner, 313 U.S. 28, 61 S.Ct. 757, 85 L.Ed. 1168 (1941), discussed at ¶ 5.03.

[4]   279 U.S. 716, 49 S.Ct. 499, 73 L.Ed. 918 (1929) (employer's payment of employee's income taxes income to the employee). See ¶ 2.01.

[5]   293 U.S. 465, 55 S.Ct. 266, 79 L.Ed. 596 (1935) (Although taxpayer complied with the literal terms of the reorganization statute, its provisions were held not to apply because the taxpayer was engaging in an artifice to avoid paying taxes). See Commissioner v. Court Holding Co., 324 U.S. 331, 65 S.Ct. 707, 89 L.Ed. 981 (1945) (which raises the closely-related question of which taxpayer sold property).

[6]   281 U.S. 111, 50 S.Ct. 241, 74 L.Ed. 731 (1930). See also Helvering v. Eubank, 311 U.S. 122, 61 S.Ct. 149, 85 L.Ed. 81 (1940) reh'g denied 312 U.S. 713, 61 S.Ct. 609, 85 L.Ed. 1144 (1941) (commissions on insurance policy renewals taxable to the person who originally sold the policies); Burnet v. Leininger, 285 U.S. 136, 52 S.Ct. 345, 76 L.Ed. 665 (1932); Poe v. Seaborn, 282 U.S. 101, 51 S.Ct. 58, 75 L.Ed. 239 (1930) (Married couple residents of state with community property law allowed to split their income. This led to a rash of states adopting community property laws, culminating in the establishment of the federal joint tax return for husbands and wives in 1948. See Bittker, "Federal Income Taxation and the Family," 27 Stanford Law Review 1389 (1975) at 1404–1414.)

in 1930.[7] This case is famous not because of the originality of *Earl's* results nor because of the brilliance of its analysis, nor even because it was the first assignment of income case (although it was). *Earl* gave to the field something far more important than any of that: it gave the field a metaphor. In dealing with a taxpayer's gratuitous assignment to a spouse of compensation income for services he had rendered, Justice Holmes, speaking for the Supreme Court, said that the income tax can "not be escaped by anticipatory arrangements and contracts however skillfully devised . . . by which the fruits are attributed to a different tree from that on which they grew."[8]

Of course, once the income was taxed to Earl, the subsequent transfer of funds to his wife would be excluded from her income as a gift.

Ironically, the metaphor was not so apt in this first case; presumably the "tree" was the taxpayer himself, and the "fruit" was his compensation income. The metaphor was more readily applicable to subsequent cases through the years.

A related case is *Commissioner v. Giannini*,[9] which dealt with a taxpayer who declined compensation for services the Board of Directors had voted him as President and Director of the company. The taxpayer told the Board that he would not accept the compensation and suggested that the Board do something worthwhile with the money. The Board thereafter granted the money to the University of California to establish a Foundation of Agricultural Economics, named after the taxpayer. The taxpayer did not report any of the $1,357,607 so transferred to the regents of the University of California as income.

The Commissioner assessed a tax on the amount. The Commissioner's argument, straight out of *Earl*, was that the actual receipt of money or property is not always necessary to constitute taxable income. A taxpayer "realizes" income when he directs the disposition of it in a manner that it reaches the object of his bounty. The taxpayer responded that he had absolutely and unconditionally

---

[7]   For an in-depth look at Earl see, Patricia A. Cain, The Story of Earl: How Echoes (and Metaphors) from the Past Continue to Shape the Assignment of Income Doctrine, in Tax Stories 275–311 (Paul L. Caron ed. 2003).

[8]   281 U.S. at 115, 50 S.Ct. at 242.

During this period the Supreme Court also used the "fruit and tree" metaphor in the wholly unrelated field of criminal procedure, barring the use of "tainted" evidence derived from an illegal or unconstitutional search or other procedure—"fruit of the poisonous tree," Nardone v. United States, 308 U.S. 338, 60 S.Ct. 266, 84 L.Ed. 307 (1939); see also Silverthorne Lumber Co. v. United States, 251 U.S. 385, 40 S.Ct. 182, 64 L.Ed. 319 (1920). Apparently the Court was in an agricultural mode during this period.

[9]   129 F.2d 638 (9th Cir.1942).

refused the property offered him. Thus it could not be "diverted" or assigned to an object of his bounty.

The court held that the taxpayer did not direct the disposition of the funds and therefore that he was not taxed on them.

A couple of revenue rulings raise similar issues, although they do not come out the same way.

In *Revenue Ruling 66–167*[10] the Service dealt with a case where a taxpayer declined to seek amounts he could have received as fees and commissions in serving as the sole executor of his wife's estate. The Service held that such waived fees and commissions were not includible in taxable income.

In *Revenue Ruling 74–581*[11] the Service addressed the treatment of payments received for services performed by a faculty member or a student of a university's school of law in their clinical programs. The policy at the school was that all fees to which the faculty member is entitled because of his work as an assigned attorney under the Criminal Justice Act would be assigned over to the law school. As a matter of practice the checks were paid by the court to the faculty member who then endorsed them over to the law school.

The Service ruled that the payments were not income to the faculty member. The ruling noted that there are a number of other similar cases in which it has ruled that the person rendering services does not have income. These include fees for representing indigent defendants where the fees are turned over to the employer, a legal aid society, and checks received by a physician from patients which he is required to endorse over to the hospital.

In 1937 the Supreme Court decided the well-known *Blair v. Commissioner*,[12] involving the assignment by a father to his children of fixed annual dollar amounts of income to be paid from his life interest in a trust. The Court held the assignments to be of property and to be valid for tax purposes. Thus the children rather than the father were taxable on the assigned income, as it was received.

Employing the fruit and tree metaphor in *Blair,* the father's life interest in the trust income would be regarded as the tree—the underlying property. Since the father did not assign a fixed amount of income for just a few years but a fixed amount of income for the full term of his life interest, the assignment was valid for tax purposes. The father, in effect, chopped down some of his fruit and some of his tree and *gave some of his fruit and some of his tree to his*

---

[10]   1966–1 Cum.Bull. 20.

[11]   1974–2 Cum.Bull. 25.

[12]   300 U.S. 5, 57 S.Ct. 330, 81 L.Ed. 465 (1937).

children. Such a "vertical cut" was effective to shift the tax liability on the assigned income to the children.

Another related case is *Estate of Stranahan v. Commissioner,*[13] which involved a decedent, Frank Stranahan, who had entered into a closing agreement with the IRS under which it was agreed that the decedent owed the IRS $754,815 for interest due to deficiencies in federal income, estate and gift taxes. In order to get the full benefit of deducting this large amount of interest the decedent accelerated the receipt of some income. He assigned his son the anticipated receipt of $122,820 in stock dividends from his Champion Spark Plug Company stock. As consideration, the son paid the decedent $115,000 by check, dated December 22, 1964. Decedent reported this amount as income on his 1964 return and was thus able to deduct his interest payments to the IRS in full.

The Tax Court held that the dividends paid to the son under this agreement in 1965 were taxable to the decedent's estate in 1965, not 1964. The Tax Court found that the agreement entered into with the son was in reality a loan by the son to the father and therefore decedent had no income in 1964 (since receipt of loan proceeds is not taxable).

The Sixth Circuit reversed, holding that the transaction was legally enforceable and not a sham. Valuable consideration was part of the transaction. Thus the transaction was economically realistic, with substance, and should be respected, notwithstanding that it concededly was entered into for the purpose of lowering federal income taxes.

The subsequent decision of the Supreme Court in *Harrison v. Schaffner*[14] in 1941 suggests this *Blair-Stranahan* analysis is correct. In *Schaffner* the life income beneficiary of a trust assigned to her children fixed dollar amounts to be paid the following year out of the income of the trust. The Court found that this assignment of income for one year was not "a substantial distribution of trust property" and hence that the assigned income was taxable to the donor rather than the donees.

Employing the fruit and tree metaphor in *Schaffner,* the donor's assignment of a fixed amount of income was not for a period coextensive in time with her own life interest but only for one year. Thus the donor in *Schaffner* can be regarded as having assigned only the "fruit," rather than a portion of the underlying property or "tree."

---

13   472 F.2d 867 (6th Cir.1973).
14   312 U.S. 579, 61 S.Ct. 759, 85 L.Ed. 1055 (1941).

The assignment was a "horizontal cut" and did not shift the tax burden to the donees.

The landmark *Helvering v. Horst*,[15] decided in 1940, was a prototype fruit-and-tree situation. Donor, the owner of negotiable bonds, detached from them negotiable interest coupons shortly before their due date and gave them to his son who collected the interest in the same year. The Supreme Court, explicitly employing the fruit and tree metaphor, held that the interest was taxable to Donor. The analysis was clear: Donor had given only the "fruit"—the coupon—rather than the "tree"—a bond. Thus the assignment was only a "horizontal cut" and therefore the income remained taxable to Donor.[16]

Thus, by 1941 the courts' theoretical approach to gratuitous assignments of income was well-established: gifts of fruit, or "horizontal cuts" in the donor's property, would be ineffective to transfer the tax on the income to the donee; gifts of the tree, or "vertical cuts" in the donor's property coextensive in time with the donor's own interest, would be effective to transfer the tax on the income to the donee. There is a rationale. To the extent the donor assigns vertical cuts the donor also loses the power to reassign income from that vertical cut. Thus the assignment will be respected for tax purposes.

Some modern applications of these principles include the case of *Susie Salvatore*[17] in which taxpayer contracted to sell her service station to Texaco and thereafter gave one-half of the service station to her children. The court held that the taxpayer was taxable on the full amount of the proceeds of the sale, not one half the amount.

---

[15]   311 U.S. 112, 61 S.Ct. 144, 85 L.Ed. 75 (1940).

[16]   Although *Schaffner* and *Horst* both involved "horizontal cuts" and therefore the assigned income was taxable to the donor, there is an interesting difference between the two cases. *Schaffner* involved an asset—the life interest in the trust income—that was in some sense wasting, or wearing out. Once the asset stopped throwing off income, because of the death of the life tenant, it would necessarily have a value of zero. The bond involved in *Horst*, however, was not a wasting asset. Once it stopped throwing off income—at maturity—the principal amount of the bond would still remain to be paid back. Putting it another way, if the life estate in the trust had been purchased from the life tenant by another (so that the purchaser would have an estate *pur autre vie*), the purchaser would be able to amortize the cost of the estate (computed by reference to the life expectancy of the seller) against the income payments. Of course the purchaser of a bond in the bond market *cannot* amortize the cost of the bond against the interest payments. What this all boils down to mean is that the assignment of income in *Schaffner*, even though it was only for one year, necessarily involved an assignment of capital or "tree" as well as income, or "fruit." The *Schaffner* court did not make this distinction between wasting and non-wasting assets. Cf. § 273, disallowing a deduction for the shrinkage in value of a life or term interest acquired by gift, bequest or inheritance. See also Early v. Commissioner, 445 F.2d 166 (5th Cir.1971), cert. denied 404 U.S. 855, 92 S.Ct. 100, 30 L.Ed.2d 96 (1971).

[17]   29 T.C.M. 89 (1970).

Also, in Revenue Ruling 69–102,[18] the Service addressed the tax consequences of the maturity and surrender for their cash surrender values of an endowment life insurance contract that taxpayer sold to a charity for less than its full value and an annuity contract that taxpayer transferred to his son as a gift. Consistent with earlier case law, the Service held that the taxpayer had ordinary income for the taxable year in which the recipients surrendered the contracts.

These principles have further found their modern incarnation in such diverse fields as income from a business, compensation for personal services, dividend income, income from property, royalty income, and income from sale of crops.[19]

¶ 5.03 ASSIGNMENTS OF INCOME FOR CONSIDERATION

The development of the case law in the area of assignments of income for consideration was much slower than for the gratuitous assignments. However the two lines of cases soon effected a dramatic merger. In *Burnet v. Harmel*[20] an advance payment or "bonus" received by the owner of property in consideration for the assignment of the right to exploit oil reserves was held to be ordinary income, in

---

[18]   1969–1 C.B. 32.

[19]   See, e.g., Rev.Rul. 55–2, 1955–1 C.B. 211 (tax on accounts receivable for personal services could not be shifted); Rev.Rul. 74–32, 1974–1 C.B. 22 (tax on income for personal services could not be shifted); Hyman v. Nunan, 143 F.2d 425 (2d Cir.1944) (L. Hand, J.) (tax on dividend income could not be shifted); Montgomery v. Commissioner, 230 F.2d 472 (5th Cir.1956) (transfer of business property to avoid liability in tort action effective to shift tax burden on subsequent income); Rev.Rul. 74–32, supra (income from sale of property could not be shifted); Commissioner v. Sunnen, 333 U.S. 591, 68 S.Ct. 715, 92 L.Ed. 898 (1948), on remand 168 F.2d 839 (8th Cir.1948) (gift of royalty payments to wife ineffective to shift tax burden where donor retained ultimate power to cancel the payments); United States v. Lawhon, 499 F.2d 352 (5th Cir.1974), cert. denied 419 U.S. 1121, 95 S.Ct. 804, 42 L.Ed.2d 820 (1975) (involving actual fruit and trees, taxpayer can be taxable on proceeds of orange sales though his children owned the orange groves); Rev.Rul. 71–130, 1971–1 C.B. 28 (vertical cut of a royalty interest shifted the tax burden to the donee).

Also a significant gratuitous assignment of income case during this period was Helvering v. Clifford, 309 U.S. 331, 60 S.Ct. 554, 84 L.Ed. 788 (1940), mandate conformed 111 F.2d 896 (C.C.A.8 1940) (Creator of a short-term trust was taxable on the trust income in view of the fact that he retained control over the investment policies and administration of the trust corpus, and the trust income was payable to his wife. Although *Clifford* is obviously in the same family of cases as those described in the text, the Court specifically declined to consider whether the case came within the ambit of *Lucas v. Earl.*)

See also Corliss v. Bowers, 281 U.S. 376, 50 S.Ct. 336, 74 L.Ed. 916 (1930) (income from a revocable trust taxed to the grantor); Burnet v. Wells, 289 U.S. 670, 53 S.Ct. 761, 77 L.Ed. 1439 (1933) (income of an irrevocable trust which was used to pay the premiums on the grantor's life insurance held taxable to the grantor).

See §§ 671–679, discussed at ¶ 5.04(3) for the present statutory treatment of *Clifford*-type trusts.

[20]   287 U.S. 103, 53 S.Ct. 74, 77 L.Ed. 199 (1932).

the nature of rent, rather than an amount received on sale of property rights yielding capital gain.

In the major case of *Hort v. Commissioner*,[21] discussed also at ¶ 4.06(3)(a)(i), a lessor received a lump-sum from the lessee in cancellation of the lease. Against the taxpayer's claim of a capital gain, the Supreme Court held that the amount received in cancellation was ordinary income, since it was a substitute for rent.[22]

Assignment of income doctrine reached its apotheosis in the case of *Commissioner v. P.G. Lake*,[23] decided in 1958. The taxpayer in *Lake* owned a working interest in an oil and gas lease—that is, the taxpayer had the right to develop and sell the oil and gas reserves on certain property over the term of the lease.[24] Since the oil and gas is inventory to the taxpayer, its sale over the term of the lease would have yielded ordinary income.[25] The taxpayer, however, assigned a portion of the anticipated future revenues from the oil and gas sale up to $600,000 to a third party in exchange for a lump sum of $600,000. The taxpayer's $600,000 assignment of income was payable out of 25% of the revenue attributable to the taxpayer's working interest; it was expected to pay out over three years (and did so); and it specified payment of 3% interest on the unpaid balance remaining from month to month. After the $600,000 plus interest was paid, the taxpayer would receive the entire gross revenues from his working interest for himself for the balance of the lease term.

In oil and gas tax law parlance, the taxpayer on these facts had "carved out" an "oil payment"—the right to receive a specific sum of

---

[21]   313 U.S. 28, 61 S.Ct. 757, 85 L.Ed. 1168 (1941), see ¶ 5.01 supra.

[22]   In characterizing the gain by reference to what the payments substitute for, *Hort* bears a close relationship to the damages field, see ¶ 3.11.

Taxpayer in *Hort* also had the temerity to assert, as an alternative argument, that the cancellation payment should give rise to a loss, since it was for less than the difference between the present value of the future lease payments and the fair rental value of the property for the unexpired period of the lease. The Court quite properly rejected that argument on the ground that taxpayer's proper tax benefit in this event simply lay in reporting less gross income in the future.

Another possible basis for the ordinary income holding in *Hort*, although it was not employed by the Court, could have been that the transaction did not constitute a sale or exchange but rather was just an extinguishment of taxpayer's claim, since the property (the lease) did not survive the transaction. Compare ¶ 4.06(3)(a)(xii) regarding the treatment of the retirement of debt instruments.

[23]   356 U.S. 260, 78 S.Ct. 691, 2 L.Ed.2d 743 (1958), reh'g denied 356 U.S. 964, 78 S.Ct. 991, 2 L.Ed.2d 1071 (1958).

[24]   In the oil and gas field the typical arrangement is that the owner of land will convey an oil and gas lease—the right to develop and sell the oil and gas reserves over a term of years—to the lessee. The consideration to the lessor is usually a royalty or fraction of the gross revenues produced (often one-eighth). See K. Miller, Oil and Gas Federal Income Taxation (1982) Ch. 13.

[25]   Section 1221 and see ¶ 4.06(3)(a)(i).

money out of the proceeds of the sale of oil and gas.[26] The question was whether the assignment of such a "carved out" interest gave rise to ordinary income or capital gain.

That the Supreme Court held the assignment of income in *Lake* gave rise to ordinary income is not so surprising; but the way in which the Court reached that result effected a quantum jump in the development of assignment of income doctrine. The first ground of the Court's opinion was that the $600,000 received was a substitute for what would have been received in the future as ordinary income.[27] Although this appeared to partake of *Hort,* this was in fact a considerable expansion of *Hort,* since the lump-sum payment made in lieu of the ordinary income in *Lake* came from a third party; whereas in *Hort* the lump-sum payment was simply an acceleration of payments from the original payor. As another way of looking at the matter, the property involved in *Lake*—the oil payment—survived the transaction and was in the hands of the third party. Whereas in *Hort,* the property involved—the lease—was extinguished by the transaction. Thus the transaction in *Lake* looked considerably more like a sale or exchange of property than did the transaction in *Hort.* Yet still the Court found the payment in *Lake* to be a substitute for ordinary income.

Striking though this aspect may have been, it was not the most significant feature of the Court's opinion. The Court went on to cite major *gratuitous* assignment of income cases, to buttress its opinion—*Clifford,*[28] *Schaffner,*[29] and most particularly *Hort.*[30] The gratuitous assignment of income cases, of course, dealt not with the character of consideration received on the assignment, but with the question of the taxable person. By introducing the gratuitous assignment of income cases into the *Lake* analysis, the Court necessarily infused the assignment of income for consideration area with the whole theoretical framework developed in the gratuitous assignment of income area—viz., "vertical cuts," "horizontal cuts," "fruit and tree," etc.

Veritably, the theory of the gratuitous assignment of income area adapted exceedingly well to the assignment of income for consideration cases. The "carved out" oil payment in *Lake* could

---

[26]   Anderson v. Helvering, 310 U.S. 404, 410, 60 S.Ct. 952, 955, 84 L.Ed. 1277 (1940).

[27]   356 U.S. at 264, 78 S.Ct. at 693.

[28]   See ¶ 5.02.

[29]   Id.

[30]   See ¶ 5.02. See *Lake,* 356 U.S. at 267.

certainly be regarded as a "horizontal cut" (and it since has been[31]) or a sale of "fruit" and not the "tree," hence giving rise to ordinary income rather than capital gain. This seems to be the clear import of the Court's opinion in *Lake*. Conversely, where a taxpayer owns a working interest or a royalty and sells a percentage of it coextensive in time with his own interest (a "vertical cut" or sale of "fruit and tree" together), the result should be a capital gain. This was in fact the Service's position in I.T. 4003,[32] quoted with approval by the Court in *Lake*.[33]

Thus since *Lake* the two types of assignment of income are subject to the same analysis; and the ripples of *Lake* are felt on a wide range of types of assignment of income down to the present time.[34] Ironically, considering *Lake*'s great importance in the field, the actual results on *Lake*-type facts were changed by the Code for transactions after August 7, 1969. After that date, an oil payment or production payment[35] carved out and sold as in *Lake* will be treated as a mortgage loan on the property.[36] This was done to eliminate tax

---

[31]   E.g. Lyon and Eustice, "Assignment of Income: Fruit and Tree as Irrigated by the P.G. Lake Case," 17 Tax Law Rev. 295 (1962).

[32]   I.T. 4003, 1950–1 C.B. 10, 11, declared obsolete by Rev.Rul. 70–277, 1970–1 C.B. 280. Although I.T. 4003 was since declared obsolete along with a number of other rulings as part of the Service's program of declaring obsolete pre-1953 rulings, see Rev.Proc. 67–6, 1967–1 C.B. 576, its spirit would seem to live on after its quotation by the Supreme Court in *Lake*.

[33]   356 U.S. at 265 n. 5, 78 S.Ct. at 694 note 5, see ¶¶ 3.05 and 4.06(3)(a)(vi) regarding the disposition of interests in licenses and patents. See also Rev.Rul. 71–130, 1971–1 C.B. 28 (Gratuitous assignment by a husband and wife of one-half of a one-eighth royalty interest to an irrevocable trust for the benefit of their minor children effective to shift the tax burden on the assigned interest to the trust—illustrating again the merger of the theories of gratuitous assignments and assignments for consideration); Rev.Rul. 55–526, 1955–2 C.B. 574 (allowing capital gain on the sale of a royalty interest, since it constitutes property).

[34]   See ¶ 4.06 for general treatment of capital gains and the several attractive rates now available to capital gains.

A variation on the theme is the assignment of future dividend, rent, or other income not for the purpose of getting capital gain but to accelerate the income into the year of the assignment when the taxpayer has a large offsetting loss. The Service's response to this has been to treat the transaction as a loan. Compare Estate of Stranahan v. Commissioner, 472 F.2d 867 (6th Cir.1973) (assignment of future dividends effective to accelerate income) with Martin, 56 T.C. 1255 (1971) (assignment of future rents treated as a loan). See also Johnston, 35 T.C.M. 642 (1976) (assignment of rental income to preserve Subchapter S status held a loan). Cf. discussion of *Arlen,* ¶ 3.05(2) where taxpayer sought treatment of advance royalties as a loan.

[35]   A "production payment" is a right to a specified share of the production from minerals in place or the revenues therefrom (thus in the nature of a royalty), but it must have an expected economic life shorter than that of the mineral interest it burdens. It may be limited by a dollar amount, quantity of mineral, or period of time. Hence the definition includes the oil payment. See Reg. § 1.636–3.

[36]   Section 636(a); Reg. § 1.636–4.

advantages arising from "ABC" and similar transactions involving interests in mineral property.[37]

¶ 5.04 APPLICATION OF ASSIGNMENT OF INCOME DOCTRINE

The principles forged in the early assignment of income cases have come to radiate out into a large number of fields today— sometimes intact, sometimes modified by subsequent cases or statute. Some of these topics have already been discussed, but it is useful to summarize them.

(1) Oil, Gas, and Other Minerals

As discussed above, under current law where a production payment is carved out of underlying mineral property and assigned for consideration, the transaction will be treated as a mortgage loan on the property. Thus the "carve out" will not give rise to income to

---

[37]   Actually an ABC transaction involved somewhat the reverse of the facts in *Lake,* although both are covered by § 636. In an ABC transaction, A, the owner of a working interest in an oil and gas lease (the right to develop and sell the oil and gas reserves over a lease term, note 5 supra), would sell that interest to B less a retained production payment (a royalty limited by dollar amount or time, etc., to being less than the underlying working interest note 19 supra). A would then sell to C the production payment. This is attractive to A because he gets capital gain on the two sales. This is because even after *Lake,* A would presumably get capital gain on the sale of the working interest, since that is the sale of the "tree," albeit he did retain the "fruit." The subsequent sale of the production payment or "fruit" should also give rise to capital gain, since A is now selling everything he has in the property. As for B, this arrangement is attractive, since he has been able to purchase the working interest for a reduced price. B also gets the attractive intangible drilling and development expense deduction (§ 263, Reg. § 1.612–4) and may qualify for percentage depletion (§§ 613, 613A). Most important also to B is the fact that the income paying off the production payment would not be included in B's income, even though the production payment has helped finance B's purchase of the working interest. C includes in income the income of the production payment but may amortize his cost of the production payment against it.

Section 636 takes the fun out of ABC transactions, particularly for B, who would have paid a premium to A for the tax advantages. Under § 636 the retention by A of the production payment, on his sale of the working interest to B, is treated as a purchase money mortgage loan. A's sale of the production payment to C is then treated as a sale of the mortgage to C (Reg. § 1.636–1(a)(2)). The income paying off the production payment is included in B's income, as a discharge of his mortgage obligation to C. B gets no deduction for the payment to C, since it is a non-deductible repayment of a loan (except for the interest).

Section 636 also removes a tax benefit that grew directly out of *Lake.* A taxpayer with a working interest in mineral property might be limited in the amount of depletion he could take either because he is running losses or because of the 50% limit of § 613. By carving out and selling a production payment, under *Lake,* he could increase current depletable income. Converting this transaction to a loan, of course, eliminates this maneuver.

See Joyce and Del Cotto, "The AB (ABC) and BA Transactions: An Economic and Tax Analysis of Reserved and Carved Out Income Interests," 31 Tax Law Rev. 121 (1976); Wilkinson, "ABC Transactions and Related Income Tax Plans," 40 Texas Law Rev. 18 (1961).

the assignor. The income used to pay off the production payment will be treated as the repayment of the loan by the assignor and the assignee. Similarly, where the underlying mineral property is sold less a retained production payment, the retained production payment will be treated as a mortgage loan on the property (this to preclude the so-called ABC transaction). Where, however, the cut is "vertical" and the assignment is, for example, of a royalty interest coextensive in time with the underlying property, the transaction will be considered a sale of property with the potential of yielding capital gain under the usual rules.[38]

The same analysis applies in a gratuitous assignment. If the gift is a "vertical cut" of the mineral interest, it will be effective to transfer the tax burden to the donee.[39] "Horizontal cuts" will not be effective to transfer the tax burden to the donee.[40]

(2) Leases

(a) Gratuitous Assignments

Consistent with the analysis developed above, a gratuitous assignment of a lease by the owner of the underlying property will in general not be effective to shift the tax burden on the rent to the donee.[41] Perhaps if the only interest the taxpayer has is the lease (i.e., the taxpayer does not own the underlying property), a gratuitous assignment of the lease would be effective to shift the tax burden. This should be the case because the taxpayer would not be engaging in a "horizontal cut" but would be assigning everything the taxpayer had.

---

[38] There is nothing in § 636 to preclude this, and see also early discussion of *Lake.* See also ¶ 4.06 for the attractive rates available for capital gains and losses.

[39] Rev.Rul. 71–130, ¶ 5.03.

[40] See ¶ 5.02.

[41] Iber v. United States, 409 F.2d 1273 (7th Cir.1969) (gratuitous assignment of lease to a 10-year trust failed to shift tax burden, notwithstanding that had the underlying property been assigned, the incidence of tax apparently would have been shifted pursuant to the grantor trust rules, the court citing *Earl, Horst,* and *Schaffner*); Rev.Rul. 58–337, 1958–2 C.B. 13 (same facts and same result); Galt v. Commissioner, 216 F.2d 41 (7th Cir.1954), cert. denied 348 U.S. 951, 75 S.Ct. 438, 99 L.Ed. 743 (1955) (gratuitous assignment of lease failed to shift tax burden where taxpayer retained reversionary interest in the property); United States v. Shafto, 246 F.2d 338 (4th Cir.1957) (assignment of five-year lease failed to shift tax burden); but see Lum v. Commissioner, 147 F.2d 356 (3d Cir.1945) (gratuitous assignment of lease was effective to shift tax burden because assignee received rights as "landlord"; questionable whether this older decision would hold up but perhaps this could be pursued by taxpayers in the Third Circuit). If the assignment of the lease fails to shift the tax burden it would seem to follow *a fortiori* that assignment of just the rent from the lease would also be ineffective, see Midwood Associates v. Commissioner, 115 F.2d 871 (2d Cir.1940).

(b) Assignments for Consideration—Cancellation of the Lease by Landlord or Tenant

Where the tenant pays the landlord to cancel the lease, it is clear that the landlord realizes ordinary income under *Hort*.[42] Where a landlord pays a tenant to cancel a business lease, the payment is generally given § 1231 treatment, since the tenant is disposing of the entire interest in the property—a vertical cut.[43] Suppose, however, the lessee sublets part of the lease and receives a payment in cancellation of the sublease. Is the taxpayer regarded as a landlord, to whom the payment is ordinary income under *Hort*, or a tenant, to whom the payment is given § 1231 treatment? This delicious issue was presented in *Metropolitan Building Co. v. Commissioner*,[44] discussed also at ¶ 4.06(3)(a)(i), where, under a rather unusual set of facts, the sublessor released the sublease to the landlord in exchange for a payment from the sublessee. The sublessee then entered into a

---

[42]   See ¶ 5.03. See also Reg. § 1.61–8(b).

[43]   Where the landlord pays the tenant to cancel the lease, the initial question is whether the transaction is a sale or exchange. Section 1241 deems the transaction to be a sale or exchange, consistent with earlier case law. Having established that there is a sale or exchange, the next question is whether there has been a sale or exchange of *property*, rather than of just income from the property—i.e., the *Lake*-type question. It is clear that a leasehold of land constitutes property to the tenant, without regard to the term of the leasehold, Rev.Rul. 72–85, 1972–1 C.B. 234. See also Reg. § 1.1250–1(e)(3) and House Report 749, Eighty-eighth Congress, 1964–1 C.B. (Part 2) 125,401 deeming a leasehold real property for purposes of recapture of depreciation (¶ 4.06(3)(a)(vii); but see Reg. § 1.1031(a)–1(c) (providing that a lease must have 30 years or more to run to be considered real estate for purposes of a tax-free exchange for other real estate) (see ¶ 4.05(2))).

Having established that a leasehold is property, the next question is whether it is the kind of property that can qualify for capital gains-type treatment. If the leasehold was not used in the taxpayer-tenant's trade or business but was, for example, of personal use property, it would constitute a capital asset in the taxpayer's hands and its sale would give rise to a capital gain, clearly implied by Rev.Rul. 72–85. See §§ 1221, 1222. (A loss on the sale of such property would not be allowed. See ¶ 4.04(2). See also ¶ 4.06(3) for treatment of sale of property not used in a trade or business but held for investment.) If the leasehold is used in a trade or business, its sale will give rise to § 1231 treatment, since the leasehold is depreciable property used in a trade or business. Rev.Rul. 72–85; see also § 1231(b)(1). If the taxpayer were in the business of selling leases, his gain on sale of the lease would be ordinary, Rev.Rul. 72–85. See § 1221. The basis of the leasehold for purposes of depreciation or sale would be its acquisition cost (see ¶ 6.03(4)).

As a further note on the sale or exchange aspect of this transaction, § 1241 allows payment made for a partial cancellation of a lease to qualify as being received in a sale or exchange, if the cancellation relates to a severable economic unit—such as a portion of the premises covered by the lease, or a reduction in the lease term, Reg. § 1.1241–1(b). Such partial cancellations have been held to involve property and hence to give rise to capital gain, Rev.Rul. 56–531, 1956–2 C.B. 983 and cases cited therein. Note that this is a somewhat more liberal approach than *Lake*. § 1241 specifically does not preempt the field, 1.1241–1(a), hence other types of partial lease cancellations could give rise to sales or exchanges and capital gain (or loss). See Rev.Rul. 56–531. See also Modiano-Schneider, Inc., 32 T.C.M. 19 (1973).

[44]   282 F.2d 592 (9th Cir.1960).

new lease on the same property with the landlord. Since the sublessor was paid for the release by the sublessee, the facts conjured up *Hort* and ordinary income. But since the release of the sublease was to the landlord, the facts also suggested § 1231 treatment as discussed above. The Ninth Circuit struggled with this problem and heroically came up with the solution that the sublessor enjoyed § 1231-type treatment, since the release of the sublease was to the landlord. The source of the payment was held to be irrelevant.

Metropolitan, however, should not be taken as standing for the proposition that the cancellation of a sublease always gives rise to a capital gain to the sublessor. The *Metropolitan* court did not speak to the question of what would happen if the release of the sublease had been to the sublessor rather than the landlord. In a case where the sublessee pays the sublessor for a release from the sublease and then does not do further business with the landlord (presumably a more common set of facts than in *Metropolitan*), the pattern is vintage *Hort* and presumably ordinary income would be the result.[45]

(c) *Assignments for Consideration—Third Party Transactions*

Where a tenant sells a lease used in a trade or business to a third party, the transaction will receive § 1231 treatment.[46] If a landlord sells a lease of underlying property, a classic *Lake* situation is presented: an interest of lesser duration in time than the underlying interest is being carved out and sold. *Hort,* although it involved an extinguishment rather than a sale of a lease, is also relevant for its concept of a substitute for ordinary income in the landlord-tenant situation. Thus the landlord would get ordinary income on the sale of a lease of the property.

Finally, in the real estate setting, the landlord might try an "ABC" type transaction, as described in ¶ 5.03 supra, relating to the oil and gas area. This would involve selling the property for cash plus a right to receive a "production payment" or a payment in the nature of a royalty up to a fixed amount, payable out of the profits of the property in future years. The theory would be that the seller had retained an economic interest in the property and hence that the buyer would not be taxed on the income attributable to the "production payment." In fact, however, a very good argument can be made that the transaction is in substance a purchase money mortgage in favor of the seller and hence that the buyer should be

---

[45]   Indeed the Tax Court held that *Hort* applied in *Metropolitan* (31 T.C. 971 (1959)) only to be reversed by the Ninth Circuit.

[46]   Rev.Rul. 72–85, and authorities discussed therein. If the lease is for personal-use property, gain on the sale will be a capital gain; a loss will not be allowed.

taxed on the proceeds of the "production payment" before paying them over to the seller.[47]

Note that the buyer and the seller of real estate have somewhat adverse interests as to whether such a transaction shall be treated as the sale of property less a retained economic interest or as a purchase money mortgage in favor of the seller. If the transaction is treated as a sale of property less a retained economic interest, the buyer is not taxed on the proceeds of the production payment;[48] the seller, however, receives ordinary income on the pay-out of the production payment. If the transaction is treated as a purchase money mortgage in favor of the seller, then the buyer is taxed on the proceeds of the production payment. When the proceeds are then paid to the seller, they will be part of the purchase price of the property and the seller will generally get capital gain on them.

In the classic ABC transaction, the best of both worlds is attained by arranging to have the seller sell the retained production payment to a third party soon after selling the property. (Whence the nomenclature "ABC", since three parties are involved). The seller can now claim to get capital gain on the sale of the production payment, since the seller is now disposing of the entire remaining interest in the property and hence cannot possibly be engaging in a "horizontal cut" or sale of fruit only. Thus does the seller get capital gain while the buyer excludes the proceeds of the production payment. The buyer of the production payment amortizes the cost against the payment proceeds, and A, B, and C each go home happy, no doubt the envy of the rest of the letters of the alphabet.[49]

These are essentially the facts of *Bryant v. Commissioner*,[50] involving the sale of a farm, in which the Fifth Circuit held that the buyer could not exclude the proceeds of a production payment, to be satisfied out of future farm profits, reserved by the seller (the seller's tax liability was not at issue). The court cited three factors that influenced it to hold that the transaction was in substance a sale of the entire property with a mortgage in favor of the seller: (1) the production payment was limited to a specific amount and was

---

[47]   As discussed in ¶ 5.03 supra, this purchase money mortgage analysis is now imposed by statute on "ABC" transactions involving oil and gas and other mineral property.

[48]   Reasoning by analogy from the old mineral interest cases, summarized in ¶ 5.03.

[49]   The transaction could perhaps be made even stronger if the seller of the property retains an already existing lease. Subsequent sale of the lease could be very strongly argued to give rise to capital gain, since it is well established that a lease is property; see Rev.Rul. 72–85. For "ABC" transactions in the mineral property area see ¶ 5.03 supra.

[50]   399 F.2d 800 (5th Cir.1968).

included in the total figure that the parties, as a factual matter, regarded as the purchase price; (2) the production payment was expected to be satisfied in a short time and for a certain sum; and (3) interest was to accrue on the unpaid balance of the production payment. Not stated as part of the court's reasoning but possibly also influencing the outcome was the fact that the seller's subsequent sale of the production payment was to a *Clifford* trust formed by the buyer. If these factors were otherwise, perhaps an ABC transaction could still be effected in the real estate area; *Bryant* certainly has not totally closed the door here.[51]

(3) Trusts

Assignment of income problems can arise in two ways in the trust area. On the creation of the trust the question is whether the transfer by the grantor of income-producing property to the trust is effective to shift the tax burden on the property from the grantor to the trust. Historically the most nettlesome problems in this area have arisen where the trust is a short-term or grantor trust.[52] The second assignment of income problem in the trust area occurs when the trust beneficiary seeks to assign rights to the trust income.

(a) Creation of the Trust

The tax consequences of the creation of a short-term trust have been a matter of controversy from the early days of assignment of income doctrine.[53]

Most significant for the purposes of this discussion is the fact that a grantor is regarded as the owner of the trust property if the grantor or the grantor's spouse retains a reversionary interest in the trust corpus or income which has a value of more than five percent of the trust property.[54]

What is the practical significance of this five-percent rule? The time value of money considerations crank out that the reversionary interest cannot take place for 39 years, assuming an 8% discount

---

[51]   See discussion of other authorities in *Bryant.*

A field closely related to this is whether there has been a sale or exchange at all or rather a license. See ¶¶ 3.05, 4.06(3)(a)(xi).

The purchase of a corporation, of course, may also be financed by income which the corporation itself produces—the so-called "bootstrap acquisition," see Boone v. United States, 470 F.2d 232 (10th Cir.1972) (purchase of a life insurance company financed by 84% of future premium income); in such corporate transactions the buyer or seller may be threatened with dividend treatment if the transaction is not structured carefully.

[52]   Also known by the sobriquet "Clifford Trust," see ¶ 5.02 supra.

[53]   See ¶ 5.02 supra, and see Henning, "Treatment of the Grantor Trust as a separate entity," 32 Tax Law Rev. 409 (1977).

[54]   Section 673(a).

rate. If the trust instrument provides, for example, that the reversion will take place after 15 years, the reversionary interest will have a value of 31% of the trust corpus or income.

If the trust instrument provides that the reversion to the grantor will take place on the death of an income beneficiary (other than the death of a minor child), the trust will automatically be treated as a grantor trust, and the income of the trust property will be taxable to the grantor.[55]

(b) Related Topics

(i)   How to Pay for Law School(?): Below-Market Loans

Another method of shifting income from higher-bracket family members to lower-bracket family members has historically been the use of interest-free loans. To take a random case, suppose Buford's mama wishes to pay Buford's law school tuition and expenses but is finding it onerous to do so. Let's say law school costs $20,000 a year. (Hey, we can dream, right?) Suppose Buford's mama has $250,000 cash investments. The maneuver is that she lends the $250,000 to Buford without requiring Buford to pay interest. Buford has two choices at this point: He could either abscond to Puerto Rico (who needs law school with that kind of coin in your pocket?), or Buford could invest the funds in corporate bonds paying 8% per year interest. That cranks out to the $20,000 Buford needs every year for law school. Buford is in a lower tax bracket than his mama. So Buford pays a lower tax than his mama would on the money. After the end of his three-year sojourn in law school, Buford will repay his mama the $250,000 (she hopes).

If all this works out as Buford's mama would like, Buford has a law degree, and she has paid for the degree with funds taxed at a reduced rate.

Before Buford writes home with this suggestion, he should be aware that Congress has taken the zip out of this one, too. It has done so in a way that is both interesting in itself and that shows the power of a tax statute to recharacterize transactions.

What the statute does is to say that if Buford and Buford's mama try this maneuver described above, they will not get the result they expect. Instead, the transaction will be deemed to something different. It will be deemed to be that Buford is paying interest to his mama at a higher than market rate (an "applicable federal rate"). Buford's mama is then deemed to be giving Buford that interest back

---

[55]   Section 673(b).

as a gift.[56] Gifts of course are not deductible. Buford is also getting interest in fact on the $250,000. Buford can deduct the interest payments he is deemed to be making to his mama against the interest he is in fact receiving on the $250,000. The interest deduction Buford takes for these deemed payments cannot exceed the interest income Buford is receiving on the $250,000.[57]

All this is sorted out in the accompanying series of graphics:

GIFT LOANS #1: WHAT BUFORD AND HIS MAMA CAN DO

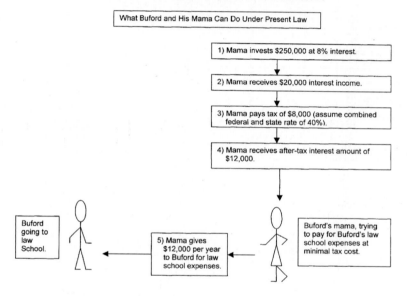

Treatment of Gift Loans with Below-Market Interest #1

What Buford and His Mama Can Do Under Present Law

1) Mama invests $250,000 at 8% interest.

2) Mama receives $20,000 interest income.

3) Mama pays tax of $8,000 (assume combined federal and state rate of 40%).

4) Mama receives after-tax interest amount of $12,000.

Buford going to law School.

5) Mama gives $12,000 per year to Buford for law school expenses.

Buford's mama, trying to pay for Buford's law school expenses at minimal tax cost.

Net family picture: Buford and his mama receive $20,000 of interest on the $250,000 and pay tax of $8,000, leaving $12,000 to Buford for law school expenses.

---

[56] Section 7872(a).

[57] Because § 163(d) limits the deduction for investment interest to the amount of investment income received.

GIFT LOANS #2: TRICKY MOVE BUFORD
AND HIS MAMA TRY

Treatment of Gift Loans with Below-Market Interest #2

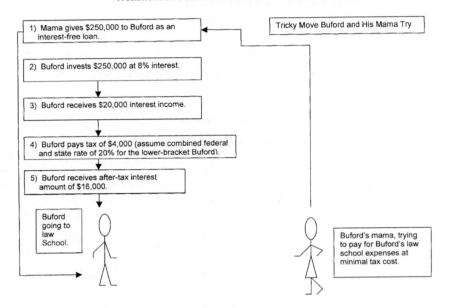

1) Mama gives $250,000 to Buford as an interest-free loan.

Tricky Move Buford and His Mama Try

2) Buford invests $250,000 at 8% interest.

3) Buford receives $20,000 interest income.

4) Buford pays tax of $4,000 (assume combined federal and state rate of 20% for the lower-bracket Buford).

5) Buford receives after-tax interest amount of $16,000.

Buford going to law School.

Buford's mama, trying to pay for Buford's law school expenses at minimal tax cost.

Net family picture: Buford and his mama receive $20,000 of interest on the $250,000 and pay tax of $4,000, leaving $16,000 to Buford for law school expenses.

GIFT LOANS #3: WHAT THE STATUTE DOES TO THE TRICKY MOVE BUFORD AND HIS MAMA TRY

Treatment of Gift Loans with Below-Market Interest #3

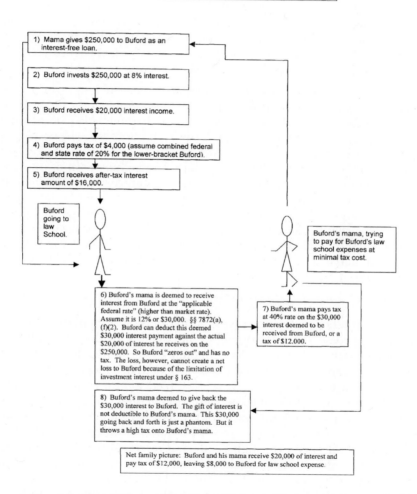

What the Statute does to the Tricky Move Buford and His Mama Try

1) Mama gives $250,000 to Buford as an interest-free loan.

2) Buford invests $250,000 at 8% interest.

3) Buford receives $20,000 interest income.

4) Buford pays tax of $4,000 (assume combined federal and state rate of 20% for the lower-bracket Buford).

5) Buford receives after-tax interest amount of $16,000.

Buford going to law School.

Buford's mama, trying to pay for Buford's law school expenses at minimal tax cost.

6) Buford's mama is deemed to receive interest from Buford at the "applicable federal rate" (higher than market rate). Assume it is 12% or $30,000. §§ 7872(a), (f)(2). Buford can deduct this deemed $30,000 interest payment against the actual $20,000 of interest he receives on the $250,000. So Buford "zeros out" and has no tax. The loss, however, cannot create a net loss to Buford because of the limitation of investment interest under § 163.

7) Buford's mama pays tax at 40% rate on the $30,000 interest deemed to be received from Buford, or a tax of $12,000.

8) Buford's mama deemed to give back the $30,000 interest to Buford. The gift of interest is not deductible to Buford's mama. This $30,000 going back and forth is just a phantom. But it throws a high tax onto Buford's mama.

Net family picture: Buford and his mama receive $20,000 of interest and pay tax of $12,000, leaving $8,000 to Buford for law school expense.

A summary of this series of graphics is to say that you can do #1. But if you try to do #2, which is much better than #1, you get #3, which is much worse than #1.

The only way the interest can be taxed to Buford instead of his mama is for her to give Buford the $250,000 outright.[58] So get on the

---

58   This payment, however, might be subject to gift tax.

phone and tell Buford's mama about this new tax ploy you've learned.[59]

Actually the below-market loan provisions are just sort of an elaborate preventive. Because of their punitive effect they just scare everyone away. So no one ever does transactions that would trigger them. That being the case, it could be said that you don't have to learn these provisions. All you have to know is that it's a bad idea to do low interest loan deals. We don't actually recommend that approach, however. We think you ought to know how it works because you're a tax lawyer. Tax lawyers fear neither complexity nor mechanics.

If the below interest loan is made from an employer to an employee, then the treatment is that the employer is deemed to receive interest from the employee at the high applicable federal rate; the employer is deemed to give back the high interest to the employee treated as wages, which is deductible to the employer but gross income to the employee. The employee's deemed payment of interest to the employer seems to be a wash with the interest received, except that it is deductible below the line and therefore may be lost. The employee is taxed on the interest received from investing the funds. If the transaction is a below-market loan from a corporation to a shareholder, the result is very unfavorable to the corporation, since it has a deemed dividend paid to the shareholder which is not deductible to the corporation.

(ii) Unearned Income of Children

As a further restriction on assigning income from higher-income to lower-income family members, the Code provides that all net unearned income (above a floor amount of $1,050 in 2016 plus the greater of another $1,050 or expenses incurred in generating the income) of a child under 14 years is taxed at the rate the income would be taxed at if the income were received by the parent. This is the case regardless of the source of the assets producing the income. Unearned income is income from investment property. Income the under-14 child earns through rendering personal services (such as babysitting or winning Wimbledon) would be taxed to the child at the child's own marginal rate. Thus the child could pay income at two different rates of tax depending on the source of his income. Indeed, the child's tax return become even more complex than the parent's.

This rule cuts back on the parents' ability to shift income-producing property to a lower-bracket child in order to lessen the overall tax on the family.[60] This provision is like the joint return in

---

[59]   For further discussion of the expenses of law school, see ¶ 6.03(3)(b).

[60]   See § 1(g).

that it moves our system closer to the idea that the taxable unit is the family rather than single individuals.

(c) Alimony

The payment of alimony and child support is another major statutory example of assignment of income. One party to the dissolving marriage is allowed to shift income to the other lower-bracket party. The subject of alimony is treated in detail at ¶ 6.02(14).

¶ 5.05 ASSIGNMENT OF INCOME WITHOUT TEARS

The trouble with assignment of income doctrine is that it is a song without end.[61] The whole area of capital gains[62] can be looked on as an application of assignment of income doctrine. That is, most any asset has value because it is capable of producing a stream of ordinary income either at the present or in the future. Hence the proceeds from the sale of that asset are in some sense a substitute for ordinary income, conceivably triggering *Lake*-type discussions of "carve-outs," "vertical and horizontal cuts," "fruit and tree," etc. Similarly, where the assignment of income is gratuitous, the problem that is raised is what is the appropriate family unit on which to impose a tax. Indeed, as discussed above, the joint return is a congressionally-sanctioned assignment of income from the wage earner to his spouse.[63] Family partnerships present assignment of income problems. The field of corporate taxation is rife with assignment of income issues ranging from the viability of the corporation as a taxable entity to questions of the character of taxable gain in the collapsible corporation area.[64]

Thus when Justice Oliver Wendell Holmes planted the tree in *Lucas v. Earl*,[65] he doubtless did not know how great a tree would grow, how far its branches would reach, and where its fruit would fall.

---

[61]   Cf. Lyon and Eustice, "Assignment of Income: Fruit and Tree as Irrigated by the P.G. Lake Case," 17 Tax Law Rev. 295 (1962).

[62]   See ¶ 4.06(2)(b)(i) for discussion of the several low rates available for capital gains.

[63]   See discussion of Poe v. Seaborn, ¶ 5.02 supra. See also Bittker, "Federal Income Taxation and the Family," 27 Stanford Law Review 1389 (1975).

[64]   Cf. § 482, allowing the Service to allocate income, deductions and credits among taxpayers under common control in order to clearly reflect income; § 341 regarding "collapsible corporations."

[65]   See ¶ 5.02, supra.

Chapter 6

BUSINESS DEDUCTIONS

Table of Sections

Para.

STRUCTURE OF FEDERAL INCOME TAXATION

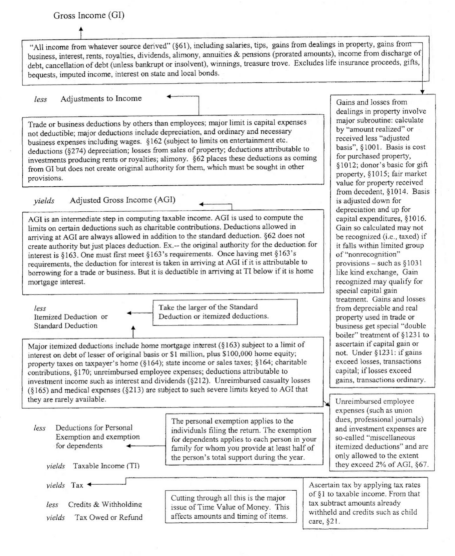

Gross Income (GI)

"All income from whatever source derived" (§61), including salaries, tips, gains from dealings in property, gains from business, interest, rents, royalties, dividends, alimony, annuities & pensions (prorated amounts), income from discharge of debt, cancellation of debt (unless bankrupt or insolvent), winnings, treasure trove. Excludes life insurance proceeds, gifts, bequests, imputed income, interest on state and local bonds.

less　　Adjustments to Income

Trade or business deductions by others than employees; major limit is capital expenses not deductible; major deductions include depreciation, and ordinary and necessary business expenses including wages. §162 (subject to limits on entertainment etc. deductions (§274) depreciation; losses from sales of property; deductions attributable to investments producing rents or royalties; alimony. §62 places these deductions as coming from GI but does not create original authority for them, which must be sought in other provisions.

yields　　Adjusted Gross Income (AGI)

AGI is an intermediate step in computing taxable income. AGI is used to compute the limits on certain deductions such as charitable contributions. Deductions allowed in arriving at AGI are always allowed in addition to the standard deduction. §62 does not create authority but just places deduction. Ex.-- the original authority for the deduction for interest is §163. One must first meet §163's requirements. Once having met §163's requirements, the deduction for interest is taken in arriving at AGI if it is attributable to borrowing for a trade or business. But it is deductible in arriving at TI below if it is home mortgage interest.

less
Itemized Deduction or
Standard Deduction

Take the larger of the Standard Deduction or itemized deductions.

Major itemized deductions include home mortgage interest (§163) subject to a limit of interest on debt of lesser of original basis or $1 million, plus $100,000 home equity; property taxes on taxpayer's home (§164); state income or sales taxes; §164; charitable contributions, §170; unreimbursed employee expenses; deductions attributable to investment income such as interest and dividends (§212). Unreimbursed casualty losses (§165) and medical expenses (§213) are subject to such severe limits keyed to AGI that they are rarely available.

less　　Deductions for Personal
　　　　　Exemption and exemption
　　　　　for dependents

The personal exemption applies to the individuals filing the return. The exemption for dependents applies to each person in your family for whom you provide at least half of the person's total support during the year.

yields　　Taxable Income (TI)

yields　　Tax

less　　Credits & Withholding

yields　　Tax Owed or Refund

Cutting through all this is the major issue of Time Value of Money. This affects amounts and timing of items.

Gains and losses from dealings in property involve major subroutine: calculate by "amount realized" or received less "adjusted basis", §1001. Basis is cost for purchased property, §1012; donor's basic for gift property, §1015; fair market value for property received from decedent, §1014. Basis is adjusted down for depreciation and up for capital expenditures, §1016. Gain so calculated may not be recognized (i.e., taxed) if it falls within limited group of "nonrecognition" provisions – such as §1031 like kind exchange, Gain recognized may qualify for special capital gain treatment. Gains and losses from depreciable and real property used in trade or business get special "double boiler" treatment of §1231 to ascertain if capital gain or not. Under §1231: if gains exceed losses, transactions capital; if losses exceed gains, transactions ordinary.

Unreimbursed employee expenses (such as union dues, professional journals) and investment expenses are so-called "miscellaneous itemized deductions" and are only allowed to the extent they exceed 2% of AGI, §67.

Ascertain tax by applying tax rates of §1 to taxable income. From that tax subtract amounts already withheld and credits such as child care, §21.

¶ 6.01 STRUCTURAL ISSUES IN GENERAL

(1) Putting the Tax Code on the Back of an Envelope

It is in the area of deductions that the "pop culture" critics of the income tax founder most egregiously. These "pop culture" critics include some politicians, a large number of journalists, and a huge number of people who horse-collar us at parties and even in nursing homes while visiting relatives to tell us how they are going to reform the federal income tax. Since we have had it up to our *keisters* with these people, will you pardon us if we get a few things off our chests?

The main thing these experts like to do is to explain how the present Internal Revenue Code and Regulations (which together constitute some 10,000 pages) can be reformed to fit on the back of an envelope. Now we would be the first to admit that the Code and Regulations run, at times, to the prolix. Nevertheless, the idea that the rules of a reasonable income tax system in a sophisticated economy such as ours could be reduced to the back of an envelope is absurd.

Let's take the typical proposal from one of these "experts." Let's say it's a well-known media correspondent. These folks usually say something like "Let's take income and just apply one flat rate of tax, say, 15%, and that'll be it." (Some politicians have thrown out ideas like this too). Already we are in limbo. The complexity of the Internal Revenue Code stems not from the progressive rate structure. That only takes a few pages in § 1.

What's complex is not the rate structure but the base to which the rate structure is applied.

This leads us to the next "reform" proposal (give me a nickel for every time we've heard this one—and we'll pay tax on all those nickels too).[1] The "expert" says: "Just put a tax on income and allow no deductions." That is rich.

Take a simple case. A neighborhood grocery store is owned by the owner as a sole proprietor. Over the course of a year the grocery store generates $1,000,000 of sales. Shall we tax that $1,000,000 at 30 or 40 percent or whatever it is? Say we tax it at 40%. That's a tax of $400,000. The cost of goods sold is $600,000. This grocery store has employees. Expenses there run $90,000. What about utilities? There's another $45,000. Rent is another $80,000. There's insurance; there's property taxes—another—another $10,000. Putting all the expenses together with the income, this business made $275,000 this year. They'll have a tough time paying tax of $400,000. You think there's a taxpayer revolt now; try presenting this business with a tax bill of $400,000.

---

[1] This is reminiscent of the 1940s song written by Buddy Kaye and Ralph Care "A Penny a Kiss—A Penny a Hug." In the song, the couple puts a penny in a jug every time they hug or kiss. They believe that if they do this they will be millionaires. As a child this seemed ridiculous, but if we consider the time value of money—who knows. Well actually, we know the couple was wrong. If a 20-year old couple kissed or hugged 100 times a day for 45 years, they would only have about $75,000 when they retired.

We simply have to allow the expenses of generating the income, or else we are just imposing a mindless tax on the volume of economic activity. Compare this to someone who sells stock he bought at $1,000,000 for $2,000,000. To whom is it more fair to give the tax bill of $400,000?

The idea of an income tax is inextricably bound up with the idea of fairness. It's based on ability to pay. Income, inherently, is a net concept. To gauge the ability to pay we must subtract from income the legitimate expenses of producing that income. As soon as the self-styled tax expert admits that, the idea of fitting everything on an envelope evaporates.

There's a lot of complex transactions out there. Suppose somebody constructs a building in 2016 for $40 million to produce rental income of $4 million per year over the next 30 years. Do we allow the deduction of the $40 million in the first year? Recall our discussion of the time value of money. Allowing that deduction up front is much more valuable to the taxpayer than spreading that $40 million deduction out over the period the building produces income. It's probably fairer to require the building to be deducted over the period it is producing income. That's depreciation. Well that takes a few rules to specify, doesn't it? Once again: poof goes the envelope.

So our expert is still struggling. The expert says, "Okay, allow business deductions. I admit there'll be some complications." But it's more than just complications. Let's say we are arguing about this matter over lunch. That immediately leads to two questions: 1) who is going to pick up the tab; and 2) can whoever picks up the tab deduct it in arriving at the amount of his taxable income?

Suppose (just to fantasize for a moment) that your tax professor picks up the tab. Isn't explaining the tax law (or fruitlessly trying to) part of a law professor's job? Or is that just too nebulous? Do we need some rules in this area? Don't we have a problem—once we decide to allow business deductions—in figuring out just what it is that constitutes business deductions? Drawing the line between deductible business expenses and non-deductible personal expenses is complicated.

How about taxing an annuity, a subject we've talked about a couple of times already (see Chapter 3). A taxpayer pays a premium in 2010 and then in 2016 the taxpayer begins receiving payments for 20 years. How do we tax that? No deduction at all for the premium? Obviously wrong. We have to deduct the premium somehow along the time that the income comes in. That gets complicated. How is that to be simplified?

The statute is always going to be complicated. That is not something to run away from. Step up to it. Enjoy it. The complexity is part of the attraction of the field.

Now even though the statute is always going to be complicated, there is some simplification we can do. We can look at the "deep structure" of the Internal Revenue Code. We've talked about this before. And we have our diagram that attempts to depict the field on one page that appears at the beginning of this book, at the beginning of this chapter, and other chapters in this book. There's a deep structure to the field of federal income taxation. It does not change, though some individual provisions change. Understanding that deep structure will help you.

(2) The Deep Structure of the Tax System

Okay, we're in a position, having fought our way through the discussion of income, to look at the deep structure of this field. A taxpayer has income. As we discussed in the introduction, income is defined as gross receipts or gross income (§ 61), less the deductions necessarily required to produce that income. That is what we mean by income.

Despite the apparent complexity of the subject, there's amazingly only two things that the taxpayer can do with his income. The taxpayer can consume it or invest it. When a taxpayer consumes income, it's in the form of an "expense." When a taxpayer invests income, it's called a "capital expenditure." Here is some welcome news: you cannot name an outlay that does not come under one of those two categories. Every outlay is either an expense or a capital expenditure.

How do we handle those two basic types of outlays? In a "pure" income tax, there would be no deductions for either consumption or saving. In a "pure" income tax, we are taxing income and we do not reduce income for expenses or capital expenditures.[2] (Section 62 provides no deduction for personal, living or family expenses; § 263 provides no deduction for capital expenditures.)

There is one further qualification, with regard to capital expenditures. To understand it first consider that the term "capital expenditure" is broader than you might think. Thus if you buy a building, you've made a capital expenditure; if you buy gold, you've made a capital expenditure; if you buy a computer, you've made a capital expenditure; if you buy stock, you've made a capital expenditure; if you spend money to produce an invention that gains

---

[2] For discussion of the consumption tax, as compared to the income tax, see Chapter 1.

a patent, you've made a capital expenditure; if you buy an annuity, you've made a capital expenditure; if you put your money in a savings bank account, you've made a capital expenditure.

What do all these transactions have in common? They all create an asset of one kind or another that produces income in the future. Now there are two kinds of capital expenditures. One kind produces a wasting asset and the other kind produces an asset that theoretically lasts forever. Consider the examples of capital expenditures in the previous paragraph. Which of them produced a wasting asset and which produced an asset that theoretically lasts forever?

The following examples are capital expenditures that produce wasting assets: building, computer, and patent, annuity. The others are assets that theoretically last forever. In both scenarios, we do not allow an immediate deduction for the cost of the capital expenditure (§ 263). On wasting assets, we allow a deduction of their cost or basis spread out over the period of their useful lives (the major example here is depreciation under § 168). How we ascertain their useful lives could be a matter of controversy, but for now we are only talking about deep structure and theory. On assets that last forever we do not allow a deduction over time for the cost or basis. This would be the case even if the asset is producing a stream of income over time. An example of this is stock that pays dividends. We do not allow a deduction of the cost of the stock over time as we hold it even though the stock is producing taxable dividends over time.

Keep this deep structure in mind. This is the real economics of an income tax system. What you want to understand is how our system at various times departs from this deep structure. If you understand this deep structure, it will also help you to understand how various deductions fit into the picture. It will also help you to understand what people are arguing about, and why particular arguments—that sound silly off the top—are made.

Let's just take one example that hits close to home. Why can you only deduct at most $4,000 of your law school tuition paid in any one year?[3] There's no doubt that is all you get. It doesn't matter who you are, what your family circumstances, what your reasons for going to law school. Best case scenario, you can only deduct $4,000 of your law school tuition paid in any one year and that is it.[4]

---

[3]   See ¶ 6.03(3)(b). The deduction will theoretically expire after 2016, but the threat of termination has long loomed over this particular deduction. See § 222 and ¶ 6.03.

[4]   See ¶ 6.03(3)(b).

What is the reason for this? The lay person—which you are rapidly ceasing to be—would think it is just another one of "those arbitrary rules." But in fact this rule grows out of the deep structure of the federal income tax. The cost of legal education prepares you for a new profession, a profession you cannot enter without this education. Thus it creates an asset that produces income over time. Thus it is a capital expense and not deductible when paid.

Now we move to the second step in analyzing capital expenditures. Is this a wasting asset or an asset that lasts forever? It would appear it is wasting—that is that your legal career cannot last beyond your lifetime. However, the Service regards it as an asset that does not waste. Thus there is no deduction for your legal education over its estimated life expectancy.

You could argue about that. You could say that the tax law ought to allow you to write off the cost of your legal education over time. Now you are making an educated argument. You know what you are talking about. (The argument loses, however, as you'll see later.)

Take some other examples. The deduction for interest on a home mortgage is a good example. The cost of borrowing for business is deductible. That's part of the cost of doing business. But the interest cost on the home mortgage is a personal consumption item. The expense should not be deductible in the pure income tax. But we do allow it to be deducted in our income tax (see Chapter 7). Why is that? We could debate that. The home mortgage interest deduction raises major policy questions. That's because it violates the deep structure of a pure income tax.

Here's another one. Employer contributions to so-called qualified pension plans are excluded from the employee's income (see Chapter 8). That violates the deep structure. You can see it clearly if you bear in mind that exclusions are equivalent to deductions. That exclusion for pension contributions is the same thing as if the employee received the amount of money and then put it into the pension fund himself and was allowed to take a deduction.

This pension contribution is savings. In effect, this treatment of pension plans gives the employee a deduction for saving. As we said before, in a "pure" income tax we do not give the taxpayer a deduction for saving. But we do in our system.

Keep in mind as we go along where we are within in the deep structure, and consider whether a particular deduction violates the deep structure of federal income taxation.

(3) The Statutory Structure of the Tax System

Once a taxpayer has ascertained the amount of gross income for a year, including items of compensation for services rendered, other items to be included in income, gains from dealings in property (including whether some of transactions and property qualify for the favorable capital gains treatment), it is time for the taxpayer to consider deductions. There are two general kinds of deductions, which are illustrated by the following schema: (you may also wish to refer to the introduction and the graphic at the beginning of this Chapter).

Steps in Computing Taxable Income and Amount of Tax Owed

1. Gross income

2. Less: deductions allowed above the line as provided by § 62

3. Yields: adjusted gross income

4. Less: the greater of itemized deductions or the standard deduction

5. Less: deductions for personal and dependency exemptions

6. Yields: taxable income[5]

7. Calculate Tax

8. Less: Any tax credits[6]

It can be seen from this schema that deductions are allowed in two sets: Those deductions in Line 2 that are taken from gross income (Line 1) to arrive at adjusted gross income (Line 3), and those deductions in Line 4 taken from adjusted gross income to arrive at taxable income. It is § 62 of the Code that directs whether particular deductions will be allowed as deductions from gross income or from adjusted gross income. Section 62 itself creates no deductions, nor does it bar any. It simply directs where particular deductions shall be taken. In popular parlance, then, it's a traffic-cop section. Deductions that are taken from gross income are said to be taken

---

[5] Sections 61, 62 and 63. A taxpayer in the business of selling goods would have a preliminary step of ascertaining gross receipts less cost of goods sold to arrive at gross income from that business.

[6] As you can see, tax credits are subtracted from your tax, not from your income. Thus, a tax credit provides a dollar for dollar reduction in your tax bill. Tax credits normally benefit lower and middle income individuals because the benefit to the individual does not depend on the marginal rate structure. Absent other phaseouts, a person in the lowest bracket and a person in the highest bracket will receive the same benefit from a credit. If both receive a deduction, the higher bracket taxpayer will receive a much larger benefit than the lower bracket taxpayer.

"above the line;" deductions that are taken from adjusted gross income are said to be taken "below the line," in the argot of tax professionals.

There are several reasons why it is important to ascertain whether a deduction is above the line or below the line. Deductions taken above the line are allowed in full to all taxpayers. Deductions taken below the line—so-called itemized deductions—are only taken if they in the aggregate exceed the standard deduction. The standard deduction is in essence a floor amount which is allowed as an itemized deduction to all taxpayers.[7]

In addition, adjusted gross income (AGI) is sometimes used to make further computations—the major ones being to ascertain a floor for the medical expense deduction, a floor for the casualty loss deduction to personal-use property, a floor for deduction of miscellaneous itemized deductions, and a ceiling for the deduction for charitable contributions.[8]

Adjusted gross income serves as a more sensible measure for limiting these other deductions than does gross income. Suppose, for example, Adelle Furgeson who owns her own auto parts business generates $100,000 of revenues but has $70,000 in expenses. She suffers, let us say, a personal casualty loss to her home of $15,000. The casualty loss deduction (as discussed in Chapter 7 at ¶ 7.01(5)) only allows casualties to personal-use property to the extent they exceed a floor of 10% of adjusted gross income. If the 10% floor were keyed to *gross income* rather than adjusted gross income, Adelle would then be able to deduct only $5,000 of her $15,000 loss. (10% of $100,000 = $10,000; hence $5,000 of $15,000 is in excess of the floor). Compare Adelle's case to that of Bennett Fargsworth who works as an accountant in a small company at a salary of $30,000 with no business deductions. If we're still using gross income and Bennett suffers a $15,000 personal casualty, he would be able to deduct $12,000 of it. This is the excess of $15,000 over 10% of $30,000 or $3,000. Thus although Adelle and Bennett have the same net income of $30,000, Adelle can only deduct $5,000 of her casualty whereas Bennett can deduct $12,000, if gross income is used as the measure.

When the casualty loss is keyed to adjusted gross income rather than gross income, this anomaly drops out. Adjusted gross income more or less takes account of Adelle's business expenses. They both have $30,000 of adjusted gross income. The 10% rule appropriately gives them each the same floor for calculating their deductible casualty loss. Thus so-called "horizontal equity" is insured.

---

[7]   Section 63(c).

[8]   See generally Chapter 7.

The concept of adjusted gross income performs this important task of insuring horizontal equity in a less than perfect fashion. As discussed at various points in this chapter and Chapter 7, the deductions allowed in arriving at adjusted gross income do not perfectly reflect the expenses of producing gross income. For example alimony payments are allowed as a deduction in arriving at adjusted gross income, although alimony payments do not generate any gross income.[9] Similarly a number of deductions, called "miscellaneous itemized deductions," are not allowed in arriving at adjusted gross income. Examples of these would include union dues, and work clothing expenses. This is the case even though these expenses have produced gross income (see Chapter 7 ¶ 7.02). Thus AGI is a little ragged in producing a concept of net income to assist in calculating various limits on deductions. But that is the main idea behind it.

To qualify as a deduction above the line, a deduction must specifically fit within § 62, otherwise the deduction is allowed only below the line. Whether a particular deduction can be taken above the line will depend on the particular facts. For example, interest on a loan is allowed as a deduction by § 163. But the deduction for interest will only be allowed above the line if the loan giving rise to the interest payment was taken for the purpose of conducting the taxpayer's own business or for producing rental or royalty income for the taxpayer. If the loan was taken to purchase a home, then the deduction for interest allowed by § 163 can only be taken below the line, since there is nothing in § 62 that allows it to be above the line. Similarly, the deduction for casualty losses can only be taken above the line if the casualty was sustained by business or investment-type property; if the casualty was to non-business or personal property, it may only be deducted below the line.[10]

It is only after it is ascertained that a particular item is deductible under one of the specific Code provisions discussed below that the item is tested under § 62 to determine whether it is deductible above or below the line.

---

[9]	Putting the alimony deduction above the line could be justified on choice of taxable person grounds, see ¶ 6.02(14).

[10]	Section 165, discussed at ¶ 7.01(5). Note that a deduction for casualties to *personal-use* property is subject to a $100 per casualty floor, and further that, as discussed above, such casualties are only deductible to the extent that in the aggregate they exceed 10% of the taxpayer's adjusted gross income.

¶ 6.02 DEDUCTIONS ARISING OUT OF BUSINESS AND PROFIT SEEKING ACTIVITY

(1) Common Business Expenses

(a) Ordinary and Necessary Business Expenses

Section 162(a) allows for the deduction of "all the ordinary and necessary expenses paid or incurred during the taxable year in carrying on any trade or business." Congress also, in § 212, provided that there shall also be allowed as a deduction "all the ordinary and necessary expenses paid or incurred during the taxable year—(1) for the production or collection of income"; (2) for the management, conservation or maintenance of property held for the production of income. . . ." Sections 162 and 212, therefore, provide for the two major types of activity as defined by the Code: activity that constitutes a trade or business; and activity that constitutes investment (or production-of-income activity that does not rise to the level of a trade or business).

Thus, a taxpayer who is an employee, or who runs a business as a sole proprietor, is engaging in a trade or business (that of either being an employee of a particular kind or of running a particular business). However, a taxpayer who buys stocks and bonds or who holds a piece of real estate for rental income is not engaging in a "trade or business" but is rather engaging in "profit-seeking" or "investment" activity.[11]

The taxpayer who is engaging in a "trade or business" deducts ordinary and necessary business expenses under § 162(a); the taxpayer who is engaging in "profit-seeking" or "investment" activity takes ordinary and necessary business expenses as a deduction under § 212. Because deductions under § 162 are often treated far more favorably than deductions under § 212, the distinction between "trade or business" and "investment" may be very important.[12] Moreover, the Code often speaks in terms of "trade or business" activity on the one hand and investment or profit-seeking activity on the other, and it is useful to know that those terms are referring to the activities described in §§ 162 and 212, respectively.[13]

The words in the phrase "ordinary and necessary business expenses" have come to be matters of great litigation. Obviously, the great mass of expenses incurred by a taxpayer in running a

---

[11]   See ¶ 6.02(2).

[12]   See ¶ 6.02(10), relating to the deduction for an office in the home.

[13]   See e.g. §§ 167(a) and 168 relating to the deduction for depreciation, discussed at ¶ 6.02(12).

business—wages, rent, utilities, repairs, etc.—are deductible under § 162(a) without question. The term "ordinary" might imply some type of test relating to the extent the expense is traditionally incurred in a trade or business. Earlier cases took a stricter view of "ordinary and necessary." For example, the Board of Tax Appeals held that a life insurance policy taken out by a stock dealer on the President of the United States was not an ordinary and necessary business expense despite the fact that the death of the President might adversely impact the stock market because it did not appear that other persons in the same business, when confronted with similar conditions, incurred such expenses.[14] Similarly, it was held that an attorney who paid hush money to an accuser whose charges were harming his professional reputation could not deduct the payments as an ordinary and necessary business expense.[15]

These cases apparently rest on the ground that the expenses in question were not ordinary and/or necessary. Thus the deduction is denied even though the expenses are legitimately incurred incident to the taxpayer's trade or business. In short, not *all* expenses related to the taxpayers trade or business are deductible. Only those which are "ordinary and necessary" are deductible.[16]

In recent years, the Services appears to have been reluctant to attack expenses on ordinary and necessary grounds unless the expense really lacked a business purpose. The Supreme Court dealt with this in the famous case of *Welch v. Helvering*.[17]

---

[14]   Goedel v. Commissioner, 39 B.T.A. 1, 1939 WL 263 (1939); to the same effect is Rev.Rul. 55–714, 1955–2 C.B. 51 (denying the manager of an entertainer a deduction for life insurance premiums on policy on the entertainer's life).

[15]   Bonney v. Commissioner, 247 F.2d 237 (2d Cir.1957), cert. denied 355 U.S. 906, 78 S.Ct. 333, 2 L.Ed.2d 261 (1957). See also Reffett, 39 T.C. 869 (1963) (contingent fees paid to witnesses in damage suit were not ordinary); But see Rev.Rul. 63–275, 1963–2 C.B. 85 (research expenses of faculty members, including travel, are ordinary and necessary business expenses—thank God for small favors).

[16]   Some mildly interesting *dicta* on what is "ordinary and necessary" is provided in Welch v. Helvering, 290 U.S. 111, 115, 54 S.Ct. 8, 9, 78 L.Ed. 212 (1933) ("life in all its fullness must supply the answer to the riddle"); Deputy v. du Pont, 308 U.S. 488, 496, 60 S.Ct. 363, 367, 84 L.Ed. 416 (1940) ("it is the kind of transaction out of which the obligation arose and its normalcy in the particular business which are crucial and controlling").

[17]   290 U.S. 111, 54 S. Ct. 8 (1933).

WELCH V. HELVERING[18]

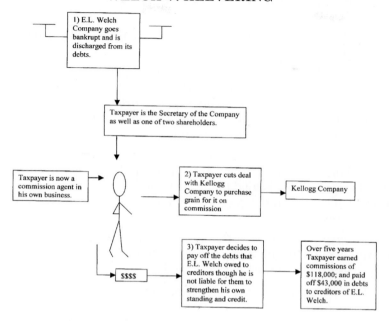

1) E.L. Welch Company goes bankrupt and is discharged from its debts.

Taxpayer is the Secretary of the Company as well as one of two shareholders.

Taxpayer is now a commission agent in his own business.

2) Taxpayer cuts deal with Kellogg Company to purchase grain for it on commission

Kellogg Company

$$$$

3) Taxpayer decides to pay off the debts that E.L. Welch owed to creditors though he is not liable for them to strengthen his own standing and credit.

Over five years Taxpayer earned commissions of $118,000; and paid off $43,000 in debts to creditors of E.L. Welch.

Facts: Taxpayer, Thomas Welch, was the secretary of a company engaged in the grain business. He and his father were the shareholders in the company. The company went bankrupt and was released from its debts. The taxpayer subsequently made a contract with the Kellogg Company to purchase grain for it on commission. In order to re-establish relations with customers that he had worked with in his previous capacity, he decided to try to pay off as many of the debts of the bankrupt company as he was able. Over five years the taxpayer earned $118,000 on commission and paid off $43,000 in debts to creditors of his bankrupt former company.

Question: Is the taxpayer's payment of Welch Company debts deductible to taxpayer as "ordinary and necessary" business expenses under § 162?

Service's argument: Payments are not deductible as ordinary and necessary but were capital expenditures for the development of reputation and goodwill.

Held: The payments were not deductible for two reasons: 1) the payments were "necessary" but not "ordinary"; 2) the payments were

---

capital expenditures establishing goodwill, agreeing with Service's argument.

Comment: The second argument concerning goodwill has come to be one for which *Welch* is famous.

Comment: Since the taxpayer in *Welch* was continuing a business in which he and his father were already engaged, he might have been regarded as just "repairing" his already existing goodwill. Therefore the payments might have been regarded as immediately deductible as "ordinary and necessary."

Comment: Note that the taxpayer's payment of debts was always substantially less than his income from commissions each year. This suggests he carefully scaled his repayments so that he always had a net profit. This might suggest the payments are deductible expenses of doing business.

Comment: Curiously, although this case is famous, the weight of subsequent cases of *voluntary debt repayment* is to allow an ordinary and necessary expense deduction.

The result in this case was that taxpayer could add the debt repayment amounts to his basis in his goodwill. Goodwill, under present rules, can be written off on a straight line basis over 15 years if it has been purchased by the taxpayer.[19] This goodwill was apparently not purchased and hence is regarded as an asset with an indefinite useful life. Thus there is no depreciation or amortization of the goodwill in this case. The only way taxpayer in *Welch* would ever get the tax benefit of these expenditures would be if he would sell his business, including the goodwill. This was, of course, something he might well never do. This had to be a bitter pill to swallow, given that the alternative result was immediate deduction of the payments. This was, essentially, a case of "now or never" for the taxpayer. Another major limit on the deductibility of expenses has to do with salaries. To be deductible, salaries or other compensation for personal services must be reasonable, § 162(a)(1). The Service is not in the business of limiting the size of salary payments as a matter of public policy. Rather, the Service uses the weapon of "reasonable compensation" to limit shifting income between related taxpayers who are trying to reduce their total tax burden. Nevertheless, given the great attention that has attended the high salaries of corporate executives in recent years, one may wonder whether the Service could use the "reasonable . . . compensation" weapon of § 162 to curb high salaries as a matter of public policy. Without a directive from

---

[19]   See ¶ 6.02(13)(d).

Congress, the Service was most unlikely to attempt this even though the approach has support in the statutory language.[20]

In 1993, Congress gave the Service just such a directive, enacting § 162(m), which applies to publicly held corporations. It denies a deduction to such a corporation for a salary in excess of $1 million if the recipient is one of the corporation's 5 highest-paid executives. If the salary in excess of $1 million is based "on the attainment of one or more performance goals," then the deduction is allowed in full. "Performance goals," under the statute are required to be developed in advance by outside directors and to be approved by a majority of the corporation's shareholders. The legislative history states that performance criteria that could be used could include the company's sales, earnings or share price.

This provision raises some interesting questions about corporate governance that are more within the gambit of a course on corporations. It sounds like an effective curb on excessive salaries to require approval by outside directors and shareholders of performance criteria. But in practice outside directors are frequently not very far "outside," and can receive many perks from management in their role as outside directors. Similarly shareholders often passively vote for whatever management proposes, often without even realizing what they are voting for. Thus perhaps the question of excessive salaries for management is a corporate governance question rather than a tax question.[21]

These ideas seem to be borne out by a study by Graef Crystal, a corporate compensation expert in San Diego. There are a number of directors who sit on many boards of the Fortune 1,000 companies at the same time. Indeed, in 1995, 68 directors of Fortune 1,000 companies sat on nine or more corporate boards, according to Directorship, a Greenwich, Conn., consulting firm. The question is how much scrutiny can a director give a company (when there are four to 11 meetings a year) sitting on so many boards? The study by Mr. Crystal looked at the performance of the 256 companies whose boards have one or more of these 68 directors and found no

---

[20]   The Service does have an older case as a weapon if it wanted to use it. In Patton v. Commissioner, 168 F.2d 28 (6th Cir.1948), the Service successfully limited the deduction of the salary of a bookkeeper to $13,000 instead of the $46,000 that was being paid. The $46,000 was paid in accordance with an arrangement that gave the bookkeeper 10% of the business's net sales. The Service succeeded even though the bookkeeper was not related to the controlling partners of the enterprise, and there was no suggestion that the transaction constituted a gift. The result was that the $33,000 disallowed amount was taxed to the partnership, since no deduction was allowed. The $33,000 was also taxed to the bookkeeper because he in fact received it. The Service made out very well indeed.

[21]   Many people are now aware of these types of problems in light of the Enron, WorldCom and other major corporate scandals.

statistically significant difference in performance. Mr. Crystal did find, however, that those 256 companies paid their chief executives and their directors more than did other companies. See generally Judith H. Dobrzynski, When Directors Play Musical Chairs.

As to closely-held corporations, § 162(m) does not deal with excessive salaries for management. In that area, the Service is still fighting with its traditional tools. Common examples of unreasonably high compensation being paid which would be subject to challenge by the Service would include: excessively high salaries paid to the controlling shareholders of a closely-held corporation for the purpose of minimizing the corporation's tax; excessive salaries paid to members of the family employed in the family business, for the purpose of deflecting income to lower-bracket family members;[22] wage payments between taxpayers who are also engaging in other transactions such as the purchase and sale of property, where a capital expense may be disguised as a deductible wage payment.[23]

The employees in these "suspect" situations may very well be rendering substantial services, in which case their employers are entitled to deduct their compensation in full. The most difficult case arises where the employee in this situation is rendering substantial services, but appears to be overpaid for those services. Then the courts and the Service must engage in the agonizing process of determining how much of the employee's compensation was "reasonable" and how much was "unreasonable," for the purpose of disallowing as a deduction to the employer the unreasonable amount. A large number of factors have been adduced by all hands concerned to try to settle this matter, and the number of litigated cases is exceedingly large. The major factors seem to be the level of compensation paid other employees in comparable jobs, whether the payments are pro rata to stock holdings, level of employer earnings, the type of work performed.

Problems can arise if the compensation is contingent on earnings, and the earnings grow to a surprising degree over the years. The result may be compensation that appears to have grown to an unreasonable level, but the regulations provide that if the contingent compensation agreement was arrived at pursuant to a free bargain between the parties, the resulting very high level of compensation will be allowed as a deduction.

Demonstrating that a contingent compensation arrangement was arrived at under a free bargain where, as is usually the case in

---

[22]   Cf. Chapter 5 on the doctrine of assignment of income.
[23]   See generally Regs. §§ 1.162–7 and 8.

these cases, the corporation is a family corporation or otherwise closely-held, can be difficult indeed.

For example, the case of *Harolds Club v. Commissioner*,[24] involved a contingent profit arrangement in a family setting. The two sons of Raymond Smith owned all the stock of Harolds Club casino. Raymond was an effective manager and his sons entered into an agreement where by Raymond would receive an annual salary of $10,000 plus 20% of the profits. Thereafter, as will come as no surprise, gambling proved to be extremely popular. Harolds Club profits increased dramatically, leading Raymond to receive as total salary under the contingent arrangement, $350,000 to $560,000 during 1952–1956. The question was whether this salary was reasonable. Competitors testified that they thought he was worth what he was paid.

The Ninth Circuit noted that under the regulations, contingent compensation, generally speaking, should be allowed as a deduction even though it is unusually large if it is paid pursuant to a "free bargain" between the employer and the individual, Reg. § 1.162–7(b), and if the contract was reasonable at the time when it was made. The Ninth Circuit affirmed the Tax Court's disallowance of the deduction on the grounds that there was no "free bargain," since it found that Raymond dominated his sons. (Apparently Raymond was a little too effective as a manager).[25]

Often on the occasion of a merger or takeover, upper-level executives may be displaced. They often land on their feet, however, assisted in their descent by a golden parachute, or large severance pay. Section 280G, however, limits the deduction of these payments when they are found to be "excess parachute payments."[26]

As previously discussed, the Service does not usually pursue an excessive compensation case unless it appears that the salary is being used to shift income between related parties trying to reduce their tax burden. In the following case, however, the Service broadened that approach.

---

[24]   340 F.2d 861 (9th Cir.1965).

[25]   See also Reg. § 1.404(a)–1(b), providing that contributions to qualified pension, profit sharing, and other deferred compensation plans may be deducted only if the contribution, when taken together with the other compensation of the employee, constitutes reasonable compensation; Kennedy v. Commissioner, 671 F.2d 167 (6th Cir.1982) (compensation arrangement was reasonable when made).

[26]   Section 280G.

EXACTO SPRING CORP. V. COMMISSIONER[27]

Facts: Exacto Spring was a closely held corporation that manufactured precision springs. It paid its chief executive, the founder of the corporation, a salary of $1.3 and $1.0 million in 1993 and 1994. The founder of the corporation held 55% of the shares of the corporation and the two major minority shareholders held 40% of the shares. The minority shareholders approved the salary payments. The Commissioner determined that the salary payments were excessive and concluded that an appropriate salary for 1993 was $381,000 and for 1994 was $400,000.

Question: Was the compensation excessive?

Tax Court decision: The Tax Court applied a seven factor test that examines "(1) the type and extent of the services rendered; (2) the scarcity of qualified employees; (3) the qualifications and prior earning capacity of the employee; (4) the contributions of the employee to the business venture; (5) the net earnings of the employer; (6) the prevailing compensation paid to employees with comparable jobs; and (7) the peculiar characteristics of the employer's business."[28] After applying the test the Tax Court concluded that the maximum salary payment should have been $900,000 and $700,000 respectively.

Held: The Seventh Circuit rejected the test used by the Tax Court and determined that the compensation was reasonable. Instead, the court determined that a better test would be the "independent investor test." Under this test, the court looks to see whether the investors are receiving an acceptable level of return on their investment. If they are, the court believes that the compensation is presumptively valid.

Comments: This case is interesting both for its substance and for its form. The court repeatedly refers to the test at issue as "the Tax Court's test."[29] It then in many ways ridicules the test and the Tax Court's analysis. It claims that the test "does not provide adequate guidance to a rational decision."[30] This would be well and good (well maybe not good) if in fact it was the Tax Court's test. But, the Seventh

---

[27]   196 F.3d 833 (7th Cir.1999).

[28]   Exacto Spring Corp. v. Commissioner, 75 T.C.M. 2522, 2525 (1998).

[29]   Exacto Spring Corp., 196 F.3d at 834 ("the Tax Court applied a test"), at 838 ("the test [the Tax Court] applied"), at 838 ("We owe no deference to the Tax Court's statutory interpretation").

[30]   Id. at 838.

Circuit has applied the exact same seven factor test in several cases. Why did the court ignore those cases?[31]

We don't know for sure. The court states that other courts of appeals have been moving toward the independent investor test but those courts refer to the test as a "lens" through which one applies the seven factor test.[32] The court rejects the need to resort to the "lens" rationale because it believes it owes no deference to the Tax Court's interpretation. But doesn't it owe deference to its own prior decisions? Strangely, the court does not even make reference to those prior decisions.[33] A panel of a court of appeals cannot overturn a court of appeals decision in the same circuit. The court must either hear the case *en banc* or hope for review by the Supreme Court.[34]

There is another interesting procedural issue presented in this case. The court indicated that the Tax Court's decision was clearly erroneous even if you applied the seven factor test. Why did the court overturn the seven factor test and ignore its prior precedent when it could have reached the same decision by merely holding that the Tax Court's decision was clearly erroneous? Who knows, maybe it really, really, really, didn't like the seven factor test.

---

[31]   Edwin's, Inc. v. United States, 501 F.2d 675, 677 (7th Cir.1974); Hammond Lead Products, Inc. v. Commissioner, 425 F.2d 31, 33 (7th Cir.1970).

[32]   Exacto Spring Corp., 196 F.3d at 838; see LabelGraphics, Inc. v. Commissioner, 221 F.3d 1091, 1095 (9th Cir.2000), quoting Elliotts v. Commissioner, 716 F.2d 1241, 1245 (9th Cir.1983) (applying a five-factor test but stating that when considering the test "it is helpful to consider the matter from the perspective of a hypothetical independent investor. A relevant inquiry is whether an inactive, independent investor would be willing to compensate the employee as he was compensated.")

[33]   The Government in its brief cited and discussed Edwin's v. United States, 501 F.2d at 677. The Government specifically argued that the Seventh Circuit in Edwin adopted the seven factor test discussed above. The court, however, makes no reference to Edwin or any other Seventh Circuit case adopting the seven factor test. See Brief for the Appellee at 20, 25, 31, Exacto Spring Corp. v. Commissioner, 196 F.3d 833 (7th Cir.1999) (No. 99–1011).

[34]   In Eberl's Claim Service v. Commissioner, 249 F.3d 994 (10th Cir.2001), the Tenth Circuit refused to overturn a factor based test in favor of the independent investor test. The court noted that it had previously approved the factor test and could not overturn it absent *en banc* consideration or a change in the law. Id. at 1003. Eberl's Claim Service involved a sole shareholder of a corporation, who worked long hours for the corporation. The employment agreement between Eberl and the corporation had no fixed amount of compensation nor a formula to set the compensation. For 1992 and 1993, Eberl's corporation sought to deduct $4,340,000 and $2,080,000 as compensation for Eberl. After applying a multi-factor test that looks at the compensation in prior years, the general economic conditions, the compensation of other employees, and the financial condition of the company, the court then concluded that Eberl set his compensation "at a level that depleted [the company] of virtually all of its profits."

Interestingly, the independent investor test probably wouldn't have saved Eberl. Unlike in Exacto Spring, Eberl was the sole owner of the corporation. He did not have independent investors that acted as a check on his corporate power. The test still might have found in Eberl's favor by looking at the hypothetical independent investor but it didn't need to do so in Exacto Spring.

With that said, the substantive question is, did the court get the test right? In that regard, it probably did. In *Exacto Spring* there were minority shareholders who approved the compensation. The founder and CEO was not using, and in many ways could not be using, compensation as a means of limiting the size of the dividend paid to shareholders. There were minority shareholders with a sizeable interest. Presumably, they could have protested, or at least not voted for, the compensation if they believed it was excessive.

Is there any reason that the IRS should be protecting minority shareholders in such a situation? Don't they have redress under corporate and securities laws if the majority shareholder abuses his position?

Now remember, the minority shareholders here were disinterested parties. They were not related to the founder, and there is no evidence that they were participating with the majority shareholder in a tax avoidance scheme. If they were related parties, the independent investor test might be suspect. What test should apply then? Isn't that a justification for keeping the seven factor test and using the independent investor test as a "lens" with which to view the seven factors?

Maybe this case stands for the proposition that the Service should not apply § 162(a) when there are independent investors.

Beyond the "ordinary and necessary" limitation, there are other very important grounds for denying a deduction under § 162(a), discussed elsewhere in this work. They are that the deduction may be denied under § 162 because the expenditure is, in fact, personal in nature,[35] a capital expenditure (which may sometimes be amortized over time)[36] or that the expenditure violates public policy.[37] Moreover, special rules are provided for particular areas such as travel and entertainment expenses, educational expenses, and fines and penalties. These special topics are discussed below.

(b) Travel and Transportation Expenses: Flowers; Hantzis; Andrews; Correll

Section 162(a)(2) allows the deduction of traveling expenses, including amounts expended for meals and lodging other than amounts which are "lavish" or "extravagant" while away from home

---

[35]   See ¶ 6.03(3).

[36]   See ¶ 6.03(4).

[37]   See ¶ 6.03(5).

in the pursuit of a trade or business.[38] Surprisingly nettlesome problems are presented by this statutory provision.

The leading case in this area is *Flowers*:

COMMISSIONER V. FLOWERS[39]

Facts: Taxpayer, J. N. Flowers, lived and worked in Jackson, Mississippi. He accepted a job as General Counsel for the Gulf, Mobile & Ohio Railroad, which was located in Mobile, Alabama. Flowers did not want to move to Jackson. Flowers and the company agreed that Flowers could continue to live in Jackson, but that he would pay his travel expenses and his living arrangements. (Luckily for Flowers, he worked for the railroad so his train ticket was free). Flowers did much of his work in Jackson, but his principal place of business was in Mobile.

Question: Were Flowers's travel expenses (including transportation, meals and lodging in Mobile) deductible?

Service's argument: "Home" under § 162(a)(2) is the principal place of business. Thus, the taxpayer was not away from home when in Mobile and hence no deduction for travel.

Held: Three-part test for determining whether a travel expense is deductible under § 162(a)(2): 1) The expense must be reasonable and necessary; 2) The expense must be incurred while away from home; 3) The expense must be incurred in pursuit of business. Taxpayer flunks third test; the expenses were not incurred in pursuit of business. It was his own choice to live in Jackson. This is just a long commute and therefore not deductible as being personal expenses under § 262.

Comment: "Travel expenses" in tax law is defined as not only expenses of travel but also meals and lodging at the destination, § 162(a)(2).

Flowers gets a lot of attention because it is a Supreme Court case. Prior to *Flowers* there was a split in authorities as to the definition of "home" under the statute. The Tax Court and the Service defined it as the taxpayer's place of business. Other cases had defined it as the taxpayer's residence. Thus the issue was squarely presented in *Flowers*. While the *Flowers* Court purported to decline to rule on this question, implicit in and necessary to its holding is the idea that the taxpayer's home for tax purposes is the taxpayer's place of

---

[38]   See Moffit, 31 T.C.M. 910 (1972) allowing deductions for meal expenses on a business trip under § 212.

[39]   326 U.S. 465, 66 S.Ct. 250, 90 L.Ed. 203 (1946), reh'g denied 326 U.S. 812, 66 S.Ct. 482, 90 L.Ed. 496 (1946).

business, agreeing with IRS. That one's home is where one's business is has come to be the principal idea in this area.[40]

Under the terms of the statute, a deduction is allowed for "traveling expenses . . . while away from home in the pursuit of a trade or business." Another case which probes the meaning of "away from home" is *Rosenspan v. United States*.[41] In this case, taxpayer Robert Rosenspan was a jewelry salesman working on a commission basis, paying his own traveling expenses without reimbursement. He traveled for some 300 days a year by car in the midwest, staying at hotels and eating at restaurants (sounds like fun). He used his brother's home in Brooklyn as his residential address. Often when he was in New York, he stayed at a hotel rather than wearing out his welcome at his brother's house. At one point he changed his registration of his automobile to the address of a cousin in Cincinnati. He did not claim that he had a permanent abode or residence in Brooklyn or anywhere else.

The court disallowed a deduction for Rosenspan's meals and lodging while in his sales territory because he did not have a home to be away from, as required by the statutory language. Rosenspan in effect carried his home on his back. He did not have any possible duplication of expenses which is part of the rationale for being able to deduct expenses while away from home in pursuit of a trade or business.

A further illustration that, perhaps, hits somewhat closer to home is afforded by *Hantzis*.

HANTZIS V. COMMISSIONER[42]

Facts: Taxpayer, Catharine Hantzis, was a second-year law student who tried unsuccessfully to find employment in Boston for the summer. She did find work at a New York-based law firm, where she earned $3,750 and had $3,204 in expenses. Hantzis's husband

---

[40] Note that Flowers could not deduct his expenses in Jackson because when he was there he was not in pursuit of his trade or business, for which the main posting was in Mobile.

Cf. Daly v. Commissioner, 631 F.2d 351 (4th Cir.1980), on reh'g 662 F.2d 253 (1981) (salesman who lived in Virginia and stayed overnight in his territory of Delaware, Pennsylvania, and New Jersey was away from home on these occasions and could deduct meals and lodging expenses). Six v. United States, 450 F.2d 66, 69 (2d Cir.1971) (home means residence); Burns v. Gray, 287 F.2d 698, 699–700 (6th Cir.1961) (same); Wallace v. Commissioner, 144 F.2d 407, 410 (9th Cir.1944) (home should be read in its ordinary way); Markey v. Commissioner, 490 F.2d 1249 (6th Cir.1974) (home held to be principal place of business); Curtis v. Commissioner, 449 F.2d 225, 227 (5th Cir.1971) (home is the abode near your principal place of business).

[41] 438 F.2d 905 (2d Cir.1971), cert. denied 404 U.S. 864, 92 S.Ct. 54, 30 L.Ed.2d 108 (1971), reh'g denied 404 U.S. 959, 92 S.Ct. 306, 30 L.Ed.2d 281 (1971).

[42] 638 F.2d 248 (1st Cir.1981), cert. denied 452 U.S. 962, 101 S.Ct. 3112, 69 L.Ed.2d 973 (1981).

was a professor at Northeastern and remained in Boston at the couple's home during the summer. The taxpayer deducted $3,204 from her tax return, representing the cost of meals, lodging in New York, and the transportation from Boston to New York.

Question: Were Hantzis's transportation, meals and lodging in New York deductible under § 162(a)(2) as traveling expenses while away from home in pursuit of a trade or business?

Service's argument: Deduction should be disallowed on grounds that 1) expenses were not incurred "in the pursuit of a trade or business;" 2) taxpayer's tax home was New York and thus she was not away from home when she incurred the expenses.

Held: No deduction. 1) Hantzis did incur the expenses in the pursuit of a trade or business, but 2) she was not away from her tax home.

Comment: Since Hantzis had no business reason to maintain a home in Boston, she could not argue that her tax home was Boston and that she was on temporary employment in New York (see discussion below).

Comment: As did the Supreme Court in *Flowers*, the court purports to say that it is not holding that the tax home is the place of business. Yet, as in *Flowers*, that is necessarily part of the decision.

Comment: The court in *dicta* mentions the necessity for duplicative expenses to gain the deduction.

Another interesting case is *Andrews v. Commissioner*[43] involving a second home that Edward W. Andrews and his wife Leona maintained at Lighthouse Point, Florida. The Andrews attempted to deduct the Lighthouse Point home as traveling expenses while away from home in the pursuit of a trade or business.

Andrews was president and chief executive officer of Andrews Gunite Co., which was engaged in the swimming pool and construction business in New England. Andrews was also engaged in business in Florida, being a large builder of swimming pools and also raising, breeding and racing horses. The horse business was profitable. Andrews used the Lighthouse Point house as his personal residence during the racing season in Florida. Andrews claimed deductibility in full as lodging expenses for the expenses of his Lighthouse Point house, including depreciation of the house and furniture as well as deducting tax, mortgage interest, utilities and insurance. All these deductions were taken in connection with his horse racing business.

---

[43]   931 F.2d 132 (1st Cir.1991).

The Tax Court found that Andrews spent six months in Florida on the race horse business and six months in Massachusetts in the pool business. The Tax Court concluded that Andrews therefore had two tax homes and was not away from either one when he was at the other one. Thus the court denied Andrews deduction of his Florida meals and lodging expenses.

The First Circuit remanded the case to the Tax Court with instructions to ascertain which home was Andrews' tax home, so that he could deduct expenses of the other as being away from home. The court noted that generally time spent at a location will be determinative of which is the taxpayer's principal place of business for deciding where is his tax home. Then expenses at the other location would be deductible. But it was now up to the Tax Court to make the excruciating decision in this case, when the taxpayer spent six months of the year at each location.

Flowers and *Hantzis* are further examples of the more general idea that inherently personal living expenses are not deductible. They are not deductible even if they are increased because of the taxpayer's work or business. In that sense *Flowers* and *Hantzis* are straight out of the book of the older case of *Smith*,[44] which held that expenses of a nurse for a child of a married couple are not deductible even though the nurse is needed so the wife could work.

Flowers and *Hantzis* may also be seen as great big commuting cases. It is well established that the cost of commuting is not deductible.[45] Most commentators regard nondeductibility of commuting expenses as an appropriate result. Commuting expenses

---

[44]   40 B.T.A. 1038, 1939 WL 83 (1939), aff'd without opinion 113 F.2d 114 (2d Cir.1940). See discussion later in this chapter ¶ 6.03(3).

[45]   Regs. §§ 1.162–2(e), 1.212–1(f). See Coombs, 67 T.C. 426 (1976), aff'd in part, rev'd in part 608 F.2d 1269 (9th Cir.1979) (employees at a nuclear test site in Nevada who were compelled to travel 65 miles to nearest lodging could not deduct their "commuting" expenses).

The bar against the deductibility of commuting expenses is lifted if the taxpayer has to carry such bulky tools and equipment that he must incur additional expenses to bring his equipment with him. Such additional expenses would be incurred if, for example, because of having to transport bulky equipment the taxpayer took his private car rather than public transportation. Fausner v. Commissioner, 413 U.S. 838, 93 S.Ct. 2820, 37 L.Ed.2d 996 (1973), reh'g denied 414 U.S. 882, 94 S.Ct. 43, 38 L.Ed.2d 130 (1973) (deduction denied to airline pilot who had to transport flight bags because he would have taken his automobile to the airport whether or not he had to transport the bags; therefore, he did not incur any additional expenses on account of the bags); Rev.Rul. 75–380, 1975–2 C.B. 59; Kallander v. United States, 526 F.2d 1131 (Ct.Cl.1975) (same as *Fausner* and same result); McCabe v. Commissioner, 688 F.2d 102, 49 A.F.T.R.2d 82–1192 (2d Cir.1982) (policeman could not deduct expenses of driving to work in order to be able to carry his revolver, as he was required to by his employer, since the necessity for driving was occasioned by where he chose to live); Cf. Green, 74 T.C. 1229 (1980) (blood donor could deduct cost of traveling between her home and hospital because her body was the container in which the blood was transported).

are seen as inherently personal and barring their deduction is a fundamental principle of federal income taxation.

However, when the matter is viewed from an economic approach, non-deductibility of commuting expenses does not make sense. Put the non-deductibility of commuting expenses against the deductibility of interest on a home mortgage and see where that takes us. From the standpoint of function, commuting and the home mortgage interest payment are substitutes for one another. The more affluent individual can live closer to work in a fancy neighborhood and is able to deduct the interest on the large home mortgage. Compare that to the lower-income individual who is compelled to live further away from work. The taxpayer is able to spend less on a house and less on deductible home mortgage interest. The taxpayer must spend more on commuting expenses which the taxpayer cannot deduct. Anyone like to go out into an outlying suburb of a major metropolitan area and defend all this?

But what about the situation where it is impossible to live near your place of business? In *Coombs v. Commissioner*,[46] the Ninth Circuit held that employees at a nuclear test site in Nevada who were compelled to travel 65 miles to the nearest lodging could not deduct their commuting expenses under § 162 as ordinary and necessary business expenses. The court denied the deductions even though the taxpayers could not live closer to their jobs. The court did allow taxpayers to deduct expenses under § 162(a), as travel away from home, if the taxpayers were required to stay overnight at the test site.[47] Thus, the court rejected the Commissioner's interpretation that one's home is the principal place of business, and instead concluded that in light of the facts of this particular case, taxpayers' homes were their personal residences.

The denial of commuting costs here seems like a close call. But what if the closest habitable area was 400 miles away? What if the place of employment was at the North Pole? Doesn't it seem rather harsh to claim that travel expenses to work in remote locations are just an ordinary commute?[48] Unlike most of the taxpayers in cases in this area, taxpayers here do not have the ability to move closer to their work. Isn't whether there is a business reason for the long commute, rather than a personal one, a better test?

---

[46]   608 F.2d 1269 (9th Cir.1979).

[47]   Id. at 1275–1276.

[48]   See also United States v. Tauferner, 407 F.2d 243 (10th Cir.1969) (denial of deduction for commuting expenses to a chemical plant even though nearest habitable land was over 20 miles away); Pilcher v. Commissioner, 651 F.2d 717 (10th Cir.1981) (rejecting deduction even though closest housing was 67 miles away).

You may think that these are just more crazy hypotheticals presented to you by crazy tax professors. Well, you're half wrong, This issue was squarely presented, although avoided by the court, in the case of *H B & R v. United States*.[49] In *H B & R*, a company hired employees to perform maintenance on oil wells in the North Slope of Alaska. Due to the harsh conditions, employees could not live on the North Slope. Instead, employees rotated and spent three weeks on the North Slope working and then had three weeks off. While at the North Slope they lived in barracks provided by the company. During their off weeks they could live anywhere they wanted. The nearest residential communities to the North Slope are Fairbanks and Anchorage and both are hundreds of miles away.[50] Although H B & R paid employees extra to live in Alaska, most employees chose to live in the continental United States. H B & R paid for the employees' flight from their homes to Anchorage and then from Anchorage to the North Slope. The substantive question was whether the trips from the continental United States to Anchorage, and the trips from Anchorage to the North Slope, were personal expenses and thus income to the employees. The actual issue in the case was whether the employer was required to withhold income and FICA taxes on transportation expenses paid to employees.

The Commissioner argued that H B & R should have withheld income and FICA taxes from the employees pay, since H B & R's payment of transportation expenses was merely a reimbursement of commuting expenses.[51] Interestingly, the Service asserted that both the transportation from taxpayer's home to Fairbanks or Anchorage, and the transportation to the North Slope was a commuting expense. The Eighth Circuit rejected this approach based on a technical reading of the reporting regulations. It did not reach the issue whether the transportation expenses were income to the taxpayers.[52]

What is interesting here is that after the district court case, the Government did not appeal the district court's finding that the trip from Fairbanks or Anchorage to the North Slope was not a commuting expense because "the employee could not be reasonably expected to live any closer than Anchorage to the work place."[53] The court determined that the policy rationale behind limiting commuting expenses is that the taxpayer should locate his home for

---

[49] 229 F.3d 688 (8th Cir.2000).

[50] Id. at 689.

[51] Brief for the Appellee (the United States) at 8, H B & R v. United States, 229 F.3d 688 (8th Cir.2000) (Nos. 99–3206 & 99–3394).

[52] 229 F.3d at 691.

[53] Brief for the Appellee (the United States) at 9, quoting unpublished district court order.

tax purposes as to minimize the amount of travel away from home.[54] In its brief, the Government argued that the taxpayer's home was, if not Deadhorse, Alaska then Anchorage, which was the nearest possible reasonable place to live.[55] Does this mean that the Commissioner recognizes that in some circumstances a commute is no longer personal, but is due to the exigencies of the business? One can only hope, because that seems like a much better rule.[56]

One last point: if a taxpayer's place of business is the home for purposes of § 162(a), then an employee traveling to the North Slope is not traveling away from home. The North Slope is the home. The Eighth Circuit had previously determined that taxpayer's home under § 162 is the principal place of business.[57] This makes the case more difficult because the taxpayer is not traveling away from home by going to the North Slope. In circuits that take a more flexible approach, a taxpayer's trip to the North Slope may be considered traveling away from home, giving rise to expenses that would be deductible under § 162(a).

But what does it mean to travel away from home? The leading case in this area is *Correll*.

UNITED STATES V. CORRELL[58]

Facts: Taxpayer, Homer Correll, was a traveling salesman for a wholesale grocery company. The taxpayer left for work extremely early in the morning, ate both breakfast and lunch on the road, drove approximately 150–175 miles, and then returned home in time for supper.

Question: Can the taxpayer deduct cost of breakfast and lunch on the road as being "traveling expenses while away from home pursuing his trade or business" under § 162(a)(2)?

Service's argument: To qualify for travel "away from home" the trip must require sleep or rest.

Taxpayer's argument: "Away from home" in § 162(a)(2) should mean outside the greater metropolitan area in which a taxpayer resides.

---

[54]   Id.

[55]   Id.

[56]   See also Edmands v. Commissioner, 58 T.C.M. 167 (1989) (the Commissioner did not seek to include in income air transportation for an oil worker who traveled to a pump station on the Alaska pipeline).

[57]   Ellwein v. United States, 778 F.2d 506, 509 (8th Cir.1985).

[58]   389 U.S. 299, 88 S.Ct. 445, 19 L.Ed.2d 537 (1967).

Held: The court adopts the Service's "sleep or rest" rule. The words "meals and lodging" together in the statute suggest that taxpayer can only deduct meals where lodging also involved on trip.

Comment: Briefs amici curiae in favor of the taxpayer were filed by the Bureau of Salesmen's National Associations, and the Manufacturing Chemists' Association.

The *Correll* case owes its place in the pantheon to the fact that it is a Supreme Court case that affirms the Service's long-held "sleep or rest" rule as a definition of deductible "travel expenses" under § 162(a)(2). It is the black letter law on the subject.[59]

This sounds like a fairly reasonable definition. However, it appears that it comes down harder on the less affluent. Correll was working some grueling hours, leaving home at 5 a.m. to get to his appointed rounds on time.

Is this the work-style of an affluent, high-paid salesman? Not likely. Why didn't Correll stay over night on the road to take some of the pressure off himself? Probably because he couldn't afford it. He was obviously paying his own expenses, or he wouldn't be litigating this matter. So another high-powered, very well-paid salesman in Correll's shoes would stay overnight on the road and as a result would be able to deduct his meals (in addition to deducting his lodging). Like in *Flowers*, a seemingly neutral principle seems to in fact come down harder on the less affluent.

Where the taxpayer travels between various business locations during the day, the taxpayer can deduct the cost of such traveling expenses (automobile expenses, public transportation expenses) as ordinary and necessary business expenses under § 162(a). Since such taxpayers would not be "away from home" they could not deduct any expenses for meals.

While it is necessary to be away from home overnight in order to be "away from home" for purposes of deducting traveling, meals and lodging expenses, it is possible to stay away from home too long, in which case the taxpayer's home will be deemed to have moved with him. In such an event, the taxpayer will not be able to deduct expenses inasmuch as the taxpayer is no longer "away from home." The Service's approach here has been to distinguish between "temporary" employment—in which case the taxpayer is "away from home" and can deduct meals and lodging expenses—and employment for an "indeterminate" period—in which case the taxpayer's home moves to the place of employment and the taxpayer cannot deduct

---

[59] See also Rev.Rul. 75–170, 1975–1 C.B. 60 (railroad employees); Barry v. Commissioner, 435 F.2d 1290 (1st Cir.1970) (napping on side of the road in car did not qualify).

meals and lodging expenses. The Service has ruled that where employment at a particular location is anticipated to be, or turns out to be, for a year or more, the employment is not temporary but permanent.

This one-year rule works out very well for law professors and other academics who visit at another institution for a year. They can deduct their transportation, food and lodging expenses because they are still deemed to be away from home. Such are the little bones we get from academic life.[60]

The final logical extreme of all these possibilities is the peripatetic or itinerant taxpayer who for reasons of business seems to have no home at all but is continuously on the road throughout the year. Where the facts demonstrate that this is the case, the taxpayer is regarded as "carrying a home on the back" and therefore cannot deduct any of meals and lodging expenses. This is a ridiculous result and demonstrates the weakness of the *Correll* approach.[61] Traveling expenses (airfare, gasoline, etc.) in such a case could, however, be deducted.

Taxpayers with two or more places of business may deduct the cost of traveling from the major business site to the minor business site.[62] Where a married couple have their business or place of employment in two widely separated locations, no deduction for living expenses at either location is allowed.[63] This rule appears rather harsh even under *Correll*; it would seem that a married couple could be regarded as having a tax home at one of the two business locations and deduct the other.

Be careful in this area. People often confuse the deductibility of commuting expenses under § 162 and the deduction for expenses

---

[60]   Rev.Rul. 74–291, 1974–1 C.B. 42; Peurifoy v. Commissioner, 358 U.S. 59, 79 S.Ct. 104, 3 L.Ed.2d 30 (1958) reh'g denied 358 U.S. 913, 79 S.Ct. 227, 3 L.Ed.2d 234 (construction workers); Wills v. Commissioner, 411 F.2d 537 (9th Cir.1969) (baseball player Maury Wills of the Los Angeles Dodgers did not meet the temporary employment test because his work was seasonal); Six v. United States, 450 F.2d 66 (2d Cir.1971) (remand of question of whether actress Ethel Merman's engagement in New York musical "Gypsy" (ironic in this context) was of sufficient duration not to be temporary). Hasselback, "Tax Implications of a Visiting Professorship," 52 Taxes 499 (1974).

[61]   Rev.Rul. 73–529, 1973–2 C.B. 37; Rosenspan v. United States, 438 F.2d 905 (2d Cir.1971), cert. denied 404 U.S. 864, 92 S.Ct. 54, 30 L.Ed.2d 108 (1971) reh'g denied 404 U.S. 959, 92 S.Ct. 306, 30 L.Ed.2d 281 (1971).

[62]   Sherman v. Commissioner, 16 T.C. 332 (1951) (acq.); Rev.Rul. 55–109, 1955–1 C.B. 261; Folkman v. United States, 615 F.2d 493 (9th Cir.1980).

[63]   Foote, 67 T.C. 1 (1976).

See generally Riepen, "Extraordinary Commuting Expenses: Deductibility of Transportation Expenses Between Residence and Temporary Place of Business," 51 S.Cal.L.Rev. 499 (1978); Chod, "Travel, Transportation and Commuting Expenses: Problems Involving Deductibility," 43 Missouri L.Rev. 525 (1978).

under § 162(a) when traveling away from home on business. Section 162 applies to travel expenses associated with your business that do not constitute commuting. For example, if you are an electrician and drive to work, the cost of the trip to work is not deductible. If you then drive from your work to various job sites, the costs of travel to those job sites will be deductible. This is all deductible under § 162. Section 162(a) only applies to travel away from home (your place of business or your metropolitan area). If you travel away from home you get to deduct your travel expenses and your meals and lodging.

It is interesting from an analytical standpoint to put the principles discussed in this section together with the principles involved in taxing meals and lodging provided by the employer, discussed at ¶ 2.02(2). Putting all these principles together, the following pattern emerges: If the taxpayer receives meals and lodging from an employer on the employer's business premises, and meets certain other requirements, the value of the meals and lodging will be excluded from the taxpayer's income. If, however, the taxpayer obtains and pays for meals and lodging some distance away from the employer's business premises, the taxpayer cannot deduct their cost, and thus the value of the meals and lodging will be included in income. If the taxpayer, however, should have to travel on business away from home and stay overnight, the cost of meals and lodging is deductible, and therefore their value in effect will be excluded from income. Finally, if the taxpayer travels away from where the house to a job location for a long period of time, the tax home will be deemed to have moved with the taxpayer to the new job location and the taxpayer will not be able to deduct the cost of meals and lodging—their value will therefore in effect be included in income. The question is whether all this really makes any sense.

(2) The Dichotomy Between Deduction and Capital or Personal Expenses

(a) Necessary Rental and Similar Payments; Starr's Estate; Fitzpatrick

The classic case of *Starr's Estate* presents a good introduction to the problems in this area.

STARR'S ESTATE V. COMMISSIONER[64]

Facts: The agreement between the parties purports to be a lease providing for 1) rental of the sprinkler system for $1,240 per year for five years ($6,200 total); and 2) option on taxpayer's part to renew the lease at the end of five years for another five years for $32 per year. The agreement was silent as to what would happen in the 11th

---

[64]   274 F.2d 294 (9th Cir.1959).

year. The contract stated that if the Company did not pay its rent, the sprinkler system installers could come in and remove the system. If the sprinkler company ever reclaimed the system, the salvage value would be negligible. (The actual taxpayer here was the estate of Delano Starr, the owner of the Gross Manufacturing Company.)

Question: Were the payments under the agreement rent or an installment purchase of the sprinkler system?

Held: For tax purposes, the payments were an installment purchase of the sprinkler system even though title did not pass under the agreement under state law. The value to the lessor in the sprinkler system was exhausted by this arrangement. The court remanded the case for consideration of interest as being deductible to taxpayer. The normal purchase price of the system was $4,960, while the total price here was $6,200, suggesting $1,240 as interest over the 5 years.

Comment: Thus the annual payments were not deductible as paid but were rather capital expenses. Depreciation would then be allowed, since the sprinkler system and the attendant building are wasting assets.

Comment: Under the numbers given, the arrangement implies that the interest rate was 7.93%, which is a reasonable rate. This further confirms that the economic reality of the situation was an installment purchase with interest.

Comment: The court stated the Commissioner allowed depreciation of $269 per year, finding that the sprinkler system had a 23-year useful life. That $269 over 23 years assumes that the purchase price is $6,200 (23 × $269 = $6,200). However, if we follow the court's approach that $1,240 of the $6,200 is interest, then the purchase price is $4,960. It is therefore only $4,960 that should be depreciated over the 23 years. That churns out to be a depreciation deduction of $216 per year. The moral of this story is that you do not add the interest to your basis for depreciation purposes.

Let us pursue the installment purchase idea a little. What are the numbers on the installment purchase theory? The interest deduction for the first year is 7.93% of the purchase price of $4,960, or $393. Interest in subsequent years would be less because the principal would be declining as it is paid off. See the appendix in general for further discussion of the treatment of interest as compounding over time. It would, in short, be wrong to just deduct 1/23 of the interest per year. After five years, when the purchase price is paid, there would be no further payments and of course no interest deduction. Looking at depreciation, the $216 deduction, which is taken on a straight-line method, would continue for the full 23 years.

This is comprised of the five years of the installment purchase agreement and the subsequent 18 years.

What do these numbers come to in the first year? In the first year the interest is $393 and the depreciation is $216. This gives a total deduction the first year if the installment purchase approach is followed of $609. That is considerably less than a deduction of the full amount of the payment under the contract of $1,240. That is what the fighting was about.

The court, however, at the end of its opinion seems to down-play the significance of this difference. How much difference does this really make? The question is what is the present value of being able to deduct $1,240 per year for five years?[65]

That's the lease theory. Then we need to compare that with the present value of deducting interest for five years and depreciation for 23 years. That's the installment purchase theory. We need, of course, a chart:

---

[65] We ignore the payment of $32 per year for the second five years as being *de minimis*.

COMPARISON OF LEASE AND INSTALLMENT PURCHASE IN *STARR*

Comparison of Lease and Installment Purchase Theory of *Starr's Estate*. Assume combined federal and state tax rate of 40%; before tax interest rate of 7.93% and after tax interest rate of 4.76%. 7.93% interest rate arrived at by computation from numbers in the case. 4.76% interest rate is the after-tax rate of interest (i.e., 60% of 7.93%).

		LEASE (TP View)			INSTALLMENT PURCHASE (IRS View)					
	Payment	Tax Savings from Ded Payment	Present Value of Ded Payment	Interest Ded	Tax Savings from Ded Interest	Present Value of Int Ded	Depre-ciation	Tax Savings from Ded Depr	Present Value of Depr Ded
Year									
1	$1,240	$ 496	$ 473	$ 393	$ 157	$ 150	$ 216	$ 86	$ 82
2	$1,240	$ 496	$ 452	$ 326	$ 130	$ 119	$ 216	$ 86	$ 79
3	$1,240	$ 496	$ 431	$ 254	$ 101	$ 88	$ 216	$ 86	$ 75
4	$1,240	$ 496	$ 412	$ 176	$ 70	$ 58	$ 216	$ 86	$ 72
5	$1,240	$ 496	$ 393	$ 91	$ 36	$ 29	$ 216	$ 86	$ 68
6							$ 216	$ 86	$ 65
7							$ 216	$ 86	$ 62
8							$ 216	$ 86	$ 59
9							$ 216	$ 86	$ 57
10							$ 216	$ 86	$ 54
11							$ 216	$ 86	$ 52
12							$ 216	$ 86	$ 49
13							$ 216	$ 86	$ 47
14							$ 216	$ 86	$ 45
15							$ 216	$ 86	$ 43
16							$ 216	$ 86	$ 41
17							$ 216	$ 86	$ 39
18							$ 216	$ 86	$ 37
19							$ 216	$ 86	$ 36
20							$ 216	$ 86	$ 34
21							$ 216	$ 86	$ 32
22							$ 216	$ 86	$ 31
23							$ 216	$ 86	$ 30
Total			$ 2,162	$1,240		$ 445	$ 4,968		$ 1,189
				$2,162					$ 1,635

Total Present Value of Treatment as Lease

Total Present Value of Treatment as Installment Sale (sum of total present value of interest deduction and total present value of depreciation).

Thus the difference between treating it as a lease and as an installment sale is $2,162 − $1,635 = $527. Small change, you say? Well calling it a lease increases the present value by 32%. Any time you can increase asset value by 32% you are doing something significant. This is the case notwithstanding that the court in *Starr's Estate* suggested that the attack on leases may not be worthwhile in terms of revenue.

Another aspect of the case is the treatment of Automatic Sprinklers, the company that manufactured and installed the sprinkler system. If the transaction is treated as a lease to Starr's Estate (attractive for Starr's Estate as we have seen), then the payments would be rental payments to Automatic Sprinklers as the lessor. These would be taxable, of course. The relevant offsetting deduction would be a deduction for depreciation of the sprinkler system, which was found in the case to have a useful life of 23 years. Thus there would be a relatively small deduction for Automatic Sprinklers each year of $216. From the point of view of the Internal Revenue Service, then, the lower taxes paid by Starr's Estate if the transaction is called a lease would be offset by the higher taxes paid by Automatic Sprinklers.

If, on the other hand, the transaction is regarded as an installment sale over five years, then as we have seen, Starr's Estate pays a higher tax. However, Automatic Sprinkler is then favored with a lower tax because on an installment sale over five years Automatic Sprinklers is allowed to offset its cost of the sprinkler over five years instead of 23 years (see Chapter 8). Thus on an installment sale Starr's higher tax is offset by Automatic Sprinkler's lower tax.

Therefore it appears to all break even for the government. It would appear that the government should allow the parties to call a transaction a lease or a sale as they like, since the revenues more or less break even. Except for what? The analysis that the tax revenues break even either way assumes that the parties are in the same tax bracket. This might well not be the case of course. If Automatic Sprinkler is running losses from the rest of its business, it will be happy to style the deal as a lease. The higher income will still not be taxable to Automatic Sprinkler and Starr's Estate will have lower income. If Starr's Estate has losses and Automatic Sprinkler has high income, then the parties will style the deal as an installment sale.

Part of the negotiation between the parties will be to split the tax gains they get by styling the deal in the most favorable way. The government cannot sit by and let the taxpayers deal to their own advantage in this way.

Having said all that, it must also be said that much of the preceding analysis is now irrelevant. This is because of the rules allowing rapid depreciation (or cost recovery) provided by the MACRS system (see ¶ 6.02(12)).

These rules allow very short useful lives for depreciation. As the *Starr's Estate* table above indicates, if depreciation occurs over 5 years instead of 23 years, the difference between the lease approach and the installment sale approach would be erased.

So under current law none of this matters very much anymore. But the principles of immediate deduction versus capital expenditure highlighted by this discussion remain important.

White v. Fitzpatrick[66] involved a transfer of property from husband to wife with a resulting lease or license back. The taxpayer was engaged as a sole proprietor in the manufacture of chokes for use on barrels of shotguns. He had a patent on the device, which he transferred to his wife for the full term of the patent for consideration of $10. The wife then licensed the patent back to taxpayer, with royalties at $1 on each device marketed. The taxpayer filed a gift tax return declaring the fair market value of the patent he transferred to be $10,000. For the next four years, the taxpayer paid his wife $60,000 as royalties.

At about the same time the wife also purchased the property on which the company was located for $16,800 and then leased it back to her husband orally. The next day the taxpayer made a gift to his wife of $16,175 to cover the purchase price and filed a gift tax for that amount. Rental payments were $1,500 a year plus a one time $5,000 "adjustment in rent."

During the tax years in question, the taxpayer deducted both the royalty and rent payments as business expenses.

It will be noted that if these two transactions are allowed to stand, the income from the patent is shifted to the wife from the husband. (Husband takes deduction and wife has income). This case arose out of tax years prior to the filing of the joint return, so the arrangement was effective in shifting income from the husband to the wife, who was presumably in a lower tax bracket.

Recognizing this, the Second Circuit affirmed the district court and disallowed the deduction of the payments to the wife. The court said that "underlying reality ... contradicts this appearance of complete assignment. Though title to the properties might reside in the wife, control rests with the husband as effectively as if he had never made the gift of the patent or the money to buy the property." Thus considerations of family relations override the form of a transaction, compare *Harolds Club* above at ¶ 6.02(1)(a). Compare also assignment of income problems in Chapter 5.

---

[66]   193 F.2d 398 (2d Cir.1951), cert. denied 343 U.S. 928, 72 S.Ct. 762, 96 L.Ed. 1338 (1952).

(b) Education Expenses

(i) The Law; Hill; Coughlin

A case illustrating the problems in this area is *Hill v. Commissioner*[67] which involved school teacher Nora Payne Hill. Ms. Hill taught school in Virginia for 27 years. For the tax year in question, she attended summer school at Columbia University in New York City, incurring expenses of $239.50, which she deducted. The laws of the state of Virginia required that to retain her teaching certificate she must either present evidence of college credits in professional or academic subjects earned during the life of the certificate or pass an examination on selected books. Ms. Hill held the highest certificate issued to public school teachers in Virginia. The court noted that to satisfy this requirement she took two courses, one on short story writing, which was in her field, and the other on abnormal psychology which, the court noted, "would be most useful to a teacher whose pupils were adolescents."

The Fourth Circuit reversed the Tax Court, which had held the expenses were personal, and found that these expenses were incurred in carrying on a trade or business and were both ordinary and necessary. The expenses also were not personal. Hence the court held the expenses were deductible. The court regarded it as irrelevant that the state requirements could be satisfied by a test instead of taking the courses. Indeed the court opined that taking the courses was a better way to satisfy the requirement (although that observation was not necessary for its decision).

Hill can be usefully compared with the case of *Coughlin v. Commissioner*[68] in which a tax lawyer attended the Fifth Annual Institute on Federal Taxation of New York University. (One day, this could be you.) In so doing, he incurred expenses of tuition, travel, board and lodging of $305. The taxpayer argued that his expenses were deductible as an ordinary and necessary expense incurred in the practice of his profession. Analogizing to *Hill*, the court held that these expenses were to enable taxpayer to keep sharp the tools he actually used in his going trade or business.

The area of education expenses is now blanketed by regulations, which provide several inter-related tests to determine the deductibility of education expenses.

Education expenses are deductible if they (1) maintain or improve skills required by the individual in his employment or other trade or business or (2) meet the express requirements of the

---

[67]   181 F.2d 906 (4th Cir.1950).

[68]   203 F.2d 307 (2d Cir.1953).

taxpayer's employer, or the requirements of applicable law as a condition to the retention by the taxpayer of his employment or rate of compensation.[69] Even if the education expenses meet either test (1) or test (2), they will still not be deductible unless further they (3) are not expenditures made by an individual for education to meet the minimum educational requirements for qualification in his employment or other trade or business; or (4) do not lead to qualifying the taxpayer for a new trade or business.[70] Thus, to be deductible, educational expenses must pass either test (1) skill maintenance; *or* test (2) required by employer or by law; and then pass both test (3) not required to meet minimum educational standards or qualifications in taxpayer's trade or business; *and* test (4) not qualify taxpayer for a new trade or business.

The theory of these regulations is that educational expenses to maintain existing skills or which are required by the employer or other state or federal law are analogous to expenses to keep a piece of machinery used in taxpayer's trade or business running. Such expenses are clearly deductible as an ordinary and necessary expense of doing the taxpayer's business. Expenses which cause the taxpayer to meet minimum educational requirements for a trade or business, or which prepare the taxpayer for a new trade or business, are analogous to capital expenses and therefore cannot be deducted.[71]

Examples of skill-maintenance educational expenses which would pass test (1) as well as tests (3) and (4) would be refresher courses or courses dealing with current developments in the taxpayer's professional field.[72] Examples of educational expenses that would meet test (2) expenses required by employer or law would be explicit (and reasonable) employer requirements that certain courses be taken from time to time for job retention or state statutes requiring professionals to take a certain number of courses to retain professional licensing. The Regulations provide some detailed

---

[69]   Reg. § 1.162–5(a).

[70]   Reg. § 1.162–5(b)(2) and (3).

[71]   A problem with this theory is that educational expenses which are treated as capital should then be amortizable over the taxpayer's anticipated career or lifetime, but such amortization has been absolutely disallowed, Sharon v. Commissioner, 591 F.2d 1273 (9th Cir.1978), cert. denied 442 U.S. 941, 99 S.Ct. 2883, 61 L.Ed.2d 311 (1979) (cost of law school and bar review course may not be amortized over taxpayer's professional life because such costs were "personal" expenses).

[72]   Reg. § 1.162–5(c)(1); Carroll v. Commissioner, 418 F.2d 91 (7th Cir.1969) (policemen studying philosophy in college could not deduct); compare Glasgow, 31 T.C.M. 310 (1972), aff'd per curiam 486 F.2d 1045 (10th Cir.1973) (minister could deduct expense of college courses in history, literature, psychology, and other liberal arts subjects on theory that such courses assisted him in serving his congregation; a questionable holding which probably should not be relied upon); Ford, 56 T.C. 1300 (1971), aff'd per curiam 487 F.2d 1025 (9th Cir.1973) (teacher of English and social studies could deduct expenses for studying linguistics and anthropology).

examples of test (3) which must be passed by all educational expenses to be deductible, namely that the expenses do not qualify the taxpayer to meet the minimal education requirements of his trade or business.[73]

Examples of the test (4) that must also be passed by all educational expenses to be deductible, namely that the expenses do not qualify for the taxpayer for a new trade or business, would be a general practitioner of medicine who takes a two-week course reviewing new developments in several specialized fields of medicine. The expenses would be deductible because they maintain or improve his skills (test (1)) and do not qualify the general practitioner for a new trade or business.[74]

An example of educational expenses that flunk test (4) would be an engineer who studies law at night and receives a law degree. This expenditure would flunk test (4) in that it prepares the engineer for a new trade or business, and may, depending on the facts, also be disqualified because it does not pass either tests (1) or (2).[75] Indeed, even if an employee is absolutely required by an employer to obtain a law degree in order to keep a nonlegal job, nevertheless, the expenses of the legal study would be nondeductible even though the employee does not intend to practice law, since the expenses do as an objective matter prepare the employee for a new career.[76] This rule has caused, for example, Internal Revenue Service agents who attended law school at night to improve their skills in their existing jobs to be unable to deduct the expenses of their legal education.[77]

The major problem with test (4) is differentiating between expenses that simply prepare an employee for a change of duties that does not constitute a new trade or business, in which case the expenses are deductible, and expenses which do qualify the employee for a new trade or business, in which case the expenses are not deductible.[78]

---

[73]   Reg. § 1.162–5(b)(2)(iii), relating to secondary school teachers.

[74]   Reg. § 1.162–5(b)(3)(i), Example (3).

[75]   Reg. § 1.162–5(b)(3)(i), Example (1).

[76]   Reg. § 1.162–5(b)(3)(i), Example (2).

[77]   See Weiler, 54 T.C. 398 (1970).

[78]   Reg. § 1.162–5(b)(3)(i). The Regulations throw a moderate amount of light on this subject by providing that all teaching and related duties are considered to involve the same trade or business and educational expenses relating to such shifts—as from teacher of one subject to another, teacher to guidance counselor, or teacher to principal—are deductible.

See also the following cases holding that education expenses were not deductible because they involved qualifying the taxpayer for a new trade or business: Davis, 65 T.C. 1014 (1976) (cost of Ph.D. for social worker); Burnstein, 66 T.C. 492 (1976) (cost of becoming a social worker not deductible to teacher of handicapped children); Sharon v. Commissioner, 591 F.2d 1273 (9th Cir.1978), cert. denied 442 U.S. 941, 99 S.Ct.

The fact that a course of educational study leads to the granting of a degree does not in itself cause the educational expenses to flunk any of tests (1) through (4).[79]

Expenses of travel for education are not deductible.[80]

(ii) The Economics: What Does It Really Cost to Go to Law School?

So what does it finally cost to go to law school? It costs you your tuition, books, travel and living expenses. Of course you would have had living expenses anyway, but perhaps they are higher at law school. What else does it cost? The standard economic analysis here is that going to law school (or any vocationally-oriented school) also costs you your "opportunity cost," to use the jargon. That is, it costs you what you could have earned had you gotten a job instead of going to law school. You are out of pocket that money, too, so the analysis goes. That analysis is OK as far as it goes, but it assumes you could have gotten a job with your B.A. in sociology or art history or whatever degree you have. But you might not have gotten a job at all if the economy is in rocky shape.[81]

The other economic aspect of legal education is the fact, as discussed in the previous section, that its cost cannot be deducted (except for up to \$4,000)[82] or amortized over time. This seems unjustified since it is creating an asset (your career) which will produce income over time. However, the tax code is treating you better than you think. As you labor to gain your legal education, you are in receipt of imputed income (as discussed in Chapters 1, 2). That is, you are performing educational services on yourself. This imputed income is not taxed. So even though you cannot deduct your legal

---

2883, 61 L.Ed.2d 311 (1979) (cost of California bar review course not deductible by New York lawyer); Antzoulatos, 34 T.C.M. 1426 (1975) (cost of intern becoming a registered pharmacist not deductible). Expenses of attending a graduate study program leading to a Master's degree in Taxation are deductible, where the taxpayer has engaged in the practice of tax law prior to the commencement of the graduate study, on the theory that such training improves existing skills but does not prepare the taxpayer for a new trade or business. However, were a taxpayer to complete law school and then immediately embark upon graduate tax study, it is likely that such expenses would not be deductible since the taxpayer would not have established the trade or business of being a tax lawyer prior to commencement of the graduate study.

[79]   Reg. § 1.162–5(a) and see authorities in note 23 supra.

[80]   274(m)(2).

[81]   See Kramer, Legal Education in an Era of Change: Will Legal Education Remain Affordable, by Whom and How?, 1987 Duke L. J. 240 (1987).

[82]   See § 222 and ¶ 6.03. Note that § 222 is set to expire at the end of 2016, though it is likely to be extended given it has been consistently since 2004.

education expenses, you also are not taxed on your imputed income.[83] Don't you feel better now? Next time your brother-in-law at a family reunion rags you around the cheese dip for being an impoverished law student, tell him you've got imputed income. That'll hold him for at least a half an hour.

(3) Expenses for the Production of Income, or for the Maintenance of Investment Property: Higgins; Gilmore; Estate of Baier; Surasky; Myer J. Fleischman; Horrmann; Lowry

As discussed above, § 212 allows individuals to deduct all the "ordinary and necessary expenses paid or incurred during the taxable year—(1) for the production or collection of income; (2) for the management, conservation or maintenance of property held for the production of income . . ." The reason it takes two Code sections to provide the deductions for expenses incurred in all of these business-type activities is that the Supreme Court in the 1941 case of *Higgins v. Commissioner*[84] upheld the Service's position that expenses incurred in profit-seeking or investment-type activity were not deductible under the predecessor of § 162. Congress nullified that holding by enacting the following year the predecessors of §§ 212(1) and 212(2).[85] Sections 162 and 212, therefore, embodying as they do the same "ordinary and necessary" language, are generally interpreted in a parallel fashion insofar as the standards that must be met for the deduction to be allowed.[86]

The same standards generally apply as to whether an expense is ordinary and necessary; and the same standards apply to determine whether an expense will be disallowed because it is personal in nature, a capital expense, or violative of public policy.[87]

There are some differences between §§ 212 and 162, however. Importantly, since the deductions under § 212 are, by definition, not attributable to a "trade or business," they are only deductible above the line if they are attributable to property held for the production of rents or royalties.[88] *Hence as an extremely important structural point, most deductions under § 212 only come off "below the line," i.e., as*

---

[83] Also, particularly if you go to a low-tuition state school, you've got a subsidy in that your legal education costs more to provide you than you are paying for it. This subsidy is not taxed.

[84] 312 U.S. 212, 61 S.Ct. 475, 85 L.Ed. 783 (1941), reh'g denied 312 U.S. 714, 61 S.Ct. 728, 85 L.Ed. 1145 (1941).

[85] S.Rep. No. 1631, 77th Cong., 2d Sess., reprinted in 1942–2 C.B. 504, 570.

[86] See Bingham's Trust v. Commissioner, 325 U.S. 365, 65 S.Ct. 1232, 89 L.Ed. 1670 (1945).

[87] See Regs. §§ 1.212–1(d), 1.212–1(f), 1.212–1(n).

[88] See ¶ 6.01.

deductions from adjusted gross income in arriving at taxable income. Moreover, those deductions under § 212 that come off "below the line" are also subject to the 2% floor on itemized deductions as described at ¶ 7.02.[89]

As one example of how all this goes together, the expenses of renting a safe deposit box in order to store stock certificates—which yield dividend income and not rents or royalties—would be deductible under § 212 but could be taken only below the line.[90] Moreover, those expenses would only be deductible at all to the extent they, together with the other miscellaneous itemized deductions of the taxpayer, exceeded 2% of the taxpayer's adjusted gross income. Similarly, the expenses of other profit-seeking activities, or investment activities engaged in by the taxpayer, which do not rise to the level of being a trade or business, which produce income other than rents or royalties would only be deductible below the line and would run the gauntlet of the 2% floor (as discussed at ¶ 7.02).[91]

For expenses to be deductible under § 212(1) or 212(2), they must be reasonable in amount and must be reasonably related to the profit-seeking activity.[92] Expenses can be deductible under § 212 even though the profit-seeking activity is fruitless and the taxpayer is in fact running losses.[93]

A major case in this area is *Gilmore.*

UNITED STATES V. GILMORE[94]

Facts: Taxpayer, Don Gilmore was the controlling stockholder in three franchised General Motors dealerships. His wife instituted divorce proceedings, claiming marital infidelity; Don cross-claimed for divorce. Don then retained expensive legal counsel in order to defeat his former wife's claims. Don needed to defeat her claims because he feared that if she was granted divorce, he might lose his controlling stock interests, which would cost him his corporate

---

[89]   Section 67.

[90]   See ¶ 7.01(1).

[91]   Another difference between §§ 212 and 162 is that § 212 expenses can be deducted only by individuals; however, corporations can apparently deduct their expenses in such investment activities under § 162 without challenge. There are also limitations on § 212 expenses with respect to the computation of net operating loss carryovers under § 172, and use of taxpayer's dwelling unit for business purposes under § 280A (see ¶ 6.02(10).)

[92]   Reg. § 1.212–1(d); Lykes v. United States, 343 U.S. 118, 72 S.Ct. 585, 96 L.Ed. 791 (1952), reh'g denied 343 U.S. 937, 72 S.Ct. 768, 96 L.Ed. 1344 (1952) (legal expenses not deductible simply because taxpayer would use income-producing property to pay the judgment if the case were lost—compare the *Gilmore* case note 20, infra).

[93]   Regs. § 1.212–1(b).

[94]   372 U.S. 39, 83 S.Ct. 623, 9 L.Ed.2d 570 (1963).

positions. Moreover, Don believed that if he were found guilty of marital infidelity, General Motors might cancel his dealer franchises. In the end of the proceedings, Don was granted the divorce and his wife's community property claims were denied in their entirety. The taxpayer incurred $40,611 in legal expenses.

Question: Are Don's legal fees deductible, under § 212(1) and (2)?

Service's argument: The entire amount of fees is nondeductible as a personal or family expense under § 262.

Taxpayer's argument: The expenses were necessary to protect his property held for the production of dividend and salary income from his wife's claims.

Held: (Harlan, J.) For IRS. The deductibility of § 212 deductions depends on the origin of the claim, which was here personal—the divorce. This limitation has been present on § 162 deductions and the same limit is followed for § 212. Characterization as business or personal depends on the origin not on the consequences of the litigation.

Comment: The legal fees were apparently larger because the taxpayer had to defend this property.

Comment: Surprisingly, Don was subsequently allowed to add the legal expenses of the divorce litigation to the basis of his property, a highly questionable treatment which is not consistent with the original *Gilmore* case.[95]

The Court said that to allow the deduction for the divorce litigation expenses means that if two taxpayers are each sued in an automobile accident the deductibility of their litigation costs would turn on the "mere" character of the assets each happened to possess. What is wrong with that? Deductibility of a particular expense always turns on the particular circumstances of a taxpayer. Notwithstanding that, the "origin of the claim" theory is regarded as a good rule in the field.[96]

But, the "origin of the claim" theory cannot be defended as logical or consistent with the "deep structure" of federal income taxation (see the beginning of this Chapter, ¶ 6.01). Rather, it should be clear that if substantial assets are held, they are going to on occasion have to be defended against the claims of estranged spouses

---

[95]   See Gilmore v. United States, 245 F.Supp. 383 (N.D.Cal.1965). See also Nadiak v. Commissioner, 356 F.2d 911 (2d Cir.1966) (applying the *Gilmore* origin-of-the-claim test to a deduction claimed under IRC § 162).

[96]   See also United States v. Patrick, 372 U.S. 53, 83 S.Ct. 618, 9 L.Ed.2d 580 (1963), a companion case to Gilmore in which the Court disallowed deduction of legal expenses of a husband in arriving at a property settlement incident to a divorce.

and others. The cost of that defense is properly deductible as a cost
of holding that property. To fail to allow the deduction is to fail to
accurately reflect the true cost of holding the asset.

The "origin of the claim" doctrine does two things which are
attractive from the Service's point of view: 1) provides a bright line
distinction as to what is deductible and what is not; and 2) narrows
the scope of the deduction.

Sections 212(1) and 212(2) allow a fairly broad range of
deductions incident to profit-seeking activity, such as investment
advisory fees, office rent, clerical help, and custodial fees with respect
to such activity or with respect to income-producing property.[97]
Brokerage fees, paid incident to the purchase or sale of stock,
securities, real estate, or other property cannot be deducted but must
instead be added to the cost of the property purchased or subtracted
from the selling price of the property sold.[98]

Subsequent examples of litigation under § 212 include *Bowers v.
Lumpkin*[99] in which the court held that legal expenses to defend title
to property are not deductible under § 212. The case of *Estate of Baier
v. Commissioner*[100] held that legal expenses incident to the
disposition of a capital asset (a patent) cannot be deducted under
§ 212 but are capital expenses and are thus deducted from the
amount realized on the sale of the asset. Thus in effect the legal fees
are deducted against favorably taxed capital gains rather than less
favorably taxed ordinary income. The rationale was that the origin of
the claim lay in the dispute concerning the disposition of the patent.

In *Surasky v. United States*[101] the taxpayer was a shareholder of
Montgomery Ward & Co. In connection with a proxy fight with
respect to the company, the taxpayer contributed $17,000 to a
shareholders' committee to help wage the fight for one side. The
taxpayer was not an officer, director or employee of Montgomery
Ward and did not seek such a position, although he did believe he
would make more money if the shareholders' committee drive was
successful. The taxpayer eventually received substantial dividends
on his stock and eventually sold his stock for a substantial capital
gain. The Fifth Circuit reversed the lower court decision and held
that the contributions were deductible even if they were not
proximately related to the production of income. Thereafter the

---

[97]   Reg. § 1.212–1(g).
[98]   Reg. § 1.263(a)–2(f)(2(ii)(I).
[99]   140 F.2d 927, cert. denied 322 U.S. 755, 64 S.Ct. 1266, 88 L.Ed. 1585 (1944).
[100]   533 F.2d 117 (3d Cir.1976).
[101]   325 F.2d 191 (5th Cir.1963).

Service, in Revenue Ruling 64–236[102] ruled that it would follow the *Surasky* opinion except to the extent that the court indicates that deductible proxy fight expenditures need not be proximately related to the production of income.

Fleischman v. Commissioner[103] presented the question of the deductibility of legal expenses incurred in defending a wife's lawsuit to set aside their antenuptial contract. The taxpayer tried to distinguish his facts from those of *Gilmore* (see above) on the grounds that the legal expenses did not spring out of the marriage relationship but from rights excluded from that relationship. Nevertheless the court found the wife's rights here were also grounded in the marriage relationship. The court found the legal expenses were not deductible, relying on *Gilmore*.

In the interesting case of *Horrmann v. Commissioner*[104] the taxpayer bought and lived in a house and then put it up for sale, intending never to live in it again. The property was held out for sale for three years. The taxpayer sold the property in 1945 for $20,800. At the time he bought the property its value was $60,000 and at the time he abandoned it as a personal residence the value was $45,000. The question was whether the taxpayer could take deductions for depreciation, maintenance and a capital loss with respect to the property. The court found that the taxpayer had attempted, albeit unsuccessfully, to rent the property during the time it was for sale. Because of the attempts to rent, the taxpayer was entitled to take depreciation with respect to the property for the three years it was held for sale.

Similarly, with respect to maintenance expenses, the court found that the property was held for the production of income and therefore the maintenance expenses were deductible. As to the question of deduction of the long-term capital loss, the court held that the standard was not whether the property was "held for the production of income," but rather whether holding the house was a "transaction entered into for profit." The court as to this issue held that the property had not been converted from personal use to a transaction entered into for profit and denied the deduction for the long-term capital loss.

Lowry v. United States[105] is a leading case regarding the deductibility and sale of real estate used at one time as a residence. The taxpayers stopped using their summer house as residential

---

[102]   1964–2 Cum.Bull. 64.

[103]   45 T.C. 439 (1966).

[104]   17 T.C. 903 (1951).

[105]   384 F.Supp. 257 (D.N.H.1974).

property in 1967 and immediately offered it for sale without attempting to rent it. The question was whether they converted it into "income producing property," thereby entitling them to deduct the maintenance expenses incurred after it was put on the market and prior to its sale in 1973. Notwithstanding the taxpayer's failure to attempt to rent the property, the court ruled that it had been converted from personal to business use. Since the house was part of a cooperative community on Martha's Vineyard, it was not practical to try to rent it. Moreover, citing Reg. § 1.212–1(b) the court said that income for purposes of § 212 deductions is not confined to recurring or rental income but applies also to gains from dispositions of property.

Indeed, the court pointed out that under that regulation, maintenance expenses of property held for investment are deductible even if the property is not producing income, there is no likelihood of current income and there is no likelihood of gain upon sale of the property. Rather the determination of whether the prior residence has been converted depends on the taxpayer's purpose in light of all the facts and circumstances. Here the taxpayers were knowledgeable in real estate and sought to take advantage of the boom in recreational real estate prices.

(4) Miscellaneous Business and Pleasure Travel Expenses: Rudolph

Often a taxpayer may be forced to attend a business meeting or convention in Acapulco, Las Vegas, or New Orleans. As the taxpayer packs and prepares to undertake the burdens of this trip, the taxpayer may wonder whether the IRS will be so rude as to question whether the expenses of the trip are deductible. This question relates to the third test set forth in the *Flowers* case,[106] namely, that the expense must be incurred in pursuit of the taxpayer's business. Obviously in this situation, there is no question of where the taxpayer's home is or that the taxpayer is away from home. But the fact that business and pleasure may very well be combined on the same trip raises some of the more nettlesome questions in the tax law.

A leading case in this area is *Rudolph*.

RUDOLPH V. UNITED STATES[107]

Facts: The taxpayer, Rudolph, was an insurance salesman for the Southland Life Insurance Company. By selling a predetermined

---

[106] See ¶ 6.02(1)(b).

[107] 370 U.S. 269, 82 S.Ct. 1277, 8 L.Ed.2d 484 (1962), reh'g denied 371 U.S. 854, 83 S.Ct. 15, 9 L.Ed.2d 93 (1962).

amount of insurance, Rudolph and his wife were qualified to attend the company's convention in New York City. Rudolph and his wife, accompanied by 150 other salesmen and 141 other wives, then traveled on a special train to New York City. In New York City all the individuals stayed in a single hotel for the two-and-a-half-day visit. One morning of the trip was devoted to a business meeting and a group luncheon, while the rest of the time was devoted to leisure activities such as sight-seeing and entertainment. The entire trip lasted one week, cost $80,000, and was paid for by the company; the portion of the trip allocable to Rudolph and his wife was $560.

Question: Was the cost of the trip income to Rudolph as a bonus under § 61? If it was income, were the expenses deductible to Rudolph as a business expense under § 162(a)(2)?

Taxpayer's argument: He was a trapped organization man compelled to attend conventions.

Held: Dismissed the writ of certiorari as improvidently granted, thereby letting the lower court findings stand. These findings were that the dominant purpose of the trip was for the company to afford a pleasure trip in the nature of a bonus. Thus it was income. From Rudolph's point of view it was a pleasure trip. Thus the expenses were not deductible.

Dissent (Douglas, J., joined by Black, J.): Other professionals are able to attend conventions without attracting tax. Why single out insurance agents?

Comment: Note the methodology: First the question of income and then the question of deduction.

Comment: One answer to Justice Douglas is that this "convention" was held out as a reward for selling a certain amount of life insurance. Nevertheless, there is no doubt conventions present one of the toughest problems around for untangling business and pleasure.

Rudolph is still good law on the income side of mixed business and pleasure travel. For purposes of ascertaining deduction, the rules are now much more complex. For purposes of deductibility, the expenses of such trips are divided into two parts: the expense of traveling to and from the destination; and the expenses of lodging, meals, and entertainment incurred at the destination. With respect to the expenses for traveling to and from the destination, the Regulations provide an all-or-nothing approach. The expenses of traveling to and from the destination are fully deductible if the trip is "related primarily" to the taxpayer's trade or business, and the expenses are not deductible at all if the trip is "primarily personal in nature." These determinations are made by reference to time spent on business or pleasure.[108]

As to the second type of expenses—the expenses incurred at the destination—the approach is to allocate those expenses. The expenses allocable to business activities while at the destination are deductible; the expenses allocable to personal activities while at the destination are not deductible. This allocation approach is followed regardless whether the expenses of getting to and from the destination were deductible or not.[109]

Since foreign travel for business purposes has been regarded by Congress with a particularly jaundiced eye, such travel must also meet the tests of § 274(c). Section 274(c) disallows deductions for that portion of the travel which is not allocable to the taxpayer's trade or business or profit-seeking activity.

Section 274(c) bites, therefore, in particular as to the travel to and from the destination. It is already true, as discussed above, that expenses incurred at the destination are only deductible to the extent they are allocable to business activities. However, where the business travel is to a foreign destination, to the extent some of the taxpayer's time at the foreign destination is spent on personal activities, some portion of the expenses for traveling to and from the destination will be disallowed by virtue of § 274(c).[110] This restriction of § 274(c) on travel to and from a foreign destination does not apply if the travel does not exceed one week, or if the taxpayer spends less than 25 percent of his total time on non-business activities.

Expenses of foreign conventions (defined as conventions held outside of the U.S. and its possessions, Canada, and Mexico) are deductible only if it is "as reasonable" for the meeting to be held outside North America as within it.[111]

The expenses of a spouse, dependent, or other individual accompanying the taxpayer are only deductible if the spouse, dependent or other individual is an employee of the person or business paying the expenses, the travel of the spouse, dependent, or other individual is for a bona fide business purpose and such

---

[108] Reg. § 1.162–2(b)(1) and (2).

[109] See also Cannon, 24 T.C.M. 1074 (1965).

[110] Section 274(c)(2); Reg. § 1.274–4(f)(5), and see Reg. § 1.274–4(g) for further qualifications.

[111] Section 274(h), as amended by HR 5973, which repealed restrictive rules enacted in 1976 regarding subsistence, expense limitations, air fare limitations, and other special reporting requirements. Expenses of a convention on a cruise ship are deductible up to $2000 per person per year, only if the cruise ship is registered in the U.S. and all ports of call are in the U.S., Highway Revenue Act, 1/6/83.

expenses would otherwise be deductible by the spouse, dependent, or other individual.[112]

Business travel expenses must meet the substantiation requirements of § 274(d) discussed infra.

(5) Entertainment, Amusement and Recreation Expenses: Sutter; Cohan; Sanitary Farms

Once a taxpayer has returned home from an invigorating business trip to the Bahamas, which the taxpayer hopes will be deductible, the taxpayer may choose to entertain some business associates and their significant others with dinner and an evening at the theater, which the taxpayer would also like to deduct. The expenses of entertaining business associates has presented one of the most difficult problems in the tax law. Obviously it is very difficult to separate the pleasure component from the business component where a taxpayer pays the bill for actual or potential customers, or other business associates at dinner, the theater, or other recreational activities.

How should we handle this? If the taxpayer is at home and just goes out to dinner alone, there is not deduction for the cost of that dinner. But if the taxpayer takes a client out for dinner, then should there be a deduction not only for the client's dinner but also for that of the taxpayer? Isn't that going too far? The taxpayer would have had to eat dinner in any case. Isn't the theoretically proper approach to the taxpayer's own dinner to allow a deduction only to the extent it exceeds what the taxpayer would have otherwise paid for dinner?

The Service took that position originally. In 1921 the Service promulgated a regulation allowing a deduction for the cost of meals and lodging away from home. That deduction was limited to the extent the cost exceeded "any expenditure ordinarily required for such purposes when at home."[113]

This is the logical approach but it proved difficult to administer. Thus to simplify matters the Treasury asked Congress in 1921 to allow a deduction for the entire amount of such meals and lodging expenses.[114] Congress responded in 1921 with language[115] that later

---

[112]   Section 274(m)(3).

See Postlewaite, "Deduction of Expenses for Conventions and Educational Seminars," 61 Minn.L.Rev. 253 (1977); Shaddock, "The Tax Consequences of a Spouse's Convention Expenses," 29 Baylor Law Review 585 (1977).

[113]   Treas. Reg. 45 (1920 ed.), Art. 292, 4 Cum. Bull. 209 (1921).

[114]   Statement of Dr. T.S. Adams, Tax Adviser, Treasury Department, in Hearings on H.R. 8245 before the Senate Committee on Finance, 67th Cong., 1st Sess., at 50, 234–235 (1921).

[115]   Section 214(a)(1) of the Revenue Act of 1921, c. 136, 42 Stat. 239.

became § 162(a)(2). This historical perspective is helpful to see why the rules in this area seem to be too generous.

If this is true for food, then what about Knicks games, the theater, The Final Four, country clubs and nightclubs? The same issue is presented there. If the taxpayer takes a client to such events on business, can the taxpayer deduct not only the client's expenses but the taxpayer's own costs? This problem was presented in the well-known case of *Sutter*.

SUTTER V. COMMISSIONER[116]

Facts: The taxpayer, Richard Sutter, was a doctor specializing in the area of industrial medicine. His clients were the businesses that employed his patients and insurance companies that insured these businesses. Sutter engaged in a wide variety of activities to promote his business, including sending flowers, candy, tickets, and other gifts to various groups, attending numerous luncheons, buying a cabin cruiser on which he entertained both colleagues and his family, and joining a yacht club.

Question: Can Sutter deduct his promotion and entertainment expenses, including maintenance and depreciation on his cruiser, under § 162 as ordinary and necessary business expenses?

Held: Giving the flowers is not deductible at all. As to luncheons, entertaining and maintenance and depreciation on cruiser, expenses are only deductible for those expenses associated with the business. Costs of entertaining taxpayer and/or his family are not deductible even in the business setting unless they are different from or in excess of what the taxpayer would have incurred for his own personal use. The burden of proof on this matter is on taxpayer, citing *Cohan*, see below.

Comment: This imposes the same rule on entertainment expenses that the Service originally attempted to impose in the meals and lodging area, as discussed above.

The same administrative difficulties that attended the Service's original rule in the meals and lodging area has caused the Service to by and large ignore the *Sutter* rule. Thus the Service has generally allowed taxpayers to deduct their own expenses in full incurred in a business setting.[117]

---

[116] 21 T.C. 170 (1953).

[117] Contra Moss v. Commissioner, 758 F.2d 211 (7th Cir.1985), cert. denied 474 U.S. 979, 106 S.Ct. 382, 88 L.Ed.2d 335 (1985) (rejecting lawyer's attempt to deduct all his lunch expenses, including those of lunches with associates in his own firm, because he thought all his lunches were in a business setting).

Another major theme in the travel and entertainment area has been the irksome problem of keeping records. Some taxpayers solve the problem by not keeping any, as illustrated in the major case of *Cohan.*

COHAN V. COMMISSIONER[118]

Facts: The taxpayer, George Cohan, was a producer of plays who often entertained actors, employees, and dramatic critics. In addition, he traveled often, many times with his attorney. These expenses were substantial and at least some of them were deductible, but the taxpayer kept no records.

Question: Given that Cohan had some real travel and entertainment expenses, can he deduct any of them given that he did not keep records.

Held: The court reversed a Board of Tax Appeals holding that in the absence of records Cohan can deduct nothing. The court remanded the case to the BTA holding that "absolute certainty in these matters is usually not possible . . . the Board should make as close an approximation as it can . . ." With the further proviso that the Board can estimate the amounts conservatively against the taxpayer given that the inexactitude is of the taxpayer's own making.

Comment: The opinion by Learned Hand noted that the taxpayer "naively" admitted to entertaining drama critics.

Comment: This case, decided in 1930, over time led to game-playing by taxpayers. Taxpayers without records would give high estimates of their business expenses, expecting to be cut down by the Service, which began to take this factor into account in cutting back the estimates. Since most returns were not audited at all, most of these inflated estimates went through unchallenged. This is an example of how the unrelenting pressure of taxpayers to lower their tax bill on an annual basis can degrade rules that are not designed to stand up to that pressure.

Those who cry for simplification in the tax system rarely address the problem of substantiating travel and entertainment expenses in the business setting. Can we take any "back of the envelope" proposal seriously unless they deal with this issue?

The net result of all these developments in the 1920's and 30's was that things were kind-of wide open in this area. As long as there was a colorable case that the meals or travel and entertainment activities had to do with "business," not only were the client's expenses deductible but so were the taxpayer's. This wide open

---

118   39 F.2d 540 (2d Cir.1930).

attitude reached its apotheosis in the famous case of *Sanitary Farms Dairy*.

SANITARY FARMS DAIRY, INC. V. COMMISSIONER[119]

Facts: Sanitary Farms Dairy was a company specializing in dairy products. Most of the stock in the dairy was owned by O. Carlyle Brock and his family. Brock was a big game hunter. He and his wife held dinners for prospective customers in which they served the game that he had killed. In addition, the taxpayer opened up a museum at the plant in which to showcase some of the game that Brock had killed. Brock and his wife then decided to gain publicity for the dairy by going on an exotic safari.

Question: Are the expenses of a big-game hunting African safari undertaken by the controlling shareholder deductible to a dairy as advertising expenses?

Held: Yes, the expenses are deductible.

Comment: You've got to be kidding!

Comment: The court in dicta said "there is a little bit of the hunter in all of us."

Comment: Not only was the cost of the trip deductible to the dairy but it was not income to Brock (an avid big-game hunter) and his wife. Just a sideline benefit of his job, like air-conditioning. You know how it goes in the dairy business. Just scuffle, scuffle, scuffle.

Comment: It was cases like this that inspired comedian Mel Brooks to style himself as a tax expert who announced he had cut his own tax bill from $90,000 to $1.40 by deducting World War II under travel expenses.

After cases like *Sanitary Farms,* it became apparent that stricter rules were necessary to qualify for these business deductions. The business nexus of such activities should be much more clear.[120]

---

[119]   25 T.C. 463 (1955).

[120]   Just so you don't think these pranks are limited to the 1950s, see Robson v. Commissioner, 73 T.C.M. 2574 (1997), aff'd by unpublished opinion, 172 F.3d 876 (9th Cir.1999). In *Robson*, the taxpayers donated game mounts to a charitable organization (whether it actual was a charitable organization is another question). They sought to deduct the cost of the game mounts from income. Since California prohibited the sale of game mounts, taxpayers argued that the fair market value should be determined based on the replacement cost (i.e. the cost of traveling to Africa and shooting another animal), not based on comparable sales. What taxpayers were attempting to do was to receive a deduction for their recreational trip to Africa. Regardless what you think of game hunting, taxpayers certainly should not be subsidizing a recreational hunting trip. Both the Tax Court and the Ninth Circuit rejected taxpayers' replacement cost approach.

Theoretically, the matter should have been dealt with under § 162, or § 212 where appropriate, in simply determining whether the particular expense was, under the circumstances, an ordinary and necessary business expense. However, in the early 1960s, the probably accurate public impression was that there were widespread abuses in the area of deductibility of business entertainment.[121] As a result, Congress enacted § 274(a), applying strict standards to business-oriented entertainment, amusement and recreation. In addition, rules for the substantiation of such expenses were required by new § 274(d), thus overruling *Cohan*. Consequently, expenses for business-oriented entertainment, amusement, and recreation must meet the usual standards of § 162 or § 212, and must further run the gauntlet of potential disallowance under § 274(a) as well as be substantiated by § 274(d).

Section 274 deploys a set of rules of stupefying complexity. It is set forth in the accompanying flow-chart. The major points of the chart are discussed further in the text.

---

[121]　See Staff of House Ways and Means Comm., 90th Cong., 1st Sess., Legislative History of the Revenue Act of 1962, Pt. 1.

§ 274: BUSINESS EXPENSES INVOLVING ENTERTAINMENT, AMUSEMENT OR RECREATION

Business Expenses Involving Entertainment, Amusement, or Recreation

Deductible as "ordinary and necessary" business expense under § 162.

Deductible as "ordinary and necessary" for production of income under § 212. Treated as trade or business for purposes of statute, § 274(a)(2)(B).

"Activities" generally considered to be entertainment, amusement or recreation. § 274(a).

Business gifts to an individual: No deduction to extent exceed $25, § 274(b).

Foreign Travel: No deduction for that portion which, under regs, is not allocable to trade or business, § 274(c)(1).

Traveling expenses including meals and lodging: No deduction unless substantiated, § 274(d)(1).

Allowed only if the item was "directly related to" the active conduct of the taxpayer's trade or business § 274(a)(1)(A).

If the item directly precedes or follows a substantial and bona fide business discussion, including business meeting at a convention, item deductible only if it "was associated with" the active conduct of the taxpayer's trade or business, § 274(a)(1)(A).

No deduction for a "facility" used with above "activities," § 274(a)(1)(B).

Allocation rules do not apply if 1) foreign travel does not exceed 1 week or 2) less than 25% of time is spent on personal travel, § 274(c)(2).

Attendance at conventions: No deduction if held outside North American area unless meeting is directly related to active conduct of trade or business and it is "reasonable" for the meeting to be held outside the "North American area" (as defined in §§ 274(h)(3)(A), 274(h)(6)) as within it. $2,000 maximum deduction. § 274(h)(1) & 2.

Restrictions do not apply to various items provided to employees and certain other items, § 274(e).

No deduction unless substantiated § 274(d)(2), (3).

Dues or fees to any social, athletic or sporting club are items with respect to facilities.

Disallowance for facilities does not apply if taxpayer establishes that the facility was used "primarily for the furtherance" of the taxpayer's trade or business and the item was "directly related" to the active conduct of such trade or business.

Conventions on cruise ships: No deduction unless business time substantiated, § 274(h)(5), and taxpayer established that 1) meeting is "directly related" to his trade or business; 2) the cruise ship is registered in U.S.; and 3) all ports of call are in U.S. or possessions, §274(h)(2).

General limit on luxury water travel: No deduction to the extent that it exceeds twice the per diem amount for executive branch employees, except for cruise ships, § 274(m).

Entertainment tickets for activities or facilities: Deduction cannot exceed face value of ticket except for certain charitable sports events, § 274(l)(1).

No deduction for seminars for § 212 purposes (such as to advise on investments), § 274(h)(7).

Luxury skyboxes leased for more than one event: Amount deductible cannot exceed sum of the face value of the non-luxury box seat tickets for the seats in the box, § 274(l)(2).

Business meals and beverages: No deduction unless expenses are not lavish or extravagant, and taxpayer or an employee of taxpayer is present at meal or beverage, § 274(k)(1).

When you get all through, there's an across-the-board limit that only 50% of meals and entertainment expenses otherwise allowable is allowed, § 274(n)(1). Minor exception is for deduction of cost of de minimis fringe benefits under § 132(e) or charitable sports events and other minor exceptions, § 274(n)(2).

There will be a quiz on this at noon.

The flow-chart depicts what can only be described as a nightmarish statutory scheme. Note, for example, that for a taxpayer to be able to deduct a luxury skybox, the taxpayer must undergo six levels of statutory analysis. (Wouldn't you rather just stay home and watch it on TV?)

As the flow-chart indicates, § 274(a) disallows deductions with respect to activities which are of a type generally considered to constitute entertainment, amusement, or recreation, unless the taxpayer establishes that the item was directly related to—or, in the case of an item directly preceding or following a substantial and bona fide business discussion, that the item was associated with—the active conduct of a taxpayer's trade or business. The two major tests here are that the entertainment, etc. item must be "directly related" to the active conduct of the taxpayer's trade or business, or that the entertainment, etc. activity must be "associated with" the active conduct of the taxpayer's trade or business, if the item directly precedes or follows a substantial and bona fide business discussion.[122] The Regulations, setting a new standard in turgidity, go on to explain the "directly related to" and the "associated with" tests, elaborate on various other terms in § 274(a), as well as give a few examples.[123] As a rough generalization, it could be said that the Regulations apply strict standards in the explanation of the rules of § 274(a).

Expenses for entertainment, amusement, and recreational facilities—such as country clubs, sporting lodges, and other entertainment clubs—are subject to severe limitations on deductibility. The general rule is that no deduction is allowed with respect to a facility used in connection with entertainment, amusement or recreation, even though such deduction would qualify as an ordinary and necessary business expense under § 162.[124] This disallowance of expenses with respect to entertainment, etc. facilities applies to dues or fees to any social, athletic or sporting club.[125] Clubs operated solely to furnish lunches in a business setting are exempted from this disallowance.[126] And in a significant further exception, if the taxpayer establishes that in the case of a club, the facility was used primarily for the "furtherance of the taxpayer's trade or

---

[122]   Expenses incurred under § 212 are treated as incurred under § 162 for the purposes of § 274, § 274(a)(2)(B).

[123]   Reg. § 1.274–2(c), (d), (e). Reg. § 1.274–2(b)(1) defines entertainment, amusement or recreation.

[124]   Section 274(a)(1)(B).

[125]   Section 274(a)(2)(A).

[126]   Reg. § 1.274–2(e)(3)(ii).

business" and that the amount paid was "directly related" to the active conduct of such trade or business, the disallowance will not apply.[127]

A number of relatively minor business-oriented entertainment expenses are exempted from these disallowance rules, including business meals, food and beverages for employees, expenses for goods, services, facilities and recreation for employees (under certain conditions), expenses for business meetings, and certain other expenses.[128]

As with expenses for travel, expenses for entertainment, amusement, and recreation which survive the gauntlet of § 274(a) can still only be deducted if they are substantiated in accordance with the requirements of § 274(d), discussed below.

(6) Limits on Deductibility of Business Meals: Sutter Lives

The rules related to the deductibility of business meals are set forth under § 274(k). Once the deductible amounts are established under § 274(k), only 50% of them may actually be deducted, under § 274(n). Under § 274(k)(1), no deduction is allowed for the expense of any food or beverage unless (A) the expense is not lavish or extravagant under the circumstances, and (B) the taxpayer (or an employee of the taxpayer) is present at the furnishing of such food or beverages. Under § 274(k)(2) these restrictions do not apply if the general restrictive rules of § 274(a) do not apply to the expense by reason of § 274(e)(2) (taxpayer treating the expenses as compensation for withholding purposes), § 274(e)(3) (reimbursed expenses), § 274(e)(4) (recreational expenses for employees other than highly compensated employees), § 274(e)(7) (items made available to the public), § 274(e)(8) (entertainment sold to customers), or § 274(e)(9) (expenses includible in income of persons who are not employees).

As also indicated in the flow-chart above, there is a broad backstop rule providing that after all the tests and computations of other entertainment, amusement and recreation rules, in any event only 50% of the established deduction is allowed in many cases.

In particular, under § 274(n)(1) only 50% of deductions otherwise allowed are allowed for any expense for food or beverages and any activity which is of a type generally considered to constitute entertainment, amusement, or recreation, or with respect to a facility used in connection with such activity.

---

[127] Section 274(a)(2)(C).
[128] Section 274(e). Reg. § 1.274–2(f)(2).

This 50% restriction does not apply to certain relatively minor expenses, under § 274(n)(2). If the employee is reimbursed for business meals, then the employee is not subject to these rules; instead the employer will be. The employer can also deduct in full the cost of food qualifying as a de minimis employee fringe benefit. Thus, little lunches, dinners, and parties for employees are deductible in full by the employer.

This general disallowance of 50% of meal and entertainment expenses may be seen as a limited reincarnation of the *Sutter* rule. In the *Sutter* case, discussed above at ¶ 6.02(5), the court allowed deduction of the taxpayer's own entertainment expenses in the business setting only to the extent the expenses exceed what the taxpayer would have paid for himself had business not been involved. Suggesting the taxpayer would have spent only 50% of the expenses on himself had business not been involved shows that, in watered-down form, *Sutter* lives.

(7) The Substantiation Requirement for Travel, Entertainment, and Business Gifts

In the leading case of *Cohan*,[129] discussed also above at ¶ 6.02(5), performer and producer George M. Cohan spent substantial amounts of money on business travel and business entertainment but had no records whatsoever to substantiate his expenditures. The Service admitted that Cohan had spent significant sums in this fashion but attempted to disallow the deductions because of the lack of any substantiation. Judge Learned Hand, speaking for the Second Circuit, held that Cohan under these circumstances was entitled to some deduction which, in the absence of documentation, would have to be estimated. The Court seemed to concede that the estimate could be relatively small in comparison to what Cohan might have actually spent, but it was wrong, in the Court's view, to disallow all expenses because of the lack of substantiation.

This relatively attractive *Cohan* rule continues to hold sway for deductions under § 162. However, with respect to travel, entertainment, and business gift expenses, the *Cohan* rule has been superseded by the stringent substantiation requirements of § 274(d).

The basic rule of § 274(d) is that no deduction will be allowed for any traveling, entertainment, amusement, or recreation expense or

---

[129] Cohan v. Commissioner, 39 F.2d 540 (2d Cir.1930). Compare Raytheon Production Corp. v. Commissioner, 144 F.2d 110 (1st Cir.1944), cert. denied 323 U.S. 779, 65 S.Ct. 192, 89 L.Ed. 622 (1944), holding that a damage award attributable to destruction of goodwill was taxable in full, inasmuch as the taxpayer failed to prove the cost of its goodwill. For discussion of damage awards, see ¶ 3.11.

any expense for business gifts unless the taxpayer can substantiate these expenses.[130]

The Regulations describe in great detail what is required to meet the substantiation standard of § 274(d). Substantiating an item by adequate records means the taxpayer must maintain an account book, diary, statement of expense or similar record in which each element of an expenditure is recorded at or near the time of the expenditure and in addition provide documentary evidence—such as receipts, bills, or similar evidence. Taken together, the account book and the documentary evidence will meet the requirement of providing "adequate records" for purposes of § 274(d).[131]

Exempted from the substantiation requirements are expenses relating to food and beverages for employees, certain expenses treated as compensation, certain items available to the public,[132] items relating to entertainment sold to customers, and items relating to recreational expenses for employees.[133]

Where an employee incurs expenses for the benefit of his employer and is reimbursed for them, the employee may omit both the expenses and the reimbursement from the tax return, if the employee makes an adequate accounting of the expenditures to the employer.[134] This shifts the requirement to substantiate the travel and entertainment, etc. expenses under § 274(d) to the employer.

The Service is empowered to promulgate rules regarding reimbursement arrangements, per diem allowances and mileage allowances which can take the place of requiring the employee to meet the substantiation standards of § 274(d), and the accounting requirement in the case of employees under reimbursement arrangements.[135]

Thus, in sum, entertainment expenses must meet the requirements of § 162 (the business expense); then meet the standards of § 274(a); and finally be adequately substantiated.

---

[130] See also Reg. § 1.274–5; Temp. Reg. § 1.274–5T.

[131] Reg. § 1.274–5(c)(2). See Dowell v. United States, 522 F.2d 708 (5th Cir.1975), cert. denied, 426 U.S. 920, 96 S.Ct. 2626, 49 L.Ed.2d 374 (1976) (expenditures must be substantiated individually). Reg. § 1.274–5(c)(3).

[132] Section 274(e)(1)–(10), also providing certain other exceptions.

[133] Reg. § 1.274–5(c)(7); Temp. Reg. § 1.274–5T. Also exempted from the substantiation and other rules of § 274 are expenses which are deductible in any event without regard to the relationship to the taxpayer's business, such as interest, property taxes, and casualty losses. See Reg. § 1.274–6.

[134] Reg. § 1.274–5(e)(4); Reg. § 1.274–5(e)(2)(i); Temp. Reg. § 1.274–5T. If the reimbursement exceeds the expenses, the employee must include the difference in his income, Reg. § 1.274–5(e)(2)(ii). See also Lewis v. Commissioner, 560 F.2d 973 (9th Cir.1977) (excessive allocation to personal use under reimbursement agreement).

[135] Reg. § 1.274–5(f); Temp. Reg. § 1.274–5T.

(8) Moving Expenses

Moving expenses incident to a taxpayer being transferred to a new job assignment present a difficult theoretical question in that both personal and business elements are present to a high degree. Obviously, the taxpayer could not take on the new job without moving to the new job location. At the same time, it may be argued that moving the taxpayer's family and personal effects is "inherently personal" and therefore nondeductible.[136] Thus moving expenses present much the same theoretical problems that travel and entertainment expenses present: they have a strong business and personal component. As we have seen, above, the matter was resolved in the case of entertainment expenses by applying the very stringent standards of § 274(a), coupled with the substantiation requirements of § 274(d). Thus the Code walks the fine line between allowing reasonable and legitimate business entertainment expenses and disallowing personal expenses for entertainment. In the moving expenses area, the approach is to allow some of the expenses in full, and impose some dollar limitations on certain other expenses incident to the taxpayer's moving to a new job location.[137]

To qualify for any deduction at all for moving expenses under § 217, the moving expenses must be incurred in connection with the commencement of work by the taxpayer as an employee or as a self-employed individual at a new principal place of work.[138] The term "commencement of work" includes the beginning of work by the taxpayer as an employee or as a self-employed individual for the first time or after a substantial period of unemployment or part-time employment; the beginning of work by a taxpayer for a different employer or, in the case of a self-employed individual, in a new trade or business; or the beginning of work by a taxpayer for the same employer in the same business at a new location.[139] To qualify as being in connection with the commencement of work, the move must bear a "reasonable proximity both in time and place to such commencement," and in general the expenses have to be incurred within one year of the date of the commencement of the work.

The new principal place of work must be at least fifty miles farther from the former residence than was the former principal place

---

[136]   See the discussion of the personal expense limitation on deductions, ¶ 6.03.

[137]   Section 217. See also § 82, which provides that amounts the taxpayer receives as reimbursement for moving expenses will be included in income, regardless of the extent to which the taxpayer's moving expenses are deductible under § 217.

[138]   Section 217(a).

[139]   Reg. § 1.217–2(a)(3).

of work.[140] The taxpayer must be a full-time employee for at least thirty-nine weeks during the twelve month period immediately following arrival in the general location of the new principal place of work.[141]

"Moving expenses" means, for purposes of the § 217 deduction: (A) moving household goods and personal effects from the former residence to the new residence; (B) traveling (including lodging) from the former residence to the new residence. Expenses for meals are not deductible under this rule.

(9) Activities Not Engaged in for Profit

One of the areas viewed with the greatest suspicion by the tax law is where the taxpayer piles up large deductions while engaging in activities that bring great personal enjoyment. While no one would question the deductibility of expenses incurred in the running of a dry cleaning business, grocery store, or investing in stocks and bonds—no matter how much the taxpayer may enjoy these business activities—there is apparently something inherently suspect about a farm to which the taxpayer makes repairs on weekends or the raising of horses for breeding or racing purposes, or any other activity which appears to partake of the sweet life.

From early in its history, the tax law has purported to be able to differentiate between business and profit-seeking activities on the one hand and activities not entered into for profit on the other, with a concomitant disallowance of losses generated by the latter activities.[142] Taxpayers' success in having deductions arising out of these fun-type activities allowed ultimately led Congress to enact § 183, which disallows deductions under certain conditions which are attributable to an "activity not engaged in for profit."

The particular limiting rules of § 183 are triggered when the taxpayer engages in an "activity not engaged in for profit." Thus a great deal turns on the definition of that phrase. The Code and Regulations set forth a large number of factors to be used in determining whether an activity is engaged in for profit. Briefly

---

[140] Section 217(c), also providing that if the taxpayer had no former principal place of work, the place of work must be at least fifty miles from his former residence.

[141] An alternative test that may be met here is that during the twenty-four month period immediately following the taxpayer's arrival at the general location of his new principal place of work, he is a full-time employee or performs services as a self-employed individual on a full-time basis in the new location for at least seventy-eight weeks, of which at least thirty-nine are during the first twelve months following his arrival in the new location. § 217(c)(2). These tests are waived if the taxpayer is unable to satisfy them by reason of death, disability, involuntary separation (other than for willful misconduct) from the service of the employer, and certain other conditions.

[142] See e.g. Thacher v. Lowe, 288 Fed. 994 (S.D.N.Y. 1922).

stated, these factors are, first, that the activity should be one other than one for which deductions are allowed under § 162 or 212. Next, one must consider the manner in which the taxpayer carries on the activity, the expertise of the taxpayer or the taxpayer's advisers, the time and effort expended by the taxpayer in carrying on the activity, the expectation that assets used in the activity may appreciate in value, the success of the taxpayer in carrying on similar or dissimilar activities, the taxpayer's history of income or losses with respect to the activity, the amount of occasional profits, if any, which are earned, the financial status of the taxpayer, and the elements of personal pleasure or recreation involved in the activity.[143] In addition to these factors, the Regulations also inform that "the determination whether an activity is engaged in for profit is to be made by reference to objective standards, taking into account all of the facts and circumstances of each case."[144]

This mélange of facts and circumstances are illustrated by several examples in the Regulations, which include deeming an inherited farm, writing and publishing philosophical pamphlets, dog and horse breeding, as "activities not engaged in for profit" when the taxpayer had other sources of substantial income.[145] On the other hand, an inherited farm operated by a taxpayer in a fairly serious fashion, an independent oil and gas wildcat driller, and a chemist with his own workshop were found by the Regulations, under the particular facts set forth, to be "activities engaged in for profit" notwithstanding that significant losses were incurred over the years.[146] The bottom line is that where the activity is "recreational," as that term is usually defined—i.e., farming or horse and dog racing, etc.—and the losses from the activity are taken against taxpayer's substantial other income, the taxpayer is very likely to be deemed to have an "activity not engaged in for profit."[147]

---

[143] Section 183(c); Reg. § 1.183–2(b). Reg. § 1.183–2(a).

[144] Reg. § 1.183–2(a).

[145] Reg. § 1.183–2(c) Examples (1)–(3). See as a significant case in this area Brannen, 78 T.C. 471 (1982), judgment aff'd 722 F.2d 695 (11th Cir.1984) (limited partnership investment in a "spaghetti western" movie found to be not engaged in for profit at the partnership level and hence individual partners' deductions barred. See ¶ 8.02).

[146] Reg. § 1.183–2(c) Examples (4)–(6). Cf. Dreicer v. Commissioner, 665 F.2d 1292 (D.C.Cir.1981), on remand 78 T.C. 642 (1982) (even though taxpayer may believe likelihood of profit is small, as long as taxpayer has intent to make profit, the activity is not within § 183).

[147] See Reg. § 1.183–2(b)(8). Cf. Gertrude Gorod, 42 T.C.M. 1569 (1981) (ten years of fruitless effort to rent lower level of a duplex in run-down area of Malden, Mass. did not constitute an activity not engaged in for profit, and hence maintenance and depreciation deductions could be taken); Miles, 45 T.C.M. 1333 (1983) (ineptly run chicken farm, where taxpayer failed to heat henhouse during winter and allowed chickens to roam freely over 45 acres so that he could not find their eggs (characterized

Once it is established that a taxpayer is indeed involved in an "activity not engaged in for profit," the rules specifying the amount and type of deductions allowed are clear. Potential deductions are divided into three categories:[148] (1) deductions that are allowable without regard to whether or not the activity is engaged in for profit—i.e., mortgage interest, property taxes; (2) deductions that would be allowable if the activity were engaged in for profit but which do not result in adjustments to the basis of the property—i.e., ordinary and necessary expenses under § 162 or 212; and (3) deductions that would be allowed if the activity were engaged in for profit but which do result in an adjustment to the basis of the property—primarily the deduction for depreciation or cost recovery.[149]

Deductions in the first category one will always be allowed in full. Deductions in the second category will only be allowed to the extent the gross income from the activity exceeds the deductions in the first category attributable to the activity not engaged in for profit. The deductions in the third category will only be allowed to the extent that the gross income from the activity not engaged in for profit exceeds the deductions from the first two categories.[150]

As an example, consider the case of a horse farm owned by an executive who has $100,000 of income from salary. The executive tends to the horse farm generally on weekends and enjoys it. Members of the family help out. The horse farm is an activity "not engaged in for profit." The horse farm generates $25,000 of gross income; there are mortgage interest and property taxes attributable to the horse farm property of $11,000; supplies and maintenance are $13,000; and depreciation or cost recovery on buildings and equipment of the horse farm is $5,000. The computation of the amount of these deductions that will be allowed is illustrated by Table 6–1.

---

by the court as "open-range chicken farming"), was an activity not entered into for profit.)

Being in a bad mood and smelling like a horse apparently will have its tax advantages. In Morely v. Commissioner, 76 T.C.M. 363 (1998) the taxpayer was a dentist who also engaged in Arabian horse breeding. When working on the horse farm, he neglected his family and, according to his wife's testimony, came home late at night in a bad mood and dirty with a certain aroma from his work. Held: Not an activity not engaged in for profit and expenses deducted in full. Is there a larger lesson here?

[148] Section 183(b); Reg. § 1.183–1(b)(1).

[149] See ¶ 6.02(12). Also allowed here would be the deduction for casualty losses to business property (which is not subject to the 10% of adjusted gross income limit, see § 7.01(5)).

[150] Reg. § 1.183–1(b).

If more than one piece of property is eligible for the depreciation deduction, the Regulations prescribe rules for allocating the depreciation deduction and appropriate basis adjustment.[151]

Table 6–1

LIMITATIONS ON DEDUCTIONS OF ACTIVITY NOT ENGAGED IN FOR PROFIT

1.	Gross income from horse farm	$25,000
2.	Level one deductions, mortgage interest, and property taxes (allowed without limit)	$11,000
3.	Gross income less level one deductions	$14,000
4.	Level two deductions, supplies and maintenance (do not affect basis)	$13,000
5.	Gross income less level one and two deductions (line three less line 4)	$1,000
6.	Depreciation on buildings and equipment	$5,000
7.	Amount of depreciation allowed as a deduction (line 6 up to limit of line 5)	$1,000
8.	Total deductions allowed with respect to horse farm (lines 2 + 4 + 7)	$25,000

The taxpayer is assisted by a presumption that if there is a profit from the activity for three of the past five taxable years, the activity will be presumed to be an activity engaged in for profit. In computing whether there is a profit, the activity is treated as though it were an activity entered into for profit, so that all appropriate deductions are taken account of in full.[152] Where the activity consists in major part of the breeding, training, showing or racing of horses, the taxpayer need only show a profit in two out of a period of seven consecutive taxable years in order to get the advantage of the presumption.[153]

This presumption suggests that taxpayers may be able to do a little planning by way of bunching up income in order to turn a

---

[151] Regs. § 1.183–1(b)(2), 1.183–1(b)(3).

[152] Section 183(d); Reg. § 1.183–1(c)(1). The net operating loss deduction of § 172 is not taken into account in computing whether a profit has been turned for the purposes of this presumption.

[153] Section 183(d), last sentence.

perhaps small profit in several years of the five- or seven-year measuring period. Thus, a few judicious sales of property might be enough to tip the scales in the taxpayer's favor in two or three years out of the appropriate measuring period. When contemplating such planning, however, it should be borne in mind that the presumption here is not conclusive; the Service may still determine that, notwithstanding a profit for the qualifying number of years, the activity is still an activity not engaged in for profit.[154] If the taxpayer were to run huge losses in the activity in two years and very small profits in the activity in three years, the Service may very well be able to rebut the presumption and impose the § 183 limitations upon the activity.[155]

Taxpayers hoping to benefit from the presumption may elect to stay a determination of whether the presumption applies and report their activities as though they were entered into for profit.[156] If over the five or seven years that the taxpayer so reports the activity the presumption does not come into effect or is rebutted, the statutory period for the assessment of any deficiency attributable to treating the activity as one not engaged in for profit is extended to cover the years in question.[157]

To the extent that deductions are allowed under § 183, they will be allowed below the line as itemized deductions, since nowhere in § 62(a) are deductions arising from an activity not engaged in for profit mentioned, see Brannen v. Commissioner, 78 T.C. 471 (1982), judgment aff'd 722 F.2d 695 (11th Cir.1984).

Section 183 has generally been unsuccessful in limiting taxpayers' attempts to treat personal hobbies as businesses. Taxpayers have sought to treat activities such as motor cross racing and dance lessons for their children as business expenses.[158] After all, their child might grow up to be a motor cross racing champion or

---

[154]   Section 183(d).

[155]   Faulconer, 45 T.C.M. 1084 (1983), judgment rev'd 748 F.2d 890 (4th Cir.1984) (small profits in profit years and large losses in loss years plus other surrounding facts allowed IRS to overcome presumption for Buck Island and Westover Farms, Virginia horsefarm.)

Where the taxpayer is engaging in more than one activity which may be arguably regarded as an activity not engaged in for profit, it may be possible to combine or fragment such activities in order to get the benefit of the presumption, or indeed to escape the reach of § 183 altogether. Regs. § 1.183–1(d) deals with these issues.

[156]   Section 183(e).

[157]   Section 183(e)(4).

[158]   See McCarthy v. Commissioner, 164 F.3d 618 (2d Cir.1998) (motor cross racing for 13 year old); Carino v. Commissioner, T.C. Summ.Op. 2002–140, 2002 WL 31427012 (dancing lessons for 14 year old).

the star in a Broadway musical. What is next? Would golf lessons be deductible if you hoped to be the next Rory McElroy?

In addition, because taxpayers are given some time to generate a profit, taxpayers often get away with improper business deductions for several years before they are audited.[159] Why don't we have a hard and fast rule regarding hobby loss deductions?[160] Some unfairness might result, but could it be any worse than the current situation?

(10) Office in the Home; Soliman

The deductibility of expenses attributable to a taxpayer using a portion of the taxpayer's home as an "office" for carrying on business or profit-seeking activities has long vexed the courts, Congress and the Service. Much as in the case of entertainment expenses (discussed at ¶ 6.02(5)), § 162's stricture that only ordinary and necessary business expenses could be deducted proved inadequate to deal with apparent widespread taxpayers' abuse in this area.[161]

Congress, therefore, enacted § 280A(a), providing relatively stringent rules. Section 280A(a) also provides rules for the treatment of the rental of vacation homes, and certain other business uses of residential property. These issues are discussed at ¶ 6.02(11).

With respect to the home office issue, it is first clear that deductions that are generally allowed without regard to whether the taxpayer has a home office will still be allowed.[162] This would include deductions like mortgage interest, property taxes and deductible casualty losses.[163] Instead, § 280A applies to deductions that are only allowed if the taxpayer is engaged in a trade or business, or profit-seeking activity—such as maintenance expenses, utility expenses,

---

[159] Rinehart v. Commissioner, 75 T.C.M. 2449 (1998) (taxpayer was not engaged in horse breeding for profit. Taxpayer, however, succeeding in deducting over $600,000 of losses prior to the audit period); Berry v. Commissioner, 79 T.C.M. 1776 (2000) (farm and horse breeding activity not engaged in for profit. Taxpayer succeeded in deducting more than $800,000 over a 13 year period); Filios v. Commissioner, 224 F.3d 16 (1st Cir.2000) (horse racing not engaged in for profit. For thirty-five years prior to the years covered by the audit, taxpayer had deducted almost $6 million in losses.) A special thanks to Travis Garrison, a student in Professor Tobin's Tax Policy class, for his work on this issue.

[160] Allan J. Samansky, Hobby Loss or Deductible Loss: An Intractable Problem, 34 U. Fla. L. Rev. 46 (1981).

[161] Cf. Bodzin v. Commissioner, 509 F.2d 679 (4th Cir.1975), cert. denied 423 U.S. 825, 96 S.Ct. 40, 46 L.Ed.2d 41 (1975) (attorney for the Internal Revenue Service not allowed to deduct rent attributable to study where he had adequate office space at work).

[162] Section 280A(b).

[163] As to casualty losses it does matter whether the taxpayer can deduct them as part of a home office business, because if a deduction is proper it will be allowed "above the line" and thus be business casualties not subject to the $100 and 10% of AGI floors.

rent, and depreciation or cost recovery. It is these deductions, then, that are at stake in the home office area.

These deductions are only allowed to the extent they are allocable to a portion of the taxpayer's residence which is *exclusively* used on a regular basis (A) as the principal place of business for any trade or business of the taxpayer; (B) as a place of business which is used by patients, clients, or customers in meeting or dealing with the taxpayer in the normal course of his trade or business; or (C) in the case of a separate structure which is not attached to the taxpayer's residence, in connection with the taxpayer's trade or business. Moreover, where the taxpayer's trade or business involves being an employee, the taxpayer may only take business deductions attributable to a home office if the use of the home office is for the convenience of the taxpayer's employer.[164]

These rules bar deductions attributable to a home office where the taxpayer does not conduct a trade or business in the home office, but is only engaging in profit-seeking activity. Thus, exclusive use of a study or den for the purpose of making investments in the stock market by a taxpayer who is not in the trade or business of investing in securities would not qualify; nor would exclusive use of a study or a den in the home by a teacher to prepare for class qualify, unless it could be shown that the employer provided no work space and required the teacher to prepare lessons at home.[165]

Taxpayers who can take business-type deductions (maintenance, utilities, rent, depreciation, etc.) attributable to their home offices are generally taxpayers who are self-employed and use the home offices as their principal place of business, or taxpayers who may have more than one trade or business, one of which is operated from the home office.[166]

Allowing taxpayers who regularly meet patients, clients, or customers in the home to also qualify as having a home office (even

---

[164] Section 280A(c).

[165] Thus, the taxpayer in Bodzin, supra, would have also lost under these new rules. Cf. Moller v. United States, 553 F.Supp. 1071 (Ct.Cl.1982), judgment rev'd 721 F.2d 810 (Fed.Cir.1983), cert. denied 467 U.S. 1251, 104 S.Ct. 3534, 82 L.Ed.2d 839 (1984) (very active securities investment qualified as trade or business for purposes of § 280A; expenses allowed for offices in two different homes); Drucker, 79 T.C. 605 (1982), judgment rev'd 715 F.2d 67 (2d Cir.1983) (concert violinist playing for the Metropolitan Opera Orchestra could not deduct room at home set aside for practice, since it wasn't the principal place of his trade or business, notwithstanding that the Met provided him with no practice space). But see Popov v. Commissioner, 246 F.3d 1190 (9th Cir.2001) and ¶ 6.02(10).

[166] Section 280A(c)(1)(A). See Edwin Curphey, 73 T.C. 766 (1980) (doctor with principal place of business at hospital had principal place of business at home office with respect to his real estate business); John Green, 78 T.C. 428 (1982) (home office deduction allowed where office was used only to receive telephone calls).

though the office may not, in fact, in some cases be the taxpayer's principal place of business) indicates that Congress will relax its standards somewhat where one can objectively show that the taxpayer makes extensive business use of a portion of the home. Allowing taxpayers business-type deductions where they have a separate structure used in their businesses, even though it may not be their principal place of business, again relaxes the standard where there is a more objective test.

It should be emphasized, however, that where the taxpayer is an employee, no business-type deductions will be allowed with respect to a home office unless it is for the convenience of the employer, as well as being the employee's principal place of business.[167]

Even if the taxpayer qualifies as having a home office by meeting one of the three alternative tests described above, the situation is no particular bargain. The business deductions attributable to such home office may not exceed the gross income derived from the use of the home office less any deductions allocable to such use which would be allowed no matter whether the taxpayer had a qualifying home office.

As an example, suppose a taxpayer generates $15,000 of gross income from a small consulting business, operated out of a den at home. If the mortgage interest and property taxes attributable to the den are $5,000, then there is a balance of $10,000 against which deductions for maintenance, utilities, and depreciation attributable to the den may be taken. To the extent the deductions for maintenance, utilities, and depreciation exceed $10,000 they will not be allowed. The Service has promulgated regulations specifying the order in which allowed deductions will be taken.[168]

The Supreme Court in the case of *Commissioner v. Soliman*[169] tightened the standards in the home office area. Although the

---

[167] Indeed, even if the employer provided the employee with no work space, the employee might arguably be denied a home office deduction because notwithstanding making significant use of the home office, the home office is still likely not to be the employee's principal place of business, if the employee transacts substantial amounts of business on the employer's premises or elsewhere. Nor is it likely that such an employee would meet clients or customers in a home office, or have a separate structure attributable to the business. Cf. Weightman, 42 T.C.M. 104 (1981) (part of room can be a home office; on these particular facts other requirements for a home office not met).

[168] The order of deduction is: (1) deductions that would be allowed regardless of use as a home office, i.e., mortgage interest and property taxes attributable to the home office; (2) deductions that do not cause basis adjustments (maintenance); (3) deductions that do cause a basis adjustment (depreciation and casualties), Reg. § 1.280A–2(i)(5); Reg. § 1.280A–3(d)(3). See generally Lang, "When a House Is Not Entirely a Home: Deductions Under Internal Revenue Code § 280A for Home Offices, Vacation Homes, etc." 1981 Utah L.Rev. 275 (1981).

[169] 506 U.S. 168, 113 S.Ct. 701, 121 L.Ed.2d 634 (1993).

decision was reversed by subsequent legislation, it is still worthwhile it look at the *Soliman* case before considering the Congressional response.

The case concerned an anesthesiologist who spent 30 to 35 hours per week administering anesthesia and postoperative care in three hospitals, none of which provided him with an office. He also spent two to three hours per day in a room in his home that he used exclusively as an office.

According to the Court the taxpayer's home office was not his principal place of business. The treatment of patients at the hospitals was more important than the administrative work he did at home.

Moreover, the hours he spent at home were insufficient to render the home office the principal place of business in light of the circumstances of the case. Thus taxpayer was denied deductions associated with the business use of his home.

Congress reversed this decision by providing that the term "place of business" includes a place of business which is used by the taxpayer for the administrative or management activities of any trade or business of the taxpayer if there is no other fixed location of that trade or business where the taxpayer conducts substantial administrative or management activities of that trade or business.[170]

The legislative history provides that the fact that a taxpayer also carries out administrative or management activities at sites that are not fixed locations of the business, such as a car or hotel room, will not affect the taxpayer's ability to claim a home office deduction. Moreover, if a taxpayer conducts some administrative or management activities at a fixed location of the business outside the home, the taxpayer will still be eligible to claim a deduction so long as the administrative or management activities conducted at any fixed location of the business outside the home are not substantial.

Nevertheless, the legislative history also states that the deduction will be allowed only if the office is exclusively used on a regular basis as a place of business by the taxpayer, and in the case of an employee, only if that exclusive use is for the convenience of the employer.

Thus, college teachers, lawyers and others who are employees who have a business office will be hard-pressed to qualify their office in the home for the deduction. The new rules are, however, a boon for the self-employed who perform their services on outside sites, and Dr. Soliman will be taking his deduction after all.

---

[170] Section 280A(c)(1).

Taxpayers whose home office qualifies will then also apparently be able to deduct expenses of traveling between that home office and other places of business. In effect, then, these taxpayers can deduct what used to be considered commuting expenses![171]

The following case provides a good example of many of the nuances presented in this area.

POPOV V. COMMISSIONER[172]

Facts: Katia Popov, her husband, and their 4-year old daughter (and sometimes a grandmother) all lived in a one-bedroom apartment in Los Angeles. Katia Popov was a violinist in the Los Angeles Chamber Orchestra and the Long Beach Symphony. She also recorded music at various studios for use in motion pictures. In 1993, she recorded music at 38 different locations. None of her employers provided her with a place to practice. Popov claimed that the living room in the apartment was a home office and that "no one slept in the living room and that her daughter was not allowed to play there."

Service's argument: The taxpayer's home was not her principal place of business under *Soliman*. In *Soliman*, the Court said that "the point where goods and services are delivered must be given great weight in determining the place where the most important functions are performed." Since taxpayer's services were delivered at the studio or concert hall her place of business was not her home. The second prong of *Soliman* looks at the amount of time spent on the activity. The IRS argued that her practice time should not count in considering the amount of time she spent on the activity because she had to practice to generally maintain her skills.

Court's holding: The living room is Popov's principal place of business. Music is not easily captured under a delivery of service rationale. The court quotes the poet Heinrich Heine observing that music "stands 'halfway between thought and phenomenon, between spirit and matter.'" It then concluded that the delivery of service prong was not helpful in this case. It then examined the amount of time spent on the activity and concluded that Popov spent more of her time at home practicing then at her performances.

Comments: Popov is an interesting case for several reasons. First, it is very difficult for people with children to believe that Popov's living room was used "exclusively" for business. She lived in a one-bedroom apartment with her husband, a four-year old and at times, the child's grandmother. How could all of these people live in a one-bedroom apartment and still claim that the living room was

---

[171]   See Revenue Ruling 94–47, 1994–2 CB 18. See ¶ 6.02(b).

[172]   246 F.3d 1190 (9th Cir.2001).

used exclusively for business? Interestingly, according to the court, Popov claimed that her child was not allowed to play in the living room and that no one slept there. That does not mean the child did not use the living room or that it was exclusively used for business. How did we even get to the principal place of business prong if the living room was not used exclusively for business? This just doesn't pass the smell test. The district court, however, found otherwise and the court of appeals noted that the IRS did not dispute the factual finding in this case.[173] Thus, we have to assume that Popov meets the "exclusive use" prong of the statute.

This leaves then only the second question, was her living room her principal place of business? In this regard, it is hard to imagine that a violinist's principal place of business is her home. Without the concert halls and the recording studios she could not make a living. Her actual performance of her job did not take place in her living room. What does the court's quotation to Heinrich Heine have to do with this case? Should musicians get special treatment because music is "halfway between thought and phenomenon"?

(11) Rental of Vacation or Other Homes

Taxpayers who rent vacation or other homes which they also use for personal purposes are limited in the deductions they may take by § 280A. The fact that § 280A also simultaneously provides rules for limiting deductions with respect to qualifying home offices and certain other business uses of residential property causes the statute here to be virtually unintelligible.

Rental homes are best analyzed, under § 280A, by dividing them into four categories:

1.   *Rental homes that are not used by the taxpayer for personal purposes at any time during the taxable year.* These are simply investment properties owned by the taxpayer and are not subject to any of the restrictions on deductibility under § 280A. The taxpayer may take deductions with respect to these properties under the usual rules under § 162 or 212, as well as §§ 167 and 168, relating to depreciation or cost recovery.

Under § 280A(d)(3), renting a dwelling to any person (including relatives according to the legislative history) for use as the tenant's principal residence shall not be treated as using the dwelling for personal purposes. This makes it possible for a taxpayer, for example, to buy a home, rent it to the taxpayer's elderly parents for fair rental and take all deductions including depreciation in full.

---

[173]   Popov, 246 F.3d at 1191 n. 1.

    2. *Rental homes used for personal purposes for a period which does not exceed the greater of fourteen days, or 10 percent of the number of days during such year for which the unit is rented at a fair rental.*[174] Taxpayers with units which fall into this category may take deductions which are allowable without regard to business use of property—such as mortgage interest (if it is qualified residence interest—see ¶ 7.01(3)), property taxes and casualty losses above the prescribed limits—in full.[175] Deductions which may only be taken if they are attributable to property used in business or profit-seeking activity—such as maintenance, utilities, depreciation and casualty losses without regard to the 10% of adjusted gross income and $100 floors—may only be taken to a limited extent, based on usage. The usage limit as to these deductions is that they may be taken only in proportion to the number of days the property is rented out, divided by the total number of days the property is used for rental and personal purposes. Thus, if property is rented out for three hundred days and used personally for twenty-five days, 300/325 of the business type deductions may be taken.[176] The passive loss rules of § 469 could also bite here (see ¶ 8.02(3)).

    3. *Rental homes used for personal purposes for a number of days which exceeds the greater of fourteen days or 10 percent of the number of days during the year for which the unit is rented at a fair rental.*[177] This is the type of unit on which the restrictions of § 280A bear most heavily; and, not surprisingly, it is the type of unit of most interest to taxpayers who wish to make some tax hay out of a vacation home of which they make substantial personal use. Taxpayer dreams of renting a little cottage by a lake in Maine and using it as a vacation home all summer, followed by a two week rental, thereupon to deduct all expenses associated with the vacation home founder on the shoals of § 280A.[178]

---

[174] Section 280A(d)(1). Thus, for example, if a vacation home were rented for 300 days during the year and used by the taxpayer for 25 days during the year, it would fall into this category since the number of days of personal use did not exceed 10 percent of the number of days it was rented.

[175] Section 280A(b).

[176] Section 280A(d) and (e). It should be noted that § 280A is a disallowance provision. It only comes into play to the extent that the taxpayer otherwise establishes allowable deductions under § 162, 212, 167, or 165, etc. See Bolton, 77 T.C. 104 (1981), judgment aff'd 694 F.2d 556 (9th Cir.1982), apparently rejecting the approach of § 280A(e).

[177] Section 280A(d) as discussed in the text supra, § 280A(d)(3), added in 1981, provides that renting a dwelling unit to any person (including relatives, according to the legislative history) for use as the tenant's principal residence shall not be treated as using the dwelling unit for personal purposes.

[178] For whatever anecdotal evidence is worth, the authors have received more requests for free tax advice from friends and acquaintances in the area of vacation homes than in any other area.

Rental home units in this category are subject to the same usage restrictions on deductions as units in category 2 described above.[179] In addition to the usage limit, units in this category are subject to an income limit. Business-type deductions, such as maintenance, utilities, and depreciation which meet the usage limit are still subject to the further income limit that they cannot be deducted to the extent that they exceed the gross rental income derived from renting the property less the deductions that would be allowed regardless of business use (such as mortgage interest, property taxes, and casualty losses that are allocable to the business use).[180]

To further complicate this issue, the IRS and two circuit courts have different interpretations on how costs should be allocated. This difficult problem was address by the 9th Circuit in *Bolton v. Commissioner*.[181]

BOLTON V. COMMISSIONER[182]

Facts: The Boltons owned a vacation home in Palm Springs, California. They rented the unit for 91 days and used it personally for 30 days. The unit was unoccupied for the remainder of the year. The taxpayers had interest and property tax expenses of $2,854, and $621 respectively. They also had $2,693 in maintenance expenses and had $2,700 in gross rents.

Question: What ratio should be used under 280A(c)(5) for determining the allocation of expenses that would otherwise be allowed to the rental use of the property? This amount is subtracted from gross rents before determining the amount of other rental expenses that can be deducted.

Taxpayer's argument: The ratio should be the number of days rented/number of days in a year.

Service's argument: The ratio is the number of days rented/number of days used. The IRS had issued Proposed Treasury Regulation § 1.280A–3(d) indicating that the days rented/number of days used ratio was the proper ratio.

Comment: As should be no surprise, the ratio used by the taxpayer allocates less of the "otherwise allowable deductions" to business use. Since those deductions are allowed even if personal, taxpayer wants these deductions to count as little as possible on the business side, thus, allowing the taxpayers to take more of their other expenses against the rental income. For obvious reasons, the IRS

---

[179] Section 280A(d) and (e).
[180] Section 280A(c)(5).
[181] 694 F.2d 556 (9th Cir.1982).
[182] 694 F.2d 556 (9th Cir. 1982).

seeks a ratio that assigns more of the "other allowable deductions" as rental expenses.

Held: The court held the regulation was not a "reasonable statutory interpretation" because 280A(e)(2) specifically provides that (e)(1) (creating the ratio used by the IRS) does not apply to deductions which would be allowable no matter whether the unit was rented. In other words (e)(2) says that (e)(1) doesn't apply to interest and taxes, so the (e)(1) ratio is not a reasonable interpretation of the statute.

What does all this mean? Basically, when a property is rented out for more than 14 days, but is still a personal residence, the deductions are limited to the income from the rental. However, there are deductions to which the taxpayer is entitled no matter whether the property is for business use. In applying the limitation that "deductions cannot exceed gross income," we need to consider what proportion of those deductions that would have been allowed absent the business use should be allocated to business use and thus subject to the limitations. Taxpayers want as little as possible (because they can deduct the rest anyway and therefore don't want these expenses to be counted toward their limit), and the IRS wants as much as possible allocated to business expenses (thus limiting additional business expenses.)

The court in this case did a great job explaining why this matters.

BUSINESS USE OF INTEREST
AND PROPERTY TAXES

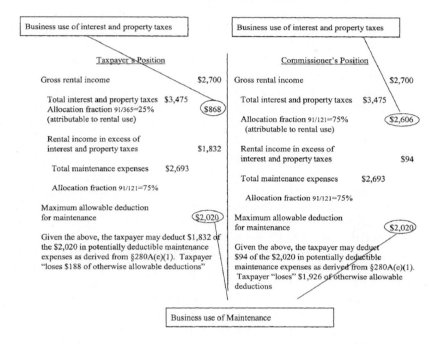

Business use of interest and property taxes		Business use of interest and property taxes	
Taxpayer's Position		*Commissioner's Position*	
Gross rental income	$2,700	Gross rental income	$2,700
Total interest and property taxes $3,475 Allocation fraction 91/365=25% (attributable to rental use)	$868	Total interest and property taxes $3,475 Allocation fraction 91/121=75% (attributable to rental use)	$2,606
Rental income in excess of interest and property taxes	$1,832	Rental income in excess of interest and property taxes	$94
Total maintenance expenses $2,693		Total maintenance expenses $2,693	
Allocation fraction 91/121=75%		Allocation fraction 91/121=75%	
Maximum allowable deduction for maintenance	$2,020	Maximum allowable deduction for maintenance	$2,020

Given the above, the taxpayer may deduct $1,832 of the $2,020 in potentially deductible maintenance expenses as derived from §280A(e)(1). Taxpayer "loses $188 of otherwise allowable deductions"

Given the above, the taxpayer may deduct $94 of the $2,020 in potentially deductible maintenance expenses as derived from §280A(e)(1). Taxpayer "loses" $1,926 of otherwise allowable deductions

Business use of Maintenance

Notice that the taxpayer's position allows significantly less of the interest and taxes to be allocated to the business use, which in turn gives the taxpayer a greater maintenance deduction. The taxpayer doesn't care that there is only an $868 deduction for interest and taxes since the taxpayer will deduct the remainder as an itemized deduction.

The Tenth Circuit has followed the Ninth Circuit but the IRS has not acquiesced in the decision.[183]

4. *Rental homes rented for less than fifteen days.* If a taxpayer makes personal use of his vacation or other rental home and does rent it but for less than fifteen days, then no deductions whatsoever attributable to the rental use (i.e., maintenance, utilities, depreciation) will be allowed. But the rental income so generated is excluded from gross income.[184] This rule simplifies calculations for taxpayers who engage in relatively short-time rentals of their property. However, it does bestow a windfall on taxpayers who can

---

[183] See McKinney v. Commissioner, 732 F.2d 414 (10th Cir.1093).

[184] Section 280A(g).

rent their vacation units for a very high rental during a short period.[185]

The provision is now famous because the producers of the former television show "Extreme Makeover: Home Edition" used it to claim that payments to participants and improvements on the renovated home are not income to the recipients.[186] Extreme Makeover is a television show where "deserving" people receive a major home renovation free of charge. The television network's accountants argued that the property provided is either excludable as a rental payment of less than 15 days or excludable as a leasehold improvement.

What are they talking about? Well, the network would rent the property for a few days while the homeowners were away on a vacation supplied by the network. The network claimed that some of the property given to the contestants are rent, and that the improvements to the property are leasehold improvements that are excludable under § 109.[187] Some commentators have argued that for liquidity and valuation reasons the IRS should let this one slide,[188] and in other contexts, scholars have argued that gain should be recognized when the time received is sold.[189] It does, however, seem like the network was pulling a fast one. If the problem is that taxpayers do not have the liquidity to pay the extra tax, the network could easily give taxpayers cash as well as property. In any event, it is clear that taxpayers (and the network) were enriched by the Extreme Makeover experience.

(12) Depreciation and Accelerated Cost Recovery

(a) Background

(i) Rationale for Depreciation

Taxpayers are entitled to take a depreciation deduction with respect to certain property used in the trade or business or for the

---

[185] An example of this would be a condominium overlooking the running of the bulls at Pamplona, see E. Hemingway, *The Sun Also Rises* (1927) *passim.*

[186] Daniel McGinn, Tax Trouble for ABC's 'extreme' Winners, Newsweek, May 17, 2004, at 12.

[187] Section 109 provides that "gross income does not include income (other than rent) derived by a lessor of real property on the termination of a lease, representing the value of such property attributable to building erected or other improvements made by the lessee."

[188] See Brian Hirsch, The Extreme Home Renovation Giveaway: Constructive Justification for Tax-Free Home Improvements on ABC's Extreme Makeover: Home Edition, 73 Cin. Law Rev. 4 (2005).

[189] Richard Schmalbeck and Lawrence Zelenak, Federal Income Taxation 203 (2003) (treasure troves should be taxed when sold, not when they are found).

production of income.[190] The rationale of the depreciation deduction is that the property the taxpayer uses in his trade or business, or profit seeking activity, is wearing out and that deterioration is a cost of doing business which is appropriately reflected on the taxpayer's tax return.

Put differently, the deduction for depreciation is simply a way of reflecting the fact that the taxpayer is always entitled to a deduction for a return on capital, and should only be taxed to the extent the income exceeds the cost of the investment. Therefore, the taxpayer may deduct an aliquot part of the cost of an asset spread out over the asset's useful life against the income generated by the asset.[191]

By the same reasoning, depreciation will not be allowed for property which does not wear out over time or through use. Thus, no depreciation is allowed for undeveloped land, securities or stocks, gold, collectibles, or goodwill. Basis is recovered on such property when it is sold or otherwise disposed of (see Chapter 4).[192] Another way of stating the same theory is that depreciation is a method for matching income produced by the asset with the cost of the asset.

In any event, this theoretical justification for depreciation is eroded in fact by a number of considerations. First, it is often true that depreciable property, in particular improved real property, goes up in value over time rather than declines in value to zero or to a hypothetical salvage value. Furthermore, the deduction for depreciation is often an instrument of national economic policy. Rapid methods of depreciation are often allowed, and artificially shorter useful lives may be used with the intention of stimulating investment in new depreciable property.

Thus, for all these reasons, the deduction for depreciation should not be viewed as an attempt to seriously represent what is happening to the value of the property being depreciated, but rather as an artificial method for the taxpayer to do what every taxpayer is entitled to do—namely, ultimately to recover the cost of an investment used in a business or other profit-seeking activity.[193]

---

[190]   Section 167(a).

[191]   Cf. Lischer, "Depreciation Policy: Whither Thou Goest," 32 Sw.L.J. 545 (1978).

[192]   The purchase price of improved real estate must be allocated between the land, which cannot be depreciated, and the improvements, which can be depreciated. Reg. § 1.167(a)–5.

[193]   Yet another way of interpreting depreciation is that it provides a "reserve" set aside for the taxpayer to reinvest in new property once the old property wears out. However, given inflation and technological change, it is not at all clear that the cost of new property the taxpayer would buy would bear any particular relationship to the cost of the property depreciated. See discussion below.

It should also be noted that publicly-traded corporate taxpayers may take accelerated forms of depreciation for purposes of computing their tax liability and

As we would expect from our discussion of time value of money issues, the taxpayer generally wants to depreciate property as rapidly as possible. This will involve choosing a so-called accelerated method of depreciation if it is available for the particular asset, and using the shortest useful life allowed for the particular asset. In taking rapid depreciation, the taxpayer benefits from a deferral of tax liability. This is usually attractive, for the tax dollars saved can be reinvested in the taxpayer's business or otherwise used by the taxpayer.[194]

The deduction for depreciation is the obverse side of the requirement that capital expenditures may not be deducted immediately.[195] Where an expenditure must be capitalized rather than deducted immediately, it may then be subject to the allowance for depreciation and recovered over a period of years. It follows, then, that as the deduction for depreciation is taken on a particular asset, the basis of that asset goes down by the amount of depreciation taken.[196] However, depreciation is not "optional" in the sense that even if the taxpayer chooses not to take a deduction for depreciation—because there may already be an operating loss for the year, say—the basis of the property involved will still go down by at least the minimum amount of depreciation allowable on the property.[197]

This basis adjustment means, of course, that if the property has not in fact been declining in value during the period the depreciation was taken, when the property is finally sold there will be a substantial taxable gain. This gain appears to just balance the books since the taxpayer has been enjoying a depreciation deduction over the time the property was held. But in fact the taxpayer may well wind up ahead of the game, because the deduction for depreciation has been taken early, whereas the gain on the sale of the property is taxed later.

Beyond that, with respect to real estate, the gain attributable to the previously taken depreciation is generally taxed at a lower rate,

---

slower or straight-line forms for computing their profits as reported to stockholders. While this ability to simultaneously tell bad news to the IRS and good news to the shareholders has been criticized, it still remains a practice that can be engaged in as long as it is disclosed. Cf. SEC Reg. SBX, 17 CFR § 210.3–16(o)(1975).

"Depreciation" as used in this discussion also covers the term "amortization," which often refers to the writing off of the cost of intangible assets, such as patents, copyrights, franchise agreements, leases. Amortization is generally done only on a straight-line basis.

[194]   For a fuller discussion of the advantages of deferral of income, see ¶ 8.02(1).

[195]   See ¶ 6.03(4).

[196]   Section 1016(a)(2).

[197]   Section 1016(a) (flush language).

25 percent, than the ordinary income against which the depreciation deduction was taken. This is because the gain attributable to previously taken depreciation is taxed at a maximum rate of 25 percent under the capital gain rules, see ¶ 4.06(2)(b)(i).

(ii) Inflation Problems

Balanced against the benefit of deferral and the possible lower rate on recapture that depreciation affords the taxpayer is the effect of inflation. Depreciation provides a deduction for taxpayer's original cost of the property. This approach fails, however, to take account of inflation. Say a company buys a machine that costs $5,000 and properly depreciates it over 10 years. Suppose also that the inflation rate is 10% a year over the ten years and that the cost of replacing the machine increases by that inflation rate. At the end of 10 years taxpayer would have taken $5,000 in depreciation deductions to fully recover the original cost. There is just one tiny problem. With the inflation rate of 10% a year, replacing the machine now costs $12,969.

Should depreciation take account of inflation? It is clear that in the inflationary environment of this example we are not adequately taking account of the taxpayer's cost of doing business. It would appear that the replacement cost of the asset is at least as relevant as the historical cost.

It would appear, therefore, that by understating the taxpayer's true cost of doing business (the replacement cost) we are overstating profits. Therefore, we are overtaxing the taxpayer. Moreover, this problem is not limited to the relatively high inflation rate posited by the example. Even if inflation is 3% over the course of the 10-year period—which is about as low as it gets over a 10-year period—the cost of replacing the $5,000 machine would be $6,720. If the useful life was 20 years, with 3% inflation, the cost of replacing the machine would be $9,031.

It is often suggested that the way to cope with this problem is to index the original cost of the machine for inflation. Then one would calculate the depreciation deduction based on that indexed cost. While this idea sounds nice in theory, it is not so clear how it would actually work. Consider the chart below:

Depreciation of an Asset That Is Indexed for Inflation

Inflation Rate = 10% Per Year

Year	Original Basis After Inflation Adjustment	Depreciation Taken St. Line
1	$5,000	$500
2	$5,500	$550
3	$6,050	$605
4	$6,655	$666
5	$7,321	$732
6	$8,053	$805
7	$8,858	$886
8	$9,744	$974
9	$10,718	$1,072
10	$11,790	$1,179
Total		$7,969

We see that by taking 10% of the indexed original cost of the asset each year for 10 years as depreciation gives us a total amount of depreciation of $7,969. Yet the replacement cost of the machine after 10 years is $11,790. While it is true that using the indexed original cost basis gave us more depreciation than using the non-indexed original cost (i.e., $5,000), this indexing procedure did not produce enough depreciation to compensate the taxpayer for the replacement cost of the machine.

There are other approaches that could be tried. It is often glibly asserted in the financial press that depreciable assets should be indexed to reflect inflation. We now see that coming up with a sensible approach there is not so simple. The tax law does not index the basis of assets for depreciation (or for any other reason) at the present time. Thus it seems fair to say that not enough depreciation is being allowed. However, this effect is offset by the fact that the present Accelerated Cost Recovery System (ACRS), discussed in the next section, allows for very rapid depreciation. This is accomplished by the use of relatively short useful lives and the use of accelerated methods of computing depreciation. These result in a large amount of the total depreciation being taken very early in the life of the asset. These large deductions early have the effect of deferral of tax. As we have learned, deferral of tax is money in the bank to the taxpayer. Hence these accelerated methods may make up (or perhaps more than make up) for the failure to index the basis of the asset for inflation.

(iii) Basic Methods of Depreciation

The basic method of computing depreciation is to deduct a portion of the asset's basis each year over a period of years. The three variables in making this calculation, as a general rule, are: the basis of the asset, the period over which the deductions are to be taken, and the method of computing how much will be deducted each year. The basis of the asset is generally determined under rules discussed elsewhere in this work (¶ 4.03(2)); usually the basis of a business asset is the cost of the asset. The period over which the depreciation deductions will be taken is determined by reference to rules promulgated by the IRS and Congress. There are various methods for computing the amount of depreciation that will be taken in each year. The ACRS system, discussed below, provides simplified, and attractive rules for making these calculations.

An illustration of the basic workings of computing depreciation can be given by the following example: an asset has a cost basis of $100.00. Reference to the appropriate rules determines that this asset is properly depreciated over a period of ten years—the "useful life." If the "straight line" method of depreciation is used, then 10% of the basis of the property will be deductible each year for the useful life of the property, leading to a deduction of the total amount of the basis of the property at the end of the ten-year period.

Thus, in this example the taxpayer would take a depreciation deduction of $10.00 per year for ten years. The taxpayer's basis would go down by $10.00 per year for ten years. At the end of ten years the adjusted basis would be zero, and there would be no more depreciation taken, even though the property might be used in further years. If the taxpayer were to sell the property after five years, the basis for computation of gain or loss on the sale would be $50.00. The rate of deduction for each year for straight-line depreciation is determined by dividing 100% by the number of years in the useful life. Thus, in the example above, had the useful life been five years, the rate of depreciation taken per year would have been 20%; a useful life of fifty years would have given rise to a rate of 2%, etc.

Instead of using the "straight-line" method described above, the taxpayer may sometimes use one of the various methods of "accelerated depreciation." One well-accepted accelerated method of depreciation is the "double declining-balance method." Using the original example above, the double declining-balance method would involve using a rate of depreciation that was twice that used under the straight-line method. Thus, the taxpayer would, in the first year, take a depreciation deduction of $20.00. In subsequent years the taxpayer would continue to use a rate of 20% but importantly, the 20% rate would be applied to the *remaining* basis on the taxpayer's property at the beginning of the year, rather than to the *original* basis. Thus, the depreciation taken in the second year under the 200% declining-balance method would be $16.00 (20% of the remaining basis of $80.00). In the third year the amount of depreciation taken would be $12.80 (20% of the remaining balance of $64.00). Thus, it can be seen that the double declining-balance method yields much greater depreciation deductions in the early years of the useful life of the property.

However, the mathematics of the double declining-balance method means that in the later years of the useful life it will yield less depreciation than the straight-line method. This is because the 20% rate of depreciation is applied to an ever decreasing basis, whereas the 10% rate under the straight-line method is always applied to the original basis. Moreover, it is inevitable that the double declining-balance method will yield smaller depreciation deductions than the straight-line method in the later years of the useful life because the overall amount of depreciation that can be taken under either method is only $100.00. To the extent that the double declining-balance method yields greater deductions in the earlier years, obviously, in the later years it will yield smaller depreciation deductions, because there will simply be less depreciation left to be taken.[198]

As a matter of fact, the problem is somewhat more complex than that. The mathematics of the double declining-balance method will actually lead to the result that not all the depreciation will be taken. The method, in short, never leads to the basis getting to zero, since it always involves computation of 20% of a smaller and smaller amount. The solution, therefore, is to switch from the double declining-balance method to the straight-line method at some point during the useful life to be able to take all the depreciation and bring the basis to zero. A comparison of the amounts of depreciation taken over a ten-year useful life with an asset with a cost basis of $100.00, including the switch from double declining-balance to straight-line, is set forth in the accompanying chart.

[198] Section 167(b).

COMPARISON OF STRAIGHT-LINE AND DOUBLE DECLINING-BALANCE DEPRECIATION

Straight-Line: — **Double Declining-Balance:**
IRC Sec. 167(b)(1) — **IRC Sec. 167(b)(2)**

Basis at Beginning of Year	Year	Amount of Depreciation Taken	Basis at Beginning of Year	Year	Amount of Depreciation Taken
100.00	1.00	10.00	100.00	1.00	20.00
90.00	2.00	10.00	80.00	2.00	16.00
80.00	3.00	10.00	64.00	3.00	12.80
70.00	4.00	10.00	51.20	4.00	10.24
60.00	5.00	10.00	40.96	5.00	8.19
50.00	6.00	10.00	32.77	6.00	6.55*
40.00	7.00	10.00	26.21	7.00	6.55
30.00	8.00	10.00	19.66	8.00	6.55
20.00	9.00	10.00	13.11	9.00	6.55
10.00	10.00	10.00	6.55	10.00	6.55
0.00	11.00		0.00	11.00	

* Switching to straight-line when it becomes more attractive, Sec. 167(e)(1).

Similarly to the double declining-balance method of depreciation, the Code also provides for a "150% declining-balance method." This method works like the double declining-balance method in that the rate of depreciation that is used is a percentage of the rate that would be employed in the straight-line method.

(iv) 50% Bonus Depreciation

Taxpayers can deduct up to 50% of the adjusted basis of certain depreciable property in the year in which the property is placed in service. Accordingly, only the undeducted half of the adjusted basis will run through the accelerated cost recovery system. This special allowance of "bonus depreciation" is available for property with a recovery period of 20 years or less, computer software, water utility property, or qualified leasehold improvement property. This provision, however, is not mandatory, and a taxpayer is not required to take the additional allowance.[199]

Under current law, the 50% bonus will drop to 40% in 2018, and again to 30% in 2019 before being repealed altogether in 2020. You'll

---

[199] See § 168(k)(2)(C)(iii); Rev. Proc. 2002–33.

want to pay attention as 2020 approaches, however, for it is common for Congress to extend legislative "sunsets" like this.

Congress passed this "bonus depreciation" starting in 2003 because of economic downturns. The argument was that these provisions would encourage investment and provide a stimulus to the economy. As you will see in the next section, we are skeptical of this.

(b) The Myth That Accelerated Depreciation Stimulates Investment in Plant and Equipment

We can use the time value of money concepts discussed previously and developed more thoroughly in the Appendix to explore the "received wisdom" that accelerated depreciation encourages investment in new plant and equipment. As the chart above illustrates, the same total amount of depreciation is taken in the straight-line method and the double declining-balance method. Nevertheless it is virtually universally believed that if machinery may be depreciated under, say, the double declining-balance method, this will stimulate investment in plant and equipment compared to limiting depreciation to the straight-line method.

In fact running the numbers shows that this effect is so weak as to be negligible.

Consider the case of Jennifer, a sole proprietor who owns a widget factory. Jennifer is considering the purchase of a widget redactor that would increase the income from her business. The machine costs $50,000. The widget redactor has a useful life of 10 years and produces income after maintenance expenses of $11,000 per year. Jennifer is in a tax bracket of 40%. Given the level of risk of the income from the widget business the relevant after tax rate of return for analyzing the present value of the income stream from the widget redactor is, let us say, 12%.[200]

The question is whether Jennifer should invest in the machine. The proper approach is to ascertain what the present value of the machine is to Jennifer, given the numbers set forth above. If the present value of the machine is more than $50,000, Jennifer should

---

[200] It should be emphasized that in this example this rate of return is a subjective matter. It depends on the point of view of Jennifer. In other examples where we have used present value analysis (in the Appendix especially) we have used an objective after-tax interest rate. That is because in those examples we were dealing with virtually risk-free returns on high-grade bonds. In this example, we are dealing with the at least somewhat risky return on a business. When risk is involved the judgment of what rate of return is required depends on the particular individual. Some people are much more risk-averse than others. Most everyone is at least somewhat risk-averse. When risk is present, people (and businesses) require a higher rate of return to make up for it.

buy the machine. If the present value is less than $50,000, Jennifer should not buy the machine.

The accompanying table illustrates the calculations:

PRESENT VALUE OF $50,000 MACHINE COMPARED USING STRAIGHT-LINE AND DOUBLE DECLINING-BALANCE DEPRECIATION

Straight-Line

Year	Income from Machine	Straight-Line Depreciation	Income After Depreciation Deducted	Tax on Income from Machine at 40%	Net Cash Flow: Income from Machine less Tax	Present Value of Cash Flow from Machine at 12%
1	$11,000	$5,000	$6,000	$2,400	$8,600	$7,679
2	$11,000	$5,000	$6,000	$2,400	$8,600	$6,856
3	$11,000	$5,000	$6,000	$2,400	$8,600	$6,121
4	$11,000	$5,000	$6,000	$2,400	$8,600	$5,465
5	$11,000	$5,000	$6,000	$2,400	$8,600	$4,880
6	$11,000	$5,000	$6,000	$2,400	$8,600	$4,357
7	$11,000	$5,000	$6,000	$2,400	$8,600	$3,890
8	$11,000	$5,000	$6,000	$2,400	$8,600	$3,473
9	$11,000	$5,000	$6,000	$2,400	$8,600	$3,101
10	$11,000	$5,000	$6,000	$2,400	$8,600	$2,769
Total	$110,000	$50,000	$60,000	$24,000	$86,000	**$48,592**

Double Declining-Balance

Year	Income from Machine	Double Declining-Balance Depreciation	Income After Depreciation Deducted	Tax on Income from Machine at 40%	Net Cash Flow: Income from Machine less Tax	Present Value of Cash Flow from Machine at 12%
1	$11,000	$10,000	$1,000	$400	$10,600	$9,464
2	$11,000	$8,000	$3,000	$1,200	$9,800	$7,813
3	$11,000	$6,400	$4,600	$1,840	$9,160	$6,520
4	$11,000	$5,120	$5,880	$2,352	$8,648	$5,496
5	$11,000	$4,096	$6,904	$2,762	$8,238	$4,675
6	$11,000	$3,277	$7,723	$3,089	$7,911	$4,008
7	$11,000	$3,277	$7,723	$3,089	$7,911	$3,578
8	$11,000	$3,277	$7,723	$3,089	$7,911	$3,195
9	$11,000	$3,277	$7,723	$3,089	$7,911	$2,853
10	$11,000	$3,277	$7,723	$3,089	$7,911	$2,547
Total	$110,000	$50,001	$59,999	$24,000	$86,000	**$50,148**

Difference in present value as percentage of cost of machine = 3.11%

On these numbers Jennifer would invest in the machine if allowed to take accelerated depreciation and would not invest in the machine if limited to straight-line depreciation. Thus these numbers seem to prove that a government policy allowing accelerated depreciation does stimulate investment in plant and equipment.

But hang on! The numbers here have been cooked to put us on the knife edge. As the chart indicates, the difference in the present value between the two methods constitutes about 3% of the purchase price of the machine. Is this a big difference? Rather than being on the knife edge as we are in this example, it is much more likely the case that the machine is either worthwhile to purchase or not regardless of the method of depreciation.

Another way of looking at our numbers is to say that if the machine costs less than $48,592, it should be purchased regardless of depreciation method and if it costs more than $50,148, it should not be purchased regardless of depreciation method.[201] Only if the price of the machine happens to fall within this 3% range between $48,592 and $50,148 does the method of depreciation have any impact on the decision to purchase the machine.

This 3% range becomes even more irrelevant when it is recalled that the numbers going into these ten-year calculations are not exactly written in stone. How do we know that the machine will produce net income of exactly $11,000 per year for 10 years? How do we know that the tax rate will remain at 40% for the next 10 years? How about this 12% discount rate—which depends on the risk of the taxpayer's business and on the prevailing interest rates in the economy? Is all that going to remain the same for 10 years? All these numbers are "soft" estimates. The sponginess of these numbers washes out this 3% differential.

For example, if the projected income from the machine is $11,500 per year instead of $11,000 per year, then the present value of the machine when straight-line depreciation is used is $50,287; and the present value when double declining-balance is used is $51,843. Thus the machine should be bought regardless of depreciation method. By the same token if the projected income from the machine is $10,500 per year, then the present value of the machine when straight-line depreciation is used is $46,897; and the present value when double declining-balance is used is $48,453. Thus the machine should not be bought regardless of depreciation method.

---

[201] If the machine does cost a little less or a little more than $50,000, that will change our depreciation numbers slightly and feed back to effect a slight change in our present value calculations. That minor effect does not detract from the point being made in the text.

What this seems to show is that we are going through a great deal of complexity in the statute with regard to these accelerated methods of depreciation in order to have a minimal impact on investment. But be warned, only an extreme minority among those interested in tax policy believe the proposition that accelerated depreciation methods provide little economic stimulus to investment.

(c) "Sinking Fund" Depreciation

We can squeeze a little more blood out of the example in the previous section. The question now before us is whether there is a theoretically "correct" way to calculate depreciation. Economists have approached the matter using so-called "sinking fund" depreciation.[202] Here is another fearless chart, derived from the chart above. We have $11,000 per year, before taxes, for 10 years income from the machine. The machine cost $50,000. This means our internal rate of return on the machine is 17.68%. Another way of putting it is that $11,000 per year for 10 years discounted at a rate of 17.68% equals $50,000.

Now as each year goes by, the machine becomes less valuable. At the beginning we could expect 10 years of income from the machine. The value of the machine at the beginning of 10 years is obviously the discounted present value of 10 years of income from the machine. After the first year is over and we have pocketed our income from the machine, there are only nine years left.

What is the value of the machine now? If we really believe that this machine was only good when we started for a total of 10 years of income at $11,000 per year, then after the first year the machine is only good for 9 more years of income at $11,000 per year. Hence the machine is after one year only worth the discounted present value of 9 years of income at $11,000 per year. What has been lost? Obviously the tenth year of income of $11,000. What is that worth? It is clearly the discounted present value of $11,000 10 years from now. Another way of saying it is that after the first year's usage, the tenth year's payment has dropped off the chart. Thus we could say that the machine has declined in value by the present value of that tenth year's payment. Then we could say that is the appropriate amount of the depreciation deduction for the first year. After the second year's usage and pocketing of income from the second year, the machine now only has eight years left on it. The machine has now dropped by the value of the $11,000 payment nine years from now. Therefore that is the amount of depreciation we would take in the second year. We continue with the back year dropping off until we have

---

[202] See e.g. Samuelson, Tax Deductibility of Economic Depreciation to Insure Invariant Valuations, 72 J. Pol. Econ. 604 (1964).

depreciated the entire value of the machine. This is depicted in the accompanying chart. The crazy lines indicate that the value of the machine each year has dropped by the present value of the last year's payment for the previous year.

To put "sinking fund" depreciation in a nutshell (suitable for exam-taking purposes), you can say that the back end payment drops off every year.

Notice that if you follow the depreciation line across you see that the amount of depreciation allowed is small in the earlier years and builds up to be large. As pointed out earlier, depreciation is "back loaded" under the sinking fund approach. If you follow this approach, then what you say is that of each $11,000 annual income, the depreciation amount as calculated in the chart is a deduction from the $11,000 and the balance of the $11,000 annually is taxable.

"SINKING FUND" DEPRECIATION

"Sinking Fund" Depreciation		Start of Year 1 Present Value	Start of Year 2 Present Value	Start of Year 3 Present Value	Start of Year 4 Present Value	Start of Year 5 Present Value
Year	Income					
1	$ 11,000	$ 9,347	$ 9,347	$ 9,347	$ 9,347	$ 9,347
2	$ 11,000	$ 7,943	$ 7,943	$ 7,943	$ 7,943	$ 7,943
3	$ 11,000	$ 6,750	$ 6,750	$ 6,750	$ 6,750	$ 6,750
4	$ 11,000	$ 5,736	$ 5,736	$ 5,736	$ 5,736	$ 5,736
5	$ 11,000	$ 4,874	$ 4,874	$ 4,874	$ 4,874	$ 4,874
6	$ 11,000	$ 4,142	$ 4,142	$ 4,142	$ 4,142	$ 4,142
7	$ 11,000	$ 3,519	$ 3,519	$ 3,519	$ 3,519	
8	$ 11,000	$ 2,991	$ 2,991	$ 2,991		
9	$ 11,000	$ 2,541	$ 2,541			
10	$ 11,000	$ 2,160				
Machine's Value		$ 50,002	$ 47,843	$ 45,302	$ 42,311	$ 38,791
Annual Change in Value or Depreciation:			$ 2,160	$ 2,541	$ 2,991	$ 3,519

		Start of Year 6 Present Value	Start of Year 7 Present Value	Start of Year 8 Present Value	Start of Year 9 Present Value	Start of Year 10 Present Value	Start of Year 11 Present Value
Year							
1		$ 9,347	$ 9,347	$ 9,347	$ 9,347	$ 9,347	
2		$ 7,943	$ 7,943	$ 7,943	$ 7,943		
3		$ 6,750	$ 6,750	$ 6,750			
4		$ 5,736	$ 5,736				
5		$ 4,874					
6							
7							
8							
9							
10							
Value		$ 34,659	$ 29,776	$ 24,040	$ 17,290	$ 9,347	$0
Depreciation		$ 4,142	$ 4,874	$ 5,736	$ 6,750	$ 7,943	$ 9,347

This is analogous to the approach that was followed with the treatment of original issue discount. You may find it helpful to review that treatment at this time.

Thus we have shown that as a matter of economic analysis, straight-line depreciation (reasonable as it seems) actually allows depreciation to go too fast. Depreciation should be back-loaded.

Consider, from that perspective, the fact that most businesses finance the purchase of their depreciable plant and equipment with borrowed funds. The borrowed funds generate of course a deductible interest payment. As we have discussed elsewhere (¶ 1.03(e)(1)), the deduction for interest is front-loaded to the borrower. Thus the business that borrows to finance the purchase of depreciable plant and equipment is winning two ways: it is able to take the deduction for interest on a front-loaded basis, and it is able to take the deduction for depreciation on a front-loaded basis.

When you add the extremely rapid methods of depreciation now allowed by ACRS (see below), you have really got a major subsidy for investment in plant and equipment. This is more or less intentional—although Congress may not have realized the full impact of the incentives it was creating.

The ACRS system is discussed in the next section.

(d) The ACRS System; Sharp

The Accelerated Cost Recovery System (ACRS) was established by the Economic Recovery Tax Act of 1981. The system was changed to the Modified Accelerated Cost Recovery System (MACRS) in 1986. MACRS continues in force today.

Under MACRS, one need not establish the "useful life" of property or the "salvage value" of property. Further, it makes no difference whether the property is new or used. The terms "cost recovery" and "depreciation" will be used in this discussion more or less interchangeably.

MACRS, contained in § 168, is mandatory, although it allows some elections to be made within the system. It applies to most tangible depreciable property. Those few types of property not covered by § 168 are covered by older § 167. Intangible property is covered to a large degree by § 197.

Recovery Periods. Under MACRS, property is assigned to one of several classes of recovery periods. Most personal property is recovered over 3, 5, or 7 years. Automobiles are specifically assigned to the 5-year class. Residential real property (like an apartment building) is written off over 27.5 years and nonresidential real property (office buildings, factories, and the like) over 39 years.

Methods of Depreciation. As to methods of depreciation, residential real property and nonresidential real property can be depreciated only on the straight-line method (as part of the attack on tax shelters, see Chapter 8). Property in the 3, 5, 7, or 10 year classification can be depreciated under the double declining-balance method, with a switch to straight line when that method yields more depreciation. Property recovered over 15 and 20 years uses the 150% declining-balance method, switching to straight line when it becomes more attractive. Property in the 3 to 10 year classes may be depreciated using the 150% declining-balance method rather than the double declining-balance method for all property within a particular class put into service in the year of the election (an election few will make). Moreover, property within the 3 to 20 year classes may be depreciated on the straight-line method for all property within a particular class (once again an election few would make, to the point that one wonders why the election is available at all). An extended useful life election is also available.

Conventions. There are certain "conventions" or rules for treating property that is acquired during the year as acquired at a particular point in the year. As a default MACRS uses the "half-year convention," which means that for administrative convenience all property is treated as though it were placed into service (or disposed of) at the midpoint of the year regardless of when it was actually put into service (or disposed of). The result is one-half year of depreciation is allowed whether an asset is placed in service on the first day or the last day of the taxpayer's taxable year. To balance off, there is a half year of depreciation at the end of the asset's recovery period as well. Assets under MACRS that are sold are also treated under a half-year convention for the year of sale.

More Bonus Depreciation: § 179. Congress keeps believing that if it throws more depreciation at taxpayers it will stimulate the economy. As a result, in addition to the very attractive depreciation rules described above investment in personal property might also qualify for the § 179 election. Section 179 allows an immediate deduction of the cost of some depreciable personal property in the year in which it is put into service. The maximum amount of bonus depreciation is $500,000.[203]

Moreover, this ceiling is lowered by one dollar for every dollar of § 179 property placed in service during the year in excess of

---

[203] This amount was increased from $25,000 to $100,000 about a decade ago. Then it jumped to $250,000 in 2008 before reaching $500,000 in 2010. See § 179(b)(1).

$2,000,000. Thus very large businesses do not get the benefit of § 179; it belongs to relatively small businesses and individuals. The basis of property depreciated under § 179 is reduced to reflect the § 179 depreciation and then such basis as is left is depreciated under the usual MACRS rules (including, remember, the 50% bonus under § 168(k).

Other Limits on Depreciation: Luxury Cars and "Listed" Property. A maximum of $12,800 (an amount adjusted for inflation for years after 1988) may be deducted with respect to cars over the usual five year period. Thereafter a maximum of $1,475 can be depreciated in each year following the first five years until basis is exhausted, under § 280F.

But Congress really placed a goodie in the Code for taxpayers who want to depreciate luxury automobiles. Automobiles used in business qualify for the § 168(k) bonus depreciation benefit.[204] Congress also provided that if you take the special depreciation allowance, you may deduct more of the cost of the car in the first year. How does this work?

Section 168(k)(2)(F) provides that if an automobile qualifies for the 50% bonus depreciation benefit, the limitation under § 280F(a)(1)(A)(i), is increased by $8,000. (Maybe the purchase of more luxury automobiles will provide the economic stimulus needed to spur economic growth). If the purchase is subject to the restrictions in § 280F, then the purchase only qualifies for a deduction under § 179 to the extent of the applicable limits contained in § 280F. See § 280F(d)(1).

Want to get really mad? The deal is even better if you buy an SUV or truck. SUVs are considered trucks so § 280F's limitations do not apply. Thus, if you buy a luxury SUV for your business, you get to deduct $25,000 of the cost under § 179, then claim the 50% bonus under § 168(k) without limit, all in the name of stimulating the economy. This only works if you can purchase the SUV as a business expense, but a lot of small business people lick their chops over this. In other words, the current provisions in the Code are actually encouraging businesses to buy luxury SUVs. Does this make any sense?

Also under § 280F, MACRS deductions are limited with respect to other "listed property" where there is a business use of 50% or less. "Listed property" includes: passenger automobiles, entertainment property, computers not used exclusively at a regular business establishment (watch that home computer), and cellular phones. Use of "listed property" by an employee is not regarded as business use

---

[204]   See ¶ 6.02(12)(a)(iv).

unless the use is for the convenience of the employer and is required as a condition of employment. Listed property which is used for business 50% of the time or less is depreciated under an alternative depreciation system.[205] This involves longer useful lives and less rapid methods of depreciation.

The computational approach to the complex rules described above is to first compute any § 179 bonus depreciation, then compute the § 168(k) bonus, then apply the regular MACRS depreciation rules and finally see if any limits of § 280F apply.

The case of *Sharp v. United States*[206] presented some interesting depreciation problems. The taxpayers, Hugh and Bayard Sharp, were equal partners in a partnership which purchased a Beechcraft airplane at a cost of $45,875. They made additional capital expenditures to the plane, bringing its total basis to $54,273.50. During the period of ownership the plane was used by the partnership 73.654% for personal use and 26.346% for business. (One rarely sees a percentage allocation out to this level of accuracy.) Thus the partnership was only allowed to take depreciation on 26.346% of the basis of the plane, or $14,298.90. So over the five years of use from 1948 to 1953, only $13,777.92 of depreciation was allowed. (Note these were based on depreciation rules that predated ACRS). The plane was sold in 1954, with the question being the amount of gain or loss realized by the partnership.

The taxpayers calculated as follows: original basis of $54,273.50 less $13,777.92 depreciation yields adjusted basis of $40,495.58. The selling price of the airplane was $35,380. Hence the taxpayers compute a loss of $5,115.58. They do not seek to deduct the loss (that would be overreaching, they say).

The Service treated the plane as though it were two assets, a business asset and a personal asset. The Service calculated the basis of the business asset was $14,298.90 less the depreciation allowed of $13,777.92, producing and adjusted basis of $520.98. The Service then also allocates 26.346% of the amount realized on the sale of the plane as attributable to the business asset. This yields $9,321.21 and thus the Service concludes that the taxpayers had a gain of $8,800.23 on the sale. Since they were equal partners, they would each be responsible for one-half the gain. (As to the personal asset portion of the plane the numbers would be: $26,058.79 amount realized less adjusted basis $39,974.60 or a loss of $13,915.81. The loss, being personal, is not deductible.)

---

[205]   Section 168(g).

[206]   199 F.Supp. 743, aff'd 303 F.2d 783 (3d Cir.1962).

The court upheld the Service's allocation theory. Otherwise the taxpayer would have been able to deduct the cost of the business portion of the plane to a greater degree than actual economic depreciation and not have to pay tax on the difference on sale.

(13) Other Business Deductions

(a) Depletion

Various Code provisions encourage the exploration for and development of natural resources. The depletion allowance is a way for owners of mineral deposits to recover their cost, which they as the owner of wasting assets are assuredly entitled to do.

There are two kinds of depletion allowances: cost depletion and percentage depletion.[207] Cost depletion, allowed for all mines, oil and gas wells, other natural deposits, and timber, is computed with respect to the taxpayer's adjusted basis in the mineral property. In particular, the computation of cost depletion involves spreading the taxpayer's adjusted basis over the amount of the mineral deposit and taking the aliquot amount of the adjusted basis as a deduction as the mineral deposit is sold. Thus, if 10% of the deposit is recovered and sold, the taxpayer can deduct 10% of the adjusted basis attributable to the mineral deposit.[208] If, after working the deposit for a while, the taxpayer determines that the estimated amount of the mineral deposit was incorrect and must be changed, the change in the estimate is made and the taxpayer's remaining adjusted basis is spread over the new estimated amount of the deposit. Once the taxpayer's basis goes to zero under cost depletion, no further depletion deduction is allowed, even though the taxpayer may continue to extract and sell more of the deposit. Cost depletion, therefore, is a reasonable way to allow a taxpayer to recover cost in a wasting mineral deposit, where it is difficult to estimate the precise amount of the mineral deposit that can be economically exploited.[209]

Percentage depletion is keyed to the taxpayer's income from the mineral property and in that sense is unique among allowances in the nature of depreciation. In particular, the taxpayer is allowed to take a percentage, varying from five to 22 percent depending on the mineral involved, of the gross income from the property as a deduction for depletion.[210] The attractive aspect of percentage

---

[207] Sections 612 and 613.

[208] Section 612.

[209] In the case of timber, this approach must be refined to take account of the fact that new trees may be growing to at least in part replace the trees that are cut. Reg. § 1.611–3(b)(2).

[210] Section 613(b). The gross income from the property against which this percentage is calculated means the taxpayer's gross income less any rents or royalties

depletion is that even after the taxpayer has recovered the cost of the mineral property involved, if the taxpayer continues to be able to exploit the mineral property and generate additional income from it, the taxpayer continues to be able to take percentage depletion. Percentage depletion, in short, is not limited by the taxpayer's basis in the property.

This exceedingly attractive aspect of percentage depletion has led to heavy criticism and has also been defended as an incentive for needed mineral exploration.[211] Congress has responded to this controversy by limiting the use of percentage depletion for oil and gas under complex rules.[212]

Taxpayers may use cost or percentage depletion, whichever yields the most attractive result for the particular taxable year.[213] There are a number of questions in the depletion area relating to whether a taxpayer has an economic interest in minerals in order to claim depletion, allocation of depletion among various owners, separation or aggregation of properties eligible for depletion, minerals which qualify for depletion, and other issues. There is rich case law and authority on these questions.[214]

(b) Intangible Drilling and Development Costs

As a further boost to the exploration for and development of oil and gas wells, taxpayers are allowed to deduct immediately so-called intangible drilling and development costs with respect to such wells.[215] Deduction of intangible drilling costs (IDCs in the argot of the trade) is optional, and a taxpayer electing not to deduct his IDCs may treat them as a capital expense to the property involved which can be recovered by depreciation. It is usually the case that the IDC deduction is available on property which is eligible for the percentage depletion allowance, the size of which is not affected by the basis of the property. Faced with this embarrassment of riches, the taxpayer

---

paid or incurred by the taxpayer in respect of such mineral property, § 613(a). This makes sense in that the rents or royalties paid by the taxpayer in connection with the property are themselves subject to depletion by the payee and therefore their exclusion prevents the same income from being depleted twice. Moreover, the depletion allowance shall not in any event exceed 50 percent of the taxpayer's taxable income from the property (computed without the depletion allowance).

[211] Cf. Galvin, "The 'Ought' and 'Is' of Oil and Gas Taxation" 73 Harv.L.Rev. 1441 (1960).

[212] Section 613A.

[213] Sections 611–613.

[214] See Burke & Bowhay, Income Taxation of Natural Resources (1983).

See ¶ 5.04(1) regarding the treatment of "carved-out production payments" in the oil and gas area.

[215] Section 263(c); Reg. § 1.612–4. The IDC deduction also applies to geothermal wells.

will, in such circumstances, almost always elect to take the deduction for IDCs immediately. A variety of questions surround the IDC deduction, including the party eligible to take the deduction, expenses which qualify for this attractive treatment, and procedures for making a valid election.

An analogous immediate deduction for mining exploration and development expenditures is also allowed.[216]

(c) Bond Premium

Because of the volatility of the credit markets, a taxpayer may pay more for a bond than its face amount. This excess amount is known as bond premium. Payments on the bond would then, as an economic matter, not all be interest; some of such payments would represent return of the taxpayer's bond premium. To recognize that economic fact, the Code allows a taxpayer to amortize any bond premium over the life of the bond.[217] In the absence of such treatment, the taxpayer with bond premium would report too much interest income and then take a capital loss when the bond is paid off.

(d) Purchased Intangibles: Section 197; Newark Morning Ledger

Section 197 allows for the straight-line amortization (i.e., deduction) over 15 years of the cost of goodwill, going-concern value, and other intangibles purchased in connection with a business. Contrast this with the financial accounting rules that permit goodwill, for example, to be written off over 40 years. To understand the importance of § 197, you must consider the extremely large numbers riding on the treatment of goodwill and other intangibles in the takeover field. For example, in the Time/Warner merger, 80% of the $14 billion Time paid to acquire Warner Bros. was attributable to goodwill, and 90% of the $13 billion Philip Morris paid for Kraft was attributable to goodwill. In these two cases the ability to write off goodwill of that magnitude for tax purposes over 15 years would result in deductions approaching $1 billion per year.

Before § 197 came into effect in 1993, taxpayers could not amortize goodwill. That rule led taxpayers to engage in evasive maneuvers to try to have various intangible assets acquired to be deemed to be something other than goodwill. The most prominent of

---

[216] Sections 616 and 617, which do not apply to oil and gas wells, which already enjoy the IDC deduction. This immediate write-off of capital expenditures is not allowed for expenditures incident to operations of a mine.

[217] Section 171, which is elective except in the case of tax-exempt securities. Market premium as well as original issue premium may be amortized. Amortization of the bond premium reduces the basis of the bond, § 1016(a)(5).

these cases was the celebrated *Newark Morning Ledger v. United States*.[218]

In *Newark Morning Ledger* the taxpayer bought eight newspapers from Booth Newspapers, Inc. for $328 million. It allocated $67.8 million of the purchase price to subscriber lists and claimed deductions for amortization of these lists. The Service took the position that amortization of the lists was not proper because the subscriber lists were inseparable from goodwill. The taxpayer's position was that once it proved the value and the useful life of the subscriber lists, it could amortize them. The taxpayer asserted goodwill is a residual concept only.

In a 5–4 decision, the Supreme Court held that the deduction was allowed. The Court asserted that "goodwill has no determinate useful life of specific duration." the Court said that in this case the taxpayer carried the burden of showing the subscriber lists have a limited useful life. The taxpayer must also be able to prove the value with reasonable accuracy.

The decision was hailed in the financial press as one that would have a multibillion-dollar effect on large takeovers where a great deal of the consideration paid is for goodwill.

In response to this and other cases, congress enacted § 197 to provide for 15-year straight-line amortization for all purchased intangibles. Such intangibles include:

- Goodwill and going-concern value

- Covenants not to compete

- Customer lists, favorable contracts with suppliers or customers (but not accounts receivable)

- Workforce in place

- Books and records and databases

- Patents, copyrights, know-how, formulas, processes

- Franchises, trademarks, trade names

- Licenses, permits, and other rights granted by government

This 15-year straight-line amortization treatment is obviously much more favorable than prior law for assets such as goodwill, which could not be amortized at all for tax purposes. But it is much less favorable than prior law for other assets. An example here would be a covenant not to compete, which generally runs no more than five

---

[218]   507 U.S. 546, 113 S.Ct. 1670, 123 L.Ed.2d 288 (1993).

years. Indeed, it would violate the law and/or public policy of most if not all states for a covenant not to compete to last as long as 15 years. But it is clear, under the statute, that even though a covenant not to compete expires after, say, five years, it must still be amortized over 15 years unless taxpayer disposes of the taxpayer's entire interest in the business before that time has exhausted, § 197(f)(1)(B).

From a policy point of view it might be argued that allowing goodwill to be amortized is questionable, given that advertising expenditures are immediately deductible. Advertising expenditures are supposed to preserve and build up goodwill. It therefore might be argued that if the goodwill is being built up by (deductible) advertising expenditures, it should not be amortizable at all. An answer to that is that one can still make deductible repairs to an asset (such as a blast furnace) that is itself being depreciated.

(e) Miscellaneous Rapid Write-Offs

A number of other types of capital expenditures are allowed rapid amortization by the Code, generally in order to encourage these expenditures as being socially desirable. Examples of such expenditures include research and experimental expenditures,[219] expenditures for pollution-control facilities,[220] newspaper, magazine, and other periodical expenditures,[221] and expenditures to remove architectural and transportation barriers to the handicapped and elderly.[222]

Also see § 195, allowing amortization of expenses in connection with starting up a business, and § 194, relating to amortization of reforestation expenditures.

(14) Alimony and Similar Payments; The Marriage Tax

(a) Alimony and Property Settlements

Breaking up is hard to do, and the tax law does not make it any easier with its complex rules governing the taxability of payments between parties incident to a divorce or a separation. While divorced spouses may hope to sever all aspects of their relationship, when it comes to their tax liability they often remain inextricably intertwined. The basic rule is that alimony payments are includible

---

[219] Section 174.

[220] Section 169.

[221] Section 173.

[222] Section 190.

in the recipient's gross income[223] and are deductible to the payor above the line.[224]

There are a couple of ways to look at the fact that the payments are deductible "above the line." It could be viewed that this is inconsistent with the idea that deductions above the line should be business-like deductions to assist us in arriving at net income or adjusted gross income. Alimony is an intensely personal deduction. Arguing the other way, the statutory arrangement here could be seen as simply a way of choosing the taxable individual. If one spouse is just a conduit for income going to the other spouse, then it is appropriate to net out the alimony above the line, so that it has no further impact whatsoever on the first spouse's return.

There are only two possibilities under the statute regarding payments in the nature of alimony: 1) the payments can be deductible to the payor and income to the payee (in which case the tax burden of the payments falls on the payee); or 2) the payments can be not deductible to the payor and not income to the payee (in which case the burden of the payments falls on the payor).[225]

It is important to understand that taxpayers are invited by the statute to engage in tax planning in this area. The underlying economics of the divorce situation are usually that the higher-income spouse makes payments to the lower-income spouse. What is usually desired by both parties and their tax advisors, therefore, is that the payments be deductible to the payor and income to the payee. This is more attractive than if the payments are not deductible to the payor and not income to the payee. The reason for this is clear: when the payments are deductible to the higher-bracket payor, it saves the estranged couple more in taxes than it costs to have the payments income to the lower-bracket payee.[226] Thus the parties have more after-tax income to divide among themselves. No matter how much the estranged couple hate each other, they can certainly get together on that great American pastime: beating Uncle Sam out of some taxes.

Not every payment the payor spouse makes to the payee spouse is deductible to the payor and income to the payee (thereby throwing

---

[223] Section 71.

[224] Sections 215, 62(a)(10).

[225] The reader might like to know if there is a possibility that a payment could be deductible to the payor and not income to the payee. The answer is: not a chance. The only two choices under the statute are those given in the text.

[226] In some unusual cases it might be that the parties prefer that the burden of the tax fall on the payor. This could be true if the payee is in a higher bracket than the payor. The payee might, for example, have responsibility for raising several children and thus be deemed by the court to require high payments from the payor even though the payee has more income than the payor.

the tax burden onto the payee, which is where we usually want it). Only payments which meet the statute's technical definition of "alimony or separate maintenance payments" are treated this way. Payments which do not meet the definition of "alimony or separate maintenance payments" are not deductible to the spouse and not income to the payee (thereby throwing the tax burden onto the payor). By choosing to have the payments come within or without the statutory definition of "alimony or separate maintenance payments," the parties can decide on whom to throw the tax burden. This is illustrated in the accompanying graphic.

THE TAX BURDEN OF PAYMENT BETWEEN DIVORCED OR SEPARATED SPOUSES

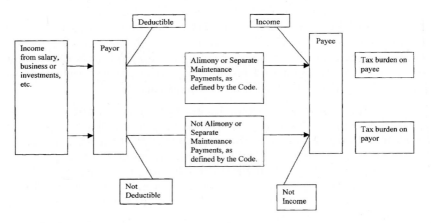

Thus the technical definition of "alimony or separate maintenance payments" is critical here in ascertaining on whom the tax burden falls. The Code here proceeds in a rather technical fashion. The Code first states that "alimony or separate maintenance payments," as illustrated above, are income to the recipient and deductible to the payor.[227] As previously discussed, this treatment is usually what the parties want. To qualify for this attractive status of being income to the recipient and deductible to the payor, the payments, as illustrated above, must meet the elaborate technical definition of "alimony or separate maintenance payments." The statute defines "alimony or separate maintenance payment" to mean any payment that:

---

[227] Sections 71(a), 215(a).

1)   is in cash;[228]

2)   is made under a divorce or separation instrument;

3)   the divorce or separation instrument does not specify that the payment is not deductible to the payor and not income to the recipient (i.e., the parties can choose to throw the burden of the payments onto the payor rather than the payee by just so specifying in the instrument, even though the requirements for alimony are met);

4)   if payor and payee are divorced or legally separated, they may not be members of the same household at the time of payment;

5)   payments must be terminable at death of payee spouse.[229]

In addition, the statute also states that if any part of the payment which otherwise meets the above definition is fixed by the divorce or separation instrument to support children, it will not be treated as alimony or separate maintenance but rather as child support. Child support, not being "alimony or separate maintenance," is not deductible to the payor and is not income to the payee (the tax burden of child support is therefore on the payor).[230] Once again we see the parties specifically able to choose who will bear the tax burden of the payments. Also, if any amount specified in the instrument will be reduced on the happening of a contingency relating to a child, then that amount will be treated as child support rather than alimony (burden on payor).[231]

As another example, *I.T. 4001*[232] dealt with a husband who paid premiums on two life insurance policies. One policy had been assigned to his former wife, and she was the irrevocable beneficiary

---

[228]   A check is of course all right. What they mean here is not "in kind," like a dozen frozen turkeys.

[229]   Section 71(b)(1).

[230]   Section 71(c)(1).

[231]   Section 71(c)(2).

In the leading case of Commissioner v. Lester, 366 U.S. 299, 81 S.Ct. 1343, 6 L.Ed.2d 306 (1961), which influenced the enactment of the present statute, the written agreement incident to the divorce provided that the payments made by the husband to the wife shall be reduced by one-sixth in the event that any of the three children marry, become emancipated, or die. Although the arrangement seemed to suggest that one-half of the payments to the wife was for child support, the Supreme Court held that the agreement did not adequately "fix" one-half of the payments for child support, and therefore the payments were entirely alimony and fully deductible to the husband. This case is notable for its discussion of the statutory scheme governing alimony and similar payments. The court stated that the statutory scheme gives the husband and wife the power to allocate the tax burden between them to their mutual advantage.

[232]   1950–1 Cum.Bull. 27.

of the policy. The other policy was not assigned to the wife but she was listed as a contingent beneficiary. The question was whether those payments are alimony (i.e. income to the wife and deductible to the husband). The Service ruled that the premiums on the policy which was assigned to the wife and with respect to which she was the irrevocable beneficiary were alimony under the statute but that the payments on the policy which was not assigned to her and with respect to which she was only the contingent beneficiary are not alimony (and thus not deductible to the payor and not includible in the income of the payee). The Regulations confirm that payments made by the payor spouse "on behalf of" the payee spouse can qualify as alimony if the other statutory requirements are also met.

There is also an odd rule that alimony payments may not be "front-loaded." The rule is that if the payments in the second year exceed payments in the third year by more than $15,000, then that excess is "recaptured" in the third year. Then if the alimony payments in the first year exceed the average of the payments in the second and third year (after reducing the second year excess payments as ascertained above) by more than $15,000, that excess amount is also recaptured in the third year. For this purpose, "recapture" means that the excess is included in the gross income of the payor and is deductible by the payee.[233]

A problem, of course, may arise if one of the parties is advised as to the tax consequences of the divorce agreement and the other party is not. This can lead to an agreement which heavily favors the well-informed side.

One very important practice note. Alimony not only ends upon the death of the payee spouse, it also ends upon the death of the payor spouse. The same is true for child support. Thus a divorced spouse with two children may be receiving $1,000 a month in alimony and $2,000 a month in child support, but upon the death of the former spouse, the payee spouse is entitled to nothing. The payments cease. Moreover, the payor spouse may have left nothing to the payee spouse or the children. (You are not required to leave anything to your former wife or your children). Many single parents have found their financial situation drastically altered by death and poor

---

[233] Section 71(f). If the payments cease during the three-year period due to the death of either spouse or the payee's remarriage, the recapture rule does not apply, § 71(f)(5).

This strange concern with front-loading of alimony payments (not regarded as a widespread tax shelter) apparently arose out of the great concern of one member of the Senate over this issue. The real problem in the field is, of course, not the front-loading of alimony but the failure to pay it at all.

financial planning. The easy solution is to buy life insurance on the payor spouse and make sure the premiums are kept up to date.

(b) *Property Settlements; Davis*

Often, instead of alimony or in addition to alimony, the parties to a divorce will enter into a property settlement. The leading case in this area is *United States v. Davis*,[234] which is also discussed at ¶ 4.02(2).

In *Davis*, the husband transferred to his estranged wife 1,000 shares of appreciated DuPont stock. In consideration the wife transferred "in full settlement and satisfaction of any and all claims and rights against the husband whatsoever (including . . . dower and all rights under the laws of testacy and intestacy").

This posed the questions: was the transfer of DuPont stock a taxable event? 2) If so, how much taxable gain resulted?

The taxpayer argued the transaction is like a nontaxable division of property between two co-owners. The Service argued the transaction is a taxable transfer of property in exchange for the release of an independent legal obligation.

The Supreme Court held that this was a realizing event, not a non-taxable division of property between co-owners. Because applicable state law provided the wife's inchoate rights in her husband's property "do not even remotely reach the dignity of co-ownership," the wife's rights are a personal liability against the husband rather than a property interest.

The Court then held that the way to measure gain to the husband is by fair market value of what was received (satisfaction of rights) less basis in stock transferred. The Court conceded it is difficult to value satisfaction of marital rights. The Court thus assumed that the parties bargained at arm's length. Hence the Court assumed that the marital rights are worth the fair market value of property transferred.

Under the Court's rationale, a division of property in a community property state would lead to a different result: no tax to the husband. This would be the case because the transaction would then constitute a division of property among two co-owners. The Court conceded that under its reasoning results would vary depending on the state.

Congress changed the law in this area in 1984. It provided in § 1041(a) that no gain or loss is recognized on a transfer of property

---

[234] 370 U.S. 65, 82 S.Ct. 1190, 8 L.Ed.2d 335, rehearing denied 371 U.S. 854, 83 S.Ct. 14, 9 L.Ed.2d 92 (1962).

to a spouse or to a former spouse (if the transfer is incident to the divorce). This overrules *Davis*. Congress then provided in § 1041(b) that the basis of the property so transferred is the transferor's basis. Section 1041 is discussed in more detail at ¶ 4.02(2).

(c)　The Marriage Tax: Once More with Feeling

Over the years, there continues to be a substantial controversy regarding status for filing a return. This is the so-called "marriage tax" or sometimes the "single person tax." Historically, this issue has oscillated back and forth depending on the particular rate schedules in place at the time. The idea is that depending on the particular rate schedules in place at the time, sometimes it appears that the tax law favors married people and sometimes it favors single people.

The tax rates that were in effect in 1992 give a particularly good example of this effect. Examine the accompanying table.

MARRIED AND SINGLE PERSONS' TAX FOR 1992

Taxable Income	Tax on Married Couple (Sec. 1(a))	Tax on Single Person (Sec. 1(c))	Difference: The Single Person Tax
$10,000	$1,500	$1,500	$0
$20,000	$3,000	$3,072	$72
$30,000	$4,500	$5,872	$1,372
$40,000	$6,982	$8,672	$1,690
$50,000	$9,782	$11,560	$1,779
$60,000	$12,582	$14,660	$2,079
$70,000	$15,382	$17,760	$2,378
$80,000	$18,270	$20,860	$2,591
$90,000	$21,370	$23,960	$2,591
$100,000	$24,470	$27,060	$2,591
$110,000	$27,570	$30,160	$2,591
$120,000	$30,670	$33,260	$2,591
$130,000	$33,770	$36,360	$2,591
$140,000	$36,870	$39,460	$2,591
$150,000	$39,970	$42,560	$2,591
$160,000	$43,070	$45,660	$2,591
$170,000	$46,170	$48,760	$2,591
$180,000	$49,270	$51,860	$2,591
$190,000	$52,370	$54,960	$2,591
$200,000	$55,470	$58,060	$2,591
$210,000	$58,570	$61,160	$2,591
$220,000	$61,670	$64,260	$2,591
$230,000	$64,770	$67,360	$2,591
$240,000	$67,870	$70,460	$2,591
$250,000	$70,970	$73,560	$2,591
$260,000	$74,070	$76,660	$2,591
$270,000	$77,170	$79,760	$2,591
$280,000	$80,270	$82,860	$2,591
$290,000	$83,370	$85,960	$2,591
$300,000	$86,470	$89,060	$2,591

Note that these calculations do not take account of the fact that above $150,000 the personal exemption is gradually phased out (see Chapter 7). This phaseout in substance causes the marginal rate (and thus the effective rate) to go up somewhat on incomes above the $150,000 level.

What does this all mean? Well, suppose Jack and Jill are unmarried cohabitants. Jack falls down and breaks his *keister* so Jill is the only one making any money. Jill's 1992 income as an advertising agency executive is $140,000. We see from our trusty table that Jill is paying a tax of $39,460. But if Jack and Jill marry that year, Jill's income is put on the married person's table, and her (their) taxes are now $36,870. So they save $2,591 in taxes. Not bad for a night's work.

Comes now Little Boy Blue. He plays a trumpet with a small jazz band. In 1992, he makes $140,000 per year. (Not a bad gig, so to speak.) Little Boy Blue pays more taxes than the married Jack and Jill. He thinks it's unfair and tells Jack and Jill exactly that.

"Pshaw," says Jack, massaging his keister. "Two can't live as cheaply as one. We should get a tax break."

"You should get a job," says Little Boy Blue.

To everyone's surprise, Jack does get a job. With his background in water-hauling, he gets a job as an upper-level manager with the Sanitary District. The salary is $70,000.

Meanwhile Jill's been taking a hit. Advertising revenues are off; the Olympics Triplecast tanked, and her salary plummets to $70,000. As a married couple with income of $140,000, their taxes are still $36,870. When they next meet up with Little Boy Blue, he says "You should get divorced." Is he right?

This supposed tax penalty of marriage arises from the fact that in the case where the husband and wife have approximately equal amounts of taxable income, the joint return tax rate schedule will impose a heavier tax on the couple than if each of them had filed as unmarried individuals. Moreover, the married couple in this circumstance cannot avoid this effect by filing separately, because the couple will then be subject to the tax rate schedule for married individuals filing separately which would impose approximately the same tax as the joint return tax rate schedule. In Jack and Jill's case, if they filed as married individuals filing separately, they would each incur a tax liability of $18,414, for a total joint tax liability of $36,828. This is approximately the same as the liability for married individuals filing jointly.

This has led from time to time to a public outcry to "do away with the tax on marriage" by allowing married persons who both have income to file as though they were unmarried individuals.

The problem with that idea is that a married couple so filing will have a smaller tax liability than another married couple where only one of the parties earns all the income—even though the two couples have the same total amount of income. Thus if Jack and Jill, each with their $70,000 of income, are each allowed to file as single individuals, they will have a tax liability of $17,760. This would crank out, as our trusty table helps us compute, to a total joint tax liability of $35,520. The problem is this would violate the principle that two married couples with the same income ought to pay the same tax. Thus if Jack Spratt and his wife earn $140,000 on the wife's salary as a chef, their tax liability is $36,870. Why should the Spratts pay more than Jack and Jill? Dispirited as we are by this conundrum, we are relegated to just sitting in a corner and eating our Christmas pie.

As can see by the above, when married couples have disproportionate incomes and one spouse makes most of the income, marriage usually causes the couple to have a marriage bonus. The reason for this is that had the lower income spouse filed separately, that spouse would not have used up all of the applicable deductions and credits. When that spouse marries, the higher income spouse gets to use up some of the lower-income spouse's unused deductions. In addition, because the standard deduction and the rate schedules for married couples are not double the amounts for a single person, two single people receive a larger deduction and pay less tax than if they got married.

But if we increase the standard deduction and that rate schedules, we will increase the bonus that one-income or disproportionate-income married couples receive. Thus a married couple with one income will be paying significantly less than a single person with that same income.

As you can probably imagine, this issue became a political hot potato. In 2001, Congress attempted to lessen the so-called marriage penalty. In doing so, however, it increased the marriage bonus for some couples and in many ways provided a "single penalty." It amended the rate schedules in § 1(a) to provide that the income range for the 15% bracket would be twice the range for individuals.[235] Congress also provided that the standard deduction for married couples should be twice that of the one provided for singles.

¶ 6.03 LIMITATIONS ON DEDUCTIONS

(1) In General

Notwithstanding the detailed treatment of a wide variety of deductible items described above, there are a number of expenditures which appear to arise out of business or profit-seeking activity whose deductibility can still be in question. There are several broad

---

[235] Section 1(f)(8).

principles that may apply to such items, which have the effect of preventing them from being deducted even though they are expenditures arising out of business or profit-seeking activity. The major principles here are that in the case of compensation for personal services, the compensation must be "reasonable"; expenditures may also be nondeductible because they are personal in nature, are capital expenditures, or violate public policy. In addition to these broad limits, there are also some more specialized disallowance provisions. Taken together, these limits on deductions cover a wide variety of expenditures and transactions as the ensuing discussion indicates.

(2) The Limit of Reasonable Compensation for Services

(a) In General

The wages of an employee, of course, are deductible as an ordinary and necessary business expense.[236] However, the wages, salary, or other compensation for personal services must be "reasonable"; to the extent that compensation for personal services is unreasonable, it will not be allowed as a deduction.[237] In the usual case, the question of unreasonable compensation does not arise, since the employer and employee are at arms length, and whatever bargain they strike will be respected for tax purposes by the Service. Where the parties are related, as by family or by virtue of other business associations, the possibility that inflated compensation is being paid to maximize the employer's tax deduction becomes real, and such arrangements draw intense scrutiny from the Service.

Detailed discussion of the area of reasonable compensation for services is given at ¶ 6.02(1).

(b) The Problems of the Double Tax on Corporate Dividends

Let us look briefly at the vexing case of the closely-held corporation. Corporations (other than so-called S-Corporations) pay a corporate tax at a top rate of 35% under § 11. Once corporate income is taxed, it then may be distributed to shareholders as a dividend. Dividends paid by corporations are not deductible to the corporation in arriving at its taxable income. Salaries paid by the corporation are deductible. Both dividends and salaries are, however, taxable to the shareholders. Under current law, corporate dividends are taxed at the preferential capital gains rate (now as high as 20%). Assuming,

---

[236] See ¶ 6.02(1).

[237] Section 162(a)(1); a similar limitation is generally held to exist for wages deducted pursuant to § 212, see ¶ 6.02(2).

for simplicity, a flat corporate rate of 35% and a flat shareholder rate of 15%, the situation may be represented by the diagram accompanying this discussion.

DOUBLE TAX ON CORPORATE DIVIDENDS

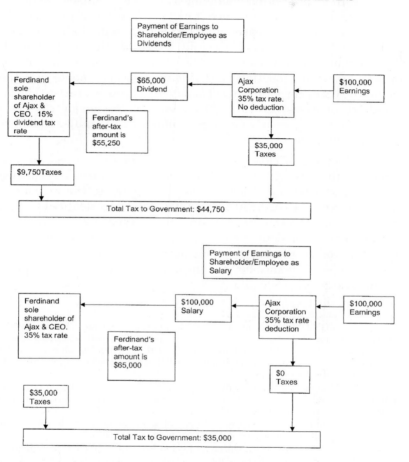

Thus the imposition of the corporate tax rate on dividends left Ferdinand with $9,750 less ($65,000 minus $55,250) than if the payment is treated as salary. The corporate tax reduced Ferdinand's rate of return. Thus we get a very vexing problem in the administration of the tax laws with regard to closely-held corporations whose shareholders also serve as executives or employees of the corporation. The corporation will make payments to these shareholder/employees. As illustrated above, if the payment is called "dividends," there is the double tax, even though the dividend is taxed at a preferred rate to the shareholder. If the payment is called "salary," there is only the single shareholder-level tax.[238]

For this reason, closely-held businesses often prefer to pay a generous amount of salary to employee-shareholders. The Service is aware of this, and often challenges excessive salary payments. (Remember Exacto Springs, See ¶ 6.02). Since § 162 provides that compensation must be reasonable, the Service will challenge salary payments that are too high and disallow the deduction for "unreasonable" compensation. The Service will recharacterize unreasonable compensation as dividends. The payments will then pick up the extra corporate tax. Taxpayers, of course, resist. There is a plethora of cases on the subject. One of the major sources of evidence in such cases is what other companies in similar industries pay for comparable services.

Shareholders of closely-held corporations also engage in other maneuvers to try to extract money out of their corporations and avoid the corporate level tax. They may rent property to the corporation and charge an excessive rent. Rent, like salary, is deductible. They may lend money to the corporation and charge a very high rate of interest. Interest is deductible. Another move is to put children or other relatives on the payroll. This again is a way to try to extract funds and also shift income to someone who may be in a lower tax bracket. The Service is vigilant.[239]

---

[238] Prior to JGTRRA, dividends were taxed as ordinary income. This produced an even larger amount of income subject to double taxation. The reduction in the amount of taxation of dividends reduces the incentive to treat dividends as compensation. As is clear from the above diagram, the problem still exists because even after JGTRRA dividends are still subject to tax.

[239] This double tax on corporate dividends is of significance to large publicly-held corporations as well. With the publicly-held corporation, you do not have the issue of executives trying to take dividend payments out as salary. Usually executives of publicly-traded companies do not own a large enough percentage of the stock. Thus substantial payments to them cannot be denominated dividends.

The problem with the double taxation of dividends in the publicly-held company is that it encourages companies to raise money by selling debt or bonds instead of stock in order to raise money. The interest payments on debt is deductible whereas the dividends on stock are not deductible. This leads to excessive amounts of debt in the economy ("overleveraging," in the argot). Companies with large amounts of debt are, of course, more likely to go bankrupt than companies without it. The payment of interest on debt is legally enforceable whereas the payments of dividends on stock is not.

This problem that the tax system encourages debt-financing has been the subject of intense study by the American Law Institute and the Treasury Department. One obvious answer is to make dividends deductible to the corporation. That has a major problem in that it causes a large loss in tax revenue. It is simply impossible to lift the double tax on dividends and not lose revenue. Making dividends deductible also could have the effect of increasing shareholder pressure for corporations to pay dividends. Corporate executives and their advisors may not like this since they would prefer to retain the funds for purposes of reinvestment.

The fact that unreasonable compensation is not deductible to the employer does not necessarily affect the taxability of such unreasonable compensation to the employee. First of all, taxpayers are taxable on *all* compensation received, whether reasonable or unreasonable. Second, if the unreasonable compensation may not be deducted by the employer on the grounds that it is, for example, a dividend, then the unreasonable compensation will be deemed a dividend to the employee. If a simultaneous sale of property is going on between the employer and the employee, the excessive compensation may be deemed a payment for the property, a result which is unattractive to the payor-employer—who therefore cannot deduct the payment—but could be attractive to the payee-employee, who might be able to treat the payment as a capital gain, taxable at several very low rates.[240]

(3) The Limit of Personal Expenses

(a) *Miscellaneous Personal Expenses: Smith*

A fundamental principle of federal income tax is that no deduction is allowed for personal, living, or family expenses.[241] This seemingly self-evident and simple proposition is, in fact, fraught with difficulty. Virtually every expenditure 'a taxpayer makes can be viewed as having both a personal or family component, and hence be regarded as nondeductible, and as having a business expense component, and hence be regarded as deductible. Even such apparently personal items as food and shelter have their business component, since obviously a taxpayer cannot work without nourishment and protection from the elements. Even such a purely personal expense as a tennis vacation could be regarded as having a business aspect, since without such recreation and incentive, the taxpayer may very well perform less effectively at a trade or business. Thus, lines must be drawn and rules must be made, to prevent all expenses of living from being deductible in full.

The leading case in trying to unpack this problem is *Henry C. Smith:*

---

[240] For elaboration of these principles see Sterno Sales Corp. v. United States, 170 Ct.Cl. 506, 345 F.2d 552 (1965) (unreasonable compensation still taxable to employee as compensation); Regs. § 1.162–8 (unreasonable compensation deemed payment for property). For general discussion, see Mayson Manufacturing Co. v. Commissioner, 178 F.2d 115 (6th Cir.1949); Hoffman "Heeding Significant Factors Improves the Odds for Reasonable Compensation," 50 J Tax. 150 (1979); Ford and Page, "Reasonable Compensation: Continuous Controversy," 5 J.Corp.Tax. 307 (1979).

[241] Section 262. See Halperin, "Business Deductions for Personal Living Expenses: A Uniform Approach to An Unsolved Problem," 122 Univ. of Penn.L.Rev. 859 (1974).

SMITH V. COMMISSIONER[242]

Facts: The taxpayers, Henry and Lillie Smith, were husband and wife and both worked. Because both the taxpayers worked, they employed nursemaids to care for their young children.

Question: Are the child care expenses deductible as an ordinary and necessary business expense?

Taxpayer's argument: A "but for" test: "But for" the nurse, one spouse would have to stay behind to care for the kids.

Held: The expenses are personal in nature, not the ordinary accompaniment of business pursuits. Thus not deductible under § 262.

Comment: The Board of Tax Appeals (the predecessor of the Tax Court) asserted that medical care, clothing and food also meet the "but for" test in that without them one cannot work. Those expenses, of course, would be incurred regardless whether the second spouse works. The child care expenses are only incurred if the second spouse works.

Comment: While the issues raised in *Smith* are still quite lively, Congress did have some pity on working couples with children by providing for a credit for child care expenses, see ¶ 10.02, as well as a general child credit, see ¶ 10.06.

The *Smith* case has come under criticism for its analysis. As the comment above indicates, the test is faulty. However, as the brief above indicates, another ground of the *Smith* case's holding was that the nursemaid expenses are personal in nature. However you feel about child care, the idea of inherently personal non-deductible expenditures is certainly a very real concept. The working person has a variety of increased expenses for food, clothing, and commuting. None of these is deductible.

Some of the cases and commentary in this area take the approach that there is something almost mystical about this concept of expenses that are "inherently personal" even if they are derived from business. In fact the tax system would not fall down if expenses of increased food, clothing, commuting, haircuts and so forth on account of employment were deductible. What would happen is that the tremendous number of people who have those kind of expenses would deduct them; the tax rate would be increased to make up for the lost revenue; and we would be back more or less to square one. In fact that is probably a superior way to handle things. That is because those people who stay home and do not have these kinds of

---

[242] 40 B.T.A. 1038, 1939 WL 83 (1939), aff'd without opinion 113 F.2d 114 (2d Cir.1940).

employment-related expenses would be hurt by a regime of allowing these deductions and increasing the tax rates. And those people should pay higher taxes, since they are not out-of-pocket work-related expenses. The people who are working should be able to deduct their increased expenses from doing so. This would more accurately reflect their true incomes.

In any event, following this "inherently personal" principle, it is clear that items such as food, clothing, shelter, are not deductible.[243] Also not deductible are other more optional but such inherently personal expenditures as haircuts (even though more haircuts may be required because the taxpayer is employed), dentures, health spa expenses, and hearing aids.[244]

See also Vitale v. Commissioner, 47 T.C.M. 1869 (1999), aff'd 217 F.3d 843 (4th Cir.2000) dealing with a Treasury department budget analysis who wrote a book about legalized prostitution titled "Searchlight Nevada." This was published and marketed. Taxpayer also researched and wrote a sequel entitled "Nevada Nights, San Joaquin Dawn." Held: taxpayer was engaged in the activity for profit and thus could deduct most of his expenses, even if they exceeded his income from the activity. Amounts taxpayer paid to prostitutes for "interviews" were not deductible because they were inherently personal.

The "inherently personal" principle has been inadequate to deal with a wide variety of expenses that contain heavy personal and business elements, such as travel and entertainment, and these expenses are subject to specialized rules, discussed earlier in this chapter.

(b) Education Expenses

Expenses for education are often barred because they are in the nature of capital expenses or personal expenses. As a result, they form a subcategory of limitations on deductions. Detailed discussion of education expenses is given at ¶ 6.02(2)(b), and ¶ 10.07.

---

[243] The cost of acquiring and maintaining uniforms is deductible as a business expense if the uniforms are specifically required as a condition of the taxpayer's employment and the uniforms are not suitable for ordinary wear, Rev.Rul. 70–474, 1970–2 C.B. 35. Cf. Sanner, 28 T.C.M. 476 (1969) (gray suit required to be worn by state driver's license examiners not deductible because it was suitable for ordinary wear); Pevsner v. Commissioner, 628 F.2d 467 (5th Cir.1980), reh'g denied 636 F.2d 1106 (1981) (Yves St. Laurent clothing bought by saleswoman to work in a boutique not a deductible expense even though she lived simply and did not wear them off the job).

[244] Reading, 70 T.C. 730 (1978), aff'd 614 F.2d 159 (8th Cir.1980) (living expenses in general); Moscini, 36 T.C.M. 1002 (1977) (food); Drake, 52 T.C. 842 (1969) (acq.); Sparkman v. Commissioner, 112 F.2d 774 (9th Cir.1940) (dentures); Rev.Rul. 78–128, 1978–1 C.B. 39 (health spa expenses); Bakewell, 23 T.C. 803 (1955) (hearing aid).

(4) The Limit of Capital Expenditures: Mt. Morris Drive-In; Midland Empire; Morton Frank; INDOPCO

It is fundamental to the federal income tax system that no deduction is allowed for capital expenditures, which are in general defined as the cost of acquisition, construction or erection of buildings, machinery and equipment, furniture and fixtures and similar property having a useful life substantially beyond the taxable year.[245] Instead of being deducted immediately, capital expenditures are added to the basis of the property involved and, if the property is depreciable, depreciated or amortized over the property's useful life.[246] If the property is not depreciable (such as stock or securities or undeveloped land), then the tax benefit of a capital expenditure will only be enjoyed upon sale or other disposition of the property, where the higher basis will result in a smaller gain or a larger loss on the transaction.

The rationale for this treatment of capital expenditures can probably be best understood as an accounting concept: where an asset produces income over a period of time, expenses incurred in purchasing that asset should be written off over that same period. Where the income-producing asset is not a "wasting" asset, then no such write-off of the expenses to produce it is appropriate. Failure to allocate expenses of producing and acquiring a capital asset in this way would constitute a failure to accurately compute income.[247]

(a) Capitalization of Tangible Assets

Despite the importance of capitalization, the Code is fairly sparse with regard to the capitalization/expense distinction. Section 263(a) provides that no deduction is allowed for amounts "paid out for new buildings or for permanent improvements or betterments made to increase the value of any property," or for amounts "expended in restoring property or in making good the exhaustion therefore for which an allowance is or has been made." The statute provides for four types of expenditures that must be capitalized: (1) new buildings, (2) permanent improvements intended to increase value; (3) restoration costs; and (4) expenditures that will give rise to exhaustion.

---

[245] Section 263(a) .

[246] See ¶ 6.02(12); § 1016.

[247] Section 446(b), requiring that the taxpayer use a method of accounting that accurately reflects income.

Treasury regulations clarify and expand this list considerably and provide separate rules for the capitalization of costs related to tangible assets and intangible assets.

Amounts paid or incurred for *incidental repairs* which do not add to the value or substantially prolong the useful life of the property are not capital expenditures and are deducted immediately.[248] Allowing the deduction for repairs is like allowing the deduction for casualty losses. (Indeed the repair may be occasioned by a casualty loss). In both the breakdown requiring the repair and the casualty loss, the property involved has undergone some unexpected damage reducing its value. In both cases a deduction is appropriate. Indeed, a breakdown which is not repaired might very well qualify as a casualty loss.

In any event, while it is usually clear whether a particular expenditure is a deductible repair or a replacement which must be capitalized, the borderline is far from distinct. There is a great wealth of litigation in this area.[249]

Note that the difference between finding something to be a repair and to be a capital expense is one of timing. The repair is immediately deductible ("currently deductible" in the argot), whereas a capital expense is only deductible at some time in the future. As we have learned, the question of timing can be of towering importance to the taxpayer (and the Government). The leading case of *Mt. Morris Drive-In Theatre Co.* illustrated the excruciating problems that can arise in trying to distinguish a repair from a capital expense.

MT. MORRIS DRIVE-IN THEATRE CO. V. COMMISSIONER[250]

Facts: The taxpayer, Mt. Morris Drive-in Theatre Co., constructed an outdoor movie theater on a 13-acre plot of land outside of Flint, Michigan. This new construction increased the water drainage onto the neighbor's land (Mt. Morris knew it would), which was used for farming and as a trailer park. The neighbor then brought suit, which was settled when the taxpayer agreed to

---

[248]   Reg. § 1.263(a)–1, see also Reg. § 1.162–4.

[249]   See, e.g., United States v. Times-Mirror Co., 231 F.2d 876 (9th Cir.1956) (cost of microfilming back issues of a newspaper deductible); United States v. Wehrli, 400 F.2d 686 (10th Cir.1968) (repairs not deductible if part of a larger plan of capital investment); Red Star Yeast and Products Co., 25 T.C. 321 (1955) (acq.) (new sewer and drains capital expenditures). Campbell v. Commissioner, T.C. Summ. Op. 2002–117 (removal of existing leaky roof and replacement with plastic sheeting and tar was a repair); Northen v. Commissioner, T.C. Summ. Op. 2003–113 (removal of existing leaky roof and replacing roof with new coating was not a structural improvement and could be treated as a repair.)

[250]   25 T.C. 272 (1955).

construct a drainage system to divert the water. This drainage system cost the taxpayer $8,224.

Question: Was the $8,224 cost of the drainage system immediately deductible or a capital expense?

Held: Capital expense. Mt. Morris knew it would have to build a drainage system when it bought the property.

Concurrence Raum, J.: This was a capital expense regardless of whether the need for it was foreseen at the time of the acquisition of the land.

Dissent Rice, J.: This expenditure did not improve the property or extend its useful life. It was a currently deductible repair.

It would appear, at first blush, that the Tax Court got it right. The drainage system would last longer than a year. But of course so does any repair. But still, the expenditure made the property better suited for its use and foreclosed a lawsuit.

As indicated in the discussion above, what was at stake in this case was the timing of the deduction for the drainage system. The $8,224 would either be deducted immediately as a repair (as taxpayer argued) or added to the basis of the property. The drainage system would then be depreciated over its appropriate useful life. The land on which the drive-in theater was built could of course not be depreciated because land is not a wasting asset. However improvements and structures to the land can be depreciated. Apparently the drainage system would fall into that category. Hence the stakes in *Mt. Morris* were that the taxpayer would take an immediate deduction for the cost of the drainage system, or write it off over time.

As we know, this timing issue is money in the bank to the taxpayer. Just to demonstrate the point once again, let us assume a combined 40% tax rate and an after-tax interest rate of 7%. Let us also assume that the drainage system is appropriately written off over thirty years at a straight-line rate. This means that 1/30 or 3.33% of the cost of the drainage system is deducted per year.

What is the present value to the taxpayer Mt. Morris Drive-In of each of these two methods of recovering the $8,224 cost? For the immediate write-off, the present value is clear: With a 40% tax rate, the deduction reduces taxable income by $8,224 and thus reduces tax by 40% of that amount, or $3,290.

Figuring the present value of writing it off on a straight-line basis over 30 years is a little more complex but nothing we can't handle after all we've been through together. If 3.33% of the cost is deducted each year for 30 years, then that means that $274 per year is deducted. That $274 per year deduction saves, at a 40% tax rate, taxes of $110 per year for 30 years. Therefore, we want to know the present value of $110 per year for 30 years with an after-tax interest rate of 7%. That present value cranks out to be $1,365. That is a difference of $3,290 − $1,365, or $1,925. That difference is 23% of the original investment of $8,224. Thus changes in tax timing amount to a 23% rate of return on the original investment.

We probably feel that *Mt. Morris* was correctly decided. It is useful to compare it to the leading case of *Midland Empire.*

MIDLAND EMPIRE PACKING CO.
V. COMMISSIONER[251]

Facts: Midland Empire Packing Co. owned a meat-packing plant. The basement of the packing plant was used by the taxpayer for curing of hams and bacon and for the storage of meats and hides. The original walls and floors of the basement were made of concrete but were not sealed to protect against water; therefore, water seeped through cracks in the walls for many years. Years after the taxpayer's plant had been opened, an oil refinery opened three hundred yards from the taxpayer's plant. Oil then started to seep into taxpayer's basement, and federal meat inspectors said taxpayer either needed to close the plant or oil-proof the basement. The taxpayer then oil-proofed the basement at a cost of $4,868.81.

Question: Is the expense of oil proofing the basement a repair or a capital expenditure?

Service's argument: The expenditure is for a capital improvement and should be recovered through depreciation.

Held: The expense of oil proofing is a repair and hence deductible immediately as an ordinary and necessary expense.

Comment: The court states that it is not required to reach the question whether the expenditure is deductible as a business loss under § 165.

Can *Mt. Morris* and *Midland Empire* be reconciled? One way to reconcile the cases is to note that the problem encountered in *Mt. Morris* (the drainage) was foreseeable, whereas the problem encountered in *Midland* (the seepage from the new refinery) was not. The only problem with that approach is that foreseeability has never been a test in the field. But perhaps it is some kind of subliminal test. Suppose we overlay the facts of *Mt. Morris* onto *Midland.* That is, suppose that when Midland bought its plant, the refinery was

---

[251] 14 T.C. 635 (1950), acq., 1950–2 C.B. 3.

already in place and generating a seepage problem into Midland's property.

It would seem that oil-proofing the basement at the time of purchase to combat a pre-existing seepage problem would constitute a capital expense. Have we discovered something in the capital expense/repair area? The secret test of foreseeability?

The Treasury has issues regulations further explaining the distinction between repairs and improvements. The following table explains the treatment of betterments, restorations, and adaptions under the Treasury Regulations.[252]

---

[252] See Treas. Reg. §§ 1.263(a)–1, 2, 3.

BETTERMENTS, RESTORATIONS, AND ADAPTATIONS

Betterments	Restorations	Adaptions
PRE-EXISTING DEFECTS. The cost ameliorates a condition or defect that existed prior to the property's acquisition or production by the taxpayer, no matter whether the taxpayer knew of this condition or defect at the time. Reg. § 1.263(a)–3(j)(1)(f).	PREVIOUS DEDUCTION OR SALE. The cost is for the replacement of a component when the taxpayer has already deducted the costs of the original item or accounted for the basis of the item as a part of a sale or exchange. Reg. § 1.263(a)–3(k)(1)(i), (ii), (iii).	DIFFERENT USE. The cost produces a change that is not consistent with the intended original use of the property. Reg. § 1.263(a)–3(1).
MATERIAL ADDITION. The cost results in a material addition, including enlargement, expansion, or extension of the property Reg. § 1.263(a)–3(j)(1)(ii).	RETURNS TO ORDINARY OPERATION. The cost returns the property to its ordinarily efficient operating condition and the property has deteriorated so much that it is no longer functional for its intended use. Reg. § 1.263(a)–3(k)(1)(iv).	
INCREASED PRODUCTVITY. The cost reults in a material increase in the property's capacity, productivity, efficiency, strength or quality. Reg. § 1.263(a)–3(j)(1)(iii).	REBUILD TO LIKE-NEW CONDITION. The cost returns the property to a new, rebuilt, remanufactured condition. Reg. § 1.263(a)–3(k)(1)(v).	
	REPLACEMENT OF A MAJOR COMPONENT. The cost replaces a substantial structural part of the property. This includes components that are a large part of the structure or that perform a discrete and critical function. Reg. § 1.263(a)–3(k)(1)(vi).	

Advertising expenses are deductible, even if they are "institutional" advertising expenses designed to create goodwill.[253]

The ability to deduct advertising expenses immediately raises some troubling questions. Take this hypothetical. Suppose Pan-World Airlines has $100 million to spend to improve its competitive position in this market. It can spend the money on a new fleet of planes that provide more reliable and safer service than its older fleet. Or it can keep its older fleet and advertise the "Great Pan-World Shuttle—Come Fly with Us!" Pan-World's management figures that both plans—the new fleet of planes or the advertising campaign—will increase before tax profits by 15%. As an economic matter the two plans are equivalent. But the advertising is deductible immediately. By contrast the new fleet of planes constitutes a capital expenditure whose cost can only be recovered over a number of years. Because of the different tax rules, the advertising is more profitable than buying the new planes. Thus it will not be surprising if management chooses to go with the advertising.

Is that the result we want? Does this have anything to do with why the air fleets in this country are aging while the advertising is the slickest in the world?

Expenses of searching for a job are deductible if the taxpayer is searching for employment in an existing trade or business. If the taxpayer has a trade or business but searches for employment in a new trade or business, expenses of searching for the new job are not deductible, even if the taxpayer succeeds in finding a job in the new trade or business. If the taxpayer has no pre-existing trade or business, job-seeking expenses are not deductible, even if the taxpayer is successful in finding a job.[254]

The case of *Frank v. Commissioner*[255] illustrates the nettlesome problems of deductibility of expenses for searching for a new business. In *Frank*, taxpayer traveled through many states to examine newspapers and radio stations for possible purchase. He had

---

[253] Reg. § 1.162–20(a)(2); see also Sanitary Farms Dairy, Inc., 25 T.C. 463 (1955) (acq.), discussed above at ¶ 6.02(5) (expenses of taxpayer's African big game photography safari deductible as advertising expense to taxpayer's controlled corporation, a dairy in Pennsylvania, no part of the cost of the trip taxable to taxpayer); cases like this give all taxpayers hope, but the opportunity has long since gone.

[254] Rev.Rul. 75–120, 1975–1, C.B. 55, also holding that unemployed taxpayers may in general deduct the expenses of search for a job in the trade or business of their last previous employer. If the break in employment is too long, however, the taxpayer may lose the deduction for job seeking expenses, see Canter v. United States, 173 Ct.Cl. 723, 354 F.2d 352 (1965) (four-year break was too long for taxpayer to get deduction).

See ¶ 2.04(4), relating to employer reimbursement of employee moving and job-seeking expense.

[255] 20 T.C. 511 (1953).

previously been employed by several small newspapers. After a substantial amount of travel he took a job with the Arizona Times in Phoenix and then traveled more, looking at newspapers to purchase. Eventually the taxpayer and his wife purchased a newspaper in Canton, Ohio. The taxpayer claimed a deduction for their traveling and telephone expenses and legal fees in the course of this search. None of these claimed expenses had anything to do with taxpayer's employment at the Arizona Times.

The court held that the taxpayer could not deduct any of these expenses of searching for the new business venture. The expenses of investigating and looking for a new business and trips preparatory to entering a business are not deductible as an ordinary and necessary business expense. The word "pursuit" in the statutory phrase "in pursuit of a trade or business" is not used in the sense of "searching for" but in the sense of "in the course of." Instead of being deductible, expenses of searching for a new business or investment are considered acquisition expenses and are added to the basis of the property acquired.[256] Under the court's analysis, if the search for a new business is not successful, the expenses are not deductible, on the theory that the taxpayer is not engaged in a trade or business and that there was no transaction entered into for profit.[257]

To clarify this area Congress enacted § 195 to deal with "start-up" expenses. Under § 195 a taxpayer can deduct up to $5,000 of start up expenses. The $5,000 amount is reduced by the amount of start-up expenditures that exceed $50,000. The remainder of start-up expenses are amortized over a 15-year period.[258] To employ § 195, the taxpayer must actually enter the trade or business.

The following chart helps explain the capitalization of startup expenses:

---

[256] Woodward v. Commissioner, 397 U.S. 572, 90 S.Ct. 1302, 25 L.Ed.2d 577 (1970).

[257] Frank, 20 T.C. 511 (1953) (as discussed in the text, unsuccessful search for a newspaper or radio station); Bick, 37 T.C.M. 1591 (1978) (same result as to expenses for investigating business possibilities in Europe); Richmond Television Corp. v. United States, 345 F.2d 901 (4th Cir.1965), rev'd and remanded on another issue 382 U.S. 68, 86 S.Ct. 233, 15 L.Ed.2d 143 (1965), on remand 354 F.2d 410 (4th Cir.1965) (expenses of preparing to start up a new business must be capitalized).

[258] Section 195(b)(1).

CAPITALIZATION OF STARTUP EXPENSES

(b) Capitalization of Intangible Assets

Capitalization rules with respect to intangible assets are far trickier than the ones surrounding tangible assets. The regulations provide significant assistance here but before in order to understand the regulations you also have to understand the Supreme Court's battle with capitalization.

INDOPCO V. COMMISSIONER[259]

Facts: Taxpayer, INDOPCO, Inc. (known during the transaction as National Starch), was a company that manufactured and sold adhesives, starches, and specialty chemical products. Another company, Unilever, expressed interest in acquiring the taxpayer. The taxpayer's largest shareholder, the Greenwalls, only agreed to transfer their shares if it could be done in a tax-free manner. Lawyers for the parties and the investment banking firm of Morgan Stanley devised a reverse subsidiary cash merger in order to make the transaction a tax-free exchange. Morgan Stanley charged $2,200,000, along with $7,586 for out-of-pocket expenses, and $18,000 for legal fees. In addition, the attorneys charged the taxpayer $490,000, along with $15,069 for out-of-pocket expenses. (Clearly Morgan Stanley knew better about how to bill clients!) Finally, the taxpayer incurred miscellaneous expenses regarding the transaction totaling $150,962.

Question: Are the expenses of planning this tricky transaction capital under § 263 or deductible under § 162?

---

[259] 503 U.S. 79, 112 S.Ct. 1039, 117 L.Ed.2d 226 (1992). For an in-depth look at INDOPCO, see Joseph Bankman, The Story of INDOPCO: What Went Wrong in the Capitalization v. Deduction Debate?, in Tax Stories 183–20 (Paul L. Caron ed. 2003).

Taxpayer's argument: Based on case law, the test for capital expenditures is whether an asset was created or enhanced. No asset was created or enhanced here. Deductibility under § 162 is the rule rather than the exception.[260]

Held: While an expenditure that creates or enhances a separate and distinct asset should be capitalized, it does not follow that only expenditures that create or enhance separate and distinct assets are to be capitalized. While the presence of a future benefit is not controlling, it is undeniably important in deciding if an expenditure is capital. The expenses of planning this merger with Unilever created substantial future benefits for National Starch, including access to Unilever's technology, synergy with Unilever's own products, and the convenience of having one shareholder rather than 3,500.

Comment: One of the reasons the tab for this transaction was so high was that a new tricky maneuver had to be invented to accommodate the desires of the Greenwalls.

Thus we see the Court in *INDOPCO* adopting a sophisticated financial approach to ascertaining what is a capital expenditure. This is to be contrasted with a literal, asset-based approach. The Court seems to have made the right choice. The asset approach would not have given a clear answer, since the concept of what is an asset is nebulous.[261]

In 2004, Treasury issued final regulations dealing with capitalization of intangibles under § 263(a).[262] In many ways the regulations overturn the significant future benefit test in *INDOPCO*, and are very taxpayer-friendly with regard to what must be

---

[260] Brief for Petitioner 16, citing *Commissioner v. Lincoln Savings & Loan Assoc.,* 403 U.S. 345, 91 S.Ct. 1893, 29 L.Ed.2d 519 (1971) (additional premiums paid by bank to federal insurers are capital expenditures because they created a separate and distinct capital asset).

[261] See Johnson, The Expenditures Incurred by the Target Corporation in an Acquisitive Reorganization are Dividends to the Shareholders, Tax Notes 463, 478 (1991).

This case has created a furor in investment banking and merger and acquisition circles, since it means that fees involved in this kind of work become more expensive to clients on an after-tax basis. See Norwest Corp. v. Commissioner, 112 T.C. 89 (1999), aff'd in part, rev'd in part 224 F.3d 874 (8th Cir.2000) (Target of a takeover incurred legal, accounting and investment banking expenses for investigating whether to accede to the takeover. Held: Expenses had to be capitalized under INDOPCO, because the costs were "sufficiently related to an event that produced a significant long-term benefit.").

[262] T.D. 9107, 2004–7 I.R.B. 447. For an excellent discussion of the new regulations see, Ethan Yale, The Final INDOPCO Regulations, Tax Notes, Oct. 25, 2004.

capitalized.[263] They regulations pay lip service to the *INDOPCO* test, but really completely undermine it.

Here is how they work. Treasury Reg. 1.263(a)–4 provides that the following intangibles must be capitalized: amounts paid to (1) acquire or create an intangible;[264] (2) a separate and distinct capital asset;[265] (3) "to create or enhance a future benefit identified in published guidance in the Federal Register."[266]

Did you see what just happened? If not, read that again. The original rule under *INDOPCO* was that an asset needed to be capitalized if it created or enhanced a significant future benefit. But the Regulations now say that such assets only need to be capitalized if they are identified in published guidance. In other words, this turns the presumption of capitalization on its head. Instead of presuming an asset that creates a long-term benefit is capitalized, we now assume it is not capitalized unless the Service has specifically indicated that it must be capitalized.

Moreover, did you see what else must be capitalized? The regulations require the capitalization of amounts paid to create a separate and distinct capital asset. This was the same test rejected by the Supreme Court in *INDOPCO* that was dicta in *Lincoln Savings*.[267]

The regulations also modify long-standing rules regarding employee compensation. The general rule was that wages paid to employees who were working on projects that created or acquired a capital asset were capitalized.[268] The regulations, however, provide that employee compensation and overhead "are treated as amounts that do not facilitate the acquisition or creation of an intangible."[269] This is true even if the employees' efforts are designed to create a new asset. Once again the justification for this is simplification. But the simplification rationale is completely destroyed by the fact that this rule applies whether or not the business treats the costs as

---

[263] In fact, some critics of the proposed regulations have indicated that the proposal is extremely similar to one made by the INDOPCO coalition, a coalition of businesses formed to overturn INDOPCO. See Lee A. Shepard, Bringing the Separate-asset Test Back from the Dead, 97 Tax Notes 1655 (Dec. 30, 2002) ("The only real goal the administration achieved was the reduction of disputes with a well-represented group of large taxpayers with live controversies before the federal courts.").

[264] Treas. Reg. § 1.263(a)–4(b)(i),(ii).

[265] Treas. Reg. § 1.263(a)–4(b)(iii).

[266] Treas. Reg. § 1.263(a)–4(b)(iv).

[267] *Commissioner v. Lincoln Savings & Loan Assoc.*, 403 U.S. 345, 91 S.Ct. 1893, 29 L.Ed.2d 519 (1971).

[268] Commissioner v. Idaho Power, 418 U.S. 1, 13, 94 S.Ct. 2757, 41 L.Ed.2d 535 (1974).

[269] Treas. Reg. § 1.263(a)–4(e)(4).

capital for accounting purposes. There is no requirement in the regulations requiring firms to take consistent positions for accounting and tax purposes.[270] What this allows companies to do is capitalize the cost for accounting purposes, thus creating higher profits, but immediately deduct the cost for tax purposes, thus creating less tax liability.

Finally, at least with regard to our discussion, the regulations provide that amounts paid to create or facilitate an intangible asset need not be capitalized if the benefit lasts less than 12 months.[271] This rule may allow companies to front load expenses and deduct those expenses in the first taxable year (even though the benefit is in the next taxable year). The company thus obtains the benefits of the time value of money for one year. This is the kind of provision that tax shelter promoters are just waiting to exploit.[272]

The Regulations are a major shift away from capitalization towards allowing for immediate deductions. This shift significantly modifies existing law and the Supreme Court's decision in *INDOPCO*. It is highly questionable whether the Treasury can overturn or seriously modify the Supreme Court's interpretation of a code provision simply by promulgating a contrary regulations. The problem here is that since this regulation is very taxpayer-friendly, it is unclear if a taxpayer will ever contest the regulation.[273] There is, in a sense, no party to protect the public fisc because Treasury has decided not to.

So why did Treasury do this? There appears to be two major reasons. The first is that there was a tremendous amount of litigation and controversy after *INDOPCO*. The IRS became fairly aggressive in its interpretation of what assets needed to be capitalized and businesses claimed that they were being treated unfairly.[274] Secondly, a coalition of business groups had been lobbying for

---

[270] The Treasury did suggest that it was thinking about limited the simplifying conventions to taxpayers that deduct the costs for accounting purposes. See Notice of Proposed Rulemaking 67 F.R. at 77707.

[271] Treas. Reg. § 1.263(a)–4(f)(1). Specifically the regulations provide that taxpayer is not required to capitalize expenses if rights or benefits do not extend beyond the earlier of "(i) 12 months after the first date on which the taxpayer realizes the right or benefit; or (ii) The end of the taxable year following the taxable year in which the payment is made."

[272] For a discussion of the problems with the 12 month rule see Calvin H. Johnson, A Fool or a Fox? The Clearly Erroneous One-Year Rule, reprinted in 97 Tax Notes 1026 (November 25, 2002).

[273] For a possible scenario, see Yale, *supra* n. 276, at 437.

[274] For a review of this issue see, John Lee, Transaction Costs Relating to Acquisition or Enhancement of Intangible Property: A Populist, Political, but Practical Perspective, Va. Tax. Rev. 273, 278 (2002). But see, Richard Schmalbeck & Lawrence Zelenak, Federal Income Taxation 595–596 (Aspen 2004) arguing that IRS did not take an overly aggressive position with regard to INDOPCO.

significant change in this area for years. It appears they finally found an sympathetic audience.[275]

(5) The Limit of Public Policy

(a) Background

A troublesome area of the tax law has been the status of bribes, kickbacks, and fines, which are regularly paid by taxpayers incident to the conduct of their businesses or profit-seeking activities. These payments may be made by taxpayers whose businesses are otherwise legal—for example a kickback paid by an optician to an eye doctor who recommends patients to him—or they may be made by taxpayers whose entire *modus operandi* is beyond the pale of law and order.[276] Since the federal income tax purports to be literally an "income" tax, not a tax on gross receipts, the argument can be made that such payments should be deductible at least if regularly made by taxpayers incident to their business or profit-seeking activities. However, allowing the deduction of bribes, kickbacks or fines for violating public health and safety regulations may be too outrageous to be countenanced.[277] Congress more or less dealt with this problem by enacting § 162(c) dealing with illegal bribes, kickbacks, and other payments; § 162(f) dealing with fines and penalties; and § 162(g) dealing with treble damages under the anti-trust laws. These are discussed in turn.

(b) Illegal Bribes, Kickbacks and Other Payments

There are three types of illegal payments whose deduction is barred under § 162(c): (1) illegal payments to government officials or employees; (2) other illegal payments; (3) kickbacks, rebates, and bribes under medicare and medicaid.

As to the first category, no deduction is allowed under § 162(a) for any payment made directly or indirectly to an official or employee of any government, or any agency of any government, if the payment constitutes an illegal bribe or kickback. If the payment is to a foreign official or employee of a foreign government, the question whether the payment is regarded as illegal will be ascertained by reference to the Federal Corrupt Practices Act of 1977. Payments to facilitate

---

[275] It is interesting that the INDOPCO coalition succeeded by having the IRS issues regulations and not by convincing Congress to amend § 263.

[276] Illegal income is subject to tax, ¶ 3.13(2).

[277] See Tank Truck Rentals, Inc. v. Commissioner, 356 U.S. 30, 78 S.Ct. 507, 2 L.Ed.2d 562 (1958) (fines paid by trucking company which consistently violated the State Highway weight regulations not deductible); Cf. Commissioner v. Tellier, 383 U.S. 687, 86 S.Ct. 1118, 16 L.Ed.2d 185 (1966). See also Mazzei, 61 T.C. 497 (1974) (taxpayer hoodwinked into putting money into a box that was supposed to reproduce money could not deduct his loss).

nondiscretionary administrative acts are deductible. Payments to foreign political figures to get business are not deductible. The burden of proof for establishing whether a payment is illegal (or would be illegal by reference to the Federal Corrupt Practices Act of 1977 in the case of foreign payment) is upon the Service.[278]

As to the second category, illegal payments to parties other than domestic or foreign government officials or employees are also not deductible. The test of illegality here is whether the payment is illegal under any law of the United States or any law of a state, but importantly, only if the state law is generally enforced. The term illegality is stretched, however, in that a payment which subjects the payor not only to a criminal penalty but also to the loss of a license or privilege to engage in a trade or business will be regarded as illegal for purposes of barring the deduction. Illegal payments specifically include a kickback in consideration of the referral of a client, patient or customer. The burden of proof of establishing that the payment is illegal rests, as in the case of illegal payments to government officials, with the Service.[279]

As for kickbacks, rebates, and bribes under Medicare and Medicaid, no deduction is allowed for such payments regardless whether the payments are illegal.[280]

Finally, there is the question of payments that are themselves legal but that may have something to do with illegal activities. The Supreme Court case of *Commissioner v. Tellier*[281] held that legal expenses incident to unsuccessful defense of prosecution for fraud in the sale of securities could be deducted.

---

[278]　Section 162(c)(1).

[279]　Section 162(c)(2). Case law has generally held that this statutory bar to deductibility does not reach illegal discounts or rebates to taxpayers customers, but only reaches illegal payments to third parties in the nature of kickbacks or referral fees. See, e.g., Max Sobel Wholesale Liquors v. Commissioner, 630 F.2d 670 (9th Cir.1980).

　　See Alex v. Commissioner, 628 F.2d 1222 (9th Cir.1980); Rev.Rul. 77–243, 1977–2 C.B. 57 (allowing customer rebates to be subtracted from gross receipts in arriving at gross income); Boucher, 77 T.C. 214 (1981), decision aff'd 693 F.2d 98 (9th Cir.1982) (fact that state does not enforce law does not make illegal payments deductible).

　　The theory of the authorities in general that allow the illegal customer discount or rebate is that such a discount or rebate is a subtraction from gross receipts in arriving at gross income, and not a deduction; therefore, the transaction is not covered by the statute, Rev.Rul. 82–149, 1982–33 I.R.B. 5 (illegal price rebates may be subtracted from gross sales in arriving at gross income).

　　See Chu and McGraw, "The Deductibility of Questionable Foreign Payments," 87 Yale L.J. 1091 (1978).

[280]　Section 162(c)(3). Under § 280E, no deduction is allowed for amounts paid with respect to illegal trafficking in drugs.

[281]　383 U.S. 687, 86 S.Ct. 1118, 16 L.Ed.2d 185 (1966).

The Court found that the payments were expenses of his securities business, citing *Gilmore*. Moreover the Commissioner conceded the expenses were ordinary and necessary. Thus the only ground on which they could be disallowed would be that allowing the deduction would be against public policy. The Court rejected that argument, asserting that the federal income tax is a tax on net income, not a sanction against wrongdoing. Indeed income from criminal activity is taxed. The Court cited *Commissioner v. Sullivan*[282] that deductions for rent and wages paid by operators of a gambling enterprise are deductible even though the business itself and the specific rent and wages payments were illegal under state law. The Court distinguished *Tank Truck Rentals v. Commissioner*[283] (disallowing deductions claimed by taxpayers for fines and penalties imposed on them for violating state penal statutes) on the grounds that allowing a deduction in those circumstances would directly dilute the punishment involved.

(c) Fines and Penalties

No deduction is allowed for any fine or similar penalty paid to a government for the violation of law, even if such fine could be otherwise established to be an ordinary and necessary business expense.[284] This codifies the *Tank Truck Rentals*[285] holding that payments for fines are not deductible no matter whether the fines arise from intentional or inadvertent violations. This statutory bar to deductibility extends also to payments pursuant to a conviction or plea of guilty or *nolo contendere* for a crime; civil penalties imposed by Federal, State or local law, including additions to tax and other tax penalties; payments in settlement of the taxpayer's actual or potential liability for a fine; payments forfeited as collateral posted in connection with a proceeding which could result in the imposition of a fine or penalty.[286]

(d) Treble Damage Payments Under the Antitrust Laws

If the taxpayer is convicted in a criminal proceeding of violating the antitrust laws, or pleads guilty or *nolo contendere* to an indictment or information charging such a violation, no deduction is allowed under § 162(a) for two-thirds of any payment for damages paid under the treble damage provisions of the Clayton Act. If the

---

[282] 356 U.S. 27, 78 S.Ct. 512, 2 L.Ed.2d 559.

[283] 356 U.S. 30, 78 S.Ct. 507, 2 L.Ed.2d 562.

[284] Section 162(f).

[285] Tank Truck Rentals, Inc. v. Commissioner, 356 U.S. 30, 78 S.Ct. 507, 2 L.Ed.2d 562 (1958).

[286] Reg. § 1.162–21. These rules, however, do not bar the deduction of legal fees and related expenses paid or incurred in defending a prosecution or civil action arising from the violation of law. Reg. § 1.162–21(b)(2).

treble damage payment arises out of a private cause of action against the taxpayer without a concomitant criminal proceeding as described above, then the entire amount of damages paid will be deductible.[287]

(e) Expenses to Influence Legislation and Elections

A long-standing rule of the tax law has been that expenses for the passage or defeat of legislation, political contributions and other lobbying expenditures are not deductible.[288] Congress has refined this principle in certain respects.

Ordinary and necessary expenses, including traveling expenses and the cost of preparing testimony, paid or incurred in direct connection with appearances before members of Congress or committees of Congress, as well as the cost of submission of statements to members of Congress or committees of Congress, are deductible if incurred in connection with the taxpayer's trade or business. Such expenditures are also deductible if paid or incurred for the purpose of communicating with any state legislative body or its members. Similarly, ordinary and necessary expenditures, including travel expenses, carried on for the purpose of engaging in direct communication between the taxpayer and an organization of which he is a member are deductible if the communication is with respect to legislation of direct interest to the taxpayer in his trade or business and to the organization.[289]

Beyond these limited allowances for deductions, Congress has codified the long-standing judicial rule that expenses for participation in, or intervention in, any political campaign on behalf of any candidate for public office are not deductible. Also not deductible are expenses in connection with any attempt to influence the general public, or segments thereof, with respect to legislative matters, elections, or referendums.[290]

---

[287] Section 162(g). In the absence of a criminal proceeding § 162(g) would not apply and the full amount of the damage payment would be deductible under the usual rules. Apparently, the reason only two-thirds of the treble damages paid is not deductible is that the amount of the actual damages paid were earlier reported in income and therefore the taxpayer is certainly entitled to a deduction when the actual damages are repaid.

[288] Cammarano v. United States, 358 U.S. 498, 79 S.Ct. 524, 3 L.Ed.2d 462 (1959) (expenses of liquor and beer dealers to defeat anti-liquor legislation not deductible).

[289] Section 162(e); Reg. § 1.162–20, providing extensive discussion. Experts, whether employees or self-employed, may deduct the cost, including travel, of testifying before legislative committees in area of their expertise, Reg. § 1.162–20(c)(2)(ii)(b)(2). It is perhaps unfortunate that although business interests and "experts" may deduct their expenses of testifying before congressional committees, an ordinary citizen who wishes in good faith to speak to a matter of public concern before a congressional committee may not deduct expenses for doing so, even if he is invited.

[290] Section 162(e)(2). See Rev.Rul. 74–407, 1974–2 C.B. 45 (corporate expenses for preparing a brochure for shareholders suggesting they contact their congressman with

Congress in 1966 enacted legislation to prevent taxpayers from circumventing the long-standing rules against deductibility of political contributions by providing that even indirect contributions to political parties will not be deductible. Such indirect contributions would include (1) advertising in a convention program of a political party, or in any other publication if any part of the proceeds of such publication benefits (or is intended to benefit), a political party or political candidates; (2) admission to any dinner or program, if any part of the proceeds of such dinner or program directly or indirectly benefits a political party or a political candidate; (3) admission to an inaugural ball, gala, parade, or concert, or similar event which is identified with a political party or a political candidate.[291]

(6) Other Limits

(a) Expenses and Interest Relating to Tax Exempt Income: Tax Arbitrage

Since interest on state and local bonds is tax exempt[292] it has occurred to enterprising taxpayers in the past that they might borrow, say, one million dollars at, say, 12 percent interest, and use the funds to buy one million dollars worth of state bonds on which the 9 percent interest is tax-free. The taxpayer uses the bonds as security for the loan. If the taxpayer is in the top bracket, the deduction for interest[293] reduces the effective rate of interest on the loan to around 7.8 percent.[294] Since the bonds pay 9 percent, the taxpayer has a sure-fire winning investment, courtesy of the Internal Revenue Code.

Congress has taken the fun out of this maneuver by providing that no deduction shall be allowed for interest on indebtedness incurred to purchase tax-exempt obligations.[295] While that simple prohibition may dispose of matters in an obvious case like the one described above, taxpayer's financial affairs may be sufficiently complex to make it difficult to determine whether taxpayer has borrowed funds to carry tax-exempt obligations, or whether taxpayer

---

respect to pending tax legislation not deductible). See Krebs, "Grassroots Lobbying Defined: The Scope of Section 162(e)(2)(B)," 56 Taxes 516 (1978).

[291] Section 276; Reg. § 1.276–1, providing extensive discussion.

[292] See ¶ 3.01(2).

[293] See ¶ 7.01(3).

[294] How, you ask? Well if the $1 million is borrowed at 12%, then interest of $120,000 must be paid. Taking a deduction for $120,000 means taxpayer's income is reduced by $120,000. Since taxpayer is in the 35% bracket, taxes are reduced by 35% of $120,000 or $42,000. Thus you could say that the net amount of after-tax interest that is paid is $120,000 − $42,000 = $78,000. That certainly seems to suggest that the after-tax interest rate on the borrowing is 7.8%.

[295] Section 265(a)(2).

has simply by happenstance incurred an indebtedness while at the same time owning tax-exempt obligations. For example, would it be argued that any taxpayer with a home mortgage should be denied a deduction for the interest on that mortgage to the extent that the taxpayer happened simultaneously to own tax-exempt bonds? A variety of other examples could be adduced in which the taxpayer has incurred mortgage or other indebtedness in connection with a wide variety of investments while at the same time owning some tax-exempt bonds.

Matters are not simplified by the fact that the statute requires a subjective test: The question is whether the taxpayer incurred the indebtedness *for the purpose* of purchasing tax exempt obligations. The Service tried to sort this matter out by issuing Rev.Proc. 72–18,[296] which discusses various methods for ascertaining whether indebtedness has been incurred for the purpose of purchasing or carrying tax-exempt obligations. If the borrowed funds can actually be traced to the purchase of the tax exempt obligations, that would certainly establish the tainted purpose. If the tax-exempt securities are used as collateral for an indebtedness, that is very strong evidence that a tainted transaction has occurred. Borrowing funds for purposes of financing a trade or business or for financing a personal transaction, such as the purchase of a house, would generally not be regarded as tainted, even though the taxpayer simultaneously owns tax-exempt securities. However, a transaction in which taxpayer ostensibly borrows funds in order to buy stock as an investment and simultaneously owns tax-exempt securities would be suspect.

These rules, while making it more difficult, certainly do not close the door on a taxpayer who wants to borrow funds to buy tax-exempt securities and is willing to go to a significant amount of effort to camouflage the transaction. In light of all these difficulties and possibilities for abuse by enterprising taxpayers, it might be better to allow borrowed funds to be used to purchase tax-exempt securities on the theory that widespread taxpayer transactions of this type would drive down the yield of such securities and deny the taxpayers their benefits.

In addition to the fact that apparently the market would cure the supposed abuse in this area, there are some other reasons to question the wisdom of § 265(a)(2). There are a variety of other ways, unimpeded by the Code, for borrowing to produce tax-exempt income. For example, anyone who has a home mortgage and an IRA (which is a lot of people) is in effect borrowing to produce tax-exempt income.

---

[296]   Rev.Proc. 72–18, 1972–1 C.B. 740.

As an economic matter the individual is borrowing money and investing in something which produces tax-free income. Indeed, you do not even have to stretch to talk about an IRA.[297]

Anyone who is borrowing money for a home mortgage is already borrowing money and deducting interest to produce tax-exempt income. The tax-exempt income in this case is the imputed income that comes from owner-occupied housing. See Chapters 1, 2 and 7. Once again anyone who borrows money and buys stock that increases in price is borrowing money, deducting the interest and getting tax-exempt income from the transaction. Consider anyone who borrows money while having a pension fund or life insurance policy that has an inside buildup of insurance value. There again is the phenomenon of borrowing and deducting interest while enjoying tax-free income.[298]

The bottom line is that § 265(a)(2) is like trying to plug up a tidal wave with a bottle cap. The economic phenomenon of "tax arbitrage"—borrowing and deducting interest for the purpose of investing for tax-exempt income—is widespread.[299]

However, before we hit the hysteria button, let us recall once again, that the market has a way of curing these things. Take owner-occupied housing. While it is true that borrowing to buy a house is in effect tax arbitrage, it is also true that this advantage is exploited by many people, driving up the price of owner-occupied housing. Thus in effect the imputed income of owner-occupied housing is reduced to an after-tax rate.

In case you think we are spinning moonbeams, consider this. Suppose we changed the tax laws so that people were taxed on their imputed income from owner-occupied housing. In other words, when you bought a house, one of the things you had to consider in your budget (in addition to the mortgage payments and property taxes) was the "imputed income tax." Once imposed, the price of housing would generally drop in the economy across the board. That shows that the lack of tax on imputed income has caused the price of housing to rise. If the price is up because of a lack of tax on imputed income, then the rate of return from getting the imputed income (i.e., the shelter of the house) is down. The bottom line is that the tax

---

[297] For discussion of the five kinds of IRAs now available, see ¶ 8.04(4).

[298] Section 264(f) bars deduction of interest on borrowing to finance the inside buildup of life insurance, but, as discussed in the text, it is hard to trace what is borrowed for what.

[299] See Shakow, Confronting the Problem of Tax Arbitrage, 43 Tax L. Rev. (1987).

arbitrage effect of borrowing to buy a house is eliminated by the market.[300]

Notwithstanding this excellent analysis, Congress does not appear to be listening. It has enacted several other provisions designed to foreclose tax arbitrage, ignoring the fact that the market will cure the problem. Some of these other "anti-arbitrage" provisions are § 264(a)(2), disallowing deduction of interest on debt incurred to carry a single-premium insurance or annuity contract. Section 163(d) limits deduction of interest on debt incurred to finance investments. The amount that can be deducted is limited to the amount of the taxpayer's investment income. (Investment income for these purposes means income from dividends, royalties, rents, interest and gains from sale of investment property).

Any amounts of investment interest disallowed are carried forward to subsequent years where they may qualify for deduction. This provision shows a concern with timing. Congress does not want to see taxpayers, for example, borrowing to buy a stock that pays no dividends (or vacant land) and getting an immediate interest deduction. Meanwhile the taxable gain from the growth stock or vacant land would occur at some later date, giving the taxpayer a time value of money advantage.[301]

Another example of anti-arbitrage legislation is the so-called passive loss rule of § 469. This provision limits the deduction of losses from "passive" or investment activities (other than portfolio investments in the financial markets). The limit is that the losses from such activities can only be deducted to the extent of the income from such activities. Once again a major focus is timing. We do not like to see early deductions producing later income.[302]

Other expenses relating to carrying tax-exempt securities—such as safe deposit boxes, investment advice—which would otherwise be deductible under § 212—are not deductible.[303] These items are not nearly as significant in amount as interest on indebtedness.

As to tax-exempt income other than interest—such as life insurance proceeds, gifts, and scholarships—expenses attributable to

---

[300] Conversely, it is reliably estimated that elimination of the deduction for interest on the home mortgage would cause housing prices to drop generally 15 percent, see ¶ 1.03(2)(h).

[301] For a general discussion of deductibility of interest, see ¶ 7.01(3).

[302] See ¶ 8.02(3).

[303] Section 265(a)(1).

such tax-exempt types of income are not deductible, regardless of under what provision they would otherwise be deductible.[304]

(b) Sham Transactions or Transactions Lacking Economic Substance: Knetsch

What happens when a taxpayer designs a transaction solely to take advantage of a technical reading of a tax provision? Should a taxpayer be able to obtain a deduction when the transaction itself has no substance except for the reward provided by the Code? In a perfect world, our answer would be "yes" when the activity is one Congress intended to encourage and "no" when a brilliant tax attorney was manipulating the Code in a manner not intended by Congress. Since brilliant tax attorneys abound, so do transactions designed solely for the tax benefits they generate.

Several doctrines have developed in order to attack transactions that appear to meet the technical requirements of the Code but also appear to be designed solely for their tax benefit. The three main doctrines are the doctrines of substance over form, sham transaction, and economic substance. Under the substance over form doctrine, the Service may look past a transaction and recast it in a different light if the substance of the transaction does not match its form. We saw this in *Starr's Estate*, 6.02(2)(a), supra, dealing with a lease entered into in a manner that indicated it was actually a sale.

The sham transaction doctrine is really divided into two parts. Those transactions that are really a sham (referred to as sham in fact). These transactions are fake transactions. For example, if you and a friend decide to create your own market for securities and trade on those markets, the IRS would argue that those transactions are shams in fact.

The second, and far more contentious type of transactions are those that lack "economic substance." These are referred to as economic shams. These transactions are real transactions, often on major markets, the sole purpose of which are to obtain tax losses. The problem with the economic substance or economic sham doctrine is that taxpayers often legally engage in transactions only for their tax benefit. You might sell stock for the loss, or buy a home solely because of the mortgage deduction. So it cannot be just your motivation that is at issue, it must be something else. The doctrine usually looks at whether the transaction had any substance, purpose or utility beyond

---

[304] Section 265(a)(1). See also § 264(a), barring a deduction for life insurance premiums in the context of taxpayer's business where taxpayer is directly or indirectly a beneficiary under the policy. Thus the deductibility of life insurance premiums is often dead twice, from § 265(a)(1) and § 264(a).

the tax benefit.[305] Courts usually look to see if there was any chance for profit and if the taxpayer was exposed to any risk when entering into the transaction.

The courts have been split on the common law economic substance doctrine. Some courts, following the lead of the Fourth Circuit in *Rice's Toyota World v. Commissioner,*[306] apply a two-part test for determining whether a transaction is a sham. Under *Rice's Toyota*, a transaction will not be considered a sham unless the court finds that "the taxpayer was motivated by no business purposes other than obtaining tax benefits in entering in the transaction, and second, that the transaction has no economic substance because no reasonable possibility of profit exits. Thus, if a taxpayer can show either that a reasonable possibility of profit exists (objective standard) or that the taxpayer intended to make a profit and had a business purpose (subjective test) the transaction will be respected for tax purposes.

Other courts have taken a much stricter approach to tax avoidance transactions and have required taxpayers to show that they had both a business purpose and that there was a reasonable possibility of profit.[307]

Courts and tax scholars continue to grapple with this issue. How much risk is enough? How much potential profit is necessary?

For an initial jump into this topic, try out the leading case of *Knetsch.*[308]

---

[305] Goldstein v. Commissioner, 364 F.2d 734 (2d Cir.1966), cert. denied 385 U.S. 1005, 87 S.Ct. 708, 17 L.Ed.2d 543 (1967).

[306] 752 F.2d 89 (4th Cir. 1985).

[307] See ACM Partnership v. Commissioner, 157 F.3d at 231 (3d Cir.1998) For further discussion of ACM see ¶ 8.02.

[308] For an in-depth look at Knetsch see Daniel N. Shaviro, The Story of Knetsch: Judicial Doctrines Combating Tax Avoidance, in Tax Stories 315–370 (Paul L. Caron ed. 2003).

KNETSCH V. UNITED STATES[309]

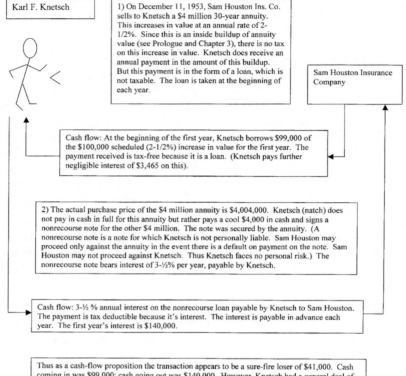

Karl F. Knetsch

1) On December 11, 1953, Sam Houston Ins. Co. sells to Knetsch a $4 million 30-year annuity. This increases in value at an annual rate of 2-1/2%. Since this is an inside buildup of annuity value (see Prologue and Chapter 3), there is no tax on this increase in value. Knetsch does receive an annual payment in the amount of this buildup. But this payment is in the form of a loan, which is not taxable. The loan is taken at the beginning of each year.

Sam Houston Insurance Company

Cash flow: At the beginning of the first year, Knetsch borrows $99,000 of the $100,000 scheduled (2-1/2%) increase in value for the first year. The payment received is tax-free because it is a loan. (Knetsch pays further negligible interest of $3,465 on this).

2) The actual purchase price of the $4 million annuity is $4,004,000. Knetsch (natch) does not pay in cash in full for this annuity but rather pays a cool $4,000 in cash and signs a nonrecourse note for the other $4 million. The note was secured by the annuity. (A nonrecourse note is a note for which Knetsch is not personally liable. Sam Houston may proceed only against the annuity in the event there is a default on payment on the note. Sam Houston may not proceed against Knetsch. Thus Knetsch faces no personal risk.) The nonrecourse note bears interest of 3-½% per year, payable by Knetsch.

Cash flow: 3-½ % annual interest on the nonrecourse loan payable by Knetsch to Sam Houston. The payment is tax deductible because it's interest. The interest is payable in advance each year. The first year's interest is $140,000.

Thus as a cash-flow proposition the transaction appears to be a sure-fire loser of $41,000. Cash coming in was $99,000; cash going out was $140,000. However, Knetsch had a general deal of other income and was paying taxes at about an 80% effective rate ("effective rate" means the average rate of all income). The top marginal rate on high amounts of income was 91% in 1953 ("marginal rate" means the rate of the highest amount of income in the progressive system). Thus deducting the $140,000 interest saved Knetsch 80% of $140,000 or $112,000 in taxes on his other income. This $112,000 tax savings offset his $41,000 economic loss, giving Knetsch a net gain on the deal of $71,000. Not bad for just sitting in an office one afternoon and shuffling papers.

In fact the deal was so good, Knetsch repeated the transaction on approximately the same numbers for two more years.

Facts: Taxpayer, Karl Knetsch, bought ten 30-year deferred annuity savings bonds with a $400,000 face value from the Sam Houston Life Insurance Company. The bonds bore interest at 2.5% compounded annually. Since this was an inside buildup in an annuity (see Chapter 3) there is no tax on this increase in value. The total purchase price for this transaction was $4,004,000, which the taxpayer paid with $4,000 in cash and signing a $4,000,000 nonrecourse loan secured by the annuity bonds. The note bore interest at 3.5%. Taxpayer then borrowed against the inside buildup

---

[309]   364 U.S. 361, 81 S.Ct. 132, 5 L.Ed.2d 128 (1960).

in the annuity (under the contract terms he was allowed to do this in advance). He borrowed $99,000 out of a possible $100,000 ($4,000,000 multiplied by the 2.5% rate). He also paid the interest he owed in advance in the amount of $140,000. The taxpayer also had to pay interest of $3,465 on the $99,000 he borrowed from his annuity. If we look at Knetsch's cash flow, he is losing $44,465 on the transaction ($143,465 interest minus $99,000 return from annuity). Despite this cash-flow loss, Knetsch continued the same type of arrangement in the next year as well.

The transaction was advantageous for Knetsch despite the loss because Knetsch had a great deal of other income and was paying taxes at about an 80% effective rate (remember this is the average rate of tax on all income). The top marginal rate in 1953 was 91 percent. Thus deducting the $140,000 interest saved Knetsch 80% of $140,000 or $112,000. This $112,000 tax savings offset his $41,000 economic loss, giving Knetsch a net gain on the deal of $71,000.

Question: Was the interest Knetsch paid on the nonrecourse note deductible?

Service's argument: The transaction was a sham. There was no economic substance to the transaction. No economic gain could be achieved without regard to tax consequences. Thus the indebtedness is not real and the interest deduction should be denied.

Taxpayer's argument: The transaction meets the letter of the law.

Held: The transaction was a sham entered into solely for the purpose of reducing Knetsch's taxes. The deduction of interest is denied.

Dissent: Justice Douglas: It is true that the taxpayer was bound to lose on the annuity. Yet as long as the transaction itself is not "hocus pocus," the interest seems deductible.

Comment: The contract called for a monthly annuity of $90,171 at maturity (when Knetsch would be 90 years old). If Knetsch had held the annuities to maturity and continued every year to borrow the net appreciation less $1,000, the amount of the annuity at maturity would be $43 per month.

Comment: Knetsch was investing long and borrowing short. That is, he was locking the insurance company into a 2.5% interest rate for 30 years. If prevailing interest rates dropped to 1%, then Knetsch could have paid off his nonrecourse loan with other funds borrowed on a nonrecourse basis at 1% and the transaction would then have been profitable to Knetsch thereafter. Is a basis of the

court's decision the taking of judicial notice that interest rates will
not fall for the next 30 years?

Comment: Suppose Knetsch had won this case. Other high-
income taxpayers would have flocked to these annuities driving down
the rate of return on them and driving up the interest rate on the
nonrecourse borrowing, to the point that the tax benefit would be
eliminated. But perhaps there were not enough high-income
taxpayers to have that effect.

Comment: This maneuver is now foreclosed by § 264(a)(2), which
was effective the year after Knetsch engaged in this transaction.

Comment: The Court may have missed the boat here and simply
misunderstood the transaction.[310] The transaction was terminated in
1956. So what was Knetsch's basis when the annuity was
terminated? The basis was $4,004,000—the amount he paid for it. At
termination, what was the annuities value? The amount of the "sale"
was the $1,000 received from the annuity plus the debt discharged
($4,307,000).[311] Remember, Knetsch kept borrowing against the
annuity and under *Tufts* the borrowing must be included in
determining the amount received at disposition. Thus, Knetsch
should have had income of $304,000 in 1956.[312]

Should this change our view of the case? Does it matter that
Knetsch did not continue the transaction forever?

This issue is not mooted by the enactment of § 264(a)(2) denying
the deduction on the particular facts of *Knetsch*. *Knetsch* has come to
stand for a general proposition that transactions without a "business
purpose" or that do not have "economic substance" may lose their tax
benefits. Rather than launching a jurisprudence of "business
purpose," would it not have been better to allow transactions that
meet the letter of the law and let Congress enact any changes it likes
(which it is doing anyway)? Maybe. (Your authors have a difference
of opinion on this one). We already have a very complex Code and
making Congress chase clever tax planners using the Code in ways
that was not intended does not appear to be the best way to address
this problem.

As a result of *Knetsch* and similar cases, the courts have evolved
significant judicial doctrines for the barring of deductions and other
tax benefits on transactions that appear to satisfy all statutory
criteria. These doctrines, known variously as sham transaction,
substance over form, step transaction, business purpose, give the

---

[310] This argument is made and developed in Klein, Bankman, Shaviro, Federal
Income Taxation 628 (Aspen 2000).

[311] Id.

[312] Id.

courts and the Service a relatively formidable arsenal to apply to carefully structured transactions where it appears that the taxpayer may be trying to pull a fast one. The problem is that the scope of these doctrines is most uncertain.

On the other hand there certainly is a broad class of transactions where taxpayers seem to be extracting tax benefits not contemplated by the statute. Perhaps the best test for whether these doctrines will apply is whether the taxpayer appears to be extracting, in a dramatic fashion, a tax benefit not contemplated by the particular statutory provision involved.

In a similar vein, in *Goldstein v. Commissioner*,[313] the taxpayer won $140,000 in the Irish Sweepstakes and, on the advice of her son, purchased $1,000,000 of United States Treasury Notes paying interest of 1.5%, borrowing $1,000,000 from two different brokerage houses at 4% to finance the transaction. The notes were pledged as collateral for the borrowing. The court denied the interest deduction on the ground that the transaction had no substance or purpose aside from the taxpayer's desire to obtain the tax benefit of a large interest deduction to offset the sweepstakes winnings.

---

[313] 364 F.2d 734 (2d Cir.1966), cert. denied 385 U.S. 1005, 87 S.Ct. 708, 17 L.Ed.2d 543 (1967). See also Lee v. Commissioner, 155 F.3d 584 (2d Cir.1998).

See generally, Bittker and Menikoff, "Restructuring Business Transactions for Federal Income Tax Purposes," 1978 Wisc.L.Rev. 715 (1978).

Chapter 7

ITEMIZED DEDUCTIONS AND PERSONAL EXEMPTIONS

Table of Sections

Para.

¶ 7.01 ITEMIZED DEDUCTIONS

(1) In General

As discussed at the beginning of Chapter 6 and in the introduction, deductions may be classified into two categories: deductions taken "above the line" and deductions taken "below the line." Deductions taken above the line are those deductions which are taken from gross income to arrive at adjusted gross income. Deductions taken below the line are deductions taken from adjusted gross income to arrive at taxable income. Deductions taken below the line are called "itemized deductions."[1] It is § 62 of the Code that provides the rules for whether the particular deductions will be taken above the line or below the line.

It should be noted that to the extent the deductions discussed in this chapter do not relate to business or profit-seeking activity, they represent an exception to the general structural principle of the Code that personal or living expenses are not deductible.[2]

These deductions, including those for interest on a home mortgage, charitable contributions, medical expenses, casualty losses, and state and local taxes, have come under criticism because they are not required for a theoretically sound income tax. Indeed they are considered "tax expenditures" that are allowed for a policy

---

[1]   As an exception to the generalization in the text, the deductions for personal and dependency exemptions are taken below the line but are not regarded as "itemized deductions," § 63(d).

[2]   Section 262.

reason and cost tax revenues to promote certain policies or assist taxpayers in some way. As discussed at ¶ 1.02(3)(c), one of the criticisms of "tax expenditures" is that they help higher-income bracket taxpayers more than lower-income bracket taxpayers.

As a partial response to this criticism, Congress enacted § 68, which limits the amount of itemized deductions that upper income bracket taxpayers may take. Section 68 is directed to taxpayers who have adjusted gross income that exceeds $300,000 (on a joint return, as adjusted upward for inflation).[3] The amount of itemized deductions such taxpayers can actually deduct is reduced by 3% of the excess of adjusted gross income over $300,000.[4] Thus for example if a taxpayer has adjusted gross income of $400,000 and itemized deductions otherwise allowable of $75,000, the itemized expenses allowed to be deducted would be reduced by $3,000 to $72,000. This is computed by taking 3% of $100,000, which is the amount that the taxpayer has in excess of $300,000. That $3,000 is then subtracted from $75,000 to yield $72,000.[5]

Also important as to deductions taken below the line is that they will only have an impact on the computation of the taxpayer's taxable income to the extent their total exceeds the taxpayer's standard deduction.[6]

(2) Expenses of Tax Advice, Attorneys' Fees, and Litigation

(a) Tax Advice and Litigation

Expenses in connection with the determination, collection, or refund of any tax are deductible.[7] This includes taxes of federal, state or municipal authorities, and includes income, estate, gift, property

---

[3]   The amount was $311.300 in 2016.

[4]   An alternate limit in the statute is that itemized deductions will be reduced by 80% of the total of itemized deductions if that is lesser than the 3% limit. This 80% limit will rarely be triggered.

[5]   In ascertaining the amount of itemized deductions for this purpose, the medical expense deduction, the deduction for casualty losses, and the deduction for investment interest are not included. These deductions are subject to their own limits as discussed elsewhere in this chapter.

[6]   Therefore, taxpayers may attempt to argue that a particular deduction should be taken above the line if they do not expect that their total deductions below the line will exceed their standard deduction. Excess itemized deductions may be subject to tax under the alternative minimum tax, see ¶ 7.05.

[7]   Section 212(3). Reg. § 1.212–1(e); see Rev.Rul. 68–662, 1968–2 C.B. 69 (legal expenses incident to unsuccessful defense of criminal tax case held deductible); compare Wassenaar, 72 T.C. 1195 (1979) (graduate of LL.M. program in taxation of New York University could not deduct a year's tuition, meals, and housing as an expense of preparing his tax return; anyone who has eaten the food at Hayden Hall for a year is probably entitled to some satisfaction but this was not the way). Merians, 60 T.C. 187 (1973) (acq.).

or any other tax. Also deductible are expenses paid or incurred for tax counsel or expenses paid or incurred in connection with preparing tax returns or in connection with any proceeding involved in determining taxpayer's tax liability or contesting his tax liability.[8] In major planning areas, such as divorce settlements (see ¶ 6.02(14)) or estate planning, that proportion of the legal advice which is properly allocable to tax planning is deductible.[9]

(b) Attorneys' Fees Generally

Attorneys' fees are deductible when they are incurred as ordinary and necessary business expenses or for the production of income. They are not deductible when incurred as a personal expense. See ¶ 6.02 for a discussion of the cases involving the deductibility of attorneys' fees. Although attorneys' fees may be deductible under § 162 or § 212, if the taxpayer is deducting the fees under the authority of § 212, or they are unreimbursed employee business expenses under § 162, the taxpayer may have a big problem. These deductions will be subject to the 2% floor on miscellaneous itemized deductions discussed in the next section and may be added back into income for purposes of the AMT.[10]

In light of these problems, Congress provides an above-the-line deduction for attorneys' fees in connection with a range of civil rights lawsuits. Covered actions include claims for unlawful discrimination under the Civil Rights Act, the National Labor Relations Act, the Fair Labor Standards Act and many others.[11]

After Congress enacted this exception, the Supreme Court upheld the IRS's position that Attorneys' fees may be subject to the floor on miscellaneous itemized deductions in certain situations, and added back into income for purposes of the AMT.[12] For further discussion of the issue see ¶ 7.05.

(3) Interest

The mortgage interest deduction functions as a major housing program. Interestingly, however, the primary beneficiaries of this housing program are wealthy individuals.

---

[8]   Reg. § 1.212–1(*l*).

[9]   Rev.Rul. 72–545, 1972–2 C.B. 179.

[10]   See ¶ 7.02 for a discussion of the floor on Miscellaneous Itemized Deductions and ¶ 7.05 for a discussion of the AMT implications.

[11]   See § 62(a)(20).

[12]   Commissioner v. Banks, 543 U.S. 426, 125 S.Ct. 826, 160 L.Ed.2d 859 (2005).

Wealthy taxpayers have bigger homes, bigger mortgages and are in higher brackets so they benefit more from the mortgage interest deduction.

This is one of the more spectacular effects of tax expenditures (see Chapter 1). Let's talk a little about the interest deductions generally and then we'll return to the intriguing subject of the home mortgage interest deduction.

The first question is whether a particular arrangement gives rise to deductible interest at all. In the leading case of *J. Simpson Dean v. Commissioner*,[13] taxpayer obtained an interest-free loan from a corporation he controlled. The Government's theory of taxation is that the taxpayer has enjoyed an economic benefit from the free use of borrowed funds (which could after all be invested to earn interest). The taxpayer's alternative to the interest-free loan was of course to borrow money at interest. By giving the taxpayer an interest-free loan the controlled corporation would have to forego earning interest on the money itself. Thus it looks like income. However, the court held the arrangement was not income because had the taxpayer borrowed the funds elsewhere he would have 1) had income from investing the funds and 2) had an offsetting deduction of the interest he paid on the borrowed funds. Since the deduction for interest paid offsets the interest earned on the borrowed funds, the court held that the taxpayer has no income on the receipt of an interest-free loan from his controlled corporation. (In this connection see ¶ 5.04(3)(b) on low interest loans, § 7872, and assignment of income.)

Interest can be deductible if it arises from business or investment activity. It is not deductible if it arises from personal activity.[14] Interest is deductible from gross income at arriving at adjusted gross income (i.e., above the line) if it is attributable to indebtedness incurred in connection with business, or for the production of rental or royalty income.[15] However, if interest is attributable to profit-seeking activity which does not produce rental or royalty income—such as interest on a stock brokerage margin account, which produces dividend income—the interest is only deductible as an itemized deduction.[16]

The way matters stack up now in the Code, there are basically four kinds of interest.

---

[13]   35 T.C. 1083 (1961).

[14]   Section 163(a).

[15]   Section 62(a)(1) and (4).

[16]   Section 62(a)(4). See ¶ 6.01 and the introduction for discussion of the significance of taking deductions from gross income to arrive at adjusted gross income, or from adjusted gross income to arrive at taxable income.

1) *Interest arising out of a trade or business.* This is where Willie Taxpayer borrows money to finance the purchase of supplies for his restaurant operated as a sole proprietorship. No doubt that is a cost of Willie doing business and no doubt that interest is deductible. Moreover, no doubt it is deductible "above the line" as a deduction from gross income in arriving at adjusted gross income.[17] Note, in the nasty department, the above-the-line deduction of trade or business interest is denied to interest incurred in the performance of services by the taxpayer. Thus, while such employee trade or business interest is deductible, it is deductible only "below the line."[18] Happily, though, this particular type of expenditure for employees rarely happens.

2) *Investment interest.* Willie also has investments in the stock market. He borrows some money against some of the stocks he owns in order to finance the purchase of other securities. He can deduct the interest on this borrowing up to the extent of his investment income, including gains on sales of his investment property. Any interest disallowed because in excess of investment income can be carried forward to the next taxable year.[19] As an override to these rules, interest on debt incurred to carry tax-exempt bonds and some other tax-exempt investments is not deductible.[20] Investment interest is deductible above the line if attributable to rental or royalty income.

3) *Interest incurred in a passive activity.* Willie borrows to invest in an apartment building which he does not actively manage. The deduction for interest on the debt incurred to buy the apartment building is limited to the amount of income derived from the investment. Disallowed amounts are carried forward.[21]

4) *Interest incurred to finance purchase of personal-use property or services.* This category breaks into two parts. Interest for personal-use purposes—typically credit card interest on personal items such as clothing, dining out, and travel—is considered to be "personal interest" and is not deductible. Interest on automobile loans is similarly not deductible. Home mortgage interest and the interest on some educational loans are the only exception here. It is

---

[17]   Section 62(a)(1).

[18]   Section 62(a)(1). This is "nasty" of course because deductions that come below the line will not get used at all unless the taxpayer itemizes his deductions (i.e., has enough itemized deductions to exceed the standard deduction).

[19]   Section 163(d).

[20]   See Chapter 6, ¶ 6.03(6)(a). Interest on borrowing attributable to the inside buildup of a life insurance policy is not deductible, § 264(f).

[21]   Section 469. Often these passive-loss or shelter-type investments are made in the form of a partnership, which passes the losses through to the individual partners. See Chapter 8.

a major interest payment item for taxpayers and it is deductible subject to certain dollar and price limits.[22]

Student Loan Interest

Up to $2,500 of interest per year may be deducted above the line on loans to finance education expenses of the taxpayer, the taxpayer's spouse and the taxpayer's dependents. This deduction phases out for married couples filing jointly with adjusted gross income from $100,000 to $130,000, and for single filers from $50,000 to $65,000.[23]

Remember: Interest arising from a trade or business (as long as you are not an employee), and interest on loans for your education (up to $2,500) are above the line deductions. Most other interest deductions are below the line.

Home Mortgage Interest

Let us discuss in a little more detail the home mortgage interest deduction. The rules allow only "qualified residence interest" to be deducted. Qualified residence interest is defined as interest on debt secured by a principal or second residence of the taxpayer. This interest is deductible notwithstanding the general rule providing that personal interest is not deductible. Qualified residence interest is limited to *acquisition debt* and *home equity debt.*

1) Acquisition debt is debt to acquire or substantially improve a principal or second residence (up to a total debt of $1 million). 2) Home equity debt is debt (not in excess of $100,000) secured by a principal or second residence which is not acquisition debt. Thus the maximum debt on which a taxpayer could deduct interest as qualified residence interest would be $1,000,000 plus $100,000, or $1,100,000.

As far as the acquisition debt is concerned, the debt must be taken to buy, build, or improve the home. A second limitation with regard to the acquisition debt is that refinancing the old mortgage will qualify only up to the amount of the balance of the old mortgage just prior to the refinancing. Thus a homeowner who has paid off part of a mortgage can only refinance (to take advantage of lower interest rates, say) up to the amount of the remaining debt balance. (The taxpayer may go above that debt by as much as $100,000 and still qualify as home equity debt). A third overall limit is that the total amount of home mortgage acquisition debt may not exceed $1,000,000. If it does, only the amount up to $1 million qualifies for the interest deduction. (To that $1 million can be added the other

---

[22]   Section 163(h). Under § 163(h), if the debt on the home (acquisition indebtedness) exceeds $1,000,000, the interest on indebtedness over $1,000,000 is not deductible. See discussion infra.

[23]   Section 163(h), 221.

debt of up to $100,000 in home equity debt, if the value of the house will support it in the eyes of the bank).

The $100,000 home equity debt provision makes possible the popular home equity line of credit, in which typically a bank lends the homeowner up to $100,000 on a second mortgage. All of the interest on the loan would be deductible regardless of the use to which the proceeds were put. § 163(h)(3). Thus, to take a nasty little example (remember we didn't make these rules), your parents could borrow on their house to finance your legal education and deduct the interest. Whereas, as pointed out above, only a small amount of interest on student loans is deductible.

Bear in mind, as mentioned above, the deduction for home mortgage is allowed not only on the taxpayer's principal residence but also on one other second residence.[24]

By and large the interest on the home mortgage is the largest single itemized deduction for taxpayers. Absent the mortgage interest deduction most people would not build up enough itemized deductions to exceed the standard deduction. The home mortgage interest deduction represents a major tax expenditure which much more heavily subsidizes the well-to-do than it does the poor. At the same time, any attempts to change or limit it appear to be politically out of the question. People build their financial lives around the mortgage interest deduction, and the authors of this book are among them.

The advantage to deducting interest on the home mortgage is even greater when one recalls that home ownership produces significant imputed income (see Chapters 1, 2, and 6.03(6)). To review the concept of imputed income briefly: if you buy a bond, it produces taxable interest income. If you buy a house it produces in-kind income—namely shelter. However, the shelter income the house produces is not taxable. We call this income "imputed income." We could also call it "in-kind income from the house the taxpayer owns."

So let's look at it. The taxpayer who has borrowed money to purchase a house has borrowed money to produce tax-free income. The taxpayer should, therefore, as a theoretical matter be barred from taking the deduction since there is no tax on the income.[25]

---

[24] This feeds into the area of deductibility of expenses of vacation homes, see ¶ 6.02(11).

[25] Cutting the other way is the argument that a homeowner who owns a home free and clear is getting an advantage of imputed income without any offsetting limitation on deduction. Thus it could be argued the mortgaged homeowner should also be able to enjoy imputed income without any offsetting limitation on deduction. However, that argument appears to be unpersuasive. That argument seems to be saying in substance that since a homeowner who owns a house free and clear is getting

Another way to demonstrate the inequity is to compare the homeowner with a tenant. The tenant pays rent which produces the imputed income of shelter from the apartment. But the tenant cannot deduct the rent.

Another take on the situation is to say that not taxing imputed income from owner-occupied housing causes resources to be directed to that tax-free source of income. Resources are therefore directed away from taxable sources of income such as corporate bonds.

Note also that it is higher-income people that benefit the most from the exclusion of imputed income from owner-occupied housing. Higher-income people have fancier houses—which generate more imputed income. And higher-income people are in higher tax brackets; hence the exclusion saves them more money. Put that together with the fact, as discussed at the beginning of this section, the mortgage interest deduction favors higher-income people and you have a powerful effect.

All of this can be easily summarized in one succinct piece of tax advice: If you are rich, buy a big house.

In case you hoped this discussion was over, may we point out that the same analysis applies to other consumer durables? But the interest deduction rules are different.

For example, interest on an automobile loan cannot be deducted. There is unquestionably imputed income with respect to cars. A car that one owns confers valuable transportation services. Thus when a taxpayer borrows money to buy a car, the taxpayer is borrowing money to acquire an asset that produces tax-free income. As we have seen from the discussion above, when one borrows money to produce tax-free income, the appropriate response at first blush appears to be to deny a deduction for the interest on the loan. This is because it is too much to allow the benefit of the deduction—which is supposed to be an expense of producing income—when the income is not taxed.

The problem here again is what about the person who owns a car outright. That person is also in receipt of imputed income but is not suffering any offsetting penalty. Thus, the argument goes, the person who has borrowed to buy the car should also not suffer an offsetting penalty and should be able to deduct the interest on the loan.

---

away with a major benefit, let us also give the benefit to the (much larger) group of homeowners who have mortgages.

What all this boils down to say is that the exclusion of imputed income from owner-occupied housing is a large tax benefit that should, as a theoretical matter, be closed but that will, as a practical matter, not be closed.

But the analysis can get away from you if you look too long at it. Consider Melanie, who borrows money from the dealer to buy a new car for $30,000. Let us say Melanie also has $30,000 worth of marketable securities, securities which she chose not to sell to buy the car outright. So Melanie's position is that she owns a $30,000 car; she owes $30,000 on it; and she has $30,000 of securities. The rule under current law, as we know, is that Melanie cannot deduct the interest on her auto loan, because that is "personal interest."[26]

Now let's consider Judy who also has $30,000 of marketable securities. Judy also wants to buy a $30,000 car. But instead of selling the securities she borrows $30,000 against them, using them as collateral for the loan.[27] She then walks over to her friendly Jaguar dealer and plunks down the cash.

What is the result? Judy, like Melanie, is in receipt of tax-free imputed income from the car. Judy, unlike Melanie, can apparently deduct the full amount of her interest on the indebtedness. This is because her indebtedness is not personal interest but rather investment interest.[28] But no, you say. Judy's interest is personal because she used the loan proceeds to buy the car.

You'd have a point. The Service in 1987 issued guidelines for allocating interest expenses in view of the varying rules on deductibility of various kinds of interest. The basic principle is that interest expense on debt is allocated in the same manner as the debt to which the interest relates. Debt is allocated by tracing the use of the proceeds of the debt to specific expenditures. The example above would clearly cause the interest to be regarded as personal.

Okay, then, how about this: Judy and Melanie each have $30,000 cash. Melanie buys a car for $30,000 borrowing the entire purchase price. She then uses her $30,000 cash to buy marketable securities. Judy uses her $30,000 in the bank to buy the car outright. She then borrows $30,000 to finance the purchase of marketable securities, using the securities to secure the loan. Is Judy's interest personal and non-deductible now? Yes. Do the debt-tracing rules work now? No.

What is the moral of this muddle? First we see here an example of why the rule used to be that interest is always deductible. As an economic matter it is really impossible to say what debt is financing

---

[26]   Section 163(h).

[27]   We recognize that Judy cannot borrow 100% of the value of the securities, unless they are T-Bills. The reader who is worried about this could just assume that Judy has $60,000 of securities and borrows 50% of their value.

[28]   Deduction of investment interest has its own limitations, § 163(d), but these limits are not triggered if the investment income is greater than the investment interest.

what acquisition. That being the case, it then becomes impossible to compare the taxpayer who has borrowed to buy a car or a house with the taxpayer who has supposedly bought the car or house outright. Unless the taxpayer who has supposedly bought the car or house outright has no other indebtedness, you cannot really say that he has bought the car, house, or anything else outright. It would appear that you have to come back to say that not taxing imputed income at least on big ticket items like houses and cars is a distortion. But it does not make a whole lot of sense to try to use the interest deduction rules— which are themselves fraught with theoretical difficulties—to try to make the distortion more even-handed. No matter what you do with the interest deduction, it is still going to be the case that failure to tax imputed income from big-ticket consumer durables is a distortion, in that income from other investments is taxed.

Policy. There is a reason for the peculiar propensity of the recent legislation to encourage borrowing against the home. The drafters of the recent legislation wanted to limit the deduction of non-business interest. At the same time, they did not want to limit the home mortgage deduction, because of the political uproar that would cause. They feared, however, that sharp-planning taxpayers, having lost the deduction for non-business or personal interest, would begin refinancing their houses for ready cash and continue to take the interest deduction. Seeing the handwriting on the wall, the drafters decided to beat the sharp-planning taxpayers to the punch by providing specific rules for second mortgages or refinancings.

Whether, as a matter of national economic policy, the tax system should favor the leveraging of the family home is another question. After all this "blood, sweat and tears," it turns out that the benefit of being able to deduct interest on the home mortgage is not at all as great as it seems. This is because the residential real estate market responds to this subsidy by a general rise in prices. Thus, the homeowner is able to deduct his mortgage interest, but he is paying more (and has to borrow more) to buy his house. So the homeowner is not really much better off due to being able to deduct the interest on his mortgage, but he is more deeply in debt.

There is no doubt this price effect from deductibility of the home mortgage occurs. We see a similar effect in a small way when home mortgage rates change. When rates are down, housing prices tend to go up. When rates are up, housing prices tend to be depressed.

As discussed in detail (you might say excessive detail) in the Appendix, interest has a special role in the tax law. It is particularly bound up with the concept of time and time value of money. This impacts even the simple question of deductibility of interest. Prepaid interest—i.e., interest paid before the time period to which it is attributed—generally must be capitalized. For example, under § 263A(b) construction-period interest must be added to the basis of the property under construction, rather than deducted immediately.

In the past, tax shelter arrangements in the real estate area would employ nonrecourse debt which is in excess of the fair market value of the property being financed by the debt. In such a case, the interest deduction may be disallowed on the theory that the indebtedness is not bona fide because the debtor, having no equity in the property, has no motivation to pay off the debt.[29] Reference here should also be made to ¶ 6.03(6)(b) relating to disallowance of deductions in connection with sham or uneconomic transactions.

Other problems in the area of determining whether a bona fide indebtedness exists include the question of debt versus equity in the closely-held corporation,[30] and leases with an option to purchase which may be deemed to be a purchase on credit.[31]

(4) Taxes; Cramer

A wide variety of taxes may be deducted. These are: real property taxes (state, local and foreign); sales taxes (state and local); personal property taxes (state and local); income, war profits, and excess profits taxes (state, local and foreign); the windfall profits tax.[32] These taxes may be deducted whether or not they are attributable to a trade or business, profit-seeking activity, or personal activity. These taxes are allowed as a deduction "above the line" under two conditions: (1) they are attributable to a trade or business carried on by the taxpayer; or (2) they are attributable to profit-seeking activity of the taxpayer which produces rent or royalty income.[33] If these taxes are not deductible above the line but only

---

[29]   Estate of Franklin v. Commissioner, 544 F.2d 1045 (9th Cir.1976) (purchase of motel by limited partnership followed by lease back of the property to the original owner financed by nonrecourse liability to be paid in installments; held on the facts taxpayer failed to carry the burden of showing the nonrecourse debt did not exceed the fair market value of the property.) Beck v. Commissioner, 678 F.2d 818 (9th Cir.1982) (same as *Franklin*). See ¶ 8.02(4).

[30]   As discussed also in Chapter 6, stockholders of a closely-held corporation generally prefer to have the investment in the corporation denominated as debt rather than stock, so as to provide their corporation with an interest deduction on payments with respect to their investment. The Service naturally has opposed these efforts, see e.g. Fin Hay Realty Co. v. United States, 398 F.2d 694 (3d Cir.1968); Plumb, "The Federal Income Tax Significance of Corporate Debt: A Critical Analysis and a Proposal," 26 Tax L.Rev. 369 (1971). See § 385.

[31]   Rev.Rul. 55–540, 1955–2 C.B. 39 (providing extensive guidelines); Cal-Maine Foods, Inc., 36 T.C.M. 383 (1977) (purported lease with option to purchase was respected).

See Green v. Commissioner, 367 F.2d 823 (7th Cir.1966) (presenting the related question of whether a sale would be treated as a loan).

[32]   Section 164(a).

[33]   For elaboration of these structural issues see ¶ 6.01; and see also § 62.

below the line, they will only benefit the taxpayer to the extent he has excess itemized deductions that exceed the standard deduction.[34]

After the American Jobs Creation Act of 2004, taxpayers may choose to deduct states sales taxes instead of State income taxes.[35] Prior to the Tax Reform Act of 1986, taxpayers could deduct state sales taxes as well as property taxes. Taxpayers could save their receipts or could claim a specific amount based on IRS generated tables. The Jobs Act re-institutes this deduction but requires taxpayers to make a choice between income and sales taxes. This provision is generally seen as a major boon to taxpayers in States that have little or no income taxes, or to taxpayers who make very large expenditures.

The deduction for taxes which are not attributable to the taxpayer's trade or business or profit-seeking activity can be criticized on the grounds that it is an unjustified erosion of the tax-base.[36] It can be defended on the ground that it effects a rough revenue sharing between the states and the Federal Government; to the extent states and localities raise property taxes, the taxpayer's federal tax bill will be decreased. The problem with this argument is that it is not necessarily those states which may be most in need of federal funds that impose higher state and local taxes.

In any event, the primary beneficiaries of the deduction for taxes unrelated to business or profit-seeking activity are homeowners who can deduct their property taxes. Moreover the deduction for property taxes on more expensive homes will send the owner over the standard deduction with respect to his itemized deductions and thereby cause him to benefit in full from other itemized deductions, such as charitable contributions, medical expenses, casualty losses, etc.

On the sale of real property, the property tax is apportioned between the buyer and seller according to the number of days in the tax year that each owns the property.[37]

---

[34]   State, local, and foreign taxes not explicitly described in the text may be deducted if attributable to carrying on a trade or a business or profit-seeking activity, § 164(a). This would allow, for example, state stock transfer taxes and unemployment compensation taxes to be deducted. Federal taxes, including income or profits and excess profits, estate and gift, and certain other taxes may not be deducted, § 275. Foreign income taxes may, at the taxpayer's election, be taken as a tax credit rather than deducted, see §§ 901–908.

[35]   This provision is applicable for taxable years 2004 and 2005.

[36]   See ¶¶ 1.02(2)(b) and (c).

[37]   Section 164(d), reversing the rule of Magruder v. Supplee, 316 U.S. 394, 62 S.Ct. 1162, 86 L.Ed. 1555 (1942), requiring the purchaser to capitalize his share of property taxes.

A tax refund is includable in gross income to the extent that the deduction of the tax in a previous year conferred a tax benefit.[38]

An interesting case in the real estate tax area is *Cramer v. Commissioner*,[39] in which the Tax Court held that 1) where a daughter paid her mother's real estate taxes, the payments were not deductible to the daughter, since she had no legal obligation to pay them and had no legal or equitable interest in her mother's property. Her payments were in substance gifts to her mother; 2) where a taxpayer had sold property and provided owner financing and retained title under state law, her payment of property taxes that the buyer let fall in arrears were imposed on her and deductible.

(5) Casualties and Other Losses

(a) Casualties

Losses are allowed to individual taxpayers if they are incurred in a trade or business or incurred in a transaction entered into for profit, to the extent not compensated for by insurance. Losses of all kinds incurred in a trade or business or profit-seeking activity producing rents or royalties are allowed above the line.

Losses incurred with respect to personal-use property are only allowed if the loss arises from a casualty and then only if the loss exceeds certain limits.[40] The limits are first that the amount of an individual loss to personal-use property is deductible only to the extent that it exceeds a $100 floor amount. The second limit is that the aggregate of all these personal-use casualties, after subtraction of the $100 floor, is only deductible to the extent it exceeds 10% of the taxpayer's adjusted gross income.[41]

An example will illustrate the operation of these limits:

Mr. Hardluck has an adjusted gross income of $50,000. He suffers three different casualties during the year to his personal residence, uncompensated for by insurance. He suffers a fire with damage of $2,000, windstorm damage of $2,500, and a theft with damage of $3,000. His casualty loss deduction would be computed as follows: After taking out the $100 floor on each of these casualties the amount of the loss that might be deductible is $1,900, $2,400 and

---

[38]   See ¶ 9.02(3).

[39]   55 T.C. 1125 (1971).

[40]   Insurance premiums on personal-use property are not deductible. If they were deductible that would mean the taxpayer would be able to take a deduction to produce the tax-free imputed income that arises from consumer durables (see Chapter 1).

[41]   Sections 165(a), (c), (h). If an area in which a taxpayer lives is declared a Federal Disaster Area, the taxpayer may deduct a casualty loss attributable to the disaster in the year preceding the year the casualty was sustained, subject to the 10% and $100 limits, § 165(i).

$2,900, respectively. Adding these amounts up yields $7,200. Ten percent of Hardluck's adjusted gross income is $5,000. Therefore the amount of his allowable casualty loss deduction is $2,200 ($7,200 − $5,000).

Note that the character of the deduction would be determined under § 1231, if the property which suffered the casualty had been held longer than one year. (see ¶ 4.06(3)(a)(iv)).

The floor of 10% of adjusted gross income was added to the Code by the Tax Equity and Fiscal Responsibility Act of 1982, effective for tax years beginning after 1982. This floor means that the overwhelming majority of casualty losses to personal-use property will not be deductible. Rare indeed will be the taxpayer who has aggregate casualty losses, uncompensated for by insurance, that will exceed 10% of his adjusted gross income. And even if that floor amount is exceeded, the deduction is good only to the extent of that excess. Moreover, if the taxpayer does finally surmount these limits to get a deduction with respect to a casualty to personal-use property, it will still only do him some good if his total itemized deductions exceed his standard deduction (see ¶ 7.03).[42]

This high floor limit on casualty losses to personal-use property will increase the pressure by taxpayers to show that a particular casualty loss was to business or investment property (deductible without regard to the 10% floor) rather than to personal-use property. Given the great stakes, vigorous litigation may be expected where the facts show a close case.

The allowance of a deduction for losses incurred in a trade or business or incurred in profit-seeking activity is consistent with the general theory of income taxation that a taxpayer should be allowed to deduct losses arising out of his business or investment activities.[43] Such business or profit-seeking activity losses, other than casualties, are discussed below.[44]

The allowance of a limited deduction for a casualty to personal-use property is an exception to the usual rule that no deductions are allowed with respect to property used by the taxpayer only for personal purposes. Thus, a taxpayer may not depreciate or take maintenance deductions with respect to property used for personal purposes, such as his home or personal-use car, lawnmower, television set, etc. However, should a casualty be sustained to any such items of personal-use property, a deduction would be allowed as

---

[42]   For more on these structural matters, see ¶ 6.01. See also ¶ 4.04(2), relating to losses on sales and other dispositions of property.

[43]   See ¶ 1.02(2).

[44]   See ¶ 7.01(5)(b).

discussed above, if aggregate personal casualties exceed 10% of adjusted gross income.

Apparently the theory underlying allowance of the limited deduction for casualties to personal-use property is that the major casualty deprives the taxpayer of disposable income in circumstances which did not yield him personal satisfaction or utility. Therefore, it could be argued, the major casualty loss is fairly deducted in arriving at a true measure of the taxpayer's taxable income. The contrary view would hold that even substantial casualty losses are part of the risks of living and it is not the place of the Internal Revenue Code to cure all the world's problems.[45] These countervailing considerations are probably what led Congress to arrive at the conclusion in 1982 that casualty losses to personal-use property could be deducted, but only to the extent they exceed 10% of adjusted gross income.

"Casualty" losses include losses from fire, storm, shipwreck, or other casualty, or from theft.[46] There is a refreshing paucity of cases litigating the question of what is a "fire," "storm," or "shipwreck," this being one of the few areas over the years on which taxpayers and the Service could agree. However, the litigation over what is an "other casualty" is ample indeed. There is also a fair amount of dispute over what is a "theft."[47]

After surveying a wide range of disparate cases, the Service attempted to get control of the question of what is an "other casualty" by ruling that "other casualties" must be analogous to fires, storms or shipwrecks. In particular, according to the Service, an "other casualty" must be "sudden" (as opposed to gradual or progressive); "unexpected" (as opposed to anticipated); and "unusual" (as opposed to commonly occurring).[48] Earthquakes and floods have been found to be casualties.[49] Losses from a severe drought may constitute a casualty.[50] Gradual deterioration from rust or dutch elm disease is not sufficiently sudden to be a casualty.[51] There was an epic battle with regard to termite damage, the Service finally ruling that the

---

[45] See ¶ 1.02(2)(b), relating to the comprehensive tax base and (c) relating to tax expenditures.

[46] See § 165(c)(3).

[47] See James A. Wilson, 43 T.C.M. 699 (1982) (theft occurred when live-in girlfriend of taxpayer stole $10,000 necklace and other articles from him, even though he did not press charges).

[48] Rev.Rul. 72–592, 1972–2 C.B. 101.

[49] Grant v. Commissioner, 30 B.T.A. 1028, 1934 WL 342 (1934); Rev.Rul. 76–134, 1976–1 C.B. 54.

[50] Ruecker, 41 T.C.M. 1587 (1981) (death of lawn and shrubbery on account of strict water rationing rules arising from a drought held to be a casualty; not clear if the fact if the area was declared a federal disaster area was essential to the decision).

[51] Appleman v. United States, 338 F.2d 729 (7th Cir.1964), cert. denied 380 U.S. 956, 85 S.Ct. 1090, 13 L.Ed.2d 972 (1965) (Dutch elm).

dietary propensities of termites are such that the damage they cause occurs too gradually to constitute a casualty.[52]

Casualties need not arise only from the vagaries of weather, fire and pestilence; they may also arise from more mundane events or even the taxpayer's own actions. Thus, in the latest of a surprisingly long line of cases in which husbands somehow manage to destroy their wives' diamond rings, it has been held that a husband accidentally throwing his wife's diamond ring down a garbage disposal was a casualty.[53] Damage to taxpayer's automobile arising even from taxpayer's own faulty driving (so long as it is not due to the willful act or willful negligence of the taxpayer) can constitute a casualty.[54]

But what happens if your property remains unharmed but your surroundings change, causing your property to lose value? For example, what if a mudslide stops at your property line, but the surrounding area is devastated. Or, what if you live next O.J. Simpson's house, and the attention surrounding the murder of Nicole Simpson causes your home to be devalued? The answer appears to depend where you live.

In *Chamales v. Commissioner*,[55] taxpayers lived near O.J. Simpson's house. They claimed that their home lost value due to the large crowds that gathered outside his home. A real estate agent estimated that their home decreased in value by between 30 to 40 percent. Taxpayers used the 30 percent figure and argued that they were entitled to a casualty loss of that amount. The taxpayers made this claim even though they made substantial improvements to the house costing over $1,000,000.

The court didn't buy it and sent the taxpayers home. It did, however, determine that penalties were not warranted. In reaching its conclusion, the Tax Court looked to the law in the Ninth Circuit. The Ninth Circuit has determined that there is not a casualty loss unless there is actual physical damage or abandonment by physical

---

[52]   Rev.Rul. 63–232, 1963–2, C.B. 97 (citing the leading authority Our Enemy the Termite, by T.E. Snyder); compare Herbert H. Nelson, 27 T.C.M. 158 (1968) (attack of voracious beetles a casualty); Rev.Rul. 79–174, 1979–1 C.B. 99 (same).

[53]   Carpenter, 25 T.C.M. 1186 (1966); See also John P. White, 48 T.C. 430 (1967) (acq.) (accidental slamming of a car door on wife's hand, breaking her ring and causing her to lose the stone, a casualty); but see Keenan v. Bowers, 91 F.Supp. 771 (E.D.S.C.1950) (flushing of wife's diamond ring down the toilet not a casualty); compare Kielts, 42 T.C.M. 238 (1981) (loss of 2.47 carat diamond from setting of ring while going about daily chores a casualty because violent blow of which taxpayer was unaware had apparently dislodged the stone).

[54]   Reg. § 1.165–7(a)(3); see also Shearer v. Anderson, 16 F.2d 995 (2d Cir.1927).

[55]   79 T.C.M. 1428 (2000).

necessity. The Tax Court reasoned that the taxpayers here had no such physical damage.

The Eleventh Circuit, however, has taken a different approach.[56] The Eleventh Circuit does not require physical damage but instead looks to see if there is a permanent devaluation due to the casualty.[57] Even under this standard, however, the Chamales's would have a hard time arguing that their property was permanently devalued.

"Theft" as a type of casualty loss has been broadly defined by the Regulations to include, but not necessarily be limited to, larceny, embezzlement, and robbery.[58] The difference between thefts and other casualties is that thefts are deductible in the year when discovered, whereas fire, storm, shipwreck, or "other casualties" are deductible in the year when sustained.[59]

The rule for determining the amount of the deduction on a casualty loss is as follows: taxpayer may deduct the lesser of (a) his basis in the property or (b) the decline in the fair market value of the property due to the casualty.[60] The amount so calculated is subject to the $100 and 10%-of-adjusted-gross-income limits discussed above where the casualty is to personal-use property.[61] If the casualty is to property used in a trade or business or property held for the production of income, and the property is totally destroyed, then the deductible loss is the amount of the basis regardless of whether the fair market value is greater or less than the basis.[62] This more liberal treatment of business property reflects the fact that business property is often subject to the allowance for depreciation and therefore the basis will be recoverable by the taxpayer even if there is never a casualty. If property is converted from personal to business or profit-seeking use before the casualty, the basis for use in computing the casualty loss is the lesser of the property's adjusted basis in the taxpayer's hands or the fair market value of the property at the time of the conversion.[63]

If a casualty does not completely destroy the property, the same principles apply, with minor modifications. The amount of the

[56]   Finkbohner v. United States, 788 F.2d 723 (11th Cir.1986) (lots demolished due to flood and authorities determined that several of the home could not be rebuilt. The resulting devaluation in the existing homes was a casualty that could be deducted as a casualty loss.).

[57]   Id. at 727.

[58]   Reg. § 1.165–8(d).

[59]   Section 165(e) (thefts); § 165(a).

[60]   Reg. § 1.165–7(b)(1).

[61]   Sections 165(c)(3), and (h).

[62]   Reg. § 1.165–7(b) (flush language).

[63]   Reg. § 1.165–7(a)(5).

casualty is still the lesser of the property's adjusted basis or the decline in the fair market value of the property.[64]

> **Example:** An automobile used in business has a basis of $3,600 in taxpayer's hands and a fair market value of $2,000. The automobile is damaged in an accident and after the accident it has a fair market value of $1,500. The amount of the casualty loss is $500 (the lesser of the decline in fair market value or the adjusted basis of the property).[65]

The amount of any deduction taken as a casualty loss on property which is not completely destroyed reduces the basis by the amount deducted.[66]

Where several related types of property are damaged by a casualty, the Regulations take two different approaches, depending on whether the property is used in a trade or business or profit-seeking activity on the one hand, and used for personal purposes on the other. Thus, for example, if damage by a casualty has occurred to a building and ornamental or fruit trees all used in the trade or business, the computation of the amount of the deductible casualty is made by reference to each individual type of property and separate losses are determined for the building and the trees. However, if the building and the trees are used for personal purposes, the value of the building and trees and the bases of the building and trees are aggregated and an overall computation is made, using the rule discussed above to ascertain the amount of the deductible casualty.[67]

Fair market value of property before and after the casualty must generally be ascertained by competent appraisal.[68] The cost of repairs is evidence, but not dispositive, of the question of the loss of value on account of the casualty.[69]

---

[64] This approach will be taken with respect to property used in the taxpayer's trade or business or profit-seeking activity, as well as personal-use property. The rule that amount of a loss is always the adjusted basis for business property only holds where the business property is completely destroyed, Reg. § 1.165–7(b)(1) (flush language).

[65] See Reg. § 1.165–7(b)(3). Example (1). This example in the text assumes no compensation by insurance. Also if the automobile were personal-use property, the $100 floor and the 10% of adjusted gross income limit would have to be applied after making this computation to determine how much (if any) of this loss is deductible.

[66] Like depreciation, this is an adjustment to basis. § 1016(a)(1).

[67] Reg. § 1.165–7(b)(2)(i) and (ii), again subject to the $100 and 10% limits.

[68] Reg. § 1.165–7(a)(2)(i).

[69] Reg. § 1.165–7(a)(2)(ii). The appraisal fees would be deductible as expenses of determining a tax liability, § 212(3); Blackburn, 44 T.C.M. 1124 (1982) (repair costs allowed as a measure of damages only if repairs are made).

To the extent taxpayer is compensated by insurance for his loss, the amount of the casualty will not be deductible.[70] Thus, in the example above, where the taxpayer's loss was $500, if he had received insurance proceeds of $300, his deductible loss would only be $200. Indeed, it is quite possible that the taxpayer would receive insurance compensation in an amount greater than his adjusted basis for the property, in which case the taxpayer does not have a casualty loss, but a casualty gain.

> **Example:** Taxpayer owns a painting with a cost basis of $5,000. It has a fair market value of $25,000. It is destroyed by a fire and the taxpayer receives insurance proceeds of $15,000. The taxpayer has a $10,000 gain on the casualty. The fact that the insurance proceeds did not compensate him fully for his loss with respect to the fair market value of the property is irrelevant. The appreciation in the value of the painting was never taken into the taxpayer's income.[71]

Where the taxpayer's loss is deductible in one year and he anticipates an insurance recovery in the following year, he may deduct the loss in the year the casualty is sustained only to the extent (if at all) it exceeds the likely recovery.[72] If a taxpayer declines to press a claim for fear that his insurance rates will rise, he may deduct his loss, even though had he pressed his claim he would have been compensated in full.[73]

(b) Other Losses

Losses other than casualty losses are only deductible if they are attributable to the taxpayer's trade or business or profit-seeking activity.[74] The allowance of a deduction for business losses relates primarily to losses on sales of property. But a business loss can arise

---

[70]   Section 165(a).

[71]   For the characterization of gains and losses on casualties, see § 1231, discussed at ¶ 4.06(3)(a)(iv). In particular, this transaction would go into the "casualty pot." If it were alone there, it would go into the "main pot." If it were alone there, it would come out a capital gain subject to the various favorable capital gain rules, see ¶ 4.06(2)(b)(i). On this transaction there would be a question whether it still retains its character as a "collectible," thus in the 28% group, or whether it is adjusted net capital gain, in the 15% rate group.

The legal fees and other expenses incurred in securing compensation for the loss are considered part of the loss, Spectre, 25 T.C.M. 519 (1966).

[72]   Reg. § 1.165–1(d)(2)(i), also providing that the balance of the loss may be deducted only upon the taxpayer establishing by objective evidence, such as the execution of a release, that he has abandoned the insurance claim.

[73]   Hills v. Commissioner, 691 F.2d 997 (11th Cir.1982), reh'g denied 697 F.2d 1094 (1983) (discussion of other authorities); contra Bartlett v. United States, 397 F.Supp. 216 (D.Md.1975) and Axelrod, 56 T.C. 248 (1971).

[74]   Section 165(c).

from other transactions, such as a breach of contract that goes uncompensated. The loss deduction should not be confused with the case where a business is running operating losses, which are produced by other deductions, such as the deduction for ordinary and necessary business expenses,[75] depreciation,[76] or bad debts,[77] etc. A net operating loss so produced has significance in that it may be carried over to other years to be deducted against taxable income in those other years.[78]

The disallowance of losses from sales of personal-use property is of major structural significance in the Code. This rule wipes out a raft of losses frequently undergone by taxpayers. For example, one virtually always has a loss on the sale of one's personal automobile. This loss is not deductible under § 165(c)(3). The sale of household effects at a garage sale for far less than their original cost also does not give rise to a deduction for the same reason. And most significantly, loss on sale of one's house is not deductible.[79] Before one bemoans the fact of the disallowance of these losses, bear in mind that if these losses, were allowed to all taxpayers, then tax rates would have to be higher to make up for the lost revenue. (There is, as has often been noted, no free lunch.)

It is at the borderline between non-deductible losses on personal use of property and deductible losses on business or investment use that we find litigation tension. This tension might particularly be expected to occur where large losses have occurred. One of the toughest areas here is losses on residential real estate that has also been used for investment or business purposes. Taxpayers of course may well have a mixed motive in buying residential real estate. They may well think about the potential for appreciation when they buy their home. If the taxpayer uses the property solely as a principal residence, the fact that taxpayer had profit potential also in mind would not be enough to sustain a deduction if the property were later sold for a loss. If some business or investment use is made of the property, the chances are better, but success is not guaranteed.[80]

---

[75]   Section 162(a).

[76]   Sections 167, 168.

[77]   Section 166. Losses on sales of property deductible under § 165 may also, of course, contribute to producing a net operating loss.

[78]   Section 172; see Davies, "The Net Operating Loss Deduction: Inequity Among Taxpayers," 10 Tax Advisor, 530 (1979).

[79]   Counterbalanced by the fact that gain up to $250,000 ($500,000 for married couples) is not taxed, see § 121 and ¶ 4.04(5).

[80]   See Gevirtz v. Commissioner, 123 F.2d 707 (2d Cir.1941) (loss deduction denied when vacant land purchased to construct apartment buildings in fact used for construction of a large personal residence); Weir v. Commissioner, 109 F.2d 996 (3d Cir.1940), cert. denied 310 U.S. 637, 60 S.Ct. 1080, 84 L.Ed. 1406 (1940) (loss on sale

In allowing losses on sales of business and investment property to be deducted, the loss deduction of § 165(a) plays an integral part in the scheme for taxing gains and losses on the sales and other dispositions of property, discussed at ¶ 4.04. In addition to losses on sales and other dispositions of property, a loss may be sustained as a result of a casualty, discussed at ¶ 7.01(5)(a). A deductible loss under § 165(a) may also arise if securities held by the taxpayer become worthless during the taxable year, discussed at ¶ 7.01(6).

Abandonment of business or investment property will also give rise to a deductible loss under § 165(a). Since abandonment is not a sale or exchange, the loss on abandonment, even of a capital asset, is deductible against ordinary income without regard to the restrictions that attend capital losses.[81]

The major areas of dispute with respect to abandonment are (1) whether the property has been abandoned or sold, given the more favorable treatment to taxpayers of abandonment[82] and (2) whether property has been abandoned or is just temporarily not being used by the taxpayer.[83] As with casualty losses, other losses otherwise deductible may only be deducted to the extent not compensated for by insurance or otherwise.[84]

Losses from gambling transactions are allowed only to the extent of gains from such transactions.[85] This appears at first blush to be a relatively liberal treatment of gambling losses; since most gamblers are not engaged in a trade or business or even profit-seeking activity but rather are simply indulging in personal recreation—for which ordinarily no deduction is allowed whatsoever. However, this relatively liberal treatment of gambling losses is balanced by the fact that any net income from gambling is taxable.[86]

---

of shares in coop apartment building in which taxpayer lived held deductible because the shares produced taxable dividend income).

[81]   See ¶ 4.06(2)(b)(ii). Abandonment of depreciable property used in the taxpayer's trade or business similarly does not come within § 1231 because it is not a sale or exchange, and therefore will not run the risk of being treated as a capital loss. See ¶ 4.06(3)(a)(iv).

[82]   Cf. Bloomington Coca-Cola Bottling Co. v. Commissioner, 189 F.2d 14 (7th Cir.1951) (plant held sold rather than abandoned).

[83]   See Reg. § 1.165–2(a). The Regulations provide rules regarding a loss deduction on account of the demolition of buildings, Reg. § 1.165–3.

[84]   Section 165(a).

[85]   Section 165(d).

[86]   Cf. ¶¶ 6.03(3), 3.13(3). See generally Epstein, "The Consumption and Loss of Personal Property and the Internal Revenue Code," 23 Stanf.L.Rev. 454 (1971).

(6) Bad Debts and Worthless Securities: Whipple

(a) Bad Debts

Any debt which becomes worthless during the taxable year is deductible, whether or not the debt arises out of the taxpayer's trade or business, profit-seeking activity, or personal activities.[87] In thus allowing a deduction for a bad debt which arises out of personal activity—such as a loan to a family member—this rule is surprisingly liberal.

As with the deductions for interest, taxes, and casualties and other losses, if the bad debt is attributable to the taxpayer's trade or business or to profit-seeking activity that produces rental or royalty income, it is allowed as a deduction from gross income in arriving at adjusted gross income ("above the line").[88] If the bad debt does not meet these tests, it will be allowed as an itemized deduction ("below the line"), and therefore will only benefit the taxpayer to the extent he has excess itemized deductions.

A major area of dispute is whether the taxpayer has a true indebtedness which can be deducted at all. This is particularly troublesome where the debt is owed to members of the family. While there may be a presumption that intra-family transfers are gifts rather than loans, that presumption may be rebutted if there is a real expectation of repayment and intention to enforce the collection of the indebtedness.[89] If amounts are invested with the expectation they will be returned, with a profit, on the happening of some contingency—such as the success of a business venture—and the contingency does not occur, then the taxpayer has a loss, deductible under § 165, rather than a bad debt.[90] If the transaction arises out of personal activities, the taxpayer is better off having it characterized as a bad debt rather than a loss since losses from personal activities are not deductible under § 165.[91]

If the transaction arises out of profit-seeking activity, the taxpayer is better off having it characterized as a loss, since losses incurred in connection with profit-seeking activities are deductible in

---

[87] Section 166(a).

[88] Section 62; See ¶ 6.01 for further discussion of structural issues.

[89] Van Anda's Estate, 12 T.C. 1158 (1949), aff'd per curiam 192 F.2d 391 (2d Cir.1951) (on facts, no valid debt to wife); compare T. Albert White, 30 T.C.M. 64 (1971) (transfer to child created a debt although deduction disallowed because the debt was not worthless).

[90] See Canelo, 53 T.C. 217 (1969), aff'd per curiam 447 F.2d 484 (9th Cir.1971) (attorney's payment of litigation costs which would be reimbursed on successful termination of litigation; held was not a debt).

[91] See ¶ 7.01(5)(b).

full;[92] whereas bad debts incurred in profit-seeking activities are generally restricted to being deducted as a short-term capital loss.[93] If the transaction arises out of the taxpayer's trade or business, it will not matter whether it is characterized as a loss or a bad debt, since both are deductible in full.[94]

The amount allowed as the deduction on a bad debt is the basis of the debt.[95] This will be the amount of money loaned, if the taxpayer is the original creditor. If the taxpayer acquired the debt by purchase, the basis will, of course, be the amount he paid to acquire the obligation—which could be less or more than its face amount. Similarly, if the taxpayer acquires the debt by gift or inheritance, the appropriate basis rule will apply.

There is a great deal of litigation concerning the tax year that a debt becomes worthless so that it may be deducted.[96] The Service will play its own version of three-card monte with the taxpayer in forcing him to pick the correct year in which the debt became worthless while the spectre of the running of the statute of limitations hangs over the taxpayer's head.[97] A wide variety of factors may be used to indicate that a debt has become worthless: insolvency of the debtor, bankruptcy, refusal to pay, death, and subordination.[98]

The taxpayer may elect to charge off part of a debt where it becomes clear that the debt will not be fully paid.[99] The *pas de deux* between the taxpayer and the Service is to a somewhat different tempo in the case of partially worthless debts. The taxpayer has somewhat more control as an initial matter since he may elect to take a deduction for partial worthlessness by charging off the unrecoverable amount on his records.[100] However, since it is not desirable to give the taxpayer unfettered discretion as to when he

---

[92] Section 165(c).

[93] Section 166(d) and see discussion below.

[94] Sections 165(c), 166(a).

[95] Section 166(b).

[96] The problems here are acknowledged by § 6511(d)(1) which provides for a seven-year statute of limitations for claims relating to bad debts and worthless securities, instead of the usual three years.

[97] See Denver & Rio Grande Western R. Co. v. Commissioner, 279 F.2d 368 (10th Cir.1960) (taxpayer failed to prove the year in which a debt became worthless).

[98] See e.g., Zeeman v. United States, 275 F.Supp. 235 (S.D.N.Y.1967), modified and remanded 395 F.2d 861 (2d Cir.1968); Schultz, 30 T.C. 256 (1958), rev'd on other grounds 278 F.2d 927 (5th Cir.1960) (running of statute of limitations not dispositive); Los Angeles Shipbuilding & Drydock Corp. v. United States, 289 F.2d 222 (9th Cir.1961).

[99] Section 166(a)(2).

[100] Reg. § 1.166–3(a)(2)(i).

decides to take a deduction for partial worthlessness, the Service must be satisfied that the debt has become partially worthless.[101]

Bad debts which are deducted and then subsequently paid must be taken into income pursuant to tax-benefit principles discussed in Chapter 9.[102]

If a nonbusiness debt becomes worthless during the year the taxpayer is entitled to only treat it as a short-term capital loss.[103] A nonbusiness debt is a debt incurred in connection with profit-seeking activity of the taxpayer, or personal activity of the taxpayer. It is not a debt incurred with respect to the trade or business of the taxpayer.[104] This treatment of nonbusiness bad debts is restrictive in the sense that a taxpayer may only claim them as a short-term capital loss; but the treatment is liberal in the sense that taxpayers may take a deduction at all for a debt which may be incurred solely with respect to personal activities—so long as the debt is bona fide.[105] Nonbusiness bad debts are also unattractive in that they may not be deducted as partially worthless, and they may not be treated by reserves.[106]

Given that business bad debts are deductible in full, whereas nonbusiness bad debts may only be deducted as a short-term capital loss, it is not surprising that there has been a substantial amount of litigation as to whether a particular debt is business or nonbusiness. The leading case in this area is *Whipple*.

WHIPPLE V. COMMISSIONER[107]

Facts: A. J. Whipple was a former construction supervisor turned entrepreneur who started numerous partnerships and corporations, including the Mission Orange Bottling Company. He owned approximately 80% of the outstanding shares of the Bottling Company when he entered into an arrangement with the Mission Dry Corporation entitling him to produce, bottle, distribute, and sell Mission beverages in various counties in Texas. The taxpayer made a number of cash advances to the company so the company could pay

---

[101] Section 166(a)(2); Reg. § 1.166–3(a)(2)(i) and (iii). See also Brimberry v. Commissioner, 588 F.2d 975 (5th Cir.1979) (in light of the Service's discretion to disallow election for partial worthlessness, taxpayer has a heavier burden of proof than in the case of total worthlessness).

[102] Where the taxpayer is using a reserves method, it may be necessary to take unused reserves back into income, where the taxpayer goes out of business.

[103] Section 166(d).

[104] Section 166(d)(2).

[105] For the restrictions applicable to short-term capital losses, see ¶ 4.06(2)(b)(ii).

[106] Section 166(d)(1)(A).

[107] 373 U.S. 193, 83 S.Ct. 1168, 10 L.Ed.2d 288 (1963), reh'g denied 374 U.S. 858, 83 S.Ct. 1863, 10 L.Ed.2d 1082 (1963).

creditors. Ultimately the company owed the taxpayer $56,975. The Bottling Company shut down its operations, and the debts became worthless.

Question: Is the $56,975 loss undergone by Whipple deductible as a "trade or business" bad debt under § 166(a) (giving rise to a full ordinary income deduction) or a nonbusiness bad debt under § 166(d) (giving rise to a very limited capital loss deduction).

Taxpayer's argument: His many activities in promoting business constituted a trade or business. Hence the loss was deducted in full as arising out of a trade or business.

Held: The loss did not arise from a trade or business. Any potential gains would have been a return on his investment and the deduction is therefore limited to a nonbusiness bad debt. It is well-established that full-time service to a corporation does not alone amount to a trade or business. That being the case, full-time service to many corporations also cannot constitute a trade or business. Taxpayer might have had an argument if he were developing these businesses for subsequent sale to others, but he was not.

Comment: Presumably taxpayer was reporting the gains on the sale of others of his other business ventures as capital gains. Thus he apparently sought the best of all worlds: capital gains on his gains and ordinary losses on his losses. This favorable treatment would give tax incentives to promoters of small businesses—which may be what we want to do. But it is obviously up to Congress to make that decision.

If you find *Whipple* a little frustrating, bear in mind that the distinction between capital gains and losses and ordinary gains and losses is fundamentally arbitrary. See the discussion in Chapter 4. *Whipple* can be viewed as another example of a case (in the loss area) of drawing that arbitrary line.[108]

Another issue regarding the bad debt deduction is whether a person actually has a basis in the debt that they seek to deduct. As we discussed in ¶ 6.02(14), alimony is normally deductible by the payor and includible in income of the payee, and child support is usually not deductible by the payor and not includible in income. But what happens when a person obligated to pay child support fails to do so? Some taxpayers have claimed that the failure to pay child

---

[108] See also United States v. Generes, 405 U.S. 93, 92 S.Ct. 827, 31 L.Ed.2d 62 (1972), reh'g denied 405 U.S. 1033, 92 S.Ct. 1274, 31 L.Ed.2d 491 (1972) (loans by an employee to a family corporation created nonbusiness debt where the taxpayer could not show that his dominant motive in making the loan was protection of his job). See also Reg. § 1.166–9, dealing with the deductibility of losses of guarantors, endorsers, and indemnitors; Reg. § 1.166–6 dealing with treatment of the mortgagee or pledgee on the sale of mortgaged or pledged property.

support should result in a bad debt deduction to the payee, and should be discharge of indebtedness income to the payor.

There are several structural problems with this theory, but it is somewhat appealing. The main problem is that the recipient spouse has no basis in the debt. She has not paid out anything to anyone.[109] Someone simply has a legal duty to pay her money.

In *Diez-Arguelles v. Commissioner*,[110] Christina Diez-Arguelles argued that she was entitled to a bad debt deduction for money her husband failed to pay in child support. Ms. Diez-Arguelles introduced evidenced that she had spent more than the child support amount on her children and claimed that this established a basis in the debt. The Tax Court rejected Ms. Diez-Arguelles's argument holding that the amount she paid to her children did not create basis in her debt.

Although this seems like the correct result, there does appear to be some justice in letting Ms. Diez-Arguelles deduct a bad debt and requiring Mr. Diez-Arguelles to include that amount in income. It does, however, pose some administrative problems for the IRS.

One of the great aspects of tax law is that there is almost always a Member of Congress willing to run with a good idea. Senators Boxer and Snowe in the Senate and Congressman Cox in the House introduced bills in the 107th Congress that would allow a bad debt deduction for unpaid child support and would require the deadbeat spouse to include the amount of the unpaid obligation in income.[111]

(b) Worthless Securities

If a security which is a capital asset becomes worthless during the taxable year, the resulting loss is treated as a sale or exchange on the last day of the taxable year of a capital asset.[112] A "security" for these purposes means a share of stock or right to receive a share of stock in a corporation, or a bond, debenture, note or other evidence of indebtedness issued by a corporation or by a government, with interest coupons or in registered form.[113]

The artificial holding period, extended to the end of the year in which the security becomes worthless, obviates the necessity of determining on what day of the taxable year the security became worthless (a great help in that it is usually difficult enough to

---

[109] See Long v. Commissioner, 35 B.T.A. 479 (1937), aff'd, 96 F.2d 270 (9th Cir.1938).

[110] 48 T.C.M. 496 (1984).

[111] See S. 2732, 107th Cong., 2d Sess. (2002); H.R. 5130, 107th Cong., 2d Sess. (2002).

[112] Section 165(g).

[113] Section 165(g)(2).

determine in what year a security became worthless let alone what day). Worthless securities are therefore treated less attractively than business bad debts, in that they wind up being capital losses.[114] This relatively unattractive treatment of worthless securities may lead taxpayers to try to assert that their loss on a worthless evidence of indebtedness should be treated under the business bad debt rule.[115] However, lest there be any doubt about it, the statute explicitly provides that the bad debt rule shall not apply to a debt which is evidenced by a security as defined under the worthless security rules.[116]

Determining when a security has become worthless presents the same problems as determining when a debt has become worthless.[117] It has been held that a taxpayer does not have to be "an incorrigible optimist" and wait until the last possible moment to deduct an investment as worthless; however, the taxpayer cannot be "a Stygian pessimist" and deduct the investment at the first sign of difficulty. This literary mouthful is not particularly helpful in the great mass of cases in which there is a significant amount of debtor difficulty but taxpayer may very well expect to be paid on his debt.[118] In such cases, it is exceedingly difficult to determine in which year the security finally becomes worthless.[119]

(7) Medical Expenses: Ochs

Amounts paid for medical care and medical insurance of the taxpayer, his spouse, and dependents are allowed as a deduction, to the extent uncompensated for by insurance or otherwise. A major barrier to getting any benefit from this deduction is that expenses for medical care are only deductible to the extent they exceed 7½% of the taxpayer's adjusted gross income. "Medical care" for these purposes covers a wide variety of medical and dental treatments and medicaments. The term is sufficiently vague to invite dispute, and taxpayers have not been too ill to litigate the matter extensively with the Service. In particular, the Code provides that the term "medical care" means amounts paid "for the diagnosis, cure, mitigation,

---

[114] For the disadvantage of capital losses, see ¶ 4.06(2)(b)(ii).

[115] See ¶ 7.01(6)(a).

[116] Section 166(e).

[117] United States v. S.S. White Dental Manufacturing Co., 274 U.S. 398, 403, 47 S.Ct. 598, 600, 71 L.Ed. 1120 (1927).

[118] Ruppert v. United States, 22 F.Supp. 428, 431 (Ct.Cl.1938), cert. denied 305 U.S. 630, 59 S.Ct. 94, 83 L.Ed. 404 (1938).

[119] See Morton v. Commissioner, 38 B.T.A. 1270, 1938 WL 165 (1938) (nonacq.), aff'd 112 F.2d 320 (7th Cir.1940) (extensive discussion); Reg. § 1.165–5(b) and (c); Austin Co., 71 T.C. 955 (1979) (sale of assets and liquidation of debtor supported claim of worthlessness). See generally Natbony, "Worthlessness, Debt-Equity, and Related Problems," 32 Hastings L.J. 1407 (1981).

treatment or prevention of disease, or for the purpose of affecting any structure or function of the body; for transportation primarily for and essential to medical care referred to above; or for insurance covering medical care."[120] Closely related to this ability to deduct premiums for health insurance is the fact that insurance premiums paid by an employer are excluded from an employee's gross income.[121] The exclusion of premiums if paid by the employer does not have to run the daunting gauntlet of the 7½% floor. Thus the message from the statute is that employer-financed health insurance is favored over employee-financed. This could be understandable as a paternalistic nudge to encourage expenditures on health insurance.[122] The Regulations further elaborate the definition of "medical care."[123]

> "Amounts paid for operations or treatments affecting any portion of the body including obstetrical expenses and expenses of therapy or X-ray treatments are deemed to be for the purpose of affecting any structure or function of the body and are therefore paid for medical care. Amounts expended for illegal operations or treatments are not deductible. Deductions for expenditures for medical care allowable under Section 213 will be confined strictly to expenses incurred primarily for the prevention or alleviation of a physical or mental defect or illness. Thus, payments for the following are payments for medical care: hospital services, nursing services (including nurses board where paid by the taxpayer), medical, laboratory, surgical, dental and other diagnostic and healing services, X-rays,

---

[120] Section 213(e)(1). Reg. § 1.213–1(e)(1); Elective cosmetic surgery is not deductible as a medical expense. See Section 213(e)(1). Reg. § 1.213–1(e)(1)(ii). See also Edward A. Havey, 12 T.C. 409 (1949) (travel to the shore and Arizona not deductible although doctor recommended the trips for the taxpayer's health; the trips were not specifically linked with a change of climate). Compare with Rev.Rul. 76–332, 1976–2 C.B. 81 (cosmetic surgery deductible; Congress has since overturned this); Rev.Rul. 73–201, 1973–1 C.B. 140 (legal abortions and vasectomies deductible); Reg. § 1.213–1(e)(1)(iii) (allowing expenditures which would ordinarily be treated as non-deductible capital outlays to be immediately deductible if they qualify as a medical expense, providing the examples of eyeglasses, seeing eye dog, artificial teeth and limbs, a wheelchair, crutches, an inclinator or an air conditioner which is detachable from the property and purchased only for the use of a sick person).

In the case of a capital expenditure, which, unlike the items described above, effects a permanent improvement to the property—such as a swimming pool that otherwise is deductible as a medical expense because of taxpayer's heart disease—the deduction is allowed to the extent the cost of the improvement exceeds the increase in value (if any) of the property as a result of the improvement. To the extent that, because of these rules, the cost of the improvement is not deductible, it will be added to the taxpayer's cost basis of his property); see Feld, "Abortion To Aging: Problems of Definition in the Medical Expense Tax Deduction," 58 B.U.L.Rev. 165 (1978).

[121] Section 106.

[122] Section 213(d)(1).

[123] Section 213(d)(9).

medicine and drugs ... artificial teeth or limbs, and ambulance hire. However, an expenditure which is merely beneficial to the general health of an individual such as an expenditure for a vacation, is not an expenditure for medical care."[124]

If the taxpayer regularly runs significant medical expenses approaching or exceeding the 7½% floor each year, he would be well advised to, if possible, put off payment of medical expenses for one year so as to bunch two or more years' deductible expenses into a single year for the purpose of exceeding the 7½% floor.

The leading case of *Ochs* illustrates the kind of borderline problem that can arise in the medical deduction area. This case came before a distinguished panel of the Second Circuit that included Augustus Hand and Jerome Frank.

OCHS V. COMMISSIONER[125]

Facts: Helen Ochs was diagnosed with cancer. After surgery, she was unable to speak above a whisper, making it very difficult for her to communicate and care for her two children, ages four and six. On the recommendation of the operating surgeon, Helen and her husband Samuel decided to put their two children in boarding school at a cost of approximately $1,456. The surgeon stated that if the children were not separated from their mother, then her cancer could reappear. During the time that the children were in boarding school, Samuel's income was between $5,000 and $6,000.

Question: Are the expenses of sending the children to school deductible as a medical expense?

Taxpayer's argument: It is medically necessary for wife to recover to send the children away from school.

Held: Children's schooling expenses were nondeductible family expenses under § 262.

Dissent by Judge Frank: This leader of the "legal realism" school asserted that the deduction should be allowed. Congress never thought of this problem when it enacted the medical expense deduction. If the wife were sent away to a sanitarium, the expense would be deductible. This is a meaningless distinction. "The cure ought to be the doctor's business, not the Commissioner's ... "

---

[124] Reg. § 1.213–1(e)(1)(ii). Cf. Rose C. France, 40 T.C.M. 508 (1980), aff'd per curiam 690 F.2d 68 (6th Cir.1982) (no medical expense deduction for dance lessons to 66-year-old widow; though the Service won't dance, it will call the tune).

[125] 195 F.2d 692 (2d Cir.1952), cert. denied, 344 U.S. 827, 73 S.Ct. 28, 97 L.Ed. 643 (1952).

Comment: It was taken for granted by all that in order to raise young children you need to be able to scream.

Medical expenses are inherently personal. But the statute allows a deduction for "medical care," defined as an expense for the "cure, mitigation, treatment or prevention of disease."[126] The expenses in *Ochs* certainly seem to fall within that definition. One way to interpret the court's opinion is to say that the expenditures were for "medical care" but that § 213 is overridden by § 262's disallowance of personal expenditures.

This holding is consistent with the idea, discussed in Chapters One and Two, that the imputed income of taxpayers' household services which they do for themselves is not taxed. It is also the case that if taxpayers pay for someone else to perform those services that payment is not deductible. Thus, in this particular situation the Code provides a disincentive for a non-working spouse to obtain paid employment. This case does nothing to change that even though the taxpayers had a medical necessity for incurring the child care expenses.

But there seems to be some wiggle room in this area. In Revenue Ruling 64–273,[127] the IRS concluded that amounts paid to a person to accompany a blind child through the school day were an expense for medical care under section 213. The Service noted that Regulation 1.213–1(e)(1)(ii) provides for the deduction of expenditures for medical care that is "incurred primarily for the prevention or alleviation of a physical or mental defect or illness." Expenses for a seeing eye dog are paid primarily for the prevention or alleviation of a physical defect.[128] The Service concluded that the sole purpose of having someone accompany the child was to alleviate the child's physical defect of blindness.[129]

If this is so, then why isn't the expense in *Ochs* designed to alleviate her condition? Or what if you have a personal assistant to help you in your home because you do not have use of your arms and legs? Is the cost of a personal assistant a personal expense or a medical one?

As an aside, the Service has recently ruled that the cost of weight-loss programs are deductible under § 213 when they are for

---

[126]   Section 213(d).

[127]   1964–1 C.B. 121, 1964 WL 12756 (IRS RRU).

[128]   Citing Rev.Rul. 57–461, 1957–2 C.B. 116.

[129]   See also Rev.Rul. 75–328, 1975–2 C.B. 88. The amount that the cost of braille books exceeds the cost of regular books is deductible as a medical expense.

the treatment of a specific disease or ailment that is diagnosed by a physician.[130]

As pointed out above, the limit imposed on the amounts paid for medical care which can be deducted is that it is only deductible to the extent it exceeds 7½% of the taxpayer's adjusted gross income.[131] The effect of this very high floor is that few people will take the medical expense deduction. Generally, only very wealthy, ill people who carry no health insurance will be taking this deduction.

The only drug expenditures that qualify for deduction are expenditures for prescription drugs and insulin.[132]

Medical expenses cannot be deducted if they are compensated for by insurance or otherwise, and this rule holds true even if the taxpayer is not reimbursed in the same year in which he pays his medical expenses. If the taxpayer does take a deduction for payment of medical expenses in one year (because, perhaps, it is unclear whether he will be reimbursed), reimbursement of those expenses in the following year must be included in his income to the extent that the expenses were allowed to be deducted under the rules of § 213.[133]

As indicated above, the taxpayer may deduct expenses for medical care of his dependents.[134] Medical expenses are considered support in ascertaining whether the taxpayer has met the support tests for determining dependency status.[135]

As a policy matter, allowing medical expenses to be deducted can be criticized as an erosion of the comprehensive tax base. The medical expense deduction can be defended on the ground that medical expenses reduce the taxpayer's discretionary income to be spent on consumption that increases his personal satisfaction.[136] In terms of tax expenditure analysis, the medical expense deduction is less vulnerable than other itemized deductions to criticism that it favors higher-bracket taxpayers, because of the 7½% percent floor.[137]

Our current system, however, is grossly inequitable. Employees may receive employer-provided medical care tax free and may even

---

[130] Rev.Rul. 2002–19.

[131] Section 213(a).

[132] Section 213(b).

[133] Reg. § 1.213–1(g)(3)(ii). The approach of the Regulations here is to attribute the reimbursed amounts first to the portion of the medical expenses that were deductible, rather than to the amounts that were nondeductible because of the five-percent floor.

[134] See ¶ 7.04 for discussion of dependents.

[135] Reg. § 1.152–1(a)(2)(i). See also § 152(a).

[136] See ¶ 1.03(2)(b).

[137] See ¶ 1.03(2)(c). See also Andrews, "Personal Deductions in An Ideal Income Tax," 86 Harv.L.Rev. 309 (1972); Newman, "The Medical Expense Deduction: A Preliminary Postmortem," 53 So.Calif.L.Rev. 787 (1980).

use flexible spending accounts to expend pre-tax dollars on medical expenses. Why should the Code provide for the equivalent of tax deductible expenditures for employees lucky enough to have employer provided health insurance, but deny an equivalent deduction to other taxpayers?

Although not particularly convincing, one reason may be that the Government is confident that employer provided health insurance is actually going to medical care. While taxpayers seeking the deduction may be seeking it for items that might not really be medical care, for example a hot tub for my aching back. Employers that provide flexible spending accounts are required to obtain documentation from employees indicating that the expenses qualify as medical expenses. In a sense, the employer is an initial screen for frivolous deductions.

There is another means by which a taxpayer can use pre-tax dollars to pay for medical care and thus avoid the 7.5% limitation. In 2003, Congress passed another provision that lets some individuals avoid the 7.5% limitation on the deduction of medical expenses, these are referred to as HSAs or Health Savings Accounts.[138] HSAs were designed to reduced health care costs by allowing patients to be better consumers. They allow individuals who are in high deductible health plans to put pre-tax dollars in an HSAs.[139] Funds in the HSA also earn tax free returns as long as those funds are spent on medical expenses.[140]

A high deductible plan is defined as a plan with annual deductibles for an individual of $1,000 or more, and $2,000 for families. In addition, the plans must not have maximum out of pocket cost that exceed $5,000 for individuals and $10,000 for families.[141]

Participants may contribute up to the amount of the deductible on their plan or $2,250, whichever is less, in each taxable year. They may contribute this amount even if they do not spend the amount in the fund. Participants who have family coverage may contribute up to $4,500.[142]

(8) Charitable Contributions

(a) *In General*

Charity may begin at home but to the extent the taxpayer supports charities outside the home, he may receive a tax deduction

---

[138]   Section 223.

[139]   Amounts contributed are an above-the-line deduction under § 62(a)(19).

[140]   Sections 223(e)(1), (f)(1).

[141]   Section 223(c)(2).

[142]   Section 223(b).

as an itemized deduction. In order to receive the deduction the gift must be to a qualified charitable organization.

Deductions for charitable contributions are subject to certain percentage limits of the taxpayer's adjusted gross income and must meet several other standards, as discussed below.[143]

The organizations that are qualified to receive a deductible charitable contribution are in general qualified organizations that are nonprofit organizations organized exclusively for religious, charitable, scientific, literary, or educational purposes, or to foster amateur sports, or for the prevention of cruelty to children or animals.

The restriction that charitable organizations cannot generally engage in lobbying was held constitutional even though veteran's groups are allowed to receive deductible contributions while carrying on lobbying.[144] The IRS may properly revoke the status of a school to receive deductible charitable contributions if the school practices racial discrimination.[145]

The taxpayer's transfer must be a contribution or gift, as opposed to a payment in consideration for value received, in order to qualify for the charitable deduction.[146] Guidance in this area can be provided by the leading case of *Commissioner v. Duberstein*,[147] holding that gifts must arise out of "detached and disinterested generosity." In *Singer Co. v. United States*,[148] the court asserted that the appropriate test is whether a substantial benefit is expected from the contribution, meaning by that that the benefit to be received would be greater than benefits that inure to the general public. One might here ask whether the widely publicized donations of Bill Gates to public libraries to foster the purchase of computers might not fail the test of deductibility, since it would be a major stimulus to these libraries buying computers that ran software produced by Microsoft. Just fostering the donor's public image would not in itself bar the deduction.[149] If the taxpayer receives consideration of a value less

---

[143]   Section 170.

[144]   Regan v. Taxation with Representation of Washington, 461 U.S. 540, 103 S.Ct. 1997, 76 L.Ed.2d 129 (1983).

[145]   Bob Jones University v. United States 461 U.S. 574, 103 S.Ct. 2017, 76 L.Ed.2d 157 (1983).

[146]   Section 170(c).

[147]   363 U.S. 278, 80 S.Ct. 1190, 4 L.Ed.2d 1218 (1960), conformed to 283 F.2d 949 (6th Cir.1960), discussed at ¶ 3.08(2).

[148]   196 Ct.Cl. 90, 449 F.2d 413 (1971) (sewing machine company's sale of sewing machines to schools at a discount was not a charitable contribution but a marketing plan, held deduction denied; bargain sales to churches, hospitals, and government agencies allowed as a charitable deduction).

[149]   Id. at 423.

than the amount he contributes, the excess can qualify as a deductible contribution.[150]

In order to be deductible within a particular taxable year, "payment" of the charitable contribution must be made within that year.[151]

The charitable contribution must be of "property;" contribution of services will not qualify.[152] If the charitable contribution is of property other than money, the general rule is that the amount of the contribution is the fair market value of the property at the time of the contribution.[153] This means that the taxpayer is generally well advised to sell depreciated property, in order to realize a loss, and contribute the proceeds, but to contribute appreciated property and not sell it and contribute the proceeds, to avoid realizing a gain.[154]

The advantage of contributing appreciated property to charity rather than selling it can be illustrated with an example:

> **Example: Contribution of Appreciated Property for Fun and Profit.** T buys stock in Xidex Corporation for $25,000. It has appreciated since her original purchase ten times and is now worth $250,000. T wishes to contribute the stock to the law school from which she graduated. T has two

---

[150] Oppewal v. Commissioner, 468 F.2d 1000 (1st Cir.1972) (payment to school deductible to extent it exceeded cost of educating taxpayer's children); Rev.Rul. 68–432, 1968–2 C.B. 104 (same approach as to membership fees of charitable organizations); Rev.Rul. 67–246, 1967–2 C.B. 104 (same approach of partial deduction for tickets to charitable events where price paid is more than value of attending the event).

[151] Section 170(a)(1); ordinarily, a contribution is made at the time delivery is effected, Reg. § 1.170A–1(b); Mann v. Commissioner, 35 F.2d 873 (D.C.Cir.1929) (pledges not deductible); Reg. § 1.170A–1(e) (transfers contingent on the happening of a precedent event not deductible unless the possibility that the transfer will not become effective is so remote as to be negligible).

[152] Reg. § 1.170A–1(g), providing, however, that unreimbursed expenditures made incident to the rendering of services to a qualified organization are deductible, including the out-of-pocket costs of transportation and meals necessarily incurred in performing donated services. See also Orr v. United States, 343 F.2d 553 (5th Cir.1965) (depreciation not allowed on automobile and airplane used by taxpayer on charitable business); Babilonia v. Commissioner, 681 F.2d 678 (9th Cir.1982) (parents of Olympic figure skater Tai Babilonia could not deduct cost of skating lessons and travel expenses of Tai and her mother as unreimbursed expenditures made incident to the rendering of services to the U.S. Olympic Committee).

[153] Reg. § 1.170A–1(c)(1); see below for an important limitation on this principle where the transfer is of property that would not have yielded long-term capital gain if sold by the taxpayer.

[154] This maneuver is possible because a gift is not a taxable event, see ¶ 4.02(1). Although the general rule is that using appreciated property to satisfy a pre-existing obligation is a taxable event, using appreciated property to satisfy a pre-existing charitable pledge does not trigger imposition of tax, Rev.Rul. 55–410, 1955–1 C.B. 297.

choices. She can sell the stock and contribute the proceeds or she can just contribute the stock directly.

What happens in each case?

Alternative 1) Sell stock and contribute proceeds: If T sells the stock and contributes the proceeds, it lays out like this: Sale of the stock yields a taxable gain of $225,000 ($250,000 FMV less $25,000 AB). If T's capital gains rate is 15% (assuming the stock is held longer than 12 months it is in the 15% group—see ¶ 4.06(2)(b)(i)), T's tax is $33,750. T has left after paying the tax $250,000 (the gross proceeds of the sale)[155] less the $33,750 tax, or $216,250. It is that $216,250. that T can contribute to her law school as a result of liquidating her investment in Xidex Corporation. T then gets a charitable deduction for contributing that $216,250 to her law school.[156] That deduction saves T (in a 35% bracket for ordinary income) $75,687. How does this all wind up? T's law school has received $216,250, and T's taxes have been reduced by $79,130. The combined benefit is $216,250 + $75,687 or $291,937.

Alternative 2) Contribute the stock: Suppose in the alternative T just gives the stock to the law school. The gift is not a realizing event, thus T does not recognize or pay tax on her $225,000 gain on the stock. Notwithstanding that, T can take a deduction for the full value of the stock, or $250,000. This deduction saves T (in a 35% bracket for ordinary income) $87,500 in taxes. How does all this wind up? T's law school has received stock with a value of $250,000. It being a tax-exempt organization, it can sell the stock for $250,000 and keep all the proceeds. Thus the law school's true benefit is $250,000. T has saved taxes of $87,500. The combined benefit is $250,000 + $87,500 or $337,500.[157]

Comment: This is a truly amazing result. It is better to contribute the property than to sell it and contribute the proceeds. The result here is often described as a double benefit. The double benefit is that T gets not to pay tax on the appreciation and yet take a deduction for the full fair market value of the property. In fact the benefit is triple. In addition to the double benefit described above, T gets a larger deduction when she contributes the unsold property than when she contributes the after-tax cash on selling the property.

---

[155] Don't get confused on this one. While T's taxable gain on the transaction was $225,000, T of course actually received $250,000 for the sale. That money is in the bank until T has to pay some of it for her taxes.

[156] This assumes T's adjusted gross income is large enough so as not to trigger limitations on charitable contributions keyed to gross income (see discussion below at ¶ 7.01(8)(b)).

[157] Some of the zip could be taken out of this transaction by the alternative minimum tax (AMT), as discussed later in this chapter.

Note that in 1) when T sells the stock, T gets a deduction of $216,250 on contributing the after-tax proceeds. But in 2) contributing the stock, T gets a deduction of $250,000, the full value of the stock.

Thus for tax planning purposes contributing appreciated property to charity is even more advantageous than is commonly realized.

As a policy matter, the question is whether it really makes sense to confer such a great advantage on the contribution of appreciated property compared to selling the property and contributing cash.[158]

This is why Congress limited the amount that can be deducted for contributions of appreciated property to 30% of the taxpayer's adjusted gross income rather than 50% (as discussed below). This is not a particularly serious limitation and in any event the excess deduction not allowed can be carried forward five years.

Where a charitable contribution is of property that would yield ordinary income or short-term capital gain if sold, the amount of the charitable contribution is limited to the taxpayer's basis in the property.[159]

One other little trick. If you give tangible personal property (like an automobile) to a charity, and the use by the donee of that property is unrelated to the entity's charitable purpose, your deduction is limited to your basis in the property.[160] For example, if you own a famous painting that has appreciated in value and donate the painting to your child's nursery school, you will only be able to deduct your basis in the painting. But, if you donate the painting to a museum, you will be entitled to deduct the fair market value of the painting. Since most appreciable tangible property given to charities are collectibles, doesn't this provision give a huge advantage to museums over other charities?

---

[158] See Daniel Halperin, A Charitable Contribution of Appreciated Property and the Realization of Built-in Gains, 56 Tax.L.Rev. 1 (2002).

[159] Section 170(e)(1)(A). Thus a broad class of assets will only give rise to a deduction of the taxpayer's basis if a subject of charitable contribution. For example, contribution of the taxpayer's inventory will only give rise to a deduction of the taxpayer's basis. See ¶ 4.06(3) for rules defining what types of property are capital assets which would be exempt from this rule if held for the long-term holding period. This rule, combined with § 1221(a)(3) denying capital asset status to, among other things, letters and memoranda of the taxpayer, means that political figures may not secure a large charitable contribution deduction for the transfer of their personal papers to a library or a museum, etc. It was the question whether former President Nixon had contributed his Vice Presidential papers before the effective date of this rule, involving backdated documents, that created his major tax problem in the old Watergate days.

[160] Section 170(e)(1)(B).

What if the painting really, really went up in value and you want to give some of the appreciation to a charity and keep some for yourself? Taxpayers often sell appreciated property to a qualified charity for less than the fair market value of the property. To the extent the sale is for less than the fair market value of the property, the taxpayer is in some sense making a charitable contribution. The problem in these bargain sales to charities, is ascertaining how much gain the taxpayer has on the transaction and what is the amount of his charitable contribution.

For determining the taxpayer's gain on the transaction, the rule is that the adjusted basis for determining gain from the bargain sale is that portion of the adjusted basis which bears the same ratio to the adjusted basis as the amount realized bears to the fair market value of the property.[161] The amount of the taxpayer's charitable contribution is the difference between the property's fair market value and the sales price to the charity. These principles are illustrated by the following example:

> **Example:** Suppose that appreciated long-term capital gain property with a fair market value of $1,000 and an adjusted basis of $300 is sold to a qualifying charitable organization for $600. The adjusted basis for computing the gain on this transaction would be $180, i.e., 60 percent of $300, since the property was sold for 60 percent of its fair market value. The gain, therefore, on the transaction is computed as $600 amount realized, less $180 adjusted basis equals $420. This $420 would be taxed as a capital gain, qualifying for the 15% group if it was held longer than 12 months.[162] The amount of the deductible charitable contribution is $1,000 minus $600 equals $400.

Note that if the contributed property had been inventory, rather than long-term capital gain property, then the computation of gain would be the same as above, but the gain would be ordinary. The amount of the charitable contribution would, however, be only $120 (that portion of the basis that was not allocated to computing the gain on the bargain sale, in accordance with § 170(e)(1)(A)).

(b) Percentage Limits

Taxpayers are subject to a wide variety of limits on the amounts they may deduct as charitable contributions, depending on the type

---

[161]   Section 1011(b).

Congress has provided complex and restrictive rules governing the contribution of remainder interests, income interests and other partial interests in property to qualified charities, § 170(f).

[162]   See ¶ 4.06(2)(b)(i).

of charity, the type of property contributed, and the type of transfer. These matters are dealt with in turn.

The various limits are expressed as a percentage of the taxpayer's "contribution base" for the taxable year. The contribution base is the taxpayer's adjusted gross income, computed without regard to any net operating loss carryback.[163]

With respect to types of charities, the Code creates two types: those to whom the taxpayer may contribute up to 50 percent of his charitable contribution base, and those to whom the taxpayer may contribute up to only 30 percent of his charitable contribution base. The so-called 50-percent charities include churches or associations of churches, schools and colleges, hospitals, medical schools or medical research organizations, organizations receiving a substantial part of their support from the state or Federal Government or the general public, the state or Federal Government, certain private foundations.[164] So-called 30-percent charities are those organizations qualified to receive deductible charitable contributions but that do not qualify as 50-percent charities.[165]

Where the taxpayer makes contributions to both 50-percent charities and 30-percent charities in the same taxable year, the amount of the contributions to the 50-percent charities are taken against the limit first. Then if the contributions to the 50-percent charities have not exhausted the limit on 50-percent charities, the contributions to the 30-percent charities, up to 30 percent of the charitable contribution base, or the remaining amount on the 50-percent limit whichever is less, are allowed.[166]

Example of Charitable Contribution Limits: Taxpayer's charitable contribution base is $100,000. He contributes $25,000 to a 50-percent charity and $35,000 to a 30-percent charity. The $25,000 contribution to the 50-percent charity is deductible in full. Only $25,000 of the $35,000 contributed to the 30-percent is deductible, since the limit to the 30-percent charities for this taxpayer is the lesser of $30,000 or the remaining $25,000 of the 50% limit.

Contributions to 50-percent charities which exceed 50-percent of the taxpayer's charitable contribution base may be carried forward for five years.[167] Contributions to 30-percent charities in excess of the allowable limit for a particular taxable year may not be carried

---

[163] Section 170(b)(1)(F).

[164] Section 170(b)(1)(A); Reg. § 1.170A–9.

[165] Section 170(b)(1)(B).

[166] Section 170(b)(1)(B).

[167] Section 170(d)(1), providing various restrictions.

forward.[168] Thus, for example, if the taxpayer's charitable contribution base is $100,000 and he contributes $45,000 to a 50-percent charity and $25,000 to a 30-percent charity, there will be no carryover because the entire contribution to the 50-percent charity is taken out first against the 50-percent limit.

As mentioned above, if the taxpayer contributes capital gain property, it may be deducted only to the extent it does not exceed 30-percent of the taxpayer's charitable contribution base.[169] "Capital gain property" means for these purposes any capital asset, and § 1231(b) asset, the sale of which at the time of contribution would have resulted in a long-term capital gain.[170] The amount of the contribution of capital gain property which is allowed under the 30-percent limit is then applied to the 50-percent or 30-percent limits, depending on which type of charity is receiving the contribution.[171] Moreover, in determining whether the 50-percent or 30-percent limits have been exceeded, contributions of capital gain property are taken account of after all other contributions.[172] To the extent that contributions of capital gain property exceed the 30-percent limit, they are carried forward for five years and treated under these same rules for the five years.[173]

Charitable contributions are allowed as a deduction only if substantiated according to detailed rules set forth in the Regulations.[174]

The burden rests with the taxpayer to establish that the charity qualifies for the receipt of deductible contributions. The Service promulgates a cumulative list of Exempt Organizations to assist taxpayers who may be making contributions to other than the very well known charitable organizations.

---

[168] Section 170(d)(1).

[169] Section 170(b)(1)(C)(i).

[170] Section 170(b)(1)(C)(iv).

[171] This restriction only applies if the contribution of capital gain property is not subject to § 170(e)(1)(B), relating to certain contributions of tangible personal property and certain contributions to private foundations discussed supra. See § 170(b)(1)(C)(i).

[172] Section 170(b)(1)(C)(i) .

[173] Section 170(b)(1)(C)(ii).

[174] Section 170(a)(1); Reg. § 1.170A–1(a)(2)(i), 1.170A–1(a)(2)(ii). When required by the District Director, a charitable contribution must be substantiated by a statement from the organization to which the contribution was made, Reg. § 1.170A–1(a)(2)(iii). See Reg. § 1.170A–13(a) and (b). (Compare ¶ 6.02(7) regarding the substantiation requirement for travel, entertainment and business gifts.)

(c) New Rules

(i) Vehicle Donations

Some of these rules are simply too good to be true. Congress believed that taxpayers were abusing the rules regarding the donation of property in order to obtain large tax deductions. For example, Congress believed that taxpayers were donating used automobiles to charities and claiming large deductions far in excess of the fair market value of the automobile. The con went something like this. Taxpayer has an old 1990 car with 150,000 miles on it. In great condition the car is worth $2,000. Taxpayer knows he can probably only get $750 for the car and then has to go through the trouble of selling it. So instead of selling the car, he gives it to charity. (You must have seen the ads). He claims the blue book value of $2,000 and deducts that from his taxes. If he is a 30% taxpayer, he saves $600 in taxes, and he didn't have to bother selling the car. The charity then sells the car at auction for $500. (The charity can't get the $2,000 because the car wasn't really worth that much and because the charity sells the car with no guarantees).

So who wins? The taxpayer received $600 for the car and didn't have to bother with selling it, and the charity received $500. It seems like a win-win situation. But don't forget, you and the rest of us are footing the bill. The car wasn't really worth the $2,000 claimed by the taxpayer.

Congress stepped in and passed new rules for donations of motor vehicles, boats and aircraft.[175] First, taxpayers are not entitled to deduct contributions unless the charity provides a contemporaneous written acknowledgment of the donation. The acknowledgment must be made within 30 days of the donation of the vehicle or 30 days of its sale. The acknowledgment must provide that the vehicle was sold at arm's length, the gross proceeds from the sale, and a statement that the deductible amount may not exceed the gross proceeds. This provision does not apply if the charity is going to use the vehicle as part of its charitable mission (i.e. to deliver meals, services, etc.). The taxpayer's deduction is limited to the gross proceeds received by the charitable organization upon selling the vehicle.[176]

(ii) Noncash Charitable Contributions

Congress also tightened the rules on noncash charitable contributions. If a taxpayer donates property over $500, the taxpayer must provide on his return a written description of the property[177] If

---

[175] Section 170(f)(12)(A).

[176] Section 170(f)(12)(A)(ii).

[177] Section 170(f)(11)(B).

the property is valued at more than $5,000, the taxpayer must obtain a qualified appraisal and provide information about the appraisal to the IRS. These rules do not apply to cash, publicly-traded securities, and vehicles that are donated to and used by charities.[178]

¶ 7.02 FLOOR ON MISCELLANEOUS ITEMIZED DEDUCTIONS

As discussed in the introduction and in Chapter 6 at ¶ 6.01, there are two kinds of itemized deductions: "miscellaneous itemized deductions" (as defined by the statute), and "the rest of them" (for want of a better term). The difference between them is that "miscellaneous itemized deductions" are only deductible to the extent that they exceed 2% of the taxpayer's adjusted gross income. Thus they are said to be deductible subject to a 2% floor.[179] The "rest of them" are deductible in full (they are, of course, subject to the current phaseout of itemized deductions).

"Miscellaneous itemized deductions" includes unreimbursed employee expenses (such as travel or professional journals) and expenses of investment advice for investing in stocks and bonds.[180]

The itemized deductions that are not subject to the floor include home mortgage interest,[181] state and local taxes on the home,[182] losses on personal-use property,[183] charitable deductions,[184] medical expense deductions,[185] and moving expenses.[186]

This statutory treatment is depicted in the accompanying graphic.

---

[178] Section 170(f)(11)(A)(ii)(I).

[179] Section 67.

[180] Investment advice for investments that produce rents or royalties would not, however, be in this category. Investment expenses related to producing rent or royalty income are taken above the line, and are thus not itemized expenses, § 62(a)(4).

[181] The deduction for home mortgage interest is subject to some limits under § 163. It is the amounts that survive those limits that can be deducted in full thereafter without regard to the 2% floor. See ¶ 7.01(3).

[182] Allowed by § 164.

[183] The casualty loss deduction for personal-use property is subject to its own limits and floors of § 165(c) and (h), see ¶ 7.01(5). The amounts (if any) that finally get through those limits are then deductible in full below the line without regard to the 2% miscellaneous itemized deduction floor.

[184] Charitable deductions are subject to their own limits in § 170, as discussed in ¶ 7.01(8). It is the amounts that survive those limits that are then deductible in full below the line without regard to the 2% floor.

[185] The medical expense deduction is subject to severe restrictions of its own as provided in § 213, see ¶ 7.01(7). It is only the amounts (if any) that survive those limits that can then be deducted in full below the line without being subject to the 2% floor.

[186] Moving expenses are subject to their own limits under § 217. It is only the amounts that survive those limits that can then be deducted in full below the line without regard to the 2% floor.

2% FLOOR ON MISCELLANEOUS ITEMIZED DEDUCTIONS

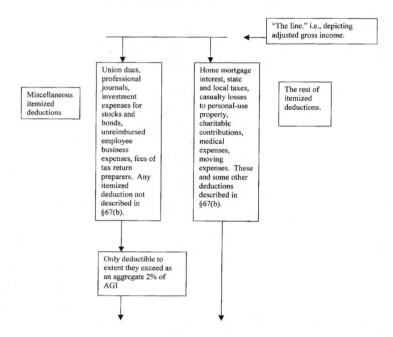

One thing that emerges from contemplating this statutory scheme is that below-the-line deductions have been a serious target of Congress in recent years. The 2% floor raises about $20 billion over five years. The deductions not subject to the floor have been subjected to their own limits. There is only one big one that stands virtually unscathed. That is the deduction for interest on the home mortgage. As discussed at ¶ 7.01(3), it is not subject to much in the way of limits in its own right and it is not subject to the 2% floor.

¶ 7.03 THE STANDARD DEDUCTION

All individual taxpayers are entitled to deduct a fixed amount from adjusted gross income in arriving at taxable income, whether or not they have any itemized deductions at all. This fixed amount, called the standard deduction, is adjusted for inflation.

Thus it is only when itemized deductions exceed the standard deduction that the itemized deductions confer a tax benefit. And then the benefit is only to the extent of that excess. This structure and how it fits together with the 2% floor on miscellaneous itemized deductions is depicted in the accompanying graphic.

2% FLOOR ON MISCELLANEOUS ITEMIZED DEDUCTIONS AND THE STANDARD DEDUCTION

Thus, taxpayers with relatively small amounts of itemized deductions are spared the agony of computation and substantiation and may simply take a free ride on the standard deduction.

As indicated in the earlier discussion on structure of the Internal Revenue Code,[187] taxpayers who do not expect to have excess itemized deductions—i.e., itemized deductions in excess of the standard deduction—prefer to have such deductions taken above the line (as deductions from gross income in arriving at adjusted gross income) so that they will get a full benefit from the deduction. Obviously, taxpayers are not free to move deductions from below the line to above the line, but must abide by the rules of § 62 in ascertaining which deductions go above the line. It is only in a close question that a taxpayer may make an attempt to argue that a deduction is above the line if he does not expect to have excess itemized deductions.

---

[187]   See ¶ 6.01.

Congress has similarly played this game when in 1976 it moved the deduction for alimony from below the line to above the line, to ensure that taxpayers would always get the full benefit of their alimony deduction.[188]

¶ 7.04 PERSONAL AND DEPENDENCY EXEMPTIONS

(1) Exemption Amount

Having worked out his itemized deductions and run the gauntlet of the 2% floor on miscellaneous itemized deductions, the taxpayer is allowed to deduct a personal exemption of $3,100, indexed for inflation, for himself and his spouse.[189] In addition he is allowed to deduct an exemption for any dependents.[190]

The idea of these deductions for personal and dependency exemptions is to assist families, as part of the "family values" that we hear so much about in the political sphere these days. In fact approximately the same result as is accomplished by personal and dependency exemptions could be achieved by altering the rate structure so that it kicks in at a higher level of income. (But that wouldn't sound so nice and "family.")

The fact that personal and dependency exemptions are simply a substitute for manipulating the rate structure is indeed recognized by the statute. Beginning in 1991, the personal and dependency exemptions are phased out for higher income taxpayers. For a joint return, total exemptions are diminished by 2% for each $2,500 that the taxpayer's adjusted gross income exceeds $150,000. The effect of this is to increase the top marginal rate of tax on higher-income people. As their income goes up above $150,000, their tax rate is going up because they are slowly losing the dependency deduction. As a result the top marginal rate on high-income people is raised above the top 35% rate stated in the statute.[191] Moreover, high-income people with large families get hit harder by this approach. This is because with larger families, they have a larger total deduction for dependency exemptions. Thus they lose more as they go over the threshold.

The reason for this bizarre approach is the same as the one for the phaseout of itemized deductions, see ¶ 7.01(1). This provision is the product of a compromise surrounding the 1990 budget agreement. Just as with the phaseout of itemized deductions, this

---

[188]   See ¶ 6.02(14). For further discussion of these structural matters see ¶ 6.01.
[189]   In 2017, the personal exemption was $4,050.
[190]   Sections 151, 152.
[191]   Section 1.

provision .is just another example where politics, and not simplification, won out. All of this is a tricky way of raising taxes on high-income people without appearing to do so. In this era when no politician wants to be caught dead suggesting that taxes should be raised (when sometimes in fact taxes do have to be raised), we may see more of the legislative legerdemain in the future.

But just as with itemized deductions, the phaseout of the personal and dependency exemptions are themselves being phased out.[192] EGTRRA eliminated the overall limitation on itemized deductions.[193] The limit is reduced by one-third for 2006 and 2007, and by two-thirds in 2008 and 2009. The overall limitation is eliminated for taxable years after December 31, 2009, but reinstated in 2011.

(2) Qualifying Child

Section 151 provides for an exemption for dependents. Section 152 defines a dependent as a "qualifying child" or "qualifying relative." The definition of qualifying child thus becomes very important. But not surprisingly, it is not just important for determining the dependency exemption. The child credit, earned income credit, dependent care credit, and head of household status all turn on whether or not there is a "qualifying child." Prior to 2004, each of these provisions had a separate definition for "qualifying child." Lucky for you, the Code now contains a unified definition for qualifying child.

There are three principal requirements for a child to be considered a "qualifying child." First, the child must have the same "principal place of abode" as the taxpayer for more than half of the taxable year, and must not provide more than half of his own support.[194] Second, the child must be the son or daughter or a descendant of a son or daughter, or a brother, sister, stepbrother, stepsister, or a descendant of one of the above. Finally, the child must meet certain age requirements.

With regard to the age requirements, the specific requirements change depending on the tax provision at issue. Section 152 provides that a qualifying depending must be under the age of 19 or a student under the age of 24. No age limit applies to people who are permanently and totally disable. Moreover, a child still must be

---

[192] Section 151(d)(3)(E).

[193] Section 68(f).

[194] Section 152(c)(1).

under age 13 for his parents to qualify for the dependent care credit, and must be under age 17 for purposes of the child tax credit.[195]

If the parents of a child are divorced or legally separated, the parent with whom the child lives for the greater portion of the year is deemed to meet the support test. The "supporting parent," however may agree in writing to allow the other parent to claim the dependency exemption. This must be done by filing a written notice with the IRS.[196] The rule allows a lower-income parent to shift the dependency exemption to a higher income parent.

¶ 7.05 ALTERNATIVE MINIMUM TAX

One of the more absurd provisions of the income tax law is the alternative minimum tax. The basic idea behind the AMT is that it is a backstop to the regular tax. We need a backstop, apparently, because all too many individuals (and corporations) are seen by Congress to cleverly wiggle through various attractive provisions of the Code. As a result many very high-income individuals and corporations contrive (with their advisors) to pay virtually no tax at all. Consider a high-income taxpayer Buford Harrington who invests heavily in state and local municipal bonds (see ¶ 3.01(2)), as well as equipment eligible for accelerated depreciation (see ¶ 6.02(12)) and deducts intangible drilling costs for oil and gas exploration (see ¶ 6.02(13)). Buford is not feeling a great deal of pain come April 15.

The basic idea of the AMT is to establish a second tax system that defines income more broadly. It includes in its base many of the items that the regular tax system exempts. For example it adds back to its base the excess of accelerated depreciation over what would be deducted using less attractive methods and longer useful lives. It also adds back to the base the inside interest build up on life insurance policies as well as benefits of incentive stock options. In addition certain deductions such as those for medical expenses and state and local taxes are diminished in computing the base. Then, in theory, the AMT applies a fairly low rate to this broader base (with the recent reductions in tax rates the "low rate" of the AMT does not seem so low). The individual caught within the maw of the AMT then in effect pays the greater of his regular tax or the AMT.

Thus the various provisions that give rise to avoiding tax remain in effect, but any individual who uses them very extensively will pick

---

[195] See H.R. Conf. Re. No. 101–696 (discussing §§ 201, 206, and 207 of the Working Families Tax Relief Act of 2004).

[196] Section 152(c)(4)(B).

up some tax under the AMT. The top AMT rate is now 28%, which is significantly less than the top statutory regular tax rate of 35%.[197]

The AMT misses a few things, though. Notably absent are the widespread advantages of the ability to deduct home mortgage interest, contributions to pension plans, employee fringe benefits, tax-free state and municipal bond interest. For capital gains, the alternative minimum tax mirrors the low rates available to capital gains and thus does not deny the benefit of the low rates (see ¶ 4.06(2)(b)(i)). Buford, if he is playing his cards right, is still feeling pretty good.

For real tax jocks, the following discussion explains how the AMT works. For the rest of you, if you buy a good computer program and have a sympathetic tax professor, you will be fine.

The first thing you do is calculate a taxpayer's alternative minimum taxable income (AMTI). To calculate AMTI you take taxable income and add back those deductions that are not allowed under the AMT (see discussion supra and sections 56 and 58).[198] You then subtract the exemption amount under section 55(d) (now $58,000 for 2005).[199] You then calculate the tentative minimum tax, by multiplying AMTI by the tax rate (either 26% or 28%). Now be careful. This is not the AMT. The AMT is actually added to the amount of tax calculated on your regular return. The AMT is therefore the tentative minimum tax minus the tax on your regular return. Are you getting a headache?

In the old days (a couple of years ago), this was not a big problem because almost no one paid the AMT. But, here is another secret that the President and Congress are hiding from you. More and more Americans are becoming subject to the AMT. It is the horror movie coming to a theater near you. Why? Two reasons. First, the exemption amount under the AMT has not kept pace with inflation.[200] Second, when Congress lowered the marginal rates, it didn't lower the rates for the AMT. This means that some taxpayers who are expecting a reduction in taxes will not receive one. Because

---

[197] Section 55(b)(1). Bear in mind that the top marginal rate for high-income people (who are the target of the AMT) is actually higher than 35% because of the phaseout of the personal and dependency exemptions, as discussed at ¶ 7.04.

[198] Section 56.

[199] Under § 55(d)(3) the exemption amount is phased out by 25% of the amount of AMTI that exceed $150,000 for joint and $75,000 for single filers.

[200] As part of the Working Families Tax Relief Act of 2004, Congress raised the exemption amount for 2005 to $58,000 for joint filers and $40,250 for single filers. The exemption amount goes back down to $45,000 for joint filers and $33,750 for single filers if Congress does not extend the higher exemption amount.

while they may owe less tax under the "regular" tax system, they owe the same tax under the AMT.

When Congress passed the AMT it provided that certain deductions would not be allowed for purposes of calculating the AMT. Included in the list are personal and dependency exemptions, state and local taxes, employee business expenses, medical expenses, and home equity indebtedness. Instead of these deductions, Congress provided for a large exemption. That exemption is now $58,000 but only for taxable years 2004 and 2005). But the AMT exemption amount has not kept pace with inflation. What this means is that more and more middle income taxpayers will be subject to the AMT. It also means that those taxpayers who do not use an accountant or tax software will have to fill out two tax forms to know their correct tax liability.[201]

If there was one provision screaming for reform as part of the last four tax bills it was the AMT. Why was the AMT not included? Who knows? But it appears that most taxpayers were unaware of the fact that they might be subject to the AMT, and that reforming the AMT was not as politically popular as lowering marginal rates (even though some taxpayers will not get the benefit of those lower rates due to the AMT).

Take the following example:

A married couple with three children. One spouse is a lawyer earning $110,000 (this could be you) and the other spouse has no income. They live in a state with a state and local tax rate of 8.186% (We like round numbers). They own their own home. They have a $200,000 mortgage ($14,000 mortgage interest) and $50,000 of home equity indebtedness used to pay off student loans ($4,000 interest). Lets see how they fared in 2004 under the regular system and under the AMT.

Under the regular system taxpayers' income of $110,000 is decreased by the $3,100 personal exemption, $12,400 dependency exemption, $14,000 mortgage interest, $4,000 home equity interest that is not acquisition indebtedness, $9,000 in state and local taxes and $5,000 in property taxes. They have $62,500 of taxable income and owe $9,106 of tax. Once the total amount of tax is calculated, you then subtract $3,000 for the child tax credit, and their total tax bill would be $6,106.

---

[201] For a discussion about the rise in the number of taxpayers who will be subject to the AMT, and the costs associated with "fixing" the problem see, Martin A. Sullivan, AMT, Estate Tax Time Bombs Set Stage for Some High-Class Warfare, 96 Tax Notes 1443 (Sept. 9, 2002).

But wait. You didn't think we would use this example if the AMT didn't apply, did you? Under the AMT, taxpayers are not entitled to deduct state and local taxes (including property taxes), nor are they entitled to deduct interest on a home equity loan unless it qualifies as acquisition indebtedness. They are also not entitled to dependency or personal exemptions. They therefore have to add $33,500 back into their taxable income. So their AMTI is $96,000 minus the exemption amount of $58,000 or $38,000. The $38,000 is multiplied by the applicable tax rate of 26% for a tax of $9,880. As we discussed previously, taxpayers' "regular tax" without the child tax credit would have been $9,106. The AMT is thus $9,880 minus $9,106 or $774.

Taxpayers must therefore pay a regular tax of $9,106 and AMT of $774. And they probably never saw it coming. Once the total amount of tax is calculated ($9,880), taxpayers may subtract $3,000 for the child tax credit, so their total tax bill will be $6,880.

Our point here is that the AMT is now not just for people who are involved in tax avoidance schemes. The reason this couple gets hit by the AMT is that they have several items that are added back in when calculating AMT. Mostly a high number of dependents (if three is high)[202] and reasonably high state taxes. But these numbers are not unusual.

One other very interesting point. Look at the couples effective tax rate. Even with the application of the AMT, the couple has an effective tax rate of 6.25%. It is up to you whether you think that is too high or too low, but our impression is that many Americans believe that their effective federal income tax rates are higher than they actually are.

One other issue that has stimulated tax litigation is the application of the AMT to attorney's fees in contingency fee cases.

COMMISSIONER V. BANKS[203]

Facts: This is a consolidated case involving two separate taxpayers, John Banks, and Sigitas Banaitis. Banks was fired from his job and sued the California Department of Education alleging employment discrimination. He signed a contingent attorney fee agreement. After trial, the parties settled for $464,000, and Banks's attorney received $150,000 of that amount.

The facts in Banaitis's case were similar to the ones above. He also sued his employer for, among other things, wrongful discharge,

---

[202] See Klaassen v. Commissioner, 182 F.3d 932 (10th Cir.1999) (unpublished), 1999 WL 197172 (taxpayer with ten children subject to AMT).

[203] 543 U.S. 426, 125 S.Ct. 826, 160 L.Ed. 859 (2005).

and signed a contingent attorney fee agreement. Banaitis settled his claim for $4,864,547, and the defendants paid Banaitis's attorney another $3,864,012.

Question: May Banks and Banaitis exclude the amounts paid to their attorneys from?

Big problem: What is the problem here? Remember *Lucas v. Earl* and the fruit falling from trees (if not see ¶ 5.02). In the Banks example it would appear the income is all Bank's, and then he has a deduction for attorneys' fees. In Banaitis's case it is at least questionable, since the defendant wrote two separate checks—one to Banaitis and one to his attorney. However, since the payment of fees to Banaitis's attorneys was on his behalf, conventional tax wisdom would include it in Banaitis's income.

The big problem here is the AMT. Since the attorneys' fees constitute unreimbursed employee business expenses under §§ 62(a)(1) & (2), they are miscellaneous itemized deductions. As such, they are subject to both the 2% floor on itemized deductions and are added back into income for purposes of the AMT. Thus for AMT purposes, Banaitis has over $8.4 million of income even though he only pocketed $4,864,547.

Arguments for taxpayer: This issue became a huge one in the tax community, and the arguments for the taxpayers broke into four main categories. The first, which was the argument adopted by the Fifth Circuit and followed by several others, was that the attorney had a lien on the award for the amount of his fee and the award was therefore not income to the taxpayer. The second, was that the attorney and taxpayer actually entered into a partnership, and the attorney fee award was the attorney's share of the partnership proceeds. Third, Professor Davenport in an *Amicus Curiae* brief argued that the attorneys' fees are deductible capital expenses since the litigation is a disposition of property.[204] Finally, Professor Cohen in another *Amicus Curiae* brief argued they were deductible as reimbursed employee business expenses under § 62(a)(2)(A).[205]

---

[204] Brief for Amicus Curiae Professor Charles Davenport in Support of Respondents, Commissioner v. Banks, U.S. Supreme Court Docket No. 03–892 (filed Aug. 18, 2004); see also Charles Davenport, Capitalization of Legal Fees: Professor Davenport Responds, 97 Tax Notes 1237 (Dec. 2, 2002); Charles Davenport, Why Tort Legal Fees Are Not Deductible, 97 Tax Notes 703 (Nov. 4, 2002); Deborah A. Geier, Attorney's Fees: Davenport Has the Right Idea, 97 Tax Notes 1627 (Dec. 23, 2002) (supporting Professor Davenport's argument). For a critical analysis of Professor Davenport's theory, see Brant J. Hellwig & Gregg D. Polsky, Litigation Expenses and the Alternative Minimum Tax, 6 Fla. Tax Rev. 811, 828–34 (2004).

[205] Brief for Amicus Curiae Professor Stephen B. Cohen in support of Respondents, Commissioner v. Banks, U.S. Supreme Court Docket No. 03–892 (filed Aug. 14, 2004). This argument was advanced by the taxpayer in *Biehl v. Commissioner*, 118 T.C. 467

Arguments for Service: The attorneys' fee arrangement is an assignment of income from the taxpayer to the attorney and therefore must be included in income.

Holding: Attorneys' fees must be included in income. They are an assignment of income under *Lucas v. Earl.* The Court rejected the argument that the attorney contributes income generating assets to the enterprise and therefore has a separate right to his fees. The Court declined to "entertain" the theories raised by Professors Davenport or Cohen. It concluded that it was "reluctant to entertain novel propositions of law with broad implications for the tax system that were not advanced in earlier stages of litigation."

Comment: The First, Second, Third, Fourth, Ninth and Federal Circuits have also held that contingent attorney's fees must be included in income.[206]

Comment: The Fifth,[207] Sixth,[208] Ninth,[209] and Eleventh[210] Circuits have held that contingent attorney's fees need not be included in income, finding that the claim is "subject to a sort of virtual co-ownership."[211] Citing *Lucas v. Earl* (remember the fruit of the tree), the Fifth Circuit claims that contingent attorney fee arrangements are not just a diversion of the fruit, but also divests clients of part of the tree.[212] Thus, the court likens the contingent attorney fee arrangement to a transfer of property, the income from which is not taxable.[213]

Comments: In our view, lower courts struggled to find some tax theory that would exclude the fees. Including them in income appears to be particularly harsh. But it is not the tax doctrine causing the

---

(2002). The Tax Court rejected the argument, and the Ninth Circuit affirmed. 351 F.3d 982 (9th Cir.2003), cert. denied, 543 U.S. 1145, 125 S.Ct. 1292, 161 L.Ed.2d 105 (2005).

[206]   Alexander v. Internal Revenue Service, 72 F.3d 938 (1st Cir.1995); Raymond v. United States, 355 F.3d 107, 113–116 (2d Cir.2004), cert. denied 543 U.S. 1145, 125 S.Ct. 1292, 161 L.Ed.2d 105 (2005); O'Brien v. Commissioner, 319 F.2d 532 (3d Cir.1963); Young v. Commissioner, 240 F.3d 369 (4th Cir.2001); Kenseth v. Commissioner, 259 F.3d 881, 883–884 (7th Cir.2001); Sinyard v. Commissioner, 268 F.3d 756 (9th Cir.2001). cert. denied 536 U.S. 904, 122 S.Ct. 2357, 153 L.Ed.2d 179 (2002); Campbell v. Commissioner, 274 F.3d 1312 (10th Cir.2001), cert. denied 535 U.S. 1056, 122 S.Ct. 1915, 152 L.Ed.2d 824 (2002); Baylin v. United States, 43 F.3d 1451 (Fed.Cir.1995).

[207]   Cotnam v. Commissioner, 263 F.2d 119 (5th Cir.1959); Srivastava v. Commissioner, 220 F.3d 353 (5th Cir.2000).

[208]   Estate of Clarks v. United States, 202 F.3d 854 (6th Cir.2000).

[209]   The Ninth Circuit held for taxpayer in *Banaitis,* and against the Government in *Sinyard, supra* n. 189. The Ninth Circuit justified this conflict based on its interpretation of state law.

[210]   Davis v. Commissioner, 210 F.3d 1346 (11th Cir.2000).

[211]   Srivastava v. Commissioner, 220 F.3d at 360.

[212]   Id. at 360.

[213]   Id.

problem, it is the statute passed by Congress. Why should contingent fees be treated any differently then non-contingent fees? The basic idea is that taxpayer receives an award and then uses the award to pay the attorney. Under tax principles, this should be included in income and then be deductible. The result may be different when the attorney has a statutory right to fees from the defendant. In such a case, there is a stronger argument that the attorney had an independent right to the fee. The Supreme Court declined to reach this issue because the fees paid in this case were not pursuant to a federal statute that authorized fee awards.

Part of the reason that courts, practitioners, and professors have struggled with this is that the result doesn't make much sense. The attorneys' fees here are really the cost of earning income, and they should be deductible from the amount received in determining how much a taxpayer should include in income.

As the Seventh Circuit noted in one of the lower court cases, *Kenseth v. Commissioner,*[214] "[a]s an original matter, in taxation's Garden of Eden, it would indeed be difficult to think of a reason why Kenseth should have been denied the normal privilege of deducting from his gross income 100 percent of an expense reasonably incurred for the production of income."[215] But Congress has made the decision that miscellaneous itemized deductions are not deductible for purposes of the AMT, and there appears to be no reason to distinguish contingent attorney's fees from other miscellaneous itemized deductions.

As part of the American Jobs Creation Act, and before the Supreme Court's decision in *Banks*, Congress stepped in and modified the treatment of attorneys' fees in certain situations.[216] Congress provided an above-the-line deduction for attorneys' fees in connection with a range of civil rights lawsuits. Covered actions include claims for unlawful discrimination under the Civil Rights Act, the National Labor Relations Act, the Fair Labor Standards Act and many others.[217] Since these deductions are above-the-line they are not added back into income for purposes of calculating the AMT and are not subject to the 2% floor of miscellaneous itemized deductions.

Banks, however, is still an important case even after the statutory change. The change only applied to contingent fees in civil rights litigation. Presumably, the same problem that occurred in

---

[214]   259 F.3d 881 (7th Cir.2001).

[215]   Kenseth, 259 F.3d at 883.

[216]   See ¶ 7.01(2)(b) for further discussion of the tax treatment of attorneys' fees.

[217]   See § 62(a)(19) listing costs for suits for unlawful discrimination as an above the line deduction, and § 62(e) defining unlawful discrimination.

Banks will continue to exists for suits not subject to the § 62(a)(19) exception.[218] Several questions still remain open when a contingent fee is not treated as an above-the-line deduction: 1) is the fee treated differently if it is awarded pursuant to a federal statute (not answered in *Banks*);[219] 2) can attorneys' fees be treated as a capital expense (the Davenport theory); and 3) are attorneys' fees deductible as reimbursed employee business expenses.

---

[218] For a description of the effects of the new § 62(a)(19), see Hellwig & Polsky, supra n. 189, at 859–61.

[219] For a discussion of this issue, see Gregg D. Polsky & Stephen F. Befort, Employment Discrimination Remedies and Tax Gross Ups, 90 Iowa L. Rev. 67, 88–90 (2004).

Chapter 8

TAX PLANNING

Table of Sections

¶ 8.01 INTRODUCTION

As the Service, the courts, and Congress, weave their web of rules regarding the taxpayer's liability, the taxpayer, of course, is not inert. The taxpayer may legitimately arrange his affairs to minimize his tax liability; indeed, at many junctures, the Code invites him to do so. While tax planning approaches are discussed throughout this work, there are certain broad areas of tax planning for individuals and corporations that merit special attention. They are the subject of this chapter.

In the 1970s and 1980s, it was individuals and not corporations, that were primarily involved in tax shelters. Congress has taken steps to limit most of the tax shelter schemes promoted during the 70s and 80s and a good deal of complication in the Code is a result of Congress's attempting to limit tax shelters. As Congress succeeded in limiting tax shelters for individuals, new and far more complicated schemes have developed for corporations. The building blocks for tax shelters, however, remain the same.

This section will first explain how tax shelters work, it will then discuss some examples of tax shelters used by individuals, and finally it will discuss the recent explosion of corporate tax shelters.

But first, to get you in the mood, a quote from an opinion by Judge Murnaghan in *Barnard v. Commissioner,*[1]

> The long and the short of it all is that the parties demeaned themselves in entering so dishonest a venture, unquestionably structured to garner for each of the

---

[1]   731 F.2d 230, 332–233 (4th Cir.1984) (internal citations omitted).

taxpayers tax advantages to which they were not entitled and devoid of any realistic business purpose. In this case we confront only risk-takers who believed they proceeded on a no-loss path; if they got away with it, well and good from their misguided point of view, and, if they did not, they would be no worse off than had they never sought the unjustified benefits in the first place. We refrain from any expression of opinion as to whether the taxpayers have exposed themselves to the risk of criminal prosecution. However, even assuming that perhaps they have not, they, by their conduct, nevertheless reveal a malaise which a healthy United States of America cannot sanction. It is a frightening prospect when our wealthy citizens, those in the highest income tax brackets, seek to take indefensible advantage of the country and their fellow citizens, especially those who have far less from which to meet their tax responsibilities.

¶ 8.02 TAX SHELTERS

(1) The Building Blocks of Tax Shelters

The following are the basic building blocks of all tax shelters:

Business Activities Combined on a Tax Return

In general, an individual files a tax return which combines all of his business activities for the year. Money lost on one activity will be subtracted from money gained on another, and the net results will be the individual's taxable income for the year. This simple truism provides one of the fundamental building blocks for tax shelters. If the individual's return were bifurcated—e.g., losses incurred in real estate could not be taken against salary earned as an executive—tax shelters would be limited.[2] The concept of a high-income taxpayer engaging in activities which produce tax losses against which he offsets his high income is central to the tax shelter.[3]

---

[2]   Cf. § 183 disallowing deductions, except to the extent of income, from "activities not engaged in for profit." While § 183 might arguably be used to attack tax shelters, Reg. § 1.183–2 has tended to limit the scope of § 183 to activities which contain a sporting, hobby, or recreational element. Cf. Goldstein v. Commissioner, 364 F.2d 734 (2d Cir.1966), cert. denied 385 U.S. 1005, 87 S.Ct. 708, 17 L.Ed.2d 543 (1967). See also ¶ 6.02(9).

[3]   Indeed barring the deduction of losses in one activity from gains in another in certain circumstances is the approach of the "passive loss" rules' attack on tax shelters, discussed below.

The Limited Partnership

The limited partnership has proved to be the ideal vehicle for constructing a tax shelter. The customary arrangement is that the general partner puts together the arrangement and provides the skills and managerial know-how for conducting the partnership business. The limited partners are investors. This form is attractive for doing tax-shelter business for several reasons. First, a project (be it a movie, apartment building, equipment leasing, farming) envisioned as a tax shelter is usually too large for any one investor to finance. By conducting the project as a limited partnership, shares can be sold. Second, from the point of view of the typical high-income investor, it is all well and good to incur *tax* losses; but no one wants real, substantial, unlimited losses. Hence, a vehicle—such as the limited partnership—which limits the liability of the investor to the amount he invests is preferred.

These two features—the possibility of selling shares in the investment and limiting the investors' liability—are characteristic of the corporation as well as the limited partnership. However, the corporation is singularly inappropriate as a tax-shelter vehicle because the tax losses incurred by a corporation cannot be passed through to the shareholders but remain with the corporation to be carried over to the corporation's other taxable years.[4] Thus the third reason that the limited partnership is the favorite vehicle for a tax-shelter investment is that the tax losses it generates are passed through to the partners.

The losses incurred by regular corporations (not S Corporations) can be carried over to other years. Indeed a corporation's net operating loss carryovers can themselves become an attractive asset of the corporation which other corporations would seek to acquire.[5]

Another advantage of the partnership is the ability to allocate losses to some investors and gains to others and change these special allocations over time. This raises some of the most complex issues in the field of partnership taxation.[6]

In order to employ the partnership for these purposes, a number of technical requirements must be overcome. These are covered in the

---

[4]   So-called S Corporations do allow losses to be passed through to the shareholders much like a partnership. However, the S Corporation does not lend itself to being a tax shelter vehicle. This is mainly because the S corporation cannot exploit debt the way a partnership can to pump up basis for depreciation purposes. See discussion below.

[5]   See D. Posin, *Corporate Tax Planning: Takeovers Leveraged Buyouts and Restructurings* Chapter 13 (1990).

[6]   See § 704(b)–(d).

partnership tax course which, if you're interested in this kind of maneuvering, you might like to take.

Increase of Basis by Nonrecourse Financing

Thus far, based on the first two building blocks, there is a high-income taxpayer buying a share in a limited partnership which will generate tax losses that are passed through to a taxpayer and against which he may offset his other income. At this point it might well be asked, "What's so great about that?" If the taxpayer has invested $50,000 in a share of a limited partnership, he will presumably only be allowed to deduct an amount equal to his basis of $50,000.[7] If the taxpayer is in the 40-percent bracket, this will only save him $20,000 in taxes—not an impressive result, particularly if the taxpayer ultimately winds up out of pocket the full $50,000!

However, the taxpayer's basis is not necessarily restricted to $50,000 even though he has only paid $50,000 for his limited partnership share. If the limited partnership purchases property subject to a purchase money mortgage (or a mortgage to a third party), even though the loan was secured only by the property itself (be it apartment building, movie, railroad rolling stock, etc.), the partner's basis can be increased by his share of the loan if certain technical requirements are met.

This result applies the rule articulated by the Supreme Court in *Crane v. Commissioner*.[8] In *Crane*, which did not involve a partnership, the Court held that when property subject to nonrecourse debt is inherited, the heir includes in her basis the amount of that nonrecourse debt. You have doubtless already encountered *Crane* at ¶ 4.03(2)(b)(ii). This rule was justified on the ground of administrative convenience. If the heir's basis were limited only to her equity interest, then her basis would change every year as she amortized the mortgage, creating nightmarish problems in the calculation of depreciation.

As discussed in Chapter 4, the *Crane* approach was later applied to property purchased subject to an unassumed mortgage.[9]

An example will illustrate the effect of employing the *Crane* approach:

---

[7]   Section 165(b). The partner's basis in a limited partnership share is the amount of money he pays for his share plus the adjusted basis of the property he contributes to the partnership. § 722. A partner only can deduct as losses an amount equal to his basis in the partnership share. § 704(d).

[8]   331 U.S. 1, 67 S.Ct. 1047, 91 L.Ed. 1301 (1947).

[9]   Parker v. Delaney, 186 F.2d 455 (1st Cir.1950), cert. denied 341 U.S. 926, 71 S.Ct. 797, 95 L.Ed. 1357 (1951).

A limited partner pays $50,000 for his 10% share of a partnership. The partnership arranges a $2.5 million loan to finance construction of an apartment building, the loan secured only by the building. If various technical requirements of partnership tax law are met, the limited partner would be entitled to increase his basis in the partnership by $250,000, to a total basis of $300,000, although he had only contributed $50,000. Such 80 or 90 percent nonrecourse debt financing is common in limited partnerships in the tax shelter field.

Early Deductions

At this point in our discussion, the tax shelter is all dressed up with no place to go. Based on the previous building blocks, there is a high income limited partner who, although he has only contributed $50,000 in the partnership, has a basis that has been "artificially" increased to $300,000. Thus he has a tremendous potential for incurring tax losses. The final step in this tableau is a lot of deductions early in the life of the investment which would create a substantial net operating loss for the partnership, these losses to be then passed through to the partners. In certain kinds of businesses, large early deductions are available—whether by government policy to encourage that business, or by happenstance. It is these businesses, then, that have been typically the subject matter of the limited partnership tax shelter.

Thus, for example (recall that the discussion here is on how tax shelters work prior to the network of restrictive legislation discussed below), in the real estate area substantial deductions for interest (including prepaid interest)[10] and taxes were available during the period the project was being constructed. Since the project produced no income during the construction period, these early deductions produced substantial losses in the construction period which passed through to the partners. When the project was operating, normal operating expenses, of course, were deducted[11] along with the deductions for real estate taxes, interest on the nonrecourse loan, and accelerated depreciation. The deductions for interest and accelerated depreciation had the attractive feature of being large in the early years of the project.

As discussed at ¶ 6.02(12), even straight-line depreciation is actually too fast from an economic standpoint ("sinking-fund depreciation" being what is appropriate). Thus accelerated

---

[10]   See ¶ 7.01(3) for restrictions on deductibility of construction interest and prepaid interest.

[11]   Section 162.

depreciation is way too fast. Where the taxpayer borrows to invest in depreciable plant and equipment, an interesting situation is created. Since the depreciation he takes on this plant and equipment is excessive, that investment is in effect producing tax-free income. As a result, one could look at the situation of borrowing to invest in depreciable plant and equipment as borrowing to invest in an arrangement that produces tax-free income. If that analysis is taken, then there are grounds for denying or at least delaying the interest deduction. This would be on the authority of § 265(a)(2), discussed at ¶ 6.03(6)(a).

In the oil and gas area, in addition to deductions for interest on the nonrecourse loan and some of the other deductions discussed above, there was the unique election to deduct immediately expenditures for intangible drilling and development costs, expenses which under the usual rules would be capitalized.[12]

In the heyday of tax shelters, where a movie was the subject of the limited partnership arrangement, a notable deduction was depreciation calculated by using the "income forecast" method, which led to an early write-off of the cost of the film.[13] An alternative arrangement in the film area—the so-called Production Company—involved a limited partnership providing financing for a film by contributing its partners' capital plus the proceeds of a substantial nonrecourse loan to the distributor or independent producer in exchange for a fee, part of which was contingent on the success of the film. The partnership then deducted currently the costs of making the film, on the theory that the partnership had no ownership interest in the film. This approach was also applied to books and records.

Similarly, the areas of farming and sports franchises were used as the subject matter for tax shelters because of the availability of rapid deductions—e.g., feed costs in livestock farming to the cash method taxpayer, player contracts in sports franchises written off over a short period of time.

---

[12] Intangible drilling and development costs include expenditures related to oil and gas property for wages, fuel, repairs, hauling, supplies "incident to and necessary for the drilling of wells and the preparation of wells for the production of oil or gas," Reg. § 1.612–4. This regulation goes on to provide a rather detailed discussion of what constitutes intangible drilling and development costs. See ¶ 6.02(13)(b).

[13] Because it is difficult to estimate the useful life of a film, the normal method for calculating depreciation was not applied. Rather, the "income forecast" method was used. Under the "income forecast" method, depreciation was calculated for a particular year as follows: The cost of the film is multiplied by the income received in the year and divided by the total estimated income of the film. Since a great percentage of the total estimated income of the film is assumed to be received in the first year or two of the film's life, this method results in a rapid write-off of the cost of the film. Rev.Rul. 60–538, 1960–2 C.B. 68; Rev.Rul. 64–273, 1964–2 C.B. 62.

Winding Up

After the project has operated for several years, the shelter effect begins to wane—largely because, as indicated in the preceding discussion, many of the key deductions have their greatest effect in the early years of the project. Thus, there comes a time when it is attractive to the investor to sell out his interest and reinvest his funds in another shelter or some other project. It is upon this sale of his interest that a tax may be incurred. This is because (as discussed in Chapter 4) *Crane* also held that when property is sold subject to a nonrecourse indebtedness, the taxpayer has an amount realized in the amount of the nonrecourse indebtedness.[14] This will often give rise to a gain because accelerated depreciation and deductions analogous to it (such as the deduction for intangible drilling costs, and film depreciation using the "income forecast method") have drastically lowered the basis of the property in question. This gain upon selling out has been subjected to varying treatment over the years and has depended also on the type of property involved. Historically taxpayers have received the favorable capital gains treatment on selling out.

Deferral

Deferral of tax is not really an additional building block of tax shelters but arises out of the operation of the other factors discussed. Deferral is still a major aspect of current tax shelters.

Consider the case where the depreciation deductions in Year 1 shelter ordinary income, and then the gain attributable to those deductions is recaptured at ordinary income rates in Year 10. That postponement of tax for ten years is of great importance for two reasons:

(1) The tax imposed ten years later may be less. This could arise for instance if, as often is anticipated, the taxpayer is in a lower tax bracket ten years hence. Moreover, if the taxpayer holds the

---

[14] Crane v. Commissioner, note 7. The "phantom gain" in these circumstances cannot even be given away, see Guest, 77 T.C. 9 (1981) (charitable contribution of property subject to a nonrecourse mortgage constitutes a bargain sale to a charity), Rev.Rul. 81–163, 1981–1 CB 433 (same).

As discussed at ¶ 4.03(2)(b)(iv), the Court in *Crane* in its celebrated "footnote 37" explicitly declined to rule on the question of what would happen if the nonrecourse debt were for a greater amount than the fair market value of the property transferred (or foreclosed upon). The Court's reservation of judgment on this matter provided grist for the mill of a great number of academic papers. As discussed in Chapter 4, the Supreme Court in Commissioner v. Tufts, 461 U.S. 300, 103 S.Ct. 1826, 75 L.Ed.2d 863 (1983), reh'g denied 463 U.S. 1215, 103 S.Ct. 3555, 77 L.E.2d 1401 (1983) resolved this question by deciding that where property encumbered by a nonrecourse mortgage is sold, the amount realized on the sale includes the amount of the mortgage notwithstanding that the mortgage exceeds the fair market value of the property.

property until death, then basis of the property is stepped up to fair market value in the hands of taxpayer's heirs, and the deferral becomes a complete exemption. § 1014, see ¶ 4.03(2)(e).

(2) More significantly, even if the taxpayer is in the same bracket ten years later, the use for ten years of the money that would have gone to pay the tax is of tremendous value.

Tax-Exempt Entities

A whole new genre of tax shelter has formed through the use of tax-exempt entities. The basic strategy here is to find a tax-exempt organization, foreign entity, or pension fund that doesn't mind being hit with large gains since they are not subject to U.S. tax. The transaction is then arranged so that the gain will be incurred by the tax-exempt entity and the losses by the entity subject to U.S. tax.[15]

(2) The "At Risk" Limitations

(a) In General

The "at risk" rules have severely limited the effectiveness of tax shelter investing. The "at risk" rules take a dead-eye aim at the single most important building block of tax shelters—the use of nonrecourse financing. The fundamental rule is that a taxpayer,[16] who runs a net loss on an activity for the taxable year, may deduct that loss against his other income only to the extent that he is "at risk" (i.e., invested with personal liability) in the activity.[17] It can be seen that this rule strikes directly at the classical tax shelter as described in the preceding section.

> **Example:** Taxpayer invests $10,000 cash in an activity and incurs a $90,000 nonrecourse liability to further finance the activity. The gross income from the activity for the first year is $3,000. The deductions of interest, depreciation, property taxes, and maintenance with respect to the activity for the first year, come to a total of $15,000. Taxpayer thus has a net loss on the activity of $12,000, only $10,000 of which may be taken as a deduction against taxpayer's other income (such as salary, dividends, etc.). The $2,000 net loss that could not be deducted, plus any net loss sustained in any future years, may be held "in suspense" and used at such time as taxpayer further invests with personal liability in the activity, or otherwise increases

---

[15]   See ¶ 8.02(5) for examples of these types of shelters.

[16]   "Taxpayer" refers in the statute to individuals, Subchapter S corporations, and most closely-held corporations, § 465(a)(1). The discussion in the text will focus primarily on the treatment of individuals.

[17]   Sections 465(a), 465(d).

his amount "at risk" as by not making withdrawals against future gross income generated by the project.[18]

Consider again the example above. Suppose early in the second year of the investment, the taxpayer distributes to himself $5,000 from the activity. A problem is now presented because the taxpayer in the first year of the investment took a deduction for $10,000, which was his amount "at risk" at that time. Now, with the distribution of the $5,000 the taxpayer has only invested with personal liability, a net amount of $5,000. Yet, he has taken a deduction from the activity in the amount of $10,000. To deal with this problem, the "at risk" rules provide a "recapture" rule. The rule is that in any year that the taxpayer comes to have less at risk than the net loss taken from the activity against other income, the taxpayer must include in his income the amount by which his cumulative net loss deductions exceed the amount he has at risk in the activity. In such a situation, the recaptured net loss deductions are held in suspense and may be used at such time in the future that the taxpayer puts more at risk in the activity.[19]

> **Example:** Taxpayer puts at risk $10,000 in an activity and also incurs a $90,000 nonrecourse debt to finance the activity. In the first year of the investment the gross income from the activity is $3,000 and the deductions attributable to the activity total $15,000. The taxpayer, therefore, has a net loss from the activity of $12,000, of which $10,000 may be deducted against other income. Early in the second year of the investment, taxpayer distributes to himself $5,000 in cash. Taxpayer also sustains in the second year of the investment a net loss of $4,000. The $4,000 net loss deduction sustained in the second year will not be allowed but will be held in "suspense" for possible use in future years. In addition, the taxpayer will include $5,000 in income in order to reduce the net loss deduction taken on the activity to $5,000, which is his net amount at risk in the property. The $5,000 net loss so recaptured into income will then be put in suspense and may be deducted in such future year as the taxpayer has more at risk in the activity. Therefore, on these facts, the taxpayer now has $11,000 of net losses "in suspense." ($2,000 from first year + $4,000 from second year + $5,000 recaptured).

If in the third year of the investment, the taxpayer breaks even and also puts $3,000 additional "at risk" into the activity, he will be

---

[18]   Section 465(a)(2).
[19]   Section 465(e).

entitled to deduct $3,000 of the suspended net losses from the activity against other income.

In any year that the taxpayer has net income from the activity, his amount "at risk" in the activity will be increased by the amount of that net income (unless he withdraws the amount of the net income).

Thus it can be seen from the foregoing discussion that the "at risk" amount is a running account which is increased by the amounts the taxpayer invests with personal liability in the property, and the net income (if any) generated by the activity, and is decreased by net losses from the activity deducted against other income and cash withdrawn from the activity.

The "at risk" amount is very much akin to a partner's basis in the partnership, which continually adjusts to reflect these transactions, and limits the amount that ultimately the partner may deduct as a loss.

It might also be noticed that the "at risk" rules bear some resemblance to the rules governing "activities not engaged in for profit" and the rules governing offices in the home and vacation homes. In all these areas lines of activity are segregated and deductions limited, to some extent, by the amount of income generated by the activity.[20]

The preceding discussion has described the basic "at risk" rules. Critical to the operation of those rules, of course, is the definition of "activity." Obviously, the degree to which "activities" for the purposes of the statute are defined broadly or narrowly will affect the extent taxpayers will be able to amalgamate losses and income, or be forced to separate them and put up more "at risk" in the loss activities to gain the loss deduction. The statute lists a number of activities which have traditionally been the subject of tax shelter investments: the holding, producing or distributing of motion picture films or video tapes; farming; equipment leasing; exploring for or exploiting oil and gas resources; exploring for or exploiting geothermal deposits.[21] Holding real estate is also covered.[22]

With respect to each of these lines of business, the statute explicitly provides that a taxpayer's activity with respect to each activity shall be treated as a separate activity.[23] This means, for example, that the income from one film or videotape may not be offset

---

[20] For activities not engaged in for profit, offices in the home, and rental of vacation homes, see ¶¶ 6.02(9), (10), (11).

[21] Section 465(c)(1).

[22] Section 465(c)(3).

[23] Section 465(c)(2).

against the loss from another film or videotape; the income from each farm may not be offset against the net loss from each farm, etc.

There are, of course, a wide variety of lines of business other than the five explicitly mentioned in the statute. The major contribution of the Revenue Act of 1978 to the "at risk" rules was to provide that the "at risk" rules apply to all activities including real estate in addition to those explicitly mentioned in the statute. In so expanding the reach of the "at risk" rules, Congress did not provide guidelines for segregating the many other areas of business in which taxpayers engage into separate activities. Rather, it authorized the Service to promulgate regulations for the aggregation or separation of activities in the areas of business not explicitly mentioned in the statute.[24]

The accompanying chart illustrate the workings of the classic tax shelter. You can see that in the chart depicting the classic tax shelter the rate of return based on cash flow is extremely high in the early years. Then things go badly in the later years, which is why the taxpayer wants to sell the burned out tax shelter. But even sale gives poor results, because under *Tufts* the taxpayer still has substantial back-end gain. The ability to take a large proportion of the deductions in the early years gives the taxpayer the advantage of the time value of money.

Congress enacted several reforms to curb these unduly attractive results. They first cut back on depreciation, allowing only straight-line for real estate. Congress also enacted the "at risk" rules, as explained above. The effect of these changes is to reduce substantially the cash flow rate of return. Things also do not go so badly at the end. The result is that the taxpayer is not able to "front load" his deductions and thus does not gain the advantage of time value of money.

---

[24]   Section 465(c)(3)(C). The legislative history makes clear that "tax shelter characteristics" will be used to help define separate activities. Such characteristics would include substantial nonrecourse financing and other novel financing techniques, accelerated deductions, mismatching of income and deductions, and the method of marketing the activity as an investment. H.Rep. No. 95–1445, reprinted in 1978–3 C.B. (Vol. 1) 181, 244. To the extent a taxpayer participates in a line of business as a trade or business in which he actively participates in the management, all activities involved in that trade or business will be treated as one activity for the purposes of the "at risk" rules.

TAX SHELTER EXAMPLE

HOW THE CLASSIC TAX SHELTER WORKED

Taxpayer puts up $10,000 and borrows $90,000 nonrecourse
She buys a building for $100,000
Here are the numbers:
1) The building has a useful life of 30 years and may be depreciated using the double-declining-balance method.
2) The loan carries an interest rate of 10% and is paid off over 30 years.
3) Annual payment on the loan (principal and interest) is $9,547.
4) The building produces rental income revenues of $15,000 per year.
5) Other out-of-pocket expenses are $3,000 property taxes; $2,000 maintenance.
6) Taxpayer is in the 50% tax bracket.

A Year	B Revenues	C Maintenance & Property Taxes	D Mortgage Payment	E Portion of Mortgage Payment That is Deductible Interest	F Depre- ciation (DDB)	G Taxable Income B-(C+E+F)	H Tax Savings 50% of G	I Net Cash Flow "=B-C-D+H"	J Cash Flow Annual Rate of Return on Initial $10,000
1	$15,000	$5,000	$9,547	$9,000	$6,667	-$5,667	$2,833	$3,286	33%
2	$15,000	$5,000	$9,547	$8,945	$6,222	-$5,168	$2,584	$3,037	30%
3	$15,000	$5,000	$9,547	$8,885	$5,807	-$4,693	$2,346	$2,799	28%
4	$15,000	$5,000	$9,547	$8,819	$5,420	-$4,239	$2,120	$2,573	26%
5	$15,000	$5,000	$9,547	$8,746	$5,059	-$3,805	$1,903	$2,356	24%
6	$15,000	$5,000	$9,547	$8,666	$4,722	-$3,388	$1,694	$2,147	21%
7	$15,000	$5,000	$9,547	$8,578	$4,407	-$2,985	$1,492	$1,945	19%
8	$15,000	$5,000	$9,547	$8,481	$4,113	-$2,594	$1,297	$1,750	18%
9	$15,000	$5,000	$9,547	$8,374	$3,839	-$2,213	$1,107	$1,560	16%
10	$15,000	$5,000	$9,547	$8,257	$3,583	-$1,840	$920	$1,373	14%
11	$15,000	$5,000	$9,547	$8,128	$3,344	-$1,472	$736	$1,189	12%
12	$15,000	$5,000	$9,547	$7,986	$3,121	-$1,107	$554	$1,007	10%
13	$15,000	$5,000	$9,547	$7,830	$2,913	-$743	$372	$825	8%
14	$15,000	$5,000	$9,547	$7,659	$2,719	-$377	$189	$642	6%
15	$15,000	$5,000	$9,547	$7,470	$2,538	-$7	$4	$457	5%
16	$15,000	$5,000	$9,547	$7,262	$2,368	$370	-$185	$268	3%
17	$15,000	$5,000	$9,547	$7,033	$2,368	$599	-$299	$154	2%
18	$15,000	$5,000	$9,547	$6,782	$2,368	$850	-$425	$28	0%
19	$15,000	$5,000	$9,547	$6,506	$2,368	$1,126	-$563	-$110	-1%
20	$15,000	$5,000	$9,547	$6,202	$2,368	$1,430	-$715	-$262	-3%
21	$15,000	$5,000	$9,547	$5,867	$2,368	$1,765	-$883	-$430	-4%
22	$15,000	$5,000	$9,547	$5,499	$2,368	$2,133	-$1,067	-$614	-6%
23	$15,000	$5,000	$9,547	$5,094	$2,368	$2,538	-$1,269	-$816	-8%
24	$15,000	$5,000	$9,547	$4,649	$2,368	$2,983	-$1,492	-$1,039	-10%
25	$15,000	$5,000	$9,547	$4,159	$2,368	$3,473	-$1,736	-$1,283	-13%
26	$15,000	$5,000	$9,547	$3,620	$2,368	$4,012	-$2,006	-$1,553	-16%
27	$15,000	$5,000	$9,547	$3,028	$2,368	$4,604	-$2,302	-$1,849	-18%
28	$15,000	$5,000	$9,547	$2,376	$2,368	$5,256	-$2,628	-$2,175	-22%
29	$15,000	$5,000	$9,547	$1,659	$2,368	$5,973	-$2,987	-$2,534	-25%
30	$15,000	$5,000	$9,547	$870	$2,368	$6,762	-$3,381	-$2,928	-29%
					$99,994				

Adj. Basis at Crossover $ 28,422

Balance of Mtg at Crossover $ 65,057

Switch to straight line   Crossover point

Sale of property at crossover point for $100,000 yields cash of $34,943 and taxable gain of $71,578. *Tufts*

It is useful to point out the relationship between the at risk rules and the limits on activities not engaged in for profit (¶ 6.02(9)). When the not-for-profit rules apply, no net loss from an activity is deductible, whether or not the taxpayer has amounts invested at risk in the activity. This is a harsher rule than the "at risk" approach, which allows net losses to be deducted against other income to the extent the taxpayer is at risk in the activity. In the case of *Brannen v. Commissioner*,[25] the Tax Court used the not-for-profit rules to bar a loss deduction even where the taxpayer had amounts invested at risk in a movie tax shelter. This case, as well as the cases discussed below at ¶ 8.02(4) show the power of the courts to reach on occasion harsher results than those mandated by the at-risk rules.[26]

(b) The Collapse of the Savings & Loan Industry

It should be noted that where financing of real estate is provided from outside lending institutions such as banks and savings and loans, the "at risk" rules do not apply.[27] Thus with regard to financing from those sources, taxpayers may continue to play the shelter game with nonrecourse debt and no "at risk" limit on their deductions.

It appears that this provision, which was enacted in the 1986 tax act, put a great deal of pressure on savings and loans to provide tax-shelter financing. These loans all looked good on the books. Note that there is a certain lack of restraint present with nonrecourse financing. The borrower is delighted to borrow more than the real value of the property on a nonrecourse basis. This can be facilitated by accommodating appraisers. The lender, particularly if it is already being run and regulated in a rather loose fashion, just likes to book big loans. Unfortunately, with the collapse of real estate values, savings and loans found themselves foreclosing on property that was now valued at far less than the outstanding debt. Since the financing was nonrecourse, S & L's were unable to proceed personally against the borrowers. It appears clear that this nonrecourse financing provision in the "at risk" rules contributed to the S & L catastrophe. This provision is still on the books.

(3) Passive Activity Losses

(a) In General

Congress continued its onslaught against tax shelters in 1986 with the enactment of a complex scheme of rules limiting deduction of so-called "passive activity losses" against other income. It is useful in understanding the relationship of the passive loss rules and the "at risk" rules to compare what they are aimed against. The "at risk" rules, discussed above, took aim at the fundamental building block of tax shelters of the use of nonrecourse debt to pump up basis for depreciation purposes. The passive activity loss rules, by contrast, take aim at the building block that taxpayers generally report all

---

[25] 78 T.C. 471 (1982), judgment aff'd 722 F.2d 695 (11th Cir.1984).

[26] Compare to this case Lemmen, 77 T.C. 1326 (1981) (acq.) (managed cattle breeding arrangement was entered into for profit, amount of purchase price allocated to depreciable herd cut back.)

[27] Section 465(b)(6).

their income and losses in various lines of business or investments together on one return. The passive activity loss rules segregate losses generated from passive activities and bar them from being deducted against other income.

A "passive activity" is defined as any activity which involves the conduct of any trade or business or § 212-type activity, and in which the taxpayer does not materially participate. In addition, "passive activities" always include rental activity, regardless of whether the taxpayer materially participates in the rental activity. Thus, no matter how actively the taxpayer may manage a piece of rental property he owns, it will still be considered a passive activity.[28]

As a limited exception to this treatment of real estate, if a taxpayer actively participated in rental real estate activities during the year, then up to $25,000 of the net losses arising from that activity may be deducted against other "non-passive" income. This $25,000 exception is phased out to 0 by 50% of the amount by which the adjusted gross income (computed without regard to passive losses) of the taxpayer for the taxable year exceeds $100,000.[29]

The losses and credits generated from all such passive activities taken together can only be taken against the income and tax liability generated from such passive activities taken together. They cannot be deducted against income and tax liability arising from other activities not deemed to be passive.[30] Any unused passive activity losses and credits are carried forward to the next year where they may be applied against passive activity income and tax liability for that year. This carryforward continues indefinitely.[31] Thus the "phantom" loss that tax shelters produce with depreciation from a basis inflated by nonrecourse debt is not usable against other income. But it does remain to offset the later phantom gain on selling the property. The phantom gain is produced by the decline in basis of the property subject to the depreciation.

Portfolio or investment income, i.e., income from interest, dividends, annuities, or royalties not derived in the ordinary course of a trade or business, is not considered to be income from a passive activity for these purposes. Expenses, including interest, properly allocable to such portfolio income is also not taken into account for these purposes.[32] The gain or loss from the disposition of property

---

[28]   Section 469(c)(2).

[29]   Section 469(i).

[30]   Section 469(a).

[31]   Section 469(b).

[32]   Interest on debt incurred to finance investment income is only deductible to the extent of investment income, § 163(d).

producing such portfolio income is also not regarded as a passive activity for these purposes.[33]

A passive activity does not include a working interest in oil or gas property.[34] An interest as a limited partner in a limited partnership is generally treated as a passive activity.[35]

If an activity changes from being passive to being active, any unused deduction allocable to such activity is offset against the income from the activity for the taxable year.[36]

If during a tax year a taxpayer disposes of his entire interest in a passive activity or former passive activity, then the following rules apply: If all realized gain or loss is recognized, any loss from such activity which has not previously been allowed as a deduction is not treated as a passive activity loss.

However, this treatment does not apply if the disposition is to a related party. Also, if the loss arising from the disposition is a capital loss, the capital loss rules will be applied before the application of these rules.[37]

(b) Relationship Between the "At Risk" Rules and the Passive Activity Loss Rules

With this tide of legislation sweeping against tax shelters, one may ask just what is the relationship between the "at risk" rules and the passive loss rules. Basically, the approach is that the "at risk" rules are applied first. Any loss that sneaks through the "at risk" rules is then clobbered by the passive loss rules. Any loss that manages to get through both is allowed.

(4) Judicial and Administrative Limitations: Franklin

In addition to the juggernaut of legislation against tax shelters over the past couple of decades, there has been substantial action on the judicial and administrative fronts. For example, the leading case of *Estate of Franklin*[38] involved a sale of a motel to a limited partnership followed by a leaseback of the property to the original owner. The purchase price was to be paid in installments over ten years, plus a balloon payment at the end, for which the partnership had no personal liability. The annual rental payments on the

---

[33]   Section 469(e)(1).

[34]   Section 469(c)(3).

[35]   Section 469(h)(2).

[36]   Section 469(f)(1).

[37]   Section 469(g).

[38]   Estate of Franklin v. Commissioner, 544 F.2d 1045 (9th Cir.1976).

leaseback just equaled the amount of the installment obligations. Thus no money was changing hands over the ten-year period, yet the partnership purported to own the property for purposes of depreciation and interest deductions.

The Ninth Circuit held, following *Crane*,[39] that such an arrangement involving nonrecourse debt could be a valid sale and therefore support depreciation and interest deductions by the purchaser. However, the Court held that in this instance the taxpayer had failed to carry the burden of showing that the nonrecourse debt did not exceed the fair market value of the property.[40] Where the nonrecourse debt exceeds the fair market value of the property, the Court stated, payments on the principal yield no equity in the property. Since the taxpayer had no equity in the property, the depreciation deduction would be denied because " 'depreciation is not predicated upon ownership of the property *but rather upon an investment in property.*' "[41]

The interest deduction also requires that the borrower have an equity in the property. The nonrecourse debt has no economic significance if it is for an amount greater than the value of the property securing it, since the borrower has no motivation to pay off the debt. Hence, since there was no bona fide indebtedness the interest deduction was disallowed. *Franklin,* therefore, resolved the question left open by *Crane* of what would happen if nonrecourse mortgage debt were used to buy property with a fair market value less than the debt. *Crane* and its progeny had held that where the value of property is equal to or worth *more* than the nonrecourse debt, the nonrecourse debt would support deductions for depreciation and interest because the taxpayer would have an equity interest in the property and hence have a motivation to pay off the debt.[42] *Franklin*

---

[39] Crane v. Commissioner, 331 U.S. 1, 67 S.Ct. 1047, 91 L.Ed. 1301 (1947) and see discussion above.

[40] Estate of Franklin v. Commissioner, 544 F.2d 1045, 1048 (9th Cir.1976).

[41] Id. at 1049 (quoting Mayerson, 47 T.C. 340, 350 (1966)) (emphasis in original). See also Narver, Jr., 75 T.C. 53 (1980), opinion aff'd 670 F.2d 855 (9th Cir.1982) (nonrecourse debt not valid where promoter bought and resold property at "inflated" price through his controlled entities): Beck v. Commissioner, 678 F.2d 818 (9th Cir.1982) (same), Thompson v. Commissioner, 631 F.2d 642 (9th Cir.1980), cert. denied 452 U.S. 961, 101 S.Ct. 3110, 69 L.Ed.2d 972 (1981).

[42] See, e.g., Bolger, 59 T.C. 760 (1973) (acq.), in which taxpayer bought property from a seller, leased it to a user and paid for the purchase by incurring nonrecourse liability to an institutional lender, secured by the property and an assignment of the lease. Lease payments were made directly to the lender. Thus, Bolger owned the property via the vehicle of nonrecourse debt, reported the lease payments as income and took the large depreciation and interest deductions. The Tax Court upheld this arrangement, following *Crane,* because the amortization of the mortgage increased taxpayer's equity in the property. See Mayerson, 47 T.C. 340 (1966) (acq.); Rev.Rul. 69–77, 1969–1 C.B. 59; see also Hudspeth v. Commissioner, 509 F.2d 1224 (9th Cir.1975); American Realty Trust v. United States, 498 F.2d 1194 (4th Cir.1974).

now held that where the nonrecourse mortgage debt is of an amount greater than the fair market value of the property, the debt will not support deductions for depreciation and interest.[43]

The question might fairly be asked, "Why would a taxpayer purchase property for nonrecourse mortgage debt in excess of the fair market value of the property?" The answer appears to be that the *Franklin* court was using the concept of fair market value of the property without regard to the tax considerations. Obviously, no sane purchaser would pay more for property, whether using nonrecourse debt or not, than the property is worth. But where the purchaser, because he is in a high tax bracket, can enjoy substantial tax advantages on the purchase of the property, it may be rational for him to pay more than the property is worth in an economic sense.

Indeed, the facts in *Franklin* suggest that this was the case. Evidence was introduced in the lower court that the motel property involved had been purchased by the seller the previous year for about half the selling price to the taxpayer.[44] Moreover, the property was insured for only about half this selling price.[45]

Franklin achieves a result similar to, but by no means identical with, the results under the at-risk rules. Under the at-risk rules, a nonrecourse liability is still considered part of the basis of property for purposes of computing depreciation and interest deductions and ascertaining basis. However, if depreciation, interest and other deductions give rise to net losses in excess of amounts at risk, such losses will not be allowed (although they may be carried over and allowed if more amounts are put at-risk).[46] Thus, under the at-risk rules, the nonrecourse liability will be included in the basis of the property and the basis will be reduced by the full amounts of depreciation taken. This is not as harsh as the *Franklin* approach of disregarding the nonrecourse liability for *all* purposes, including computation of depreciation, and deduction of interest, where the amount of the debt exceeds the fair market value of the property.

---

[43] The other end of the *Crane* transaction—namely the sale of the property subject to a nonrecourse indebtedness—has been the subject of great controversy, where the amount of the nonrecourse indebtedness exceeds the value of the property. For discussion, including the decision of the Supreme Court in the *Tufts* case on this question, see discussion above and ¶ 4.03(2)(b)(iv).

[44] Estate of Franklin v. Commissioner, 544 F.2d 1045, 1048 n. 4 (9th Cir.1976).

[45] Id. The *Franklin* court did not in fact make a substantive finding that the property had been purchased for more than its economic fair market value. Rather the court simply held that the taxpayer had failed to carry the burden of showing that the purchase price including the nonrecourse debt did not exceed the economic fair market value of the property.

[46] See ¶ 8.02(2).

Franklin is therefore of great significance. All that is required to achieve its draconian results is for the Service to assert successfully that the taxpayer has failed to carry his burden of showing that the nonrecourse liability is not greater than the economic fair market value of the property. Since tax considerations tend to bid up the price of real estate shelter property beyond its economic value, the threat *Franklin* poses looms large indeed.[47]

The Service, never one to procrastinate when a favorable decision is rendered, issued a ruling hard on the heels of *Franklin,* applying its rationale to a film tax shelter financed with nonrecourse debt.[48] The film shelter originated in 1974 and thus was not subject to the at-risk rules. Employing the same rationale as *Franklin* and citing it, the Service said that the nonrecourse note used to purchase the film would be disregarded in determining depreciation and interest deductions because the note was for an amount significantly greater than the economic fair market value of the film.

In addition to *Franklin* and rulings issued pursuant to it, the Service has maintained a steady administrative pressure on tax shelters by using audit procedures to highlight them, aggressive litigating postures toward them, proposed practice rules to limit tax shelter opinion letters and the like.

(5) Corporate Tax Shelters

Over the years, Congress and tax shelter promoters have been playing cat and mouse. Congress keeps trying to legislatively stop tax shelters and promoters keep looking for new way to exploit the Code. Congress has done a pretty good job in limiting tax shelters for individuals, so promoters have now turned to corporations. In recent years, there has been a significant increase in corporate tax shelters. These shelters usually work by creating a partnership between two entities, one that is taxable in the United States and one that is not. The shelter is designed so that the nontaxable entity absorbs the gains (also referred to as "the sponge" entity) and the other party receives the economic losses.[49]

---

[47]   Would the Service have the temerity to try to apply *Franklin* even in areas where the "at risk" and passive loss rules do apply in an attempt to achieve *Franklin's* harsh results?

[48]   Rev.Rul. 77–110, 1977–1 C.B. 58, see also Rev.Rul. 79–432, 1979–2 C.B. 289. See also Narver, 75 T.C. 53 (1980), aff'd 670 F.2d 855 (9th Cir.1982) (where property re-sold by a promoter for a price far in excess of fair market value, financed by a nonrecourse note, court held there was in substance no sale and the depreciation and interest deductions were disallowed.).

[49]   For an interesting discussion of corporate tax shelters see James S. Eustice, Abusive Corporate Tax Shelters: Old "Brine" in New Bottles, 55 Tax.L. Rev. 135 (2002) (discussing abusive corporate tax shelters and possible solutions to the problem);

Let's take a look at some of the classics.

ASA INVESTERINGS PARTNERSHIP
V. COMMISSIONER[50]

Facts: AlliedSignal sold its interest in an oil and gas company and anticipated a large capital gain on the sale. It sought to reduce that gain by investing in a tax shelter partnership with foreign corporations that were not subject to U.S. tax. The transaction involved the installment sales provisions of the Code,[51] which provide that when a selling price cannot be determined, but the period over which the payments are received can be determined, the basis must be allocated in equal annual increments over the known period. By using the installment sales provisions, transactions that were basically a wash were reported as having large gains in the first year and large losses in subsequent years. The large gains were allocated to foreign entities that were not subject to U.S. tax and the losses were allocated to corporations in the United States.[52] Merrill Lynch received over $7 million for setting up this transaction.

The court simplified the facts into the following hypothetical.

A sells property to B worth $1,000,000 for $500,000 cash plus a variable rate five year debt instrument. Under the installment sales rules the basis of the property is recovered over five years, so A may recover his basis at a rate of $200,000 a year for five years. In the first year, A has proceeds of $500,000 and basis of $200,000, so he recognizes a gain of $300,000. If A sells the note in year 2 for $500,000 (presumably it is worth if the original property was really worth $1,000,000), he has a loss of $300,000 ($800,000 remaining basis minus $500,000 for the sale). In this example, there is a $300,000 gain in the first year and a $300,000 loss in the second year. This transaction is worse than a wash because taxpayer must pay tax on the $300,000 in the first year and does not get the deduction until the second year.

But, what if A can allocate the gain to another party—one not subject to tax—and keep the loss for himself? Here is how the D.C. Circuit described the transaction:[53]

James A. Doering, The Battle Over Corporate Tax Shelters Moves to the Appellate Courts, Taxes, May 2002, at 23.

[50]　201 F.3d 505 (D.C.Cir.2000), cert. denied 531 U.S. 871, 121 S.Ct. 171, 148 L.Ed.2d 117 (2000).

[51]　See § 453.

[52]　ASA Investerings Partnership v. Commissioner, 201 F.3d 505 (D.C.Cir.2000), cert. denied 531 U.S. 871, 121 S.Ct. 171, 148 L.Ed.2d 117 (2000).

[53]　201 F.3d at 506. These are very complex transactions and this material is designed to give you a general introduction to these very complicated shelters. The

A forms a partnership with a foreign entity not subject to
U.S. tax, supplying the partnership with $100,000 and
inducing the "partner" to supply $900,000. The
"partnership" buys for $1,000,000 property eligible for
installment sale treatment under § 453, and, as the ink is
drying on the purchase documents, sells the property, as in
the last example, for $500,000 in cash and an indefinite
five-year debt instrument. The cash payment produces a
gain of $300,000, 90% of which goes to the nontaxable
foreign entity. Then ownership adjustments are made so
that A owns 90% of the partnership. In Year 2 the
instrument is sold, yielding a tax loss of $300,000, 90% of
which is allocable to A. Presto: A has generated a tax loss of
$240,000 ($270,000 loss in Year 2, offset by $30,000 gain in
Year 1), with no material change in his financial position—
other than receipt of the valuable tax loss.[54]

Question: Is AlliedSignal entitled to the capital loss deductions
created by the ASA transaction or does the transaction lack economic
substance?

Service's argument: The partnership is a sham and should not
be respected for tax purposes.

Taxpayer's argument: The partnership had a business purpose.

Holding: The foreign entity in the partnership had no risk of
loss. If all a partner's risk is insured by another partner, the entity
does not meet the definition of a partnership. The court then upheld
the Tax Court's conclusion that the partners did not intend to form a
real partnership.

Comment: The court here avoided the "economic substance"
question and instead determined that the partnership itself would
not be recognized.

Comment: The important lesson to learn from *ASA* is a basic
understanding of the shelter. The foundation of this shelter is that
the transaction creates a large gain in the first year, and losses in
subsequent years. The sponge partner (the nontaxable entity) takes
a majority of the gain and then is bought out. Why is the sponge
willing to take the gain? Because for some reason, either because it
is a foreign corporation not subject to U.S. tax or because it is a
nontaxable entity, it doesn't have to pay tax on the gain. Then when
it is bought out, it goes away with a smile and a profit. The remaining

D.C. Circuit did an excellent job simplifying the facts. We therefore present its version
to you.
[54]   Id. at 507–508.

partner is then left with the losses. These losses can then be used to offset other gains.

The Third Circuit took a different approach to a shelter involving basically the same facts in ACM Partnership v. Commissioner.[55]

ACM PARTNERSHIP V. COMMISSIONER[56]

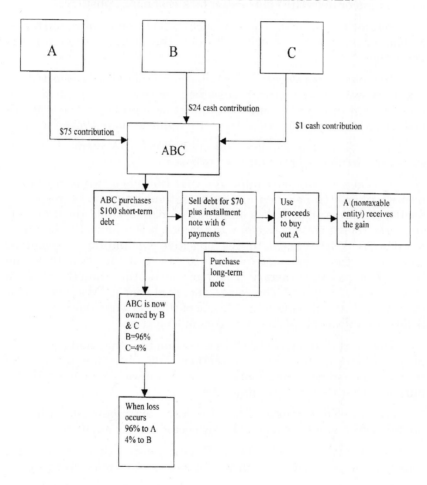

This chart is based on simplified facts used in the court opinion. The actual transaction was far more complicated.

Facts: The shelter was basically the same as the one in *ASA*, so we will not recount the basic facts again. The corporate taxpayer

---

[55]   See also Saba Partnership v. Commissioner, 273 F.3d 1135 (D.C.Cir.2001).

[56]   157 F.3d 231 (3d Cir.1998).

seeking to avoid tax in this case was Colgate-Palmolive. In 1988, Colgate sold a wholly-owned subsidiary and reported long-term capital gains of $104,473,250. Colgate entered into the partnership in order to offset its large gain.

Question: Is ACM (really Colgate since they own 94% of ACM) entitled to the capital loss deductions created by the ACM transaction or does the transaction lack economic substance?

Service's argument: The transaction lacks economic substance. It had no substance or utility beyond the attempt to obtain tax deductions.

Taxpayer's argument: The transaction should be respected for tax purposes because the transaction on its face satisfied each requirement of a contingent installment sale provision, and ACM's deduction arise from a straightforward application of those rules.

Held: The transaction did not have sufficient economic substance to be respected for tax purposes.

Reasoning: The court indicated that there is a two-part inquiry into whether a transaction has sufficient substance to be respected for tax purposes. The first is an objective evaluation of the economic substance of the transaction and the second is the subjective business motivation. With regard to the objective evaluation of economic substance the court noted that courts look to "whether the transaction has any practical economic effects other than the creation of income tax losses."[57] The court concluded that ACM's investment in notes and its subsequent quick sale of the notes had only "nominal, incidental effects on ACM's net economic position."[58]

The court also rejected ACM's assertion that they had a business purpose for entering this transaction. The court found that the transaction had no useful nontax purpose and was a scheme with "no purpose other than tax avoidance."[59]

Dissent: The transactions here were legitimate sales in the nontax sense, and they should be respected for tax purposes.

Comment: Notice the Third Circuit, unlike the D.C. Circuit, relied on the fact that the transaction lacked economic substance.

Comment: In addition to understanding the way the shelter works (which you should have gotten from ASA), there are two main lessons to take from ACM. The first is the Third Circuit's restatement

---

[57] 157 F.3d at 248, quoting Jacobson v. Commissioner, 915 F.2d 832, 837 (2d Cir.1990).

[58] Id. at 249.

[59] Id. at 256, quoting United States v. Wexler, 31 F.3d 117, 124 (3d Cir.1994).

of the economic substance test. The Third Circuit concluded that the transaction must have sufficient substance to be recognized for tax purposes, and that the substance is measured with both an objective economic substance and a subjective business purpose test.

The next lesson is that you never know what will happen with tax shelters. Many commentators believed that this was a clear case. In fact, this shelter was rejected by both the Third and the D.C. Circuits. This transaction smelled and it certainly was entered into only for its tax benefits. But notice that there was a dissent in the ACM opinion. At least one Third Circuit judge believed the transaction was okay. This makes it very hard to subject ACM to penalties, and some attorneys will use the dissent to justify recommending similar schemes.

For another creative scheme let's look at Compaq v. Commissioner.[60]

COMPAQ V. COMMISSIONER

Reprinted from the Government's brief on Appeal in the Compaq case. See, Brief for the Appellee, Compaq v. Commissioner, No. 00-60648.

Facts: Stock in foreign corporations are often not sold on U.S. stock exchanges. Instead, the foreign stock is deposited into a U.S. trust, and the trust's trading units (referred to as ADRs) are traded on U.S. exchanges. Twenty First Security, an investment firm, set up the following transaction for Compaq. Compaq purchased ADRs of Royal Dutch Petroleum (RDR). Twenty First Security picked both the size and prices of the trades and the identity of the company that would sell the ADRs to Compaq. The key to this transaction is that a stock is worth more, cum dividend (before it paid a dividend) than it

---

60   277 F.3d 778 (5th Cir.2001).

was ex dividend (after a dividend). Economically, once a dividend is paid the value of the stock should drop by the amount of the dividend and the transaction costs.

The Netherlands, however, imposes a 15% withholding tax on dividends, so if RDR declares a $100 dividend, the U.S. shareholder only receives $85. The U.S. shareholder must report the full amount $100 even though it only receives $85. Federal tax laws then allows the U.S. shareholder a foreign tax credit. If the owner of the shares is a nontaxable entity (for example a pension fund), the credit has no value to the shareholder. The Netherlands, of course, does not refund the amount withheld. Since the nontaxable entity has no use for the credit, it loans out its ADRs so a taxable entity can receive the dividend and thus the credit.

Compaq bought 450,000 ADRs cum dividend, received the dividend, and then immediately sold the ADRs. The transactions were to a party picked by Twenty First but they were made at the market rate. The aggregate purchase price was $887.6 million (cum dividend), the sale price was $868.4 million (ex dividend). Compaq received a dividend of $22.5 million, and about $3.4 million in tax was withheld from the dividend. Compaq received the net dividend of $19.2 million.

On its tax return, Compaq reported $20.7 million in capital losses (it had sufficient gains to offset the loss), $22.5 million in dividends and a $3.4 million tax credit. The end result was that Compaq had a profit of $1.6 million.

Service's argument: The transaction lacked economic substance.

Taxpayer's argument: The transactions were real transactions made on established markets and thus had economic substance.

Held: The transactions had economic substance and a business purpose and should be recognized for tax purposes. The benefit to Compaq was the gross dividend (before taxes). Since the gross dividend was greater than the drop in price after the payment of the dividend, the transaction produced a profit. With regard to business purpose, the court held that Compaq sought the benefit it would get from the dividend.

Comment: Come on. It is obvious that Compaq only entered into this transaction for its tax benefit. Isn't this a scam? On the other hand, who cares if tax motivation was the sole reason for Compaq's actions if the transactions were legal? Isn't the reason that Compaq could engage in these transactions that the market was not adequately pricing stock cum and ex dividend? Compaq got away with this tax arbitrage because the price of the stock was not dropping by the full amount of the dividend. (This is probably because some entities cannot take the foreign tax credit so there is not a dollar for dollar reduction in the price of the stock once the dividend it paid.) From an economics perspective, Compaq is just helping fix a discrepancy in the market.

Comment: Even if that is true, Compaq bought and almost immediately sold the ADRs, and it did so only to receive a tax deduction. In a sense, Compaq made a profit on our backs. Is this really okay?

In addition to *Compaq*, other controversial corporate tax planning techniques have been upheld by the courts. In *United Parcel Service v. Commissioner*,[61] the circuit court reversed the Tax Court's determination that a transaction entered into by UPS lacked economic substance. As part of its business, UPS sells insurance on its packages. Luckily for UPS it does not damage many packages so its insurance business is very profitable. UPS sought to avoid paying tax on this profit by restructuring the transaction as insurance provided by an overseas affiliate. In a complicated set of transactions, UPS managed to continue the insurance program, and incur no profit in the United States. The Tax Court found the transactions were anticipatory assignments of income and lacked economic substance. The circuit court reversed, finding that the transactions at issue in UPS were real and created legal obligations between the parties. It thus concluded that the transactions should be respected for tax purposes. In other words, the circuit court was less concerned that UPS had almost completely eliminated its risk of loss, and instead focused more on whether there were legally binding obligations.

As you can see, courts and judges often differ as to whether a transaction should be respected for tax purposes. Some of this difference may be explained by judicial philosophy. Some judges may be willing to uphold a transaction as long as it fits within the letter of the law, and believe that if a fix is necessary it is Congress's job, not the court's, to fix the problem. Others judges may implement more of a smell test. If the transaction stinks, and everyone knows its only purpose was to manipulate the law to achieve tax benefits, the transaction need not be respected.

(6) Other Tax Avoidance Techniques

(a) Corporate Inversion

In addition to tax shelters, there are other methods that corporations and individuals use to avoid paying tax. Corporations have started to change their place of incorporation to foreign

---

[61]   254 F.3d 1014 (11th Cir.2001).

countries, thus avoiding tax on their income outside the United States. This has been referred to lately as corporate inversion. While an in depth discussion of corporate inversion is outside the scope of this book, a very basic summary is provided here. Under the United States system of taxation, a corporation is taxable on its world wide income, not just the income it earns in the United States. If a company reincorporates in another country, the other country's tax rules, not ours apply. So if a corporation reincorporates in a foreign country that does not tax world wide income, the company is not subject to our world wide system.[62] The company would still be required to pay tax on income earned in the United States, but if it is a large multinational corporation with significant income outside the United States, reincorporating in another country may save the company millions of dollars.

(b) Corporate Owned Life Insurance

Life insurance, an often used tool in tax avoidance schemes, is being used by major corporations to defer taxable income. Corporations often insured their top executives, believing that the death of a top executive would impact the companies' bottom line (referred to as Corporate Owned Life Insurance or "COLI").[63] But starting in the 1980s, companies started insuring their rank and file employees. Why would they do this? As we have discussed previously, the inside build-up in a life insurance policy is not taxed. It is not taxed when it is earned and it is not taxed when it is paid upon the death of the insured. But the inside build-up is reported on corporate balance sheets. So what a company does is buys life insurance on its employees and designates itself as the beneficiary. Each year the corporation pays premiums on the policy. These premiums are deductible. Part of the premium is an insurance component and part is an investment component. The company then reports the investment component on its books as income, but does not have to pay tax on this deferred gain. Companies also use various techniques to borrow against the cash value of the life insurance policy. If they cannot do so, then they simply wait until the insured has died and collect the benefit.

Too good to be true? Well companies have been doing it and getting away with it for years. The IRS does require that there be some business purpose for the insurance (companies often argue the

---

[62]   Under our laws, the corporation may be entitled to a credit if they pay tax to a foreign country on income earned outside the United States. But if that income is not taxed abroad, it is taxed at home.

[63]   See Ellen E. Schultz and Theo Francis, How Corporations built Finance Tool out of Life Insurance, Wall Street Journal, Dec. 30, 2002., at A1, A8.

purpose is to provide benefits to employees) and has recently been cracking down on corporate owned life insurance.[64]

(c) Foreign Credit Cards

Another tax avoidance technique that has become popular among individuals is the use of foreign credit cards to get access to money hidden abroad. To be clear, it is not against the law to have a foreign credit card. It is against the law to earn income, hide it abroad, and not pay tax on it. It appears that people are using trusts and foreign entities to hide income that is subject to tax in the United States. It does no good, however, to hide money if you can't use it. People have, therefore, been using foreign credit cards to purchase items. They then use money in their foreign accounts to pay the foreign credit card bill. The individuals hope that using foreign cards will make it difficult to trace the transactions.

The IRS has taken aggressive action to uncover fraud involving foreign credit cards. The IRS obtained John Doe summonses against American Express, Visa, and MasterCard, which were designed to obtain information regarding United States participants who hold credit cards issued by banks in Antigua, Bermuda, the Bahamas, and the Cayman Islands.[65] As a result of these summonses, the IRS estimates that one to two million Americans may be using offshore credit cards.[66]

(7) Tax Shelters Without Tears

What is the problem? Why are we having so much trouble with tax shelters? Historically, we see the decision in the *Crane* case,[67] followed by the flowering of tax shelters followed by the huge, complex outpouring of legislative, judicial and administrative actions against tax shelters. It is fair to say that the system of administration of the tax laws has been engaged in a massive campaign against tax shelters for several decades.

The question is whether it had to be this way. Once *Crane* was decided the way it was, could the response to tax shelters have taken a different course?

It seems clear that things could have been different. As we have seen, the amount of depreciation allowed in the early years of an investment is, from the point of view of economic analysis, always

---

[64]　See e.g. Winn-Dixie v. Commissioner, 254 F.3d 1313 (11th Cir.2001)(finding corporate owned life insurance program was a sham transaction).

[65]　See IRS News Release, IRS Sets New Audit Priorities, September 2002 (FS–2002–12), 2002 WL 31053874 (I.R.S.).

[66]　Id.

[67]　See ¶ 4.03(2)(b)(ii).

overstated. Even straight-line depreciation overstates the amount that should be allowed in the early years (and necessarily understates it in the later years). See ¶ 6.02(12). This leads to deferral of income which is the essence of tax shelters.

As our discussion of depreciation has shown, the economically correct method of depreciation is "sinking fund" depreciation. It will be recalled that under that method, depreciation is backloaded—with small amounts of depreciation in the early years and large amounts in the later years.

If that method of depreciation had been applied historically, the strength of the tax shelter type of investment would have been seriously if not mortally impaired. There would have been no deferral. We would not have had to enact the massive phalanx of anti-tax shelter rules that we now have. The tax law would have been much simpler.

There was a better way once, but it's too late now.

¶ 8.03 DEFERRED PAYMENT SALES: *LOGAN*

(1) In General

Where a taxpayer sells property for deferred payments to be paid over a period of years in the future, he is automatically put on the installment method of reporting, unless he elects otherwise.[68] The installment method of accounting for such sales in effect spreads the taxpayer's gain out over the period for which he will receive the payments. This approach is generally attractive because it results in deferral of gain and is used by most taxpayers. As we have pointed out at great length elsewhere, deferral of gain is money in the bank to the taxpayer. See the Appendix and ¶¶ 1.032(2)(e); 3.08(4)(b); 6.02(12).

The question may be asked whether it is appropriate to defer gain in this situation and thereby put money in the pocket of the selling taxpayer. The idea behind installment sales treatment is that the seller who has taken back a note from the buyer does not necessarily have the funds to pay the tax. The buyer's notes cannot be easily sold for cash. That does make sense, but if that is the problem, then it would be appropriate to charge the seller interest on his deferred tax liability. It is one thing to be concerned about the seller's liquidity; it is another to put money in the seller's pocket just because he has chosen to use the installment method of reporting.[69]

---

[68] Section 453(d)(1). For rules barring the installment method on sales between certain related parties, see discussion below.

[69] The statute does impose an interest charge on the deferred tax liability in the case of sales for a price above $150,000, where the buyer has a total face amount of

Without an interest charge on the deferred tax liability, the statute encourages sellers to use the installment method of reporting even if they do have the funds (say from other sources) to pay the tax on the sale immediately. This misallocates resources. We are encouraging the seller to keep his funds loaned to the buyer rather than perhaps put his funds elsewhere based on financial market conditions.

If the deferred payment sales arrangement is not reported on the installment method, then the so-called closed method approach is used. The fair market value of the deferred payment claims is included in the cash basis taxpayer's amount realized in the year of the sale. The amount realized so computed will be taken against the taxpayer's basis in the property to ascertain taxpayer's gain or loss in the year of sale.[70]

In the rare case, the claims are so speculative in value that no fair market value may be placed upon them. The payments could be difficult to value because they are contingent on events based in the future that are hard to predict. For example the payments could be a percentage of the royalties produced by a copper mine in an era when copper prices are volatile. The payments could also be difficult to value because the debtor is staggering on the edge of bankruptcy. In such cases the transaction may be reported as "open." Under "open" or *Logan* treatment, the payments received as the years go by will first be applied against the basis of the property and no gain will be reported until the year in which the cumulative payments exceed that basis. Payments in excess of that basis will be reported as capital gain if the underlying property sold was a capital asset.[71]

---

obligations from such sales exceeding $5 million, § 453A. In addition, borrowing against such obligations is considered to be a payment, triggering tax. This provision was enacted to combat what was perceived as sharp tax planning in the case of the Campeau/Federated Department stores leveraged buyout. See D. Posin, *Corporate Tax Planning: Takeovers, Leveraged Buyouts and Restructurings* Chapter 3 ¶ C (1990).

[70] If the property sold is a capital asset, the gain (or loss) will be capital (which leads to the possible application of one of several attractive rates, ¶ 4.06). If the claims are subsequently paid at face, the difference between the face amount and the fair market value will be treated as ordinary income, regardless of whether or not the underlying property sold was a capital asset.

If any claim is not paid off (or paid off at less than the amount at which it was valued), then the taxpayer has a bad debt loss, which will generally give rise to a short-term capital loss, unless the sale of the property was incident to the taxpayer's trade or business. See Warren Jones Co. v. Commissioner, 524 F.2d 788 (9th Cir.1975), rev'g 60 T.C. 663 (1973) (land contract included in amount realized notwithstanding its fair market value was steeply discounted from its face amount); § 166(d) (short-term, capital loss on nonbusiness bad debts); see also ¶ 7.01(6) for bad debts and worthless securities generally.

Accrual method taxpayers are treated similarly except that the initial valuation of the installment notes to the accrual method taxpayer is at their face amount.

[71] Cf. Burnet v. Logan, 283 U.S. 404, 51 S.Ct. 550, 75 L.Ed. 1143 (1931), see graphic below.

This "open" treatment is, therefore, attractive in that gain is deferred until basis is recovered. In Congress's view, "Only in rare and extraordinary cases will property be considered to have no fair market value."[72]

The issues involved in "closed," "open" and "installment" treatment are illustrated by the classic case of *Burnet v. Logan*.

BURNET V. LOGAN[73]

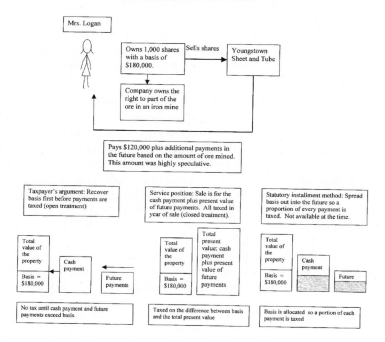

Facts: Mrs. Logan owned 1,000 shares of Andrews & Hitchcock Corp (A & H), with a basis of $180,000. A & H owns the right to part of a very rich iron mine. In 1916, Logan sells her shares to Youngstown Sheet & Tube. Youngstown payed Mrs. Logan $120,000 cash plus additional payments in the future based on the amount of ore that A & H mined. This amount was highly speculative.

---

[72] Reg. § 1.1001–1(a); Senate report accompanying Installment Sales Revision Act of 1980, page 24; McCormac v. United States, 191 Ct.Cl. 483, 424 F.2d 607 (1970) (contingent payments valued); compare Wiggins' Estate, 72 T.C. 701 (1979) (open transaction allowed for contracts that lacked ascertainable fair market value). See also United States v. Davis, 370 U.S. 65, 82 S.Ct. 1190, 8 L.Ed.2d 335 (1962), reh'g denied 371 U.S. 854, 83 S.Ct. 14, 9 L.Ed.2d 92 (1962) (value of extinguishment of marital rights determined by reference to value of property given up; discussed on other issues at ¶ 4.02(2)).

[73] 283 U.S. 404, 51 S.Ct. 550, 75 L.Ed. 1143 (1931). The facts in this graphic have been simplified from the original case.

Question: How are the payments to be received in the future taxed? The options are: 1) The payments are untaxed until basis is recovered first, 2) The cash payment and the present value of the future payments are taxed in the year of sale; or 3) A possibility not considered by the *Logan* Court is the installment method of the current statute, discussed below.

Taxpayer's position: Use open treatment. No gain in year of sale nor until basis recovered. She argues that the $120,0000 cash should be offset by her $180,000 basis in the stock. She further argues that she should have no taxable gain until she receives another $60,000 (the remaining basis) from A & H. Amounts received after the $180,000 basis is recovered will be taxable.

Service's position: Use closed treatment. Estimate future payments will come in at $9,000 per year for 45 years, based on the amount of ore supposedly left at the deposit. These payments had a present value of $100,000. This $100,000 present value plus the $120,000 cash payment gave Mrs. Logan an amount realized in the year of sale of $220,000. Taking that $220,000 against Mrs. Logan's basis of $180,000 gave her a gain in year of sale of $40,000.

Held: Open treatment should be used. The arrangement is too speculative to be valued. Thus nothing is included in income for 1916, the year of sale.

Comment, the three methods: Note the extreme difference between the Service's approach and the taxpayer's approach. The Service's approach gives the gain as early as possible and the taxpayer's approach gives the gain as late as possible. The installment method approach gives a result in between the other two. It provides for ratable inclusion of income as payments are made. These are the three major approaches to contracts for future payments. As discussed further below, the open treatment has pretty well gone out with the buggywhip. The installment method is by far the most widely used. The closed method is rare but can be elected under the statute.

Comment, time value of money analysis applied to Logan: What happens as each payment for the next 45 years comes in under *Logan?* The total of $9,000 per year for 45 years has been valued by the Service as being worth $100,000 on a present value basis.[74] Note that without discounting the total worth of the payments is 45 × $9,000 or $405,000. Since the total value of the payments on a present value basis is $100,000, then each payment, having been valued at its present value, would take a basis of its present value at

---

[74]   This implies an interest rate of 8.8%. These numbers have been simplified from the actual numbers of *Logan*. The principle is the same.

the year of the sale. Then as each payment came in at $9,000, the excess of $9,000 over the basis of the payment would be income. This is shown in the accompanying chart.

TIME VALUE OF MONEY ANALYSIS
APPLIED TO *LOGAN*

Present Value of $9,000 Payments Paid Annually for 45 Years.

Year	Amount of Payment	Present Value or Basis of payment	Amount Included in Income as Payment Rec'd
1	$9,000	$8,272.06	$727.94
2	$9,000	$7,603.00	$1,397.00
3	$9,000	$6,988.05	$2,011.95
4	$9,000	$6,422.84	$2,577.16
5	$9,000	$5,903.34	$3,096.66
6	$9,000	$5,425.87	$3,574.13
7	$9,000	$4,987.01	$4,012.99
8	$9,000	$4,583.65	$4,415.35
9	$9,000	$4,212.91	$4,787.09
10	$9,000	$3,872.16	$5,127.84
11	$9,000	$3,558.97	$5,441.03
12	$9,000	$3,271.11	$5,728.89
13	$9,000	$3,006.54	$5,993.46
14	$9,000	$2,763.36	$6,236.64
15	$9,000	$2,539.86	$6,460.14
16	$9,000	$2,334.43	$5,665.57
17	$9,000	$2,145.61	$6,854.39
18	$9,000	$1,972.07	$7,027.93
19	$9,000	$1,812.56	$7,187.44
20	$9,000	$1,665.96	$7,334.04
21	$9,000	$1,531.21	$7,466.79
22	$9,000	$1,407.37	$7,592.63
23	$9,000	$1,293.53	$7,706.47
24	$9,000	$1,188.91	$7,811.09
25	$9,000	$1,092.75	$7,907.25
26	$9,000	$1,004.36	$7,995.64
27	$9,000	$923.13	$8,076.87
28	$9,000	$848.46	$8,151.54
29	$9,000	$779.84	$8,220.16
30	$9,000	$716.76	$8,283.24
31	$9,000	$658.79	$8,341.21
32	$9,000	$605.51	$8,394.49
33	$9,000	$556.53	$8,443.47
34	$9,000	$511.52	$8,488.48
35	$9,000	$470.14	$8,529.86
36	$9,000	$432.12	$8,567.88
37	$9,000	$397.17	$8,602.83
38	$9,000	$365.04	$8,634.96
39	$9,000	$335.52	$8,664.48
40	$9,000	$308.38	$8,691.62
41	$9,000	$283.44	$8,716.55
42	$9,000	$260.51	$8,739.49
43	$9,000	$239.44	$8,760.88
44	$9,000	$220.08	$8,779.92
45	$9,000	$202.28	$8,797.72
Total:	$405,000	$100,000.00	$305,000.00

$9,000 minus basis of payment

Adds to $405,000.

Did the Service and the taxpayer handle open treatment this way in *Logan*? We don't know, but we doubt it. We have only been applying sophisticated time value of money techniques to taxation from the last decade or so. *Logan* was decided in 1931. Probably what the taxpayer and the Service did was to divide the $100,000 that was reported as income from these payments in the year of sale by 45, yielding $2,222. Then they would have said that $2,222 was the basis of each payment as it came in. That would then give income in each year of $9,000 – $2,222, or $6,778. 45 years of income of $6,778 gives us $305,000. So this straight-line method also gives us a total of $305,000 income reported as the payments come in. But we know from the Appendix and other areas where we have discussed time value of money that the straight-line method is the wrong way to do it.[75]

Comment, estate taxes: One of the confusing aspects of this case was that this future payment contract was, in the facts of the case, valued in the estate of Mrs. Logan's mother. But, the Court said, that valuation had to be accomplished for estate tax purposes.

Comment, planning for closely-held businesses: When a closely-held business is sold, there can be great dispute about what the value should really be. By definition the stock is not publicly traded, so the valuation problem can be acute. One technique for accomplishing such a sale that the buyer and seller might both agree upon is to make part of the consideration a percentage of gross revenues for a period of years.[76] This is then a contingent payment contract which might be difficult or easy to value depending on how volatile the revenues of the business are.

Comment, open treatment under current law: You can't hardly get it any more. If the payment is for a contingent amount and the maximum payment is not fixed but the period of time is fixed, then the Service can compel the basis to be recovered ratably over the fixed time period. If the maximum amount of the payback is fixed but the time period is not fixed, then each payment received will be taxed in the same proportion that the maximum payment on the contract bears to the seller's basis.[77] If both the maximum price and the period of payments are not fixed, then the regulations spread the basis recovery out more or less arbitrarily over a period of 15 years.[78] With all of these techniques, if it comes out wrong at the end of the contract, the seller simply takes a further deduction for loss or reports more income for gain to even things up.

Can the seller under a contingent payment deal avoid these techniques and still get the old attractive *Logan* deal? The seller

---

[75] See also e.g. ¶ 6.0(12)(c), discussing "sinking fund" depreciation and ¶ 1.032(2)(e), discussing recovery of capital.

[76] Keying the royalty percentage to *net* income would not be a good idea, since games can be played in arriving at net income.

[77] Regs. § 15a.453–1(c).

[78] Senate report to accompany Installment Sales Revision Act of 1980, pp. 23–24, also admonishing once again that only in rare and extraordinary cases may the "open" or *Logan* method of reporting be used.

might try to say that he is "electing out" of these techniques in the same way that the seller under the usual installment method (which is not contingent) can elect out of installment treatment.

See if we can keep from getting confused on this one. The normal sale for fixed payments over a fixed period of time can be reported either under the installment method or—if the seller elects out of the installment method—it can be reported as a closed transaction. (Review the graphic above on *Logan*). Transactions with a contingent selling price are treated the same way. They are either on the installment method (using the techniques described above) or the seller can elect out of the installment method. What happens to contingent deals where the seller elects out of the installment method? The philosophy of the statute is that they should be then reported on the most unattractive method of being closed in the year of sale. However perhaps the seller on a contingent payment deal— particularly if selling price and pay-out period are both not fixed and the payments are hard to estimate—might hope to get the most attractive treatment of all, open (*Logan*) treatment. Given the legislative history, and the attitude of the Service, the chances of that are not good. If the facts of *Logan* came up today, they would not get *Logan* treatment.

(2) The Installment Method of Reporting

As we have described in the previous section, the installment method of reporting involves spreading the seller's gain out over the period in which the payments are to be made. This section discusses the installment approach in more detail, since it is used in the overwhelming majority of deferred payment sales.

An "installment sale," under the statute, is a disposition of property where at least one payment is to be received after the close of the taxable year in which the disposition occurs.[79] The installment method may be used where only a single payment is to be made, provided that payment is made in a year following the close of the year of sale.[80] In an installment sale, the taxpayer is on the

---

[79] Section 453(b)(1). This discussion pertains primarily to casual sales of real and personal property; dealers who sell property on the installment method use analogous rules. See § 453(b)(2).

[80] Applying the installment method to such a one-payment sale does not spread the taxpayer's gain over more than one year, but it does have the effect of deferring the gain until the year in which the payment is actually made. Absent the installment method, such a sale with one deferred payment would probably be valued and taxed to the taxpayer in the year of the sale. See text above. Prior to the Installment Sales Revision Act of 1980, two or more payments were required in order to qualify for installment method treatment. See also Rev.Rul. 82–227, 1982–52 IRB (using installment method on year-end stock sale to choose which year to be taxed on sale).

installment method of reporting automatically, unless he elects out of it.[81]

The computation of the installment method is as follows: The proportion of each payment that is received is taxed as the proportion that the gross profit bears to the total contract price.[82]

> **Example:** T sells a plot of vacant land for $100,000 to be paid in five installments: of $20,000 in the year of sale, and $20,000 in each of the four following years. Adequate interest is separately stated and paid. The basis of the land in T's hands is $40,000. To compute the installment method for this transaction, it is first determined that the gross profit on this transaction is $60,000. The ratio of the gross profit to the contract price ($60,000/$100,000) is 60 percent. Therefore, 60 percent of each $20,000 payment, or $12,000 is taxed to T on the receipt of each payment. When the five payments have been made, T will have been taxed on his $60,000 of gain.

If the property is sold subject to a mortgage of the seller's, either with or without personal liability, only the excess of the mortgage, if any, over the seller's basis will be considered a payment in the year of sale. For purposes of computing the ratio, the contract price will exclude the mortgage except to the extent the mortgage exceeds the seller's basis.[83]

> **Example:** T sells a plot of vacant land for $50,000 plus the assumption by B of a $50,000 mortgage on the property. The $50,000 purchase price is to be paid in five installments: of $10,000 in the year of sale, and $10,000 in each of the four following years. Adequate interest is separately stated and paid. The basis of the land in T's hands is $40,000. To compute the installment method for this transaction, it is first determined that the gross profit on the transaction is $60,000 ($50,000 cash plus being relieved of $50,000 mortgage yields total amount realized of $100,000 less the basis of $40,000, gives a gross profit of $60,000). The contract price is $60,000 ($50,000 purchase price plus $10,000 excess of mortgage over basis). Thus $60,000/$60,000 or 100% of each payment will be taxed to T.

The payment in the first year is $20,000 ($10,000 cash plus $10,000 excess of mortgage over basis). The payment in each of the

---

[81]   Section 453(a) and (d).

[82]   Section 453(b) and (c).

[83]   Reg. § 1.453–4(c). The contract price is reduced by commissions and other costs of the sale under the usual rules. See ¶ 4.03(1).

next four years is $10,000. Thus the total amount taxed to T will be $60,000, which is the amount of his gain. The higher percentage applied to the payments (compared to the example above) makes up for the fact that in this example being relieved of the mortgage in the year of sale was for the most part not taxed.

This procedure not only establishes the timing for the reporting of a taxpayer's gain, but it also establishes the basis in the installment notes that the taxpayer holds. The rule is that taxpayer's basis in his installment notes is the face amount of the note less the amount which would be reportable as income were the note satisfied in full.[84] Thus, should the taxpayer sell the note before it is satisfied, he can calculate his gain (or loss) since the installment method has established his basis in each note.[85]

The installment method may be employed where some gain is recognized in a tax-free exchange. In such a transaction the approach is to apply the installment sale rules to the taxable part of the transaction. Thus, the gross profit is the recognized gain and the contract price is the total amount of the consideration received less the fair market value of the non-recognition property received. In making all these computations, the installment obligations are valued at face.[86]

With respect to the new rules on capital gains (see Chapter 4), final regulations were published providing that if the capital gain from an installment sale consists of both 25% gain and 20/10% gain, the taxpayer must take the 25% gain into account before the 20/10% gain as payments are received (T.D. 8836, Aug. 23, 1999). Presumably, this rule now applies at the 15/5% rate.

¶ 8.04 DEFERRED COMPENSATION: A SURVEY

(1) In General

Employee compensation can take a wide variety of forms, as indicated in Chapter 2. In addition, employee compensation may be in the form of various deferred arrangements. This is an area in which taxpayers and their employers may engage in significant planning to defer the employee's current tax liability, provide the employer with a tax deduction and ensure retirement security for the employee. A complete treatment of this complex subject is beyond the

---

[84]   Section 453(b).

[85]   Not only will sale of the note trigger gain or loss but so will distribution, transmission, gift, or other disposition, § 453(a).

[86]   Senate report accompanying the Installment Sales Revision Act of 1980, page 19.

scope of this work; only an outline of the planning possibilities in this area will be presented.

The difference between qualified and nonqualified deferred compensation plans is fundamental to this area. Qualified plans are so-called because they meet a variety of explicit rules relating to employee participation and benefits. When these rules are met, qualified plans receive the attractive treatment that the employee is not taxed when his benefits are earned, but only when they are received; the earnings of the plan are not subject to tax as they are accumulated, but only when distributed; and the employer gets a current deduction for contributions to such plans.

Nonqualified arrangements do not have to meet these broad requirements with respect to employee participation, benefits and funding, but the price they pay is a somewhat less attractive tax treatment as a result. Nonqualified or contractual deferred compensation plans are particularly useful for compensating the executive, or other highly compensated individual—such as an entertainer or athlete—where the employer may be willing to undergo a tax disadvantage to confer unusual benefits on the object of its bounty.

For more detailed discussion, see ¶ 8.04(2)(a) below.

(2) Non-Qualified Plans

(a) Current Razzle-Dazzle Executive Compensation Techniques

Using the nonqualified technique described above, John Welch Jr., chief executive officer of General Electric in 1995 deferred taxes on $1 million of salary. By so doing he will increase his compensation substantially within five years. Mr. Welch was not alone. J.F. McDonnell, the chairman of McDonnell Douglas corporation deferred $2.5 million. Michael H. Jordan of Westinghouse deferred $1.8 million. John L. Clendenin of BellSouth has nearly $10 million in his deferral accounts.[87] There is no ceiling on how much money can be sheltered using these nonqualified techniques. Roberto C. Goizueta, the chief executive officer of Coca Cola has accumulated $1 billion in Coca Cola stock that will not be taxed until after he retires. Readers of this book need no introduction to the extremely attractive effect of deferring large amount of tax for a significant number of years.

The size of this movement should not be underestimated. Many large companies, such as I.B.M., Tenneco, and Merrill Lynch have

---

[87] The anecdotal information in the text comes from Christopher Drew and David Cay Johnston, Special Tax Breaks Enrich Savings of Many in the Ranks of Management, The New York Times, October 13, 1996, A1.

expanded their plans to include as many as hundreds or even thousands of employees. Owners of small business are setting up nonqualified plans, which are allowing them to save for their retirement without including their employees. The employees would have to be part of any § 401(k) plan or qualified plan set up.

The total number of employers who had notified the IRS that they have nonqualified plans has swelled from less than 1,000 at the beginning of 1982 to over 24,000 at the end of 1996. And there are a number of employers who have established plans who have not notified the IRS.

A major reason the number of nonqualified deferral plans has exploded is the increased restrictions Congress has enacted with respect to qualified plans. Congress enacted ERISA which was intended to expand and protect the retirement funds of workers. ERISA, and subsequent legislation limited how much executives could save in qualified plans. In particular Congress in 1986 cut the maximum that one person could contribute to a 401(k) or supplemental retirement program from $30,000 to $7,000, because of the large amounts of tax the Government was losing with these deferral plans. In 1988 and 1993, Congress cut the amounts that executives could receive from regular pension plans from up to $250,000 to $150,000. These changes substantially lowered the federal budget deficit. Then, Congress began to raise marginal tax rates, with signatures from President Bush and President Clinton, from a maximum of 28% in 1991 to a maximum of 39.6% in 1993.[88] This was coupled with the denial of deduction to the employer for annual executive salaries about $1 million. All of this spurred the rush to nonqualified plans.

It should be noted that because these are nonqualified plans, as discussed above, the setting aside of this money for deferred taxation to the executive does not result in deferred taxation to the employer. The corporate employer and its shareholders pay taxes on the money and thus the employer and it shareholders are subsidizing the executive's tax deferral.

The Government has not challenged this practice on the theory that the money set aside and its growth is taxed to the company, so that the Treasury is not losing tax revenues. The idea is that it is not for the Treasury to police how the company and its employees distribute the tax burden. The problem with that theory is that many companies are now buying life insurance policies on their employees to fund these plans. Since the inside buildup of life insurance is not

---

[88] As we have discussed often, as part of EGTRRA and JGTRRA the top marginal rate falls from 39.6% to 35%. It will rise again to 39.6% in 2011.

taxed,[89] see ¶ 3.06, the arrangement, taken altogether is costing the Treasury substantial revenues. According to one survey about 300 of the largest 1,000 companies are now using life insurance to finance their nonqualified deferred compensation arrangements. There are several techniques that employ life insurance. The major one operates as follows: the company takes out a policy on its employees. The company pays the premium and names itself as a beneficiary. The company keys the policy's investment return to fixed interest rates or to mutual funds. When the employee is ready to withdraw his deferred money, the company borrows from the policy or cashes it in for its cash surrender value. Another option is for the company to pay the deferred money out of its own funds and hold the policy until the death of the employee, at which time it collects the proceeds tax free.

Moreover, companies are not required to inform their shareholders how much compensation top executives are deferring.[90] These plans appear to amount to a pay raise to top management and as such, critics say, should be reported. It appears that the rise of the use of nonqualified plans has significantly changed the way executives are compensated. It is estimated that in 1980 executives at large companies received 90% of their retirement benefits from regular qualified company pension plans, participated in by most employees and limited as to amounts (as discussed above). But by 1996, astonishingly, only about 30% of executive retirement benefits came from company plans and the rest came from nonqualified plans that only top management participates in. Indeed, under federal rules, only top management can participate in these plans. Since the amounts in nonqualified plans are subject to the claims of general creditors, federal law does not allow rank and file employees to participate in these plans. Also these nonqualified plans are not backed up by the federal pension insurance fund.

A survey of the 1,000 largest public companies by Compensation Resource Group Inc. showed that 74% of the companies offered nonqualified plans for top executives. Sometimes executives are allowed to defer the money for just a few years, rather than for retirement. This is to be compared with IRA's and §§ 401(k) and 403(b) plans which require a penalty of 10% on withdrawals before age 59 1/2. Beyond that, the deferred money is often awarded a very

---

[89]   However, interest attributable to borrowing to fund the inside buildup is not deductible, § 264(f).

[90]   In light of the accounting scandal surrounding WorldCom and Enron, Companies appear to be moving in the direction of disclosing deferred compensation agreements.

high interest rate by the company. BellSouth has paid interest rates to its deferred amounts of from 8 to 22 percent over the last 10 years.

To return to Mr. Welch, he received an interest rate of 14% on the deferred $1 million of his $2 million salary. After 5 years at that rate the $1 million would have compounded to $1,925,415. Receiving that amount at a 40% tax rate five years later would leave Mr. Welch with $1,155,249. If he had taken the deferred $1 million immediately and paid taxes, he would have had only about $600,000. The best, after tax, secure interest rate he could hope to receive on that $600,000 would be, say, 5%. After five years the $600,000 would compound, at that interest rate, to $765,769. Thus the gain from being able to defer and receive the artificially high interest rate is $389,480 ($1,115,249 less $765,769). Since deductible compensation is capped at $1 million (see ¶ 6.02(1)(a)), these maneuvers also preserve the companies involved the possibility of being able to deduct the payments later, when they are paid. Thus by choosing to defer payments with nonqualified plans, executives save their companies taxes. For example a company in the top corporate bracket of 35% saves $350,000 by being able to deduct $1 million in deferred salary. Companies can be willing to give some of these tax savings back to the executive who agrees to defer some of his salary. Companies may also pay the cost of insurance that eliminates the risk of using nonqualified deferred compensation plans.

Using these techniques has enabled a great many top management people to defer a great deal of income, as indicated above. But the unquestioned giant in the field of executive compensation is the late Roberto C. Goizueta, the chief executive of the Coca-Cola Company. He had by all accounts done an excellent job as the chief executive officer of Coke. His accomplishments in the deferred compensation field, though, are the stuff of legend. Mr. Goizueta was born in Cuba and educated at Yale. From 1979 through 1996, according to company proxy statements, Mr. Goizueta received total compensation of more than $1 billion. Not counting stock options. And one might want to count stock options, since Coca-Cola's stock price appreciated 52 times under his stewardship. The $1 billion does not count his § 401(k) plan and his regular pension which was worth $3 million a year. But the really interesting part is that he paid taxes on this billion dollar package at a rate of 5%. This makes a nice comparison with a typical middle class family with $50,000 of income and two children, which pays 17% of its income in taxes.

Basically, Mr. Goizueta employed § 83, discussed at ¶ 2.03. He received a total of 17.2 million Coke shares on the condition that he not sell them or borrow against them before he retired. He also received two cash payments based on the price of Coke stock. The restrictions on the stock did not affect his power to vote the shares or receive dividends on them (which amounted to $4.9 million in 1995). As long as the restrictions were not lifted, Mr. Goizueta did not have to pay taxes. With the stock trading around $50 in late 1996, Mr. Goizueta checked in at right around $1 billion of deferred compensation. As we know, deferral of tax is like money in the bank. Mr. Goizueta's accomplished a great deal as chief executive officer of Coke. His career also demonstrated that deferred compensation goes better with Coke.

Another aspect of these nonqualified plans is that they take top management out of the same pension plans as the rest of the employees. As Sylvester J. Schieber of Watson Wyatt Worldwide, a benefits consulting group, said, "Senior management is no longer in the same puddle with the rest of the work force, and if the puddle dries up, senior management is not much affected."[91] Although nonqualified plans supposedly do not have the safeguards of qualified plans, the fact is that the power of top management is such that their nonqualified plans are protected in bankruptcy proceedings even as the rank and file's § 401(k) plans, in which they may be required to invest in the company's stock, go broke.

An example is the widely publicized bankruptcy of Morris Knudsen construction company. The company had a distinguished reputation for building major projects in difficult places, such as the 726 foot Hoover Dam across the Colorado River and the Trans-Alaska oil pipeline. It also had an outstanding reputation for taking care of its employees. But soon after Mr. William J. Agee (the ex-corporate raider with Bendix who had a widely publicized relationship with Mary Cunningham, a former Bendix executive whom he eventually married) took charge of the company, the company fell on hard times. Workers' regular pension benefits were frozen and further years of service did not count toward future benefits. Instead, only a § 401(k) plan was available for retirement for new employees. Mr. Agee, meanwhile, moved the company headquarters from its traditional location in Boise Idaho to Carmel, California, closer to Mr. Agee's mansion in Pebble Beach. Thereafter, the board set up a deferred-compensation plan for Mr. Agee and 100 of his top executives. Six months later, the company reported surprising losses on its new mass-transit manufacture contracts, that had been initiated by Mr. Agee. In February, 1995, the board demanded Mr. Agee's resignation. For about a year the company resisted its creditors but eventually it

---

[91]   The anecdotal information on treatment of pension benefits in bankruptcy is based on Diana B. Henriques and David Cay Johnston, Managers Staying Dry as Corporations Sink, The New York Times, October 14, 1996, page A1.

filed for protection of the bankruptcy laws in connection with a purchase of the company by another smaller construction company. The company's stock shrank virtually to $0, and the § 401(k) plans that had bought mostly the company's stock similarly dissolved. A year before the bankruptcy filing, however, the company's creditors agreed to let the company pay Mr. Agee and its other executives the $4.4 million in their supposedly more risky nonqualified plan.

Another story is presented by Carter Hawley Hale. The Carter Hawley Hale § 401(k) was different from the Morris Knudsen in that the employees of Carter Hawley Hale could only buy the company's stock in it. Through the 80's, as the company's stock soared. More than 14,000 employees participated in the § 401(k), as a supplement to their relatively small regular pension plans. Ultimately the company went bankrupt and was eventually purchased by Federated Department Stores, with rank and file employees losing at least 90% of their value in their 401(k)'s. The supplemental pension and savings plans set up for Philip M. Hawley, the president and chief executive officer and other top executives had more options than just the company's stock, including an account that paid 10% interest. During the bankruptcy these supplemental pensions and deferred compensation plans of top management were preserved.

Still another example is the recent Enron Bankruptcy. It appears that Enron executives were selling their stock and divesting their interest in the company while employees were unable to do so. Employees, who owned large amounts of Enron stock in their 401(k) plans, found their retirement savings decimated.

These cases are not unique. Giving the lie to the idea that nonqualified benefits go to the end of the creditors line are the bankruptcy filings of R. H. Macy & Company, now owned by Federated; Dow Corning, the silicon-products company combatting liability claims for breast implants; Am International, a manufacturer of graphics and mailroom equipment; First American Health Care, the leading home health care provider; Insilco, the manufacturer of Rolodex office products; Federated Department Stores and its sister chain Allied Stores. In all these cases, according to bankruptcy records collected by New Generation Research of Boston, all or substantial amounts of supplemental or deferred nonqualified compensation for top executives were preserved or reinstated in connection with the bankruptcy proceeding.

In addition to relying on the top management's own bargaining power in the bankruptcy proceeding, other devices are being employed to safeguard nonqualified deferred compensation. A popular device is the so-called "rabbi trust," (the model was created for a rabbi of a Jewish congregation in Brooklyn). Under a rabbi trust, the company sets the executive's deferred money aside in a separate account. Although the money still belongs to the company and is subject to its creditors, the account is nonetheless considered to be safer than relying on just the company's promise to pay. In addition, executives can purchase insurance to protect deferred compensation or supplemental benefits from a company's unwillingness or inability to pay in the future. Some companies may even reimburse the executive for the cost of the insurance. Executives of PG & E and CSX corporation have purchased such insurance.

The upshot of these trends is that life seems to be getting tougher for middle management and rank-and-file employees. In the bankruptcy setting, top management may negotiate for its own benefits as the rank-and-file are being squeezed. Also the heavy use of § 401(k) plans that encourage or require investment in the company's stock means that middle management and rank-and-file employees may have their retirement funds too heavily invested in the stock of one company. One interesting turn may give employees some hope in the future. During the Enron bankruptcy, the United States Trustee approved a separate creditor's committee for employees. This separate committee gives the employees far more say than usual in how the assets of the company will be distributed.

The original thesis of the pension law was to provide that if management wanted to save for their retirement on a tax-deferred basis, they had to develop a plan that covered most employees. With these nonqualified plans, that link is being broken and less provision is now being made for rank-and-file employees.

It can be argued that by limiting the amounts that executives can save in regular pension plans, the Government created this problem and perhaps those limits should be liberalized. Another approach would be to remove the tax advantages of deferred compensation, through, for example, legislatively imposing the doctrine of constructive receipt on nonqualified arrangements (see ¶ 9.03(2)(b)).

(b) Incentive Stock Options

A stock option is a right granted by a company to an employee to purchase the stock of the company from the company at a particular price for a particular period of time. If the company's stock rises to a price above the option price, the employee has a sure-fire winning deal. This is a form of compensation.

Under the incentive stock option there is no tax on the grant or the exercise of the option. When the employee sells the stock he receives on exercise of the option he is taxed at a capital gains rate.

See ¶ 2.03(2) for a discussion of the treatment of incentive stock options.

To qualify for this attractive treatment, the incentive stock option arrangement must meet a series of conditions at the level of the corporate employer, and the employee must satisfy certain holding period requirements.

With respect to the employer, the option must be granted under a plan which is approved by the stockholders within 12 months before or after the plan's adoption by the employer. The option itself must be granted within 10 years of the date that the plan is adopted or approved by the shareholders, whichever is sooner. The option must be exercisable only within a period of ten years after the date it is granted. The option price must equal or exceed the fair market value of the stock to which it is subject when the option is granted. The option must be not transferrable other than at death and it may be exercised only by the employee during his life. If the employee owns more than 10% of the company's stock he is not eligible for the option unless the option price is at least 110% of the fair market value of the stock, and the option may not in this case be exercised more than 5 years after it is granted. The option cannot be exercisable while there is an outstanding incentive stock option that has been granted to the employee in an earlier year. Employees may be granted incentive stock options for stock per year for no more than $100,000 fair market value of the stock, plus a carryover of one half of the amount of stock options that could have been granted in a previous year (the unused carryover amount may be carried over for 3 years).

At the employee level the employee who has acquired stock by exercising an incentive stock option must hold the stock for at least one year and cannot dispose of the stock within two years after the option was granted, in order to qualify for capital gains rates on disposition of the stock.[92] If either of these holding period requirements is not met, the gain on disposition of the stock will be taxed at ordinary income rates. The gain, whether capital or ordinary, on the disposition of the stock is measured by the amount realized on the sale of the stock and the price paid for the stock pursuant to the option.[93] To the extent the gain on the disposition of the stock is ordinary, because of failure to comply with the holding period requirements, the employer will be entitled to a deduction.[94]

---

[92] See ¶ 4.06(2)(b)(i).

[93] Section 422.

[94] Section 421(b).

(3) Qualified Plans

A pension, profit-sharing, or stock bonus plan which meets a wide variety of rules receives the attractive tax treatment that employer contributions to the plan are immediately deductible to the employer and not includable in the income of the employee until the benefits are received. Moreover, earnings on the amounts contributed by the employer to the plan accumulate tax-free until distributed to the employee. See the Appendix for a numerical example of the immense benefits that are conferred by qualified plans.[95]

In order to qualify for these attractive tax benefits the plan must be "qualified", which means it must meet requirements related to the following areas:

Minimum participation standards must be met; this requires that while not every employee must be covered, a certain minimum number must be covered to insure that the plan confers relatively broadly based benefits and does not just benefit a few highly-placed employees.[96] The plan must not involve any discriminatory contributions or benefits; this again is to insure that highly-placed or highly-compensated employees do not obtain excessive benefits under the plan.[97] Benefits must vest within certain time periods to prevent an employee working for a long period of time and receiving no benefits.[98] In addition to vesting pursuant to specified schedules, benefits must also accrue according to specified schedules; accrual is necessary first before benefits can vest. Accrual applies only to defined benefit plans.[99] There are limits on the benefits and contributions that may accrue to participants in qualified plans. The particular amounts are adjusted upward by the Service.[100] To ensure employer ability to pay benefits, minimum funding standards are also provided.[101]

Employees are taxed only the receipt of the benefits from the plan, and they have various options as to how they will be taxed on them. For example, the employee may choose to roll over a distribution from his pension plan into another qualified plan, an annuity plan, or an IRA.

---

[95]   Sections 404(a) (employer contributions); 402(a)(1) (employees).

[96]   Sections 401(a)(3), 410.

[97]   Section 401(a)(4).

[98]   Sections 401(a)(7), 411. This was an important result of The Employee Retirement Income Security Act of 1974 (ERISA).

[99]   Section 411(b)(1).

[100]   Section 415.

[101]   Section 412.

In addition employees may make deductible contributions up to certain limits depending on income to so-called § 401(k) and 403(b) plans. The earnings on these plans accumulate tax free and the contributions and earnings are taxable on withdrawal.

(4) Festival of IRAs

There are now more Individual Retirement Accounts (IRAs) out there than you can shake an accountant at. Here is the festival of IRAs:[102]

(a) Deductible IRA

Taxpayers who are not covered by a qualified plan, described above, can make a deductible contribution of up to the contribution amount ($4,000 in 2005–2007; $5,000 in 2008)[103] of their annual earnings to an IRA, regardless of their income. If a taxpayer's annual earnings do not exceed the contribution amount, taxpayer's deduction is limited by the amount of compensation includible in taxpayer's income for the taxable year.[104]

In addition, taxpayers who participate in a qualified plan can make an annual contribution of up to the contribution amount, but the eligible amount of the contribution phases out based on adjusted gross income limits. The AGI phaseout for single taxpayers starts at $50,000 for 2005 and gradually phases out from $50,000 to $60,000. The AGI phaseout for a married taxpayer filing jointly who actively participates in a qualified plan starts at $70,000 and phases out by $80,0000.

The earnings on the contributions are not taxed (and thus enjoy the benefit of compounding). Withdrawal of the original contribution and earnings are taxed. Distributions before age 59 1/2 are generally subject to a 10 percent penalty. Two exceptions to the penalty for early withdrawal are withdrawals for education and withdrawals of up to $10,000 for first-time home-buying. Distributions must begin at age 70½.

(b) Roth IRA

Taxpayers may also contribute to a Roth IRA. Contributions to the Roth IRA are not deductible. Earnings are not taxed. Distributions of both the contributions and earnings are not taxed, if the account is at least five years old and the account holder is at least 59½, dead or disabled. There are the same exceptions as the

---

[102] Section 219.

[103] This amount is adjusted for inflation after 2008. See § 219(b)(5)(c). However, as part of EGTRRA this amount goes back to $2,000 in 2011.

[104] Section 219(b)(1)(B).

deductible IRA from penalties for early withdrawals for education and first-time home-buying. Distributions do not have to begin at age 70½.

In 2005, single taxpayers may contribute up to $4,000 to a Roth IRA if their income is below $95,000. The eligible amount is reduced as income rises, and with the amount dropping to zero as income hits $110,000. Married taxpayers filing jointly can make contributions to the Roth IRA,[105] with the eligible amount of their contribution phasing out at a combined AGI of $150,000 to $160,000. Single-filing taxpayers may make contributions to the Roth IRA with the eligible amount phasing out at an AGI of $95,000 to $110,000. Married taxpayers may each be able to make the $4,000 IRA contribution. See 8.04(4)(d).

(c) Nondeductible IRA

Anyone with enough income to cover the contribution can make a contribution up to the contribution limit to a nondeductible IRA. The contributions are not deductible. The earnings are not taxed. Withdrawals of the original contribution are not taxed (since the original contribution was not deductible); withdrawals of the earnings are taxed. The other rules are similar to those of the deductible IRA.

(d) Spousal IRA

A working taxpayer not covered by an employer-sponsored retirement plan may now have a deductible IRA even if his spouse is an active participant in an employer sponsored retirement plan. The amount of the eligible contribution is phased out if their combined AGI is between $150,000 and $160,000. A nonworking taxpayer and his spouse may contribute up to the contribution amount as long as the working spouse earns at least that much.

The eligible working spouse may choose either a deductible IRA or a Roth IRA. The eligible nonworking spouse may have a deductible, Roth or nondeductible IRA, depending on the couple's income and job retirement plans.

> **Example:** Wilhelmena is an active participant in a retirement plan but her husband Harry is not. Their combined AGI is $130,000. Since Harry is not an active participant, he can make a deductible contribution, because the combined AGI is less than $150,000.

---

[105] Section 408A. The Roth IRA is named after Senator William Roth, (R. DE) Chairman of the Senate Finance Committee.

Wilhelmena, however, cannot make a contribution because the couple's combined AGI exceeds applicable dollar amount for an active participant filing jointly ($50,000–$80,000 in 2007, see deductible IRAs above).

(e) Education IRAs (Now Referred to as Coverdell Education Savings Accounts)[106]

Contributions of up to $2,000 per child under 18 may be made each year. If the contributor's income exceeds $95,000 for single or $190,000 for joint filers the allowable contribution is phased out (phaseout range $95,000 – $110,000 for single and $190,000 – $220,000).[107] This can be referred to as the grandparents' rule (although it applies to anyone). As long as the grandparent does not have AGI over these amounts, he or she can contribute to the grandchild's IRA. The contributions are not deductible. The earnings are not taxed. On withdrawal, the original contribution is not taxed (since it was not deductible) and the earnings are not taxed, if they are used for qualifying educational expenses. Money that is not spent on education or rolled over to another family member's IRA must be paid to the beneficiary at age 30 and is subject to tax and a 10 percent penalty.

The Coverdell IRA may be used for qualified elementary or secondary education expenses,[108] or for higher education.[109]

Two important points to recognize with regard to Coverdell IRAs. The first is that the income limits are higher for Coverdell IRAs than for other IRAs. Thus parents may be able to contribute to a Coverdell IRA even if they are foreclosed from contributing to a Roth IRA. Secondly, anyone can contribute to the child's Coverdell IRA, even the child. Thus, a parent could give their child $2,000 and the child, making a wise investment, could contribute that money to a Coverdell IRA.[110] Thus, the income limits on the Coverdell appear to be insignificant. Most children do not have AGIs exceeding $90,000 (and if they do, they do not need to save for college).[111]

For other, also small, assistance with college expenses, see the discussion of education credits at ¶ 10.07.

---

[106] Named after Senator Coverdell.
[107] Section 530.
[108] Section 530(b)(4).
[109] Section 530(b)(2).
[110] See IRS Notice 97–60, 1997–2 C.B. 310, 1997–46 I.R.B. 8, 1997 WL 708559.
[111] The income limits here are also insignificant in light of another deferred option for college savings, namely section 529 plans. See ¶ 8.04(4)(g).

(f)   *Strategies for Investing in IRAs*

If income is too high for a deductible IRA, the Roth IRA is far superior to the nondeductible IRA, because the earnings on the Roth IRA are forever tax-free, whereas they are only tax-deferred in the nondeductible IRA.

The tougher question is if the taxpayer is eligible for both the deductible IRA and the Roth IRA. If the taxpayer is in the same bracket at the time of contribution and withdrawal, then the deductible IRA and the Roth IRA deliver the same results. This is contrary to the advice given by such pillars of the investment community as The New York Times Business Section,[112] and Money Magazine.[113] What this pop financial advice fails to consider is that the taxes saved by the deductible IRA can be reinvested, whereas the Roth IRA does not put that extra cash in hand at the beginning. If the tax savings from the deductible IRA are invested in assets that deliver a comparable tax-free return to the assets invested in the Roth IRA such as in tax-free municipal bonds, then the results will be the same as the Roth. This can be demonstrated in the table below, assuming assets invested in both types of IRA and with after tax funds accumulate tax free at 6% and that the taxpayer is in the 25%[114] bracket at the beginning and the end.

---

[112]   "Roth earnings will deliver more money over time to the account than will a deductible IRA," Jan M. Rosen, "Allure, and Mystery, in the New I.R.A.'s," The New York Times, November 23, 1997, p. BU 4.

[113]   ". . . if you think you have a good chance of maintaining or even boosting your income in retirement, then the Roth wins hands down," Malcom Fitch, "How to Pick the Best IRA," Money, January, 1988 p. 75 at 78.

[114]   We use 25% because it is the rate that would apply to the maximum income level for which a taxpayer is eligible for a deductible IRA.

Comparing the Roth IRA and the Deductible IRA

Type of IRA	Contribution/ Investment	Accumulation After 15 Years @ 6%	Taxes Due @ 25%	After-Tax Amount
Roth	$2,000	$4,793.12	$0	**$4,793.12**
Deductible	$2,000	$4,793.12	$1,198	$3,595
Tax Savings from Deductible IRA Invested in Tax-Free Municipal Bonds Paying 6%	$500	$1,198	$0	$1,198
Combined Results of Deductible IRA and Tax Savings from Deductible IRA	$2,500	$5,991.35	$1,198	**$4,793.12**

If the after-tax savings of the deductible IRA are invested in an asset that attracts tax, then it's return would have to be higher than the return in the Roth IRA to pay for the tax.

One advantage of the Roth IRA, however, is that distributions from a deductible IRA must begin at age 70½, whereas distributions need not commence at that time for Roth IRAs. In addition contributions may continue to be made to Roth IRAs even after age 70½. Thus the Roth IRA can lead to a large build up of the estate that could be passed on to heirs.

However, the taxpayer's tax bracket at various stages can affect the decision between the deductible IRA and the Roth IRA. Consider the tax bracket at retirement. The tax free withdrawal of the Roth IRA is worth more to the person in a high bracket at retirement than the person in a low bracket.

Consider the tax bracket at the time of contribution. Compared to the deductible IRA, the cost of making a contribution to a Roth IRA is higher for people in high tax brackets than in low tax brackets. This is because the non-deductibility of the Roth contribution costs the high-bracket individual more taxes.

What this boils down to is that a person in a high bracket at time of contribution and a low bracket at withdrawal should favor the deductible IRA, whereas the person in a low bracket at contribution and a high bracket at withdrawal should favor the Roth IRA.

The only problem with that analysis is that typically taxpayers make contributions to IRAs over many years and may very well make withdrawals over many years. In that setting it is almost impossible for a taxpayer to tell whether, in advance, when you put it all together, what tax bracket he is in at the time of contribution and at the time of withdrawal.

From this point of view, the Roth IRA confuses the IRA concept.

Beyond these considerations, it should also be recalled that, as discussed above at the end of ¶ 8.04(3), employees may make deductible contributions up to certain limits to so-called § 401(k) and 403(b) plans. Sometimes employers match the contributions to these plans and where that is done, contributing to these plans would be preferable to contributions to an IRA. After taking account of all these issues, in general probably the most attractive account is the Roth IRA, if eligible, followed by the deductible IRA and then the nondeductible IRA.

The education IRA is not as attractive. The annual maximum contribution is low. Children are in a low tax bracket anyway; thus a direct gift to children of investible funds may be superior, without the restrictions that accompany the education IRA. But for some who cannot participate in either a deductible or Roth IRA, the Coverdell IRA may have advantages. The main advantage of a Coverdell IRA over giving the money to your children is that if you do give the money to your children it is their money. They can decide to go to college with it or to take a trip around the world. The Coverdell IRA money may only be used for education.

(g) Section 529 Plans—Qualified Tuition Programs

This is probably one of the biggest tax deferral options for anyone saving for a child's education. A qualified tuition program is a savings device usually maintained by a state government or state agency (they are often managed by private parties.) The programs allow participants to save for higher education through a tax deferred device. Programs either allow participants to purchase tuition credits that entitle the beneficiary to a waiver of tuition payments in the future or allow participants to make a contribution to an account that is for the beneficiary's education.[115]

Amounts paid to a qualified tuition program on behalf of a beneficiary are not included in the beneficiary's income. Contributions to the program are considered gifts to the beneficiary. But section 529(c)(2) provides that a donor may elect to spread the contribution over a five-year period for gift tax purposes.[116] Thus, a married couple may contribute up to $110,000 at one time to a section

---

[115] Section 529(b).

[116] Section 529(c)(2)(B).

529 plan. Or, grandparents with a large estate can give up to $110,000 per grandchild without being subject to gift or estate tax.

The 529 plans have therefore become a favorite tax planning device of the wealthy. Unlike IRAs it is available to them regardless of their income, and they can place large amounts of wealth in a tax deferred device. The tax subsidy here is huge.

¶ 8.05 A BIRD'S EYE VIEW OF SOPHISTICATED ESTATE PLANNING

While the subject of estate planning is beyond the scope of the basic course in federal income taxation as it is usually conceived, it seems that it is useful to convey to beginning students some of the sophisticated techniques that are employed in the estate planning area. These are matters that the student is likely to run into with respect to parents or other relatives. Also, the tax avoidance in this area raises policy questions of interest to a student of the field of federal taxation. An informed attorney should have some knowledge of the basic principles of estate planning (or as the late Professor David Kadane used to say "never let your client get out the door without asking if he has a will.")

Although an extensive discussion of estate and gift tax is outside the scope of this book, EGTRRA made major changes to the estate and gift tax provisions and at least a brief understanding of these changes is important.

The basic principle is that if one dies with an estate above $5,490,000 in 2017, a 40% tax is levied on that excess.

The gift tax provisions somewhat parallel those of the estate tax. The estate and gift tax law allows individuals to give tax-free gifts of up to $14,000 per year (indexed for inflation) to as many people as they want. A married couple can give $28,000 (indexed for inflation) annually to as many people as they want. Moreover, under current law, there is a "unified credit." What this means is that in addition to the yearly $14,000 gift-tax exclusion, you can use up some of your estate tax exemption on gifts that you make during your lifetime. You can make up to $5,490,000 of gifts that will not be subject to gift tax. So if you want to give your child $114,000, the first $14,000 is exempt and the remaining $100,000 merely reduces your $5,490,000 lifetime gift tax credit exclusion amount. After you have exceeded $5,490,000, gifts you make during your lifetime are taxable.

The basic maneuvering in the field is to keep assets out of the estate so that they do not trigger the tax. There are a large number of techniques available to the well-advised for doing that.

Corporate executives, for example, are able to transfer millions of dollars of stocks and stock options to their children and not pay estate tax on them. Investors can put a wide variety of property, including stock and vacation homes into partnerships for their children, causing the property to be valued for taxation purposes at 30% to 70% less than their fair market value. Moreover, further appreciation in the value of these assets in the partnership does not attract the estate tax. A taxpayer can purchase a share of his children's inheritance which protects the inheritance from the estate tax. Moreover, some taxpayers can put their financial affairs together in such a complex fashion that the Service may sometimes give up trying to penetrate the legal miasma to collect the taxes.

The estate tax is easy to avoid; indeed, less than one percent of adult deaths triggers payment of the estate tax. The rest of adult deaths are of either people who were too poor to trigger it or were sufficiently well-advised to avoid it.

One of the basic estate planning techniques is to set up a trust that holds property and avoids having the estates of the husband and wife put together when one spouse dies and leaves property to the other. Thus the couple can pass on $2 million in assets without subjecting those assets to the estate tax.

In the executive compensation area, a major device is the transferable stock option. Stock options have long been a way to compensate executives, giving them the option to buy the company's stock at less than market value, see discussion above. Indeed if the company's stock appreciates greatly, this right to buy stock at a low price becomes extremely valuable indeed. Where the stock option has the feature that it is transferable to the executive's children, either directly or in trust, it can become a powerful means to transferring great amounts of wealth without triggering gift or estate tax. The Service has not provided guidelines on how to value stock options, so taxpayers are, not surprisingly, valuing them at virtually no value. Once the option is transferred the child can exercise the option to great profit, and no further gift or estate tax is triggered to the parent. It is the case that the exercise of the option causes the parent to have to pay income tax, under the assignment of income doctrine, see ¶ 5.02. That in itself can be an estate planning technique as the payment of income taxes by the parent enriches the child who does not have to pay the tax and reduces the parent's estate for estate tax purposes.

As an example of this technique, Eugene M. Isenberg chief executive of Nabors Industries, a Houston oil drilling and exploration company, transferred options to buy 2.25 million Nabors shares to trusts for his two daughters and grandchildren. In October and

November of 1996 these options were exercised and produced a gain of $29.7 million. Mr. Isenberg did have to pay income tax on the gain. The transfer of these options had conditions attached that made it less valuable for gift tax purposes, so that a lesser gift tax was paid. The condition was that over the term of the trusts, Mr. Isenberg must get back the value of the assets he transferred plus a rate of interest.

The house as real and tax shelter. Another maneuver has withstood IRS challenge for some time. This is transferring the family house or a vacation home to a trust with the donor parent holding a life interest and the (usually minor) children with a remainder interest. The trust lapses, say, in 30 years. The value of the house to the children for gift tax purposes is calculated as only the present value of their remainder interest. When the children eventually come into ownership of the house in fee simple, they pay no further tax. During the life of the trust, they get no income from the house (conveniently ignoring the fact that they are living in the house and thus receiving shelter income). The children's remainder interest in a $500,000 house 30 years from now is $49,689 (assuming an 8% interest rate for the calculation). That is all that is charged for gift tax purposes. The gift is valued at the time it is made. Obviously the house has a fair market value of far more at the time of the gift and will be much more valuable 30 years from now when it actually passes to the children. If the parents die before the 30 year term of the trust, the value of the house would be included in their estate. Much of the advantage of the maneuver is then lost, but as the saying goes, there is no harm in trying. One maneuver is also to set up the term of the trust for a period that is substantially less than the life expectancy of the grantor, or person setting up the trust. When the trust period lapses on the home, the children then own the home. The parents can still stay in the home and pay rent. Or they can move out, at a time when the children are grown and that is something they just might want to do.

All of this can be done twice in that the Service permits two personal residence trusts; so the family vacation home can also be transferred this way and avoid estate taxes.

Another problem dealt with by the estate planning is the case of the small family business that has become immensely profitable and is now extremely valuable. An example is the Telect Company, located in Spokane, Washington, started by Bill and Judi Williams.[117] which manufactures fiber optic telephone equipment. Starting as a very small business the company now has 700 employees and annual

---

[117] Anecdotal information in this discussion is based on Christopher Drew and David Cay Johnston, For Wealthy Americans, Death is More Certain Than Taxes, The New York Times, December 22, 1996, p. A1.

revenues of $72 million. The question for the family is how to pass on the family business to their children without incurring a tax so large it would cause them to have to sell the business to outsiders to pay it. To solve the problem, the family engaged in a current hot estate planning technique.

The approach allows a those who own a family partnership or corporation to give minority interests in it away and have the value of the gifts discounted by as much as 40%. The reason the Service has grudgingly accepted this technique is that it is the case that a minority interest in a closely-held business is less valuable than its proportionate share because the minority lack control and can be exploited to some extent subject to somewhat loose standards of fiduciary duty. For the same reason some people will pay a "control premium" to gain control of a company, a minority interest can be discounted. The Service has long accepted this analysis in valuing minority interests when unrelated people own the business, the Service has resisted it for family members, because of the obviously possibility of collusion (say for example to avoid gift taxes).

The issue of valuing transfers of minority interests in family corporations was litigated for several decades and the Service started losing cases recently. They kept fighting until they incurred the ire of the Tax Court and were forced to pay a taxpayer's legal expenses. Thereafter the Service ruled, in 1993, that transfers of minority interests in family partnerships and corporations could be discounted for estate and gift tax valuation purposes.

This ruling, in turn, has led to some aggressive tax planning. Many taxpayers are creating partnerships, transferring vacation homes, securities, and other investments in to them and then giving minority interests in the partnership to their children, discounting the value by 30 to 70 percent.

In the early 1990s, then-91-year old Charles C. Clark of San Antonio put $2 million of securities into a partnership. He then gave ownership interest in the partnership to 11 relatives, including children, in-laws and grandchildren. For estate and gift tax purposes he discounted the value of the gifts by 30%. The Service disallowed the discounts arguing that Mr. Clark had no valid business reason for the transfers. The Service asserted the transaction was a sham, undertaken only to obtain tax advantage. One flaw in the taxpayer's approach would seem to be that the stocks in the portfolio transferred are publicly traded (indeed including such major companies as Microsoft, Coca-Cola and Walt Disney). Thus the discount rationale, which applied originally to the illiquid shares of a closely held business, does not hold up. Similarly the minority-ownership-in-business rationale also does not seem to apply to vacation homes or primary residences.

As a further spin on this technique is to have the wealthy patriarch of the family transfer his assets to trusts in the Bahamas in favor of children or other relatives. This has the further virtue from the taxpayer's point of view of making it hard for the Service to get records, given the Bahamian bank secrecy laws. If the Service cannot reach the records in full, it is likely to throw in the towel in a case.

Chapter 9

TAX ACCOUNTING

Table of Sections

¶ 9.01 IN GENERAL

The term "tax accounting" is somewhat misleading. Tax accounting is not like financial accounting (you will be relieved to hear), with balance sheets and income statements. Rather, the subject of tax accounting is really timing. The question in the field of tax accounting is just *when*, i.e., in what year, is an item included in income or deductible. Thus the field of tax accounting might better be termed tax timing.

So to be absolutely clear about that matter (not to say tedious), the field of tax accounting is not concerned with the validity or amounts of income or deduction items. The only question in tax accounting is in what year does the item properly occur.

At first blush, it sounds like *when* something is included in income or deductible is no big deal. But you know much better than that. As you know, timing in federal income taxation can be of immense significance, particularly where long periods of time are involved. Since this chapter's focus is on timing. it should be considered to be closely related to the Appendix. The difference is that in this chapter we focus on the particular statutory and case law rules regarding timing. In the Appendix we focused on the broader economic significance of timing and the time value of money.

Another difference between this chapter and the Appendix is that timing can be important because marginal and/or effective rates of tax[1] change from one year to the next. These changes can occur from change in the law or changes in the taxpayer's income. This is not something that we pay much attention to in the Appendix (where we just happily ran numbers on out to the horizon). Thus the matter

---

[1]   See Chapter One for discussion of marginal and effective rates of tax.

of timing can be of great significance if the effective rate of tax is different between the two years.

The Code attempts to get a grip on the elusive topic of timing by providing as an opening statement that taxable income shall be computed under the method of accounting on the basis of which the taxpayer regularly computes his income in keeping his books.[2] Thus while the Code does not directly employ financial accounting concepts on the issue of timing, it will borrow some of the concepts of financial accounting. After the Code borrows some of these principles, it alters them for its own purposes.

This creates a major tension in the financial world. Tax accounting and timing principles often diverge from financial accounting and timing principles, even for major publicly traded corporations.[3]

Having in its opening statement given the taxpayer the right to ascertain timing questions based on the taxpayer's method of financial accounting, as discussed above, the Code then characteristically takes some of what it promises back. It says further that if the method of accounting used by the taxpayer does not "clearly reflect income" (major words in the field), then the Service may use some other method that does clearly reflect income.[4]

Given the large stakes on the question of timing, one could easily expect substantial conflicts between the Service and taxpayers on the timing of income or deduction items. And it is true that this area of the tax law is no less devoid of litigation than any other area.

It is interesting to note that in financial accounting, the precise timing of borderline items into one year or the next does not result in any change of liabilities to the corporation. But the choice of taxable year for a borderline item in the tax field can have a direct effect on increasing or decreasing the taxpayer's tax liability. Thus one might suppose that the problems of timing in the financial world are less intense than in the tax world. This would be especially so because footnotes on a company's financial records can explain why certain timing decisions were made.

However, one can make too much of this difference between tax and financial accounting. While allocation of borderline items on the financial books does not literally have a direct effect on a company's liabilities, it can have a significant effect on the profits the company reports. This in turn can have a significant effect on the company's

---

[2]   Section 446(a).

[3]   As an example of this growing out of the S & L catastrophe, see the *Cottage Savings Ass'n* case in Chapter 4.

[4]   Section 446(b).

stock price. The variation in the stock price can affect the company's cost of capital, or the level of dividends it must pay to support its stock price. Thus timing principles in the financial world are rather well developed, and the tax law makes some use of them.

¶ 9.02 TRANSACTIONAL PROBLEMS

There is a fundamental tension in the field of tax accounting. It is between the legal rule that taxable income is reckoned up on an annual basis and the economic fact that many complex business transactions span more than one year. We explore the implications of this tension in the following material.

(1) Annual Accounting: Sanford & Brooks

Most individual taxpayers compute their income on the basis of the calendar year.[5] Alternatively, we could wait until the individual dies and then collect all the income taxes due on the individual's income for his lifetime at his death. But the Government, as is well known, does not like to wait (time value of money and all that). By nailing the taxpayer every year, however, certain distortions are created. Business transactions are not always organized to fit neatly within one year. But the overall thrust of the law in this area is not transaction-oriented. Instead, it's an annual accounting concept. This keeps things simple. Except when there are exceptions. Which make things complicated. This is all illustrated nicely by the leading case of *Sanford & Brooks*.

---

[5]　　Section 441(a) and (b). Business firms often use a fiscal year, say September 1 through August 31 of the following year. The fiscal year may be geared to the company's seasonal business. Thus Toys R Us would have a fiscal year ending January 31.

BURNET V. SANFORD & BROOKS CO.[6]

Facts: On a subcontract from Atlantic Dredging Company, Sanford & Brooks engaged in dredging the Delaware River for the United States. Through the years 1913 to 1916, the taxpayer incurred net losses on the contract in the amount of $176,272. In 1915, the taxpayer abandoned the job and in 1916 Atlantic Dredging Company brought suit for breach of warranty of the character of the material to be dredged. In 1920, Atlantic Dredging Company won the lawsuit, and Sanford & Brooks received $192,578, comprised of the $176,272 in net losses on the contract plus $16,306 in interest.

Question: Should an annual accounting concept be applied and therefore the $192,578 is income in 1920; or should a transaction accounting concept be applied and therefore the $192,578 is offset by the $176,272 losses and $16,306 interest in earlier years?

Comment: A clear implication of the annual accounting concept is that the losses in the earlier years would then stand. If the transaction approach is applied, then there would be no income in 1920 and no losses in the earlier years. Taxpayer would file amended returns to eliminate those losses.

Comment: Taxpayer preferred the transaction approach because it was not getting immediate benefit from the losses in the earlier years but would have to pay taxes on the damages in 1920. The Service preferred the annual accounting approach for the same reason.

---

6   282 U.S. 359, 51 S.Ct. 150, 75 L.Ed. 383 (1931).

Held: Apply annual accounting concept. Receipts from the conduct of a business are included in the taxpayer's return regardless of whether the particular transaction results in net profit. Annual accounting was a familiar concept at the time of the adoption of the 16th amendment providing for the income tax. The Sixteenth Amendment does not require transaction accounting.

The taxpayer obviously had a strong argument on the grounds of equity. But if we are going to be that fair to each individual taxpayer, exploring the implications over several years of each transaction undertaken, we are going to have a very complex tax code indeed.

After *Sanford & Brooks,* Congress did act to deal with such problems. It enacted § 172, which now allows losses incurred in one year to be carried back 2 years and then forward 20 years.[7] The provision is much broader than anything needed by Sanford & Brooks. The losses under § 172 need not arise out of transactions that are related to profitable results in later years. Rather, any losses incurred in one year may be carried to a total of 22 other years and taken against any profits in those other years.

Thus we begin to understand the roots of complexity of the tax statute. By attempting to treat taxpayers like *Sanford & Brooks* more fairly we enact a provision which makes the statute more complex. But perhaps this is worthwhile. By allowing the losses to be carried to the income years, we make the treatment of the cyclical firm more akin to that of the firm which enjoys steady income over the years.

For example, Variable Corporation has the following income and loss pattern over a four year period:

Year 1 $50,000 loss

Year 2 $200,000 gain

Year 3 $50,000 loss

Year 4 $200,000 gain

The total net income over the four year period is $300,000. Without a provision like § 172 allowing carryover of losses, Variable Corporation would have incurred $56,250 in tax liability in years 2 and 4 (using the corporate tax rates of § 11). This would mean a total tax liability over the four-year period of $112,500. Compare that to Stochastic Corporation, which has income of $75,000 per-year for the

---

[7]   Under the Job Creation and Worker Assistance Act of 2002, P.L. 107–147, Congress increased the NOL carryback to five years for losses incurred in 2001 or 2002. See § 172(b)(1)(H).

four years. That also comes to $300,000 of income over the four years. Using again the corporate tax rates of § 11, we find that Stochastic's annual tax is $13,750. Stochastic's total tax over the four-year period is $55,000. Though the two companies have the same amount of income over the four-year period, Variable's total tax is $112,500 and Stochastic's total tax is $55,000, a staggering difference of $57,500! Should Variable really be taxed more than Stochastic? Of course not, you say.

Do we cure the problem by allowing Variable to carry its $50,000 losses forward to its $100,000 income years? You might think so, but let's run the numbers. By carrying forward its losses Variable now has $150,000 of income in each of years 2 and 4. That of course still cranks out to be total income of $300,000. Under § 11, we find that Variable's income in each of years 2 and 4 is $39,250. That's a total tax over the period of $78,500. That's still $23,500 more than Stochastic pays! So allowing the carryover improved the situation. But we still have a significant problem!

Why is that? Why has the carryover not solved the problem? Anybody that can answer that is excused from the exam. Think about it; the answer is in the footnote.[8]

Comment: We have to a significant extent abandoned the simplicity of the annual accounting method by enacting § 172. But even with the addition of that complex provision, we still have not managed to treat Variable the same as Stochastic. Thus we got the worst of all worlds: still not treating the two companies the same and a complex statute.

Section 172 may only be used by businesses (including sole proprietors). A salaried employee generally does not incur expenses greater than his income. But if he does, he cannot carry them over to other years.

Another change to the Code also ameliorates the problems encountered by the taxpayer in *Sanford & Brooks*. This is § 186, enacted in 1969, which provides that damages for breach of contract or fiduciary duty or antitrust violations will be excluded from income if the loss giving rise to the damages did not generate a tax benefit.

---

[8]   Hi. We are sure you don't need this help but here it is anyway. While allowing the losses to carry over to the income years ameliorated the problem, we still have a progressive rate structure. Even with allowing the carryover of losses, Variable's income is still bunched up compared to Stochastic's. Being bunched up punched Variable up into the higher progressive corporate rates, causing Variable still to have to pay a higher corporate income tax over the four-year period.

(2) Claim of Right: North American Oil; Lewis

North American Oil is the leading case illustrating transaction problems.

NORTH AMERICAN OIL CONSOLIDATED V. BURNET[9]

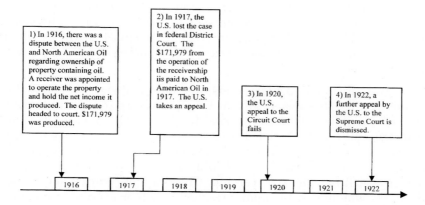

Facts: North American Oil Consolidated operated a number of oil properties, one of which had a legal title which stood in the name of the United States. In 1916, the United States also claimed beneficial ownership of the property, brought suit against the taxpayer, and secured an appointment of a receiver to operate the property and to hold the net income the property produced. In 1916, the property produced $171,979. In 1917, the taxpayer won the case in U.S. District Court and received the money in dispute. The United States then appealed, and in 1920 the Circuit Court of Appeals affirmed the District Court judgment. Finally, the United States Supreme Court dismissed a further appeal by the United States in 1922.

Question: In what year is the $171,979 from the operation of the property by the receiver included in income to North American Oil?

Taxpayer's argument: The money is taxable in 1916. If not taxable in 1916, it is taxable in 1922.

Service's argument: The money is taxable in 1917.

Comment: In this ambiguous set of facts, do you think that the taxpayer and the Service arrived at their respective conclusions as to when the money is taxable based on their respective views of the integrity and underlying jurisprudence of the federal income tax? If

---

9   286 U.S. 417, 52 S.Ct. 613, 76 L.Ed. 1197 (1932).

not, then how *did* they arrive at their respective conclusions as to year of taxability?

Comment: Three guesses and the first two don't count. The taxpayer was in a much higher bracket in 1917 than in either 1916 or 1922. 1917 was a very high bracket year. See the discussion of *Old Colony Trust* in Chapter 3.[10] Thus taxpayer comes up with the conclusion that the taxable year is anything but 1917. Conversely, the Service arrives at the conclusion that 1917 is the right year. Having decided ahead of time what their conclusions will be, they then construct their argument. Tax law is no different from any other practice of law.

Held: (Brandeis, J.) The funds were not taxable as income to the company in 1916, because at that time there was no assurance that the company would receive the funds at all. There was no "constructive receipt" (see below) in 1916, because at no time in that year could the company demand the funds. The company was taxable on the funds in 1917, the year when the District Court entered a final decree vacating the receivership. It does not matter for these purposes whether the company was on a cash or accrual method of accounting (see below). The funds were not income in 1922 when the litigation was finally terminated. "If a taxpayer receives earnings under a claim of right and without restriction as to its disposition, he has received income which he is required to return [i.e., report on his tax return], even though it may still be claimed that he is not entitled to retain the money, and even though he may still be adjudged liable to restore its equivalent." If in 1922, the Government had ultimately prevailed and the taxpayer were obliged to refund the money received in 1917, it would then properly take a deduction for 1922.

Brandeis in *North American Oil* invented a concept, the "Claim of Right," that had not been in existence prior to this case. But after all, he was Louis Brandeis. The apparent elements of this new concept are that 1) the taxpayer actually receives the funds and 2) the taxpayer does not concede that there is any other valid claim to the funds, even though in fact others may dispute the taxpayer's right to the funds. These elements would distinguish this transaction from borrowing money, where an obligation to repay is of course recognized by the recipient of the funds. When funds are received under a claim of right, the taxpayer is in receipt of income which may then be taxed. If an adverse claim later proves valid, the approach is to take a deduction in the year the funds are repaid.

---

[10]   Also note that the top bracket on corporations in 1916 was 2%. In 1917, at the height of World War I, the top bracket on corporations ranged up to 60%. In 1922, the top corporate bracket was 12.5%.

As in *Sanford & Brooks*, we see here the annual accounting concept prevailing over transactional analysis in the courts. From the point of view of administering the tax laws, it appears the Service should not have to wait until this interminable litigation finally drags to a conclusion before it collects its taxes.

Beyond that, if we take the transactional approach in this particular case, the question could arise as to just when is the litigation over. Even after an appeal to the Supreme Court is dismissed, who knows what other judicial or legislative moves the Government might try which would keep at least a minor cloud hanging over the ultimate resolution of the underlying dispute. Rather than sitting around trying to decide whether there is still life in this controversy or not, it is more efficient to employ the claim-of-right doctrine and then take a deduction later if necessary.

The *North American Oil* analysis sounds good, but would there be any problems if North American did have to pay back the funds in 1922. Would that be so simple to deal with? While that did not happen in the *North American Oil* case, we do have a case where that did happen. The case is *Lewis*.

UNITED STATES V. LEWIS[11]

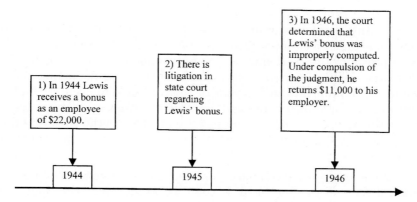

Facts: Ellis Lewis received an employee bonus of $22,000 in 1944. He used this money during the taxable year thinking that he was entitled to it. In 1945, there is litigation regarding Lewis's bonus. In 1946, taxpayer is compelled to return $11,000 to his employer.

Question: Should taxpayer take the deduction for the repaid $11,000 in 1944 or in 1946?

---

[11]　340 U.S. 590, 71 S.Ct. 522, 95 L.Ed. 560 (1951), reh'g denied 341 U.S. 923, 71 S.Ct. 741, 95 L.Ed. 1356 (1951).

Service's argument: Taxpayer should deduct the $11,000 in 1946.

Taxpayer's argument: He should deduct the $11,000 in 1944, by filing an amended return with his recomputed taxes.

Comment: Obviously Lewis was in a higher bracket in 1944, so the deduction meant more to him then. That is why the Service and Lewis squared off the way they did.

Held: (Black, J.): Relying on *North American Oil*, the amount is deductible in 1946. The bonus was held by taxpayer under a claim of right. Nothing in the holding of the *North American Oil* court permits an exception just because a taxpayer is mistaken in his belief as to his claim of right. Income taxes must be paid on an annual accounting method, citing *Sanford & Brooks* (see above). The claim-of-right doctrine is a rule of finality and "is now deeply rooted in the tax system."

Comment: This does not seem to really be a claim-of-right case. The claim-of-right doctrine described by the Court in *North American Oil* seemed to contemplate that there were adverse claims to the funds at the time they were received by the taxpayer. But the taxpayer did not concede their validity. In the case of *Lewis,* there was no adverse claim to the money he received at the time he received it.

In any event, assuming as the Court does that Lewis received the funds under a claim-of-right, as in *North American Oil*, the *Lewis* case presents the next question: what happens on repayment? In *dicta* the *North American Oil* Court said that the deduction there would be appropriate in the year of repayment. This would employ the annual accounting method instead of transactional analysis. Since the annual accounting method is embedded in the statute,[12] the Court properly applied it rather than improvising new transactional analysis theory.

It can be useful to compare this area to the assignment of income area, discussed in Chapter 5. It could be argued that the Supreme Court was willing to improvise there and formulate rules restricting the ability of taxpayers to shift income to lower-bracket members of the family. Yet the Court is not willing to improvise in the assignment of income area. But one factor explains the Court's approach in both these lines of cases: They came out against the taxpayer.

We could have lived with the results in *North American Oil* and *Lewis.* When an amount has to be repaid in a different year (which does not happen that often, let's face it), sometimes the annual

---

[12]   See the discussion above at ¶ 9.02(1).

accounting approach would help a taxpayer and sometimes hurt him. This would of course depend on the applicable tax rates when the taxpayer receives the money and when he has to repay it. The annual accounting approach would not always be biased against taxpayers. So we could have lived with this simple approach. But naturally we don't.

The result in *Lewis* was seen to be a problem. If there is a problem, then with good old American know-how we can fix it. And a statutory provision was enacted to fix it. But the price to pay was increasing the complexity of the statute.

Three years after the decision in *Lewis*, Congress enacted § 1341. This allows a taxpayer who receives an amount under a claim-of-right which he must later repay to reduce his taxes in the year repaid by the larger of the following: 1) the tax savings if the deduction is taken in the year repaid or 2) the tax savings if the deduction were taken in the year the amount was received.[13]

The accompanying graphic illustrates the operation of § 1341 by showing how it would work in *Lewis*.

APPLICATION OF § 1341 TO *LEWIS*

A case construing § 1341 was *Joseph P. Pike*.[14] The taxpayer, an attorney who practiced insurance law, in 1957 sold stock he owned in the Cardinal Life Insurance Company for a gain of about $20,000. A

---

[13]   There is a *de minimis* rule that none of this kicks in unless the amount involved exceeds $3,000.

[14]   44 T.C. 787 (1965).

special counsel of the state of Kentucky came to the conclusion that, for various reasons, the $20,000 properly belonged to the Cardinal Company. Taxpayer did not agree with this result, but to protect his reputation in the insurance industry, he paid the $20,000 to the Cardinal Company in 1958. He then sought to employ § 1341 to take the tax savings as if the deduction were taken in the year of receipt of the $20,000, 1957. The court held that § 1341 was not available to the taxpayer because it was not "established" under the terms of § 1341(a)(2) that the taxpayer did not have an unrestricted right to the item. He was not compelled by legal process to repay the item. Rather, taxpayer repaid the item out of his belief that the continued controversy would damage his reputation. Hence the $20,000 was deductible in 1958 as an ordinary and necessary business expense under § 162.

It might be noted that this case also conjures up the case of *Welch v. Helvering*[15] on the question whether a payment to safeguard one's reputation is deductible at all.

Section 1341 was also interpreted by *Van Cleave v. United States*.[16] Taxpayer was president and majority stockholder of VanMark Corporation which adopted a by-law requiring corporate officers who received from the corporation income determined by the IRS to be excessive and therefore not deductible to the corporation (i.e. unreasonable compensation, see ¶ 6.02(1)) to pay the amount deemed excessive back to the corporation. In addition, the taxpayer had a separate agreement with the corporation to repay nondeductible compensation. In an audit, the Service determined that $57,500 of taxpayer's salary for tax year 1974 was excessive and disallowed it as a deduction to the corporation. Taxpayer paid this amount back in 1975. The Service on audit of 1975 allowed the deduction in 1975 but disallowed the use of § 1341 to take the deduction against 1974's income.

The district court disallowed the use of § 1341 because the payment was voluntary in the sense that taxpayer was the controlling stockholder of the employer and thus could have caused the corporation to abrogate the repayment agreement. The Government did not pursue this argument, which appears to be flawed. There was a valid agreement with the employer, a separate legal entity, that the compensation should be repaid.

The Government's argument was that § 1341 only applies if it appeared that the taxpayer had an unrestricted right to the excess salary. The Government asserted that taxpayer had more than an

---

[15]   See ¶ 6.03(4).
[16]   718 F.2d 193 (6th Cir.1983).

appearance of an unrestricted right but actually had an unrestricted right, contingent on the happening of an event in a subsequent year. The court rejected the argument and held that § 1341 was available to the taxpayer. The fact that taxpayer's ultimate right to the compensation was not determined until the occurrence of a subsequent event does not mean that he had, in the statutory sense, an unrestricted right to the compensation when he received it.

(3) The Tax Benefit Rule

(a) In General: Alice Phelan Sullivan Corp.

There is another transactional pattern that gets into tension with the annual accounting concept. It is kind of the reverse of *Lewis* and similar to *Sanford & Brooks.* A taxpayer may recover an item for which he took a deduction in an earlier year. Thus a loan previously deducted as a bad debt[17] may in fact be paid in a later year, or an amount deducted for medical expenses[18] may be reimbursed by insurance in a later year. Ordinarily repayment of a loan or health insurance payments do not give rise to income.[19] On equitable principles, however, it would appear that the fact that these transactions gave rise to earlier deductions should cause the later recovery to be included in income. If so, what is the appropriate treatment on recovery where the earlier deduction produced no tax benefit because the taxpayer, on account of other losses, had no taxable income in the year the earlier deduction was taken?

The problems in this area are exemplified by the case of *Alice Phelan Sullivan Corporation.*

---

[17]   Deductible under § 166. See ¶ 7.01(6)(a).

[18]   Deductible under § 213 above certain limits. See ¶ 7.01(7).

[19]   The interest on loans will, of course, be income. See ¶ 3.01.

ALICE PHELAN SULLIVAN CORP.
V. UNITED STATES[20]

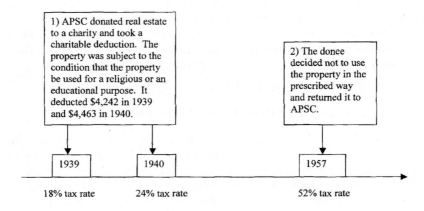

1) APSC donated real estate to a charity and took a charitable deduction. The property was subject to the condition that the property be used for a religious or an educational purpose. It deducted $4,242 in 1939 and $4,463 in 1940.

2) The donee decided not to use the property in the prescribed way and returned it to APSC.

1939	1940	1957
18% tax rate	24% tax rate	52% tax rate

Facts: Alice Phelan Sullivan Corporation donated one parcel of real estate in 1939 and one parcel of real estate in 1940, claiming both as charitable deductions. These charitable deductions totaled $4,243 in 1939 and $4,463 in 1940, yielding the taxpayer a total tax benefit of $1,877. Both of these donations were made subject to the condition that the property be used for either a religious or educational purpose. In 1957, when the tax rate was 52%, the donee decided not to use the gifts of real estate anymore and reconveyed them to the taxpayer.

Question: Should Alice Phelan Sullivan Corp. take the return of the property in 1957 back into income?

Service's argument: The entire amount of $8,707 that was previously claimed as a charitable contribution in 1939 and 1940 should be added back into taxpayer's income in 1957, generating taxes of $4,528.

Comment: Since the applicable corporate tax rate was much higher in 1957 than in 1939 and 1940, adding the same amount back in 1957 generates more taxes ($4,528) than were saved by the deductions in 1939 and 1940 ($1,877).

Taxpayer's argument: The present assessment can be no more than the tax saved on the original deal, or $1,877, relying on the *Perry* case which had held to that effect.

Held: 1) A transaction which returns to a taxpayer his own property cannot be said to give rise to income. 2) But the principle is well-engrained in our tax law that the return of property which has

---

[20]　381 F.2d 399 (Ct.Cl.1967).

been the subject of a deduction must be treated as income in the year of recovery. 3) This latter principle is limited by the "tax benefit rule," which holds that the returned item may be excluded from income to the extent that the initial use as a deduction did not actually provide a tax saving. 4) But where the full use of a deduction was made, giving rise to a tax saving, then the amount of the saving is immaterial. The recovery is viewed as income to the full extent of the deduction previously allowed, basing the opinion on § 111 and the regulations thereto, which have broadened the tax benefit concept beyond the statutory limitations. Using the annual accounting concept of *Sanford & Brooks* (see above), the taxpayer takes the full amount of the deduction back into income at the higher current rate.

Comment: The taxpayer's basis in the property once it has been returned would equal the amount included in income, or $8,707.

Comment: There is a third alternative, which is to have the property come back into income not at the value used when it was deducted—but at its current value. This could well be different from the $8,707 value that it had at the time it was donated. Neither the parties nor the court appeared to consider this possibility. But it would seem highly relevant if the property were now worth $75,000 or $25.

The tax benefit rule is one of the venerated principles in the field of federal income taxation. In the early controversies on the matter, the Service took the hard-nosed position that the recovery of previously deductible items gave rise to income, and the recovery did so regardless of whether the earlier deduction had produced a tax benefit.[21] Section 111, however, whose predecessor was enacted in 1942, has now pre-empted the field and takes the more reasonable view that recovery of such deductible items gives rise to income only to the extent that the earlier deduction produced a tax benefit for the taxpayer. This is the essence of the tax benefit rule: that recovery of a previously deductible item gives rise to income only to the extent the previous deduction produced a tax benefit.

The tax benefit rule is sometimes viewed as having two aspects: the inclusionary aspect and the exclusionary aspect. They are really two sides of the same coin. The inclusionary aspect states that if a deduction in an earlier year generated a tax benefit, then the later recovery will be taxed, as in *Alice Phelan Sullivan*. The exclusionary aspect states that if a deduction in an earlier year generated no tax benefit (because there would have been no taxable income even without the deduction), then a later recovery of the item will be excluded from income.

---

[21]   G.C.M. 22163, 1940–2 C.B. 76.

Reasonable as it sounds, the tax benefit rule still leads to anomalous results. This is curious given that it is an equitable principle. The anomaly of the tax benefit rule of § 111 and *Alice Phelan Sullivan* is highlighted when it is compared with its sister provision, § 1341, discussed above. The tax benefit rule "looks forward"—an amount deducted in an earlier year that generates a benefit is included in income in a later year, when it is recovered. § 1341 "looks backward"—dealing with the problem of an erroneous inclusion of income in an earlier year which must be deducted in a later year, when it is paid back. Rather than focusing on the amounts includible and deductible, § 1341 focuses on the tax liabilities involved, giving the taxpayer the option of selecting the tax result in either the year of inclusion or the year of deduction, whichever is more favorable.[22] Thus, under § 1341, the taxpayer gets the best possible deal regardless of the tax rates in the two years involved. By contrast, the taxpayer in the maw of § 111 and the tax benefit rule is playing a lottery. He may do well or poorly depending on the tax rates in the years involved in his transaction.

The Regulations are clear that the tax benefit rule does not apply to deductions for depreciation, depletion, or amortization.[23]

Thus suppose for example business property is depreciated for several years, but the depreciation deductions produce no tax benefit because the taxpayer, on account of other losses, has no taxable income for those years. On a subsequent sale of the property for an amount in excess of its depreciated basis, the entire amount of the gain will be income notwithstanding that the depreciation deductions produced no tax benefit.[24] Taxpayer's only solace here would be the net operating loss carryover rules (if applicable), discussed above.

The tax benefit need not and usually does not occur in the year the deduction is taken. Thus if a deduction for a bad debt, etc., is taken in a year in which the taxpayer already has operating losses,

---

[22]   Both of these provisions are related to §§ 1311–1314, which allow for adjustments to be made in tax liability for years barred by the statute of limitations where, generally, for an open year the taxpayer or the Service has successfully maintained a position inconsistent with a position taken in the barred year. See Coleman, "Mitigation of the Statute of Limitations—Sections 1311–1314," 31 N.Y.U.Inst.Fed.Tax 1575 (1973). See Stone v. White, 301 U.S. 532, 57 S.Ct. 851, 81 L.Ed. 1265 (1937), reh'g denied 302 U.S. 777, 58 S.Ct. 260, 82 L.Ed. 601 (1937) (defense of equitable recoupment available to Service or, presumably, taxpayers.) See also Ames, "The History of Assumpsit," 2 Harv.L.Rev. 53 (1888).

[23]   Section 1.111–1(a).

[24]   This example suggests the possibility that the taxpayer might try to elect not to take the depreciation deduction during the loss years. However, depreciation is essentially not elective, although various methods of depreciation may be elected. Under § 1016(a) (flush language) the basis of property subject to the deduction for depreciation must go down by at least the minimum amount of depreciation allowed regardless of whether the deduction is actually taken or does any good. See ¶ 6.02(12).

the deduction would produce no tax benefit in that year. However the deduction could increase the taxpayer's operating loss carryovers to other years.[25] Thus, where a deduction increases an unexpired carryover, which *might* benefit the taxpayer in another year, recovery of the deducted item produces income. (Net operating losses can be carried back two years (which can be waived) and forward 20 years.)

The tax benefit rule has also been held specifically to apply to deductions and subsequent recoveries of casualty losses,[26] embezzled funds,[27] and bonuses,[28] among many other items.[29] The tax benefit rule is an outstanding example of how a narrowly-drawn statutory concept has, through judicial, administrative and legislative elaboration, come to be broadly applicable.

Section 186 has extended the theory of § 111 to provide that damages for breach of contract or fiduciary duty or antitrust violations will be excluded from income if the loss giving rise to the damages did not generate a tax benefit.

(b)　Equitable Applications: Hillsboro

As discussed in the preceding section, the tax benefit rule has a life of its own. It has grown from a narrow conceptual base to encompass transactions far beyond those originally imagined. It has spawned substantial case law, broad regulations, and additional legislation. And the vigor is still there. In a recent pair of cases, the Supreme Court raised the ante once again, applying the tax benefit rule as a broad equitable principle to rationalize transactions that would have otherwise led to an unjustified advantage to taxpayers.

Thus in the case of *Hillsboro National Bank v. Commissioner*,[30] the taxpayer corporation had paid certain taxes that were imposed on its shareholders and had properly taken a deduction for them, under § 164(e). In a later year the taxes were refunded directly to the shareholders. In that later year the Service then attempted to make the corporation take the amount of the refund back into income. The corporation's argument was that it had not received the refund.

---

[25]　See discussion above at ¶ 9.02(1).

[26]　Reg. § 1.165–1(d)(2)(iii).

[27]　Tennessee Foundry & Machinery Co., 48 T.C. 419 (1967), aff'd on other grounds 399 F.2d 156 (6th Cir.1968) (receipt of insurance proceeds includible in income because in substance a recovery of previously-deducted embezzlement loss.).

[28]　Larchfield Corp. v. United States, 373 F.2d 159 (2d Cir.1966) (bonus recovered as settlement of a derivative suit).

[29]　In the case where an insolvent accrual method taxpayer is discharged from an indebtedness he previously deducted, income will result only to the extent the taxpayer is solvent following the discharge. Haden Co. v. Commissioner, 118 F.2d 285 (5th Cir.1941), cert. denied 314 U.S. 622, 62 S.Ct. 73, 86 L.Ed. 500 (1941). See ¶ 3.10(2).

[30]　Decided with United States v. Bliss Dairy, 460 U.S. 370, 103 S.Ct. 1134, 75 L.Ed.2d 130 (1983), on remand 704 F.2d 1167 (9th Cir.1983).

Hence application of the tax benefit rule was inappropriate since the rule only taxes "recoveries," in the terms of the statute.[31]

The Court, however, described the rationale of the tax benefit rule more broadly, characterizing its purpose as being the achievement of "rough transactional parity in tax . . . and to protect the Government and the taxpayer from the adverse effects of reporting a transaction on the basis of assumptions that an event in a subsequent year proves to have been erroneous . . . when . . . the later event is indeed fundamentally inconsistent with the premise on which the deduction was initially based."[32]

¶ 9.03 ACCOUNTING METHODS

(1) Overview

In general taxpayers may elect to use any method of accounting that clearly reflects income and is regularly used in keeping their books. The two major methods of accounting are the cash method and the accrual method.

Taxpayers using the accrual method of accounting generally accrue items as income when all the events have occurred that establish the right to receive the income and the amount of income can be determined with reasonable accuracy. Taxpayers using the accrual method of accounting generally may not deduct items of expense in a year prior to the time of economic performance.

More detail on the two methods of accounting and variations on the theme is set forth below.

(2) The Cash Method

(a) In General

Taxpayers using the cash method of accounting generally recognize items of income when they are actually received or deemed to be received (constructively received). Under the cash method items are deducted when paid. This is the system used by most individuals. The conventional wisdom is that the cash method is simpler than the accrual method but that the accrual method is more accurate than the cash method. In fact, when time value of money issues are paramount, the cash method may well also be more accurate than the accrual method as well as being simpler.

---

[31]   Section 111(a).

[32]   It should be pointed out that the above approach by the Court to the tax benefit rule was strong *dicta*. It actually decided the case based on an interpretation of § 164(e) that the corporation should not be taxed on the refund because it had not actually received it.

This is not to say that the cash method is without its difficulties. One major problem with the cash method is that it does not mean what it says. Suppose, for example, that a migrant farm worker is paid by his employer with a bushel of apples. Does the worker have income notwithstanding that what he received was not cash? There is not a shadow of a doubt that the worker has income in that setting under the cash method. Under the cash method of accounting "all items which constitute gross income (whether in the form of cash, property, or services) are to be included for the taxable year in which actually or constructively received."[33]

This causes a bit of a muddle right off the top. Suppose that our migrant farm worker, instead of receiving apples, receives a promise from the owner to pay him at a later date. Is this worker now in receipt of income on the receipt of this piece of paper? If he is, then what is the meaning of the accrual method of accounting?

Note also that the Regulations allude to "constructive" as well as actual receipt of income. Thus apparently a taxpayer can have income on the cash method even though he has not *actually* received any income. He may *constructively* receive it.

So it would seem that what the Regulations are telling us here is that under the cash method the taxpayer might have income even though he does not receive cash and/or does not receive anything at all. We will struggle some more with these problems.

For example, the case of *Charles F. Kahler*[34] presented the excruciating question of when did a cash basis taxpayer realize income represented by a check delivered December 31, 1946 after banking hours?

The court held the check was income in the year it was received, asserting that, according to the regulations, all items of gross income shall be included in the taxable year in which received by the taxpayer, and that where services are paid for other than by money, the amount to be included as income is the fair market value of the thing taken in payment. Thus the court treated the check like it was a bushel of apples. The court felt that it was immaterial that the check was delivered too late to cash.

Why are taxpayers and the Commissioner fighting about in what year is something income, in these cases? Because the taxpayer is clearly fighting to put the item in a low-bracket year, and the Commissioner is fighting to put it in a high-bracket year.

---

[33]   Reg. § 1.446–1(c)(1).

[34]   18 T.C. 31 (1952).

In *Jay A. Williams*[35] taxpayer was a cash basis timber broker who received on May 15, 1951, as compensation for his services an unsecured, non-interest-bearing promissory note in the amount of $7,166.60, payable 240 days thereafter. At the time the note was issued, taxpayer knew that the maker of the note would be unable to pay anything on it because he was short of funds. Upon receipt of the note, taxpayer attempted on 10 or 15 occasions to sell it to various banks or finance companies, but he was unable to do so. Eventually he received $6,666.66 from the maker of the note in 1954.

The court held that it is unquestioned that promissory notes or other evidences of indebtedness received as payment for services constitute income to the extent of their fair market value. Taxpayer argued that the note was not received as payment but merely as an evidence of indebtedness.

The court asserted that a note received only as security, or as an evidence of indebtedness and not as payment may not be regarded as income at the time of receipt. Moreover, the court said, even if the taxpayer had failed to show that the note was not intended as payment, in fact because the maker was without funds, bore no interest, and was unsecured, it did not have a fair market value and thus it is not the equivalent of cash in the year of receipt. It would appear that this latter argument about lack of fair market value is sounder than arguments that draw from something as possibly amorphous as the intent of the maker of the note.

In *Cowden v. Commissioner*[36] the Fifth Circuit gave a very helpful discussion of the cash method. The taxpayer in April 1951 in entered into an oil, gas and mineral lease under which he would be paid various amounts over 1951–1953. The payor was willing and able to make the payments immediately and it was Cowden who negotiated to delay some of the payments. The Tax Court held that since the payor was willing and able to make the payments, the contract rights to receive the payment were income in the year they were negotiated. The Fifth Circuit said that while it is true that the parties may enter into any legal arrangement they see fit even though the form they use is selected with the hope of reducing taxes, it is also true that if the consideration which one of the parties receives is the equivalent of cash, it will be subject to tax. Thus the question is whether the undertaking by the lessee to make future bonus payments was, when made, the equivalent of cash. The court said it is not necessarily the case that only negotiable instruments are cash equivalents—in fact some negotiable instruments are not if the maker's solvency is in question. On the contrary, according to the

---

[35]   28 T.C. 1000 (1957).
[36]   289 F.2d 20 (5th Cir.1961).

court, if a promise to pay of a solvent obligor is unconditional and assignable and is of a kind that is frequently transferred to lenders or investors at only a normal discount for the time value of money, such promise is the equivalent of cash and taxable as cash. Thus the court remanded for the Tax Court to consider whether the lessee's undertaking was a cash equivalent, primarily a fact question.

(b) Constructive Receipt

The doctrine of constructive receipt speaks to the situation where the taxpayer has the choice of receiving income in a particular year or delaying it.[37] In that situation, the doctrine of constructive receipt holds that a taxpayer may not avoid paying tax on income in a particular year by declining to choose to receive it. For example, suppose royalties on the sale of a book have been earned in Year 1 and are due and payable in Year 1. The publisher offers to send the money to the author in December of year 1. The author may respond that he would rather wait until January of Year 2 before receiving them. In that event the royalties would be deemed to have been received by the author in Year 1.[38] To take another case, suppose a lawyer bills a client for services rendered in Year 1. The client is slow to pay (as they often are) and so does not pay until Year 2. This would *not* be a case of constructive receipt inasmuch as the lawyer did not have the power to receive the money in the earlier year.

The doctrine of constructive receipt serves a useful purpose in buttressing the annual accounting concept for cash method taxpayers. Without this doctrine, taxpayers and their controlled or related payors would be able to unjustifiably gain the advantage of deferral of tax. Other taxpayers, who are employees of larger institutions, would probably not have such choices.

But how far does this doctrine really reach? Is an individual who is the chief executive officer and controlling shareholder of a small corporation in constructive receipt of the corporate earnings, because he has the power to pay all the earnings out as dividends to himself?

The answer to that one is no.[39] The doctrine does not reach that far, although it is troublesome why it does not. What it would take would be for the chief executive officer and controlling shareholder of the closely-held corporation to bring about board action to authorize or set aside the funds for the payment of dividends. If he then

---

[37] We have discussed at length the benefits of delaying tax. For further discussion see the Appendix.

[38] This assumes the Service finds out about this little informal arrangement. One of the problems in this field is the difficulties of finding out what taxpayers and their controlled or friendly payors are up to.

[39] See Amend v. Commissioner, 13 T.C. 178 (1949), acq., 1950–1 C.B. 1.

declined to take the set-aside funds at that point, he would apparently be in constructive receipt of the dividends.[40]

The doctrine, therefore, can be easily avoided by the controlling shareholder of a small corporation so that he may time the payment of dividends to a year when he is in a lower bracket.

An interesting constructive receipt case was presented in *Hornung v. Commissioner,*[41] involving one of the great football players of the late 50's and early 60's. Hornung, a triple-threat player (both on and off the field), was an All-American quarterback at Notre Dame, and then played for the Green Bay Packers in their heyday. On December 31, 1961, Hornung played in the National Football League championship game in Green Bay, Wisconsin, between the Green Bay Packers and the New York Giants. He scored 19 points and established a new NFL scoring record. After the game, at 4:30 p.m., Hornung was informed he had won the Sport Magazine award as the outstanding player in the National Football League and would be awarded a new Corvette automobile. The editor of Sport Magazine did not have the key or the title to the Corvette with him. Hornung did not demand immediate possession of the car but he did accept the award. The car had been purchased by Sport Magazine and was in New York in the hands of the Chevrolet dealer. As far as Sport Magazine was concerned, the car was available to Hornung. However, it was Sunday and the New York City Chevrolet dealer was closed. Hornung was informed on December 31, 1961 that there would be a luncheon in New York the following Wednesday at which time he would receive the car. He attended the luncheon, posed for photographs and received the car. He was not required to attend the luncheon or pose for photographers to receive the car. For his 1962 income tax return Hornung reported the acquisition of the car, and the sale of the car for $3,331.04, but he claimed that there was no gain on the sale. He did not report the fair market value of $3,331.04 of the car as income in 1961, 1962 or any other year.

Hornung argued that he should have the value of the car as income in 1961, under the doctrine of constructive receipt. He was in a lower tax bracket in 1961. The doctrine of constructive receipt is ordinarily asserted by the Commissioner against the taxpayer to accelerate income into an earlier year. Thus it was somewhat unusual for a taxpayer to assert it in order to change the year that he himself had earlier reported income. Indeed one would think the doctrine should be unavailable to the taxpayer on some grounds of

---

[40]   The minority shareholders of the corporation would not be in constructive receipt of their dividends, since they do not have the power to receive their dividends at will.

[41]   47 T.C. 428 (1967).

estoppel. However, the court held that the doctrine could, in principle, be asserted by the taxpayer.

Nevertheless, the court held that in this case Hornung did not have unfettered control over the automobile in 1961, since the car was still in the hands of a dealer in New York. Moreover, at the time the award was announced in 1961, nothing was given or presented to Hornung to evidence his ownership of the car. Hence the car was income in 1962.

The other side of the coin, when is a year-end item deductible, was explored in *Revenue Ruling 54–465*[42] in which the Service ruled that a charitable contribution in the form of a check is deductible (under § 170(a)) in the taxable year in which the check is delivered provided the check is honored and paid and there are no restrictions as to time and manner of payment. In fact the rule has come to be that the payment is deductible in the year that one puts the check in the mail,[43] provided that it is subsequently honored and paid in due course. Amounts charged on a credit card are deductible when they are charged on the card.[44]

The case of *Vander Poel, Francis & Co., Inc.*[45] also offered some ideas on the related subject of "constructive payment." It quoted with approval a passage from the highly regarded Mertens, Law of Federal Income Taxation which said in substance that a payment which is found to be constructively received in an earlier year than it actually was may not actually also be constructively paid in that same earlier year. The jurisprudence of the statute is that it tries to reach all income, whereas deductions are a matter of legislative grace. Thus, it could occur that a payment would be constructively received in an earlier year but not be regarded as constructively paid in that earlier year.

(c) Accounts Receivable

It is clear that bills, or amounts due from employers, customers or clients are not income to a cash-method taxpayer. These items only become income when they are received in cash or in kind. Were these bills or accounts receivable income to the cash-method taxpayer, the difference between the two methods of accounting would be eliminated in a major respect.

If the taxpayer is on the accrual method, then accounts receivable are regarded as income even though the cash or its

---

[42]   1954–2 Cum.Bull. 93.

[43]   Witt's Estate v. Fahs, 160 F.Supp. 521 (S.D.Fla.1956).

[44]   Rev.Rul. 78–38, 1978–1 C.B. 68; Rev.Rul. 78–39, 1978–1 C.B. 73.

[45]   8 T.C. 407 (1947).

equivalent has not been received. The amount of income is the face amount of the accounts receivable.[46] When the money comes in on the receivable, there is no further income to the accrual-method taxpayer, since he has already been taxed on the item. If the receivable is ultimately not paid (there are a few deadbeats out there), then the accrual method taxpayer takes a deduction for bad debts (see Chapter 7).

(d) Application: Executive Compensation Arrangements

The basic principles of cash-method accounting we have been discussing are used to undergird some high-powered arrangements for compensating top executives, athletes and other high-income individuals on salary.[47]

What is interesting about these arrangements for highly-compensated individuals and their tax advisors is that they do not have to be made available to rank and file employees (and generally they are not).

These particular executive compensation arrangements are called "nonqualified" arrangements. This distinguishes them from ordinary pension plans which are (and must be) available to rank and file employees. A nonqualified executive compensation arrangement is a highly attractive arrangement with excellent tax advantages for the recipient.

The basic structure of a nonqualified arrangement is that there is a contractual agreement to make payments to the executive in the future. However—and this is the key—the agreement is not represented by notes or secured in any way. Thus the arrangement cannot be said to be the equivalent of cash (it's not apples, to use our farm worker example above). The arrangement does not give rise to taxable income to the employee until the payments under the contract are made.[48] This result is important because it might have been thought that under the doctrine of constructive receipt such an arrangement might have given rise to taxable income to a cash-basis taxpayer upon being entered into. However, where the contractual arrangement is not evidenced by notes, or funded or secured in any way, the cash-basis taxpayer has not received "cash or its equivalent"

---

[46] There can be a deduction of some amount as a "reserve" for bad debts (not all accounts receivable are ultimately paid).

[47] See also Chapter 8, which discusses pensions and other deferred compensation methods.

[48] Rev.Rul. 60–31, 1960–1 C.B. 174, modified by Rev.Rul. 70–435, 1970–2 C.B. 100.

and is therefore not taxed on the arrangement at the time it is entered into.[49]

If the deferral under such a contractual arrangement is to be for a substantial period of time, an interest or earnings element is generally included in the arrangement. This may take the form of ordinary interest which is credited to the employee's account, or so-called "phantom stock plans" and "stock appreciation rights" may be used in which amounts are credited to the employee's account based on the performance of the employer's stock or an index of the general stock market.

The attractiveness of these contractual, nonqualified arrangements to the employee is balanced by the fact that the employer may not take a deduction for compensation paid or accrued under such nonqualified plans until the amounts are includable in the gross income of the employee.[50]

Thus, it is difficult to shift income from one taxpayer to another,[51] but it is easier to shift income from one year to another. Should it not be the other way around?

For examples of razzle dazzle executive compensation techniques, see ¶ 8.04(2).

(e) Prepaid Expenses

As discussed in Chapter 6, taxpayers are very anxious to deduct expenses early to gain the advantages of deferral. Cash-and accrual-method taxpayers follow the same rules with regard to capital expenses (see Chapter 6). They also follow the same rules with respect to deductibility of expenses that are paid early—so-called prepaid expenses. These include items such as rent, salaries, insurance premiums. Such prepaid expenses are deductible only to the extent the service paid for is used during the taxable year.

A heavy item here is interest. Taxpayers like to prepay interest on a loan in a year when their other income is high in order to knock down their tax bracket. With a literal application of the cash method, this technique would work. The Code now chills out that maneuver with § 461(g), which provides that cash-method taxpayers must

---

[49]   Rev.Rul. 60–31, 1960–1 C.B. 174. See also Rev.Rul. 72–25, 1972–1 C.B. 127 (where the employer funded its deferred compensation liability with an annuity contract; held the deferred compensation agreement does not create an escrow account or trust or fund or any other form of asset segregation and therefore the employee is not currently taxable on the arrangement).

[50]   Section 404(a)(5). While this rule is to be expected for a cash-method taxpayer it is a significant restriction on an accrual-method taxpayer. Most employers of any significant size would be on the accrual-method of accounting.

[51]   See Chapter 5.

capitalize prepaid interest. To "capitalize" prepaid interest means not to deduct it but treat it as a capital expense. Then the taxpayer may deduct the interest over the period of time to which it is allocable.[52]

An example of the problems in the prepaid expense area is the case of *Commissioner v. Boylston Market Ass'n*,[53] which held that a taxpayer who prepaid his insurance premiums in one year to cover several years could take these payments as deduction prorated over the several years life of the policy. The court rejected the Commissioner's weird argument that the taxpayer could not take the prorated amount in a particular year of the proration because the taxpayer had not made a cash payment of sufficient size in that year. Thus *Boylston Market* illustrates the point that a taxpayer can create an asset, in that case prepaid insurance premium, by the expenditure of cash. Then the expenditure is written off over the life of the asset.

Similarly *Cathcart*[54] dealt with the question of whether taxpayer was entitled to deduct points withheld from mortgage proceeds in the year taxpayer obtained his mortgage. The court recognized that, by revenue ruling and statute, taxpayers who prepay points on their home mortgages with funds not obtained from the lender are entitled to deduct the entire amount in the year paid. But the court said that where the points are *withheld* from the mortgage proceeds by the lender, they are not deductible in the year the mortgage was obtained but must be prorated over the life of the mortgage.

The results in *Cathcart* were elaborated on in *Revenue Ruling 87–22*,[55] in which the Service dealt with case in which a taxpayer refinanced his old home mortgage with a principle balance of $80,000 with a new mortgage loan of $100,000, the extra $20,000 to be used to pay for improvements on his house. The Service ruled that $80,000 of the new mortgage loan was not incurred in connection with the purchase or improvement of the taxpayer's principal residence and $20,000 of the new mortgage loan was incurred in connection with the improvement of the taxpayer's principal residence. Thus 80% of the points on the new mortgage loan were not immediately deductible but rather had to be prorated over the life of the loan and 20% of the points on the new mortgage loan were immediately deductible, under § 461(g)(2).

---

[52]   "Points" incurred in acquiring a home mortgage are excepted from this rule and may be immediately deducted, § 461(g)(2). Once again that home mortgage interest lives a charmed life.

[53]   131 F.2d 966 (1st Cir.1942).

[54]   36 T.C.M. 1321 (1977).

[55]   1987–1 Cum.Bull. 146.

(3) The Accrual Method

(a) In General

As indicated above, the accrual-method of accounting generally involves accruing items as income when all the events have occurred that establish the right to receive the income and the amount of income can be determined with reasonable accuracy.

The conventional wisdom is that the cash method is fine for individuals and some small businesses. However, when businesses become larger and more sophisticated, the more accurate accrual method is needed. After our discussion of time value of money issues, this conventional wisdom could be questioned. Some of the tricky taxpayer maneuvers discussed there were made possible by accrual-method accounting and were cured by cash-method accounting.

The weakness in accrual-method accounting is that, in the phrase, it "does not follow the money." Since it "does not follow the money," it is weak on dealing with transactions that extend over longer periods of time.

It is the essence of accrual-method accounting to recognize income items before they are received and recognizing expense items before they are paid. Rather, items like accounts receivable (see discussion above) and accounts payable are recognized at the time the rights with respect to the item become fixed, even if no cash has yet changed hands.

For example in *Spring City Foundry Co. v. Commissioner*[56] the Supreme Court addressed a case where an accrual method taxpayer had sold goods in 1920 on credit. Before the purchaser could pay, it went bankrupt and it was clear before the end of the year that the taxpayer would not be paid in full. The taxpayer argued, among other things, that the partial worthlessness of the purchaser's obligation reduced the amount that the taxpayer need report in gross income. The Court held that in the accrual method the total amount which the taxpayer has a right to receive is included in gross income. If some part of the obligation subsequently becomes uncollectible, that is something which may be deducted under the appropriate statutory section.

Similarly in *Revenue Ruling 70–151*[57] the Service dealt with the situation that an accrual method taxpayer instituted suit against the United States in the Court of Claims for damages for alleged breach of contract. The taxpayer was awarded a judgment in 1968 and the

---

[56]   292 U.S. 182, 54 S.Ct. 644, 78 L.Ed. 1200 (1934), rehearing denied 292 U.S. 613, 54 S.Ct. 857, 78 L.Ed. 1472 (1934).

[57]   1970–1 Cum.Bull. 116.

United States filed a petition for writ of certiorari in 1969 and it was denied in 1969. Congress made no appropriation for the amount of the judgment in 1969. The Service ruled that the right to receive the sum due as a result of the judgment became fixed in 1969 and thus was properly included in the taxpayer's income in 1969 even though Congress did not in 1969 appropriate funds to pay the sum. While one can understand the principle of this ruling, it seems particularly hard on the taxpayer when it is the United States itself that is not paying its debt in a timely fashion.

(b) Income

There is a significant override to accrual-method accounting. That concerns the case where the accrual-method taxpayer receives the cash in advance of when it is due. In that case, the taxpayer is put on the cash method and taxed in full on the amount received.

To take an example, suppose rent on property is paid 3 years in advance. The lessor would have to take the full amount received into income immediately, even though he is on the accrual method. The accrual method lessee, however, would not be able to deduct the entire amount in the year of payment. Rather he would be required to treat the advance payments as a capital asset which is amortized over the three years of the advance payment at 1/3 per year. This is a heads-the-Service-wins-tails-the-Service-wins approach to this transaction. Well, after all, we have to raise some money, don't we?

See for example *New Capital Hotel, Inc.*[58] in which the Tax Court dealt with a $30,000 advance payment received by the petitioner lessor, an accrual method taxpayer. The payment was received in 1949 but was to be applied as rent in 1959. The Court held the payment was includible in income in 1949. The Court stated that the $30,000 was paid as advance rental for the year 1959; it was not a security deposit. It was intended to be rent, was described in the lease as rent and was primarily rent. Since it is received in 1949, it is taxable in 1949 even though the rent is to be applied for use of the property in 1959.

But how far can the concept be pushed? Like the cash method (see discussion above), the accrual method can only be pushed so far. What happens if a sale of property for a particular price is booked by the taxpayer in Year 1, but the closing date or date of title passing is in Year 2. Does accrual-method accounting mean that the sale price is taken into income in Year 1?

The short answer is no. The accrual of income is not allowed or required until the property contracted for has been transferred. This

---

[58]   28 T.C. 706 (1957), affirmed per curiam 261 F.2d 437 (6th Cir.1958).

is the case even though a binding contract for the transfer of the property has been entered into in an earlier year. The same principle holds for services. Suppose the taxpayer in Year 1 enters into a binding contract to perform services in Year 2. This taxpayer is not taxed on the fee for the services until they are performed.[59]

While this seems to violate the accrual method, this approach could be explained on a realization basis. That is, it could be said that the gain was not *realized* until title passed. See Chapter 4 for discussion of the realization requirement. Whether it makes one feel better to bottom one's treatment of this transaction on the artificial accrual-method accounting approach or the artificial realization requirement is a matter of personal taste. We refer to these methods as artificial because neither actually reflects the economics of what is happening in this transaction. Under economically-accurate time value of money analysis, the taxpayer should be taxed on the present value of the payments to be made in the future. That is the most economically accurate approach, but we are nowhere near adopting it.

Since we decline to follow the economically accurate approach, we are left to haggle about legal rules that may not seem to have too much point. But that's what lawyers do, isn't it?

See ¶ 9.03(3)(e) below for further specialized treatment of the prepaid income area.

(c) Deductions: General Dynamics

Under the accrual method, expenses are deducted when "all the events" occur which fix the taxpayer's liability. In particular under the "all events test," two issues must be established: 1) the fact of liability; and 2) the amount of the liability can be determined with reasonable accuracy.[60]

For example in the case of *Schuessler v. Commissioner*[61] the accrual method taxpayer was in the business of selling furnaces with a guarantee that he would turn the furnaces on and off each year for five years. The taxpayer in 1946 took a deduction of $13,300 as a reserve to represent the estimated cost of carrying out this guarantee for furnaces sold that year. The court upheld the deduction on the grounds that it more accurately reflected income than a system in which taxpayer would sell equipment in one year, be taxed on an

---

[59]   Lucas v. North Texas Lumber Co., 281 U.S. 11, 50 S.Ct. 184, 74 L.Ed. 668 (1930).

[60]   Section 461(h)(3)(B). See also United States v. Anderson, 269 U.S. 422, 46 S.Ct. 131, 70 L.Ed. 347 (1926) (munitions manufacturer incurred a profits tax on munitions manufactured in 1916 which was due and paid in 1917; held: tax deductible in 1916).

[61]   230 F.2d 722 (5th Cir.1956).

inflated price because he obligated himself to provide services and then take a deduction in the later years when he performed the services.

A leading Supreme Court case in this area is *General Dynamics*.[62] In this case, a major defense contractor, General Dynamics, an accrual-method taxpayer, provided health benefits to its employees as a self-insurer, paying its employee health benefits out of its own funds. The company still employed a private carrier to administer the plan.

Since the filing and processing of claims took time, there was a delay between the providing of health services and the payment of those claims by General Dynamics. Thus some of each year's claims would not be paid until the following year or two, because some claims would not be filed until after the year the services were provided. General Dynamics asserted it could deduct the amount of claims which were not filed in the year they were incurred. The company estimated the amount of those claims based on its actuarial experience.

The Supreme Court, speaking through Justice Marshall, held that these delayed claims could not be deducted in the year incurred because the "all events" test was not satisfied. Claims which have not yet been filed, in the Court's view, might never be filed. This could be due to employees' error or procrastination, or confusion over the coverage or fear of disclosure to the employer of the nature or type of services rendered. The Court did not wish to accept statistical evidence as a basis for allowing a deduction to an accrual-method taxpayer. Historically it has been true that the courts and the Service have not accepted statistical evidence to support additions to reserves for estimated expenses.

The stakes in this case may seem relatively minor—a delay of a year or two in taking a deduction. But recall that an accrual-method taxpayer taking the full face amount of a deduction years in advance of when the item has to actually be paid can gain some outstanding benefits. If large amounts are involved even a one-or two-year difference can mean significant tax savings.

In the interesting Supreme Court case of *Hughes Properties*,[63] the Court held, in contrast with *General Dynamics*, that an accrual-basis casino can accrue its liability at the end of the year for

---

[62] United States v. General Dynamics Corp., 481 U.S. 239, 107 S.Ct. 1732, 95 L.Ed.2d 226 (1987).

[63] United States v. Hughes Properties, Inc., 476 U.S. 593, 106 S.Ct. 2092, 90 L.Ed.2d 569 (1986).

progressive slot machine jackpots which had not yet been won by any player.

(d) Current Law: Economic Performance

Schuessler, General Dynamics and *Hughes* were decided on the "all events test." After these cases, the statute was amended to toughen up the standards for ascertaining when an accrual-method taxpayer may take a deduction. In particular the statute now provides that the "all events" test shall not be treated as met any earlier than when "economic performance" occurs with respect to the item in question.[64] Under these new rules, taxpayer in *Schuessler* and *Hughes* would now lose. Moreover, these new economic performance rules prevent some of the wild abuses in the time value of money area that are described in the Appendix. Thus under these rules it is clear that reserves for estimated future expenses such as personal injury claims, refunds, maintenance and service contracts, and cancellations may not be taken.[65]

In particular the "economic performance" standard provides that:

> *Services provided to the taxpayer:* If the liability of the accrual-method taxpayer arises out of providing services to the taxpayer, economic performance occurs when the person provides such services. Thus even though the taxpayer is contractually liable to pay or in fact does pay for the services in an earlier year, economic performance (and thus deductibility) occurs only in the later year when the services have been provided.[66]

> *Property provided to the taxpayer:* If the liability of the accrual-method taxpayer arises out of providing property to the taxpayer, economic performance occurs when the person provides such property. Thus even though the taxpayer is contractually liable to pay or in fact does pay for the property in an earlier year, economic performance (and thus deductibility) occurs only in the later year when the property has been provided.[67]

> *Property used by the taxpayer* (i.e., rented): If the liability of the accrual method taxpayer arises out of providing the use of property to the taxpayer, economic

---

[64]   Section 461(h)(1).

[65]   Taking such reserves is a standard practice in financial accounting, so once again we see a discrepancy between financial and tax accounting.

[66]   Section 461(h)(2)(A)(i).

[67]   Section 461(h)(2)(A)(ii), thus codifying the result in the older Supreme Court case of Lucas v. North Texas Lumber, 281 U.S. 11, 50 S.Ct. 184, 74 L.Ed. 668 (1930).

performance occurs when the taxpayer uses the property. Thus even though the taxpayer is contractually liable to pay or in fact does pay for the use of the property in an earlier year, economic performance (and thus deductibility) occurs only in the later year or years when the property is used.[68]

Services and property provided by the taxpayer: If the liability of the accrual method taxpayer requires him to provide services or property to someone else, economic performance occurs when the taxpayer provides such property or services. Thus even though the taxpayer is contractually obligated in an earlier year to provide property or services, there is no deduction of expenses of providing the property or services until the year these are provided.[69]

Workers' compensation and tort liabilities: If the liability of the accrual method taxpayer requires a payment to another person arising out of a workers compensation act or a tort claim, economic performance occurs as the payments to such person are made. Thus the taxpayer is put on the cash method. The accrual-method taxpayer cannot gain the huge advantage of taking an up-front deduction for the full face amount of a workers compensation or tort claim that is to be paid out over time.[70]

The Service is also given the power to promulgate regulations dealing with other items.[71]

(e) Prepaid Income: American Automobile Association; Schlude

The economic performance rules described in the preceding section govern the case of advance deductions for the accrual-method taxpayer. But what of the case of advance income for the accrual-method taxpayer? From a tax accounting standpoint it is awkward

---

[68]   Section 461(h)(2)(A)(iii).

[69]   Section 461(h)(2)(B).

[70]   Section 461(h)(2)(C). See the Appendix.

[71]   Section 461(h)(2)(D).

There are some exceptions. Economic performance is not required where it occurs within the shorter of (1) a reasonable period after the close of the tax year in which the expense is accrued or (2) 8 1/2 months after the close of that year. In addition, (a) the item is recurring in nature and the taxpayer consistently treats items of the kind as incurred in the tax year in which the all events test (not including the economic performance test) is satisfied, and (b) the item is either not a material item or its accrual in the year before economic performance results in a more proper match against income than would accruing it in the year of economic performance. § 461(h)(3).

when an accrual method taxpayer is paid in advance of the time that all the events have occurred to fix his liability.

The statutory scheme under which the Service operates here gives it a great deal of discretion. It is a discretion the Service has not shrunk from exercising.

Section 446(b) provides, as discussed above at ¶ 9.01, that if the method of accounting used by the taxpayer "does not clearly reflect income," the computation of taxable income shall be made under the method as in the opinion of the Service does clearly reflect income.

The Service, has historically argued that advance payments to accrual method taxpayers are income when received, even though the payments have not yet been earned. One of the leading cases in this area is *American Automobile Association*.

AMERICAN AUTOMOBILE ASSOCIATION V. UNITED STATES[72]

Facts: American Automobile Association provided a variety of services to its members in return for payments in the form of dues. Dues from members were paid one year in advance, although the payments and subsequent membership renewal or commencement could occur in any month of the year. The membership dues, when received, were deposited in the taxpayer's bank accounts without restriction. For accounting purposes, the taxpayer treated the dues as income received ratably over the 12-month membership period. The payments representing membership months occurring beyond the year of receipt were considered unearned income. This method used by the taxpayer was in accord with generally accepted accounting principles.

Question: In what year are dues paid in advance reportable as income by American Automobile Association?

Service's argument: The entire amount of advance dues should be reported as income in the year received.

Taxpayer's argument: The proration system they used comported with generally accepted accounting principles, as proven by expert testimony.

Held: The taxpayer's proration of dues did not necessarily correspond to the times when members might need services. Thus the taxpayer's method did not clearly reflect income. The exercise of the Service's discretion in rejecting the Association's accounting system was not unsound.

---

[72]   367 U.S. 687, 81 S.Ct. 1727, 6 L.Ed.2d 1109 (1961), reh'g denied 368 U.S. 870, 82 S.Ct. 24, 7 L.Ed.2d 70 (1961).

This is an example of hardball by the Service, with the Court not stopping it. There might be a number of approaches of clearly reflecting ·income for advance payments for the accrual-method taxpayer. But plainly, requiring the full inclusion of advance payments does not reflect income. It is plain that a variety of expenses incurred by AAA (utilities, rent, local taxes) that are fairly attributable to these advance payments would not be deductible until later years. Thus the Government's approach clearly does not reflect income.

This issue came up again in the well-known case of *Schlude*:

SCHLUDE V. COMMISSIONER[73]

Facts: Mark Schlude and his wife operated an Arthur Murray dance studio. The taxpayers' customers signed contracts for dance lessons that stated that (1) the dance students would pay tuition for the lessons in a certain amount, (2) the students should not be relieved of their obligation to pay the tuition, (3) no refunds would be made, and (4) the contract was noncancellable. The contracts in question prescribed a specific number of lesson hours ranging from five to 1,200, and some contracts provided for lifetime courses. These payments on the contracts were considered by the taxpayers as deferred income when initially received, although the payments were put into the studio's general bank account. The taxpayers only included the advanced payments into income as the lessons were taught. Advanced payments were also considered income when a customer failed to take a lesson after a year.

Question: Was it proper for the Service, exercising its discretion under § 446(b), to stop the music and reject the studio's accounting system as not clearly reflecting income and to include as income in the year received the advance payments for dance lessons?

Held: Relying on the *American Automobile Association* case, the Court invokes the "long-established policy . . . in deferring, where possible, to congressional procedures in the tax field," and, as in that case, cannot say that the Commissioner's rejection of the studio's deferral system was unsound.

Also the system employed by the taxpayer was artificial, as it was in *American Automobile Association,* in that the advance payments related to services which were to be performed only upon customers' demands without relation to fixed dates in the future.[74]

---

[73]   372 U.S. 128, 83 S.Ct. 601, 9 L.Ed.2d 633 (1963).

[74]   See also Commissioner v. Indianapolis Power & Light Co., 493 U.S. 203, 110 S.Ct. 589, 107 L.Ed.2d 591 (1990) (cash deposits made to public utility by less creditworthy customers were not advance payments of utility bills taxable under *AAA* and *Schlude* but rather were in essence non-taxable loans to the utility).

Comment: This case would seem to follow consistently from *American Automobile Association.* It suffers from the same problem in that it appears that there are a number of expenses allocable to performing under the contract in future years which cannot be deducted in advance, to match the advance payments.

Consider once again the asymmetry of the treatment of advance receipts and advance expenditures. Suppose that one of the customers in the *American Automobile Association* case was a limousine company that wished to have AAA protection for its vehicles. The company pays its dues 3 years in advance. After the AAA case, AAA must take that 3 years' advance payment into income in the year received. However, the limousine company cannot deduct the three years dues up front but must wait until "economic performance" has occurred. This would mean that it could deduct the advance payments for the AAA protection only in the year to which the dues are attributable—i.e., write the advance payment off over three years.

As another example, *Artnell Co. v. Commissioner*[75] addressed the question whether prepayments for services (proceeds of advance sales of tickets for Chicago White Sox baseball games and revenues for related future services) must be treated as income when received or whether inclusion in income can be deferred by the accrual method taxpayer until the games were played and other services rendered. The court in *Artnell,* running counter to the previous cases in the field, such as *Automobile Club of Michigan, American Automobile Association* and *Schlude* (see above), concluded that there must be situations where the deferral technique will so clearly reflect income that the Supreme Court will find an abuse of discretion if the Commissioner rejects it. The court thus remanded the case for a further hearing in the tax court to ascertain whether the taxpayer's deferral method of accounting did clearly reflect its income.

On remand indeed the Tax Court held that the taxpayer's method of accounting was more supportable than that of the Commissioner and upheld the taxpayer's method of deferring income. The Government did not petition for certiorari in *Artnell.*

Subsequently, the Commissioner propounded *Rev. Proc. 70–21*[76] in which it held that if there is prepayment of income for services to an accrual method taxpayer for services to be rendered within the current and a succeeding year, income must be included in the current year only to the extent that services are rendered in that year. However, no deferral is allowed if the prepayment is for services

75　400 F.2d 981 (7th Cir.1968).
76　1970–2 Cum.Bull. 501.

to be rendered beyond the reach of the succeeding year ("the two-year rule"). In that latter case, immediate inclusion is required for prepaid income for services to be rendered.

A couple of narrow exceptions to this stringent treatment of prepaid expenses have been enacted over the years. Congress overturned the holding on the particular facts of *American Automobile Association* with § 456, which allows deferral of prepaid dues of some membership organizations. And § 455 allows the deferral of prepaid newspaper and magazine subscriptions.

Chapter 10

CREDITS

Table of Sections

¶ 10.01 IN GENERAL

Once a taxpayer has computed his tax liability, his task is still not done (remember the introduction?). He may be entitled to certain credits against the tax liability that he owes. Credits are subtractions directly from the tax bill; whereas deductions, by contrast, are subtractions from income. Thus, a credit of $100 reduces the taxpayer's tax liability by $100. A deduction of $100 reduces a 35-percent bracket taxpayer's tax by $35.00 and a 15-percent bracket taxpayer's tax liability by $15. If the taxpayer has no taxable income, neither a credit nor a deduction will do him any good unless (as is sometimes the case) it can in effect be carried to other taxable years. Also a credit may be constructed to pay a refund and become in effect a negative income tax for poor people, see the Earned Income Tax Credit and Child Tax Credit, discussed at ¶¶ 10.05 and 10.06.

Because credits provide dollar-for-dollar tax savings, they are often seen as more equitable than tax deductions, whose impact depends on the taxpayer's tax bracket. However, that would be an overly simple view of the issue. As a practical matter, taxpayers are rarely given a credit of 100 percent of any particular expenditure that they might make. Obviously, if a 100-percent credit were available for, say, child care, every taxpayer would make the expenditure, since he would get *all* his money back from the Government. See, as a fascinating example of a 100% credit and some of the bizarre results that come from it, the Hope Scholarship Credit, enacted by the Taxpayer Relief Act of 1997, discussed at ¶ 10.07.

Credits are always keyed to a percentage of amounts expended for the particular activity in question. However, the ability to undertake a level of expenditure great enough to take advantage of the credit will depend on the taxpayer's income. Therefore, credits, as well as deductions, can often be best taken advantage of by those with higher incomes. This effect can be resisted by phasing it out for higher income levels, as happens with the child care credit, discussed below and the child credit, discussed at ¶ 10.06.

¶ 10.02 CHILD ETC. CARE CREDIT: *SMITH*

This section discusses the Child Care credit. It is not to be confused with the much larger Child Credit, discussed below at ¶ 10.06.

In the leading case of Henry C. Smith (as discussed at ¶ 6.03(3)(a)),[1] a husband and wife employed nursemaids to take care of their young child so that both could work. The Board of Tax Appeals held that the couple could not deduct the expenses of the nursemaids on the grounds that such expenses were inherently personal, and "of a character applicable to human beings generally" and therefore not deductible. *Smith* has been criticized on the basis that the expenses for child care would not have been incurred had not both parents been working. However, the court's reasoning that such expenditures are non-deductible, personal expenditures appears to be sound. Granted that additional expenses were incurred on account of the wife's working, this could also be said about a variety of personal expenses incident to the holding of a job: such as more haircuts, finer clothes, commuting expenses, lunches out. The position that all incremental increases in personal expenses incident to holding a job should be deductible would not appear to be tenable.

The question of the treatment of child care expenses can also be seen as part of the larger issue of imputed income. Consider two couples: the Joneses and the Garcias. In the case of the Joneses, Judy Jones, works and makes $50,000 per year; Willie Jones does not work but stays home and takes care of the children and the house. In the case of the Garcias, Manny Garcia works and makes $50,000 per year. Ana Garcia also works, making $15,000 per year, and they hire a housekeeper to take care of the children and the house at an annual salary of $10,000 per year. As an economic matter, the Garcias are $5,000 per year better off than the Joneses. But the Garcias are taxed in full on the $15,000 earnings of Ana. If the Garcias are in the 40% bracket (combined federal and state rate), the tax on Ana's earnings is $6,000. Subtracting the $6,000 tax and the $10,000 child care

---

[1]   Henry C. Smith v. Commissioner, 40 B.T.A. 1038, 1939 WL 83 (1939), aff'd per curiam 113 F.2d 114 (2d Cir.1940).

expenses from Ana's earnings, we find that the Garcias are actually losing $1,000 a year from Ana's job.

Thus does the tax system discourage the lower-earning spouse from going to work. If historically and culturally women are usually the second lower-income wage earner in the family, then the effect can be seen as a women's issue: the tax system discourages women from working outside the home.

We can push the analysis further. Let us say that the value of Ana Garcia's work in the home is worth $10,000 (reasonable given what the Garcias pay for a housekeeper/babysitter). Thus in terms of value to society, it is better if Ana works outside the home where her services are worth $15,000 rather than in the home where her services are worth $10,000. Yet the taxation of Ana's earnings coupled with no deduction for child care expenses means that Ana will stay home. Economists call this a "deadweight" loss to the society. The tax system has distorted Ana's behavior so that she works in a lesser-valued activity.

Lest you think this is all just some more idle chatter, Congress has actually tried to respond to this problem. While the response is not complete, it shows some thinking along these lines.

The response was a child care credit if the childcare is necessary for (or incident to) taxpayer's employment. In other words, you can't take the credit if you don't have a job. The credit is 35% of employment-related expenses for taxpayers with adjusted gross incomes of $15,000 or less. The percentage credit decreases by 1% for each $2,000 (or fraction thereof) increase in adjusted gross income. The credit does not decrease below 20%. Therefore, taxpayers with adjusted gross income of $43,000 or more receive a credit of 20% of employment-related expenses.[2]

The following table illustrates the amount of the percentage credit at various levels of adjusted gross income. The credit is 35% for adjusted gross income of $15,000 or less.

---

[2] Section 21 as amended by EGTRRA. As with other provisions in EGTRRA, this provision sunsets in 2011. In 2011, the child care credit will return to pre-EGTRRA levels.

AGI Over	% Credit
$15,000	34%
$17,000	33%
$19,000	32%
$21,000	31%
$23,000	30%
$25,000	29%
$27,000	28%
$29,000	27%
$31,000	26%
$33,000	25%
$35,000	24%
$37,000	23%
$39,000	22%
$41,000	21%
$43,000	20%

The maximum amount of employment-related expenses that may be taken into account in computing the credit is $3,000, if there is one child or other qualifying individual in the home and $6,000 if there are two or more children or other qualifying individuals in the home.[3] For example, a taxpayer with an adjusted gross income of $24,000 and one child in the home who incurred $3,100 of employment-related expenses would get a credit of $900 (30% of $3,000). If this same taxpayer had two qualifying individuals in the home, the credit would be $930 (30% of $3,100).

A "qualifying individual" for these purposes means (A) a dependent of the taxpayer who is under the age of thirteen and with respect to whom the taxpayer is entitled to a dependency deduction;[4] (B) a dependent of the taxpayer who is physically or mentally incapable of caring for himself; (C) the spouse of the taxpayer if physically or mentally incapable of caring for himself.[5]

---

[3]   Section 21(c).

[4]   It is possible for an individual to be a dependent of a taxpayer without the taxpayer being entitled to a dependency deduction for that individual. A "dependent" of the taxpayer is one who is in one of the generally familial relationships with the taxpayer described in § 152(a), and for whom the taxpayer provides more than half the support. For the individual to give rise to a dependency deduction to the taxpayer, he not only has to be a "dependent" but must meet several other tests. See ¶ 7.04. Section 21(e)(5) provides a special test for divorced parents and states that the custodial parent is entitled to the credit even if he or she does not provide half of the child's support.

[5]   Section 21(b).

"Employment-related expenses," to which the credit is keyed, means amounts paid to enable the taxpayer to be gainfully employed which are for household services and expenses for the care of a qualifying individual whether the expenses are for care inside or outside the home, as long as the qualifying individual regularly spends at least eight hours a day in the taxpayer's household.[6]

The amount of the employment-related expenses incurred during any taxable year which may be taken into account in making this computation cannot exceed, in the case of an unmarried taxpayer, the taxpayer's earned income; or in the case of a married couple, the earned income of the spouse with the lesser amount of earned income.[7] This rule is relaxed where one spouse is a student or incapable of caring for himself. In either of those events, such spouse shall be deemed to be gainfully employed and to have earned income of not less than $250 per month, where there is one qualifying individual in the household; or $500 a month where there are two or more qualifying individuals in the household. Thus, for example, if one spouse is working and earning $25,000 a year and the other spouse is incapable of caring for himself, and they have two ten-year-old children in a day care center, the spouse incapable of caring for himself will be deemed to have earned income of $500 per month for the purpose of the earned income limit. (There would be two qualifying individuals in this instance—the child and the spouse incapable of caring for himself.) In this case up to $6,000 of employment-related expenses could be taken into account in computing the credit (assuming the expenses were in fact incurred).[8]

No credit is allowed for amounts paid by the taxpayer to a person for whom the taxpayer is allowed a dependency deduction or who is a child of the taxpayer under the age of nineteen.

¶ 10.03 OTHER CREDITS

The statute provides other credits. They are an interesting grab-bag. They include: credit for the elderly and the permanently and totally disabled,[9] adoption expenses,[10] foreign tax credit (of great importance to large companies doing business abroad),[11] credit for

---

[6]   Section 21(b)(2). A liberal result in this area was reached by the Tax Court in finding that the expenses of sending a child to camp for eight weeks, plus one-third of the cost of a school trip to Washington, D.C., qualified as employment-related expenses, Zoltan v. Commissioner, 79 T.C. 490 (1982). This result was reversed by the statute, § 21(b)(2) flush language.

[7]   Section 21(d)(1).

[8]   Section 21(d)(2).

[9]   Section 22.

[10]   Section 23.

[11]   Sections 27, 901.

clinical testing expenses for certain drugs for rare diseases or conditions,[12] credit for producing fuel from a nonconventional source,[13] certain uses of gasoline and special fuels,[14] alcohol used as a fuel,[15] credit for increasing research activities,[16] low income housing credit,[17] enhanced oil recovery credit,[18] expenditures to provide access to disabled individuals,[19] targeted jobs credit.[20] If the business credits cannot be used in the taxable year, they can be carried back three years and forward 15 years.[21]

¶ 10.04 SPECULATIONS ON AN INVESTMENT TAX CREDIT

Tax ideas come in cycles. Periodically there surfaces the idea of bringing back the investment tax credit to stimulate the economy. Historically, the investment tax credit has worked roughly as follows: business firms get to subtract 10 percent of the amounts they invest in new plant and equipment from their tax bill.

It is strange that people want to bring the ITC back because the results with the credit when it was in place beginning in the late 1970's were not particularly good.

There are two kinds of credits: a one-time credit and a permanent credit.

The problem with a one-time credit is that businesses do not have time to plan for the investment before the credit runs out.

The problem with a permanent credit is that it distorts investments by directing them into the areas favored by the credit. Most particularly, it directs investments into plant and equipment instead of into worker retraining. One would think that the decision as to whether to invest in plant and equipment or worker retraining ought to be made by the market rather than have the decision biased by the tax code to favor plant and equipment.

Another problem with the credit is that in many cases it pays firms for doing what they are already doing, investing in new plant and equipment. To combat this problem, some economists, including

12 Section 29.
13 Section 29.
14 Section 32.
15 Section 40.
16 Section 41.
17 Section 42.
18 Section 43.
19 Section 44.
20 Section 51.
21 Sections 38, 39.

those advising the President, have favored an "incremental credit." This would provide a credit for investment in plant and equipment only above a certain threshold level. This seems to have the attractive feature that it encourages spending in new plant and equipment at a much smaller cost then a credit for all such expenditures.

But as the policy-maker employs an incremental credit, he begins to see that he has a tiger by the tail. One problem is to establish the "base year," the year against which the "incremental" expenditures will be measured. Whatever year or period is chosen, companies who happen to have made large investments during that period will be unfairly penalized. Moreover, as the economy expands, the "base" becomes smaller relative to overall investment. Thus the size of the credit swells, adding to the budget deficit.

To combat this problem, a "floating base" might be tried. But a floating base gives perverse results. In a boom year, when the economy is expanding, firms rapidly outrun the floating base. As a result, the credit throws off large benefits to business firms. But in a recession year, firms stay near the base. As a result, the credit's benefits diminish sharply. The credit thus magnifies the business cycle, stimulating investment in boom years and depressing investment in recession years. This is not exactly what we want.

An incremental credit also invites game-playing by business firms and their sophisticated advisors. How is the incremental credit, with or without a floating base, to be handled in the case of mergers or split-ups of companies?

Also, when coupled with accelerated depreciation, and deduction of interest on borrowing to purchase plant and equipment, the credit can yield benefits that may exceed the original price of the plant and equipment.

Putting these conceptual problems together with the credit's indifferent historical record, it may be safe to say that the investment credit is an idea whose time has come and gone.

¶ 10.05 EARNED INCOME CREDIT ("EIC")[22]

The Revenue Reconciliation Act of 1993 greatly enlarged the Earned Income Tax Credit (now referred to as the Earned Income Credit.)[23] The thrust of the EIC is to help lower income working people. The EIC provides for a credit against taxes owed. The maximum amount of the credit is $4,140 (in 2002). If on the taxpayer's particular numbers the credit exceeds the taxes owed, the

---

[22]   This was originally referred to as the Earned Income Tax Credit ("EITC").

[23]   See § 32.

balance is paid to the taxpayer as, in effect, an income subsidy. The amount of the credit depends on the amount of income earned and the number of children in the household.

While the precise calculation is complex an example may be helpful. In the typical case of a taxpayer with two children the income subsidy is paid for taxpayer's wages up to $10,350, where the taxpayer receives the maximum subsidy of $4,140. The subsidy then remains at the maximum up to $14,550 of earnings. Then the subsidy diminishes as earnings go higher, ultimately becoming zero at earnings of $34,178. At $25,000 of earnings, the taxpayer's tax liability would be zero under normal computations (taking account of the standard deduction, personal exemptions, and child tax credit), and the taxpayer would receive an EIC credit of $1,622. At $30,000 of earnings, the taxpayer's tax liability would be around $741. The subsidy or credit would be diminished at this higher level of earnings to about $675. Thus by earning $5,000 more, the taxpayer is only $2,422 better off (and this does not account for state and local taxes or social security taxes). This is why some people claim that there are very high marginal rates for low-income taxpayers as the EIC is phased out.[24] This is clearly true. But this will always be the case as a benefit is phased out. This occurs because the taxpayer is, at the same time, earning more money and thus paying higher income taxes, and losing a portion of the EIC benefit.

The Earned Income Credit is a very interesting and powerful technique. It employs the relatively efficient tax system to mount a welfare program. This is much more efficient than employing the bureaucracy of welfare agencies. The recipients just fill out a tax return. While the computation of the credit is complex, the IRS can do it for them automatically once they fill out their returns.

In making these calculations, if a taxpayer has more than $2,200 of unearned income (i.e., interest, dividends, net rental, royalty, net passive income and net capital gains), no credit is allowed.[25] For calculating the phaseout of the credit losses from these items are not used to reduce income.

The odd structure of the credit is designed to encourage work. The amount of the subsidy rises with wages. Then it remains constant over a wide range of income. It is then phased out as income rises above a certain threshold. But the way the subsidy phases out, there is little incentive to cut back on work to increase the subsidy.

---

[24] See e.g., Daniel Shaviro, The Minimum Wage, The Earned Income Tax Credit, and Optimal Subsidy Policy, 64 U. Chi. L. Rev. 405 (1997).

[25] Section 32(i).

Even though you may be subject to high marginal rates as the benefit phases out, you are always better off making more money.[26]

The EIC has become THE major income support program in this country. It shows the power of the tax system to reach out and control behavior and deal with issues far beyond what one would normally consider to be taxation.

¶ 10.06 CHILD TAX CREDIT

The Taxpayer Relief Act of 1997 enacted a per-child tax credit of $500. The tax credit was raised to $1,000 as part of Under EGTRRA, JGTRRA, and the Working Families Tax Relief Act of 2004, the per-child credit was increased to $1,000. It is now $1,000 per child through 2010.

But as you know, we are not done in 2010.

Like other provisions in EGTRRA, this increase in the child credit sunsets in 2011 and the credit returns to its pre-EGTRRA levels. If this seems absurd to you, you are not alone.

In general, the way the credit works is that after a taxpayer has figured his tax liability, he subtracts $1,000 for each dependent child[27] under 17 from that tax liability. Thus if a taxpayer in 2003 has three children and his tax was $4,000 without regard to the per-child credit, the taxpayer would subtract $3,000 from his tax liability to yield a net tax liability of $1,000.[28] For taxpayers with modified adjusted gross income (adjusted gross income with some rare modifications)[29] above certain levels, the credit is phased out in the following fashion: The credit is reduced (but not below zero) by $50 for each $1,000 (or fraction thereof) by which the taxpayer's modified adjusted gross income exceeds the specified threshold.[30] The threshold amount is $110,000 for a joint return, $75,000 for an

---

[26] It is possible that when other welfare programs are taken into account this will not always be true.

[27] The term "qualifying child" includes a son, daughter, stepson, or stepdaughter, eligible foster child, or a descendant of a brother, sister, stepbrother, or stepsister if the taxpayer cares for the person as the taxpayer's own child. See § 24(c), referencing § 32(c)(3)(B).

[28] Section 24(a).

[29] Modified adjusted gross income is adjusted gross income increased by any amount excluded under the following: § 911 (exclusion of income of U.S. citizens or residents living abroad); § 931 (exclusion for bona fide residents of Guam, American Samoa, and the Northern Mariana Islands), or § 933 (exclusion of income of residents of Puerto Rico), § 24(b)(2)(A).

[30] Section 24(b).

unmarried individual, $55,000 for a single person filing a separate return.[31]

> **Example:** In a 2004, a couple with two children who file jointly are entitled to a credit of $1,900 if their modified adjusted gross income is more than $110,000 but less than $111,000. They lose their credit entirely if their modified adjusted gross income is more than $134,000.

Since the phaseout occurs in $50 jumps, a taxpayer whose income moves up by $1 from a threshold, say, from $1,000 to $1,001 over the threshold will incur an increase in tax liability of $50.

One slight problem with the Child Credit, as it was originally conceived, was that it depended upon the fact that the taxpayer was otherwise paying taxes against which a credit could be taken. Thus, without more, the benefit would redound to the great middle class but not to the lower class. (The upper class would lose the credit because of the phaseout tied to modified adjusted gross income).

Since Congress, after some debate, decided to also help lower income families as well, the Child Credit as ultimately enacted, also provided, through some fairly complex calculations, benefits to low income families. The result is that the Child Credit is also a refundable credit (remember this means you get the credit or a portion of the credit even if you have no taxable income). The refundability of the Child Credit was increased as part of the Working Families Tax Relief Act. For 2004 through 2010, the Child Credit is refundable to the extent of 15 percent of taxpayer's income that exceeds $10,750 (this amount is adjusted for inflation). So if the taxpayer makes $11,700, and is not subject to income tax, the Child Credit is refundable up to 150 (15% of $1,000 (the amount of taxpayer's income that exceeds $10,750)).[32]

The credit is also refundable for taxpayers with 3 or more children to the extent that the taxpayer's social security taxes exceed what the taxpayer receives under the EIC.[33] Thus if taxpayer pays $3,500 in social security taxes and receives $3,000 under the EIC, up to $500 of the credit is refundable. The theory is that the credit goes to offset any remaining social security taxes paid by the taxpayer.

The relationship between the EIC and Child Credit is complex. The approach for putting all this together is that the Child Credit first reduces or eliminates income tax liability. Then the EIC, if it applies, eliminates income tax liability and then reduces FICA

---

[31]   Section 24(b)(2). These threshold amounts are not indexed for inflation, an unattractive result for taxpayers.

[32]   Section 24(d)(B)(i).

[33]   See § 24(d)(B)(ii).

liability. Thereafter the child credit reduces any remaining FICA liability. The Child Credit cannot reduce FICA liability to increase the refundable aspect of the EIC.[34]

In short, poor people need to be really good at math to get this credit.

What we have, therefore—and it is not the first time (see the EIC itself)—is an extremely complicated calculation that must be undertaken by low income people in order to take advantage of the credit. They will be paying a not insignificant amount of their benefit in tax preparation assistance, assuming they are aware of the credit and attempt to take advantage of it at all.[35]

¶ 10.07 RECAP OF TAX ASSISTANCE TO EDUCATION

Prior to the Taxpayer Relief Act of 1997, the following tax breaks were available to assist with the cost of college education.

- Deductibility under § 162 of the cost of education that maintains or improves a skill that is required in the taxpayer's business or meets express requirements of the employer or of the law, ¶ 6.02(2)(b).

- Exclusion by employees of up to $5,250 annually for education expenses paid pursuant to a qualified educational assistance program provided by the employer. After June 30, 1996, the exclusion is not available for graduate level courses, § 127.

- Deductibility of interest on Series EE bonds issued after 1989, provided that the bond proceeds are used to pay higher education expenses, § 135.

- Exclusion by degree candidates of qualified scholarships used to pay for tuition, fees and books at any primary, secondary or postsecondary educational institution, ¶ 3.09(2).

- Cancellation of debt is not triggered by the forgiveness of certain student loans if the forgiveness was

---

[34] For a discussion of the child tax credit, the EIC and the marriage penalty, see Allan J. Samansky, New Developments in Marriage Penalties and Bonuses, 96 Tax Notes 1745, September 23, 2002.

[35] The legislative history concedes this paradox by providing that "The conferees anticipate that the Secretary of the Treasury will determine whether a simplified method of calculating the child credit, consistent with the formula described above, can be achieved." Pending this great event, the best that can be done on the subject is Martin J. MacMahon Jr., The New Child Credits: Explainable Mechanics, Unfathomable Policy, 76 Tax Notes 1625, September 22, 1997.

conditioned on the student working for a certain period in specified professions, particularly applicable to law school graduates working for public interest organizations, § 108(f).

- Tax deferral on earnings from amounts paid into qualified state pre-paid tuition programs. The tax is triggered when the funds are distributed for the purpose of paying the tuition, but is taxed to the student at a presumably low rate, § 529.

- Exclusion of the benefit of low or zero tuition at state-funded institutions. While there is no statutory provision that addresses this matter, the fact that students can go to state-financed institutions and pay either no tuition or much less than the cost of their education is a major in-kind benefit. Since in general, the tax law taxes in-kind benefits, see ¶ 1.02(2)(b) relating to the Comprehensive Tax Base, this exclusion is notable.[36]

This collection of offerings was meager to say the least. But the Taxpayer Relief Act of 1997 and subsequent legislation added several more offerings.

(1) Deduction for Qualified Tuition

The first, and most important, because it applies directly to many of the people reading this book, is a deduction for higher education expenses. This deduction could pay for the cost of this book many times over so pay attention. Although this is a deductor, not a credit, we discuss it here with the educational credit because it serves the same purpose. Through 2016, taxpayers could deduct, above the line, a portion of their "qualified tuition."[37] Because this deduction is above the line, qualifying taxpayers may deduct educational expenses even if they take the standard deduction. Taxpayers with adjusted gross incomes that do not exceed $65,000 ($130,000 for joint returns) receive up to a $4,000 deduction, and taxpayers with adjusted gross incomes not more than $80,000 ($160,000 for joint returns) may deduct up to $2,000.[38] There is no phaseout for this deduction so taxpayers pay a particularly high price for exceeding the income thresholds.

---

[36]   While the text discusses this benefit in terms of public institutions, it may well also be the case that tuition at private schools, high though it may be, is less than the true cost of educating the student. Were that the case, then even students at such private institutions would theoretically have in-kind income.

[37]   Section 222.

[38]   Section 222(b)(2)(B).

Qualified tuition and related expenses has the same meaning that it has under § 25A, discussed infra. It is defined as "tuition and fees required for the enrollment or attendance of the taxpayer, [spouse, or dependent] at an eligible educational institution for courses of instruction."[39]

You cannot claim both the deduction and the § 25A credits. Moreover, qualified tuition does not include tuition or fees paid for by funds from a section 529 plans and Coverdell IRAs.[40]

The § 222 deduction expired at the end of 2016. Given that it has been extended many times before, one should not be surprised if Congress opts to extend the deduction further.

(2) Deduction of Interest on Educational Loans

Of equal importance to many readers is the deductibility of student loan interest.[41] Up to $2,500 of student loan interest is deductible from income. The eligibility for this deduction phases out from modified adjusted gross income of $50,000 to $65,000 for singles ($100,000 to $130,000 for joint returns). The loan must be a qualified educational loan, defined as "indebtedness incurred by the taxpayer *solely* to pay qualified higher education expenses.[42] And qualified education expenses is defined as the 'cost of attendance . . . at an eligible educational institution.' "[43] Once again, qualified educational expenses is reduce by the amount excluded from gross income under a section 529 plan or a Coverdell Education IRA.[44] (See ¶ 8.04(4)(g) for discussion of section 529 plans and ¶ 8.04(4)(e) for Coverdell Education IRAs.)

(3) The American Opportunity Tax Credit and the Lifetime Learning Credit

The American Opportunity Tax Credit is available for tuition and related expenses incurred during the first four years of postsecondary education.[45] The student must attend school on at least a half-time basis, and the credit is lost if the student is convicted of a felony drug offense. The credit includes tuition, fees, and course materials. The credit is available dollar for dollar for the first $2,000 of expenses, then 25% of the next $2,000. So a student with $3,000 in

---

[39]   Section 25A(f).

[40]   Section 222(c)(2).

[41]   Section 221.

[42]   Section 221(d).

[43]   Section 221(d)(2).

[44]   Section 221(d)(2).

[45]   Section 25A(i)(2).

eligible expenses would receive a $2,250 tax credit. Up to 40% of the credit is refundable.

The American Opportunity Tax Credit is phased out for higher income earners, but the income limits are much higher than those set for the former Hope Scholarship Credit or the Lifetime Learning Credit. The phaseout for the American Opportunity Tax Credit starts at $80,000 ($160,000 for joint filers) and is fully phased out at $90,000 ($180,000 for joint filers).

The credit applies to "qualified tuition and related expenses," defined as the tuition and fees paid at most colleges and universities for the taxpayer, the taxpayer's spouse, or the taxpayer's dependent. The credit expressly does not include student activity fees, athletic fees, insurance costs, or expenses for room and board.

As its name implies, the Lifetime Learning Credit is not limited to the first four years of postsecondary education. Qualified tuition and related expenses remain creditable as long as they relate to a course of instruction designed to develop or improve job skills. As with the American Opportunity Tax Credit, the credit applies to instruction received at most colleges and universities.

The Lifetime Learning Credit is limited to 20% of the first $10,000 in qualified tuition and related expenses, meaning the maximum credit is $2,000. Expenses claimed under the American Opportunity Tax Credit may not also be claimed for the Lifetime Learning Credit. The Lifetime Learning Credit phases out as income exceeds $40,000 ($80,000 for joint filers), though these amounts are adjusted annually for inflation (in 2017, for instance, the amounts were $56,000 and $112,000, respectively).

Chapter 11

ETHICS

Table of Sections

¶ 11.01 GENERAL COMMENTS

With recent corporate scandals and the increased use of questionable tax transactions by corporations and individuals, there is an ethical tax crisis facing attorneys, accountants, and our nation as a whole. What is the role of a tax lawyer when giving tax advice? Is our obligation solely to our client, or do we have some obligation to society? How aggressive can we be when we recommend a client take a particular tax position? These questions are at the center of the ethical obligations of tax lawyers.[1]

In a famous opinion, *Gregory v. Helvering*,[2] the Court stated "[t]he legal right of a taxpayer to decrease the amount of what otherwise would be his taxes, or altogether avoid them, by means which the law permits, cannot be doubted.' "[3] If it is legal for a taxpayer to avoid tax by means which the law permits, why can't a lawyer aid taxpayers in doing so? In *Gregory v. Helvering*, however, the Court found against the taxpayer. The Court noted "the question for determination is whether what was done, apart from the tax motive, was the thing which the statute intended."[4] In other words, the Court faced the same quandary that we still face today. How do we differentiate between taxpayers who are legally trying to reduce their taxes, and taxpayers who are pushing the envelope too far and using creative arguments to avoid paying tax?

---

[1]   For a general discussion of tax ethics see Bernard Wolfman, Deborah H. Schenk & Diane Ring, Ethical Problems in Federal Tax Practice (5th ed., Wolters Kluwer 2015).

[2]   293 U.S. 465, 55 S.Ct. 266, 79 L.Ed. 596 (1935).

[3]   Id. at 469.

[4]   Id.

In many ways, a tax lawyer's role is unique in our legal system. Because we have a system of taxation that is based on voluntary compliance, and because audit rates are so low (around 1 to 2 percent), the system itself depends on honest reporting by taxpayers.[5]

Generally, a lawyer has an obligation not to file a claim or take a position if the claim or position is frivolous. But if this standard applied in the tax field, attorneys would have every incentive to recommend that clients take very aggressive tax positions. After all, only a few returns are ever audited, and it is easy to justify a position as "not frivolous."

Tax lawyers have two different functions, and the ethical standards are different depending on the role of the attorney at the time. Sometimes lawyers act as advisors. In this role, the lawyer may advise a client whether a position is justified, how to set up a transaction, or how to take advantage of a loophole in the tax law. The lawyer may even be part of a company that creates and sells "tax preferred"[6] packages designed to reduce the client's tax bill. Since, as we will see later, reliance on an accountant or an attorney may shield a taxpayer from penalties, the attorney plays a role here as a check on abuse. Lawyers provide, in a sense, a seal of approval. When a lawyer is acting in this capacity, it may be fair to require that the attorney have a higher level of certainty when recommending a tax position.

A tax lawyer, however, may also be the taxpayer's advocate. After the IRS disputes an item on a taxpayer's return, the taxpayer enters into adversary proceeding with the IRS, first, usually with an IRS agent or an appeals officer, and later in court. This can happen in several different ways but usually takes one of two tracks. First, a taxpayer files a return and the return is accepted as filed by the IRS. The IRS later (it generally has three years) questions that position. If the IRS and the taxpayer cannot agree on the treatment of the position after an audit, the taxpayer may pay the tax and sue for a refund (either in district court or the Court of Federal Claims) or it may file an action in Tax Court without paying the tax.

---

[5]   See Linda Galler, The Tax Lawyer's Duty to the System, 16 Va. Tax. Rev. 681 (1997) (reviewing Wolfman, Holden, and Schenk, Ethical Problems in Federal Tax Practice (3d Ed. 1995)); David J. Moraine, Loyalty Divided: Duties to Clients and Duties to Others-the Civil Liability of Tax Attorneys Made Possible by the Acceptance of a Duty to the System, 63 Tax Law. 169 (2009).

[6]   This term refers to plans sold by accounting, legal, and consulting firms designed to reduce a person's tax. The Service no doubt refers to these plans as tax shelters. While the terms are often used interchangeably, in this book the term "tax shelter" is reserved for abusive tax preferred schemes.

Once the taxpayer's position is questioned by the IRS, the attorney's role changes (in fact it may be a different attorney). The attorney is now an advocate for the client. Once the tax lawyer is an advocate, the lawyer has the same ethical responsibilities of every attorney to be honest to the court and to not take any position that is frivolous. The lawyer has, however, no greater ethical responsibility than any other attorney representing a client in court.

There are several organizations and governmental bodies that have attempted to provide ethics rules for tax advisors. The ABA, Treasury, Congress, and the courts, have all grappled with this difficult issue.[7]

¶ 11.02 STANDARDS FOR ADVISING TAXPAYERS ON RETURN POSITIONS

One important ethics problem facing tax lawyers is the extent to which a lawyer may recommend a taxpayer take a position on the taxpayer's return. An attorney's opinion that a transaction is proper has two very significant implications. First, it puts a stamp of approval on the transaction, and makes the taxpayer more comfortable in taking the position. Second, reliance on an attorney is often a defense to various penalty provisions in the Code. If a taxpayer is protected against penalties, then there is a significant incentive to take very aggressive tax positions. After all, absent penalties the only consequence of being audited and losing is having to pay the tax plus interest. As we know from our time value of money discussions, the requirement that a taxpayer pay interest really only eliminates the benefit the taxpayer received from not having to pay the tax.

A tax lawyer must be concerned about several different rules (ABA opinions interpreting the Model Rules of Professional Conduct, a lawyer's state rules of professional conduct, statutory provisions, and Treasury Regulations) in determining whether to advise that a taxpayer take a specific position on the return.

(1) ABA Formal Opinion 85–352

Formal Opinion 85–352 sets out the ethical standards for attorneys advising clients regarding tax positions that they may take on their returns.[8] Opinion 85–352 provides that a lawyer can advise that a client take a position on his or her return as long as: (1) the lawyer has a good faith belief that the position is "warranted in existing law or can be supported by a good faith argument for an

---

[7]   See revised Circular 230, 31 CFR part 10, TD 9165 (December 20, 2004); American Jobs Creation Act of 2004, P.L. 108–357, 118 Stat 1418, § 822.

[8]   Formal Opinion 85–352, reprinted in 39 Tax Law. 631 (1986).

extension, modification or reversal of existing law" and (2) "there is some realistic possibility of success if the matter is litigated."[9]

The Formal Opinion clearly takes the position that a tax lawyer's obligations are not unique, and that the ethical standards governing tax lawyers are similar to those governing a lawyer's conduct outside of the tax area.[10] The Formal Opinion gives lawyers a green light to push the envelope very, very far.

In a report on the opinion, commentators attempted to tighten the rule slightly. The commentary indicates that the good faith standard is an objective one, and that good faith requires that there be some realistic possibility of success.[11] But how do we define "realistic possibility of success"? The commentary states that "position having only a 5 percent or 10 percent likelihood of success, if litigated, should not meet this standard," and that a position closely approximating one-third should do so.

The commentary indicates that in determining whether there is a realistic possibility of success, the chance of audit cannot be taken into account. But the vagueness and leniency of this standard certainly encourages taxpayers to play the audit lottery. Moreover, since the commentary is not part of the official opinion, it is unclear how much weight it should be given.

The rule itself only requires a good faith belief and a realistic possibility of success. The ABA implies a good standard would be a one in three chance of success but it is unwilling to set that as the standard. The commentary at least tries, but it sets a very low bar and then says "should not meet this standard." So even a 5 percent or 10 percent likelihood of success might be enough.

But the ABA makes the weakness of the standard particularly clear when it states in its opinion:

> Thus, a lawyer may advise reporting a position on a return even where a lawyer believes the position probably would not prevail, there is no "substantial authority" in support of the position, and there will be no disclosure of the position in the return.

In other words, in the balance of trying to determine whether the lawyer, as an advisor, has a duty to someone besides the client, the ABA falls squarely on the side of the client. It appears that the basis for this decision is that "a lawyer must realistically anticipate that the filing of the tax return may be the first step in a process that

---

[9] Id. at 633.

[10] Id. at 632.

[11] Task Force Report, 39 Tax Law. 635, 636 (1986).

may result in an adversary relationship between the client and the IRS."[12] Thus, according to the formal opinion, it is okay to take very aggressive positions, even ones without substantial authority, and it is okay to do so without disclosure, as long as you, as an attorney, believe that you have between a 10 and 33 percent chance of success. This doesn't seem like a very high bar for the bar.

Since audit rates hover around one to two percent how likely is it that tax advice should realistically be viewed as the first step in an adversarial process? We do not generally make this assumption in other areas of the law. For example, a political candidate's filing with the Federal Election Commission or a business's filing with the Securities and Exchange Commission is not generally thought to be the first step in an adversarial process with the Government.

The ABA Section of Taxation proposed a stricter version of the ethics rule to the ABA. The Tax Section proposed that attorneys not advise taxpayers to take a position unless it was meritorious.[13]

What does a lawyer do if a client wants to take an aggressive position? Under the ethics rules there are two options. First an attorney can simply resign as the taxpayer's attorney.[14] Second, the taxpayer can pay the tax, and then sue for a refund. In the pleading the taxpayer must set forth in detail the grounds upon which the claim for refund is based. In this instance, an attorney may still not bring a claim that is frivolous, but may bring one that the attorney believes is not frivolous but which does not meet the realistic possibility of success standard.

In addition, there is some confusion whether an attorney may advise a taxpayer to take a position that does not have a realistic possibility of success as long as the position is disclosed with the return.[15] The prevailing view appears to be that the lawyer may do

---

[12]   Formal Opinion 85–352, 39 Tax Law. 631 (1986).

[13]   See ABA Section of Taxation Proposed Revision to Formal Opinion 314, May 21, 1984, reprinted in Wolfman and Holden, Ethical Problems in Federal Tax Practice 71–73 (2d Ed. 1985); ABA Section of Taxation Proposed Revision to Formal Opinion 314, May 21, 1984, in Paul J. Sax, Ethics in Tax Practice, 38 Tul. Tax Inst. (1988). The Tax Section proposal also argued, unlike the ABA final opinion, that a tax return is not a submission in an adversary proceeding. See Wolfman and Holden, at 71. See also Theodore C. Faulk, Tax Ethics, Legal Ethics, and Real Ethics: A Critique of ABA Formal Opinion 85–352, 89 Tax. Law 643, 644 (1986).

[14]   Faulk, supra n 13,. at 638.

[15]   Compare Standards of Tax Practice Statement, Committee on Standards of Tax Practice of the Section of Taxation of the American Bar Association, 54 Tax Law. 185, 187 (2000) (believing it is ethical to do so as long as it is disclosed and not frivolous), with Frank J. Gould, Giving Tax Advice-Some Ethical, Professional, and Legal Considerations, 97 Tax Notes 593 (2002) (noting that the Report of the Special Task Force states that an attorney cannot advise taxpayer to take a position that does not meet the realistic possibility of success standard even if the taxpayer's position is

so as long as the position is disclosed and is not frivolous. This position is consistent with the penalty provision in § 6662 (accuracy related penalties).[16]

(2) Section 6694

Section 6694 provides for a penalty for the preparer of a return when there is an understatement on a taxpayer's return. Specifically, if there is an understatement of liability on any return or claim for refund, and that understatement is due to a position on the return for which there was not substantial authority, the preparer is subject to a penalty of the greater of $1000 or 50% of the income derived by the preparer.[17] The preparer is not subject to the penalty if there is reasonable basis for the position and the position is disclosed.[18] The preparer is only subject to the penalty if he knew or had reason to know the taxpayer took such a position. The preparer is subject to an increased penalty of $5,000 or 75% of the income derived by the preparer under § 6694(b) if the understatement was due to willful or reckless conduct, or to an intentional disregard of rules or regulations.[19]

A tax practitioner may rely on the reasonable basis standard if the position is disclosed as required by § 6662(d)(2)(B)(ii). Under § 6662(d)(2)(B)(ii) a position will be considered disclosed if the relevant facts affecting the item's tax treatment are "adequately disclosed in the return or in a statement attached to the return."

Treasury Regulation § 1.6662–4(d) defines substantial authority as being an objective standard involving the application of the law to the facts. The standard requires less than the more likely than not standard (50% likelihood of success on the merits) but more than the realistic possibility of success standard (33% chance of success).

The regulations further explain how to determine the weight of the authority, the nature of the analysis and the types of authority. In short, the regulations explain that the weight of authority is determined by both the type of authority and its timeliness.[20] The nature of analysis requires the type of analysis that lawyers engage in on a regular basis. One must examine how similar the facts are to a particular case. Moreover, authority with more explanation may be

---

adequately disclosed); Paul J. Sax et al., *Report of the Special Task Force on Formal Opinion 85–352*, 39 Tax Law. 635, 639 (1986).

[16]   Id.

[17]   See § 6694(a).

[18]   See § 6694(a)(2)(B).

[19]   See § 6694(b)(1).

[20]   See Treas. Reg. § 1.6662–4(d)(3)(ii).

more persuasive than authority that merely states a conclusion.[21] The regulations also list the types of relevant authority, with authority ranging from statutes and regulations to IRS press releases. Law review articles and treatises like this one are not considered substantial authority but the authorities underlying the analysis may give rise to substantial authority.[22]

In *Chemtech Royalty Associates v. United States*,[23] the court determined that Dow Chemical's reliance on two Tax Court opinions was insufficient to meet the substantial authority threshold. The court noted that while the cases cited by Dow provided some support, they were "materially distinguishable on their facts." The Dow transactions were designed more as tax avoidance transactions and the cases cited by Dow where not "contribution-leaseback transactions. Nor did they possess a mechanism that would have allowed the managing partner or real party in interest to make the sharing of profits illusory."[24] Furthermore, the court explained that both cases cited by Dow were Tax Court cases and that "one [was] old and the other unpublished."

With regard to other authority, the court noted that another case cited by the Commissioner was strongly on point, and was within the same circuit and involved a similar transaction. The court thus concluded that there was not substantial authority for Dow's position.

Disclosure of a position that might lack substantial authority significantly protects a preparer from penalties. Section 6694 provides that the preparer will not be subject to penalty under § 6694 if the position was disclosed as provided in § 6662(d)(2)(B)(ii). Under § 6662(d)(2)(B)(ii) a position will be considered disclosed if the relevant facts affecting the item's tax treatment are "adequately disclosed in the return or in a statement attached to the return." Treasury Regulation 1.6662–4(f)(2) provides that adequate disclosure is made by filling out form 8275 or 8275–R and attaching the form to the return. In addition, the Commission may prescribe rules regarding when disclosure on the return will satisfy the standard.

In *Lair v. Commissioner*,[25] taxpayer leased his farm to his son and later guaranteed his son's indebtedness incurred in farming. Taxpayer's son did not give him either cash or property as

---

21   Treas. Reg. § 1.6662–4(d)(3)(ii).

22   Id.

23   823 F.3d 282 (5th Cir. 2016).

24   Id. at 291.

25   95 T.C. 484 (1990).

consideration for the guarantee. Taxpayer then paid $141,000 to his son's creditor in satisfaction of the guarantee. The taxpayer claimed a capital loss deduction on account of the worthless debt. The court held that there was inadequate disclosure since the taxpayer failed to disclose critical facts. While the taxpayer disclosed that the capital loss involved the guarantee of a farm loan, he did not disclose that the recipient of the loan was his son or that he entered into the guarantee agreement without receiving consideration from his son.[26]

In *Accardo v. Commissioner*,[27] another case considering "adequate disclosure" in the context of a penalty for a substantial underpayment of taxes under § 6661, the court determined that a mere declaration of a deduction falls short of the disclosure of relevant facts required under § 6661(b)(2)(B)(ii).[28] Accardo stated on his return that the deduction at issue was for "Legal fees re conversation [sic] of property held for production of income." In rejecting the notion that this was sufficient disclosure under § 6661, the court also noted that "[p]articularly where taxpayer lacked substantial authority for his position and where he appeared to think that his deduction presented a novel legal issue, the mere declaration of a deduction does not entitle taxpayer to a reduced penalty."[29]

A final point to consider in this section is whether the above rules even apply to what you are doing. How broad are the terms "preparer" and when are you advising on a "return position"?

Under the regulations, an income tax preparer is anyone fitting the definition contained in § 7701(a)(36). Under this definition, a return preparer is a person who prepares a substantial portion of an income tax return for compensation, or a person who provides advice about "the existence) characterization or amount" of any entry on a return, if the entry constitutes a substantial portion of the return. But the regulations also make clear that providing tax planning

---

[26] Lair actually involved a penalty under § 6661 of the code. Section 6661 was repealed for taxable years after 1989. The provisions for understatement of tax liability are now found in § 6662. Thus, cases decided under § 6661 provide guidance for how the courts will deal with this issue under § 6662.

[27] 942 F.2d 444,453 (7th Cir, 1991).

[28] Ironically, taxpayer's deduction was for legal fee incurred in the defense of a criminal prosecution under the RICO Act. Taxpayer asserted that the legal fees were necessary to protect against the forfeiture of assets.

[29] 942 F.2d at 453; see also Little v. Commissioner, 106 F.3d 1445 (9th Cir. 1997)(taxpayer's disclosure failed to provide sufficient information to determine the true nature of the transaction); Reinke v. Commissioner, 46 F.3d 760, 764 (8th Cir. 1995)(mere reporting of amounts not sufficient to adequately disclose nature of transaction); But see Jaques v. Commissioner, 58 T.C.M. 1026 (1989) (holding adequate disclosure when taxpayer did not disclose that (1) the loan was from a company of which he was the sole owner; (2) he had only paid back $48,000 of a $1,220,000 loan; (3) the loans were unsecured).

advice about a future activity does not make a tax advisor a preparer.[30]

Recent decisions have called into question the Service's regulation of return preparers, at least with regard to the Service's efforts to require preparers to meet certain requirements. In *Loving v. IRS*,[31] the court invalidated regulations requiring tax return preparers to pass competency tests and meet educational standards. The court held that the Service did not have statutory authority to regulate tax return preparers because they are not practicing before the IRS.

One last piece of advice; lying is bad. Lying to the Government is really really bad. An attorney, or any person for that matter, who willfully aids, advises or causes the preparation of a return with material false information is subject to criminal penalties.[32] In *United States v. Akaoula*,[33] the defendant helped prepare tax returns that falsely claimed: (1) head of household status for the taxpayer even though the taxpayer was married and living with his or her spouse; (2) exemptions for dependents who did not exist or who did not receive support from the taxpayer; (3) inflated deductions for medical and other expenses; (4) earned income credits to which the taxpayer was not entitled. The preparer claimed that his clients provided him with false information, but the court determined that the evidence clearly showed that the preparer knew the information on his clients' return was false.

(3) IRS Circular 230—Best Practices and Other Standards[34]

Congress has provided the Treasury with the authority to regulate the practice of representatives before its various entities, including the IRS.[35] Circular 230 sets out the requirements for attorneys and other agents wishing to practice before the IRS. An

---

[30]   Treas. Reg. 301.7701–15(a)(2).

[31]   917 F. Supp. 2d 67 (D.D.C. 2013), *affd*, 742 F.3d 1013 (D.C. Cir. 2014). See also: Ridgely v. Lew, 55 F. Supp. 3d 89 (D.D.C. 2014) (court found the IRS doesn't have the authority to regulate the preparation and filing of ordinary refund claims by CPA tax return preparers).

[32]   Section 7206(2). A person who violates § 7206 is guilty of a felony and subject to a $100,000 fine and three years imprisonment. See United States v. Sassak, 881 F.2d 276, 278 (6th Cir. 1989).

[33]   United States v. Akaoula, 172 F.3d 879 (10th Cir. 1999) (unpublished table decision).

[34]   See 31 C.F.R. §§ 10.33–10.37.

[35]   31 U.S.C. § 330.

attorney who violates these requirements may be fined, suspended, or disbarred from practicing before the IRS.[36]

Circular 230 was amended in 2011 and the regulations move away from the realistic possibility of success standard contained in the previous regulations towards a more nuanced analysis that follows the standards contained in the statutory penalty provisions in § 6694. Many commentators advocated that the Service move to a reasonable basis standard that the ABA applied in its opinion discussed in the previous section. The Service rejected this approach and determined that a practitioner who through willful, reckless, or gross incompetence violated § 6694 should be subject to discipline. In previous version of Circular 230, the Service did not examine the mental state of the practitioner. Instead it was an objective approach. The new standard has a *mens rea* requirement so it is now possible that a practitioner will be in violation of § 6694 but will not be subject to discipline under Circular 230.

The standard under Circular 230 provides that a practitioner may not advise a taxpayer to take a position on the return if the position: 1) lacks substantial authority; 2) is a willful attempt to understate tax liability; or 3) is reckless or an intentional disregard of rules or regulations. A practitioner may advise a taxpayer take a position that lacks substantial authority if there is a reasonable basis for the position and the position is disclosed.[37]

In addition, a practitioner is not subject to discipline unless the above actions were willful, reckless, or through gross incompetence. If a practitioner makes a reasonable and honest mistake, there would be no discipline even if there was a violation of the above standards.

¶ 11.03 TAX SHELTER RULES

The ethical standards with regard to advising a client required us to balance the interests of our client with the interests of the system or the public fisc as a whole. In this regard, the ABA came down strongly on the side of the client. But the problem is far more complex when a lawyer is asked to provide an opinion regarding the validity of a tax shelter. Once again, the lawyer's opinion acts as a seal of approval. In the tax shelter situation, the seal of approval influences third-parties. Statements that a particular shelter will produce particular results obviously impact a third-party's decision

---

[36] See American Jobs Creation Act, American Jobs Creation Act of 2004, P.L. 108–357, 118 Stat 1418, § 822.

[37] 26 C.F.R. § 10.34(a)(i),(ii). Section 10.34(a)(i)(B) and (ii)(B) reference an "unreasonable position as described in section 6694(a)(2). A position must either have substantial authority or have a reasonable basis and be disclosed.

whether to invest in the shelter. In this situation, the ethics rules take a harder line.[38]

(1) ABA Opinion 346[39]

What generally happened during the wild tax shelter days of the late 1970s and early 1980s was that promoters would create fanciful tax shelter schemes. In doing so, shelter creators would often overvalue assets or make unrealistic factual representations. They would then claim, based on those assumptions, that huge tax benefits would result. Shelters often provided for 4 to 10 dollars in tax benefits for every dollar invested.[40]

The promoters would then seek an attorney to issue an opinion that the tax benefits from the transactions were based on a reasonable interpretation of the law. In these opinions. lawyers often assumed the facts were as they were represented by the promoter. So if a shelter was based on an overvalued asset, or on the claim that certain trades or exchanges were taking place, the lawyer would assume that fact to be true.

As it turned out the valuations were often outrageously over stated, and the factual assumptions made the promoters were often false. The attorneys claimed that their opinion was correct based on the facts as represented by the promoter, and they claimed that they had no duty to "audit" the promoter's claims.

The ABA, in Formal Opinion 346, however, indicated that a lawyer does have, at least some duty, to ensure that the factual assumptions upon which he bases his decision are correct. The opinion indicated that an attorney cannot ignore or minimize serious legal risks or misstate facts (it is amazing that this had to be stated). The opinion, however, further indicated that a "lawyer who accepts as true the facts which the promoter tells him, when the lawyer should know that further inquiry would disclose that these facts are

---

[38]　The ABA Rule specifically recognizes that third-party reliance means that the attorney's responsibility is not solely to the client. A third party has an interest in the integrity of the evaluation and the legal duty "therefore goes beyond the obligations a lawyer normally has to third persons."

[39]　ABA Comm. on Ethics and Professional Responsibility, Formal Op. 346 (Revised) (1982) [hereinafter cited as Opinion 346] (available in Westlaw).

[40]　See e.g. Rice's Toyota World v. Commissioner, 81 T.C. 184 (1983), aff'd in part, rev'd in part, 752 F.2d 89 (4th Cir. 1985) (ratio of $3.1 of tax benefit for every $1 invested); Charlton v. Commissioner, 60 T.C.M. (CCH) 324, 1990 WL 106668 (1990), aff'd 990 F.2d 1161 (9th Cir. 1993) (Continuing Medical Education (CME) video tape tax shelter had almost $4 of tax benefits for every $1 invested); Zfass v. Commissioner, 118 F.3d 184 (4th Cir. 1997) (upholding penalties for CME shelter); Barnard v. Commissioner, 731 F.2d 230 (4th Cir.1984) ($3 of tax benefit for every $1 invested for book manuscript shelter); Shotkin v. Commissioner, 65 T.C.M. (CCH) 1091 (1988) (5 to 1 ratio in medical product licensing shelter); Hodges v. Commissioner, 63 T.C.M. (CCH) 3198 (1992) (ratio of 5 to 1 in gold mining shelter).

untrue, also gives a false opinion." In other words, you cannot check your common sense at the door.

(2) Circular 230[41]—Tax Shelter Opinions

Prior to 2014, Circular 230 contained detailed rules regarding tax shelter opinions. The new rules are far simpler and less complicated. In providing written advice on a tax matter, the practitioner must base the advice on "reasonable factual and legal assumptions," "reasonably consider all relevant facts and circumstances, and "use reasonable efforts to . . . ascertain the facts."[42] They may not consider the possibility of an audit in evaluating the position.[43]

(3) I.R.C. § 6700—Abusive Tax Shelters

In addition to the ethical duties discussed above, a lawyer who organizes or assists in the organization of an entity may also be subject to penalties. Section 6700 is designed to penalize shelter creators and promoters who make false representations or who provide a gross overvaluation of any material matter.[44] But it also applies to an attorney involved in creating a shelter, if the attorney assisted in the organization of the entity and either makes or acquiesces in the false representation. The penalty for each violation is $1,000 per activity (and each sale is considered an activity). If the person knew or had reason to know of the false representation, then the penalty is 50% of the gross revenue derived from the person in question.[45] This could be a substantial sum of money for tax shelter promoters.

One of the past problems in this area was that the promoters often made large amounts of money despite the fact that their clients ended up have significant tax liabilities when the shelters were discovered. This provision at least provides real penalties for promoters when the make false representations in marketing the shelters.

What kind of false representations will get you in trouble? In *United States v. Buttorff*,[46] the defendant was the promoter of an equity trust, which he claimed would "enable its purchaser to avoid probate, significantly reduce income tax liability, and keep financial

---

[41] Circular 230, 31 C.F.R. § 10.33–10.37.

[42] Circular 230, 31 C.F.R. § 10.37(a)(2).

[43] Id.

[44] 26 U.S.C. 6700(a)(1), (2).

[45] 26 U.S.C. 6700(a)(2).

[46] 761 F.2d 1056 (5th Cir.1985).

dealing private.[47] The defendant advised his clients to transfer all their property (including their homes, cars and furniture) to a trust. He then claimed that they could claim the expenses associated with the property as a deductible trust expenditure.[48] Taxpayers were therefore able to deduct almost all of their personal living expenses.

The promoter, however, did not tell his clients that similar schemes had been rejected by the courts. Moreover, he specifically counseled his clients against getting an outside opinion from lawyers or accountants. The court concluded that the defendant knew or had reason to know that representations he made to his clients about the tax benefits of his shelter were false and misleading. The court noted that the legislative history surrounding § 6700 defined a matter as material if "it would have a substantial impact on the decision making process of a reasonably prudent investor."[49] Since the investors indicated that they would not have purchased the shelter had they known that other similar promotions had been rejected by the courts (do you believe them), the misleading statement was material.

---

[47]   Id. at 1057.

[48]   Id. at 1058.

[49]   Id. at 1061, quoting S. Rep. No. 97–494, at 267 (1982).

Appendix A

THE TIME VALUE OF MONEY

By The Late Professor Daniel Q. Posin

Table of Sections

Para.

¶ A1.1 CORNERING THE VIRGINIA LOTTERY

In February of 1992, a syndicate based in Australia attempted to corner the Virginia lottery. The lottery payoff had reached $27 million over the course of several weeks because there were no winners. The Virginia lottery requires the player to correctly pick 6 numbers from 1 to 44. The number of possible number combinations is seven million. The syndicate's idea was to buy seven million $1 tickets and select all possible combinations. Thus is would have a sure thing: a net profit of $20 million.

This attempt caused a sensation, gaining international press coverage. Many Virginia residents complained that these massive block purchases were unfair to the small player. The Virginia Lottery Board considered proposals to Governor L. Douglas Wilder to limit block purchases of lottery tickets.

What does all this have to do with federal income taxation?

A great deal, as we will see.

Was this scheme by the Australian syndicate a good idea? Let us think about this problem in a hard-nosed way.

Consider the numbers on such a scheme: At first blush, it looks like a lead-pipe cinch. You pay $7 million, you get $27 million.[1] But,

---

[1]   Because of logistical difficulties, the Australian syndicate actually only managed to purchase 5 million of the 7 million tickets needed to win. To keep the discussion clear as a matter of principle the text discusses the case where 7 million tickets are purchased.

as in the case of most lotteries, it turns out you do not really get your winnings up front. The Virginia lottery pays its winnings out at a rate of $1.35 million a year for 20 years. Is that still a good deal? Once again at first blush it still looks good. $1.35 million for 20 years equals $27 million.

But it turns out there are some complications. There's a tax bite. Assume a tax rate of 40%.[2] To what will this 40% bite be applied? It appears at first that it would be applied to the $1.35 million per year. But the $7 million payment for tickets is deductible since gambling losses are deductible against gambling winnings.[3] The $7 million is certainly a legitimate expense of this venture. Let us assume this $7 million deduction is also spread out over the 20 year period in which the income will be paid. This is almost certainly what the IRS would require.[4] Seven million dollars spread out over 20 years is $350,000 per year. Therefore, instead of $1.35 million per year the *taxable* amount of the payment is $1 million. Note that in order to ascertain a sensible amount on which to impose the tax we need to allow deduction of the reasonable expenses of buying the tickets. * * *

With that said we can see that the tax per year will be 40% of $1 million per year or $400,000. Thus the after tax amount of **cash** coming in each year is $1,350,000 minus $400,000 or $950,000.

We are now in a position to make a cash flow analysis (as they say in business school). As a matter of cash going out and coming in here is what happened: In the first year $7 million went out and

Apparently one reason the syndicate selected the Virginia lottery was the relatively small number of tickets that needed to be purchased. Because of the peculiarities of the laws of probability, Virginia's 7 million possibilities on a 44 number game are half that of Florida's 14 million possibilities on a 49 number game. California has 51 numbers and New York has 54.

The discussion in the text assumes that the lottery winnings are subject to tax either in the U.S. or in Australia. In fact in a subsequent lawsuit the Australian syndicate hit the jackpot again, successfully arguing that the United States and the state of Virginia cannot withhold taxes on the $27 million lottery jackpot, because of the provisions of the U.S.-Australian income tax treaty. Article 7(1) of the treaty provides that the business profits of an enterprise of one contracting state are taxable in that state only if the enterprise carries on business in the other contracting state through a permanent establishment. Thus federal and state withholding on the lottery winnings was permanently enjoined. The state of Virginia decided not to appeal. The winnings were still subject to Australian tax, however. See *International Lotto Fund v. Virginia State Lottery Department*, 800 F. Supp. 337 (E.D.Va. 1992).

For pedagogical purposes the text assumes the syndicate was a U.S.-based syndicate of law students, therefore subject to U.S. federal and state tax.

[2]   The Virginia lottery does withhold federal and state taxes from the annual payouts.

[3]   § 165(d).

[4]   The taxpayer might wish to argue that the losses should be deducted sooner, but the IRS could be expected to maintain that the deduction should be spread out over the period of the winnings.

$950,000 came back in. In the next 19 years $950,000 comes back in. Another way of saying it is that the syndicate pays $7 million out up front and gets $950,000 per year for 20 years.

Is that a good deal? Another way to phrase it is to say what is $950,000 per year for 20 year[s] worth? At first blush it appears to be worth simply $950,000 X 20 or a cool $19 million.

But is $950,000 per year really worth $19 million right now? If the syndicate had $19 million right now, it would certainly grow to be worth a lot more than that over the years in that it would earn interest.

A simple yet profound insight is that an amount to be received in the future is not worth as much as that amount in the present. Because the amount received in the present can be invested to earn interest. The amount to be received in the future cannot be (since we don't have our hands on it yet).

The process of determining the value of a stream of payments to be paid in the future is called "present value analysis." In order to perform present value analysis (explained in detail below) on the $950,000 per year we need to have a realistic interest rate to use in our calculations.

Since the annual payment is backed by the state of Virginia, it may be regarded as almost as good as Treasury Bills issued by the federal government. (States, however, have been known to threaten to default on their obligations, [and] Virginia has been in financial difficulty from time to time.) A reasonable interest rate taking into account the high degree of security of this payment is 9%. Since we are dealing with after-tax results, we will want to take the after-tax interest rate based on that 9%. We have agreed that the combined federal and state rate is 40%. Thus the after-tax interest rate based on 9% is 5.4% (i.e. 60% of 9%). Employing an after-tax interest rate of 5.4%, the present value of $950,000 per year for 20 years can be calculated (using a computer).

That present value is about $12 million. From a cash flow perspective the syndicate puts out $7 million and winds up with a deal worth $12 million, after all taxes and time value of money considerations are taken care of. Thus we seem to have a profit of $5 million. This is a lot less than the profit of $20 million that this venture appeared to offer at first blush. Applying tax and time value of money principles to this venture showed it to be worth substantially less than it appeared to be, albeit it still was profitable. A "sure thing" worth a $5 million profit on a $7 million investment is a lot different from a "sure thing" worth $20 million profit on a $7 million investment.

There are various practical risks to this venture that do not appear in the probability numbers. These risks loom a lot higher if the profit is only $5 million instead of $20 million. For example, there is the sheer logistical problem of buying seven million $1 lottery tickets. The syndicate may not be able to acquire that many. The syndicate might not know that it failed to get them until it had already spent 4 or 5 million dollars.

Indeed, that is exactly what happened to the syndicate. They actually only managed to acquire 5 million tickets in the Virginia lottery. Thus they were in for $5 million and still had 2 million possibilities not covered. In fact they did win.[6] They were lucky. So instead of a sure thing win of $20 million they were lucky to win $7 million[7]—and lucky not to lose $5 million.

Moreover, there is a further problem. That is, there may be more than one winner. Let us say there is another winner besides the syndicate. Not someone who also bought $7 million of tickets but someone who just got lucky buying one ticket. That is how one normally wins lotteries after all, getting lucky. If there were one other winner, then that winner and the syndicate split the jackpot. In that event the syndicate's payoff (before tax) is $675,000 per year for 20 years. Subtracting the $350,000 annualized expenses of the $7 million ticket purchase produces a taxable amount of $325,000. Paying a tax of 40% on that produces a tax on each payment of $130,000. Thus the after-tax cash payment is $675,000 − $130,000 = $545,000.

We therefore come to the nub question of what is the value of $545,000 per year for 20 years, with an after-tax interest rate of 5.4%. The computer cranks out the answer of $6.9 million. Now we are losing about $100,000. If there were two other winners, so that the syndicate gets one-third of the $27 million jackpot, a similar set of calculations cranks out a present value of $5.2 million. Thus $1.8 million is lost on the venture because of multiple winners. Where does the $1.8 million go (not an inconsiderable sum)? Part of it fattens up the pot for the other multiple winners, who let us say bought just one or a few tickets. The rest of the $1.8 million goes to Virginia.

What are the chances of multiple winners? The larger the jackpot, the more tickets will be bought. The more tickets will be bought, the greater the likelihood there will be multiple winners. Of the 16 jackpots in the Virginia lottery worth over $10 million between 1990 and February 1992, 3 were shared. As our calculations above

---

6   The winning numbers were 8, 11, 13, 15, 19 and 20.

7   The $7 million is roughly the $12 million present value less the $5 million spent on tickets. This calculation ignores the syndicate's other administrative expenses and the amounts of lesser prizes that might be won.

indicate, if it were shared by several people there would be a several million dollar loss to the syndicate.

Thus the arrangement, which appeared at first blush to be a sure thing, was highly risky.

There is a larger lesson here. Note the critical importance of understanding the time value of money. It was time value of money analysis that enabled us to see that the syndicate's strategy was misguided. In sophisticated financial transactions, one wants to be able to make this same sort of analysis for clients. And time value of money analysis has come, in recent years, to be of major importance in the field of federal income taxation. In the sections that follow we learn how to do it. And we see some more examples of its miraculous effects.

¶ A1.2 BACKGROUND ON TIME VALUE OF MONEY

There's some stuff [here] you're just not going to believe. * * * It all has to do with timing. In other fields of law, except for statute of limitations purposes, it does not really matter too much when a particular tort, contract, or crime occurs. But in tax, *when* something happens is of signal importance. And these effects are not just of academic interest. There are results * * * that can make you and your clients some very big money. Let's start out by looking at some of the basic ideas. Once we get through them, you're going to see some stuff you're just not going to believe.

¶ A1.3 BASIC CONCEPTS: GROWTH OF CAPITAL

One of the most fundamental concepts in the field of federal income taxation is the time value of money. The question in the field is not only how much is income or how much is deductible, the question is also when is the item income or deductible. To the student first approaching the field, it would not seem to matter especially much in what year something is income or deductible. But, as the discussion below will show, the timing of an item of income or deduction can have an astonishing impact.

As a way of approaching this subject, consider that it is a fundamental economic fact of life that capital grows. Consider in particular—an example economists frequently use—a grove of trees that will produce lumber. If you buy the grove for $100,000 and the trees grow annually at 7%, the grove will have a value of $107,000 at the end of one year. Since you can always have this deal, why invest in something that does not grow?

We can expand this idea to include all of agriculture. Since agricultural crops and farm animals grow, why invest in something that does not grow, since the agricultural option is always available? Thus the value of an investment in an industrial activity must grow over time or it will not receive attention from investors. Of course, there are short-term fluctuations in the values of investments and some companies go broke, but over the longer term overall investments in industrial productions produce positive returns.

This return on investment can be in the form of interest, dividends, or increase in the value of the investment. The example of the trees growing by 7% is an example of increase in the value of the investment. If the 7% of the trees were cut and sold at the end of the year, with the proceeds used to pay stockholders in the company owning the trees, then the growth would be represented by dividends. If the proceeds of the cut trees were used to pay interest to those who had lent money to the tree-growing business, then the growth would take the form of interest.

It is this inevitable growth of capital over time that is fundamental to our study of time value of money in taxation.

While, as discussed above, capital growth can take the form of dividends, interest, or capital appreciation, in the tax field we focus primarily on interest. This is because the nature of the obligation to pay taxes to the government is one of debt. When the payment of debt is deferred—as it often is in the tax field—we become concerned about the concept of interest. Also, interest is the most convenient way to focus on the impact of time on capital growth. We can speak of a risk-free rate of return (generally the interest rate on short-term government bonds). When we speak of dividends or capital appreciation, there will inevitably be some risk involved. When risk is involved people need a higher rate of return to make up for the risk. So the risk factor complicates the analysis. Also the variable returns in riskier investments make our calculations cumbersome.

Thus when we speak of the time value of money, we will usually be talking about relatively secure short-term interest.

¶ A1.4 INTEREST

(1) Present Value Analysis

If you were offered $100 today or $100 one year from today, which would you take? Think about this one for a while. Don't just plunge ahead reading in a hurry before you go to class. Which would you take? The answer is in the next paragraph.

Clearly the $100 today is more valuable, because it can be put in a savings account at, say, 6% interest and grow to $106. So if you take the $100 today, you will have $106 one year from now instead of $100 a year from now. * * * So, $100 today is worth $106 a year from now, whereas $100 a year from now is, of course, worth $100 a year from now.

Having said that, we can now push things just a little further. We're going to take one more step. We're going to get somewhere now. If you take this next step, you've got the rest of this course made in the shade. Well, that's probably an overstatement—but the next part is important.

We have already figured out what $100 today is worth one year from now—namely $106. Let us instead figure out just what $100 one year from now is worth today. Get me? What would you pay today for the right to get $100 a year from now. Suppose (with an interest rate of 6%) somebody offered you the right to receive $100 a year from now. Suppose he said you could have that right for 37 cents? Would you take the deal? You'd jump at it right? You don't need a Ph.D. in mathematics to figure out that that's a heck of a deal. Suppose he offered it to you for $90? That's less clear, but just eyeballing it, it looks like a good deal. Suppose he offered it to you for $103? Would you take that? You know that's wrong. $103 this year will grow to be worth over $109, as our analysis above has already indicated.

What is the right price for the right to get $100 one year from now (with a prevailing 6% interest rate)? That right has got to be worth less than $100. Let us formulate the question. What is the question to be asked here? Try it. The appropriate question is in the next paragraph.

The appropriate question is what amount of money today would grow, at 6% interest, to $100 one year from today. That is the question. It may be a little tricky to make the computation, but the principle is clear. It looks like something like $94 or $95. * * * [We could] set up the equation like this, if X is the amount we're looking for:

$$X \quad \times \quad 1.06 \quad = \quad \$100$$
$$X \quad = \quad \$100 \quad \times \quad 1.06$$
$$X \quad = \quad \$94.34$$

There, that didn't hurt too much. We have just done something that people go to business school for two years to try to learn to do (and many never do get it). We have "discounted a future payment to its present value." This jargon is just another way of saying that we have asked ourselves what is the amount now that would grow to $100 in one year at 6% interest?

This is a surprisingly powerful computation. We have valued the present value of a payment of money at some time in the future. We have figured out that $100 a year from now, with a 6% interest rate, is worth $94.34 now.

Thus, in the preceding section, when you were offered $100 today or $100 a year from today, what you were really offered (given 6% interest) was $100 today or something worth $94.34 today. The choice was clear.

(2) Simple and Compound Interest

Suppose you leave the $100 we were talking about in the preceding section in the bank for two years instead of one. Suppose further that you leave the interest of $6 in the account as well. The bank will then compute the 6% interest they will pay in the second year based on the $106 rather than $100. Why will they include the extra 6% in their computation? They have to or lose your business, that's why.

If they do not do it, you will take the $6 out and put it in another bank in a savings account. That $6 may be interest as far as the first bank is concerned, but it is principal as far as the second bank is concerned. The second bank will then give you 6% interest on your $6. The first bank knows you will do this. So rather than lose your business they will calculate the second year's 6% interest on the full $106 (no use everybody running around redepositing their interest payments as principal in other banks). Six percent interest on $106 cranks out to be $112.36.

What is the most powerful part of that number—the $112 or the 36 cents? Think that one over. This is another big-time concept in this field. The answer is once again in the next paragraph.

The $112 is certainly a lot more money than the 36 cents. But it's the 36 cents that is the power. With that 36 cents you have a tiger by the tail. The reason that the second year's computation gave us $6.36 instead of just $6 was that we were getting interest on the previous year's interest as well as interest on our original principal. The extra 36 cents may not seem like much, but try leaving that $100 in place compounding at 6% for 40 years and see what happens.

As a matter of fact, let's see what happens if you do just that. What happens is that the $100 grows to a cool $1,028.57, more than a ten-fold increase. This is demonstrated in the accompanying figure:

GROWTH OF $100 AT 6% FOR 40 YEARS

Notice the particularly powerful effects of compounding in the later years. Indeed, the interest on the accumulated amount for the 41st year is $61.71, more than 60% of the original principal. You are now getting more than 60% interest on your original principal. Forty years is a long time, of course, but on the other hand you have not had to do anything with it. You could have been drunk the whole time (although I don't recommend it). You've just let this money sit.

To juice it up a little bit, let us look at the investment if it pays 18% interest rather than 6%. How much larger will the $100 be when compounded at 18% rather than 6%? Take a guess. The 18% is, after all, triple the 6%. So would we be talking about the principal growing to around $3,000, about triple the principal grew to at 6%? Maybe a little more? Well, it turns out that $100 compounded annually at 18% for forty years blossoms to a nifty $75,037.83.

Although the interest rate was only triple, the amount the principal grew to was 75 times as much as it grew to when compounded at 6%. It grew to be over 750 times larger than the original principal. This is demonstrated in the next figure, where we compare the 6% interest compounded and the 18% interest compounded.

GROWTH OF $100 AT 6% AND 18% FOR 40 YEARS

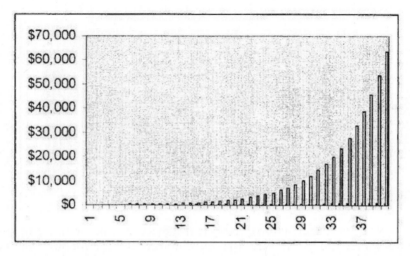

You will recall how impressive that 6% compounding looked from the first chart (and indeed it was impressive). Nevertheless, when compared to the 18% compounding in the second chart, you can hardly see the 6% compounding.

As another example of what happened, note that for the 41st year, the 18% interest on the $75,037.83 would amount to $13,506.81. This interest payment is 135 times larger than the original principal. This gives us a feel for the raw power of compound interest. We do have a tiger by the tail. I don't mean to knock other courses, but you don't come across something like this in torts, contracts, or procedure.

Compare this compound interest to simple interest. Suppose we had collected simple interest—that is just interest on the principal—for 40 years at 18%. That would amount to 18% of $100 for forty years or an unimpressive $720. That $720 is not even as much as you get with compound interest at 6%. And it is a lot less than the over $74,000 in interest we collected when interest was compounding. Thus, a little piece of financial advice: if anybody offers you simple interest, laugh in his or her face.

Having learned our basic lessons about time value of money, it is now time to have some fun with it.

¶ A1.5 A FEW STUNTS

(1) General Implications

It will surprise you how often time value of money comes up in taxation. When it comes up, the foregoing analysis always tells you what is going on. For example, taking a deduction is better sooner than later. This is because it saves you taxes sooner rather than later, and you therefore get your hands on the tax money saved sooner rather than later. You can then earn (compound) interest on your money sooner rather than later and it will grow to more. Paying tax on an income item is better later rather than sooner, because you have to part with your money later rather than sooner. Keeping the money allows you to earn (compound of course) interest on the money and it will grow to more. Another way of looking at it is to say that if you are paying later, you need to set aside less than the full amount of tax due and the amount set aside will grow in time to the amount actually due.

But enough of this pedantic stuff, let's have some fun:

(2) Stunt No. 1: How to Eliminate Tax

This is a truly astonishing result. What we are going to show here is that the simple ability to change the timing of paying tax on an investment has two amazing effects: (1) the tax on the income from the investment is eliminated; and (2) the *pre-tax* rate of return on the investment is actually increased. Talk about pulling a rabbit out of the hat! Consider the following example:

> **Example 2.1:** T, in the 50 percent bracket,[9] invests $100 in a drill bit for an oil well. A special provision in the Internal Revenue Code allows an immediate deduction of the full $100, saving T $50 in taxes.[10] T invests that $50 in the same kind of asset. Deducting immediately that $50 saves T $25 (assuming T's income is so high that he remains in the 50 percent bracket despite these deductions) which he can then reinvest in an identical asset. T continues to deduct immediately and reinvest until a full $100 is invested. At that point T will own *and have fully paid for* assets worth $200. Where did the extra money come from? The tax

---

[9]   The 50% figure is used for mathematical convenience. If the rate is lower than that, the effects described in the text will not be quite so powerful. If the rate is higher than that, the effects described in the text will be even more powerful.

Historically, the maximum marginal rate on individuals has ranged up as high as 90%. * * * Under current law, the maximum rate is in the 39% area. Combined with the income tax imposed by many states, the maximum rate on individuals frequently reaches 50%.

[10]   Such a deduction is available for investment in the costs of drilling an oil well (so-called "intangible drilling costs"). See § 263(c); Treas. Reg. § 1.612–4(a) (1965). The ability to take this deduction immediately is very favorable to the oil drilling industry. Ordinarily the expenses of creating a major income producing asset such as an apartment building or a factory are deductible over the life of the asset as depreciation * * *. Thus the ability to deduct immediately the expenses of digging an oil well, which is an asset that produces income over a long period of time, is highly attractive to the oil industry. Just how attractive is illustrated in the text.

savings from the deduction in effect gave T an interest-free loan from the government of $100. Let us assume these assets appreciate 10 percent a year (compounded annually). Since the asset is going up in value but not paying any interest or dividends, the annual increase is not taxed until the end of the 10 years when the asset is finally sold.[11] Thus this investment benefits in a second way from deferral of tax. Not only is the initial investment immediately deducted but the increase in value is not taxed until the asset is finally sold. With a 10% rate of return compounded, at the end of ten years T will be able to sell out for about $519. His tax cost would have been $0 because he deducted the amounts he invested * * *. Thus his tax gain would be $519. The $519 would be taxed at the 50% rate, yielding a tax of $259.50. Thus under these conditions when the dust clears, T's $100 grew to $259.50. That's an after tax gain of $159.50 ($259.50 minus the original $100).

Here's the corker, kids. That gain of $159.50 is what T would get with an annual rate of return of 10% with no tax. *T, by being able to deduct his investment and resulting tax savings in full, was able to in effect eliminate the tax.* This was true even though he made up for taking the deduction at the beginning of the investment by being taxed on the full amount of the sales proceeds at the end. As they say in figure skating, timing is everything.

Taking the polar opposite example, suppose T had invested his original $100 in a U.S. government bond that paid 10% interest. Holding that bond gives T no depreciation deduction at all.[12] In addition T is taxed at a 50% rate on the 10% interest each year when he receives it. He then reinvests the after-tax proceeds. At the end of ten years with this bond investment (certainly an investment most people would consider to be perfectly reasonable), T would have the princely sum, principal and interest, of $163. This is a total after tax gain of $63.

Note that the tax rules under which T operated were the same in both cases except for timing. With the first asset, T did take a deduction for the amount of his investment at the beginning, but he took that amount back into income at the end. So as a net matter there was no deduction for the investment. Also T did not pay tax every year on the appreciation of his investment but rather only paid tax on his gains from the investment at the end.

---

[11]   This is because under basic tax rules there has not been a realizing event.

[12]   Holding a bond in the financial market does not generally give rise to a deduction in the nature of depreciation or amortization because it is not tangible property subject to wear and tear.

With the second asset T did not take a deduction for his investment at the beginning and therefore of course did not take the amount of his investment back into income at the end. So as a net matter there was no deduction for the investment. T also paid tax on his income from the investment but did so every year rather than at the end. These apparently innocuous timing differences led to the amazing differences in results.

In both cases T did nothing more or less than pay tax at the same rate on the income from his investment. Nevertheless the gain on the first asset was $159.50 and the gain on the second was $63.

Thus, "mere" deferral has increased T's after-tax gain by 253 percent in the first asset over the second asset.

What is happening here? How is this possible? See if you can answer this question yourself. If you cannot answer, the answer is given in the footnote at the end of this paragraph. Try to answer it first—the answer has been alluded to in the preceding discussion.[13]

By contrast, the *after tax* return on the U.S. government bond (where there were no up-front deductions and interest was taxed annually) was a measly 5%.

But, you scoff, this is nice work if you can get it, but unless you're an oil-driller (see note above) you cannot get it. Answer: wrong. This leads us smoothly into our next stunt.

(3) Stunt No. 2: How You Can (and Probably Will) Become a Multimillionaire

All you need to do to get this is get a job which has a type of pension called a defined contribution plan. This type of plan is pretty widespread. Alternatively, you can use voluntary plans yourself to

---

[13]   I take it you are looking here to confirm your analysis. You are right. In the first investment, T was able to delay paying tax by both taking an early deduction and deferring tax on gains from the investment. This delay or temporary tax savings put extra funds in T's hands which T was able to also invest in the same tax advantaged fashion. In effect, T was able to enjoy an interest-free loan from the government. Naturally if you have an interest-free loan and are able to invest it for a profitable return, you are going to make money.

If T had been required to pay interest on his temporary tax savings he enjoyed in the first investment, his return on the first investment would have been the same as his return on the second. This is easily demonstrated. The extra $100 of temporary tax savings earned 10% per year. But if the government were charging T 10% interest, T would just have principal left after each year. T would not get compound interest. Indeed, T would not even be able to keep any interest at all. T would just be holding principal and then giving it back to the government, with no gain (or loss either) from holding it for 10 years. Thus he now has no advantage over the bond.

A similar analysis can be made with regard to the 10% per year appreciation in the value of the first investment. If T had to pay tax on the 10% per year at a 50% rate, T's after tax return would be 5% compounded for 10 years. That is exactly what T was getting on the bond.

achieve the same result.[14]   To see how this gravy train works, we need to have a quick run-through of how pension plans work (no problem).

Dry Explanation: Pension Plans

In general, employers may establish qualified pension, profit-sharing, or stock bonus plans, which are tax favored in a number of ways.

There are two kinds of plans: defined benefit and defined contribution. Defined benefit plans require amounts to be put in that will be sufficient to produce a specified annual retirement amount after the expected number of years. Defined contribution plans just provide that the employer puts in a particular fixed amount every year and whatever it grows to is what the employee gets. Frequently the employee can decide what kind of investments to make with the defined contribution plan. Amounts paid into either type of plan are not taxed to the employees even if the employee rights are "vested." Vested means the benefits are payable even if the employee quits or is fired before retirement. Employees are taxed only when they actually receive payments on retirement.

Employers deduct amounts paid into the plan immediately, even though the employee is not taxed until retirement. That being true, the employer should be equally happy to pay salary to an employee directly or to put it into a plan. The employer will put it into a plan, because the employee prefers to get the benefit. Giving the employee the extra benefit may mean that the employer can then actually bargain to pay lower salary. After all, many employers say, you get this salary and look at all your benefits.

Earnings on funds paid into the plan are not taxed and they compound tax free. This leads to the kind of stunning results we have been talking about. * * *

The benefit from these pension plans sounds OK, but at first blush you would think it is nothing spectacular. But you're past the first blush now. You've lost your innocence. You know this could be big time. Let's take a look at some numbers.

Suppose that your employer pays into a qualified defined-contribution plan, on your behalf, $12,000 per year for 40 years. Let's

---

[14]   § 401(k) for business employees and § 403(b) for employees of educational institutions. Also IRAs.

say these funds earn an annual return of 10 percent.[16] This will be tax free compounding. At the end of 40 years, the total of the contributions and the earnings will be $5,311,111. They call that being a multi-millionaire. But let's go further.

Let us say that at this point you retire and begin to receive payments. Assume your life expectancy at retirement is 20 years; assume also the amounts to be paid to you still earn 10 percent per year. The annual payment to you will be $623,841, all of which is taxable. All is taxable because none of it was taxable initially when it went into the plan. If you are taxed at a rate of 30 percent on the entire amount, the amount left after tax will be $436,689 annually.

Suppose that we now take away all the tax benefits. The employer pays an extra $12,000 each year directly to you. You are taxed on it at a 30% rate. That is a tax of $3,600. Thus you have left after tax $8,400. Let's assume (just for the sake of argument) that you don't blow this money but invest it at a pre-tax rate of return of 10%. The rate of return after tax will be 7 percent. This gives you, therefore, an investment of $8,400 per year which has a rate of return of 7 percent per year. That gives you a total accumulation at the end of 40 years of $1,676,935. Let us say this amount is used to buy an annuity. The payout is calculated assuming a rate of return of 10 percent. Again, let us say a life expectancy at retirement is 20 years. The payment each year will be $196,972. Of this annuity payment, $113,125 will be taxed, the rest being a return of what you invested. How is this calculated? By spreading the investment in the contract of $1,676,935 out over 20 years, under the annuity rules [of § 72]. That means a basis of $83,847 per year. * * * Taking the $83,847 from the $196,972 per year received gives you $113,125. $113,125 is taxed. If we assume a tax rate of 30 percent, you have a tax of 30% of $113,125, or $33,937. Thus your after tax amount is $196,972 less the tax of $33,937, leaving an after tax amount of $163,035 each year. This is 37 percent of the $436,689 after tax that you received when you had a qualified plan with the same numbers.

Note that all of this is due to deferral and compounding over long periods of time.

So get yourself a qualified plan and you will become a pension multimillionaire. There are plenty of people out there who are. Recall this was done on our numbers. Only a measly $12 thousand a year compounded over forty years leaves you with over $5 million. You get after tax pension annual payments for the rest of your life over

---

[16]   Note that the 10% figure for annual appreciation that I use for investments over long periods of time is well justified. Over the period 1960–1990, the S&P Stock Market Index appreciated 10.2% per year, see Slater, Long-Haul Investing: Riding Out the Risk in Stocks, The Wall Street Journal, December 16, 1991, p. C1.

$436,000. As mentioned, similar effects, for less money per year, can be accomplished with employer sponsored § 401(k) or § 403(b) plans as well as the various kinds of IRA's now available to everyone.

You are putting in $12 thousand a year and coming out after tax with $436 thousand for the rest of your life. Not a bad gig.

(4) Stunt No. 3: Personal Injury

We now discuss a most extraordinarily useful stunt. Understanding this stunt takes you a step toward major insight into the mysteries of time value of money. It is illuminating not only in itself but also because of the light it sheds on the field in general.

Consider Baxter Trucking Corporation, an accrual method taxpayer. Being on the accrual method means that items of income and deduction are given effect in the year when the right to them becomes fixed, even though cash has not changed hands. * * * An inevitable part of Baxter's business is that it runs over and injures pedestrians from time to time. It insures itself with respect to these accidents. In 1978 Baxter runs over a teenager, Eileen Trabert, severely injuring her. In settlement of the ensuing lawsuit Baxter agrees to pay Eileen compensatory damages of $10 million. However, under the terms of the settlement agreement, Baxter will pay the money out as $250,000 cash per year for the next 40 years.

Let us assume a combined federal and state flat tax rate of 45%, which applies both to Baxter and Eileen, and a prevailing interest rate of 12%, which is available both to Baxter and Eileen.

The amount of any compensatory damages received by virtue of personal injuries or sickness is excluded from the income of the victim.[20] Since Baxter is on the accrual method, its obligation to make the payment is now fixed. It therefore takes a $10 million deduction (even though it pays no cash out at that time). Under the law at that time the position was probably sustainable under accrual method accounting.[21] This $10 million deduction to a corporation in the 45% bracket saves it $4.5 million. Baxter takes this $4.5 million and

---

[20] See § 104(a)(2) and Regs. § 1.104–1(c). The policy behind this is apparently some idea of sympathy for the victim, or else that on balance the victim is not really "enriched" by the entire experience.

[21] See Ohio River Collieries Co. v. Commissioner, 77 T.C. 1369 (1981) (the full amount of surface mining reclamation costs that could be estimated with reasonable accuracy was properly accrued when the surface soil was removed); Treas. Reg. § 1.461–1(a)(2) (amended in 1967); Crescent Wharf & Warehouse Co. v. Commissioner, 518 F.2d 772 (9th Cir. 1975) (the full amount of the liability for uncontested workers' compensation claims could be deducted in the year in which the injury occurs notwithstanding that medical services might be rendered and disability might occur in the future); New York City Bar Ass'n, Transactions Involving Deferred Payment of Accrued Liabilities, 20 Tax Notes 699 (1983); McGown, Structured Settlements: Deduct Now and Pay Later, 60 Taxes 251 (1982).

invests it in intermediate U.S. bonds that pay interest of 12% per year. After the 45% tax bite Baxter's annual return will be 6.6% compounded.[22]

Now to understand Baxter's situation completely, we have to consider how Baxter is going to fund the obligation pay Eileen $250,000 per year for the next 40 years. An illuminating way to look at that is to say that Baxter sets aside a fund which is large enough so that when it grows at the after-tax rate of 6.6%[23] compounded for 40 years it will be just large enough to pay $250,000 per year over 40 years. At the end of 40 years the fund should be exhausted. How much does Baxter need now to set aside to accomplish this goal under these conditions? The answer is $3,724,648.[24] Another way of interpreting this number is to say that $3,724,648 is the present value of a stream of payments of $250,000 per year for 40 years with a 6.6% interest rate.

Now let's look at Baxter's complete situation using a cash flow analysis over time: In the first year, the year of settlement, Baxter is out of pocket up front $3,724,648 in the sense that it has to set that money aside, can't use it, and can't use the interest from it (otherwise it will fail to have the money for Eileen and get sued again). * * * However, Baxter takes a deduction of $10,000,000. This saves Baxter $4,500,000 in taxes. Thus, Baxter is ahead on this deal in the first year in the precise amount of $4,500,000 − $3,724,648 = $775,352. Once out in front, Baxter stays there. Baxter invests this $775,352 for the after-tax return of 6.6% compounded for 40 years. This winds up to be a cool $9,995,099. In short Baxter, as a result of incurring a liability for running over Eileen, is ahead $9,995,099.

What could Baxter have done to come out even better than this already sensational result? You doubtless will recognize from the foregoing that Baxter made a serious error in its negotiation with Eileen's lawyer. It should have held out to pay $500,000 annually over 50 years instead of $250,000 annually for 40 years. In that event it could take a deduction for $500,000 times 50, or $25 million. Deducting this amount immediately would have saved it $11,250,000 in taxes. Since it has to set aside a fund to finance payments of $500,000 per year over 50 years instead of $250,000 over 40 years, it

---

[22]　This is, of course, 55% of the 12% return; we are subtracting the 45% tax bite. Baxter reinvests the interest at the continuing after-tax 6.6% rate.

[23]　Baxter of course is taxed on funds that it has under its control, regardless of the fact that it may have earmarked the funds to finance a future liability.

[24]　The calculations in this example assume that payments and tax savings occur at the beginning of the year for which they are due. If they were made at the end, the numbers would be slightly different but the principles under discussion would, of course, remain the same. This is a complex financial calculation which requires a computer or high-powered calculator.

will have to set aside a larger fund. The present value of payments of $500,000 per year over 50 years with a 6.6% interest rate (i.e. the amount Baxter has to set aside) is $7,745,142. Once again setting aside this fund to take care of Eileen, it has leftover the following: $11,250,000 (tax savings of 45%) − $7,745,142 (Eileen fund) = $4,501,386. Investing this amount at the after-tax compounded return of 6.6% for 50 years leads Baxter to wind up with a stupendous $85,611,215. To make the 40 year and 50 year cases comparable, we need to take Baxter's 40 year amount in the previous hypo and let it accumulate at 6.6% for another 10 years, so that we've got 50 years in both deals. Doing that to Baxter's 40 year accumulation of $9,995,099 brings it out to $18,939,092. It's not bad. But it is still a staggering $66,672,123 less than Baxter winds up with when it has to pay Eileen $500,000 for 50 years instead of $250,000 for 40 years.

How can such mind-bending results occur? The problem, as you probably have ascertained, is that Baxter is getting much too large a deduction for this structured settlement. When you get a deduction that is larger than justified and take that deduction against other high income and the situation prevails over long periods of time, you are going to make out like gangbusters.

Our analysis has precisely calculated the excessive amount of Baxter's deduction. Let us concentrate on the 40-year deal (we can rest assured the 50-year deal will be even more egregious). We ascertained that the present value of $250,000 per year for 40 years was $3,724,648. An accurate accrual method of accounting would have limited the deduction to that amount, rather than allowing $10,000,000 to be deducted. Had only that $3,724,648 amount been allowed as a deduction, the tax savings would have been $1,676,092. Notice, very interestingly, that Baxter is not in a negative position in the first year. It needs to set aside $3,724,648 to fund Eileen's payments. Its tax savings are $1,676,092. So it is negative in the year of the settlement in the amount of $2,048,556. That is, of course, the normal situation. Any time you have a deductible expense, the deduction, under normal circumstances, cannot save you more in taxes than the expense itself but will save you less. Thus a deductible expense of $100 at a tax rate of 45% saves you $45. The other $55 is still out of your pocket. It is only taxpayers like Baxter in the original hypothetical, playing this lunatic game of taking deductions far in excess of what is justified, that turn a deductible expense into fabulous profits.

Looking at the situation where we have limited Baxter's deduction to the present value of the stream of payments, we see that Baxter appropriately has a loss: *Baxter gets nothing out of this situation now or 40 years from now!* You cannot invest a loss. The structured settlement, together with the proper limited deduction, has put Baxter out of pocket up front. Therefore it has nothing to invest as a result of the transaction.[27] By getting the right amount of deduction for Baxter, we have picked its pocket of its entire $9,995,099. It's actually much worse than that. Baxter is actually out of pocket $2,048,556. As well it should be. Maybe that will encourage its drivers to be more careful from now on.

It turns out to be highly useful to carry the analysis to the bitter end. We calculate how much this out-of-pocket amount in the first year is going to cost Baxter in terms of foregone interest income over 40 years. Our inquiry here then would be what would the $2,048,556 that Baxter is out of pocket have earned over 40 years had Baxter not gotten into this mess and had to pay off. $2,048,556 over 40 years at 6.6% interest is $26,408,301.[28]

What did Congress do to prevent these fabulous profits from redounding to tort-feasors? Congress's cure for this problem was interesting. Under the law as it was amended in 1984, the dazzling results we saw above are no longer possible. In effect Baxter is put on the cash method, allowed only to deduct its payments as they are made.[29] What does this mean for Baxter? Is this the right answer?

Our present-value analysis will tell us. Under Congress's rule Baxter is on the cash method and can only deduct payments as they are actually made. That is, Baxter is not allowed to deduct the full amount up front and is also not allowed to deduct the discounted present value up front.

So, what happens to Baxter under Congress's rule? Baxter still has to set aside the $3,724,648 in the first year. Baxter still has to figure out a way to make the payments. However, Baxter cannot deduct that amount. Instead Baxter can only deduct the $250,000 out of that $3,724,648 it actually pays to Eileen in the first year. That $250,000 payment saves Baxter 45% of it in taxes or $112,500.[30] Thus Baxter's cash flow position in the first year is as follows: negative $3,724,648 + $112,500 = negative $3,612,148. In the remaining 39 years, Baxter's cash flow position is + $112,500: the amount

---

[27]   Some readers (not you of course) might argue that Baxter could still invest the $1,676,092. And so it could. The trouble is that it has had to set aside $3,724,648 plus accumulated interest on this amount in order to be able to make this investment. A couple more deals like this and Baxter will be broke.

[28]   This is not lunch money. Thus, to beat the thing to death, we can say that limiting the deduction to the right amount cost Baxter over the course of 40 years the positive $9,995,009 plus put it in the hole $26,408,031. Getting the deduction right, instead of wrong then, gives Baxter a total negative swing of $36,403,136.

[29]   Section 461(h)(2)(C).

[30]   The $250,000, of course, comes out of the $3,724,648, so we do not give Baxter an additional negative cash flow hit of $250,000.

deducting $250,000 saves it in taxes. Note that from a cash flow standpoint, we do not go negative the $250,000 payment each year. We have already set aside the $3,724,648 to cover the $250,000 and thus need set aside no more cash. Baxter does enjoy the cash benefit of the deduction on our tax return when it sends her the check for $250,000, however. * * * Where does this experience leave Baxter at the end of 40 years? Baxter winds up with a loss of $23,282,713. That is exactly the amount that Baxter was behind using our approach of deducting the full $3,724,648 present value of the arrangement up front, as the discussion accompanying note 27 above indicated.

So, Congress got it exactly right here as to Baxter. Limiting Baxter to the cash method on its deductions did not overtax or undertax Baxter. It gave Baxter the same result as allowing Baxter to deduct in the first year the discounted present value of its payments. And the result from deducting the present value in the first year is economically accurate.[32]

And what of Eileen?

To understand Eileen's situation, we take as a given that for policy reasons Eileen is allowed to exclude a payment for a personal injury in a tort suit. But what was the real amount of that payment to Eileen? To ask that question is to ask what is the present value of $250,000 per year for 40 years with the after-tax rate of 6.6%. That happens to be (as we have said a number of times) $3,724,648.

That amount is the amount of the payment to Eileen that should be excluded because, as a policy matter, we exclude payments on account of personal injuries. That is the present value of her deal. We can understand that. If she had in fact negotiated to have her payment up front (for whatever reasons she may have preferred it), Baxter would have been willing to pay her $3,724,648. That is the

---

[32]   Structured settlements are usually put together using three companies to get a tax free rate of return on the money set aside to pay the claim. Thus less money need be set aside. The technique involves three companies: the casualty insurance company makes a deductible lump sum payment to a structured settlement company, which assumes the liability to make the payments. The structured settlement company purchases an annuity (an agreement to make payments over time * * *) from an annuity company that specializes in annuities for damage awards. The structured settlement company takes a deduction for that purchase which offsets the income from the original insurance company. The annuity company takes a reserve (or deduction) on its books equal to the amounts received. When the annuity company makes the payments, the structured settlement company deducts them. By shuffling things back and forth this way, the three companies produce among themselves the effect of a deduction for the money being set aside originally plus a deduction when each payment is made, when only one or the other of those deductions is justified. This in effect causes the earnings on the money set aside to fund the payment to be earning income at the pre-tax rate. Incidentally, some years ago my father was the recipient of a tort award and the companies involved were very anxious to set it up as a structured settlement of this kind.

amount, as we have demonstrated, that Baxter would have had to set aside to earn enough at the after-tax rate of return of 6.6% to be able to make the $250,000 annual payments to Eileen and come out even after 40 years.

Now, what is Eileen's actual picture with the structured settlement? She receives $250,000 per year for 40 years. She can exclude the full amount of each of these payments by virtue of § 104(a)(2) as amplified by Rev.Rul. 79–220.[33] Eileen reinvests the $250,000 payments at the same pre-tax rate of 12% as Baxter. Her after tax rate is the same 6.6%. After 40 years of this deal Eileen winds up with $48,014,605. Is this the "right" result for Eileen?

We can see by referring once again to economic truth. That is, let us see what happens if the parties had negotiated to make the payment up front. Suppose Eileen had indeed received her $3,724,648 up front and excluded it. Let us say she then invested this amount in a government bond with a pre-tax interest rate of 12% and yielding her 6.6% after tax. Note that she is taxed on her investment earnings after she gets her tax-free payment. She is not getting any further special breaks. At the end of 40 years Eileen's amount would then have grown to $48,014,605. This is the same result Eileen gets if she receives the payments stretched out over 40 years.[34]

What this shows is that the treatment of Eileen is absolutely accurate. Once you have decided to exclude the damage payments for personal injuries to Eileen, it is correct to exclude the full amount of payments made pursuant to a structured settlement. * * * The numbers above demonstrate this. This is what present value analysis really means. If the present value is the same thing (not identical of course but the same thing the way $100 worth of apples is the same things as $100 worth of oranges) as the larger future value, then if you do not tax one, you should not tax the other.[36]

---

[33] 1979–2 C.B. 74, which holds that the full amount of payments received under a structured settlement are excluded under § 104(a)(2), not just the discounted present value of them.

[34] You may wonder why Eileen gains more ($66,241,946) than Baxter loses ($36,433,067). This is a result of the fact that by virtue of this arrangement, the parties have eliminated the tax on the stream of income used to make the payments to Eileen. Baxter deducted the amounts and Eileen did not enter them into income. This is true regardless of how the parties structure the timing of the transaction.

[36] The reason the Treasury prefers the deferred deduction approach (i.e., deduct as the payments are made) of the 1984 legislation is that it does not require advance knowledge of the payment date, the payment amount, or the discount. See Hearings on S. 237 and S. 1006 before the Subcommittee on Energy and Agricultural Taxation of the Senate Committee on Finance, 98th Cong., 1st Sess. (statement of William S. McKee, Acting Deputy Assistant Treasury Secretary for Tax Policy), reprinted in *Daily Tax Report* (BNA) No. 100, at J-5 (May 23, 1983).

(5) Stunt No. 4: Original Issue Discount—The Big One

This is the biggest stunt of all. It is of major importance in the field of federal income tax. This stunt has got it all. It deals with the subject of "original issue discount" (whatever that is, don't worry, we'll talk), which is the leading subject in the time value of money area. And the time value of money is the most important topic in the field of federal income tax. So you see the importance there. Original issue discount is also a marvelous illustration of time value of money and deferral principles, what deferral really means and why it is so important. Original issue discount also is a topic of importance in advanced corporate financial transactions. * * * This stunt requires a little work, but you will be amply rewarded for it.

Here's Stunt No. 4. Let us go back to the mid-1970s, an era of high interest rates. Birdsill Corporation, a major manufacturer of outdoor birdfeeding devices and traded on the New York Stock Exchange, wishes to raise some money in the financial markets in order to make an acquisition. It wishes to acquire Beeport Corporation, a maker of beekeeping equipment and protective devices. The companies expect to get "synergies" from this transaction by putting together the birds and the bees.[38]

To get some up-front cash for this transaction, Birdsill does something rather curious. It proposes to issue some long-term debt in the marketplace with a face amount of $100 million, payable in forty years. Birdsill, being a major corporation traded on the New York Stock Exchange, should have no trouble marketing this debt. There's just one weird thing about this debt. It does not provide for the payment of any interest. No interest at all. Shocking.

Suppose your best client Irving called you and asked whether he should take a slice of this action: Pay $10 million for the privilege of getting $10 million back in forty years. Irving asks you what you think of this investment. Seems reasonable to him. Put in $10 million, get $10 million back. At least you're not losing anything, he says. Having read the earlier part of this chapter, you are in a strong position to advise your client on this matter. You could tell him that it is one of the three or four dumbest ideas you have ever heard.

However, you as an adviser might be able to do better than that. After all, we don't want to inform our most well-heeled client that he is dumb as a post for even broaching the subject. That's not what we call the intelligent practice of law. So, like any savvy practitioner, you say, "Let's talk about it." You might not want to pay, you inform

---

[38] Okay, this is not Letterman. Just keep reading, please.

Irving, a full $10 million for $10 million face of debt that pays back principal in forty years with no interest. But maybe paying less than $10 million might work for the right to get $10 million in forty years. How much we would pay is, of course, a matter that would take some calculation. We can see just eyeballing it that we know we'd pay more than 65 cents for it.

But what is the right number? We don't expect you, sitting in the student lounge with some cold coffee, to come up with this major calculation. But formulate the question. What is the question? Think about it. The answer is in the next paragraph.

As you ascertained, the relevant question is: What is $10 million forty years from now worth now? The 1970s had some very high interest rates. Birdsill, with its business being highly subject to the weather, is a risky company. Let us say, therefore, in this environment of high interest rates and a risky company, that the rate of interest that Irving needs in order to make his investment in Birdsill worthwhile, compared to other investments with similar risk, is 9%.

That is, of course, the after-tax interest rate, which is the rate that is relevant to Irving. If we assume a tax rate of 40%, then this 9% after tax rate implies a pre-tax rate of interest of 15%. What we are saying here is that 40% of the interest Irving gets is taxed to him leaving him with 60% left. Sixty percent of 15% is 9%. It is the pre-tax interest rate that must be used to figure out how much Irving would be willing to spend to get the right to receive $10 million forty years from now. The tax consequences of receiving the $10 million 40 years from now will be taken care of when the amount is received, as we have formulated the problem.

Thus our question now is: what amount invested now would grow at a 15% rate compounded annually to equal $10 million? That can be computed using the approach demonstrated above. The answer is $37,332. This is a surprisingly small number. But forty years is a very long time. This demonstrates once again the power of compound interest over long periods of time. What we are saying, then, is that $37,332 at 15% compounded annually grows to $10 million after forty years.[39] Thus after discussion with Irving considering relevant interest rates to use and so forth, you come to the conclusion that, yeah, buying $10 million face amount of this non-

---

[39] You can verify this one yourself, if you like. Take a simple calculator. Enter $37,332. Then multiply that by 1.15. Multiply the resulting number by 1.15 (you are compounding). Do that forty times and see if you don't hit in the area of $10 million. You won't hit $10 million right on the nose because of rounding but you'll be within a thousand or so of it.

interest bearing paper is a good idea after all. Just pay $37,332 for it. You're a pretty sharp guy, Irving. Let's do lunch.

But wait! Will Birdsill sell $10 million of forty year debt for that price?

Yes, it will. Because everyone else is making the same calculation that you and Irving made. So everything is jake now. Irving's got his Birdsill bonds; Birdsill's got its up front money; and (last but far from least) you've got your substantial fee for explaining all this to Irving.

Now, how does this deal play out over the course of the next forty years? Let's say, to keep the calculation simple, that Irving bought the bonds on January 1 of 1976. What happens as far as Irving's taxes are concerned in 1976? He actually gets no interest during the course of the year. All that's actually going to happen, under the terms of this bond trust indenture, is that he will get $10 million on December 31, 2015.

Does Irving therefore pay no taxes until 2015? No. Congress, while not as sharp as you and Irving, has been at this problem a lot longer and by 1969 had come to similar conclusions. These bonds are said to have "original issue discount." This is because the bonds were originally issued at a discount from their face amount of $10 million (see this field's not so tough). To show you're in the know, you don't say "original issue discount," you say "OID."

Now just what is OID? Well, we already know. Birdsill is selling this paper at $37,332 in 1976 and paying back $10,000,000 at the end of 2015 in order to pay Irving for the use of his $37,332 for forty years. That difference of $10 million minus $37,332 is equal to $9,962,668. That was paid for the use of the original $37,332, plus the use of the interest that Birdsill owed each year but did not pay. That sounds a lot like compound interest. And that's how you and Irving analyzed it, too. You viewed it as interest. In the lexicon, if it walks like a duck, talks like a duck and quacks like a duck, there's a high probability it is a duck. We've got interest here.

Interest accrues over time. That's a fundamental fact of economic life. Starting in 1969, after decades of struggling with the subject, Congress purported to tax original issue discount as interest accruing over time. Before we talk about what Congress did in 1969, let's consider the problem ourselves. How would we go about taxing the deal we have? We understand that there is interest. How much interest per year? Let's look at the first couple of years:

Year	Principal	Interest
1976	$37,332	$5,600
1977	$42,932	$6,440
1978	$49,372	$7,406
1979	$56,777	$8,517
1980	$65,294	$9,794

This is the deal that Irving will get for the first five years. What is really going on here? What is going on is that Irving loans Birdsill (by buying Birdsill's paper) $37,332. Birdsill then pays Irving $5,600, constituting 15% interest on that money. Except that, given the type of paper that Irving bought, in effect Irving, immediately upon receiving the $5,600, relends it back to Birdsill. Thus the total outstanding debt at the beginning of 1977 that Birdsill owes Irving is $42,932 (i.e., $37,332 + $5,600). Thus, Birdsill has to pay 15% on that increased amount for 1977. Once again, when the $6,440 interest is paid in 1977, Irving relends it back to Birdsill, and the loan balance increases to $49,372 ($42,932 + $6,440). Birdsill then pays 15% interest on that amount, and so it goes. How long does it go on? Well, for forty years. And what is the outstanding loan balance at the end of 40 years? Ten million dollars, of course, give or take a little due to rounding. This process is, of course, exactly the process suggested in a footnote earlier, multiplying $37,332 by 1.15 40 times.

This is what is happening as an economic matter when a bond carries no interest and is sold at a discount. As an economic matter, the holder of the bond is relending the interest back and receiving further interest on the increased balance.[43]

So, you'd expect Congress to tax you on these amounts of interest every year, noting that the amounts increase each year due to compounding. But Congress was not that smart when it enacted the rules in force in the 1970s. Congress instead took what we might call a "dumbo" approach. Congress said that the total amount of interest in this deal is $10 million − $37,332 = $9,962,668. Then, Congress said (in its 1969 rules), for a forty year bond, we'll tax the investor on one-fortieth or 2.5% of that total interest in each of the forty years.

---

[43] It is mildly instructive to compare this with what would happen if Irving bought an interest bearing bond from Birdsill. If the bond offered had promised to pay $10 million in 40 years and promised to pay in cash 15% per year (i.e., $1.5 million per year) then, assuming that was the appropriate market interest rate, Irving would have given Birdsill $10 million for the bond and collected his $1.5 million per year, which he could have invested or spent. This illustrates one side-line point about OID bonds: they in effect lock you in to a pattern of relending the interest. Of course, if it is a marketable bond, which it very well could be, it could be sold at any time, thereby relieving any liquidity lockup.

For Irving, this cranks out to be 2.5% of $9,962,668 or $249,067 in each year.

In year 1, is this kind of a shock to Irving? Bet your bottom dollar. In year 1, Irving (after your lengthy explanation to him of how original issue discount is really interest) would expect to be taxed on the real amount of interest accrued in year 1, namely $5,600. Instead, he's hit with $249,067. (And he has no cash from the deal to pay.) Is he mad, or what? At a tax rate of 40%, his taxes are $99,627. This is instead of the 40% of $5,600 or $2,240 that he expected. Boy, is he mad! Taxes were more than expected by $99,627 − $2,240 = $97,387. Wow!

Where did Congress come up with this straight line treatment for OID in 1969? By not understanding the underlying transaction. You should understand that this approach of taking the total interest paid and dividing it by the number of years is not economically meaningful. That is not what happens with interest. That is not economically what was going on in our deal, as we discussed above.

So what happens now? What happens is that Irving would not buy this bond after all. Because he would not want to get hit with this freako amount of interest in the early years of the deal. So what happens with this OID bond, under the 1969 rules? Does that mean no one would buy it? Nope. Someone would buy it who does not care about receiving a freako amount of interest up front. Do you have any ideas as to who might not care about that? See if you can think of something. The answer is in the next paragraph.

How about a pension fund? Pension funds, funds set aside for investment for employee pensions. The funds are not taxed on their current income, as part of the attractive deal for establishing employee pension funds, as we discussed in Stunt No. 2, above. Also some foreign investors at that time.

Okay. Here's the thing. Let's stop talking about Irving. Other than being very wealthy, he's not that interesting. What's interesting in this whole deal is not what happens to Irving but what happens to Birdsill. It's really going to start cooking now.

Now Birdsill may have a stupid little product line, but their financial people are on top of the situation. Birdsill's numbers are the same as Irving's with one important difference: Birdsill is paying the interest rather than receiving it. Thus Birdsill's overall numbers are that it received $37,332 at the beginning of year 1 and promised to pay back $10 million at the end of year 40.

Thus the total interest Birdsill is in effect paying out on this deal over the forty years is $10,000,000 − $37,332, or $9,962,668. And under the 1969 rules, Birdsill is regarded as paying this out on a straight line basis for forty years, or 2.5% of it per year. This, as we know from talking about Irving, is $249,067 per year. Now Birdsill is subject to a 40% tax. So Birdsill, still following the 1969 rules, deducts this $249,067 each year against its other income. This saves Birdsill 40% of that amount, or $99,627 in taxes per year. Note that Birdsill is saving that amount in taxes in each of forty years.

Now let us say that Birdsill reinvests the amount it has saved in taxes each year at the same prevailing pre-tax interest rate of 15%. If Birdsill is in the 40% bracket, that means Birdsill's after-tax rate of return is 9%. Thus Birdsill winds up with 1.09 times $99,627 after one year as a result of this. This comes to $108,593. Birdsill can keep compounding this amount at 9% a year for 40 years. What does Birdsill wind up with then? It's a cool $36,691,740.

Now that's just the results from reinvestment of the tax savings in year 1 compounded for forty years. Birdsill can also reinvest the $99,627 tax savings from year 2 at an after-tax return of 9% and do so for 39 years. That result cranks out to be $33,562,520. Naturally that is less than year 1 because we're only doing it for 39 years instead of 40. Birdsill can do this for year 3 and year 4 on down through year 40.

What do all those tax savings and compounded reinvestments add up to for 40 years? Well, it's $396,114,090. Take a look at the OID accrual chart on the next page.

ORIGINAL ISSUE DISCOUNT ACCRUAL: COMPOUND AND STRAIGHT LINE INTEREST COMPARED

OID ACCRUAL: COMPOUND INTEREST AND STRAIGHT LINE
INTEREST COMPARED
DEDUCTING EACH AMOUNT OF INTEREST AND INVESTING
THE TAX SAVINGS
15% Interest Rate; 40% Tax Rate; Savings Invested @ 9% After
Tax Rate

Year	Principal	Compound Int	St. Line Int	Tax Saved Cmp. Int.	Tax Saved St.Ln Int.	Future Value of Tax Saved Cmp Int	Future Value of Tax Saved St.Ln. Int	Annual Gain Using St. Ln. Instead of Cmp Method
1976	$37,332	$5,600	$249,067	$2,240	$99,627	$824,944	$36,691,740	$35,866,796
1977	$42,932	$6,440	$249,067	$2,576	$99,627	$867,778	$33,562,520	$32,694,742
1978	$49,372	$7,406	$249,067	$2,962	$99,627	$912,583	$30,691,676	$29,779,092
1979	$56,777	$8,517	$249,067	$3,407	$99,627	$959,411	$28,057,874	$27,098,406
1980	$65,294	$9,794	$249,067	$3,918	$99,627	$1,008,305	$25,641,542	$24,633,237
1981	$75,088	$11,263	$249,067	$4,505	$99,627	$1,059,303	$23,424,724	$22,365,421
1982	$86,351	$12,953	$249,067	$5,181	$99,627	$1,112,432	$21,390,945	$20,278,514
1983	$99,304	$14,896	$249,067	$5,958	$99,627	$1,167,708	$19,525,094	$18,357,386
1984	$114,199	$17,130	$249,067	$6,852	$99,627	$1,225,134	$17,813,303	$16,588,169
1985	$131,329	$19,699	$249,067	$7,880	$99,627	$1,284,693	$16,242,853	$14,958,161
1986	$151,029	$22,654	$249,067	$9,062	$99,627	$1,346,348	$14,802,073	$13,455,726
1987	$173,683	$26,052	$249,067	$10,421	$99,627	$1,410,038	$13,480,257	$12,070,279
1988	$199,736	$29,960	$249,067	$11,984	$99,627	$1,475,670	$12,267,582	$10,791,911
1989	$229,696	$34,454	$249,067	$13,782	$99,627	$1,543,118	$11,155,035	$9,611,917
1990	$264,150	$39,623	$249,067	$15,849	$99,627	$1,612,211	$10,134,350	$8,522,139
1991	$303,773	$45,566	$249,067	$18,226	$99,627	$1,682,731	$9,197,942	$7,515,212
1992	$349,339	$52,401	$249,067	$20,960	$99,627	$1,754,398	$8,338,852	$6,584,455
1993	$401,740	$60,261	$249,067	$24,104	$99,627	$1,826,866	$7,550,697	$5,723,831
1994	$462,000	$69,300	$249,067	$27,720	$99,627	$1,899,707	$6,827,618	$4,927,911
1995	$531,300	$79,695	$249,067	$31,878	$99,627	$1,972,400	$6,164,243	$4,191,843
1996	$610,996	$91,649	$249,067	$36,660	$99,627	$2,044,313	$5,555,642	$3,511,329
1997	$702,645	$105,397	$249,067	$42,159	$99,627	$2,114,685	$4,997,292	$2,882,607
1998	$808,042	$121,206	$249,067	$48,482	$99,627	$2,182,607	$4,485,045	$2,302,438
1999	$929,248	$139,387	$249,067	$55,755	$99,627	$2,246,996	$4,015,093	$1,768,097
2000	$1,068,635	$160,295	$249,067	$64,118	$99,627	$2,306,566	$3,583,945	$1,277,379
2001	$1,228,930	$184,340	$249,067	$73,736	$99,627	$2,359,797	$3,188,396	$828,599
2002	$1,413,270	$211,990	$249,067	$84,796	$99,627	$2,404,898	$2,825,507	$420,610
2003	$1,625,260	$243,789	$249,067	$97,516	$99,627	$2,439,762	$2,492,582	$52,820
2004	$1,869,049	$280,357	$249,067	$112,143	$99,627	$2,461,918	$2,187,145	($274,772)
2005	$2,149,407	$322,411	$249,067	$128,964	$99,627	$2,468,472	$1,906,929	($561,543)
2006	$2,471,818	$370,773	$249,067	$148,309	$99,627	$2,456,042	$1,649,849	($806,103)
2007	$2,842,591	$426,389	$249,067	$170,555	$99,627	$2,420,681	$1,413,996	($1,006,685)
2008	$3,268,979	$490,347	$249,067	$196,139	$99,627	$2,357,791	$1,197,617	($1,160,174)
2009	$3,759,326	$563,899	$249,067	$225,560	$99,627	$2,262,018	$999,105	($1,262,913)
2010	$4,323,225	$648,484	$249,067	$259,393	$99,627	$2,127,139	$816,983	($1,310,156)
2011	$4,971,709	$745,756	$249,067	$298,303	$99,627	$1,945,927	$649,899	($1,296,028)
2012	$5,717,465	$857,620	$249,067	$343,048	$99,627	$1,709,994	$496,611	($1,213,384)
2013	$6,575,085	$986,263	$249,067	$394,505	$99,627	$1,409,618	$355,979	($1,053,638)
2014	$7,561,347	$1,134,202	$249,067	$453,681	$99,627	$1,033,530	$226,960	($806,571)
2015	$8,695,549	$1,304,332	$249,067	$521,733	$99,627	$568,689	$108,593	($460,096)
Totals	$9,999,882	$9,962,550	$9,962,680	$3,985,020	$3,985,072	$68,267,220	$396,114,090	$327,846,870

Principal
Amount

Same amount of total
interest paid. (Minor difference due to rounding)

Same am't of tax
saved

Total Gain Using St. Line
Instead of Compound
Method is $396,114,090
− $68,267,220   =
$327,846,870

    We have already talked about a lot of the numbers on this chart, so it really shouldn't be intimidating. Let's talk about each column, going from left to right:

- The left-most column is the years over which this OID note is outstanding.

- The column "principal" shows how the principal increases when the compound interest (from the next column over) is added back to the principal each year. This is Irving or whoever holds the note "relending" the interest back to Birdsill. We see ultimately the principal accumulates up to about $10 million (we lost $118 in rounding).

- The "Compound Int" column is, of course, the amount of interest that is due each year—which increases because the previous year's interest is being added on to the principal, as we have discussed. We see the total of that interest ultimately paid down at the bottom, as $9,962,550. That amount plus the original amount of the note of $37,332 adds up to approximately the $9,999,882 face amount of the note due at the end of 40 years.

- The "St. Line Int" column is the erroneous Congressional solution as to how to treat this transaction. This takes the $9,962,550 total interest and divides it by 40, giving $249,067. This is the amount of interest Congress deemed would be deductible to Birdsill every year under the 1969 rules. You can see that, comparing it to the economic reality of the Compound Interest column, it vastly overstates the amount of interest deductible to Birdsill (and included in the income of whoever holds the note) in the early years and vastly understates the amount of interest deductible to Birdsill (and included in the income of the holder) in the later years. You see that ultimately (and not surprisingly, given the way it was calculated), the same total amount of interest is deductible under the straight line method as under the compound method. This illustrates that the only difference between the two methods is the *timing* of the deduction of the interest. The total amount deducted is the same.

Now we get to the intrigue. What does the fact that the timing is different come to mean? You will strongly suspect from our earlier discussions that it means a lot.

- The "Tax Saved Cmp. Int." column in our numerical chart shows the amount of tax saved by Birdsill if it deducts the amount of interest under the economically realistic compounding method. Thus in 1976 the tax saved is 40% of $5,600, or $2,240. In 1977, the tax saved is 40% of $6,440, or $2,576. We will see what Birdsill does with these amounts momentarily.

- The "Tax Saved St. Ln. Int." column, it will not surprise you to learn, is the amount of tax saved by Birdsill if it deducts the amount of interest under the straight line method, as we have discussed above. That is 40% of the same amount of $249,067, or $99,627.

- The "Future Value of Tax Saved Cmp. Int." column can be explained by looking, say, at 1976. The tax saved that year, using the economically accurate compound method, is $2,240. If that amount is invested at a 9% after-tax compound rate of return for 40 years, it grows to $824,944. If the 1977 tax saved using the compound method of $2,576 is invested at 9% compound after-tax return for 39 years, it grows to $867,778. Note that this amount is greater than the year 1976 amount. This is because, while the number of years of compounding is less, 39 instead of 40, the amount you start with is larger ($2,576 instead of $2,240). Observe how, for this same reason, the amounts in this column grow every year until 2005, at which point the effect of having less years left begins to dominate over the fact that the amount you start with is increasing and the amounts you accumulate decline through the end of the 40 year period. The total future value of all these amounts of tax saved and invested is given at the bottom of the column as $68,267,220.

- The "Future Value of Tax Saved St. Ln. Int." column, of course, performs the same computation for the straight line method. The amount (always $99,627) is compounded at 9% after tax interest in 1976 for 40 years, then in 1977 for 39 years and so forth. We would expect to see these accumulations just decline all the way from 1976 through 2015, since we are always starting with the same amount but compounding for less years. And so we see the accumulations behave as expected. The total future value of all these amounts of tax saved and invested using the straight line method is given at the bottom of the column as $396,114,090.

The totals of the "Future Value of Tax Saved Cmp. Int." and "Future Value of Tax Saved St. Ln. Int." columns tell the final story.

The total for the compound interest method is $68,267,220, which is stunningly less than the total for the straight line method of $396,114,090. As indicated in the chart, the difference is $327,846,870. Dwell on this comparison for a moment. Note also the stupefying fact that the amounts accumulated for the first two years, 1976 and 1977, in the straight line method add up to more than is accumulated in the entire 40 years in the compound method.

Thus though the total *amounts* of interest deducted were the same, the fact that the straight line method allowed much larger amounts to be deducted early puts monster money in Birdsill's pocket, compared to the economically accurate compound method. Indeed the difference was a staggering $327,846,870. Given that the face amount of the underlying obligation in this transaction was $10 million, it is positively mind-boggling that the simple matter of the difference in timing of when the total amount of interest is deducted can put over $327 million in the pocket of Birdsill (and out of the pocket of the government). This is over 30 times more than the face amount of the original obligation. Such is the raw power of the time value of money. And such is the incredible price to the government of getting the rules wrong.

For do you think that corporations and their high-powered tax counsel were aware of this effect after Congress enacted the 1969 straight line rules? Do you think that corporations, on the advice of their high-powered counsel, issued deeply discounted long term bonds as a financing tool? Does it rain in Indianapolis in the summertime?

Congress, after getting its pocket picked by this technique for a number of years, finally figured it out and went to Smart City. Congress enacted rules in 1982 that compute OID by reference to the economically accurate view that the note holder is receiving the interest and then relending it back to the issuer of the note at further interest. Thus, on our deal, the deduction allowed for obligations issued after 1982 would be calculated based on the compound amount, rather than the straight line amount.

So this particular OID game is no longer available. But the analysis is still there. It was the enactment of the OID rules in 1982 that ushered in the time value of money era in federal income taxation. Once the analysis was made there, and people began to understand the enormous implications of timing in taxation, the analysis began to be applied widely in other areas of federal income taxation. This type of analysis will stand us in good stead as we examine a variety of other transactions in this field.

Appendix B

CAPITAL GAINS RATES

CAPITAL GAINS RATES

Rate	Category
0%	This is the regular long-term capital gains rate for assets, excluding collectibles, if taxpayer is subject to a 10% or 15% marginal rate.
10%	Taxable rate for collectibles if taxpayer has room in the 10% bracket.
15%	General rate for long-term capital gain (held for more than 1 year) if the taxpayer is subject to a marginal tax rate higher than 15% but less than 39.6%. In addition, if taxpayer is taxed at 15% marginal rate, this category includes collectibles and real property (to the extent of depreciation) held for more than 1 year.
20%	General rate for long-term capital gain (held for more than 1 year) if the taxpayer is in the 39.6% bracket.
25%	If a taxpayer has previously depreciated real property, the gain that results from the previously taken depreciation is taxed at 25%. This is also the rate for collectibles and § 1202 gain if the taxpayer still has room in the 25% bracket.
28%	Gain on collectibles held over one year.

Table of Cases

Table of Internal Revenue Code Sections

Table of Treasury Regulations

Table of Rules

Index

References are to Pages
